CHINA

People and Places
in the Land of One Billion

CHINA

People and Places
in the Land of One Billion

Christopher J. Smith
SUNY–Albany

Westview Press
BOULDER ■ SAN FRANCISCO ■ OXFORD

Copyright © 1991 by Westview Press, Inc.

Published in 1991 in the United States of America by Westview Press, Inc., 5500 Central Avenue, Boulder, Colorado 80301, and in the United Kingdom by Westview Press, 36 Lonsdale Road, Summertown, Oxford OX2 7EW

Library of Congress Cataloging-in-Publication Data
Smith, Christopher J.
  China: people and places in the land of one billion/Christopher
J. Smith.
    p. cm.
  ISBN 0-8133-0853-4 — ISBN 0-8133-0854-2 (pbk.)
  1. China—Geography. I. Title.
DS706.7.S65 1991
951—dc20   90-46688
                                                                                 CIP

Printed and bound in the United States of America

The paper used in this publication meets the requirements
of the American National Standard for Permanence of Paper
for Printed Library Materials Z39.48-1984.

10   9   8   7   6   5   4   3   2   1

CONTENTS

v

T A B L E S & F I G U R E S

P R E F A C E

In a preface an author has a chance to apologize for not writing the book the publisher was expecting. I would like to take this opportunity, therefore, to explain why I decided to write this book in the first place and why it came out the way it did. When I began this project, I was full of enthusiasm about the changes that were occurring in China. I was convinced that a completely new China was emerging and confident that political reform was just around the corner. After the events of 1989 my views toward the Chinese government changed dramatically, and I had to reevaluate many of my earlier conclusions. It was obvious that the final product would be very different from what I had set out to write.

In June 1989 I had almost finished the book, but as I watched the tanks rolling into Tiananmen Square, I realized I was faced with a dilemma. How should I write about a country I thought I knew quite well, when all of a sudden I discovered that I had understood very little about it? How should I respond to the emotional roller coaster of feeling a great fondness for a country and its people, only to be repulsed by the cynical attitudes and brutal behavior of the government toward those same people? I was not at all certain that I could continue with the book, but if I did, I knew that almost everything I had written would need to be revised. It was not so much that the facts had changed but that the entire intellectual context in which I had been operating had shifted. The earth had moved from under my word processor, and it was time to go back to square one.

The book was (and still is) about the ordinary people of China and the places in which they live and work. It deals primarily with the impact of the reforms that had been sweeping through China since the late 1970s. In April 1989 it seemed to me that the reforms introduced by Deng Xiaoping had changed people's lives and landscapes so dramatically that, to use Lynn Pan's words, we were witnessing a "New Chinese Revolution."

By the middle of the summer, after watching the Chinese authorities' crackdown on the demonstrators, it was clear that use of the term *revolution* had been premature. The pace of the reforms had been furious at times, but the events of 1989 made it clear that the relationship between the people and the state in China had not changed. Political reform is inevitable, but the Communist party was not ready to discuss the transition in 1989. For the time being, China remains a solidly Leninist state, in the sense that the Party still dominates all aspects of life.

In the early 1990s outsiders will be able to do little more than look for signs of change. The early evidence points to more retrenchments in the economic sphere as well as further restrictions in personal freedoms. The difficulty for the government is that in many respects the progress that was made in the 1980s cannot be reversed. The Chinese people came to expect something more out of their lives. They had been able to peer around the corner at a new era, and they obviously liked what they saw. Many of them had more money to spend than ever before. There were more goods to buy, more places to go, more things to do. The people were enjoying the fraction of independence they had been allowed to experience, and not surprisingly they wanted more. The bolder ones hoped for greater freedom of speech; the more timid simply wanted to be left alone after three decades of Communist bullying. The Chinese people were tired of being told whom they could vote for, when to have children, where to plant trees, and what they could grow in their fields. Many of them had already witnessed a new way of life, and the desire to experience it could not be turned off like a faucet.

The "big picture" had not changed, in the sense that political reform had not occurred, but there had been a partial revolution in attitudes. The Chinese people had readied themselves for the future. Their desire for change was reflected in their extraordinary outbursts on the streets of Beijing and other cities in 1989. The strength of their convictions could be measured by their refusal to retreat even though recent history made them fully aware of the possible consequences of their behavior.

In 1990 the desire for change is greater than ever, and China is poised to explode again. The only real questions are how long it will take before the struggle rises to the surface and who the architects of the rising will be the next time it occurs. Neither question can be answered at this time, although there are many different opinions on the issue. The activists who are living in exile in various parts of the world are waiting for a spontaneous eruption from the people, to which they hope they will be able to respond quickly. Another possibility, and one that is currently being whispered about by a small group of Chinese intellectuals, is that political reform will begin from inside the Communist party. If this happens, the dissidents who have already left the country will probably have a very limited role in the future events.

Even before the tragedy of 1989 one of my most important goals in writing this book was to shine some light onto the dark secret of human rights abuses in China. I had been persuaded by reading the work of Simon Leys, a Belgian who wrote under a nom de plume to protect his identity. Leys had argued in the early 1970s that it was impossible, perhaps immoral, to talk about contemporary China without addressing the issue of human rights. Even after the Cultural Revolution (1966–1976) thousands of people were still languishing in the labor camps for "political crimes"; basic freedom of speech was denied to millions of people; and grotesque miscarriages of justice were being perpetrated in the name of the Party. Throughout the 1980s these facts were overlooked by the majority of the academics who were studying in China as well as by the governments and the corporations that were seeking friendships (and profits). What happened in Tiananmen Square and in other parts of China in June 1989 guaranteed that such complacency could never again be justified. After what was witnessed by viewers around the world the human rights issue in China was placed firmly on the international agenda.

The sad truth is that what happened after the Tiananmen massacre in 1989—the swift purges, the quick trials, the harsh sentences, and the parading of "criminals" in the streets—represented nothing new in postrevolutionary China. All of this had been seen many times since 1949, and in 1989 the government was simply going about its business as usual. As far as the Chinese Communist party was concerned, this was an internal affair, one into which others had not been invited to meddle. The outrage felt all around the world simply illustrated how far apart we are from the Chinese on the issue of human rights. In a recent interview Jiang Zemin, the general secretary of the Party, reaffirmed that the Chinese government considered its actions to be both necessary and fully justified, in spite of the fact that its opponents were unarmed: "We do not regret or criticize ourselves for the way we handled the Tiananmen event, because if we had not sent in the troops I would not be able to sit here today."[1]

Before 1989 most Westerners were hoping that the Chinese would move gradually to correct the most egregious of their human rights violations. The climate of opinion was overwhelmingly in favor of China. This international goodwill was partly a result of China's apparent willingness to embrace some of the principles of capitalism and partly a response to the extensive liberalizations that had been granted during the 1980s to the Chinese people and to foreigners wanting to trade with China. Outsiders had been lulled into a false sense of security that everything would turn out right. We had been persuaded, both by the Chinese themselves and by our own need to believe, that major moves in the direction of political and judicial reform were imminent.

It appears that we were mistaken. The Chinese government clung to its own interpretation of the events in Tiananmen Square, and our former friends became our enemies again. We could not understand what had happened. For their part the Chinese failed to grasp why we were so outraged. To make matters worse, the government offered a ludicrously biased interpretation of the events and accused the foreign media of not only grossly exaggerating but also incorrectly reporting the events. The Chinese government managed to wipe out most of the goodwill in the international community that it had worked so hard to foster for more than a decade.

Before the traumatic events of 1989 this book had been largely shaped by my academic requirements as well as my overwhelmingly positive feelings toward China and its people. For a few years I had been trying to introduce both the concepts of modern geography and an understanding of contemporary China to successive waves of undergraduate students. I had been struggling with this twin task in New York state, where most of the students had never heard of geography as an academic discipline, and also in New Zealand, where the students were considerably more conscious about geography. I had traveled extensively in China; I had taught there; and I had read as much as I could. I felt that it was time to write something down.

The idea for a book was first suggested in 1987, when I realized that no ready-made text was available for the course I wanted to teach. The best book of its type had been written a few years earlier by Cliff Pannell and Laurence Ma and was entitled *China: The Geography of Development and Modernization*, but that book was already out of print. In a desperate scramble to find something suitable I contacted the presses that specialize in China books. At Westview I encountered Susan McEachern, who suggested that I write a book about China.

The die was cast, but not without some reservations on my part. Writing a regional geography book went against the grain for me. It was counter to everything I had ever considered to be the valid territory of academic scholarship. However, there were some points in favor of the project. In the first place, writing such a book represented a tremendous challenge and would be a marvelous learning experience. Second, it seemed to me that a text that could successfully introduce students both to China and to geography was, in spite of the traditional academic snobbishness about writing textbooks, an admirable goal. I decided that in pedagogical terms my enthusiasm for China was an excellent vehicle for introducing geography to students. As I argue in Chapters 1 and 2 of the book, China is a country so rich in variety, so full of interesting people and places, and so redolent with drama that it simply cannot fail to bring geography alive to an initially unaware and skeptical audience.

When I finally began to write the book, I was determined to offer the reader a multidimensional view of China. My first goal was to review and simplify some of the Western scholarship that is currently available on China. Using a combination of firsthand observations in the field, Chinese sources of data, and personal interviews, Western social scientists have produced a wealth of research documents about life and landscapes in the new China. The volume of these works increased considerably in the 1980s as the new openness made it easier for foreigners to travel in China and for researchers to gain access to sources of information that had earlier been unavailable. Most of these works are highly specialized, and consequently their coverage is too narrow and their level of detail too great for introductory purposes. What was needed, therefore, was a synthesis, offering a representative sample of the best of Western scholarship on contemporary China.

A second goal was to provide a "lighter" and more "humane" perspective than was normally available in the academic social sciences literature. This suggested the use of nonscholarly, or popular, books, which I had noticed were usually preferred by students as introductory reading materials. Some of the books written about China by journalists, novelists, and travel writers are considerably more entertaining than even the best academic books on the market. Perhaps the only common thread among the authors in question is that they have been fascinated with China and have written about it with passion, although not always with objectivity. I had started to read these books even before I first went to China. I was deeply moved, for example, by some of the books written by American journalists in the prerevolutionary era—books that have become classics—including Jack Belden's *China Shakes the World*; Edgar Snow's *Red Star over China*; and perhaps the most impressive of all, Graham Peck's *Two Kinds of Time*, an account of life in south China during the Japanese occupation. In addition to these gems, some books about China written by journalists and travel writers in the past few years have been both engaging and informative. From my perspective, among the most useful of these and the best written are the books by Orville Schell (*To Get Rich Is Glorious* and the later *Discos and Democracy*), Lynn Pan (*The New Chinese Revolution*), Fox Butterfield (*China: Alive in the Bitter Sea*), David Bonavia (*The Chinese*), and Tiziano Terzani (*Behind the Forbidden Door*).

Two recent books written by established travel writers have helped to expand the level of awareness about China among the general literary public. Paul Theroux's *Riding the Iron Rooster* became a best-seller in spite of the author's obvious contempt for many of the people he encountered in his travels. My personal favorite is the exquisitely written book by Colin Thubron, entitled *Behind the Wall*. Thubron took the time to learn enough of the language to get by in China on his own. He traveled and was lodged unconventionally and introduced himself to a vast assortment of characters. The result is a book of great beauty, a true masterpiece, and one that cannot be improved upon by academic objectiveness. I now assign Thubron's book as compulsory reading for all students who take my China courses.

I also wanted to incorporate into my book some of the flavor of everyday life that can be gleaned from modern Chinese writers, of whom a number began publishing in English in the 1980s. Much of this new literature has been written by members of the so-called lost generation—the young people who were "sent down" to the countryside from the cities in the 1960s and 1970s. In the increasingly liberal atmosphere of the 1980s, and in a time of greater contact with the West, these writers began to provide a new and often critical view of everyday life in China. This was a refreshing change from most of the patriotic pulp that had been produced under the watchful eyes of the Communist party since 1949.

At the extreme end of this genre were the exponents of a new literature of dissent, much of which is still not available to readers in the mainland. Some of this work has been summarized and excerpted in English-language sources, including the books written by Simon Leys and the remarkable collection edited in 1986 by Geremie Barmé and John Minford, called *Seeds of Fire: Chinese Voices of Conscience.* In my opinion two of the new authors stand head and shoulders above the others not only for their political bravery but also for their eloquence: Zhang Xianliang, with his largely autobiographical novel *Half of Man Is Woman,* and Yu Luojin, whose *A Chinese Winter's Tale* was published only after she finally left China to live in Europe. There have been many more pedestrian but nevertheless illuminating exposés written about the excesses of the Cultural Revolution years in China. Some of these, like Gao Yuan's *Born Red*, Dai Houying's *Stones of the Wall,* and the books written by the husband-and-wife team Liang Heng and Judith Shapiro (including *Son of the Revolution*), have been widely read in the West.

At the less overtly political end of the spectrum is a group of novelists and short-story writers upon whom I have drawn heavily for case studies and "slices of life" stories to illustrate different themes throughout the book. With the help of English-language publishers in China, such as Panda Books in Beijing, and Western distribution outlets, such as China Books and Periodicals in San Francisco, the works of these authors (who include such figures as Wang Anyi, Jiang Zilong, Gu Hua, Cheng Naishan, Zheng Yi, Chen Ruoxi, and Zhang Jie) have become increasingly available to readers in the West. Although many of the stories appear to lose something in translation, they provide an interesting glimpse into some of the everyday occupations and frustrations of the Chinese people.

All of this suggests a book with a variety of formats. In the first place it is intended to be conceptually based. I have also tried to provide facts that are as accurate and up-to-date as possible. The book is also peppered with vignettes and stories from a wide variety of subjective sources, both academic and nonacademic, Chinese and non-Chinese. Some readers will question the use of such sources in an academic book. The observations of novelists, journalists, and travel writers are definitely not scientific; in fact they are often biased and highly selective. In defense of my choice to use such subjective sources, I argue that they clearly have a place in a book that is intended to be about ordinary lives and landscapes in China. The "facts" themselves, in addition to their questionable status, are often unable to tell us much about what life is actually like in China. It is realistic to assume that there is no infallible source of data when it comes to China, no single avenue to the absolute truth, and no one person with a total monopoly on knowledge about what is currently going on. In that case I feel quite comfortable drawing on a wide variety of sources in an attempt to piece together a realistic view of everyday life.

After the events of 1989 some of the academics who had spent the majority of their professional careers dealing with China openly reported that they were baffled by the recent turn of events. One exception was longtime *New York Times* correspondent Harrison Salisbury. In the introduction to his book about Tiananmen Square, Salisbury made what I think is an outrageous claim when he said, "I think I know China as well as, if not better than, any member of the Standing Committee of the Politburo."[2] Harrison Salisbury notwithstanding, it is difficult for any outsider to interpret the current situation in China with any confidence. This is particularly true when we listen to official statements made by representatives of the Chinese government; when we read the official publications intended for foreigners such as *China Daily, China Reconstructs,* or the *Beijing Review;* and even when we try to grapple with the official statistics published in the *State Statistical Abstracts.* Although the situation has been improving in recent years, we need to remember that in these interactions with the Chinese we are seeing, not what is really there, but what the Chinese want us to see. In the introduction to his book *Chinese Shadows,* Simon Leys warned of the dangers involved in trying to describe "reality" in China: "Those who think they can do something serious when reporting their Chinese experiences, or who pretend they describe Chinese realities when they are in fact describing the Chinese shadow play produced for them by [the] authorities, either deceive their readers or, worse, delude themselves."[3]

After the Tiananmen Square incident and the subsequent crackdown, it seemed to me that the changes we had been witnessing all through the 1980s were also part of the shadows. By focusing our attention on the shadows, we temporarily ignored the fact that the essential character of the Leninist system of government in China was not changing at all during the 1980s. Simon Leys, in what amounted to a remarkably prescient statement, had already pointed this out as early as 1974:

> Only observers [of China] who lack a sense of historical perspective can entertain the illusion that at such and such a time the regime turned a new leaf or started in a new direction. In fact its choices are severely limited by its very nature: in a totalitarian system where authority is held by a military-bureaucratic class, and where power expresses itself through periodic military coups, it is inevitable that times of stress will be followed by times of *relative relaxation;* it would be absurd to take one or the other of those cyclical phases for a new development.[4]

What happened in 1989 can be interpreted as another of the "military coups" that Leys was describing. We can assume that after the purges are finally over and the status quo is restored, presumably some time in the early years of the 1990s, China will enter another period of "relative relaxation," and at that time the whole cycle will begin again. Eventually, and who can say whether it will be sooner rather than later, a radical change—a revolution—will break the cycle, and the Chinese people will finally be able to point themselves in a new direction.

Christopher J. Smith
Delmar, New York

1. "Our Democracy Is the Best," a conversation with Jiang Zemin, general secretary of the Chinese Communist party, *U.S. News and World Report*, March 12, 1990, pp. 50–54, quote from p. 51.
2. H. Salisbury, 1989, *Tiananmen Diary: Thirteen Days in June* (Boston: Little, Brown), pp. 3–4.
3. S. Leys, 1977, *Chinese Shadows* (Harmondsworth, UK: Penguin Books), p. xiv.
4. Ibid., p. 33 (emphasis added).

ACKNOWLEDGMENTS

Under the circumstances, it is not appropriate for me to mention by name any of the Chinese people, living both in China and elsewhere, to whom I am indebted. I assume they will know who they are, but I do not want them to be associated with my views, at least not publicly. Without their help this book would not have been possible.

I am also deeply indebted to my family. Carolyn and Martyn gave a lot of time out of their lives to come to live in China with me. Jennifer also kept me company on another visit, in deep mid-winter, when we traveled together across China by train, boat, and plane. In addition to being my companion, Jennifer cheerfully assumed her other roles—as interpreter and as a constant source of attraction to the Chinese people we met en route. I would like to dedicate this book to her.

I must also thank the people I have worked with at Westview Press. Susan McEachern had confidence in the project from the beginning—probably more than I did—and without her encouragement I would not even have begun. I have enjoyed working with Jane Raese and Marian Safran, who worked miracles with the disks I sent them. I wish I had them around on a regular basis to tighten up my prose and keep me to deadlines.

Jeanette Megas did a marvelous job typing the manuscript or, in these high tech times, preparing the disks so that I could edit them. She also produced all the tables, a job that sorely stretched her patience and our friendship. I am not sure if Jeanette will ever again want to work for me, but I would give her a glowing reference.

C. J. S.

CHINA

People and Places
in the Land of One Billion

Introduction: Geography and the Middle Kingdom

the Yangtze . . . marks the immemorial divide between a soldierly, bureaucratic north, and the suave, entrepreneurial south. Men dwindle in size and integrity as they go south (say the northerners) and the clear-cut Mandarin of Beijing becomes a slushy caress. The dust of the wheat and millet-bearing plains dissolves to the monsoons of paddy fields and tea plantations. The staple of noodles becomes a diet of rice, and the low cabbages and symmetrical northern streets twist and steepen into labyrinths of whitewashed brick.

—Colin Thubron[1]

FINDING A PLACE FOR GEOGRAPHY

When the British travel writer Colin Thubron first crossed the Yangtze River, he was not prepared for the differences he was to encounter between northern and southern China. A master-craftsman with words, he could describe in a simple but richly evocative manner the everyday lives and landscapes he saw. Unlike travel writers, social scientists rarely feel comfortable making such sweeping generalizations about people or places. To present a reasonably comprehensive and objective picture of a place, the academic writer usually feels the need for an artillery of discipline-based facts to present all possible sides of each issue.

In a country as large and as complex as China, where change has been occurring so rapidly, it is difficult to get at these "facts." Much of the official data provided by the Chinese government is unreliable and impossible to evaluate. Even if we are confident about how the numbers are collected and what they mean, the facts themselves may tend to cloud the view of the novice reader, effectively preventing him or her from seeing the forest apart from the trees. It is useful,

therefore, to begin not with facts but with concepts, in an attempt to interpret the flow of events in contemporary China.

There can be no doubt that geographical factors have influenced the pattern of human settlement in China over the centuries. This is a country where distance still acts as a major constraint on social interaction; where the population is so vast that the demand for resources outstrips the supply almost everywhere; where regional variations have produced a richly interesting mosaic of human and physical characteristics; and where people have developed a strong sense of place that is based on an almost fanatical attachment to their native soil.

Four decades of socialism have altered the character of some of these geographical imperatives, but for the most part the same forces are still at work. Collective agriculture has tied the Chinese peasants more strongly to the land than was ever the case in the past. The restrictions on migration and the nature of work in the new collectives meant that most of China's peasants were legally bound for life by the state to residence in tiny production units. They were not allowed to leave their units, and if they did, their

1

food supply was jeopardized. For all intents and purposes the peasants were imprisoned in what Mark Selden referred to as "a community of destiny that structures . . . [their] life opportunities and incomes."[2]

In spite of the obvious relevance of geography to the pattern of human settlement, it is essential for the reader to appreciate the dominance of *culture* and *politics* in shaping almost all aspects of everyday life. Therefore, this book adopts a realistic view of geography. Geographical factors are considered to be important, but they operate and should be considered in conjunction with historical, political, cultural, social, and economic forces. The constraints of physical geography have markedly influenced human activities in China over the centuries—dictating where people could live and what they could grow. The more abstract properties of geography, such as distance and accessibility, have also helped to shape the course of regional development over time. In both of these cases geography exerts a powerful force; in fact it may constitute or determine human activity. In most instances, however, geography works in a more subtle and less direct way, to constrain or mediate human activities. The place for geography, therefore, is alongside the forces associated with the other social science disciplines. This book is not intended to be a "geography *of* contemporary China." It is an interdisciplinary book *about* China, in which the patterns of everyday life are interpreted through the eyes of a geographer.

SOME GEOGRAPHICAL "FACTS OF LIFE"

The book contains many facts, but the reader, bearing in mind their source and the possibility that they will be outdated before the book is published, is encouraged to develop a critical, not to say cynical, view of them. It is also appropriate to consider the facts themselves as secondary to the underlying concepts, be they geographical, political, or cultural. Before exploring these concepts in Part 1 of the book, however, it is useful to begin by considering a small set of geographical "facts of life" that can not be ignored in any discussion of China. The first of these is China's *regional context* within East Asia. China is encircled by mountains and deserts to the west and north and by the vast expanse of the Pacific Ocean to the east. As a result, the country remained in virtual isolation until relatively recently, trading little with the outside world, and caring even less for the opinions and values of foreigners. The Chinese consider their country to be the "middle kingdom" (*zhong guo*). All other countries are, by definition, peripheral, and their residents are assigned to the status of "barbarians" (see Figures 1.1 and 1.2).

Over the centuries the Chinese became complacent about their self-sufficiency and overconfident of their supremacy. The intellectual stirrings of the Renaissance bypassed China completely; the industrial revolution that swept through Europe and North America in the eighteenth and nineteenth centuries had virtually no impact in China at the time.

In spite of its isolation China was able to cultivate a rich civilization of its own, as demonstrated by the early development of art and philosophy and the long list of technological innovations usually attributed to the Chinese. The result, in the words of John King Fairbank, was that "China achieved a cultural superiority over all other East Asian regions, the after-effects of which have lasted to this day."[3] This sense of superiority made it all the more difficult for the Chinese to endure their lack of development in modern times and the loathsome interference of foreign powers. In the 1990s the harsh reality of economic backwardness relative to almost all of their East Asian neighbors is a cruel blow to the proud Chinese, especially in light of the economic successes of their own offshore (but temporarily estranged) territories in Hong Kong and Taiwan.

China's isolation has also guaranteed that when the time finally came for modernization, it would be a peculiarly tortuous experience. Modernization in the United States was a relatively painless process forged by recent immigrants who had already shed the tough skins of their culture. In China, by comparison, modernization has required the moving of a mountain of cultural baggage. To quote Fairbank again, modernization for the Chinese amounts to the moral equivalent of Americans rejecting "the Virgin Mary and the Founding Fathers . . . [and] a denial of the values of one's grandfather."[4]

The *size* of China is the second geographical fact of life. Everything about China is large:

Figures 1.1 and 1.2   Two views of the townspeople in Binxian, in Northern Shaanxi Province, in 1986, enjoying their first-ever view of foreigners ("experts," students, and English-language teachers) passing through on a sightseeing and goodwill bus trip from Xian.

its land area, its population, its resource base, and its landforms. Distances are immense, and they have worked historically to lessen spatial and social interaction between China's regions. China is the third largest country in the world, stretching well over 5,000 kilometers from both north to south and east to west. China is larger than the United States, and both countries span lines of latitude from the frozen north to the subtropical south. The latitude of the most northerly point (in Heilongjiang Province) is approximately the same as that of James Bay in Canada; the latitude of the southernmost point (in Hainan Province) is close to that of Jamaica.

China's *location* is also a geographical fact of life. Like the United States, much of China lies in the midlatitudes; hence both countries have the physical attributes needed to support large populations, especially the moisture to grow crops abundantly and moderate temperatures to make life tolerable. China and the United States both have access to a warm-water sea. The major difference between the two countries in geographical terms is that China has no California. Instead of an ocean on its western flank, China is separated from the rest of Asia by inaccessible mountains and inhospitable deserts.

China's vast *population* is a fact of life that no one can ignore. In 1989, Chinese sources placed the population at 1.1 billion, which represented more than 20 percent of the world's total. Some individual Chinese provinces would be among the world's largest countries if they were independent. Sichuan, with 104

million people, is more populous than Bangladesh, which has the ninth largest population in the world; and Shandong Province, with close to 80 million people, is larger than Mexico. To support all these people, China has less than 15 percent of the world's land area, but more important, it has only about 7 percent of the world's cultivable land. The obvious outcome is a tremendous conflict over space. What is used for building roads, houses, and factories is taken out of cultivation, and this ultimately threatens the food supply.

Another geographical fact of life in China, notwithstanding Thubron's oversimplified categorization, is the staggering amount of *diversity* between the regions of China. The weather map shows astonishing variations in rainfall, from the moisture-deficit areas of the northwest, to the lush tropical wetlands of the southeast. From west to east the land descends in a series of steps from the Tibetan plateau all the way to the sea-level plains in the Yangtze basin. The spatial variations in China's physical geography are matched by the variations in its human geography. There are more than sixty million minority (non-Han) people in China, representing more than fifty different ethnic groups. In terms of language groups and ethnic practices, no two parts of China are alike, and this works to reduce spatial and social interaction even further.

One final geographical (and political) fact of life involves the current situation in *Taiwan*, the Republic of China. According to the People's Republic of China (PRC), Taiwan is still officially part of China. The PRC government holds out hopes that reunification is possible in the near future, under the guarantee of "one country, two systems." The government and the people in Taiwan are understandably nervous about such a prospect, especially after the events of 1989. From the perspective of the PRC, the issue is made all the more difficult by the economic "miracle" that has been achieved in Taiwan since 1949 and the obvious evidence that capitalism has brought to the people of Taiwan a level of personal wealth far in excess of what has been possible in the mainland. Although the Chinese are constantly aware of its presence, in both symbolic and material terms, Taiwan will not be dealt with as a separate topic because of the thematic organization of this book. In fact, as far as the PRC is concerned, Taiwan is just another province, albeit a very rich one.

CHINA IN THE 1990s: A QUESTION OF FIFTHS

Much of the book focuses on the changes that occurred in China during Deng Xiaoping's leadership in the 1980s. The revolution has now reached middle age; in fact the new China has entered its fifth decade, and it has become clear to outside observers that a mid-life crisis is occurring. The changes have left us outsiders with many unanswered questions. How do the Chinese manage to provide enough food on a daily basis for what amounts to one-fifth of the world's population? This is a particularly important question now that the security of the collective provision of food has been abandoned in favor of privatized agriculture in the Chinese countryside.

We have also been curious about how the Chinese are coping with their attempt to restructure the socialist economy. Deng Xiaoping launched a personal crusade to lead the country toward the Four Modernizations (of industry, agriculture, science and technology, and defense). In spite of the obvious successes, some of the economic experiments have backfired, producing a serious bout of inflation and a devastating rate of unemployment. In the face of the four decades of deprivation the Chinese people have already endured, it will not be easy for the government to convince them that the struggle must continue into the 1990s.

The most important question of all is what the 1990s will hold in store for the rights of the long-suffering Chinese people. Will the fifth decade of the People's Republic of China see, at last, the introduction of the *"fifth modernization,"* the extension of ordinary human rights to more than a billion people? After what happened in Tiananmen Square in 1989, it is difficult to be optimistic about the future, but the "Peace in Beijing" poster expresses a sentiment that is shared around the world (see Figure 1.3).

AN OUTLINE OF THE BOOK

This book has four major goals: (1) It is intended to provide an introduction to the lives of the Chinese people and their landscapes, the places where they live and work. (2) It attempts to introduce a small number of geographical concepts that can be used to describe and interpret the events that have been occurring in contemporary China. (3) The book introduces the reader to the economic reforms that swept through China's urban and rural landscapes during the 1980s. (4) It attempts to evaluate the extent to which the reforms had significantly altered the lives and landscapes of the Chinese people by the end of the 1980s.

Many books written about China begin with a consideration of the effect of geographical variables on social and economic events. The discussion is usually brief, limited to a few pages in the first chapter, and the issues raised are rarely referred to again in the body of the text. In most cases the effect of geography is considered at a simplistic level—usually involving the influence of physical variables such as climate and topography on the conduct and pattern of human affairs. This book goes beyond the deterministic approach, to illustrate some of the more subtle influences of geography.

Part 1 provides the conceptual underpinning for the exploration of everyday life in contemporary China. Chapter 2 begins by considering some of the concepts of modern geography that can provide a useful framework for interpreting lives and landscapes in China. These include:

- Spatial interaction and the role of distance

Figure 1.3 Peace in Beijing: Banner hanging in downtown Auckland on June 5, 1989, on the route of a silent march in mourning for those massacred in the Tiananmen Square crackdown.

- The two-way relationships between human beings and the physical environment
- The importance of place for human activity and sentiment
- The spatial organization of urban and rural structures
- The demarcation of territory into regions

To present a realistic picture of contemporary China, Part 1 also introduces the reader to the overarching influence of *culture* (in Chapter 3) and *politics* (in Chapter 4) and illustrates some of the ways the Chinese have been shaped by these influences over the centuries.

Part 2 deals with the spatial organization of life in contemporary China. The discussion revolves around the organization of production, distribution, and consumption in the countryside (Chapter 5) and in the cities (Chapter 6). The focus here is on the economic reforms that have so dramatically altered the lives of the Chinese people and their landscapes in the 1980s. Both of these chapters are pivotal for the book, because so much of

the discussion in the subsequent chapters is based on the impacts of the economic reforms. Closely tied to the economic issue is the critical problem of China's population, and Chapter 7 describes and interprets the recent population policies and examines some of the contradictions that have emerged between the economic sphere (production) and the current birth-control policies (reproduction).

The next two chapters deal with the restructuring of space in China, at the city level in Chapter 8, and at the regional level in Chapter 9. At the end of this section, Chapter 10 investigates the relationship between development and environmental degradation in China and the emergence of a rudimentary environmental consciousness by the end of the 1980s.

Part 3 attempts to narrow down the aperture of the study to look at some specific aspects of everyday life in China, particularly in the cities. Chapter 11 deals with the gender issue, which is one of the pieces of unfinished business of the Chinese revolution. The delivery of urban services is discussed in Chapters 12 and 13, and this includes a consideration of food supplies, housing, and a range of other factors that influence the quality of life in a Chinese city. This leaves a consideration of law-and-order issues to the last, but not the least important, chapters of the book. Crime and punishment are covered in Chapter 14; and Chapter 15 shifts attention to the crucial issue of human rights in China. The events of 1989 sent a clear message from the people to the government—unless real progress is made on the issue of freedom and democracy, the economic gains of the previous decade will have amounted to nothing. At the time of this writing (late 1990) the streets of China's cities are quiet again, but history suggests that the quiet is only the lull before the next storm.

China: Geography, Culture, and Politics

■ ═══ ■

Geographical Concepts in the China Context

In Xinjiang . . . even a beggar must ride on a donkey. Otherwise, having eaten his fill in one village, he will starve to death before he reaches the next.

—Zhang Xianliang[1]

INTRODUCTION: GEOGRAPHY AT THE CROSSROADS

One of the most important challenges for modern geography is to move beyond the public perception of it as a purely descriptive discipline. The announcement of a National Geography Awareness Week in the United States in October 1987 provided a real opportunity for academic geography. It is painfully obvious that most Americans have a fundamental lack of knowledge about geography, so the Awareness Week was a much needed public-education campaign. However, what sort of geography should the public know about? Could it be that people in the United States think about geography, not as an academic discipline, but as a category in a television game show? At one level geography *is* about trivia and spatial facts. It deals with where things are; it provides details about the names of rivers, mountains, cities, and continents. All educated people should be familiar with such basic facts, and it is reasonable to assume that anyone who does not know where Beijing is does not know very much else about China. But modern geography can take us much further than the whistle-stop tour of place names and spatial facts. There are a number of concepts within the discipline that provide a unique way of looking at the world and its constituent parts.

Geographers hope that with this way of looking comes a more complete understanding of contemporary China. Before talking about China in a thematic way, therefore, it is useful to review some of these concepts.

DISTANCE AND SPATIAL INTERACTION

The major difference between geography and the other social sciences is that geography is the "where" discipline—it asks questions about where phenomena are located in space, why they are where they are, and what the consequences of their location are. All human phenomena have a unique location, and it follows that the interaction between two people or two places is a function of the distance separating them. A person living in the same neighborhood as her parents is likely to visit (interact with) them more frequently than someone separated by 1,000 miles. Similarly, two cities adjacent to each other will have more trading and travel linkages (interactions) than cities on opposite coasts.

In other words, distance acts as a friction on social interaction. During the Ming Dynasty (1368–1644) it could take as long as six or seven weeks for the imperial courier to arrive in the far southwestern reaches of China. To maintain contact with all of the provinces, the emperor had to build a complex infrastructure of couriers: teams of horses, fleets of boats, and hundreds of foot runners operating between specially provided relay stations.[2] This helps to explain why local officials in China have generally acted more independently the further they were from Beijing. In his book about Tibet, Tom Grunfeld suggested that the vast distance between Lhasa and the nation's capital has contributed to the conflict and lack of understanding between the two. The ancient saying "Heaven is high and the Emperor is in Beijing"[3] reflects a sentiment that has obviously contributed to centrifugal tendencies in Tibet and other remote parts of China. The distance from central authority has allowed people in the far-flung regions of China more room for individual initiative, even evoking a sense of the frontier spirit found in the American West. In Xinjiang Autonomous Region, for example, in-migration rules have continually been stretched to allow in people without official residence permits, contributing to the region's wild-West outlaw character.[4]

As transportation links were made across China, travel times were reduced significantly and people were able to move beyond the confines of their home territory. Personal travel horizons expanded, as did other forms of interaction, especially trading and the circulation of ideas. This effectively reduced the size of the Chinese landmass, although as most visitors to present-day China can still attest, travel across the country remains arduous and time consuming.

It would be wrong, however, to imply that spatial interaction is simply a function of distances and travel times in China, and it is always important to remember the influence of two sets of factors, namely culture and politics (see Chapters 3 and 4). From a cultural perspective, most Westerners are surprised to find that even great distances sometimes do not inhibit human interaction. Chinese families seem to be much more willing than Western families to live apart. Students traveling abroad to study often leave behind new spouses and children, sometimes for years. Couples unable to find work or residence permits in the same location often live apart permanently, with perhaps a two-week vacation together every year. To some extent this represents an adaptation to situations over which people have no real control, but

the Chinese appear to accept stoically what for Westerners would be an extraordinary hardship. Is it possible that Chinese couples can bear to be apart because so many of them marry for functional rather than romantic reasons? This conclusion is supported by the cool, almost offhand, way people announce their separation and by the apparent lack of affection displayed in public between spouses.

As we shall see throughout this book, however, such gross generalizations about Chinese values most often turn out to be oversimplifications. Western conclusions about relationships between the Chinese are probably both presumptuous and erroneous. It may simply be that distance matters very little in a Chinese relationship. The couple separated by thousands of miles may show little outward evidence of unhappiness; and the couple on their honeymoon may act as if they have been together for decades. An ancient Chinese folk saying provides some insight into this puzzling phenomenon: "Karma unites people from a thousand li's apart; the lack of it separates them face to face."[5] The operative word here is "karma," translated from the Chinese word *yuan*, a Buddhist term implying a predestined relationship. Distance per se may not be an important factor in human interactions because of the strongly held belief that relationships are cemented in previous incarnations and are only temporarily reactivated in this life.

Politics plays a major role in all aspects of life in China, so it should come as no surprise that it often perverts normal patterns of spatial interaction. Since 1949, for example, the Chinese government has implemented a number of measures to slow down the growth of cities and to hinder rural-to-urban migration (see Chapter 8). One of the most controversial of these measures was the "sending down" of educated youth from the cities to the countryside in the 1960s and 1970s. This policy not only prevented individuals from making their own decisions about where to live but also physically directed them to specific destinations. The program was intended to reduce the demand for jobs in the cities and expand the educated work force in the countryside, thereby helping to eliminate the dichotomy between city and country in China. In the countryside the youths were expected to be "purified" and freed from all of the "spiritual pollution" from the West:

To revolutionize themselves, educated youths must first turn themselves into laborers. Going to share the bitter and the sweet with the laboring people in the countryside, educated youths can gradually cultivate the habit of doing labor eagerly, establish a correct attitude towards physical labor, [and] reform their nonproletarian thoughts . . . an important guarantee for preventing themselves forever from being corrupted.[6]

The "sending down" of educated youths interfered with traditional patterns of spatial interaction, but geographical factors were important determinants of which youths were chosen. Between 1968 and 1975 an estimated twelve million young people (about 10 percent of the existing urban population) were dispatched to the countryside, but an individual's chances of being sent down were not geographically random. Some cities appeared to send down a much larger proportion of their youth than others. It is difficult to explain such variations without knowing in detail what happened in each city, but it is reasonable to expect that the rates varied with city size, the degree of industrialization, and the extent of Westernization, which would indicate to the Communist party a city greatly in need of revolutionary purification.

Assuming that one of the major goals of the sending-down policy was to provide a stimulus for rural development, we would expect to find that the majority of the youths in question were sent to the most remote and poorly developed parts of China. This happened in many cases, and modern Chinese literature is filled with stories about the plight of youths eking out a miserable existence in faraway places and squabbling with the local peasants (who were usually no happier to receive them than the youths were to be sent). The evidence suggests, however, that the majority of sent-down youth did not end up in the areas most in need of development; in fact, the counties most likely to receive them were the ones closest to provincial capitals and generally the richest and most modernized; they also tended to be at lower altitudes and have good railway connections. In other words these were not the remote and mountainous areas of China; there was a clear tendency for the sent-down youths to end up in nearby destinations. Perhaps this was a compromise that resulted from the over-whelming unpopularity of the policy. Instead of the youths' being sent where they were most needed, many of them were allowed to go to places where they could keep in touch easily with their families.[7]

THE HUMAN-ENVIRONMENT INTERFACE

It is undeniable that the physical environment of China has, over the centuries, acted to influence, and sometimes to determine, the course of human actions. In this sense much of the history of China can be thought of as a human struggle to overcome the constraints of geography and to adapt to the dictates of the environment. The constant shortage of cultivable land and the vicissitudes of the climate have shaped much of the human endeavor of the Chinese peasants.[8] The result is a massively modified landscape made up of countless microgeographies—a mosaic of humanized localities that have emerged from the continuous struggle between the Chinese people and their unyielding land.

In response to the constraints presented by the physical environment, human beings appear to have an unlimited capacity for modifying the territories they inhabit. From the earliest times and the establishment of rudimentary shelters to the development of tools and the selection and crossbreeding of plants, the major theme of human life has been change and adaptation. Wherever they have lived, people have found it necessary to tinker with almost everything in an effort to make life more agreeable for themselves. As a result, in each locality landscapes gradually evolved reflecting the cultural values of the inhabitants. In China the presence of more than fifty ethnic-minority groups helped to produce through the centuries a patchwork of cultural landscapes that reflected intimate details of the values of the people who lived on the land. This was true even of the very earliest hunters and gatherers in China. Peking Man, for example, who appeared in the Middle Pleistocene epoch, perhaps 300,000 to 500,000 years ago, knew how to use fire. He was probably the first hominid in China to alter the landscape significantly:

He had habitual campsites; he wore paths out from them that became bordered by trailside weeds that took advantage of the added sunlight and tolerated tramping and other disturbances. Seeds and roots were dropped along the trails . . . and some of them grew and reproduced themselves. Kitchen refuse, thrown out about the camps, enriched the soil with ashes and nitrogenous matter, and new combinations of plants found advantage in the altered soil . . . if fires were set . . . at first to facilitate collecting and then as a hunting device, a most potent aid to vegetative modification was assured.⁹

After nearly four thousand years of occupancy and continual modification, the Chinese land has become perhaps the most humanized in the world. As one geographer noted, "More people have lived in China than anywhere else. Upward of 10 billion human beings have moved across her good earth; nowhere have so many people lived so intimately with nature. A thousand generations have left their indelible impressions on soil and topography, so that scarcely a square foot of earth remains unmodified."¹⁰

The changes inflicted on the landscape by Peking Man, and subsequently by millions of peasants scratching away at the soil with little more than their hands, were slow to take effect. By comparison, the changes that occurred during the twentieth century with the industrialization of the Chinese countryside have produced landscapes that differ by quantum leaps from those of only a few decades ago. The pace of change during the past century can be illustrated by considering the evolution of an unpromising corner of the Qing Empire lying off the southern coast of Guangdong Province. It was more than 2,400 kilometers from Beijing—two-to-three weeks' journey even by the fastest courier. In 1840 there were no settlements larger than small market hamlets; the place had precious few resources; and most of the land was too mountainous to farm. The climate was miserably hot and humid most of the year, and vile diseases like malaria, cholera, and typhoid were endemic. Human life and landscape there had changed very little for centuries, but the place was alive with wildlife of all types. "There were leopards, tigers, badgers, Chinese otters, pangolins, wild cats and boars . . . there were also crab-eating mongooses, an unusual variety of newt, two hundred kinds of butterfly and thirty-two kinds of snake, including the flower-pot snake, the

white-lipped viper and the rock python, which grew up to sixteen feet long and could swallow a dog."¹¹

Most people in China, except for the few ethnic-minority groups who called it home, considered the little area just described too peripheral to worry about, and there was scarcely a murmur in 1840 when it was surrendered to the British in a treaty that ended a period of hostility in Chinese waters. During the next 130 years, however, that place would undergo a transformation of stupefying proportions. A godforsaken corner of the empire became the place known to the world as Hong Kong. By the 1960s it had become a futuristic metropolis—the busiest, richest, and the most extraordinary of all Chinese cities.

This was a remarkable change of landscape in such a short time, and today Hong Kong sits at the foot of the PRC, in sharp contrast to the drab "producer" cities of socialist China. Hong Kong was created by the urges of European, Chinese, and American enterprise, and the productive city-state that we see today symbolizes capitalism at its most successful.

As the example of Hong Kong suggests, the way a landscape is fashioned depends on both the physical characteristics of the environment in question and the cultural values of its inhabitants. In the far-northwestern regions of China, where the land is mountainous, the soils are thin and sandy, and the weather alternates between hot and dry and cold and dry, the landscape modifications will be quite different from those possible in the humid lands of southeast China. There are also many differences in the types of people who inhabit these contrasting lands. The explorer or the gazetteer may seek out the wilderness corners of northwest China to experience the exotic beauty of the landscape. For such a traveler, places are valued mostly for their aesthetic beauty, for the physical sensation they can impart, or even for the information they provide in the compendium of geographical knowledge.

The Chinese peasants, however, would probably view the same landscapes very differently. Their entire lives may be spent within a few miles of the places where they are born. Their involvement with the land is, by force of circumstance, total. They depend on the land for their survival but they care little for how it looks. By contrast, to the artists and intellectuals in China's past, the landscape was a magical place. For them the environment was a special commodity to be shaped, teased, and manicured into gardens and parks. The landscape was not just something to be looked at: It was in fact "an enveloping atmosphere [into] which the scholar-official [could] escape for a short period of time."[12] The ancient reverence of the Chinese gentry for the landscape contrasts starkly with the utilitarian view dominant in socialist China, where the environment is perceived mainly as a resource to be exploited, without regard for the consequences (see Chapter 10). In the Maoist version of Marxism, for example, the Chinese people are embroiled in an almost constant struggle to transform nature through their own labor—either to make it work for them or to make themselves safe from its ravages.[13]

Chinese history demonstrates that relations between people and their environments are often contradictory, in that the environment is both a resource for and a constraint to development. In the struggle to resolve this contradiction, humans usually manage to "defeat" the environment.[14] A tree is generally seen as a provider of wood for fuel or furniture, rather than as an aesthetic object. When a tree is cut down, however, far more than a visual and physical resource is used up—its ability to provide shelter against wind and water erosion, and to put nutrients back into the soil, is lost forever.

Mao Zedong's views on the struggle between people and the environment were illustrated in his version of the ancient fable of Yu Kung, the "Foolish Old Man Who Removed the Mountain." Mao altered the original story to apply it to the class struggle of the Chinese proletariat. The physical environment (to be struggled with) represents the two "mountains" of feudal and capitalist opposition. The Old Fool, in spite of being ridiculed by his neighbors, finally managed, through his incredible determination, to move the two mountains outside his home. He said, "When I die, my sons will carry on; when they die, there will be my grandsons, and then their sons and grandsons, and so on to infinity."[15] Mao was suggesting that the Chinese people could, if they were sufficiently motivated and effectively organized, move their own mountain, accomplish miracles, and remake their own history.

To some people, Mao's views reveal a tyrannical and domineering attitude toward the Chinese environment: It must at all times be subservient to human needs. Although this appears to be the case, such a view was by no means new with Mao Zedong or the Chinese Communists—in fact the Chinese have historically gone in for spectacular transformations of nature, as with the Great Wall and the Grand Canal. Since the Stone Age, Chinese peasants have "struggled to transform nature and remove mountains, not to mention forests."[16] It is ironic that Mao's views toward nature may have stemmed from his intellectual roots in Confucian reformism. Most Westerners associate Confucianism only with the well-documented esoteric reverence for and stewardship of the environment, but there was also a much more practical side to Confucianism in the nineteenth century, one that involved an attempt to promote modernization and national integration.[17] It was from this branch of Confucianism that Mao received his early inspiration, long before he had even heard of Marxism.

THE IMPORTANCE OF PLACE

Space is the territory that separates human phenomena. This means that space, in addition to having physical characteristics, is an abstract concept: All phenomena are located in space and can therefore be defined in spatial terms. Thus a Chinese village can be described either by its latitudinal and longitudinal coordinates (absolute location) or by its distance from the capital city (relative location). The spatial coordinates tell us very little about the village, other than providing a rough idea of what the ˙climate is like and indicating some of its broad regional characteristics.

Most of the habitable space in China (that which is not too mountainous, too dry, or too frozen to live in) has been occupied for centuries and transformed by human activity. The ground has been trampled on by millions of people, and although there are older lands in other parts of the world, "none have developed a more mature adjustment between man and environment."[18] As this process of humanization continues, spaces gradually become shaped into places. From an abstraction, a piece of territory becomes a center of human meaning, a place where humans live. Thus the essential importance of a place is not its location or the functions the location serves—it is the meaning it has for its residents.

> There is virtually for everyone a deep association with and a consciousness of the places where we were born and grew up, where we live now, or where we have had some particularly moving experiences. This association seems to constitute a vital source of both individual and cultural identity and security, a point of departure from which we orient ourselves in the world. A French philosopher, Gabriel Marcel . . . has summarized this simply: "An individual is not distinct from his place; he is that place."[19]

It has been suggested that the tendency for humans to identify with their home place has been stronger in China than in most other parts of the world. It is impossible to verify this statement, but there is ample evidence that Chinese people are strongly rooted to the place of their birth. For the peasants this intense localism has not been a matter of choice. Their traditional position on the bottom rung of the social ladder has consigned them to spending most of their working lives engaged in agricultural production to support the landed elite. Peasants simply have not had the time, money, or energy needed to look beyond their village and its immediate marketing area or to think about traveling to other regions. Naturally this has produced in many parts of China an extreme level of isolation and backwardness. In his travels across China in the late 1940s, the U.S. journalist Jack Belden found some pockets of isolation even in the densely populated provinces of the North China Plain. He asked the reader to consider what life must have been like in a Chinese village.

> Almost completely outside the influence of modern science and twentieth century culture, the peasant was a brutal, blundering backwoodsman. He had never seen a movie, never heard a radio, never ridden in a car. He had never owned a pair of leather shoes, nor a toothbrush and seldom a piece of soap. And if he was a mountain man, he perhaps bathed twice in his life—once when he was married and once when he died—not because he so much enjoyed wallowing in the dirt, but because water was scarce and could be spared only for drinking.[20]

The situation for women was much worse than it was for men because women were rarely allowed to leave their husband's village once they had married. Missionary Arthur Smith met a woman who told him that in her next life she wanted to be a dog because she would have more freedom. Smith wrote, "Most Chinese girls [at the end of the nineteenth century] never go anywhere to speak of, and live what is literally the existence of a frog in a well. Tens of thousands of them have never been two miles away from the village."[21]

The strong sense of attachment to locality has contributed to the centrifugal tendencies within China over the centuries. For the relatively few people who did travel beyond their homes, this attachment provided them with an identity. Two people meeting for the first time would introduce themselves by ascertaining each other's native place, which was usually more important than their surnames. If a person moved away from home, it was taken for granted that he would sooner or later return to his native place. "The normative pattern was clear: a young man who left to seek his fortune elsewhere was expected to return home for marriage, to spend there an extended period of mourning on the death of either parent, and eventually to retire in the locality where his ancestors were buried."[22]

The strength of the attachment to one's home place is illustrated by the desire among people who have permanently left their homes to be buried in their native soil. In most cities in the late imperial times, there were associations of these "sojourners" from different parts of China. The members of the groups would maintain cemeteries so that people who were unable to go back home to die could at least be buried close to others from their home districts.[23]

In life the strength of the attachment to home place was equally strong. For example, among the businessmen from Ningbo who moved to Shanghai in the nineteenth century and experienced great financial success, hiring practices were based predominantly on geographical principles. The first to be hired would be kinsmen from Ningbo (sons, then nephews, then other relatives); next would be people from the same city; then the same county; then the same region of the province.[24]

The businessmen were also likely to endow their home place with some of the profits they had amassed. "Successful emigrants were expected to expand their family estates back home, to endow their lineages, and to invest in community property . . . [many] also retired to their native places, having ensured the continuity of their businesses abroad by grooming kinsmen or fellow natives for management."[25]

People who had moved involuntarily to a new place would work hard to attach themselves to that place. In Zhang Xinxin and Sang Ye's book *Chinese Lives*, Old Lady Zhang describes her life in a tiny village in a remote corner of Shanxi Province. She moved there in a marriage swap arranged by her parents, and when she arrived she was distressed to find her new home was not even marked on a 1:100,000 map; it had no water, no electricity, and no paved roads! Nevertheless, as she said, "People are like grass. They grow where the seed drops and that is where they belong."[26] After the seed has taken root, it is almost as if the meaning of one's home place is stamped indelibly in a person's brain, to such an extent that a separation becomes a painful experience. The length of time spent away from one's "true" home may not be important. Arthur Smith, for example, told of a man who had been gone from his native village for twenty years. He finally returned unannounced and immediately went about his business as if he had never been away. "[He] . . . enters his house, throws down his bundle and without a question or a greeting to anyone, proceeds to take a solacing smoke. He may have been away so long that no one recognizes him, and perhaps he is taken for a tramp. . . . But he merely replies 'Why should I not make myself at home in my house?' and resumes his smoking, leaving [the] details to be filled in later."[27]

The attachment to one's native soil is often strong enough to overcome even the most successful of transplantations in "foreign" lands. Describing Chinese village life, Martin C. Yang wrote about some of the men who had moved to Manchuria and established profitable farms, married local women, and started families. In spite of their successful lives they longed to return to their beloved Shandong. As Yang pointed out, such men still had "a deep-rooted passion for the place

of their ancestors. They . . . [could not] resist the idea of coming back home."[28] When they finally returned, they often found that very little had changed—usually people were doing almost exactly what their ancestors had been doing hundreds of years earlier.

Over the centuries the occupants of any patch of land change the landscape. In this way the fields and villages come to look uniquely Chinese. Some people believe that different cultures are able to imprint their values in a unique way, effectively leaving a permanent "signature" on the landscape. René Dubos, for example, felt that his fellow Frenchmen would, if transplanted onto the Russian steppes, sooner or later produce a uniquely French-looking landscape, given modifications for climate and topography.

In a similar way, many travelers to China are convinced that they have seen and can readily identify unmistakably Chinese landscapes, for example, in Chinatowns all around the world. Although such places are uniquely Chinese, they are in fact highly manufactured landscapes; morevoer, what we generally identify as "Chineseness"—the noise, the neon signs, and the crowdedness—are in fact mainly symbols of capitalist Chinatowns (especially Hong Kong), and they bear little resemblance to the cities in mainland China (with the exception of "Old Town" in Shanghai, which is preserved mainly as a tourist attraction).

This is not to deny that there are some quintessentially Chinese landscape characteristics. Outsiders are most likely to define as "Chineseness" the "lived-in" quality of the landscape, whether it is urban or rural. The process of making a space into a place and imbuing it with human meaning usually takes centuries, but in some cases it may happen very quickly. For example, a new town in suburban Hong Kong, near the PRC border, may begin life as little more than a collection of vapid high-rises. After occupation, however, they are quickly transformed into "Chinese" places. The British travel writer Jan Morris has described this incredible transformation.

Hardly have the first Chinese families moved into their apartments, still smelling of paint and cement, than everything changes. Almost overnight, that monolithic cheerlessness is dispelled. The first lines of washing appear, the first advertising signs go up, the first street stall opens for business, the first restaurant announces its opening night—and next time you go back, all that cold new place is made real and vivid by the organic energy of Chinese life, its fructifying untidiness, its boisterous lack of privacy, its comforting pandemonium and its inescapable air of purpose.[29]

For the Chinese, according to Morris at least, it is easy to create places, but we should recall that it is also easy to destroy them through carelessness or even deliberate vandalism. During the Cultural Revolution there was a strong urge to remove from the landscape everything that was old and "feudal." In Beijing this meant replacing the imperial symbols and landmarks with others that would stress the city's role as a new socialist capital.[30] Outsiders have viewed this transformation harshly. After nearly four decades of socialist city planning, Beijing, according to one traveler, has been turned into "an anonymous conglomerate of roads, buildings and squares that one can hardly call a city . . . a capital which is neither Chinese nor socialist, unless socialism must mean monotony, desolation, lack of fantasy and of vitality."[31] After Liberation, Beijing's planners began to dismantle the city's triumphal arches of marble and painted wood that had straddled the streets for hundreds of years and had been originally built to honor people and events. The excuse given was that they hindered the flow of traffic on the city streets, but perhaps they were eliminated because they were reminders "of old virtues and values which the new regime did not want the people to treasure any more."[32]

Just as the meaning of places can be deliberately destroyed, it is also possible for people deliberately to avoid assigning meaning to places. Colin Thubron met a young man in Qinghai Province, for example, who had been exiled there during the Cultural Revolution. He hated the place, despised its isolation, and was perplexed by its ethnic people. Sitting gloomily in his bare one-room apartment, he longed for his native Shanghai. "He glanced around at his botched walls dribbling loose plaster, pitted with nail holes for vanished scrolls or posters. In protest or hope, he had done nothing to the place since his arrival. To clothe it would make it more permanent."[33]

REGIONS AND REGIONALIZATION

The spaces and places of a country as large as China need to be organized conceptually, and to achieve this the geographer establishes boundaries and creates (or identifies) regions. To the geographer the region is a way of bringing some intellectual structure to the study of localities. When boundaries are drawn, territory is delimited and it becomes possible to organize the study of the spaces within. Thus at the aggregate level, China can be mapped by its physiographic regions, within which there is some degree of continuity in terms of climate and topography. Economic regions describe territory within which there are identifiable patterns of spatial interaction, usually measured by trading and other economic activities. Superimposed onto such regions, often without coinciding exactly, are cultural regions defined by patterns of language or ethnicity. At yet another level we find political regions, often drawn along geographical boundaries, to delimit administrative chunks of territory—and again, there may be little or no correspondence between these boundaries and those of the other types of regions.

The vast human and physical diversity across the Chinese land has produced some easily identifiable regions. At many times in the past, the forces favoring such regional demarcations have been a considerable obstacle to national integration. Thus, instead of developing into one huge interacting and interconnected whole, China has historically been subdivided into a number of clearly identifiable and independent regions that tend to have little interaction between them. Perhaps the best known of the regional subdivisions are the eight "macroregions" identified by Skinner.[34] Although the boundaries of these regions are drawn largely along physiographic lines such as rivers or mountain ranges, Skinner argued that within each region integrated socioeconomic systems have developed over time. Specifically, Skinner suggested that in each of the regions separate urban systems developed. As a result, China had not (by the twentieth century at least) developed a single, integrated urban system. Instead there was a mosaic of regional systems, each of which was only marginally connected with its neighbors. This lack of cross-regional interaction was largely a result of the great distances involved and the high costs (in time and money) of long-distance transportation.[35]

Skinner's regions provide a more accurate picture of the pattern of social and spatial interaction in Late Imperial China than do the provincial boundaries (see Figures 2.1 and 2.2). His boundary lines have provided a conceptually coherent way of evaluating the evolution of Chinese economic life, and they have been particularly useful for helping to explain why China, as a whole, did not experience the level of economic development and technological transformation that occurred elsewhere.[36] It seems that over the centuries the economic fortunes of China have evolved largely at the regional level, and what happened in one region has not necessarily had much to do with what happened elsewhere, even in adjacent regions.

It is an elementary fact of political life that large pieces of territory need to be divided into smaller areas for administrative purposes. The world is divided into nation-states, and each of these is subdivided, in different ways, into successively smaller territorial units, all the way down to the family and individual level. There are two major justifications for this division of territory. From the perspective of the national government, dividing up the territory eases the business of government by creating spatial units that are administratively more manageable. In a country the size of China this division helps the government to exercise control over its territory and to stand fast against the natural centrifugal tendencies in the provinces. From the perspective of the citizens, dividing up territory provides individuals and communities larger groups to identify with, thereby helping them to represent themselves and their wishes and to protect their best interests. Ideally the spatial units selected can fulfill both sets of functions harmoniously, satisfying the government and the people. In many cases, however, this does not occur, as when religious or ethnic-minority groups find that their best interests are clearly not being served by the existing regional divisions of territory (as in the case of present-day Tibet).

Chinese governments have historically experienced great difficulty organizing their far-flung territories. To remain in power, a government has to prove to its people that the tasks of government can be carried out. Local needs have to be satisfied; law and order must be maintained; and the government's policies need to be implemented. In China, however, the size of the country, its regional variations in physical and human terms, and the difficulty of moving across the land have all added to the difficulties in achieving such goals. In the face of such obstacles it is remarkable that from the Qin Dynasty (221–207 B.C.) all the way through to the end of the Qing Dynasty in 1911, a succession of governments was able to establish centralized control of Chinese territory and thereby legitimate themselves.[37]

During this 2,000-year period the urban system gradually evolved. Across the nation there was established a series of towns that were the administrative outposts of the central government, providing the political linkages needed to hold the vast Chinese land together. The result was a system of cities in China that was unlike anything in other countries at the same time. China had cities at all levels in the spatial hierarchy, all the way from the capital to the county level. In other countries the system was usually far less "mature," with a typical pattern of "primacy" developing, in which there was one vast city (or possibly two), and thousands of small towns, with very little in between.[38]

By comparison, the Chinese landscape was dotted, at least in the densely populated areas, with a network of county (or *xian*) towns. The result was that few people were very far away from an urban center of some size, and from such cities the central government's policies could be administered.

After 1949 the Chinese Communist party (CCP) instituted a series of changes in the regional division of Chinese territory. The changes reflected both the reality of the times and the needs of the CCP in establishing its legitimacy. The basic element of the new system was a division of territory into twenty-one provinces (see Figure 2.2). In addition, the characteristics and needs of two other types of areas dictated the formation of special administrative units: (1) The country's three largest cities (Beijing, Tianjin, and Shanghai) were designated as special municipalities; and (2) five autonomous regions (ARs) were created in peripheral areas that had high proportions

Figure 2.1 Skinner's macroregions of agrarian China: Regional core areas are shaded; boundaries between regions are natural features, mostly rivers and mountain ranges. Reprinted from The City in Late Imperial China, *p. 214, edited by G. William Skinner, with the permission of the publishers, Stanford University Press. © 1977 by the Board of Trustees of the Leland Stanford Junior University.*

of ethnic-minority people. Although they were referred to as "autonomous," these new territories were not politically independent from Beijing, but they did receive different treatment in a number of policy areas. This first tier of spatial organization was supplemented by a system of prefectures, autonomous prefectures, and counties (see Figure 2.3).[39]

Geographical subdivisions below the county level vary depending on whether the region in question is primarily urban or rural in character. In the countryside the counties are now subdivided into townships, which administer their constituent villages (or production teams). Between 1958 and 1980, however, the counties were divided up into

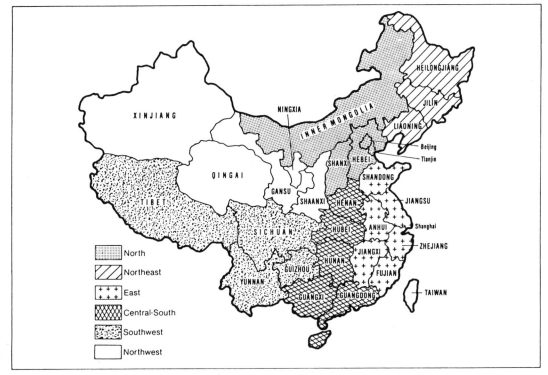

Figure 2.2 China's provinces and geographical regions, including Taiwan, still considered a province by the PRC government. Hainan Island became a province in the late 1980s. Source: S. Goldstein, 1985, "Urbanization in China: New Insight from the 1982 Census," Papers of the East-West Population Institute, No. 93 (July), Honolulu, p. 22; reprinted by permission.

communes, for administrative and political purposes, with production occurring at the lower levels of production brigades, production teams, and work groups. As a result of the agricultural reforms in the 1980s, much of this collective organization in the countryside has now been dismantled, and the majority of the communes' functions have been shifted back to the township (Figure 2.3).

SPATIAL ORGANIZATION

The CCP, when it began to orchestrate China's economic and political recovery, approached the cities with some trepidation. Triumphant as they were in 1949, the Communists found chronic food shortages in the cities, poor or nonexistent services, and a chaotic administrative system. After an initial period in which the major focus was to establish military control, concerted efforts were made to install a working civil administration in each city.

The Communists had a utopian view of the sort of city they wanted to see developed in China, a view in sharp contrast to the teeming decadence they found in the Western-influenced "Treaty Port" cities along the east coast. The latter were the coastal and inland river port cities that had been opened up for foreign trade and development in the latter part of the nineteenth century. To help introduce the necessary changes, the Communists established a new pattern of spatial organization within all the larger cities. Through this tightly knit system it would be possible to administer the policies of the central government all the way down to the household level.

To begin building the new socialist city, the Party wanted to ensure that all individuals and families were functionally connected to an organizational structure subordinated to the Communist party. No one was to live in

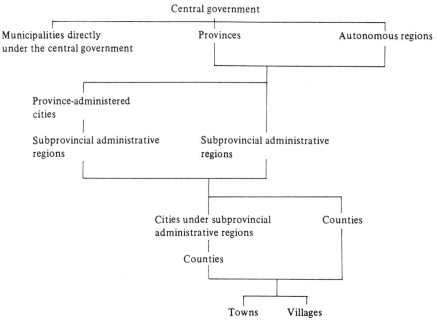

Figure 2.3 *The spatial organization of urban and rural territory, post-1984: The communes have been virtually disbanded, and most of the prefectures have disappeared. Source: R. Kojimo, 1987,* Urbanization and Urban Problems in China *(Tokyo: Institute of Developing Economies, Occasional Paper Series No. 22), pp. 102–103; reprinted by permission.*

an isolated family—everyone was to become part of a local group of citizens. Such arrangements were not unfamiliar to the residents of China's cities; in fact in the past many people had belonged to autonomous guilds or neighborhood associations, but in most cases these old groups had been established by local activists to perform certain tasks. Moreover, membership in them was usually voluntary.

The new system of urban spatial organization was unusual in that it was created, not in an ad hoc fashion, but deliberately, from above, and it was meant to be a fully integrated network of local territories at all levels in the hierarchy. The organizations at the bottom would, in other words, be connected with the higher-level organizations, all the way to the very top, in Beijing. The intention was for this top-down administrative system to facilitate the flow of authority downward from the government to the people.

This pattern of spatial organization was very different from the sort of bottom-up structure that could typically be found in a U.S. city. In the United States we might expect to see a loose collection of grass-roots local

groups, usually operating at the neighborhood level, each one focusing on a specific task.

The fundamental goal of the new urban structure was to assist the government in establishing law and order and to carry out government policies. It was also hoped that the new structures would provide a vehicle for mobilizing the population and raising political consciousness at the local level. Another potential goal was to provide an outlet for the people to express their views about the government's policies and to help the people develop their own initiatives. In actual fact this sort of decentralization was rarely possible—and for most of the time since 1949 the flow of information and the chain of command have remained solidly unidirectional (downward). In addition to the major law-and-order function and the implementation of central policy, the new neighborhood-level organizations were involved in the provision of a variety of local services, which will be described more fully in Chapter 12.[40]

From the very beginning the activities of the new neighborhood organizations overlapped significantly with those of the police; in fact the first organizations began by expanding the role of the local police stations to take on civil administrative functions. In the early 1950s there were experiments in Tianjin and Shanghai to create totally new organizations. Residents' committees were established as the first step in an effort to supplement the activities of both the local police station and the various local ad hoc groups that had sprung up naturally. The goal was to provide a more uniform and integrated structure of local organizations. The new committees were intended to assist the city's district-level operation of government and extend the activities at the local level. Their tasks included such activities as dispute mediation, sanitation works, and local educational campaigns.[41]

After a few years of experimentation, the residents' committees were extended to all cities in 1954 by government directive.[42] In the following years two types of local organizations emerged: one based on employment or production units (the work unit, or *danwei*); and the other based solely in residential areas. The functions of the two were different, and some people had to belong to both, for example, if they worked in a specific unit but happened to live in a totally different neighborhood.

The new system of spatial organization greatly facilitated the task of urban government. The residents' committees, with the help of the local police stations, were involved primarily in mediating disputes between residents and providing security at the local level. Over time, however, the committees have taken on numerous other functions, for example, local clean-up efforts, tree-planting campaigns, and, beginning in the 1970s, family-planning activities.[43]

The spatial organization of a typical Chinese city involves the following hierarchy (see Figure 2.4 for the specific example of Beijing in 1980):

- There are a small number of very large urban districts, each with several hundred thousand residents (10 districts in Beijing and 6 in Guangzhou, for example).
- Each district is divided into urban neighborhoods, with from 2,000 to 10,000 families. At both the district and urban-neighborhood levels, officials are appointed from above.
- Each neighborhood is divided into residents' committees, which include between 100 and 800 families;
- Each residents' committee is further subdivided into residents' courtyards or residents' buildings, usually containing between 15 and 40 families.
- At the lowest level there may be small residents' groups, with 8 to 15 individuals in each one, working on specific tasks.

In this way, or with slight variations on this basic model, the Chinese city came to have a highly structured spatial organization, strengthened (in terms of government-control functions) by the affiliation with the police. In many cases the neighborhood-affairs office is located close to, and in fact often next door to, the Public Security Bureau (the police station). The police are usually local residents who are well known to everyone in the neighborhood. They maintain up-to-date records on everyone who is legally registered to live in the neighborhood, and more important, they know who does not belong in the neighborhood.[44] A policeman or -woman may be designated to supervise one or two residents' committees: His or her jobs might include keeping the register up-to-date, watching out for suspicious activities, and generally keeping their ears close to the ground.

Officials at all levels of the hierarchy report to the next highest level. For example, at the neighborhood level there is a director of the neighborhood office who reports to the mayor. Once a decision is made at the top, by the Party, it can therefore be executed immediately through all levels of the geographical hierarchy. In this way the CCP has been able to strengthen its hold over the cities, and at the same time it has provided a mechanism (at least in theory) for people at the local level to get involved in running their own affairs.

In spite of the overall efficiency of this system of spatial organization, there is widespread evidence that the residents' committees generate very little enthusiasm, and often outright hostility, among the locals. This is largely because of the social-control function they perform, which requires excessive amounts of local-level surveillance and "busybodying." It is precisely this constant watchfulness that helps to make the system work— there are very few surprises in an urban

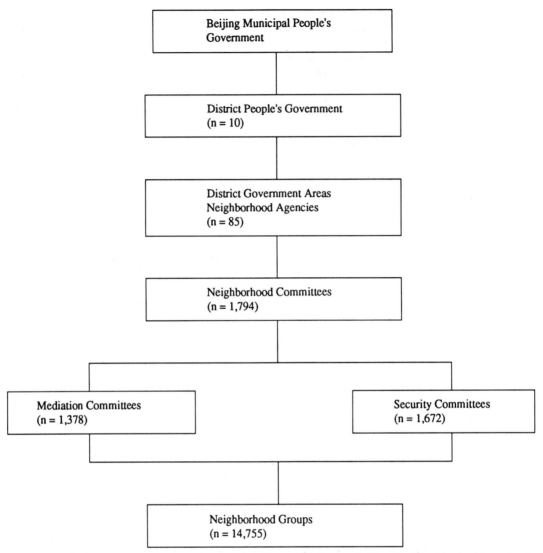

Figure 2.4 The spatial organization of the city of Beijing, 1980. Source: Beijing Review, No. 44 (November 3, 1980), p. 19.

neighborhood, and the presence of a newcomer or anyone doing something out of the ordinary quickly becomes common knowledge through the local information network. There are dozens of pairs of eyes and ears, all of them finely tuned to monitor untoward activities.

For ordinary citizens, however, the pervasiveness of the local-surveillance activity is tiresome and often infuriating. This is nicely illustrated in Zhang Jie's short story called "The Ark," which revolves around the lives of three divorced women who live together in an apartment. Partly because they have politically questionable backgrounds, but also because they are divorcées, they find themselves constantly under the watchful eyes of Mrs. Jia, the head of their courtyard committee. One day Mrs. Jia pays them a visit, on the pretext of looking for her cat, but probably just to snoop around to see if they are doing anything she should know about. During the conversation it becomes clear that she suspects the divorcées of some (unspecified) immoralities.

"Has our cat by any chance come over to your place?" [Mrs. Jia says].

"No," Jinghua [one of the divorced women] replied quickly. "Why should it come here?"

"Oh dear, Comrade Cao. Don't you know? Your cat has been paying court to all six of our toms." And she tittered sarcastically.

"Could single cats [the divorced woman thought] really evoke the same disapproval as single women? Perhaps they ought to marry Maotou [the cat] off as quickly as possible!"[45]

At this point Mrs. Jia retreats, unable to find any evidence to put into the files. She is of course more convinced than ever of the lax moral standards of single women, so lax that their behavior could even rub off onto the cat.

The unpopularity of the residents' committees has been compounded by their role in helping to administer some very loathsome campaigns at the local level. In the 1960s and 1970s, for example, they were called on to recruit the local educated youth who would be sent down to the countryside. The unpopularity of this campaign is easy to comprehend, in the sense that the residents were being required to send their own children away from home, often permanently. It is no surprise to discover that many corrupt practices emerged as families tried to find ways to wriggle out of their responsibilities.

The net effect of the extension of the top-down organizational structure is that many people live in a state of constant fear. A knock on the door could be the local security officials, often referred to within the neighborhoods as the "policemen with small feet."[46] The local police have extensive powers to search and seize. No one is safe, even in his or her own home, because the police "can at any time enter people's homes, inquire about what's cooking in the pot, and look under the bed, allegedly to check whether the family abides by the rules laid down by the hygiene campaign, but actually to check whether anything or anybody is hiding underneath."[47]

There is no doubt that the local organizations have performed valuable services in implementing difficult and highly unpopular policies, none more so than the widely detested one-child-per-family policy, as well as the very difficult task of controlling crime. These are jobs that probably could not have been performed without the constant face-to-face interaction and surveillance made possible by this complex of local-level organizations. Nevertheless, they are a constant reminder that no one has a right to privacy. In China one's home is certainly not a castle: "Through the unit where he works, through the street committee where he lives, every Chinese is constantly under scrutiny, under the control of the one organization, the Public Security Bureau, that presides over his whole life and sets the range of the path within which he can move."[48]

A COGNITIVE MAP OF THE BOOK

This chapter has introduced some of the important concepts within modern geography and has illustrated how they might be significant in the context of contemporary China. In the rest of the book the reader should be able to see the importance of these concepts for interpreting specific events and phenomena and how the concepts are illustrated by such events and phenomena. To provide a guide for that intellectual process, Table 2.1 acts as a "cognitive map" for the remaining chapters of the book, pointing out some of the instances in which the different concepts can be applied.

Table 2.1 Geographical Concepts in the China Context: A Cognitive Map of the Book

Chapter Number and Title	Distance and Spatial Interaction	Human/Environment Interaction	The Importance of Place	Regions and Regionalization	Spatial Organization
3. The Changing Shape of Chinese Cultural Values	Apparent tolerance for high-density living among the Chinese Reduction of social and spatial inter-action networks during the Cultural Revolution	Ambivalent attitudes toward the environment in China, producing degradation	Knowing one's place in Confucian China (esp. important for women, children, and peasants) Importance of the place of ancestors' birth to the Chinese	"Mapping" of cultural traits to produce contiguous regions	
4. The Changing Nature of Chinese Political Values	The importance of politics in distri-bution of wealth and power (who gets what, when, and where) Guanxi as the science of developing connections and improving inter-actions Increased urban and rural interaction as Chinese cities develop agriculture and the countryside indus-trializes "Sending-down" of political opponents and potential troublemakers	Homogenization of Chinese landscape as the countryside indus-trializes and the cities develop agri-culture Spatial and environ-mental influences and determinants on the etiology of poverty in rural China	The forced attachment to home place among China's millions of poor peasants in prerevolutionary times	Communist "base areas" in the remote rural regions, easy to defend, remote from the enemy Regional impacts of changes in political/economic strategies of development Spatial comparative advantage	The peoples' communes as the new level of spatial organization in the countryside

Chapter Number and Title	Distance and Spatial Interaction	Human/Environment Interaction	The Importance of Place	Regions and Regionalization	Spatial Organization
5. Agriculture in China: Feeding a Billion	Geographic constraints (size, transport, population) on agricultural development	The shortage of cultivable land in China as the result of climatic and topographic influences and urban encroachment The role of the agricultural responsibility system in environmental degradation	Peasant attachments to place, based on centuries of subsistence agriculture, are altered by the new collectivization in the 1950s and the move to develop the commune system	The spatial pattern of high grain yields and multiple cropping The mosaic of agricultural practices across the Chinese territory	The evolution of different socio/spatial/administrative structures from land reform through to the household responsibility system The commune as the lowest level of central government and the highest level of rural organization
6. Economic Restructuring: The Chinese Perestroika	Very little inter-regional and core-periphery interaction (trade and population flows) in ancient and recent China Conflicts between center and periphery dealt with by decentralization of decisionmaking after 1978 Changing patterns of rural-to-urban migration and its impacts on city growth Location of new Special Economic Zones vis-à-vis Hong Kong and Taiwan (influence of proximity in selection process?) The influence of China's chronically poor transportation system on economic development	The potential for environmental degradation that results from a rapid push for industrial development	The impact of changing political and economic policies on the extent to which China's rural and urban residents are tied to their existing home places	The traditional regional imbalance in ancient and modern China Regional specialization and comparative advantage Local self-sufficiency during the Maoist era Breakdown of the function of administrative regions after economic reform and replacement with more "natural" or "market" regions The establishment of new (functional) city regions with the urban annexation of rural counties	The Communist-inspired spatial organization of administrative territory is altered by the new market socialist reforms in the 1980s

25

Chapter Number and Title	Distance and Spatial Interaction	Human/Environment Interaction	The Importance of Place	Regions and Regionalization	Spatial Organization
7. China's Population: Production, Reproduction, and the Role of the State	The diffusion of population across Chinese territory

Spatial organization allows intimate (face-to-face) contact to spread both the idea and the technology of birth-control

The diffusion and adoption of new contraceptive methods across space

Out-migration of young unmarried women in the countryside prevented by agricultural reforms | Spatial variations in the ability of the Chinese land to support human populations at high density

Variations in adoption rates and success of birth-control policies influenced by spatial and environmental factors | Constant population pressures on both the rural and urban land produce attenuated ties to localities in the post-1949 era | The spatial variations in population density

Regions with high rates of poverty and/or minorities receive exemptions from birth-control policies | The role of spatial administrative/organization in implementing the birth-control policies (comparisons between cities and the countryside) |
| 8. The City in China | The lack of spatial interaction at the national and inter-regional levels in traditional China

Intraregional and intra-urban interaction only (Skinner's "macroregions")

Economic reforms result in new patterns of trade and migration | Maoist planning to rebuild Chinese cities in the image of socialism

New moral landscape of the socialist city

Post-1978 economic reforms eventually produce a new "landscape of consumption"

Environmental issues and city "beautification" become important issues for city planners | Planners in the Maoist period attempt to eliminate class-based identification with specific territory and places

The new city was intended to reflect the new values of socialist China | Skinner's "macroregions"

Regional self-sufficiency in terms of food

Concentric agricultural zones at the urban fringe

Regional inequality begins to widen as a result of economic reforms | The reorganization of territory to create new city-led structures; and the annexation of rural counties |

Chapter Number and Title	Distance and Spatial Interaction	Human/Environment Interaction	The Importance of Place	Regions and Regionalization	Spatial Organization
9. Spatial Inequality and the Redistribution of Wealth in China	Limiting rural-to-urban migration maintains inequality "Sending down" policies reverse the traditional pattern of rural-urban migration Rural reforms result in greater urban-rural interaction (jobs, trade technology transfer, etc.)	Long-standing geographical and environmental reasons for endemic poverty in certain parts of China The landscape of capitalism (e.g. tourism, new housing, etc.) HRS and agricultural reforms likely to produce great environmental change and damage; e.g. industrialization of the countryside	Pervasive locality characteristics (cultural and ecological) result in unique sets of circumstances regardless of collectivization of the countryside HRS and agricultural reforms in rural areas are changing ancient patterns of attachment to place and locality	New economic measures allow the development of local and regional comparative advantage; produces greater levels of spatial inequality The "old" and the "new" Chinas become increasingly evident	Land-use conflicts at the urban fringe produce new administrative solutions to create new city regions Entirely new organizational structures are emerging out of the economic reforms, based on market, not political, forces Cadres, communes, and old Party organizational structures are being replaced
10. Politics and the Physical Environment		Changing concepts of landscape, as artifact, habitat, utilitarian Ecological significance of forest cover and the damaging results of deforestation Environmental consequences of HRS and agricultural reforms Human and environmental influences on the water supply in Beijing	The threat to ancient human/environment ties resulting from the depletion of soils and the destruction of local ecosystems, due partly to political and partly to environmental causes		

27

Chapter Number and Title	Distance and Spatial Interaction	Human/Environment Interaction	The Importance of Place	Regions and Regionalization	Spatial Organization
11. Women's Place in the New China	The tradition of patri-local marriage meant women had to leave home, often permanently Women are very restricted in their spatial mobility, like "frogs in a well"	Women in pre-revolutionary China were forced to inter-act with their local environment	Women have come to "know their place" in Confucian China, which also has a spatial component The rootedness of women has barely changed in postrevolutionary rural China The desire to return home remains very strong even after people leave to get wealthy The significance of "home" and family in times of political insecurity		The dominance of work units and residential organizations over people's patterns of everyday life, e.g. socializing, dating, entertainment, shopping
12. The Delivery of Urban Services	Level of service provi-sion appears to be greatest in larger cities; this helps to account for overwhelm-ing desire of the Chinese to live in cities and to acquire residence permits The lure of the big city for itinerant bands of semi-skilled laborers (tinkers, tailors, cobblers)	The emphasis on pro-duction over consump-tion and services pro-duced an ugly, drab urban landscape Increasing traffic con-gestion, pollution, and other urban environmental hazards in the wake of moderni-zation and economic reforms	In spite of the drabness of cities and housing in China, people are still able to identify with their homes and create them into centers of meaning The role of the danwei and local residential organizations in fostering a sense of community and identity in China's cities		The vital importance of the newly implemented (post-1949) adminis-trative structures in the Chinese city for delivery of services The importance of the work unit in service provision

Chapter Number and Title	Distance and Spatial Interaction	Human/Environment Interaction	The Importance of Place	Regions and Regionalization	Spatial Organization
12. (Con't.)	The new demand for travel, leisure, mobility as a result of growing wealth and Westernization				
	The problem of how to dispose of the growing volume of solid waste in China				
	Residence in the work unit reduces the need for commuting				
	The importance of the residence permit in migration flows				
13. Food and the Comforts of Home in the Chinese City	The role of urban annexations of rural territory in increasing rural/urban interaction patterns	Geographic and ecological advantages of urban-fringe areas for intensive vegetable production	In the Chinese city the home is not a secure place as it is in the West; but ties between people and their homes do develop	The establishment of new city regions, post-1958	Annexations of rural counties to establish new regional structure for urban administration
	The changing pattern of land uses and employment at the urban fringe		Work units and residential organizations help to increase local identity and sense of community		The spatial organization of food production and and distribution in Shanghai
	Free markets help to increase rural/urban interactions		Rising threat of homelessness and displaced persons in the wake of economic reforms		
	Economic reforms greatly increase spatial mobility of peasants				

Chapter Number and Title	Distance and Spatial Interaction	Human/Environment Interaction	The Importance of Place	Regions and Regionalization	Spatial Organization
14. Crime and Punishment in a Revolutionary Society	Limitations placed on human movement in post-1949 Canton, after the Civil War	The geographical and environmental characteristics of the Chinese city that help to reduce crime levels (active and passive constraints)	Sense of alienation, no sense of place in the modern Chinese city may help to increase crime rates	In the Chinese city high-crime regions are less likely to develop, in comparison to Western (especially U.S.) cities	Urban administrative structures greatly facilitate local security and surveillance operations
	Various measures to reduce rural in-migration to avoid the concentration of poor in cities that can help to "breed" crime and social unrest				
	Return migration of formerly sent-down youths and the effect on crime rates				
	Vast increases in poor peasants from the country produces social problems				
	Convergence between East and West in crime rates and criminal justice procedures				
15. Human Rights and the Crime of Dissent in China	The role of Democracy Wall as a focal point for dissidents, 1978-1979	The use of China's fringe territories for housing its dissident population (the Chinese Gulag)	The stark and barren landscapes of the Chinese Gulag; in spite of this some "prisoners" manage to carve out a home and attach themselves to their new landscapes	Certain provinces and regions become associated with prisons and camps, e.g. the great northern wilderness (Heilongjiang) and Qinghai Province	The role of local security and administration structures in surveillance and rooting out "counterrevolutionaries"
	After the crackdown in 1989, the exile of dissidents to break up the Democracy Movement (the "Chinese diaspora")				

Chapter Number and Title	Distance and Spatial Interaction	Human/Environment Interaction	The Importance of Place	Regions and Regionalization	Spatial Organization
15. (Con't.)	The Chinese Gulag isolated to cut off prisoners totally from mainstream life				
	The role of communications and global media in the 1989 demonstrations				

The Changing Shape
of Chinese Cultural Values

Better to have superficial tranquility even if you're a volcano inside.[1]

INTRODUCTION

The epigraph, an ancient saying, refers to the time-honored ability of the Chinese to hide their feelings. A daughter who hates her mother-in-law must put on the mask of inscrutability and behave with respect. By not letting her true feelings show, she is exhibiting one of the Five Confucian Virtues, namely *xin*, which can be roughly translated to mean "sincerity." Masking personal feelings is usually interpreted by Westerners as the opposite of sincerity—in fact we might see it as deceitful. Westerners tend to think badly about the Chinese person who nods and smiles, giving the impression of sincere friendship, but then acts in a contrary way. He or she is not to be trusted.

This chapter looks at the cultural values of the Chinese, in an attempt to understand why they are so different from us. Why, for example, are they obsessed with controlling their emotions? And why do they have such fundamentally different views on the importance of "being an individual"? In trying to answer such questions we shall also be considering how the Chinese behave toward each other, their homes, their country, and the world around them. Finally, a question that it is central to the theme of this book will be posed: whether Chinese values in the final part of the twentieth century have been changing significantly in response to modernization pressures, and if they have, whether the age-old differences between "us" and "them" are finally disappearing.

THE FUNDAMENTAL CONFUCIAN
VALUES OF THE CHINESE

Every Chinese, educated or illiterate, growing up on the Analects *as a text to be studied or as the stuff of daily speech, has felt perhaps as if he lived with Confucius peering over his shoulder.*[2]

An ancient folktale serves to remind us of some of the cultural imperatives that have preoccupied the Chinese for centuries: A famous marksman, known throughout the land for his prowess with the bow and arrow, left home to serve his master in battle. He bid his fond farewells to his newly pregnant wife and was not repatriated for more than twenty years. On his return to his home territory, he came upon a young man boasting of his ability as a marksman and challenging him to a contest. The older man agreed to the challenge, but at the first available opportunity he shot an arrow through his opponent's heart, killing the young man instantly.

True to the form of Chinese morality tales, the boy turned out to be the son the warrior had never seen. Naturally the father was stricken with remorse. He had killed his only son. Many Chinese fathers would rather die than bear such a burden, but in this case the father's grief was tempered by the fact that the younger man had violated some ancient Chinese cultural imperatives. He had not recognized his father and therefore had not shown the required level of filial piety. He had also committed the cardinal sin of challenging an elder, thereby impugning the accepted social order. A son should behave at all times with due respect to his elders, and particularly to his father. This tragic story reveals two important messages about traditional Chinese society. In the first place, the Chinese are obsessed with social order and the need to "do the right thing." In families this required the children, no matter how old, to remain fanatically loyal to their parents; and in society at large it required individuals to serve others before themselves. In the same way, a newly wed woman must submit to her mother-in-law. "The girl may hate her mother-in-law's guts, but sincerity calls for her to deliver the kowtow with no revealing imperfection. If she let her true feelings slip . . . her position in the family would be destroyed. She would be beaten to death or ignominiously returned to her family of origin."[3] The story also implies that social harmony is possible only if everyone accepts the way things are. Every person needs to know his or her place in the social hierarchy and stay in it at all times.

These beliefs can be traced back directly or indirectly to the teachings of the sage known as Kung Fuzi, or in the latinized form, Confucius (551–479 B.C.), whose ideas became the basis of Chinese social and political life for more than two thousand years. Confucius lived in northeast China, in the state of Lu (present-day Shandong Province). His family belonged to the elite minority, but had fallen upon hard times and was actually quite poor during his lifetime. Although he was well educated, Confucius never held any high office; neither did he realize the full impact of his teachings. In fact it was not until several centuries later that Confucius was recognized as a great teacher. He was not a scholar who engaged in sustained philosophical argument of the Socratic type; in fact, his thoughts are recorded only in brief, often random statements. There are no essays written by Confucius, and as a result, his followers were required to produce posthumous collections of his most famous pronouncements (such as the *Analects*). Nevertheless, by the time of the Han Dynasty (206 B.C.–A.D. 220) his works had become the basis of the Chinese edu-

cational system and, as a result, the system of government. A Confucian education was intended to train people for public service, but nevertheless, it emphasized the broad liberal arts. Such an education began with the venerated books and the ritual texts and was supplemented by studies of language and literature, history, ethics, music, and athletics. This unspecialized Confucian education was not unlike that received by the sons of the English gentry in the eighteenth and nineteenth centuries, who were expected to use what they had learned to govern the British Empire. "Men so educated have been expected to meet any need that public life might bring— quell rebellion, build canals, devise fiscal measures, record the histories of their times. Until very recently, when governments began to meet the more complex needs of modernizing societies, this education sufficed."[4]

Confucius's ideas and those of his followers penetrated to the core of the lives of ordinary Chinese people, effectively defining for them what it meant to be human and acting as the guiding principles of Chinese social life. For a man who made such an impact on the course of events in China, Confucius was unpretentious, preferring to describe himself as a "mere transmitter" of ideas. He was obsessed with learning and with the teacher-student relationship. When asked by one of his students what he would like to have written on his epitaph, he replied: "He is the sort of man so intent upon enlightening those eager for knowledge that he forgets to eat, and so happy in so doing that he forgets his sorrows, and does not realize that old age is creeping up on him."[5]

The Cardinal Relations

The core of the Confucian value system was a set of hierarchical relationships between people, with the senior members exercising a wide range of prerogatives over the junior members. In traditional Chinese society, harmony could only be achieved if all people adhered to their position in the hierarchy, whether it be high or low. The essence of this system, known as the Cardinal Relations, was that everyone was unequal. Each person's status was ascribed relative to that of everyone else. Thus the sovereign was dominant over his subjects; the father over his sons; the husband over his wife; an elder brother over his younger brother; and an older friend over a younger friend. Although superiors were expected to treat their inferiors in a humane way, this inherently unequal system obviously legitimated many abuses. This was particularly the case for women, who found themselves subservient to their husbands, their fathers, and after marriage, to their mothers-in-law. The norm for women, in other words, was compliance.[6]

In Confucian China all individuals belonged in a network of relationships with other people, some relationships in which they were dominant, some in which they were subservient. This meant that people were related to each other in a "tapestry of dualities . . . which may call forth seemingly incompatible patterns of behavior of superordination and subordination from the same person."[7] A harmonious social system could be attained only if everyone adapted to these complex requirements and learned to accept his or her responsibilities. The result in China was a group-dominated society, with the group cemented by the hierarchical relationships between the members. The strongest group of all was the family, and complete devotion to parents was expected (usually referred to as filial piety, or *xiao*). Younger brothers were expected to be subservient to their elder brethren (fraternal submission, known as *ti*). Just as parents were treated with reverence, so was the ruler or any high official. Herein lay the connection between family relationships and the relationships within government. The ruler was to be afforded the equivalent of filial piety and fraternal submission.

The Constant Virtues

The relationships between people formed the basis of the so-called Constant Virtues, which could be realized if and only if people adhered to the Cardinal Relations. The most important of these virtues was known as *ren*, crudely translated as "true personhood" or "humaneness." The Chinese character for *ren* has two components, one illustrating a human being, and the other the number two. As this implies, *ren* refers to the way people relate to each other in society. Confucius was vague about what *ren* actually meant, and he refused to apply the label to any living person, preferring to suggest that certain individuals fell somewhat short of *ren*. He indicated that

although most people are not far from achieving *ren*, very few people could reach the goal permanently. The essential idea of *ren* involves individuals finding their true selves, although not in the modern sense of individual self-gratification.

Achieving *ren* had a social meaning in that it was defined by one's behavior in group situations. Confucius believed that to be a "real man," one needed to start out by being a good son, daughter, or brother, and a good citizen of the realm.[8] This implied that all people were created equal in terms of the goodness in their hearts, and all, in theory, were able to reach the Confucian models of perfect virtue. When applied to government, a ruler with *ren* was one who cared for the basic needs of his people and thus did not have to resort to the use of law to maintain social order.[9]

Ren could only be achieved if people followed a prescribed set of rules of conduct, generally referred to as *li* (ritual, or politesse). The term *li* suggested a code of conduct that had to be adhered to if social harmony was to be produced. In simple terms *li* was the external manifestation of *ren* in concrete social situations.[10] As the Master himself remarked, "Do not look at what is contrary to li; do not listen to what is contrary to li; do not say what is contrary to li; and do not make any movement contrary to li."[11] It is important to point out that as a code of conduct *li* was expected only among the Chinese elite. Only they "are responsible for conserving the structure of the Great Society."[12] For the peasants there were no similar expectations. "Penal law, or 'fa,' is reserved for peasants . . . [because] they have no stake in the imperial cause."[13]

A third virtue was *i*, which can be roughly translated as righteousness, propriety, or justice. *I* provided a standard by which the appropriateness of moral behavior could be evaluated. In effect, it acted like a "spring" to control the tension between *ren* and *li*. It defined proper behavior, so it was in one sense universalistic, but it also allowed for exceptions in particular situations. In certain circumstances the proscribed ritual behavior (*li*) could be dispensed with. The best-known example of this is usually attributed to Mencius, who pointed out that although *i* demanded that men and women should not touch each other in public, if a woman were drowning in a lake, a man would be behaving like an animal if he did not offer her a helping hand. In this case *i* would have mitigated *li*, but it also manifested *ren* because it was a truly humane act.

The Confucian Legacy

From an outsider's perspective, the whole of the Confucian hierarchy appears to be fundamentally inegalitarian. Apart from the servitude it implied for anyone low down in the hierarchy (particularly women), the hierarchy has also acted to inhibit the development of individual thought and behavior among the Chinese. For two thousand years it was drummed into people that relationships, especially those within the family, were all-important and the individual per se was unimportant. A Chinese person, from birth, is enmeshed within a network of interpersonal relationships. This network, whether it is the family, the work unit, or the Party, acts like a collective "womb," with the result that "man, in the sense of man with a strong ego, has never been born in China."[14] This sentiment reflects one of Lu Xun's famous statements, made in the 1920s: "True manhood has not yet been created in the Chinese world."[15] In psychological terms, the suggestion is that the individual Chinese person "does not possess the capability to 'unfold' his own potentialities fully, to give himself a willed shape. . . . He is unaware of himself as having a 'purpose' . . . and . . . regards himself as an instrument of others."[16]

Naturally such sweeping generalizations should not go unchallenged, either inside or outside China. There is evidence that in spite of the overriding emphasis on group values and family orientation, Confucianism has produced many self-directed scholars. Central to Confucian thought, for example, is a voluntaristic view of the individual. This is crystallized in the concept of self-cultivation (*xiu-ji*), which can be achieved only through a lifetime devoted to study. In the *Great Learning*, for example, Confucius said, "From the Son of Heaven [the emperor] down to the mass of the people, all must consider the cultivation of the person as the root of everything."[17] This emphasis on individual development was at the root of all intellectual thought in ancient China. In spite of the Confucian emphasis on moderation, there was also a role for nonconformist behavior, and this was particularly important when there was a need to campaign against a tyrannical ruler.[18] Countless Chinese people living in different parts of the world have also exhibited aggressively individualistic and eccentric behavior, typified by the savvy of the Chinese businessperson in Hong Kong and Singapore, in fact, in any Chinatown.

In spite of these observations, the consensus remains that over the centuries the Confucian principles of social order have produced an excessively dependent person in China, one who is rarely encouraged to think solely of him or herself. This, it can be argued, fits well with the overall conservative nature of the Chinese national character. To be too conspicuous only invites trouble, hence the saying that the Chinese "fear fame as much as pigs fear getting fat."[19]

The poorly developed concept of self in China has been used to explain (but not to justify) the apparent refusal of the current Chinese government to take the issue of human rights seriously.[20] Perhaps partly as a result of Confucian teachings the Chinese consider that the needs of the state must take precedence over the rights of individual citizens. It is difficult to say to what extent this is a Confucian or a Leninist trait, but whichever it is, it helps to account for the large number of people still serving lengthy sentences in Chinese labor camps and the shocking denial of ordinary human rights in the Chinese criminal justice system (see Chapter 14). Similarly, the development of social movements stressing the rights of individuals has often met with little success in China. The demands of groups arguing for women's rights or ethnic self-determination have not been made forcefully, in part because they are still attacked as examples of "individualism" and "spiritual pollution" imported from the decadent West.[21]

Some Western psychologists have suggested that as a result of the Confucian traditions, many Chinese people do not mature in a healthy way—they simply get older without passing through the normal developmental stages. Chinese children may as a result be robbed of the learning that comes during adolescence. The result, according to some, is that in later life Chinese men and women may be totally unable to interact with each other as two adult human beings. It follows that many adolescents grow up without knowing very much at all about sex.[22] This can produce some serious traumas, particularly for inexperienced women who are thrust into marriage without knowing what is expected of them. In a controversial novel written about her own life, Yu Luojin described in harrowing detail the pain and humiliation of her own wedding night, after which she took a pair of scissors to her husband, threatening to kill him if he ever touched her again. In a later moment of calm, Yu blamed the prudishness of Chinese society as a whole for her inexperience. "We [women] were like simpletons as far as sex was concerned . . . we learned nothing . . . either from our parents or from our schools. The very word was something shameful and immoral, to mention it was almost a crime."[23] What struck Yu most of all was how unfair this was. "Why should any understanding of it [sex] be hidden and secret from us? Why should a motley collection of men be left to initiate us . . . each in his own particular fashion?"[24]

The Confucian legacy—if one may consider it in a somewhat lighter vein—may also have contributed to an oral fixation among the Chinese. Instead of being obsessed with sex, as most Westerners appear to be, the Chinese, as Colin Thubron suggested, are obsessed with food and eating. Nowhere can this be seen as strikingly as it is in Canton, the gastronomic epicenter of China. "In Canton the national obsession with food ascends to a guzzling crescendo. At night the porticoed pavements become a chiaroscuro of celebrants munching snacks or hunting down eating places."[25] Thubron was convinced that the Chinese, especially the Cantonese, can get as high on food and chatter as we in the West can get on alcohol and sex. He watched people in Canton's restaurants getting themselves worked up to a fever pitch. "Shoulders are squeezed, forearms patted. Cigarettes are passed from hand to hand in a voluble ritual of offering, disclaiming, submitting. The men slap their knees with delight at every joke. The women pinch each other's cheeks or leave an affectionate arm curled around a friend's waist. . . . [But] nobody touches the opposite sex."[26]

To evaluate the overall legacy of Confucius, it is important to measure the criticisms against some of the more positive attributes. For example, Confucianism has helped to provide a set of well-understood rules of conduct—rules that dictated how resources should be allocated during times of scarcity and that also taught people to accept the consequences, whatever they were.[27] Needless to say, for the peasants at the bottom of the hierarchy, this often meant a blind acceptance that in the hard times they would have to continue providing for their superiors. The peasants represented what Leon Stover called the "sink of death"—an entire class of expendable persons whose only destiny was disease, starvation, and early death.[28] In a society that continually produced more people than it could feed, a harshly realistic and adaptive view of the future became an asset of sorts. If a Chinese woman was unable to move out from under the yoke of her husband and could not get along with her domineering mother-in-law, she had only two choices: to keep quiet or to take her own life.

At the level of government these stoic values helped to produce a system that was based on loyalty and submissiveness, one that was able to survive largely intact for nearly two thousand years. After the chaos of the Warring States epoch, the Confucian principles were used to lay out the structure of a new form of autocratic government, with an emphasis on status and obedience that was first seen in the Han Dynasty two hundred years before Christianity. Since that time Confucian ideology has required the Chinese people to serve their leaders with dispassionate loyalty. Through times of great deprivation Confucian values taught everyone (but especially the peasants) to act with restraint and to put on a good "face."[29] These traditional attributes may also help to explain to Westerners how the Chinese have been able to tolerate their relative deprivation, even after 1949, when in spite of the promises for a better future they continued to experience hardships, spiced with few luxuries.

One question that Westerners are fond of asking is how Confucian scholars managed to attain their legitimacy—how was it that generations of rulers and consequently millions of ordinary people have followed their teachings? John K. Fairbank, the doyen of American China scholars, has suggested that the ascendancy of Confucian thinkers is a direct result of the relationship the Chinese have with nature. The conduct of human affairs was strongly influenced by the spirits of land, wind, and water. In this sense human life is just one part of the natural order, and it followed that if people behaved improperly the harmony between life and nature would be destroyed, and nature would somehow seek revenge on humankind. This could only be prevented by timely interventions from the ruler, who, as the Son of Heaven, stood between heaven above and the people below. It was the ruler, therefore, who maintained the harmony between people and nature. Only by acting appropriately along the lines set out by Confucian scholars could the ruler ensure that nature's wrath would not be vented on humankind. It was therefore the scholar, and only the scholar, with "his knowledge of the rules of right conduct [who] could properly advise the ruler in his cosmic role."[30] As the sole interpreters of *li,* the rules of proper conduct, Confucian scholars took on a role that must have been analogous in some ways to our present-day technocrats or economists. They made themselves indispensable to the ruler. "They became technical experts, whose explanations of natural portents and calamities and of the implications of the rulers' actions could be denied or rejected only on the basis of the classical doctrines *of which they were themselves the masters.*"[31]

In other words Confucian scholars had the skills needed to deal with any situation that might arise, so they were able to maintain a position in the ruling elite of great strategic importance. They not only provided technical advice to the emperor, they also provided a rational and ethical sanction for the exercise of his despotic authority. There is no doubt that this was an impressive innovation at a time when most other rulers around the world relied entirely on religious sources of legitimation. In addition to their usefulness, Confucian scholars were usually trustworthy. Indoctrinated by the need for loyalty and integrity, and taught to believe in the value of reform through moral persuasion rather than through revolution, Confucian scholars must have seemed far less dangerous to generations of rulers than many of the others who might have taken their places.[32]

LOCATING THE CHINESE CROSS-CULTURALLY

After almost two thousand years of immersion in Confucian values and codes of behavior, the Chinese have developed a identifiable cluster of cultural values that dominates their social and cultural life. Almost every traveler to China has commented on the gulf between Chinese cultural values and those that rule life in the Western world. One of the most obvious differences revolves around the patterns of human interaction. This difference manifests itself in all aspects of publicly observable life, but particularly in the relationships between the sexes. In the United States, for example, "there is a constant, pervasive innuendo of sexuality in almost all of our relationships . . . we are exhorted to define and perceive ourselves through a sexual image; through clothes, manner, body shape, facial features . . . we are a nation slavishly devoted to sexual success and failure."[33]

Most of the Americans who visited China in the 1970s and spent any time with young people were impressed by what they found. "The most striking feeling in being with young people in China is the absence of focus on intimate feelings . . . there is virtually no pressure for pairing off, and little sexual game playing going on."[34]

In the past decade some visitors reported that things have changed considerably in China in this respect. Lynn Pan, for example, has noticed a far greater consciousness about sex in Chinese public life, in films, novels, and newspapers. Classes on sex education are being added to school curricula, and clinics have opened to counsel couples on ways to improve their sex lives. In spite of all this activity, Pan concludes that most young people in China still "have only a dim notion of sex . . . [and] wide-eyed innocence characterizes the general approach to lovemaking."[35]

Empirical Studies of Chinese Personality

The colorful and perceptive accounts of Chinese social life written by travelers and journalists have been supplemented by scientific works conducted by psychologists and other social scientists. Although these accounts are considerably less titillating to Westerners, they probably come closer to identifying the major dimensions of social relationships in China.[36] Five themes appear in the literature as "prototypically Chinese characteristics"[37] (see Table 3.1), and each of them can be traced back to the Confucian values discussed earlier in this chapter.

These characteristics appear to have persisted over time and across space; in other words, they are common to Chinese people living in the PRC as well as to "overseas Chinese," living in Hong Kong, Singapore, Taiwan, and countries all over the world. They are traits that have been modified but not significantly changed by political systems or by travel to faraway lands. In a body of literature that is already vast (and growing rapidly as Chinese social scientists enter the field), numerous attempts have been made to quantify these traits, in studies using Chinese respondents.[38] For the most part these studies have validated the stereotypical notions about Chinese characteristics.[39] Psychological testing conducted in the PRC, for example, has shown that the Chinese, in comparison to Westerners, tend to be "emotionally more reserved, introverted, fond of tranquility, overly considerate, socially overcautious . . . [and] habituated to self-restraint."[40] In assessing such conclusions we need to remember that until recently most studies using "Chinese" respondents had to be conducted exclusively in Hong Kong or Taiwan, partly because psychology as an individually oriented discipline was held in low esteem in socialist China. It is difficult to say how accurately the results of such studies can be generalized to people in the Chinese mainland.

With psychological testing still in its infancy in the PRC, cultural bias is also a problem. Most of the tests in current use have a strong Western bias. A specific personality trait may measure what it purports to measure in the United States, but in China, the concept may have an entirely different meaning. This was evident with the McClelland Achievement Tests measuring "nAch" (the need for achievement), using schoolchildren's books in the PRC.[41] The tests showed that Chinese children scored significantly higher than the world average, which contradicted the usual assumption that, compared to Americans, Chinese children would be low in "nAch." Part of the discrepancy here was a result of the political propaganda found in children's books after Liberation, depicting heroic revolutionary struggles to overcome all manner of adversity. In addition to this, the achievement tests were probably biased by a Western view of what "nAch" means (in other words, individual as opposed to group or social achievements). It follows, therefore, that the results of any tests should be interpreted with great caution.

The Geography of National Character

If one bears in mind the hazards involved in generalizing across cultures, it is intriguing to consider whether there are empirically identifiable and distinct aspects of national character. The results of a study conducted in the early 1980s using more than 100,000

Table 3.1 The Dominant Characteristics of Chinese Personality and Social Relationships

An overriding sense of duty and responsibility to the family as the fundamental unit of society

The development and maintenance of very close bonds between parents and their children

The overwhelming importance of other people and relationships within the social network, as opposed to individualism

The ability to control or to hide emotions and feelings, and the cultivation of high moral standards

A strong, almost fanatical emphasis on education and achievement for the children

Source: Modified from G. C. Chu, 1985, "The Emergence of the New Chinese Culture," pp. 15-28 in Tseng Wen-Shing and D.Y.H. Wu (eds.), *Chinese Culture and Mental Health* (Orlando, Fla.: Academic Press), pp. 16-17.

respondents in 53 countries suggested that there are clusters of values that can be associated with specific countries.[42] Two clusters of values were strongly associated with Chinese personality traits. The first was called "power distance," which measured the extent to which individuals accept that power in society is distributed unequally; the second was called "individualism," which expresses a preference for individualistic over collectivistic social structure.[43] Both of these dimensions are conceptually related to the age-old Confucian values, and as we might expect, the Chinese respondents scored high on the power-distance dimension and low on the individualism dimension.

In a follow-up a group of international scholars calling themselves the Chinese Culture Connection attempted to reproduce these findings.[44] To minimize the Western bias inherent in all such studies, the researchers used a set of values generated by Chinese respondents. Again the analysis produced dimensions that made it possible to discriminate among national characteristics. One of the most interesting of these dimensions was called "Confucian work dynamism," which measured the extent to which people agreed that the world of work should be one in which there is a definite ordering of relationships by status. At the country level scores on this dimension were strongly correlated with economic growth. In other words, countries where "Confucian work dynamism" was high had been economically very successful in the past two decades. In this respect capitalist Asian societies like Japan, South Korea, Hong Kong, Taiwan, and Singapore are clearly distinguished from other capitalist societies such as the United Kingdom, Australia, New Zealand, Canada, and the United States. Here we have some empirical support for the widely held belief that there is an "oriental" work ethic that has helped to account for the recent astonishing economic successes in the so-called newly industrializing countries (NICs) in Asia. The results of this study support a "post-Confucian" hypothesis of economic development,[45] which suggests that the inhabitants of the NICs share similar cultural values in their approach to the issue of work. "The Confucian ethic—the creation of dedicated, motivated, responsible, and educated indi-

viduals and the enhanced sense of commitment, organizational identity, and loyalty to various institutions—will result in all neo-Confucian societies having at least potentially higher growth rates than other cultures."[46] It is possible to conclude from such studies that cultural values can effectively be "mapped" on a global scale, which demonstrates that there is a geography of national character. Some of the characteristics associated with centuries-old Confucianism are still evident in Chinese societies today, in spite of vast differences in economic, social, and political systems in the countries involved and the sweeping changes that have occurred in such countries during the twentieth century.

The Geographical Implications of Confucianism

On another scale entirely, it is also possible to generalize about the impact of Confucian values on spatial behavior in China. Based on the work of such authors as Robert Sommer, Edward T. Hall, and Erving Goffman, it would appear that there are clear-cut cultural differences in the way people from different societies organize themselves in space and respond to the world around them.[47] The way the Chinese behave territorially may be more a matter of necessity than conscious choice. As noted earlier, over the centuries the Chinese have developed an impressive array of strategies to cope with adversity. In modern times the Chinese appear to have drawn deeply from this cultural reservoir to help them survive the years of political chaos and the all-round austerity during the socialist transformation.

In geographical terms Confucian values of restraint might have contributed to the tolerance the Chinese appear to have for living at high densities, far higher in cities like Shanghai, Canton, and Hong Kong than most Westerners would usually find acceptable. Confucian values about individualism may have contributed to the abilities of the Chinese to live collectively in the cities and the countryside and to share territory, possessions, and even everyday household facilities such as kitchens and bathrooms. Traditional Confucian acceptance of the status quo and the lack of concern with individualism may also have helped the Chinese to adjust to the surveillance and invasion of privacy that has been the norm since 1949.[48]

The Chinese world is a human world dominated by social relationships, and this Confucian principle may, over the centuries, have colored Chinese attitudes toward the physical environment. Many Westerners have been startled by the starkness, even ugliness, of the landscape in both urban and rural China. To some extent this is a force of circumstance—when there are barely enough resources to make ends meet, there is little left over to beautify the landscape. Beyond this, however, it seems to us on the outside that the landscape itself does not have any intrinsic value to most Chinese people, other than in a purely functional sense in providing shelter or producing food. One consequence of this is that only when places are significantly bound up with human relationships do they take on an importance for the Chinese. For a place to mean something to a particular person, it must be where he or she has ancestors, or at the very least she must know someone who lives there, or have been there with someone else who is important to her.

This might help to account for the tendency among the Chinese to eschew scenes that are, to Western eyes, of great beauty. Most Chinese tourists seem to prefer a crowded pavilion to a lonely vantage point, and for them a landscape is not complete until it has somebody important sitting or standing in its midst.[49] The ever-observant Colin Thubron commented on this phenomenon at Confucius's birthplace in Qufu. "The flurry of Chinese snapshots was directed not on this beautiful . . . [place] but exclusively at one another. A place seemed to take its meaning only from a person's presence there. Sometimes I received the overwhelming impression that these snapshots were really statements of identity, and that to be commemorated with a famous site was to be touched by its manna."[50] Chinese people are puzzled to see Westerners traveling alone, automatically assuming that being on one's own is the same thing as being lonely. They find it difficult to accept that anyone would *choose* to be alone rather than be part of a group. Of course what really baffles them is how people traveling alone are able to take satisfactory photographs!

MODERNIZATION, CULTURE CHANGE, AND THE POLITICS OF PERSONAL RELATIONSHIPS

It is intriguing to ask how the unique set of Chinese character traits have been forged out of the ecological, social, economic, and cultural crucible that has existed in China for such an extended period.[51] From the literature that is available on the topic it is possible to pinpoint three sets of influences: (1) the constraints and demands placed on society of an agriculturally based economy operating (at the best of times) only marginally above the subsistence level; (2) the dominant moral and religious and quasi-religious thoughts or doctrines, such as Confucianism, Taoism, and Buddhism; (3) genetic traits (morphological, physiological, and behavioral) of the ancient Chinese people.[52] As the model illustrated in Figure 3.1 suggests, over the centuries these influences have combined to produce a social structure with the characteristic features we have already noted: a hierarchical structuring of society based on age and seniority; a collectivist organization at the village and neighborhood level with individuals subservient to the large group; and a tightly knit social network, with a strong emphasis on the extended family.

These characteristics, in turn, have influenced the socialization practices unique to traditional China, including the emphasis on dependency, conformity, modesty, self-suppression, self-contentment, and parent-centeredness, as well as the relational characteristics so familiar to Chinese life, including the orientation toward others and submissiveness.

In the twentieth century, and especially since 1949, modernization has produced some changes in these personality traits. The quintessentially "Chinese" traits—the need for deference, the need to seek social approval, and the preference for social restraint and self-control—are now significantly less in evidence. Other traits, typically identified as "non-Chinese," have become more noticeable—the need for autonomy and achievement, a preference for self-indulgence and sensuous enjoyment, and an inclination toward individual relationships (see Table 3.2). We might be tempted to conclude from such observations

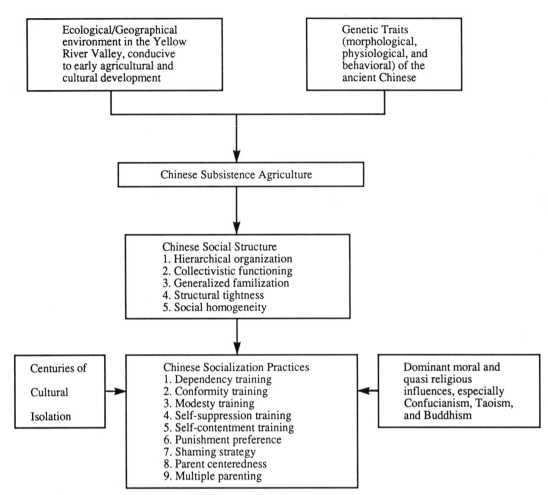

Figure 3.1 A cultural-ecological model of the development of Chinese personality and social characteristics.
Source: Adapted from Yang Kuo-Shu, 1986, "Chinese Personality and Its Change," in M. H. Bond (ed.), The
Psychology of the Chinese People *(Hong Kong: Oxford University Press).*

that there has been a significant amount of cultural convergence between Chinese societies and the West—in other words, "they" are becoming more like "us." This suggests that the drive toward modernization "makes the Chinese become gradually more like people in a modern industrialized society such as the United States, where the individually-oriented type of achievement motivation prevails."[53]

It is not clear to what extent these conclusions can be generalized to mainland China, but it seems reasonable to assume that personality traits might move in the same direction if China continues with its open-door policies and economic reforms.[54] It follows, therefore, that any discussion of social and personality traits in mainland China is incomplete without a consideration of politics. To conclude this chapter, therefore, it is useful to speculate on the way politics has influenced human relationships in China since Liberation in 1949. For this purpose it is useful to divide the period up into three eras: the immediate post-Liberation phase; the Cultural Revolution; and the post-Mao experiments with market socialism.

The Post-Liberation Era: The Shift from "Friendship" to "Comradeship"

When the Chinese Communist party returned victoriously to the cities in 1949, it

Table 3.2 The Impact of Modernization on Chinese Personality Traits

Decreasing Traits	Increasing Traits

Motivational Characteristics

Decreasing Traits	Increasing Traits
Deference	Exhibition
Order	Autonomy
Abasement	Intraception
Nurturance	Heterosexuality
Achievement (socially oriented)	Achievement (individually oriented)
Social approval	

Evaluative-Attitudinal Characteristics

Decreasing Traits	Increasing Traits
Preference for inner development	Preference for achievement (activity)
Preference for collectivist relationships	Preference for individualistic relationships
Preference for social restraint and self-control	Preference for self-indulgence and sensuous enjoyment
Theoretical value	Aesthetic value
Social value	Internal-control beliefs
Religious value	Democratic attitudes
External-control beliefs	
Authoritarian attitudes	

Temperamental Characteristics

Decreasing Traits	Increasing Traits
Self-restraint and cautiousness	Sociability-extroversion
Friendliness and harmoniousness	Ascendance and dominance
Conscientiousness	Flexibility
Perseverance	Tolerance
Femininity	Masculinity

Source: Adapted from Yang, Kuo-Shu, 1986, "Chinese Personality and Its Change," in M.H. Bond (ed.), *The Psychology of the Chinese People* (Hong Kong: Oxford University Press), p. 161.

was hoping to be able to remold human relationships in the new utopia. The Communists were convinced that life in the capitalist cities had degenerated to an all-time low. Nowhere was the decadence more evident than in the Westernized coastal cities of eastern China, such as Tianjin, Guangzhou (Canton), and especially Shanghai. The Communists suspected that in the capitalist city, the traditionally strong ties existing between people in agrarian societies had been eroded. They hoped that socialism could remedy this situation by replacing the individual struggle for economic survival with a new sense of collective purpose. In this way, they thought

it would be possible to rekindle the traditional solidarity of family and group life.

The CCP predicted that the new socialist consciousness, superimposed on the traditionally low mobility and high cohesiveness of Chinese social life, would help to ward off the alienation so common in the modern industrial city. Some early accounts of life in the new socialist cities seemed to confirm at least parts of this prediction.[55] In the area of personal friendships, for example, a new set of norms for interpersonal relationships emerged. Instead of having particularistic ties with specific friends, the new socialist society made possible a potentially universalistic congeniality—a transition that Ezra Vogel referred to as a shift from "friendship" to "comradeship."[56] All citizens (in theory) had equal status under the law, which freed them from centuries of submissiveness. In the new climate of socialist morality, the Communists were hoping to see the development of a new type of social relationship, one in which there would be no need for individual competitiveness. People would be civil to each other, helping each other out in times of need. The socialist transformation would ultimately replace the materialistic basis of social activity, and without a private ethic there would be no need to cultivate special friends to be used for economic gain (the *guanxi* network).

It is difficult to test such a hypothesis empirically, but some support was generated by the findings of a study conducted among PRC emigrés living in Hong Kong.[57] Interviews with the emigrés indicated that life in the Chinese Communist cities was clearly more comfortable and harmonious than life in Hong Kong. Some of the differences were obvious, in that Hong Kong was a fast-paced, highly competitive city, with a tremendous diversity between the "haves" and the "have nots." In comparison, life in most PRC cities has been tranquil (at least until the late 1980s). The pace of work was much more leisurely; there has been job security and income equality; and most services have been collectively provided—all of which appear to have produced significantly greater levels of mutual helping and social interaction. It seemed that the new socialist Chinese city had reproduced some of the "gemeinschaft" qualities of traditional communities that have been so revered and mourned by Western social scientists. The new socialist city was by no means a utopia, but, as Whyte and Parish observed, "life in cities with minimal mobility, minimal income or consumption gaps, minimal competitiveness, and many organized neighborhood activities has a distinct impact on the nature of interpersonal relations, creating far more mutual concern and assistance among neighbors and friends than occurs in other cities around the world."[58]

Unfortunately for the CCP, the Hong Kong respondents reported some rather disturbing trends about life in the Communist city. Although Chinese city dwellers usually had close ties with immediate family members, there had also been a significant loss of contact with both kin and friends living outside the neighborhood. Some of this was the result of job and housework pressures, which reduce the amount of time available for visiting beyond the neighborhood. With virtually no private automobile ownership, it has always been difficult to get around in the Chinese city, and the absence of personal telephones makes it difficult to keep in touch with friends. With few recreational alternatives, the natural tendency in a residentially stable neighborhood is for people to sit around chatting in their leisure time.

There is a more sinister component, however, in that most urban Chinese families since 1949 appear to have cut down seriously on the number of persons with whom they interact. The norm has been for them to shrink the size of their social network, both geographically and numerically, limiting themselves to the selection of a few very close friends. The major reason for this has been fear. In a society riddled with informants and fanatical about surveillance, it becomes difficult to know whom to trust. Zhang Xianliang, who was himself imprisoned for his dissident political views, argued that this was a deliberate goal of the Communist party, a none-too-subtle form of "divide and conquer." "They've put great efforts in these past two decades not into improving relations between men, but tearing apart the bonds that bring men together. I consider that to be the greatest crime they have perpetrated. They've destroyed a sense of trust among men. Instead of building good intentions and a readiness to help one another, they've made men into wild animals."[59]

As a response people had to be extremely selective in their choice of friends because they never knew whether their private thoughts would be reported to the authorities. It became common for friends to "turn each other in" because of an attitude or a belief that one or the other thought was politically dangerous. Rather than give someone the benefit of the doubt, they might choose to let it be known publicly that they were no longer friends. This situation faced the Chinese poet Yue Daiyun, who found herself being criticized in her work unit (a university) for holding "wrong" political views. A man she thought was her friend stood up at the criticism session to add fuel to the fire. In her book *To the Storm*, Yue tried to understand why he acted the way he did.

> He had just graduated. He hoped to stay at university as a teacher, and knew that the competition for these coveted places was keen. Future teachers would be chosen partly because of their academic achievements, but more importantly, because of their political reliability. I understood why he was speaking out against me. After I was rehabilitated, Lao Lin told me he regretted having been so obedient to the leaders, but I knew that precisely because of our former closeness, he had felt compelled to draw a line between himself and me after I was declared an enemy.[60]

During an intense political campaign the geography of social interaction became entrenched. People were unlikely to venture outside their neighborhoods or work units in search of friendships. They were nervous and frightened, looking over their shoulders and whispering. Life in such a pressure-cooker environment, where everyone knows you and knows your business, can be both stressful and tedious, and to cope with such an alien situation it was helpful to withdraw into a tightly knit social network. The three divorced women in Zhang Jie's short story "The Ark" were considered pariahs in their neighborhood, but their friendships provided them with some solace from a hostile world of busybodies and moralizing gossipers:

> The friendship between the three of them was one area of their lives that was clean and untarnished. They knew such friendships, those that had been cemented through struggle and hardship, were hard to come by in this vast world. And, indeed, the bond had taken work and, at times, cost each of them dearly. Experience had taught them the risks as well as the value of friendship, and now that they were entering middle age and had lost their youthful vigor, it turned out to be the only solid element in their lives. When Socrates was building himself a house, people had said to him, "It is too small." But Socrates replied, "That is of no matter, so long as it can contain true friends."[61]

The Cultural Revolution Era: The Shift (Back?) Toward Instrumentality

In China, people are always smiling, and you don't know why. . . . Outwardly, people are smiling . . . but inwardly, everyone is throwing stones.[62]

As the discussion in the preceding section has shown, the shift from "friendship" to "comradeship" was only a partial shift. Life in the Chinese socialist city was certainly not always comradely, and during the Cultural Revolution matters got much worse. Personal relationships began to turn away from the universal comradeship that Vogel had predicted and back toward individual friendships, but in most cases they were not the sort of friendships that either the socialists would have hoped for or the Confucianists would have expected (see Figure 3.2).

In the Cultural Revolution the attempts to transform social relationships and to create a wholly "new socialist man and woman" were pushed to extremes. At the best of times life was chaotic, with shortages of everything—jobs, food, housing, and services. At the worst of times people seriously began to fear for their safety. The "ultraleftists" within the Party had strongly discouraged any bourgeois emphasis on consumption, and it had become standard practice to tighten all controls over channels of distribution and consumption. For ordinary citizens it became more important than ever to develop regular channels of access to goods and services. Everything was in short supply, and to acquire anything over and above the bare essentials, one needed to have a wide network of connections. In this sort of milieu, friends were selected for purely instrumental purposes.

What was happening was a new affirmation of the old Chinese custom of "going through the backdoor" and developing ties based on *guanxi*. This is a system in which an individual develops a series of acquaintances for whom favors are done in the expectation of returned favors at some time in the future. Having good *guanxi* proves to be an extremely useful way of getting things done in a resource-scarce environment. It takes on many forms, varying all the way from perfectly legal "string pulling" with small gifts and favors, to outright corruption involving bribery and criminal actions. *Guanxi* reveals a thorough lack of respect for the regular channels for getting things done. It is, in other words, almost the complete opposite of *li*, the prescribed set of rituals to be followed to ensure virtuous behavior. Nevertheless, *guanxi* works for those who know how to use it, and it is usually much more efficient than going by the rules.

Figure 3.2 Cartoon depicting the evolution of a friendship: As fellow workers, two men greet each other warmly; when one becomes department head, they shake hands; when that one becomes section chief, he waves in a cursory gesture to his old friend; and as bureau chief, he barely recognizes him. Source: R. Crozier, 1983, "The Thorny Flowers of 1979: Political Cartoons and Liberalization in China," in Bulletin of Concerned Asia Scholars (eds.), China from Mao to Deng: The Politics and Economics of Socialist Development (Armonk, N.Y.: M. E. Sharpe, Inc.), p. 36.

To many Chinese *guanxi* itself is not a crime; the only crime is to be caught. In a society where virtually everything is in short supply, *guanxi* provides the operating rules. The people who control the distribution of scarce resources—the drivers of work-unit vehicles, ticket sellers, shopkeepers, shop stewards, and office managers—become enormously powerful within such a system. Even tourists in China have to submit to this power system. Anyone who has visited China will have experienced "the petty tyrants who decline

to notice you trying to catch their attention . . . the taxi driver who refuses to understand that you are in a hurry . . . each of these people rules over something he doesn't own, and from which he derives, not direct monetary benefit, but a power he can exercise in his relations . . . with others.[63]

During the Cultural Revolution the normal pattern of social relationships had broken down. Party officials acted in an increasingly arrogant way toward the rank-and-file members and the ordinary people. In the cities, normal patterns of law and order in the family had virtually ceased to exist because many teachers and parents had been sent down to the countryside. All pre–Cultural Revolution standards of social behavior were heavily criticized, and it was clear that there were new norms for what was considered appropriate—in fact, as Mao had said, "to rebel is justified."[64]

There appeared to be no relationship between what the Party officials (the cadres) preached and what they practiced in public. It was ironical that in the name of Maoist egalitarianism many of them became increasingly autocratic. As a matter of survival, social relationships became more politicized than ever before. Extraordinary things were happening: Marriages were arranged between two people because they were politically well suited; husbands turned in their wives for political offenses, and vice versa; and children informed on their parents. One of Ann Thurston's respondents described such a situation at a mass rally held at Peking University in the early years of the Cultural Revolution. "Lu Yaohua . . . publicly denounced her father as a '100 percent collaborator with imperialism.' Her action in 'drawing a clear line of demarcation' from her father presaged a new age in Chinese family relations, as children were called upon so frequently to denounce their elders that many parents feared to discuss politics with their children, yielding the task of political socialization almost entirely to school and state."[65] It should come as no surprise to find a fundamental lack of trust among people in today's China. They have seen, on countless occasions, how yesterday's friend can become tomorrow's informer.

The mass campaigns, the eradication of the private sphere by an insistence on the political character of all human relationships, and the setting of one group of citizens against another in the name of class struggle, have left a legacy of *suspicion*, hatred and cynicism. They have left family ties stronger, but loyalties more ambiguous. The state of distrust and dissembling in which many have existed through the years has left a long trail of deep *immorality*.[66]

It would prove to be immensely difficult for the Chinese government to restore the country to any semblance of normality after the chaos of the Cultural Revolution years. The Party was in disarray and its prestige was at an all-time low. People were thoroughly tired of politics and probably also a little afraid that all the madness might start up again. The Party had to do something to improve its overall image as well as to try to get the economy moving again. It was in this context that the period of economic reforms began in the late 1970s. The reforms would produce another marked shift in the nature of interpersonal relationships, one that may have moved the Chinese closer than ever to the individualism generally considered to be more prevalent in the Western world.

The Post-Mao Market Socialism Era: The Commodification of Personal Relationships

Since 1978 there has been a concerted effort to put the Chinese economy into high gear. This was partly intended to keep China on course toward modernization, but it can also be interpreted as an effort to right the wrongs of the Cultural Revolution by improving the lot of the Chinese people. It was hoped that by increasing production and generating an economic surplus, the overworked *guanxi* system would no longer be needed and would become little more than a memory from the past. Most important, however, the new reforms were seen as part of the attempt by the Party in a crisis to improve living standards, thereby improving its own legitimacy.

A detailed discussion of the reforms will follow in Part 2 of this book, so it is sufficient to say here that the economic reforms represented a dismantling of the collective efforts of the previous three decades and the implantation of a certain amount of capitalist-based enterprise into the economy. A variety of efforts were made to raise human productivity and increase competitiveness on the farms, in the factories, and even in the streets. As a result, personal autonomy has been enhanced and the right to make and keep a monetary surplus has increased. The economy, in essence, has been privatized, operating on the simple premise that some people will be allowed to pioneer the drive toward profit making. As Orville Schell pointed out in his book *To Get Rich Is Glorious*, all across the country there are countless examples of the new breed of Chinese capitalists showing how this can be done.[67]

One of the most significant impacts of the reforms has been to negate what little success the socialist government had in trying to foster a caring, mutually reinforcing society. Rather than fading from view, the instrumentality of the *guanxi* system has now become more important than ever. "The emphasis on income tied to efforts, productivity, efficiency, and specialization is establishing new hierarchies, occupational and economic strata, as well as a division of labor that will reinforce instrumental relationships."[68]

It is ironical that two very different eras, with policies oceans apart, the Cultural Revolution and the period of economic reforms in the 1980s, produced such similar results. They both reinforced a Chinese tendency to put the clock back in terms of the conduct of personal relationships. Ties between people in the era of no-holds-barred free enterprise were more than ever based on considerations of "who can do the most for me?" The only difference was that in the 1980s the majority of new relationships made were cash based, as opposed to earlier times of scarcity when all that was available to be peddled was power and influence. Once again society erected a marked hierarchy, but this time the wealthy were on the top and the poor on the bottom. During the Cultural Revolution the politically well-connected were able to lord it over the rest; in "feudal" China the Confucian intellectuals had been the elite group.

The new private ethic in China has resulted in an increasing proportion of social relationships being conducted through a cash nexus. This was especially true in the countryside, where higher levels of agricultural productivity have allowed families to increase their profits. In the new contract responsibility system, the sky is the limit—the farmer is on his own, and his personal relationships are more than ever guided by considerations of profit. From his extensive observations of the Chinese countryside, William Hinton has suggested that the enthusiasm with which the peasants have embraced the new responsibility system can be traced to their deep resentment of the commune cadres and the tight control under which they were kept in the collectives:

> Functionaries in China just assume that they have a right to run everything, down to the smallest details of people's lives. This tradition is deeply "feudal." It is . . . resented down below and that is one of the reasons for the extraordinary attraction that a free-market economy . . . has for ordinary Chinese citizens. For people suffering under feudal restraint, the cash nexus seems to promote a radical liberation where ability and not influence . . . count[s].[69]

After the landlords had been removed from the scene, control over the peasants was passed on to the collectives and to the Party cadres. In this sense the peasants saw the new agricultural reforms as a sort of "second Liberation." In the 1950s they had managed to rid themselves of the landlords, and in the 1980s "they were absolutely delighted to get the cadres off their backs."[70]

There are some other trends in contemporary China that provide further evidence of this pervasive shift toward the commodification of personal relationships. One of these is the increasingly mercenary attitude toward marriage (see Chapter 11). Brides are once again demanding comprehensive wedding gifts, and many young women are looking at prospective husbands from a purely instrumental perspective. A survey of newlyweds in small county towns in Jiangxi and Fujian revealed the average cost of weddings in 1988 to be 3,000 yuan (Y 3,000), and it could be as high as Y 7,500 (one-fifth of this was generally spent on the wedding banquet, the rest on fitting out the new home).[71] Lynn Pan told a story of a Shandong woman who conducted open competitive examinations to help her find a suitable husband. The winner was a soldier who averaged 94 percent on all the tests that were set for him. Ironically, as Pan noted, this represents a return to the ancient methods of selecting mates, but with a slight twist, in that "in Chinese stories the happy ending only comes with the groom passing the imperial examinations."[72]

Some observers have suggested that a new level of public immorality has resulted from the reforms—not only the well-publicized economic corruption and crime but also public behavior on buses, in shops, and on the streets—all of which further sounds the death knell for "comradeship." "China has reestablished and is reinforcing the material basis and private ethic for relations based on instrumentalities, the cash nexus and particularistic commitment to family, friends and fellow party members. . . . The only common goal at the moment [is not comradeship but] is individual wealth, everyone enjoying a 'bit of prosperity.' "[73]

It appears that the clock has been turned back and some ancient Chinese characteristics have started to resurface in contemporary China—notably, a renewed reliance on family ties, made necessary by the fear of overextending oneself socially; a recommodification of marriage; a greater deference to authority; a marked lack of civility; and a pervasive atmosphere of corruption. The *guanxi* system is as important as ever. What makes you important to someone else in a business relationship is not who you are, but whom you know. "In China one is always having to use irregular channels, because the regular ones are so clogged by red tape and bumbledom . . . although many a guanxi rests on bonds of true friendship, one is often left wondering how far one is valued for oneself, and how far for one's power or usefulness."[74]

CONCLUSION: REVOLUTIONS AND REFRIGERATORS

There is certainly not much evidence in contemporary China of the "comradeship" Vogel predicted a quarter of a century ago. The socialist goal of transforming interpersonal relationships into a new utopia characterized by universal morality and mutual trust has not come about. The shift back to some of the traditional values has brought with it the worst of both worlds: The negative aspects of Confucianism—the old hierarchies, authoritarianism, and the commodification of human relationships have returned, but no longer are they tempered by the positive side of Confucianism—the emphasis on morality, humane behavior, and the importance of virtue. The bonds between people that were seriously damaged during the Cultural Revolution have not been healed. In fact the scars are in danger of becoming wider, with the new emphasis on individualism and the monetary basis of most relationships in the 1980s.

It is tempting to conclude that the contemporary Chinese have precious little to believe in anymore. The goals of a universal socialist morality have been suspended; there is no religion to speak of and no moral principles of Confucianism to cling to. Many people are left floundering, searching for something in their lives to hang on to. This was evident in the stories Anne Thurston reported in her powerful book *Enemies of the People*, which is based on conversations with intellectuals who were badly treated during the Cultural Revolution. One of Thurston's respondents told her: "There is an identity crisis in China now . . . norms have been shattered, and there are no substitutes so we are facing a period of anomie, especially the younger generation. People are not sure what they are after. . . . They want change, but as to what kind of change is adequate, they are not so sure."[75]

Some older people in China might now be looking back quite fondly to earlier days when the old Maoist revolutionary zeal gave them, especially the young, a sense of purpose and something to believe in. In those days, "the young thought they were the vanguard of a revolutionary movement that would sweep the world," but in the new era of competitive striving for economic wealth this is no longer the case. As a former Red Guard put it, "For the revolution we could die . . . [but] how could we die for a refrigerator?"[76] This has turned out to be a prophetic statement, because by the late 1980s many of China's youth had once again found a cause they could believe in. The difference was that this time they were sharply at odds with the leadership and they were demanding political changes that the Party was not ready to make. The result was that in the summer of 1989 many of them did in fact die for their beliefs. Others, in numbers we can only guess at, have disappeared. They have been executed, forced underground, or exiled to the Chinese Gulag.

The Changing Nature of Chinese Political Values

In the fifties we helped each other,
In the sixties we killed each other,
In the seventies we feared each other,
In the eighties each one thinks for himself.[1]

INTRODUCTION: THE PRIMACY OF POLITICS IN CHINA

Observers of the political scene in post-Liberation China point out the inherently cyclical nature of politics in China. From one decade to another, and sometimes even more frequently, the winds of change sweep through the country, leaving Chinese and outsiders alike bewildered. This was reinforced dramatically in spring 1989, when the world first marveled at the apparent tolerance of the Chinese Communist party during April and May, only to be repelled a few weeks later at the brutality meted out to the demonstrators in Tiananmen Square.

At the level of everyday street interactions, many foreigners are convinced that the Chinese are unable to deal with one another in a cool, detached fashion. To outsiders, it often looks as though Chinese people are constantly embroiled in controversy. Even the most ordinary conversation can quickly become overheated. The Chinese seem to be almost always in conflict: arguing, scheming, making mountains out of molehills. The travel writer Paul Theroux commented on this: "The most common mode of conflict is the screaming out-of-hand row—two people screeching at each other, face-to-face. They are long and hard, and they attract large crowds of spectators."[2]

Earlier travelers reported similar reactions to this constant haggling. In his book *Two Kinds of Time*, about wartime China, Graham Peck concluded that it is almost a hobby for the Chinese to complicate situations in everyday life.[3] Why they do this is anyone's guess. Perhaps it is to enrich an otherwise dull existence, or maybe it is simply in their nature. For example, Peck noticed that in a bus station, instead of sitting around silently staring at each other, the Chinese prefer "to thrust themselves upon one another, if only in inconvenience. Theirs . . . [is] a civilization based on the belief that the interplay of personalities . . . [is] most important."[4]

Why do the Chinese spend so much of their time squabbling with each other? We think of it as a failing, but perhaps they are enjoying themselves. We should also remember that as long as the Chinese are arguing with each other, we have nothing to fear from them. Maybe this is a blessing in disguise. As one Chinese writer has reminded the rest of the world: "God knows that there are a billion of us, and if we ever managed to get it together, you'd never be able to handle us. God has been merciful to you by making it impossible for us to join forces."[5] Most of the rancorous arguments miraculously stop just short of physical abuse, but to save face the combatants usually have to wait for a third party to come to the rescue by mediating the dispute. Outsiders who observe all of this are led to the conclusion that everything in China is politics, even the most mundane of matters. It appears that everything has to be negotiated—simple things like buying a ticket to go to the movies or a pound of tofu in a street market are quickly mired in intrigue, and most Chinese people understand the importance of being well connected. As we saw in Chapter 3, *guanxi* remains the key to success in most walks of life.

At a different level there is also evidence that Party politics still dominates everyday life in China. Membership in the Communist party started to rise again in the mid-1980s, after almost a decade of decline and political apathy. In spite of the student demonstrations in recent years, many of China's educated youth realize the advantages that accrue from Party membership.[6] In 1986 more than 20 percent of the graduating seniors at China's universities applied to join the Party, compared to about 1 percent in 1981.[7] They may no longer believe in communism, but they continue to believe in the power of politics and the wisdom of joining the Party. A recent graduate explained why he had joined: "The party is the dominant institution in Chinese life. If you're ambitious and want to get to the top, you must join. . . . The party is like a fast bus. If you join . . . it's like taking the bus to your destination."[8]

The Party leaders were probably relieved about this newfound willingness to join, but even they would have to agree that much of the revolutionary zeal of the Maoist days was missing. One Party member reported, "We still have plenty of slogans, long reports, and long articles, but now the people's responses are cold."[9] Both before and during the demonstrations of 1989, many Western journalists reported that the Chinese people appeared to be thoroughly disgusted with the cynicism and corruption that is considered to be endemic within the Party and that was a major complaint voiced by the demonstrating students.[10]

At all levels, from the streets to the corridors of power, politics in China is preeminent. It is clear, however, that politics at both levels is no longer about beliefs or about ideology; it is primarily about *distribution*. In a society with too many people and too few resources, politics helps to determine how the meager pie will be divided—in other words,

Figure 4.1 *Cartoon showing how the fish is divided (Chinese equivalent of the pie): A large slice is diverted to relatives; another for work-unit leaders; one for Party delegates; and one for the fish vendor himself. Only the head and tail are left for sale to the public. Source: R. Crozier, 1983, "The Thorny Flowers of 1979: Political Cartoons and Liberalization in China," in Bulletin of Concerned Asia Scholars (eds.), China from Mao to Deng: The Politics and Economics of Socialist Development (Armonk, N.Y.: M. E. Sharpe, Inc.), p. 36.*

politics is about "who gets what, when, and where" in Chinese society (see Figure 4.1).

This is true in all aspects of life but perhaps nowhere so much as in the workplace. Jiang Zilong illustrated the importance of politics in his short story called "The Diary of a Factory Clerk" (1985). The hero of the story, Lao Wei (old Wei), is a shop-floor worker in a chemical factory. One day he was invited to an important meeting at the municipal headquarters of the chemical bureau. He went with the factory Vice-Director Jin, and at the meeting he received an object lesson in how to "press the flesh" effectively. Halfway through the meeting Wei was left to take notes—Jin had much more important work to do.

Director Jin was going from floor to floor paying everyone a visit . . . he went from room to room, everywhere acting as if he were walking into the home of old friends. He warmly greeted every section chief and every cadre, laughing and talking with them. Wherever he went he took expensive cigarettes from his pocket, liberally pressing them on people who smoked. From time to time he'd pick up someone else's cup of hot tea and drink from it freely, as one does with old friends.[11]

As Jiang's story illustrates, the constant jockeying for position in the hierarchy is a fact of life in the workplace, as well as in the neighborhoods and villages all over the country. For four decades the egalitarian principles of Chinese socialism have placed tight controls over the traditional indicators of prestige, such as personal wealth and individual possessions. In the West it is easy to trumpet one's relative standing in the community by buying a new car or a bigger house. But in China there has been only very limited access to such status symbols. The solution, therefore, was to fight to place yourself well in the complex web of *guanxi*. As we shall see in Chapters 5 and 6, the new economic reforms in China have changed the stakes somewhat in recent years, but the *guanxi* game remains essentially the same as ever. Officials and well-connected Party members use their influence to take advantage of the new reforms in the open-market economy.[12]

MARX, LENIN, AND SINIFIED MARXISM

Marx sits up in heaven, and he is very powerful. He sees what we are doing, and he doesn't like it. So he has punished me by making me deaf.
    —Attributed to Deng Xiaoping[13]

In the epigraph, Deng Xiaoping was joking about his deafness, which predates the current reform era, but his statement might reflect the guilt he felt about the "capitalist road" he has led China along since Mao's death. Neither Marx nor Mao would approve of Deng's economic policies in the 1980s, so the deafness can be interpreted either as Marx's punishment or more simply as Deng's way of turning his back on Marx.

The Chinese revolution itself was not predicted by Marx, who believed that a successful revolution could only be led by an urban-based industrial proletariat. This meant that revolution must follow a prolonged period of industrial capitalism, in which the proletariat had become sufficiently alienated to seek major changes in the political system. Lenin did not agree with this completely, and to that extent therefore, Mao Zedong was more of a Leninist than a Marxist.[14] In the twentieth century Lenin had the advantage of hindsight, and it was clear to him that a revolution in China could not be led by an urban proletariat because industrial capitalism was still in its infancy.

For China to have a successful revolution, Mao argued, it would have to be based in the countryside, supported by the masses of peasants. At this point Mao diverged sharply from the majority of Soviet political thinkers, including Lenin. Mao considered the Chinese peasants to be hopelessly naïve and totally unprepared for the revolution, but he was convinced that they could be educated and forged into revolutionary action. The standard wisdom of the Soviets was much less sanguine about the role of the peasants. Even Trotsky, who himself came from humble rural origins, agreed with Marx that the peasants would never be able to lead a revolution. Marx had generally been scornful of the peasants, describing them as "the class that represents barbarism without civilization."[15] This antipathy came to a head during Stalin's bloody purges of the kulaks, who resisted collectivization and paid dearly for their stance.[16] Stalin never really took the Chinese Communist party seriously because of its heavily rural membership; in fact in 1944 he described them as "margarine Communists" who would never amount to very much.[17]

Time proved that Mao, rather than Marx or the Soviets, had a good feel for the revolutionary potential of the Chinese peasants. In the formative years of the Chinese Communist party, however, Mao was not a very important figure. In fact, until 1927 the CCP was not a revolutionary party at all, and it had chosen to ally itself with the bourgeois Nationalist party led by Chiang Kai-Shek (the Kuomintang, or KMT). Lenin had approved of this alliance because he felt that in the absence of an urban proletariat, the CCP had few other options. He also felt that the Nationalist party, in its anti-imperialism phase, was a reasonable surrogate for a revolutionary party. Trotsky, in contrast, was violently opposed to the CCP-KMT alliance, because to join forces with Chiang Kai-Shek was, in his opinion, like making a pact with the devil.[18]

Trotsky's jaundiced view turned out to be a realistic one, when in 1927 Chiang Kai-Shek double-crossed the Communists and almost wiped them out completely in Shanghai.[19] At about this time Mao's voice was also becoming a stronger force within the party. He had been arguing for a break with the KMT and suggesting that the Communists move the base of their operations away from the cities and into the countryside.

Mao's thoughts on the revolutionary potential of the peasant masses were most clearly expressed in the report he wrote about the uprising in his home province of Hunan. In a moment of wishful thinking Mao predicted that there would soon be a successful but violent uprising in the Chinese countryside.

In a very short time, in China's central, southern and northern provinces, several hundred million peasants will rise like a mighty storm, like a hurricane, a force so swift and violent that no power, however great, will be able to hold it back. They will smash all the trammels that bind them and rush forward along the road to liberation. They will sweep away all the imperialists, warlords, corrupt officials, local tyrants and evil gentry into their graves.[20]

In Mao's view the revolution would be powered largely by the peasant masses. This meant that China did not need to wait for the urban proletariat to organize the revolution, and in fact Mao strongly believed that China's cities were centers of bourgeois conservatism that would continually stand in the way of the revolution.

Mao's view of the revolution also differed from the traditional Marxist emphasis on internationalism. Instead of situating the revolution within the broader context of worldwide socialism, as Lenin and Trotsky had attempted to do, Mao appealed solely to popular Chinese sentiments. In a country that had been humiliated by foreign intruders for more than a century, this was both a realistic and an effective sentiment.[21] In more ways than one Mao viewed the revolution as a war for national independence as much as a Marxist-guided struggle for class upheaval.[22]

The version of socialism that Mao was advocating represented a significant break with both the economic traditions of "feudal" China

and the cultural traditions of Confucian China. It is instructive, therefore, to examine some of the ways that Maoist political economy signaled a break with the Chinese past.

The Leap from Capitalism to Socialism

The basis of a capitalist economy is a system with minimal government interference. This allows all individuals in the society, whether they are acting as entrepreneurs, workers, or consumers, to pursue their own interests freely. In terms of production it implies that actions are driven primarily by the profit motive; whereas for consumption it means that individuals are able to shop around until they maximize their overall utility.

At the global scale capitalism has been amazingly successful. The seductive power of material incentive has allowed millions of people to raise their living standards to previously unimaginable levels. This happens as a result of the workings of the "invisible hand" of market forces. The factors of production are used efficiently, output increases, and national wealth expands almost inexorably.

In China capitalism was not working this way in the first decades of the twentieth century. Although a new bourgeois class was emerging in the 1930s and 1940s, it was unable to establish the infrastructure needed for the successful development of capitalism.[23] China was suffering from some of the centrifugal tendencies that had threatened to tear the country apart for centuries, and the bourgeois class appeared to be unable to replace the chaos of feuding regional warlords with a nationally unified government.

In the countryside, poverty, misery, and starvation were endemic. As the British historian R. H. Tawney described the situation in the early 1930s, "Over a large area of China, the rural population suffers horribly through the insecurity of life and property. . . . There are districts in which the position of the rural population is that of a man standing permanently up to the neck in water, so that even a ripple is sufficient to drown him."[24]

The devastating poverty that Tawney observed can be attributed partly to politics and partly to geography. China had been overrun for more than a century by imperialist powers. Superimposed onto that was almost constant civil strife: first to remove the dynastic legacy, then between the regional warlords. In addition to this perpetual chaos, life in rural China, which was marginal at the best of times, was prone to seasonal disasters brought on by floods and droughts, as well as the occasional earthquake. In agricultural terms much of China's territory was unusable, for reasons of topography and climate.

The cause of poverty in prerevolutionary China lay in the ownership of the forces of production. A tiny elite group ruled supreme over the masses, extracting from them their very lifeblood. This group—the emperor, regional warlords, bureaucrats, landlords, moneylenders, and military officials—took what they wanted from the peasants and left them with barely enough to live on. From the standpoint of the elite there was no incentive to change the way things were. Its members (particularly the landlords) monopolized the ownership of land and virtually all of the productive resources in the countryside (as the cartogram in Figure 4.2 illustrates). For

the elite poverty was "a pre-requisite for their . . . accumulation of wealth, their privileges, and their social, political, and economic domination."[25]

In his travels through war-ravaged south China in the early 1940s, Graham Peck recorded the deadly consequences of the drain on the peasants caused by the incessant demands of the landlord class. Even in wartime, with the normal supply lines cut and production drastically reduced, the landlords kept up their demands—in fact, Peck discovered, rice was being smuggled out of the countryside by local entrepreneurs to sell to the enemy (the Japanese). In 1943 all of this misery was compounded by a serious drought in Guangdong Province, which caused rationing of food and a sharp increase in grain prices. In spite of this the peasants had to continue paying their tithes and taxes to the landlords, and to do this many of them were forced to sell off what little land and property they owned. To eat, they were forced to buy back some of the rice they had paid as taxes to the

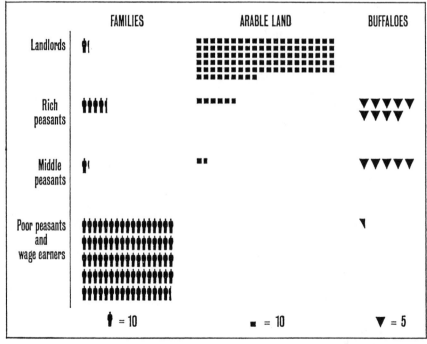

Figure 4.2 Cartogram illustrating the pattern of inequality in ownership of the means of production in a North Jiangsu rural community in prerevolutionary China. Source: K. Buchanan, 1970, The Transformation of the Chinese Earth: Aspects of the Evaluation of the Chinese Earth from Earliest Times to Mao Tse-tung (London: G. Bell and Sons), p. 119.

landlords. When their money ran out, they had to resort to eating leaves, but after a drought-affected poor harvest the leaves were soon all gone, and the peasants were left with only bark or clay to eat. Later still some of them were forced into even more desperate measures. "They would eat their seed-grain, kill and eat their beloved farm animals . . . destroying their hope of ever farming again without new debts."[26]

To save money peasant families were forced to bury their dead naked and without coffins, which was a devastating blow to people who revered their ancestors. Soon they were too weak and too poor to bury their dead at all, electing to drag the corpses out into the fields. Some people turned to banditry, others had to resort to the degrading trade in human flesh. "Some would begin by selling the less useful members of their families . . . women and children were sold by the pound even when they were sold as slaves, not food, and the day when the price of a pound of human flesh sank below that of a pound of grain could be taken as the point at which the famine had settled into its final stretch."[27]

Added to all of this was the inability of the peasants to do anything to alter their own situations. The high rates of illiteracy in the countryside; the lethargy borne of constant malnutrition; the centuries of blind Confucian acceptance of the status quo; and the tendency to seek refuge in spiritual explanations of adversity—all contributed to an acceptance of the way things were. It was clear that it would take a cataclysmic force to awaken the peasantry, make them aware of their oppression, and give them the confidence needed to challenge the elite groups. Centuries of passivity and a chronic lack of organization would need to be swept away.

The Maoist version of Marxism offered such a solution to the Chinese peasant masses. A radical restructuring of rural society would give the peasants a chance to overcome their powerlessness and bring about real changes in the centuries-old patterns of inequality. The way to achieve this was through *land reform*, which had already been carried out in the old Communist base areas before the revolution. To heighten the class struggle and mobilize the masses, the peasants had to be educated about their rights to the land and encouraged to denounce their landlords. If

necessary, the landlords would be executed and the peasants would take possession of their land.

The essential first step in this process was a careful study of class relationships, to identify the poor peasants who would then have a crucial role to play in the revolution. According to Mao's definitions, the poor peasantry represented about 70 percent of the rural population. Some of them owned land, but often there was barely enough to provide food at even the subsistence level. Most of them were tenants, small handicrafters, shop assistants, peddlers, and beggars. These were the marginal groups in the Chinese countryside "whose only hope of improved living conditions lay in the complete remolding of the social and economic order."[28]

The major goal of land reform was to raise the level of human potential in the Chinese countryside, with a focus on all of the people rather than just the best and most productive. At the grass-roots level this process would require some fundamental changes in human character. Mao Zedong believed that people would have to make great sacrifices to bring about any permanent changes, committing themselves to many years of hard work and self-denial. He hoped that the new "communist man" (and woman) would, through frugal living and constant struggle, eventually be able to "move the mountain," as the character in the Old Fool story had done (see Chapter 2).

It is significant that at the end of his version of the Old Fool story, Mao modified the original to read as follows: "We must work persistently, work ceaselessly, and we too may be able to touch God's heart."[29] As this suggests, Mao knew that the Chinese people would need some help from higher sources. In light of his revulsion toward Christianity, it is ironical that Mao left in his version of the story the reference to God in the traditional folktale. There are some other parallels between Maoism and Christianity—for example, the values of Mao's new "communist man" were similar in some ways to the asceticism that followed the Protestant Reformation and to the values associated with the rise of capitalism. Bearing in mind some of the often violent opposition to communist principles among Christians in the West, it is interesting to note some of the similarities: For example, both the Protestant ethic and Mao's call for self-discipline focused on hard work and self-sacrifice among the populace.

Marx himself actually considered the dominance of ascetic values to be inherently repressive. Although self-sacrifice would be necessary for the revolutionary proletariat during the early stages of capitalist industrialization, in the long run, Marx hoped, such asceticism could be dispensed with as the communist utopia was achieved. This suggests another fundamental divergence between Maoism and Marxism, in that Mao's new "communist man" had essentially bourgeois values, which Marx assumed would have been "relegated to the 'dustbin of history' with the transition to a socialist society."[30] In Mao's revolution this did not happen; in fact Mao hoped that instead of disappearing, the ascetic values of the spiritually remolded person would continue to set an example for the masses by demonstrating the value of "plain living and hard work."[31]

The Leap from Confucianism to Socialism

After the account of Confucianism in Chapter 3, it should come as no surprise that the CCP was violently opposed to the traditional Confucian value system in China. At various times after 1949 the Party launched anti-Confucius campaigns. At one level the campaigns were symbolically directed at political moderates like Zhou Enlai; but at another level they also involved virulent attacks on Confucian values. Mao felt that the Five Constant Virtues were symbolic of the rigid class system that existed in "feudal" China.[32] The Communists also felt that excessive loyalty to the family, although traditionally Chinese, detracted somewhat from loyalty to the Party and the state.

Mao also considered the Confucian education system to be fundamentally unjust, giving unfair advantages to intellectuals and to book learning. As a self-educated son of a peasant, he was determined to break down the Confucian meritocracy and to reward manual labor at an equal if not a higher rate than mental labor. The true Maoist hero would be the educated youth who goes to the countryside to learn from the peasants. If successful, such a person would emerge "with a dark skin and a red heart,"[33] proof that he

or she valued hard work and was politically reliable.[34]

The Communists probably also blamed the Confucian value system for the stultification of Chinese economic development and the stagnation of its culture. Unlike the utopian socialists, traditional Confucian scholars had very little to say about the future. They emphasized social harmony but basically accepted the world as it was. Confucius himself had no concept of a paradise that could be attained on earth, although he did yearn for a return to the peace and plenty of the "Golden Age" in China during the Zhang and Zhou dynasties.[35]

The frequent attacks launched on Confucianism by the CCP proved to be only partially successful, and as we saw in Chapter 3, not only have Confucian values refused to die in postrevolutionary China, they have actually reemerged vigorously in recent years. Critics of communism argue that this was because no consistent set of social or moral values has emerged as a viable alternative to Confucianism in China. In addition there has not been enough development in the material base to support the emerging values of socialism. As Mao had predicted, class struggle and hard work continued well into the 1980s for the majority of the Chinese people, but it has proved difficult, if not impossible, for the leadership to convince the people that they should rally around such austere values.

The Maoist utopia, in which there would be no class divisions, no differentiation between city and country, and equality between men and women, has clearly not been achieved. There are still hierarchies in the new China, but they are based on political savvy rather than on Confucian learning. It seems that after so many centuries of having rigid status differentiations within society, the Chinese have learned to tolerate a certain amount of inequality.

Another interpretation of the persistence of Confucianism is related to the breakdown of social and economic order that occurred during the Cultural Revolution years (1966–1976). During this period there was a return to the sorts of chaotic conditions that fostered the development of Confucian values centuries ago. As one observer has suggested: "The old patterns . . . [of Confucianism], never eradicated, re-emerge strongly under such chaotic conditions and prove how functional they are for muddling through. . . . As long as nothing viable has appeared to supplant them, they will not go away."[36]

There are some similarities in the value systems of Confucianism and Mao's version of socialism that help to explain why so many Chinese intellectuals were prepared to support socialism, and why the old Confucian values have stayed so close to the surface during the socialist era. The most obvious similarity is that both socialism and Confucianism have a vision of a good and moral society without the presence of a god or a godlike symbol. In addition they both emphasize group over individual values, although the socialist group (the collective) generally operates at a larger scale than the traditional Confucian family.

There is also an emphasis in both socialism and Confucianism on the notion of sacrifice. For the greater good of society, individuals are expected to sublimate their personal aspirations. Under socialism the sacrifice would be necessary to achieve a better world in the future. The consensus among the Chinese people by the end of the 1980s was that after four decades the struggle had not been worthwhile, and it was time (for some of them at least) to look for a viable alternative. We saw in June 1989 that the elite within the CCP was not ready to share its power with anyone, and they were willing to go to any lengths to silence opposition. In a subsequent section we shall explore the different phases of this four-decade-long struggle to bring about a socialist transformation in China, from the glory days of the revolution to the desperation of the late 1980s. Before that exploration it is necessary to introduce briefly some of the key elements of Chinese political economy since the Communist takeover in 1949.

CHINESE POLITICAL ECONOMY

The fundamental difference between a socialist and a capitalist economy is in *the ownership of the means of production.* Until the 1980s the vast majority of the productive forces in China were owned and operated either by the state or by collectives—subgroups of the population such as production teams, neighborhoods, communes, or even whole counties. Most of the "heavy" industry is still state owned, but "light" industry is usually collectively owned and operated, and in recent years it is increasingly likely to be owned "privately," either by specialized households or by new economic cooperatives (see Chapter 6).

One of the most visible differences between China's economic landscape and that of other nations is *the convergence between city and country.* Since 1949 there have been persistent efforts to introduce industry into the countryside, to such an extent that it is often impossible to differentiate between urban and rural landscapes. Small towns all over China are bristling with industry; in fact by 1983 rural collectives were responsible for more than three-quarters of China's industrial enterprises, making up over one-fifth of its total industrial output.[37] The buildup of rural industries created jobs and incomes for people who were not needed on the land. In addition, rural industry helps to supply the manufactured inputs to agriculture, such as farm machinery and fertilizer, thereby reducing transportation costs and increasing local self-sufficiency.

Foreign visitors to China are always surprised by the amount of agriculture that takes place within the city, sometimes within walking distance of the city center. In a country with such an unfavorable land-to-people ratio, it makes good sense to use all available plots of land for growing food. As we shall see in later chapters, urban agriculture also helps to reduce the dichotomy between the city and the countryside, a goal that the CCP has clung to doggedly for four decades.[38]

Another feature of the socialist economy until the 1970s was *the highly centralized system of state control* over all economic decision-making. This was most evident immediately after Liberation in 1949, when decisions came directly from the "center" all the way down to local farms and enterprises. Since these early years the Chinese Communists have experimented several times with a more decentralized decision-making system. This began during the Great Leap Forward in 1958, when control of much of the country's light industry was shifted down to the provincial level, with the state dealing only with defense and basic industries, such as steel and coal mining.

After returning to a more centralized planning system in the early 1960s, the country's economy was thrust into turmoil during the Cultural Revolution years (1966–1976), and the struggle to win control over industry became highly politicized. It was not until the era of economic reforms after 1978 that the first significant attempts to decentralize down to the enterprise level were made.

At the center of a socialist economy is usually a *regulated price system*. Floating prices could of course create havoc for a country where the major emphasis is on capital accumulation rather than private consumption. It has also been important for the government to guarantee the people access to basic commodities and services at reasonable prices. In the cities, for example, cheap food was made available by pricing agricultural products significantly lower than industrial output (this is the infamous "scissors effect," which occurs when economic planners favor industry at the expense of agriculture).[39]

After the initial transformation from what Mao called "semifeudal capitalism" to socialism, the ultimate goal of the CCP was to steer a course toward communism. In preparing for this transformation, the state would need to develop its "economic base," composed of the "forces of production" and the "relations of production."[40] The focus on these two components in postrevolutionary China, and their relative importance, would vary over time as different theories were embraced by the leadership. In the prerevolutionary days and immediately after 1949, the Communists set about to dismantle the existing relations of production in the countryside, which they did in the land-reform era by dispossessing the landlords and giving their land to the peasants. Thus at first it appeared that all they had done was to replace one form of private landownership with another (more democratic) form.[41] Only after this process was successfully completed was it possible to focus on the forces of production in the countryside by trying to increase agricultural output through collective production methods. This is what Mao Zedong meant by "putting politics in command." It was essential to win the class struggle by developing first the relations of production before attempting to develop the economy by building up the forces of production.

As this example illustrates, however, even before the political struggle can be contested,

the consciousness of the peasants had to be raised significantly. This began before the revolution in the Communist-controlled parts of rural China, where the new Red Army (the Eighth Route Army) worked diligently to instill revolutionary zeal into the peasants, using a combination of education and propaganda, backed up by force. The Red Army was different from any other army that had ever been seen in the Chinese countryside. The peasants were encouraged to speak out about their oppression for probably the first time ever, in the "speak bitterness" campaigns. With the army behind them, the peasants could realistically envision a new future for themselves, and for the whole of China. The Red Army, in other words, was not so much an army as "a people in arms. . . . To millions of peasants, soldiers and civilians alike, the Red Army brought the immediate promise of a new existence, of liberation from all the evils of the old society."[42]

The Communists realized that before the system of landownership could be challenged, it was necessary to change the way the peasants thought about themselves and their ability to challenge the status quo. To do this it would be necessary to alter fundamentally the society's "superstructure": its dominant ideology, its systems of thought, and the institutions that legitimate the existing form of government.[43] Changing a society's superstructure is a process rather than a onetime event, and as Mao predicted, the struggle to reform the superstructure would probably continue indefinitely.[44]

THE SOCIALIST TRANSFORMATION

To describe the flow of events in China after the revolution in 1949, it is helpful to outline three major phases in the attempt to bring about the socialist transformation, namely: the Stalinist, or Soviet, era, which lasted from 1949 to about 1957; the Maoist era, from 1958 to 1976; and the Dengist era, from 1978 to 1990 (see Table 4.1).

The Stalinist, or Soviet, Era: 1949–1957

Immediately following the revolution, the CCP was faced with the overwhelming task of developing the national economy. To do this it was necessary to put in abeyance much

Table 4.1 Strategies of Socialist Development (1949-1989)

	Stalinist/ Soviet Era	Maoist Era	Dengist Era
Major area of focus for political/economic strategies	Social system (nationwide infrastructure)	Individuals (producing the "new communist man")	Production units (enterprises, individuals, families)
Structural point of policy initiative	Center	Intermediate level (commune)	Production unit
Economic base/ superstructure emphasis	Mainly forces of production -- less emphasis on relations of production	Mainly relations of production and superstructure	Forces of production
Economic sector emphasized	Heavy industry	Simultaneous development of industry and agriculture	Agriculture and light industry (consumption emphasis)
Type of incentive offered	Individual, material incentive	Moral incentive at individual level, material incentive at group/collective level	Individual, material incentive
Role of the Communist party	Centralized rule from "top down"	Social mobilizer as process of continuous revolution	Contradiction between economic decentralization and Party political power
International economic relations	Integration with USSR and socialist economies	Self-reliance	Integration into the world market economy

Source: Adapted from P. Van Ness and S. Raichur, 1983, "Dilemmas of Socialist Development: An Analysis of Strategic Lines in China, 1949-1981," in Bulletin of Concerned Asia Scholars (eds.), *China from Mao to Deng: The Politics and Economics of Socialist Development* (Armonk, N.Y.: M.E. Sharpe, Inc.), p. 83.

of the prerevolutionary politics that had helped the Communists to win the support of the peasants in the base areas. The pragmatic solution was to follow the model of their close allies in the Soviet Union. At this point, the major objective was to develop the forces of production, in other words, to get the economy moving as rapidly as possible. Thus, in 1953, a series of Five Year Plans was adopted, focusing on the development of heavy industry, somewhat at the expense of agriculture. This was a highly centralized "command" economy, largely dependent on Soviet finance, technology, and personnel.

In economic terms this phase of development was highly successful: Between 1953 and 1957 industrial production grew at an average rate that exceeded 25 percent each year.[45] Agricultural production, however, grew at a much slower rate, perhaps as little as 5 percent or less each year during this period.[46] The Chinese adopted the Soviet model of development because they had few other choices in the 1950s, but it is likely that many of the country's leaders, especially Mao Ze-dong, did so with considerable feelings of ambivalence. The focus on heavy industry in the existing centers of economic strength was sharply discordant with the Maoist goals for geographical equality between the regions, between the city and the countryside, and, most important, between industry and agri-culture. It was not surprising, therefore, that by the late 1950s, a marked shift to the "left" was observable, and a set of economic policies more closely aligned to Mao's political thought emerged.

The Maoist Era: 1958–1976

In spite of the successes of the First Five Year Plan, Mao believed that the task of building socialism called for a return to some of the principles that had led the Communist party to its victory in 1949. Mao felt that the centralized economic and political system de-veloped during the First Five Year Plan was much too conservative. It needed an injection of dynamism and a greater level of partici-pation by the masses. In recommending a change of strategy, Mao was arguing that economic development was a dialectical rather than a scientific process. The transformation to socialism in China had produced its own set of contradictions, and these required some radical changes in strategy. It occurred to some of Mao's critics that his economic de-velopment strategies were not so much a set of well-worked-out plans as a process of discovery, or more accurately, a process of trial and error.[47]

What Mao advocated in the late 1950s was in some ways a swing back toward the suc-cessful mass-mobilization campaigns con-ducted in the prerevolutionary Communist base areas. Mao argued for a gigantic collective effort in which individuals would be exhorted to "serve the people," and by doing so, also serve themselves. This began with the Great Leap Forward (1958–1960) and the continuing efforts to collectivize Chinese agriculture on a vast scale (see Chapter 5). Compared to its status during the Five Year Plan era, heavy industry would be relatively deemphasized, and agricultural development would be stressed. The economy would be learning how to "walk on two legs," emphasizing industry and agriculture about equally. Mao dreamed

that the new basis for spatial organization in agriculture and industry would be the people's commune, which in his words was "the best organizational form for carrying out the two transitions, from socialist . . . to all-embracing public; and from all-embracing public to com-munist ownership."[48]

In this era the emphasis had shifted again, from the forces of production to the relations of production. The prerevolutionary concen-tration on class struggle was to be renewed; the last vestiges of private ownership were to be purged from the landscape; and Mao's new "communist man" would be exhorted to lead the way. The Great Leap Forward was intended to bring about a major transfor-mation toward socialism and economic mod-ernization.

With the advantage of hindsight, most commentators agree that the Great Leap failed because it was based too heavily on the radical politics of the prerevolutionary base area.[49] These strategies had worked well when China was struggling to repel the Japanese and the Communists were embroiled in a bitter civil war with the Nationalists, but they were not realistic for peacetime in the late 1950s. China was relatively secure from foreign occupation, and the people were ready to experience some major improvements in their material living standards. They were tiring of the revolu-tionary struggle, and most of them were prob-ably not looking forward to the prospect of prolonged austerity that Mao had predicted.[50]

In the early 1960s there was a retreat from the extreme radicalism of the Great Leap, and this helped somewhat with the economic re-covery from the disastrous years of 1959 to 1961. Mao Zedong was temporarily diverted from his radical course, and he interpreted this period as one in which the Party was essentially back-pedaling away from social-ism. To prevent this Mao launched an all-out campaign to revitalize the class struggle by enhancing the revolutionary consciousness of the peasants and workers.

Applying the terminology introduced ear-lier in this chapter, this meant that Mao was trying to shift the focus of the nation's political economy, in an attempt to alter the super-structure, which at that time he felt was a prerequisite for changing the relations of pro-duction. The result, by the latter part of the

1960s, was the Great Proletariat Cultural Revolution, which began in 1966. Mao was anxious to revive what he considered to be a faltering revolution by changing the thinking of those who favored the "capitalist road" to economic development. To outsiders the Cultural Revolution was a baffling and chaotic era. What hit the headlines most prominently was the clash between the "leftist" thoughts of the Maoists and the "rightist" thoughts of his opponents, who were usually characterized as the followers of Premier Liu Shaoqi. The Cultural Revolution degenerated into a mass movement in which Mao and his supporters, including the infamous Red Guards, struggled to remove their opponents from power. Not surprisingly, during this period very little progress was made to transform China's economy in the direction of communism.[51]

The Dengist Era: 1978–1990

In more ways than one 1976 was a traumatic year in China. In January the people mourned the death of their beloved premier, Zhou Enlai; in the summer the old revolutionary army veteran Zhu De died; and in September Mao himself died. In between there was a devastating earthquake in Tangshan, killing a quarter of a million people. The struggle for Mao's successor heated up after 1976; four of his supporters (the Gang of Four) were arrested and awaited what would become the most comprehensive and certainly the most public trial since the founding of the PRC.

Deng Xiaoping, as a result of the changing winds of fortune in Chinese politics, had already been purged twice and rehabilitated, and in 1978 he was called upon again; this time he would open up a new era in China's history. Deng seized on a theme that had been introduced by Zhou Enlai, the Four Modernizations, which involved an ambitious plan to turn China into a powerful socialist country by the beginning of the twenty-first century, with modern agriculture, industry, national defense, and science and technology.

The new strategy was adjusted numerous times as circumstances altered, but the general patterns of it had become fairly clear by the middle of the 1980s (the details of the economic reforms will be dealt with in greater detail in Chapters 5 and 6). The emphasis had clearly been shifted away from the relations of production and back toward the development of the productive forces. This was to be achieved by a combination of market mechanisms working within an overall state plan. The new strategies have emphasized more autonomy for production units at the local level; they have made possible much greater levels of material reward and have allowed higher levels of personal consumption than was the case at any previous time since 1949.

In spite of all these changes, the leaders of the CCP have continually insisted that China is still a socialist country. In 1979, the rising star of the CCP, Zhao Ziyang, argued that China must continue to emphasize public ownership of the means of production and a socialist distribution system based on the principle of "to each according to his work."[52] By 1987, however, Zhao had risen to the position of premier and he had changed his tune considerably. At that time he was clearly advocating the coexistence of public and private ownership in China and arguing for distribution systems based on, among other things, incomes earned from shares and profits.[53] This dramatic shift, according to Zhao, was justified by China's unique situation in the 1980s. It was no longer possible, he argued, to adhere rigidly to Marxist theory or even to follow the examples of other socialist nations who were attempting economic reforms. What China needed was to apply the basic principles of socialism to its own specific circumstances, to build what would become widely known as "socialism with Chinese characteristics."[54]

In 1987 Premier Zhao took the unprecedented step of criticizing the economic policies of the past, hinting that some elements of traditional socialism had hampered China's ability to develop its economy. Although Zhao's words were heavily guarded, his message was clear: "Undue emphasis was placed on a single form of ownership, and a rigid economic structure took shape. . . . All of this seriously hampered the development of the productive forces and of the socialist commodity economy."[55]

The shift toward market socialism was seen as necessary by the more pragmatic leadership that had taken over in China after Mao's death. In this sense the developments of the

1980s can be interpreted as a retreat from the traditionally egalitarian socialist views on the issue of the ownership of land and capital; in other words the relations of production were no longer being emphasized as much as they had been in the Maoist era. Throughout the 1980s the emphasis was clearly on developing the forces of production, using the power of material incentive as the motivating force.

Taking the "capitalist road" in this fashion has allowed some individuals and households to "get rich," thereby once again opening up the inequality gap in China. In 1988 outsiders were speculating about how the CCP would respond if it suddenly decided that market forces had gone too far and the entire reform process needed to be halted. As we saw clearly in the early summer of 1989, the leadership was willing to go to extreme measures to halt *any* movement considered to be contrary to its own best interests. The sails of the emerging Democracy Movement were sharply trimmed, and it remains to be seen whether the Party will also try to shift away from the economic reforms toward a more hard-line, or "leftist," stance on economic development. Although most Western economists argue that China can not afford to abandon its impressive reform agenda, it is apparent that, as usual, the CCP will continue to steer its own course.

The tragedy of 1989 has brought home the close relationship between the issues of economic and political reform in contemporary China. It is reasonable to suggest that the loosening of China's economy during the 1980s helped to generate the calls for political reform that produced the "Beijing spring" of 1989.[56] After the brutal clampdown on the Democracy Movement in 1989, China faced an economic crisis even greater than the one it had encountered in 1988 (the year of "hyperinflation"). Those people who had taken the "private road" in an attempt to better themselves could no longer be certain that the government would continue to support their actions in the 1990s. In addition to this, confidence among China's trading partners was at an all-time low level, and the threat of investment withdrawals was a real one. The extra pressure caused by such developments will further complicate the already delicate future of the economic reform movement in China.

Evaluating the Record, 1949–1990

It is difficult to evaluate the success of the socialist economy in post-Liberation China, partly because of the shortage of useful indicators and partly because of the political biases among the observers. In historical terms, however, there is little doubt that Chinese socialism brought an end to the destitution of the 1930s and 1940s. By the 1980s China was able to feed, clothe, and shelter its people considerably better than many of the world's poor countries.[57] The growth of the gross domestic product (GDP) in China in the 1980s was higher than anywhere else in the world: For example, between 1980 and 1986 China's annual growth rate averaged 10.5 percent, which was three times higher than the average for all of the world's developing countries. What is more amazing is that China's growth has even outstripped that recorded in the newly industrializing countries in Asia (Japan, South Korea, Taiwan, Singapore, and Hong Kong; see Table 4.2).

One may conclude from the indicators shown in Table 4.2 that China has significantly outperformed the other Asian developing countries along a number of dimensions. The birthrate in China is far lower than the average for developing countries and as low as it is in some of the NICs. On another measure of the overall quality of life, the per capita availability of doctors, China is better placed than all the other counties in question with the exception of Japan. Nevertheless, in comparison to the NICs, China lags far behind Asia's developed nations in some important areas, most notably in terms of average income levels, the proportion of the work force engaged in service occupations, and the level of infant mortality.[58]

It is interesting to speculate on Mao Zedong's attitude toward such achievements. He surely would have been proud to see that China was able to "stand up" in the world community; but he would not have approved of the way the economic gains were made in the 1980s. It is also a safe bet that Mao, like his counterparts at the head of the CCP in 1989, would not have tolerated the scenes that were broadcast around the world from Tiananmen Square in April and May of that year. No doubt he would have evaluated his old adversary, Deng Xiaoping, very negatively for his part in the reform process, but he

Table 4.2 Demographic, Social, and Economic Indicators: China, Asian Developing Countries, and Asian Newly Industrializing Countries, 1986

	Population Doubling Time, in years	Birthrate per 1,000	Per Capita Income (U.S. $)	% Avg. Real Growth of GNP	% Work Force in Services and Commerce	Doctors per 1,000	Infant Mortality per 1,000 Population
China	53	21	250	7.80	12.2	1.36	61.0
Bangladesh	26	44	128	3.80	16.4	0.16	128.0
India	31	35	220	3.50	12.3	0.28	110.0
Philippines	28	33	535	-0.57	30.3	0.88	51.0
Pakistan	25	43	334	6.50	25.9	0.44	120.0
Japan	107	13	8,316	5.80	53.1	1.50	6.2
South Korea	43	23	1,954	6.80	42.0	1.30	30.0
Taiwan	47	20	3,142	6.40	34.8	0.90	8.9
Singapore	64	16	5,847	5.10	62.9	1.00	9.4
Hong Kong	72	14	6,311	5.00	36.2	0.90	9.2

Source: Adapted from Far Eastern Economic Review, 1988, *Asia Yearbook: 1988* (Hong Kong: Review Publications Co.), pp. 6-9.

would probably have approved of the hard-line solution to the student demonstrations.

These speculations provide a way of putting present activities into their historical context. Obviously we will never know what Mao would have thought about Deng, but we do not have to speculate about what Deng and his cohort at the top of the CCP have thought about Mao since his death, because most of it has been a matter of public record. In the final section of this chapter we shall briefly examine that record.

MAO ZEDONG: LOOKING BACK ON A LEGEND

Everyone in his life has wished at one time or another for someone he disliked to be trundled off to shovel shit—especially an uppity person who had never gotten his hands dirty. Mao carried this satisfying little fantasy to its nasty limit.
—Paul Theroux[59]

On one of his train journeys across China, Paul Theroux thought to himself how nice it would be to banish someone you did not like to a remote corner of the realm to work as a peasant. This sort of thing had become commonplace in the PRC in the 1950s, and it was developed into a fine art during Mao

Zedong's Cultural Revolution. Theroux's fantasies were deflated quickly when he realized that as an "intellectual," he would probably have been one of the first people to be exiled by Mao!

Since 1976 the Chinese Communist party has on a number of occasions attempted to put the record straight on Mao Zedong and the Cultural Revolution. Cynics have referred to such actions (with some justification) as attempts to falsify or reinterpret history to fit better with contemporary beliefs. In the late 1970s the CCP wanted to rebuild the country's morale and, more important, to regain the popular support of the Chinese people. The Party's legitimacy had reached an all-time low as a result of more than ten years of chaos, and some serious bridge building between itself and the people was needed. The major difficulty was to devise a strategy that could gently point out some of Mao's errors without criticizing the Party or the entire system of government that had allowed such errors to occur.

The chosen strategy began by very gently demythologizing Mao.[60] The campaign was conducted on several fronts: for example, by recirculating some of his more moderate speeches; pointing out instances in which he had made mistakes, thereby challenging his omniscience; demoting leaders associated with Mao in the past and promoting Dengist replacements, such as Zhao Ziyang and Hu Yaobang; and rehabilitating some of Mao's former foes, most notably Liu Shaoqi (for whom the event occurred posthumously).

In 1981 this campaign was accelerated and the party moved toward a major reappraisal of Mao Zedong. Mao's ideas and his philosophy were criticized and judged to be neither Marxist-Leninist nor in keeping with China's situation; and a number of his specific policies were also criticized. He was accused of becoming an elitist and acting in an arbitrary fashion.[61] In a document that became known as the Authoritative Assessment of Mao's "Left Error," the party described the case against Mao in no uncertain terms: "Chief responsibility for the grave 'Left error' of the Cultural Revolution does indeed lie with comrade Mao Zedong . . . he began to get arrogant. . . . He gradually divorced himself from the masses . . . he committed gross mistakes during the Cultural Revolution."[62]

To preserve some "face" for both Mao and the CCP, he was at the same time hailed as a great proletarian revolutionary and theorist, and the document concluded that "if we judge his activities as a whole his contributions to the Chinese revolution far outweigh his mistakes."[63] This suggests that the leadership was split in its evaluation of Mao Zedong, which may be a result of either genuine ambivalence toward Mao or (more likely) political opportunism. The new leaders have shown themselves to be nothing if not pragmatic, and the mixed reviews of Mao may simply have been a way to leave the doors open for themselves should the winds of fortune ever blow again in Mao's direction.

Although that is an unlikely scenario, we would do well to remember that nothing about Chinese politics is simple or obvious for outsiders to interpret. Deng Xiaoping himself, twice purged by Mao's wrath, but always the quintessential pragmatist, has actually reinterpreted some of his own actions to show that Mao would probably have approved of them. Of his activities in the 1980s, Deng said, "In many respects . . . we are doing things . . . that comrade Mao suggested but failed to do himself."[64] Ironically, and almost absurdly in an Orwellian sense, the conclusion to be gained from the Authoritative Assessment is that Mao, in committing his "leftist" errors, was actually in violation of Mao Zedong Thought, which in spite of Mao's fall from grace has remained one of the guiding principles of Chinese socialism.

In spite of Deng's vacillation, 1981 saw the start of the "de facto demise of Mao Zedong thought."[65] Mao's "leftist" tendencies were criticized, and an attempt was made for the first time to downplay the significance of the 1949 revolution. Several prominent "former Nationalists" were subsequently appointed to the Chinese People's Political Consultative Conference (CPPCC), people who had been active Chiang Kai-Shek supporters during the Civil War. The CPPCC is only a consultative body with no executive power, but these appointments signified a thawing of relationships between Taiwan and the PRC and a gradual rapprochement with the Kuomintang. Consistent with the market-oriented reforms there has also been a relaxation in the party's attitude to "former capitalists," people who were vilified by the Maoists because of their "bad class backgrounds." In Deng Xiaoping's words, "most of [them] . . . no longer exist as a class and have been transformed into working people earning their own living."[66]

From all accounts the reinterpretation of Mao Zedong in the 1980s was not accompanied, as it might have been in the past or in the Soviet Union, with extreme purging activities, although it is abundantly clear that the government is still willing to employ such tactics. There was, during the early 1980s, a certain amount of pruning to remove the hard-line Maoists from the higher echelons of the Party, but on balance the attitude within the Party was conciliatory.[67]

In 1986 Deng Xiaoping's overall assessment of Mao Zedong was that "his contributions are primary and his mistakes secondary." Deng promised that Mao, as the founder of the Party and the state, would always be revered by the people and that "we will forever keep Chairman Mao's portrait on Tiananmen Gate as a symbol of our country."[68] In an average year there have been an estimated ten million visitors to Mao's mausoleum in Tiananmen Square, most of whom agree with the official line that Mao's mistakes have now been rectified. In an attempt to kill two birds with one stone, a *Beijing Review* reporter suggested that Mao had built the

Figure 4.3 Statue of Mao Zedong, outside the Luoyang tractor factory, still standing in 1986. Many similar statues have disappeared, but according to rumors, some were reerected in the period after the Tiananmen Square crackdown.

foundations on which Deng Xiaoping was able to implement his much needed reforms (see Figure 4.3).[69]

A far less sanguine view of Mao Zedong has been emerging in the West. In the late 1970s some Western academics began to draw analogies between Mao's China and Stalin's Soviet Union. The official reassessment of Stalin began with Nikita Khrushchev's famous "secret speech" in 1953, which praised Stalin, but pointed out the negative consequences of his personality cult, and then began to lambaste his ideology and actions.[70] Until the 1980s most Western scholars were satisfied that China's socialist transformation had differed sharply from Stalin's in the Soviet Union. As we saw earlier in this chapter, beginning in the late 1950s Mao consciously tried to divorce himself from Soviet economic policies,

particularly in the emphasis on heavy industrialization led from the center and the vilification of the peasantry. According to these earlier accounts Mao tried to implement policies that Stalin had considered far too utopian; for example, Mao emphasized decentralized development and a cooperative relationship with the peasants. The orthodox view at that time was that Mao had tried genuinely to tackle the typical deficiencies of Marxist-Leninist political systems, most notably the drift toward bureaucratic elitism and the lack of popular participation.[71]

Beginning in the early 1980s, however, a number of China scholars have pointed out the essential similarities between Maoist and Stalinist policies.[72] This campaign has been launched on many fronts, suggesting that Mao's China, like Stalin's Soviet Union:

- Gave absolute priority to heavy industry and "squeezed" the peasants, effectively ignoring agriculture
- Produced a society dominated by a cynical, abusive, and privileged bureaucracy
- Was dominated by terror and repression, associated not only with the much publicized rampagings of the young Red Guards but also with an all-embracing "Soviet-style" police state[73]

In a later development of this argument, Andrew Walder suggested that Western academics created a straw man in their earlier appraisals of Mao Zedong.[74] Walder argued that the view of Maoism as a doctrine based on populist and egalitarian themes was "a rationalized, heavily edited reconstruction by Western scholars, for Western consumption, designed to appeal to Western sensibilities."[75] The implication is that sympathetic Western scholars "constructed" a positive view of Maoism to fit what they hoped was going on inside China under Mao. The reality, according to Walder, was much different, and the "actually existing Maoism" experienced by the Chinese people was another story (see Table 4.3).

A number of similar attacks on Mao Zedong have been made in recent years, and they have produced the expected wave of rebuttals and counterarguments.[76] The strong criticism voiced by Walder was by no means the most vitriolic. Others, motivated by a desire to

Table 4.3 Comparing the Western Views on Maoism with the Chinese Experience of Maoism

Western Distillations of Maoism	Actually Existing Maoism
Dissatisfaction with the "Soviet" model of development	A paranoid political worldview that sees China riddled with conspirators and traitors
A concern for equality	A tendency to ostracize and imprison individuals for opposing Maoist principles or not showing enough enthusiasm
Opposition to bureaucratism and corruption	A treatment of enemies as essentially "non-humans"
Idealizing ascetic life-styles	Slavish conformity to a single dictator's vision
Denial of individual selfishness	A definition of democracy that implies total uniformity of thought and behavior
Championing mass criticism and the right to dissent	Imprisonment and purging of dissenters

Source: Adapted from A. G. Walder, 1987, "Actually Existing Maoism," *Australian Journal of Chinese Affairs*, No. 18 (July), p. 158.

brand not only Maoism but all socialist governments, have taken a much harder line.

> Mao is no longer a hero to anyone who knows of the vigilante violence actually wrought by the Cultural Revolution or of the 20 plus million innocents who died as a result of Mao's Great Leap Forward. Although the government of China continues to censor . . . revelations of the horrors of the Mao era . . . the evidence that has leaked out persuasively establishes that the communist fundamentalism that Mao propagated was taking China down a bloody road, a "disastrous" one.[77]

Paralleling this all-out offensive on Mao Zedong during the middle of the 1980s was a widespread attempt in the Western media to document the bankruptcy of Communist ideology in contemporary China and the crisis in confidence then facing the Party.[78] Until 1989 the Party had been improving its image with the Chinese people as a result of the gains in prosperity made possible by the economic reforms. But toward the end of the decade, according to the Hong Kong–based *Far Eastern Economic Review*, the Party was once again losing ground and was "becoming increasingly irrelevant to people's lives," which

suggests that the resurgence in interest in the Party described at the beginning of this chapter was destined to be short-lived.[79] The argument being portrayed in the media was that although the new market socialism was helping the economy and some people were indeed starting to become (relatively) rich, there was no longer any ideological commitment in China: "The reforms are secularizing the Party and gutting its core belief structure. There is nothing comparable to put in its place."[80]

One of the lessons to be learned from all that happened in China in the late 1980s is that everything—ideas, policies, and personnel—can change like the wind. Deng Xiaoping's choice in the early 1980s to lead the new drive to modernization, Zhao Ziyang, appeared to be on a meteoric rise to fame, both at home and abroad. He was, like the official that William Hinton wrote about in *Shenfan*, a "helicopter cadre."[81] In 1987 Zhao told the gathered assembly at the 17th Party Congress that the new "commodity economy" would last for a hundred years, which suggested that China should abandon the idea of communism for the foreseeable future.[82] But by October 1988 Zhao's credibility was in question. He had apparently been blamed for the problems in China's economy, which culminated in a disastrous inflation rate and a spate of panic withdrawals from savings banks all across China. He was probably demoted at that time, and he all but disappeared from public view. It seems that Zhao's attempts to modernize China's economy were moving too rapidly for the Party leaders. Once again this demonstrated that an individual could be criticized for making mistakes, leaving the larger structure of power essentially untouched, as the demythologizing of Mao Zedong had illustrated. However, it may have been desirable for Zhao himself to drop out of the limelight, especially as the economic reforms were beginning to sputter and the search for a scapegoat accelerated.

What little credibility Zhao still had left was used up by the summer of 1989, when he fell out of favor in the political realm after showing some sympathy to the demonstrators and hunger strikers in Tiananmen Square. When the Party leaders emerged after the crackdown, claiming a victory over the "thugs" and "counterrevolutionary" forces, Zhao was conspicuously absent. In the fall of 1989, official Chinese newspapers were still criticizing Zhao, even though he had not been seen or heard from for several months. By October 1989 Zhao had been clearly and publicly labeled a "splittist," mainly for his conciliatory role with the students during the demonstrations. In addition he continued to be castigated for pushing too hard for economic changes—in other words Zhao, on top of everything else, was still being made the scapegoat for the economic disasters of 1988.[83]

What Chinese people and Westerners alike were hoping would come out of the peaceful demonstrations all over China in spring 1989 was a sign that change was at least possible in the near future. A significant move to separate the Party and the government functions, effectively replacing the Party's informal power networks with formal systems of laws and regulations, was needed as well as a new level of concern for individual human rights. As we shall see in Chapter 15, until 1989 these demands had been made several times, although usually fairly quietly, since the Democracy Movement began in the late 1970s. In 1986 and 1987 student-led demonstrations resurfaced briefly, but they were dealt with peacefully. In 1989 the CCP's worst nightmare was realized, when the student and worker demonstrations for greater democracy were captured in minute detail by the world's media and were broadcast live around the world. It is impossible to predict what might happen next in China, but the prospects still look grim for those who dare to express their dissent in public.

PART TWO

The Spatial Organization of Production, Distribution, and Consumption in China

CHAPTER FIVE

Agriculture in China: Feeding a Billion

Even to this day I cannot memorize any quotations from Mao Zedong. But I did have class feelings, and I knew that we did not have enough people to do all the work that needed to be done. We had to get together and we had to work together. And when we did that we transformed our lives.

—Chen Yung-Gui, leader of the Dazhai Brigade in Shanxi Province[1]

INTRODUCTION: AGRICULTURE THROUGH THE AGES

Dazhai was a wasteland in the mountains of Shanxi Province, abandoned by all but a few former beggars. Life was dominated by the "three poors" (poor people, poor land, and a poor village) and the "five manys" (many shepherds, many hired hands, many beggars, many children sold, and many suicides).[2] In the 1950s the peasants took the collective road, and together they managed to "move the mountain" and unlock the riches of the barren slopes of Dazhai. From that time on, the Dazhai miracle was used across China as the model of "socialist efficiency." Peasants everywhere were urged to "learn from Dazhai" and follow its example.

The basic premise of the Communist party's stand on agriculture was that only by shifting from individual to collective work in the countryside could China's peasants emerge successfully from centuries of poverty. In addition to the oppressive domination by the landlords, China had always suffered from a shortage of good cultivable land. As a result of the country's topography, no more than about one-tenth of the land has been suitable for intensive agriculture, which explains why every available square inch is under cultivation (see Figure 5.1). The climate has added

to the burden of the Chinese peasant. The monsoon often brings too much rain in summer and not enough in winter, but a worse problem is the variability in rainfall from one year to the next.

Since 1949 the government has employed a range of strategies to improve China's ability to feed its vast population. In the second and third decades of the People's Republic there was a strong push to collectivize Chinese agriculture, which lasted, with some interruptions, until the late 1970s. Since that time there has been a dramatic shift back to individual-household agriculture and a virtual dismantling of the collective structures in the countryside.

During the long march toward collectivization the Chinese tried hard to increase the amount of land available for agriculture. To some extent this was possible: through the reclamation of land in peripheral regions; field consolidations; and the removal of grave sites, which occupied as much as 3 percent of the cultivable land in some areas. By 1963 these efforts had helped to increase the supply of cultivable land by 11.5 percent, from 94 million hectares in 1949 to 110.6 million hectares in 1963.[3] Since that time, however, the gains have been more than offset by the loss of agricultural land—to urban and industrial uses, the creation of new lakes and dams to conserve water and help prevent flooding,

Figure 5.1 Peasant house in rural Shaanxi Province, where the steep slopes of the foothills of the Qinling Mountains provide a continuous challenge to the local population.

and the afforestation of marginal farmlands.[4] By 1978 the total amount of cultivable land had fallen again to less than 100 million hectares, a 10 percent reduction since 1963, and during that time the population had risen to more than 950 million.[5]

The only alternative for the Chinese was to increase the productivity of the land that was available. This was possible by the use of irrigation, the provision of more fertilization, and the use of higher-yielding strains. A significant increase in the effective amount of cultivable land was achieved by multiple cropping. Although this was much easier in the subtropical areas of south China, where three crops a year were possible, in some parts of northern China winter wheat could be planted after the summer crop had been harvested. In spite of this in large parts of the country only one crop was possible each year (see Figure 5.2). Although multiple cropping has always been a feature of Chinese agriculture, it was stepped up significantly after 1949, to such an extent that the regional cropping index increased from 130 (for the whole of China) to 150 in 1979 and was in fact as high as 200 in some parts of the Yangtze basin (100 = one crop per year). The geographic pattern of grain yields reveals the extent of the underlying variations in the productivity of the Chinese land. As Figure 5.3 illustrates, the basic pattern of grain yield is one in which output declines sharply as one moves north, northwest, and west from the most productive areas in the Yangtze Valley and in south China.

As a result of improvements in farming methods and the spatial reorganization of production in the countryside associated with collectivization, significant increases in grain harvests were recorded. Output increased from 164 million tons in 1952 to 318 million tons in 1980.[6] As impressive as these statistics are, they should be considered in conjunction with the growth in China's population during the same period. As the statistics demonstrate, per capita farm output had increased only slightly by the mid-1970s (see Table 5.1). The

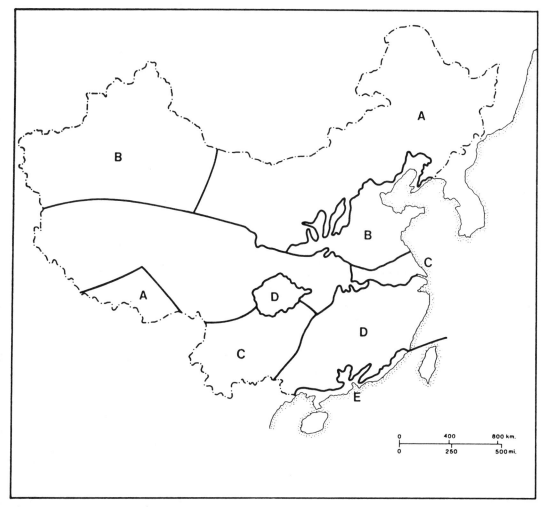

Figure 5.2 Cropping systems in China: A = one crop grown annually; B = two crops annually or three crops every two years; C = two crops annually, including rice; D = two rice crops annually, plus a third crop; E = three rice crops annually. Source: F. Leeming, 1985, Rural China Today *(Harlow, Essex: Longman Group Ltd.), p. 14; reprinted by permission.*

major factor accounting for the higher yields in the agricultural sector was the spectacular increase in inputs, particularly of machinery, fertilizer, and irrigation power (see Figure 5.4). This was in effect the Chinese version of the "green revolution," and it represented the first widespread employment of modern factors of production in agriculture.[7]

Throughout the period in question (which represents the collective era in Chinese agriculture), industry consistently performed significantly better than agriculture (Table 5.1). Farm output increased by 2.4 times in the first three decades after Liberation, compared to a 19-fold increase for light industry, and

a 90-fold increase for heavy industry. This reflects the Soviet-style emphasis on industry-led development, with agriculture taking a backseat (see Chapter 4). The ratio of investment in agriculture to investment in industry fluctuated between 1:4 and 1:6 during the 1950s. The sluggish performance of agriculture during this period was used as ammunition by Mao Zedong's opponents within the CCP. They argued that the move toward collectivization had been too hasty and that the gains of a system based largely on moral incentives were too meager.

In spite of such criticisms, by the early 1980s it was evident that the age-old problem

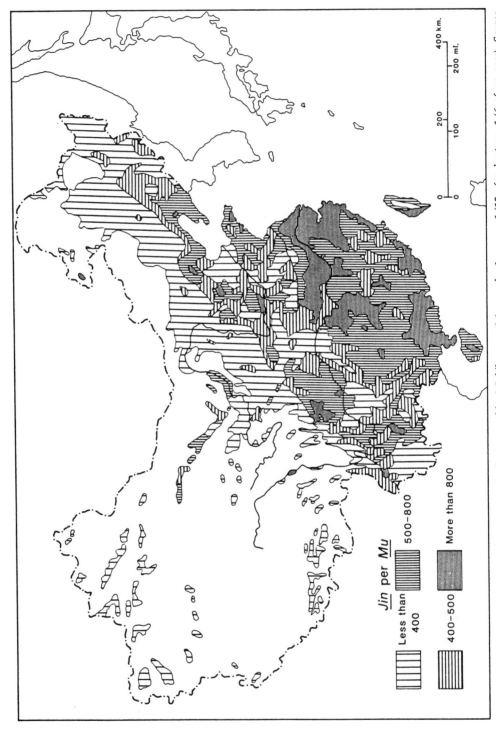

Figure 5.3 Map of grain yields per unit area (1 jin = roughly 0.5 kilogram, 1.1 pounds; 1 mu = 1/15 of a hectare, 1/6 of an acre). Source: Geographical Resource Institute, Publication No. 121 (Beijing: Sciences Press).

Jin per Mu

Less than 400

500-800

400-500

More than 800

Table 5.1 People's Republic of China: Various Rural Economic Indicators, 1952-1980

	1952	1957	1965	1976	1980	Increase 1952-1980 (%)
Total output of industry and agriculture by value (Y100 mill.)	827	1,241	1,984	4,579	6,619	700
Total output of agriculture by value (Y100 mill.)	484	537	590	1,317	1,627	236
Total population	568	641	750	925	982	73
Outputs from farming						
Grain (mill. tons)	164	195	195	286	318	94
Urban grain supplies (average, jin per person)	395	406	366	381	428	8
Pig population (mill. head)	90	146	167	287	305	239
Urban pork supplies (average, jin per person)	12	10	13	14	22	83
Cotton (1,000 tons)	1,304	1,640	2,098	2,056	2,707	108
Vegetable oil (1,000 tons)	4,193	4,196	3,625	4,008	7,691	83
Urban vegetable oil supplies (jin per person)	4	5	3	3	5	25
Inputs to farming						
Tractors (excluding small tractors) (1,000s)	1	1	7	40	75	7,400
Powered irrigation (mill. hp)	0.1	0.6	9	54	75	75,000
Artificial fertilizer used per mu (jin)	0.1	0.4	3	8	17	7,000
Artificial fertilizer (mill. tons)	--	0.2	2	5	12	12,000[a]

Note: jin = roughly 0.5 kg.
[a] 1957-1980.

Source: Adapted from F. Leeming, 1985, *Rural China Today* (Harlow, Essex: Longman Group Ltd.), p. 16, Table 2.1.

of famine, which had reappeared after the Great Leap Forward, was a thing of the past. The overall achievements can be assessed by comparing China's per capita nutrient availability in the early 1980s with that of other countries around the world (see Table 5.2). China still lagged behind the world's developed countries but was significantly ahead of many developing countries, especially in grain availability and protein per capita.[8] Incomes in the countryside increased fourfold between 1957 and 1983, although, as we shall see later in this chapter, the most dramatic changes did not occur until the Dengist reforms after 1978.[9] The flow of events since 1949 demonstrates that China's agriculture has taken a number of different turns, and in the following section some of the major phases in the evolution of modern Chinese agriculture will be outlined.

Figure 5.4   Vegetable fields in January in Xian, with early crops covered by plastic sheets.

Table 5.2 Daily per Capita Nutrient Availability, People's Republic of China and Selected Countries, 1982

	Grain		Meat Products		Total	
	Kilocalories	% of Total	Kilocalories	% of Total	Grams of Protein	Grams of Fat
PRC	2,181	80	158	6	70	40
Bangladesh	1,606	87	67	4	40	14
India	1,411	69	104	5	50	33
Pakistan	1,387	64	231	11	56	43
Sri Lanka	1,368	61	95	4	44	47
Indonesia	1,820	77	53	2	49	39
Malaysia	1,355	54	353	14	56	52
Philippines	1,605	67	228	9	54	32
Tanzania	1,262	65	146	7	42	30
Brazil	1,196	46	383	15	59	51
United States	765	21	1,316	36	106	168
Japan	1,309	46	590	21	89	81
USSR	1,504	45	871	26	100	96
Asia avg.	--	--	206	9	58	40
Developing countries avg.	--	--	213	9	58	41
World avg.	--	--	429	16	69	63

Source: A. Piazza, 1986, *Food Consumption and Nutritional Status in the PRC* (Boulder, Colo.: Westview Press), p. 99, Table 4.10. Reprinted by permission.

THE SPATIAL ORGANIZATION
OF CHINESE AGRICULTURE, 1949–1990

It was inevitable that any attempt to develop and modernize China's agriculture after 1949 would be hampered by the geographical constraints that had existed for centuries. The vast size of the country, coupled with the rudimentary nature of the transportation system, would continue to favor local self-reliance in food production rather than encourage the development of highly specialized cash crops in specific regions of the country. Over the centuries the enormous cultural differences across the Chinese landscape, in addition to the topographical and climatic constraints, had produced a variety of agricultural practices that were well suited to local conditions. These adaptations were harmonious at the local level, but it was clear that what worked in one area would not necessarily work elsewhere. There was some doubt, in other words, about the wisdom of trying to superimpose a uniform organizational structure onto this ancient but effective agricultural mosaic.

The critics also argued that collectivization would slow down the country's economic development. In spite of such counterarguments it was "politics first" in the countryside until Mao's death, and herculean efforts were made to restructure Chinese agriculture along utopian socialist goals. Nevertheless, what looked from the outside like a monolithic policy for agriculture actually concealed a lack of a consensus on collectivization within the CCP.[10] Only after long and bitter struggles between opposing factions in the party were Mao's plans for the socialist construction of agriculture implemented, and as we shall see later, they have been virtually erased since his death.[11] It was also clear that Chinese agriculture would never be able to shake free from its own past. What happened at any one time was the result of a blend, or more often a hodgepodge, of different policies superimposed onto the same landscape. Supporters of Mao, for example, have suggested that the speed with which "capitalist" farming returned to the countryside in the 1980s demonstrated that the remnants of private ownership had never fully disappeared from the landscape even during the high point of collectivization. Therefore, agricultural developments must be interpreted in their historical context, and what we see at any one time is not nearly so simple as it looks. In its extreme form, this argument implies that, as Mao Zedong predicted, the class differences that reemerged in the countryside in the 1980s were extensions of class differences that were never totally eliminated.[12]

The Socialist Transformation
of the Countryside

The first stage of the socialist transformation of Chinese agriculture was land reform, a process that had already begun in the "liberated" areas before 1949. The typical procedure began with the work of a local Land Reform Work Team, whose job it was to raise the consciousness of the peasants. The team prepared the ground for mass meetings at which the landlords would be publicly accused, their holdings revealed, and the extent of their past exploitations exposed. The property in question would then be seized and redistributed among the peasants. Overall the land-reform program was highly successful, and by 1952, 42 million hectares (106 million acres) of land had been redistributed to 300 million peasants. The share of China's cropland held by the tiny landlord class fell from 29 percent to 2 percent; whereas that held by the poor peasants and hired laborers (who represented 57 percent of the households) increased from 24 percent to 47 percent of the cultivated land.[13]

Land reform was accompanied by substantial increases in agricultural production, but the major gains were political rather than economic. The primary goal of land reform was to set the peasants free from the shackles of China's "feudal" landownership system. In that sense land reform was more of a social movement than a production system. The landlord class was largely destroyed, but more important, a source of political leadership emerged at the grass-roots level, and an entirely new set of local political institutions was established, including associations of poor peasants, peasant militias, women's associations, and youth leagues. In this sense the revolutionary action itself was used to revolutionize the revolutionaries (as Marx would have predicted)—not only by dispossessing the dominant class of its major source of power (land) but also by successfully challenging their political control over the peasantry. Two thousand years of Confucian submissiveness had instilled into the peasantry a pervasive sense of helplessness, but in mass meetings held all over the countryside there was now visible evidence of an entirely new order.

Land reform, in spite of its obvious successes, also created some problems that would contribute to a call for the next phase in the socialist transformation. The tenant-landlord relationship had been broken forever, but the nature of the individual farming economy had not been significantly changed. Most peasants still had too little land to do much more than subsist. This also stymied investments in rural infrastructure; therefore the building of new roads and irrigation schemes and the use of large-scale machinery were considerably behind schedule. Land reform also specifically protected the rich peasants. Individuals who owned land were guaranteed the so-called four freedoms to help them develop the countryside: the freedom to buy, sell, or rent land; to hire labor for wages; to lend money at interest; and to set up private enterprises for profit.[14] In the spirit of a slogan popular at the time, the newly landed peasants were given the opportunity to "enrich themselves." This allowed and even reinforced social and geographical inequalities within the rural population. Some families prospered but the majority continued to struggle. "If some families bought land other families must sell. If some families hired labor others must hire out. . . . For every family that went up the economic ladder, several must go down."[15]

The landlords were gone, but China faced the prospect of a new class struggle; the poor and middle-range peasants against the emerging class of rich peasants. For some peasant families the revolution and the struggle associated with it was over, and they felt it was time to "bury their heads in production."[16] One such family in Long Bow village was headed by Li Chuan-Chung, known locally as Li-the-Fat. "Li-the-Fat did so well with new animals and new land . . . [bought with his newfound prosperity] that he was soon in a position to buy more houses. He bought six sections in his home courtyard from a poor peasant . . . who could not make ends meet . . . [and he] continued the expansion of his holdings by setting up a small flour mill."[17]

The net effect of land reform was that in the early 1950s China faced a problem similar in some ways to that in Russia in the 1930s: the development of a rich peasant (kulak) class that according to Mao was "standing in the way" of the socialist transformation. The solution in Mao's China would be very different from the brutality wrought by Stalin across the Soviet countryside. In China, the poor peasants were to organize themselves into *mutual-aid teams* for production purposes. These were groups that shared their labor, tools, and farm animals, but each of the contributing families took home its own crops. Later on, these would become full-fledged cooperatives in which both the crops and the resulting income were pooled and redistributed equally.

Most of the leaders of the CCP agreed on collectivization as the goal for Chinese agriculture, but they disagreed on the pace of the program and the best way to achieve it. Mao Zedong was eager to push the process along rapidly by establishing huge communes, as a way to increase production and to centralize power in the countryside. Opposing him was a more pragmatic group within the CCP, favoring small collectives over mass organizations and allowing production to be guided by material incentives for individual peasant families. In the short run Mao's views predominated, and mutual-aid teams were promoted to reduce class exploitation of the poor by the rich peasants. A team usually consisted of six or seven households in a permanent collective. The successful production teams, such as the ones in Dazhai, demonstrated to others models for raising rural productivity. Rich peasants were excluded from the teams in an attempt to isolate and destroy them as a class. At the same time, state monopolies unifying the purchase and distribution of grain were introduced so that peasant families would be protected by the state from the vagaries of a private market in grain. This, in addition to the establishment of rural credit cooperatives, helped the poorer peasants to avoid becoming financially dependent on their richer neighbors.

By the mid-1950s Mao had convinced his opponents that it was time to combat further class inequality by eliminating what was left of the rich peasantry—this amounted to a rapid drive toward full collectivization. In spite of the gains that had already been made, Mao was worried that a relapse into capitalist agriculture was still a distinct possibility: "The spontaneous forces of capitalism have been steadily growing . . . with new rich peasants springing up everywhere . . . [while] many poor peasants are still living in poverty."[18] Mao set a target for the creation of 1.3 million cooperatives within a year (1954–1955), but even his wildest dreams were exceeded, and by 1956, 92 percent of all peasant households belonged to elementary, or lower-stage, agricultural producers' cooperatives (APCs). The co-ops usually contained about thirty households, and they corresponded wherever possible to existing hamlets or rural neighborhoods. They were larger than the mutual-aid teams, and all of the members' productive resources were pooled. This was only a "semisocialist" system, however, because the families that had brought more into the cooperative than others owned more shares. Partly as a result of dissatisfaction with this situation, and partly because of a wave of contagious enthusiasm for cooperatives, the idea of higher-stage cooperatives soon caught on. In spite of initial apprehensions, the richer peasants realized that if they did not join quickly, people would start to suspect their class backgrounds, branding them as possible "counterrevolutionaries" or "capitalist roaders."

The new cooperatives were much larger than their predecessors, and they were fully socialist in the sense that distribution was based solely on work done rather than on previous ownership of land or capital. The richer peasants were dealt a further blow because those who were allowed to enter the new cooperatives lost their land forever and were reclassified as ordinary peasants.

By this time many infrastructural improvements had already been carried out in the Chinese countryside. Field size had increased, making economies of scale and the efficient use of tractors possible. New water-conservancy projects were constructed, and a small amount of the cooperatives' resources could be allocated to agricultural risk taking—none of which could have occurred to the same extent under an individual-household economy. In Long Bow village, for example, the cooperative was able to borrow Y 8,000 to buy a water wheel, which irrigated vast stretches of land that could never have been reached in the old days.[19]

To some of the peasants the drive toward cooperatives produced mixed emotions. They were required to give up the land they had dreamed so long of owning and had struggled so hard to acquire. They had never really owned the land, but in the co-ops they essentially surrendered the rights to decide how their land would be used and their exclusive use of it. For many families this was a cruel blow. They were truly nostalgic about their land and could hardly believe they were losing it again after so short a time. One villager in Long Bow complained that after his bitter struggle to *fanshen* (stand up), he had been thrust right back into "feudalism": "My donkey works for everyone and here I am laboring in the fields with nothing at all just as I did in the past." Another peasant voiced a similar concern: "I had the best manure in the village, but now it's all on someone else's land. All my life I worked for the landlords. Then Mao Zedong gave me land and a house. But with this co-op I have nothing left. No land. No manure. What is going to happen to me?"[20]

The opponents of collectivization pointed out that the peasants' loss of their land and their decision-making power was unprecedented in China.[21] The higher-stage cooperatives were in some ways like Soviet collective farms in that the peasants had become little more than agricultural wage earners, although many had been able to keep a small "private" plot of land on which to grow fruits and vegetables. It was clear that Mao had succeeded over his opponents, although his success was to be short-lived. By 1957 there were nearly 800,000 higher-stage cooperatives in China, with from 200 to 700 persons living in each one.

The Great Leap Forward to Disaster?

The early stages of socialist construction had been largely completed by 1957. The landlords and the rich peasants had been removed or co-opted, and the organization of agricultural production had been radically restructured. There had been much local enthusiasm for the cooperatives, but at the national level all was not well. As usual the problems were largely political, but there was also evidence of structural problems in the long-term production capabilities of Chinese agriculture.

With the advent of the higher-stage cooperatives a new tier of cadres forced the grassroots leaders who had emerged during land reform to take a backseat. In addition, all buying and selling was done in the cooperatives, and this largely eliminated the independence of individual families. Many peasants felt that the co-ops made excessive demands on them, and as a result they were not inclined to work as hard as they might have otherwise. It also had proved very difficult to come up with an equitable system of work points to remunerate peasants with very different levels of skills and abilities. The basic principle was "he who works more gets more," but at the end of each day it was difficult to reach agreements about this. In Long Bow, for example, there was an argument about a peasant who had been lagging in the fields all day. "If we allow this then everyone will start to dawdle. We must give him less [work points]. He came out late and he never caught up with the rest of the group all day."[22]

On the larger scale the major problems facing Chinese agriculture at this time were low labor productivity and chronic underemployment. There were simply too many mouths to be fed and too many hands to be kept at work. Although local agricultural practices had, over the centuries, produced a relatively efficient system of production, it was clear that yields could not be increased significantly without the introduction of vast inputs of modern technology. Chinese agriculture was still essentially "premodern," and output levels could not be increased until agriculture was able to use the new agricultural technology that was just starting to diffuse from the West.

At the political level, factional infighting continued at the top of the CCP, and the deterioration of relations with the Soviet Union created great uncertainty about the future. Mao's opponents favored the continuation of a development strategy based on the Soviet model (see Chapter 4), which would essentially favor the development of heavy industry, with a lesser emphasis on agricultural growth. Mao, however, was ready to make a clean break with the Soviets. He wanted the Chinese economy to "walk on two legs," with an equal emphasis on industry and agriculture. He hoped to eliminate the distinction between city and country so that the agricultural inputs for the "green revolution" could be produced locally, rather than imported either from abroad or from other parts of China. He also wanted to see China rely more on its major asset, labor, rather than on capital, which was in short supply. To achieve all of this Mao envisioned massive mobilization campaigns across the nation and a shift away from centralized to local-level decision-making.

In the countryside Mao's dreams were to be put into effect by merging the cooperatives into people's communes. At first there was some real enthusiasm for communes at the grass-roots level, especially after a very good harvest in 1958 and the obvious successes of many of the higher-stage cooperatives. The communes were originally intended to be much larger than the cooperatives, at first averaging 5,000 households; but then in 1959 the average size was reduced to 1,600 households, which was still about ten times larger than the co-ops. The plan called for the communes to take over all aspects of political, social, and economic life; they were to provide local social services such as health care and education; and they were also to build their own factories to produce agricultural inputs and small machinery.

There was a brief courtship in 1958 with a truly pristine form of communal living, which was probably the closest China would ever come to true communism, but by 1960 the norm had shifted back toward smaller communes with a three-tier structure: *production brigades*, which corresponded roughly to the higher-stage cooperatives; *production teams*, which were about the same as the lower-stage cooperatives; and *work groups*, at the lowest level. The principle of distribution was now fully socialist, with rewards allocated according to work done. The brief experiment with the larger communes and with rewards allocated entirely according to needs was generally judged to have been a mistake.[23] Socialism had changed many aspects of the Chinese agricultural landscape, but in some ways very little had changed. From a historical perspective, for example, even in the communes the spatial organization of administration and production remained at the local (village) level, where it had been for hundreds of years before socialism.

The beginning of the 1960s proved to be the zenith of radical socialism in China. There were communes covering most parts of the Chinese countryside. Rural industry was humming, and mass-mobilization campaigns began to construct large infrastructure projects such as dams and irrigation ditches. "It was a time of genuine enthusiasm and very high hopes. New horizons opened up on all fronts, as many peasants gained their first experience outside farming or outside the narrow confines of the village of their birth."[24]

These great hopes were soon to be dashed. In the enthusiasm of the times there were many instances of overreporting of harvest yields, which actually obscured the harsh reality—that output levels had dropped to dangerously low levels, sometimes below where they had been in 1950. There were three disastrous harvests, in 1959, 1960, and 1961, in which crops were decimated by droughts or floods. In production terms grain output declined by an average of 26 percent per year between 1958 and 1961, and there was an annual decline of 71 percent in meat production.[25] Because of the size of the communes and the organizational greenness of the new cadres, production efficiency in many communes was nowhere near the level that had been anticipated. In addition to their basic food rations, the peasants were being paid collectively, in the form of free services, and according to the critics this was seriously damaging the incentive system. Again the specter of spatial inequality came back to haunt the communes, which in many areas had amalgamated both poor and rich cooperatives. The people from poorer villages naturally felt they were protected by the security blanket provided by the richer areas; whereas those from richer areas saw little point in working hard only to subsidize their poorer neighbors. The net effect was that agricultural productivity fell to an all-time record low level in 1960.[26]

High Collectivism

After the catastrophic effects of the Great Leap Forward, it was time for a searching evaluation of the policies that had created it. Retrenchment was the order of the day, and to boost agricultural production the most significant change was a return to local-level decision-making. The power to organize production, manage accounts, and share income was given back to the production teams (20–30 families). The larger production brigades still undertook important infrastructure projects and organized health-care and social activities as well as providing political leadership. Thus the brigades (roughly corresponding to the old villages) became more fully integrated with government at the regional and national levels. In terms of production, however, control had shifted markedly "downward" to the local level, which threatened some of the economies of scale that had been promised for the communes. By 1973 there were about 50,000 communes in China, covering more than 90 percent of the available land, more than twice the number in 1964. The commune could cover from 25 to 130 square kilometers, with an average of 15,000 members, although this number ranged from 8,000 to 80,000, depending on the nature of the terrain and the richness of the soils. The commune was the lowest level of the central government (in that it was the most localized), but it was the highest level of spatial organization in the countryside. All the administration for the commune was to be concentrated in the market towns, where the commune's banking, tax collection, buying, and distribution were headquartered.

In spite of the egalitarian goals of the commune movement, in the 1960s there was a resurgence of social and spatial inequality. Some of the more efficient peasant families, including those in the formerly "rich peasant" class, were still critical of the collective drive, and they showed how production could be best served by following their example. Inequality within the same commune (in other words, at the team level) was seen in a more positive light than it had been in the more radical days because differences in wealth could provide incentives to the entire team to work harder, thereby earning more for everyone. It is not surprising that the persistence of these and other spontaneous "capitalist" tendencies in the countryside worked to keep alive the smoldering feud between Mao and his opponents (notably Liu Shaoqi and Deng Xiaoping) about how to guide China's future agricultural development.

During this period of "high collectivism" (1963–1978) several problems continued to plague commune officials all over the countryside. Although the commune was responsible for the collective provision of services such as education, health care, and welfare benefits (usually referred to as the "five guarantees"), it was evident that some material incentives were needed at the local level to make the peasants work harder. Small private plots of land had been reallocated to the peasants; thus in Mao's terms this was only partial collectivization. This remnant of privatization would continue to cause contention within the Party leadership.

Privatized Agriculture: The Household Responsibility System and the New Rural Reforms

The critics of collectivism argued that the state's interference with the production process kept local entrepreneurship in the countryside at an artificially depressed level. This resulted in consistently low incomes—in fact, average per capita incomes increased by only Y 10.5 between 1965 and 1976.[27] In addition to collectivization there were other factors contributing to the poor performance of China's agricultural economy at that time, most notably Mao Zedong's excessive emphasis on growing grain at the expense of the production of specialized crops in certain areas. The strong central control over rural markets, and the restrictions on commercial trading between production teams, also worked to lower the incentives of the peasants—without the promise of financial rewards there was no reason to become more efficient. In spite of such counterarguments it was the collectives themselves that received the brunt of criticism from the new leadership after Mao's death, perhaps mainly because they symbolized the old Maoist egalitarianism that was no longer in vogue. Once the new agricultural reforms were introduced after 1978 and productivity and incomes started to rise, critics got on the bandwagon, attacking the collective system in general.

During the 1978–1990 period systematic attempts were made to dismantle the structure of agricultural administration that had been painstakingly erected in the countryside from the early 1950s. The transformation, however, is best interpreted as neither socialist nor capitalist but as a combination of the two. As a result of the agricultural reforms, the peasants are now able to contract with the collective for land over a long time period. These contracts are not typical capitalist contracts, however, because in many cases the collective still specifies which crops are to be grown on the land, and the contracts are not usually drawn up at market values. Notwithstanding these differences, the peasants have in fact been allowed to behave like small capitalists in a number of ways; for example, they can own capital equipment like trucks and tractors; they can hire labor and start up businesses; and they can sell their surpluses on the free market for a profit.

The collectives themselves have not totally disappeared. In some regions they still own and operate local enterprises and they still run some schools and provide local social services. In the area of production, however, the collectives are no longer dominant in rural China. There are no work points to be decided anymore, and most peasants spend all day working on their own plots of land, which means there is no longer a need for collective meetings for production purposes. In spite of this there is still evidence of collective politics in some aspects of rural life, such as dispute mediation. For historical reasons collective debate remains common in the Chinese countryside, and to some extent this is to be expected because the land that is being contracted out is in fact property that was developed as a result of several decades of collective effort.

The critics of Maoist agricultural policies argued that reform was essential by the late 1970s to return to the peasants what collectivization had taken from them, namely "power" (quan), "responsibility" (ze), and "payoff" (li).[28] Under the new guidelines, output and land were to be contracted out to households. It is possible to argue that, at least in the beginning, the reform was intended to be simply a more efficient way to organize collective agriculture rather than a wholesale negation of collectivization. The people who argue this way are implying that large-scale collectivization, beginning in the 1950s, produced a situation in which the new "relations of production" (membership in the new collectives) were too far ahead of the "forces of production." This meant that the level of development in agriculture was too low to justify the radical shift in ownership from individual to collective farming. In the 1950s Mao Zedong had likened his critics, the ones who were reluctant to move ahead rapidly with collectivization, to "women with bound feet." In the late 1970s Mao's critics were able to turn his metaphor around, suggesting that collectivization had forced agriculture to "put on shoes that were too big so that she [agriculture] couldn't move. It was now high time, they argued, to find 'shoes that fit.' "[29]

The actual reforms can be divided into two categories, although they are closely interrelated. In the first place there has been a legitimation of the household-based contracts (HRS—the household responsibility system), which amounts to a return to private landownership in the countryside. The second set of reforms, made necessary by the first, has proved to be much more controversial and far more difficult to implement. In a series of stages, attempts were made to allow market forces to regulate the distribution of China's agricultural produce. This started in 1979 with a 20 percent increase in grain prices for the summer harvest, a 50 percent increase for all sales above the quota, and an average price rise for all agricultural produce of 22 percent.[30] In 1984 it was announced that the state's thirty-year-old monopoly over the buying and selling of agricultural products would be gradually abolished, thereby allowing market forces, rather than the state, to influence the distribution of foodstuffs.[31]

Beginning as early as 1978 in some parts of the country, attempts were made to introduce the HRS into Chinese agriculture. The basic idea was to allow the peasants, as individuals, families, or groups of families, to sign contracts with the collectives that would increase their incentives to expand output. Under the socialist slogan of "to each according to his work," peasants would be able to accumulate a surplus by working harder and raising their productivity.

Many different types of contracts have been signed since 1978, and this diversity was intended to match contract systems with local conditions. At first, small groups of peasants or even single families could contract with the production team to fulfill specific tasks, and they would be repaid in work points, with bonuses for overfulfilling their contracts. This was only a minor break with the past, and it kept the essential ingredients of collectivism intact (planning, the ownership of machinery and animals, and most important,

land, remained collectively owned by the production team). The major innovation was that a closer link had been established between work done and rewards received. Although this was supposed to be a new system, similar arrangements had in fact already appeared in the 1960s as a result of peasant opposition to collectivization and the disastrous harvests following the Great Leap Forward.

Later contractual developments would allow families to use a particular piece of land to produce their output. In these arrangements production was privatized but distribution remained collectivized—essentially households contracted a fixed amount of their output to the production team for an agreed-on number of work points. Although they could dispose of their surplus any way they chose, the actual value of their work points was still dependent on the total output of the production team. Planning and the ownership of machinery and animals also remained in the hands of the collective.

The third stage in the evolution of contract systems resolved this tension between private production and collective distribution by eliminating work points altogether. Families could dispose of their output however they wished, after they had handed over the prearranged quota to the state, paid their taxes, and contributed to the collective's fund for investment and welfare programs. In addition to giving the households de facto control of their land, this system enabled them to contract for all of the farm inputs (machinery and animals). The production team, in other words, now retained control in only a few areas, for example, in the matter of overall planning and in setting sales quotas for the individual households. In 1983 households were allowed even more freedoms, including the ability to hire labor, buy their own vehicles and machinery, and transport produce for sale across prefectural and provincial boundaries. Contracts could be extended to fifteen or even thirty years, which worked to reduce householder's uncertainties about how long they would be allowed to have exclusive use of their land. By 1984 almost all of China's production teams had adopted some form of the household responsibility system, mostly of the latter type (*baogan daohu*).[32]

Peasant families could now choose to produce whatever they could grow and sell most efficiently (see Figures 5.5 and 5.6). Not surprisingly, this resulted in a huge increase in crop diversification and a corresponding rise in family incomes. Many families branched out into "sideline" activities such as poultry farming or fish hatching; others got out of agriculture altogether and started small businesses in catering, construction, or manufacturing. New farmer-entrepreneur families, known as "specialized households," began to appear, and many of them managed to do well. In Daqing township, in Liaoning Province, for example, there were 40 such households (out of a total of 2,500), with total incomes that were four times higher than the local average.[33]

EVALUATING THE AGRICULTURAL REFORMS

By most objective standards of evaluation, China's rural reforms since Mao's death can be judged as a major success. Although it is difficult to find anyone in China who would not agree with this assessment, there are some who feel that the new reforms have "sold out" the revolution and that the three decades of socialist transformation in the countryside were all for nothing. To understand this debate it is important to begin by viewing the household responsibility system as one of a broader set of policies intended to restructure the operation of Chinese agriculture—rather than simply as a way to increase the incomes of China's long-suffering peasants. It was hoped that the new system would combine the best of collective and individual endeavors, with the responsibility for overall planning and management tasks, the running of welfare programs, and large-scale infrastructure projects remaining at the collective level. In many parts of China, however, collective work has now entirely broken down or has been replaced by new producer cooperatives or specialized households. In 1982 the peoples' communes ceased to exist formally and their political and administrative functions were returned to the townships and the villages.

Although nominally the peasants still do not own the land for which they contract, there has essentially been a privatization of property rights under the new arrangements. In addition, although the original intent of the reforms was to maintain collective ownership of the forces of production (other than land), there was in fact an official sanction of private ownership in the 1980s, which was strengthened by the extension of bank credit to individual households. By 1983 most of

Figure 5.5   Street market in Chongqing, Sichuan Province, where food is plentiful since the reforms of the 1980s. Stall sells only peppers, a well-known feature of Sichuanese cooking.

Figure 5.6 A tofu stand in a street market. In the absence of meat or other forms of animal protein, the Chinese have been able to work wonders with the versatile soybean product.

China's farm machinery was either owned outright or managed by private households.

In light of the evidence it is difficult to avoid the conclusion that the reforms have broken with the three-decade-long drive toward collective ownership of the forces of production. Although there are some similarities with what occurred in the mutual-aid teams and the lower-stage producer cooperatives in the 1950s, the major difference is that "private" landownership at that time was seen as a transitional stage in a transformation toward a more advanced form of collectivization. The current developments cannot be interpreted in the same light and are, in fact, heralded by the political "left" as a backward step in history, to a rural economy that is once again dominated by rich peasants and bourgeois households. According to this argument, the HRS is similar in some ways to a tenant-farming system in which the collective is nominally the landlord but is playing only a minor role. The "rent" paid by households to the collectives is fixed (agricultural taxes plus contributions to investment and welfare funds), whereas what the households can earn by selling their surplus is limited only by the peasants' willingness to work hard and the productivity of their land.

The result is that the new system is far removed from the traditional socialist principle of "to each according to his work." Deng Xiaoping had suggested that some people would be allowed, even encouraged, to become wealthy, and (presumably) as a result of "trickle down" economics, their greater wealth would benefit the whole community and ultimately the entire country. The Chinese press and television networks and foreign journalists from around the world have shown us that many people took Deng at his word, embracing the traditional Chinese saying that "to get rich is glorious."[34] The new superheroes in China are the so-called 10,000 yuan householders (*wanyuanhu*), easily identifiable by their new possessions and/or their private homes. In one sideline enterprise, for example, a peasant's wife in north China took out a bank loan to breed minks for their skins. Soon, as other families started to "get rich" as well, she was able to sells the skins for Y 300 yuan each. In an interview with this couple, while they were flaunting their newfound wealth in an expensive Tianjin restaurant, Zhang Xinxin and Sang Ye, in their book *Chinese Lives*, reflected on some of the dreams and problems of the newly rich in China. The wife is talkative, in love with her new wealth, and very acquisitive; but her husband is taciturn and much more cynical. She makes no bones about her crass love for money: "Sometimes my mink kittens die. It makes me cry. It really cuts you up—it's worse than losing your own father. That's good money dying on you."[35] The money they earn buys them most of what they want. They have all of the expensive consumer goods so much coveted by long-deprived Chinese families, and they own their home. While she is talking, her exasperated husband reminds her that she has no education, to which she scoffs in reply that all anyone in China needs these days is the first three years of middle school!

To die-hard socialists in the West, as well as to Mao's supporters in China, the dangers inherent in a system that allows such income inequalities to reappear are plainly obvious.[36] Such critics point out the futility of dismantling the organizational system that had taken three decades to build up. They are also fond of pointing out that many of the present-day gains in agricultural productivity are in part the result of earlier collective efforts: the terraced fields, the irrigated lands, and the transportation infrastructure in the countryside.[37]

Moreover, there has been some pure irony in the reforms, because in the 1980s actions were officially sanctioned that had been illegal at various times in many parts of the countryside since 1949. What once was rewarded with harsh criticism, imprisonment, or even worse fates can now help to elevate somebody to the status of a local hero. The tragedy of such a situation is illustrated by Gu Hua in his story "Pagoda Ridge." Gu described how poor peasants in a remote village tried to circumvent the "ultraleftist" egalitarianism associated with Maoist agriculture during the Cultural Revolution. In despair, the villagers drew lots to elect a new team leader. A recently demobilized soldier, Tian Faqing, won the unenviable task, and he decided to institute a production system very similar to the present-day contracting arrangements, one that allowed relatively lucrative "sideline" activities. Within a year the whole county was buzzing with the news of the successes at Pagoda Ridge and Tian was praised as a hero in the commune. Cadres came from all around to view the "miracle." Only later when a work team came to investigate the village did one of the peasants, under the influence of drink, gave the game away, admitting that "Pagoda Ridge was a fake. Had built itself up not by learning from Dazhai but by stealing state trees, profiteering, farming individually and taking the capitalist road."[38] Most of those activities are commonplace today and are officially sanctioned by the state, but in 1971 they verged on conspiratorial. Tian was labeled a "counterrevolutionary" and was jailed in a labor camp. When he subsequently returned to Pagoda Ridge, the new reforms had taken hold. All across China people were being encouraged to do what he had been jailed for, and they were getting rich doing it!

It is relatively easy to appreciate why the post-Mao leadership felt it was important to reform the country's agriculture. The most commonly aired problems were the consistently low prices in the agricultural sector—which resulted in low rural incomes, making it impossible for the peasants either to spend or to save (thereby limiting rural investment funds)—and low labor productivity and associated poor levels of agricultural output. It was necessary to diversify agricultural production, partly to raise local incomes but also to improve the quantity and quality of Chinese diets. In objective terms the official data released from China indicated that significant improvements had been recorded in these areas by the mid-1980s. The value of agricultural output grew at an average of 9 percent per year between 1978 and 1986, although this figure is actually inflated by the shift by many farmers from grains to higher-value crops and to lucrative sideline activities (which accounted for close to 20 percent of total rural-output value by 1984).[39] This resulted in more varied diets for many Chinese people, with more protein and fat available.[40] Again the opponents of reform have pointed out that growth rates of this magnitude suggest that before the reforms there were serious misallocations of resources and considerable amounts of rural inefficiency. They also imply that the gains now being made may be very short-lived.

Rural incomes more than doubled between 1979 and 1984, which allowed a 51 percent increase in per capita consumption.[41] The net effect is that the traditional discrepancy between urban and rural incomes may have changed in favor of the countryside. Although Mao had hoped to reduce the urban/rural dichotomy, in fact the gap probably expanded during his lifetime, as we shall see in Chapter 9. For example, the ratio of urban to rural consumption levels for food and nonfood items increased from 1.9:1 in 1957 to 3.2:1 in 1975 and 3.1 in 1979.[42] After a few years of the agricultural reforms, this situation changed significantly. Between 1978 and 1987, for example, urban sales per capita (a proxy variable for consumption) increased from Y 434 to Y 491; while sales in rural areas increased from Y 103 to Y 581 (see Table 5.3).[43] As they were promised, the peasants had more money either to spend or to save by the latter part of the 1980s. The rate of "commoditization," which is the proportion of their produce the peasants have left over to sell privately, was nearly 60 percent in

Table 5.3 Retail Sales (Total Value and per Capita) of Consumer Goods in Urban and Rural China

	1978	1981	1984	1987
Total value of urban sales (bill. Y)	74.8	102.6	137.7	247.0
Urban population[a] (millions)	172.5	201.7	330.1	503.6
Per capita urban sales (1978 Y)	433.7	454.1	347.7	490.7
Total value of rural sales (bill. Y)	81.0	132.4	199.9	335.0
Rural population (millions)	790.1	799.0	704.7	577.1
Per capita rural sales (1978 Y)	102.5	148.0	236.4	580.5

[a]There was a rapid urbanization during this time period, but it is important to remember that the growth of cities was enhanced artificially by the change in definition of what constitutes a town in 1984 (see L.J.C. Ma and Cui Conghuo, 1987, "Administrative Changes and Urban Population in China," *Annals of the Association of American Geographers* 77, No. 3 [September]).

Sources: Adapted from C. Riskin, 1987, *China's Political Economy: The Quest for Development Since 1949* (London: Oxford University Press), p. 295, Table 12.4, and *China Statistical Yearbook 1988* (Beijing: State Statistical Bureau of the PRC, 1988), p. 612.

1984; and the money in peasant bank accounts increased from 26 percent of the national total in 1978 to more than 36 percent by 1984.[44]

The productivity of the inputs to agriculture has also recorded some impressive gains since 1978, in comparison to the previous two decades. Whereas labor productivity in the countryside increased only 10 percent from 1957 to 1975,[45] there were very significant increases for farm inputs after 1979 and an annual growth rate of agricultural output per unit of input of 5.7 percent per year (see Table 5.4).[46]

There is no doubt that the reforms boosted peasant initiatives, enhanced savings for investment, and expanded lucrative sideline activities. The reforms in the distribution system also allowed and reinforced regional crop specializations. However, it is important not to overlook the expanded role of technology in Chinese agriculture and the more efficient use of agricultural inputs, especially chemical fertilizers (Table 5.4). These improvements, in addition to the obvious advantages of several bumper harvest seasons in the early 1980s, occurred largely independently of the household responsibility system. The statistics themselves also show that agricultural output began to grow very rapidly in both 1978 and 1979, which was before either the price reforms or the HRS had really had time to take hold (in 1980, for example, only about 1

percent of China's households had adopted any form of HRS). On balance, therefore, it would be wrong to assume that all of the agricultural gains that have been recorded have been the result of the reforms.

CONCLUSION: THE CONTRADICTIONS OF REFORM

The agricultural reforms produced some significant changes in the relationships between households and collectives in the Chinese countryside. From the perspective of the peasants these new relationships were predominantly positive, in that they resulted in greater levels of political and economic freedom than had been the case during the collective era.[47] It would be a mistake, however, to conclude that the reforms and their consequences have been met with universal approval either by the Chinese themselves or by outsiders. It is apparent that the impact of the agricultural reforms overlaps with several crucial aspects of life and landscape in contemporary China. Some of these issues will be dealt with in the later chapters of this book; for example, in spite of the success of the reforms, there are a number of inherent conflicts between the HRS and some of the other modernization policies. In Chapter 7 we shall look at the conflict between the production policy inherent in the new HRS

Table 5.4 Average Annual Growth Rate of Farm Outputs and Inputs, 1979-1983

	% Change per Year
Outputs:	
GVAO (gross value of agricultural output)	7.9
Food grain (in tons)	5.0
Inputs:	
Agricultural labor	2.0
Land (sown area)	-0.8
Farm machinery	9.0
Draft animals	4.1
Chemical fertilizer	13.6
Aggregate input	2.9
GVAO per aggregate input	5.7

Source: C. Riskin, 1987, *China's Political Economy: The Quest for Development Since 1949* (London: Oxford University Press), p. 297, Table 12.5. Reprinted by permission.

and the reproduction policies designed to lower the birthrate—an issue of crucial importance in China. As opportunities for side-line activities opened up and jobs in rural enterprises became available, many families realized that their combined incomes in the future could be increased by having more than one child.

In Chapter 8 we shall look at some of the consequences of the HRS on China's cities. With greater agricultural efficiency the surplus rural population has grown considerably, and there has been a tendency for those displaced from the land to move into the cities, bringing with them higher rates of unemployment and some of the social problems so familiar to cities in poor countries all around the world. The need to develop medium-sized and small cities, and to plan satellites and new towns, will become greater than before as the Chinese seek ways to avoid some of the worst aspects of overurbanization.

In Chapter 9 we shall look at the controversial issue of regional inequality, which appears to be increasing as a result of the HRS, thereby conflicting with the previous policies designed to bring about regional equality. Chapter 10 considers some of the consequences of the HRS for China's beleaguered environment, as the incessant push to build housing and factories in the countryside not only reduces the amount of cultivable

land available but also adds to the potential pollution of air and water in the countryside. When collective land was reparceled out to individual households, many collective assets, including invaluable forests, were destroyed for fuel or building materials, compounding the long-term problems of soil erosion and deforestation. As the HRS evolved, there was also a tendency for many households to develop a predatory view of the land they had contracted, seeing it not as a long-term resource but as an input to be exploited to the full, often with serious consequences for its future productivity. In addition, the expansion of output achieved largely through the input of massive amounts of chemical fertilizer is bound to have important consequences in a country already seriously lacking in potable water.

The agricultural reforms have also had a significant effect on patterns of everyday life in China, which is the theme of the third and last section of this book. For example, in Chapter 11 we shall look at the impact of the HRS on women in China, to examine the extent to which it has been a liberating or a subjugating force. In a number of ways the demise of the collective appears to threaten Chinese women. The gains made by women under collective agriculture are now being challenged as the household once again becomes the key economic unit in the countryside, thereby reinforcing the traditional pattern of male domination within the family.

In Chapter 14 we shall look at an issue that the Chinese government is currently taking very seriously, the huge increase in economic crime and corruption in the countryside (as well as in the cities). As the drive to "get rich" was ushered in by the reforms, reports of tax evasion, theft, and large-scale corruption have been widespread in the media. As income inequality increases, it is reasonable to assume that the growing body of unemployed (and perhaps unemployable) peasants will have to leave the land and seek work elsewhere. They will look enviously at the precedent set by the families that have become rich and longingly at those lucky enough to be able to live in the cities. It remains to be seen what consequences these unfulfilled aspirations will have for crime and other social problems in contemporary China.

Economic Restructuring:
The Chinese Perestroika

Production is like war . . . to be wounded or die is unavoidable.[1]

INTRODUCTION: ECONOMIC PERFORMANCE IN THE "TWO CHINAS"

By the time of Mao's death in 1976 nearly three decades of socialism had produced some impressive economic achievements. Although growth rates had fluctuated, often dramatically, industrial production expanded at an average rate of more than 9 percent per year between 1953 and 1980 and the gross national product (GNP) had grown by an average of 6.2 percent.[2] As impressive as these statistics were, it was painfully obvious to the new leaders of the CCP that the strength of the economy in the "other China" (the Republic of China) had far surpassed that in the mainland. Capitalist Taiwan had significantly outperformed Communist China, and as a result the people were much better off than their counterparts in the People's Republic. The growth of GNP in Taiwan had consistently been close to 50 percent higher than it was in the PRC, and by the 1980s per capita incomes in Taiwan were more than ten times higher.[3]

Taiwan's economic transformation has been hailed around the world as a "miracle." The government in the PRC hated to admit it, but it was fairly obvious to partisans on both sides that the dynamic partnership between the private and the public sectors in Taiwan had produced bountiful results. After consolidating its power, the post-Mao leadership began to implement some dramatic changes in its industrial policies, parallel to those that

had already been introduced in the agricultural sector. This chapter investigates and evaluates China's economic restructuring, which is referred to as the "Chinese perestroika" (even though it occurred before its counterpart in the Soviet Union). To set the stage for this discussion, and to put the reform era into its historical and political context, the chapter begins with a brief description of the socialist transformation of the Chinese economy after 1949.

THE SOCIALIST TRANSFORMATION

After 1949 the Chinese Communist party moved fairly cautiously toward the transformation of China's industry.[4] The Party had no experience in national government and little in urban administration. The country had been ravaged by four decades' of civil, revolutionary, and foreign wars, and after a century of imperialism the economy was in a shambles.

Unemployment and inflation were at an all-time high level, and there were deep structural defects in the country's economic system: a chronic shortage of investment in industry, a dearth of skilled labor, and relatively few competent managers. In Guangzhou (Canton), for example, the major problem was to transform a city that was famous for its small enterprises into a more efficient system that could be made amenable to centralized planning. "Local officials responsible for planning economic activities had become painfully aware of the difficulty of guiding tens of thousands of private enterprises, each trying to outwit the government. . . . The task of directing thousands of pushcarts and tiny handicraft shops and millions of tiny farms . . . created headaches for officials everywhere."[5]

In preparing for a shift from private to public ownership of the forces of production, the CCP focused on the issue of "thought preparation," in which the goal was simultaneously to weed out "counterrevolutionaries" and to win support for the socialist transformation. The Party tried to achieve this by a skillful mix of threat and persuasion, avoiding as much as possible the excesses associated with the collectivization drive in the Soviet Union.

In addition to economic and political difficulties there was a notorious geographical imbalance in China's economy—a developed "core" along the coast and in the northeast, and an undeveloped "periphery" in the western, northwestern, and southwestern regions. The roots of this spatial imbalance were partly environmental, partly cultural, and partly political. The peripheral regions tended to be areas where climatic and topographical characteristics were favorable neither to agricultural development nor to dense settlement patterns. Superimposed onto this was the influence of the foreign powers in China during the previous century and the development of the Treaty Ports in eastern and southern China. In the first of these ports to be developed, especially cities like Tianjin, Shanghai, and Canton, Western commercial development helped to produce bustling economies. Later on, the northeastern provinces of China (Manchuria) were occupied by Japan, and there was considerable investment in mining, industry, and infrastructure.

In the first two decades of the People's Republic, serious efforts were made to counteract this regional imbalance in China, with the establishment of newly industrialized cities in the interior, including Xian, Zhengzhou, Taiyuan, Chengdu, and Lanzhou; and policies to encourage new industrial development close to resource-rich locations in the more remote regions of the country. It became obvious, however, even to Mao Zedong, committed as he was to regional equality in China, that it still made good economic sense to concentrate development in China's most efficient areas, in other words, in the east coast provinces.

Unlike the relatively swift dispossession of the landlords in the countryside, many of China's urban bourgeois class were allowed to stay in business after 1949. Nationalization was carried out only in certain economic sectors, and economic decision-making was centralized relatively gradually. The government took over the assets of the Kuomintang (KMT) elite who had fled to Taiwan with Chiang Kai-Shek, and most of the foreign-owned companies. This was in fact the industrial core of the economy, accounting for most of the heavy industry and mining, and more than three-quarters of the fixed capital, but it represented only about one-third of the nation's total industrial output.[6]

The bulk of the country's light industry was owned by what the Communists called the "national capitalists," a group that had not traditionally been closely tied to the Kuomintang. Instead of expropriating the members of this class, the CCP decided to co-opt them into a newly formed coalition, in the understanding that the country badly needed their technical and managerial skills. The net effect was that China's economy came to be dominated by petit bourgeois enterprises; in fact the number of privately owned firms had increased sixfold to 150,000 by 1953, making up almost one-fifth of China's output value.[7] With the passage of time, significant efforts were made to weed out those members of the bourgeoisie who could not be relied on to support the CCP and the pursuit of socialism, but even these campaigns were relatively mild, compared to the attack on the landlords in the countryside.[8]

The economy was recovering relatively well, largely as a result of careful management by the CCP and by the existing bourgeois class's being allowed to continue their operations.[9] Industrial output was restored to the level of the 1930s, but it was clear that a major economic propulsion was still required to bring about the socialist transformation.

Nationalization

The model of development chosen for this purpose was based on the Soviet Five Year Plans (see Chapter 4). Although this strategy was a realistic way to build up the economy and the Soviets willingly provided massive amounts of technical and financial aid, it represented a fundamental departure from the geographical principles of Chinese socialism. Planning was to be highly centralized, effectively reducing the emphasis on local and regional self-reliance that had been so successful in the revolutionary base areas prior to 1949.

There was a marked priority given to industrial development over agriculture, and because the bulk of investment funds was generated by peasant agriculture, it was evident that the countryside was being "exploited" to support China's industry.[10] This represented a transfer of resources away from the countryside and into the cities, which was in direct contradiction to Mao Zedong's avowed principles for economic development. Most of the country's economic growth during this period was focused on the existing centers of strength, which meant the urban areas in the northeastern and eastern provinces of China. Their further development threatened to open up a still wider gap between the nation's richest and poorest regions.

During the First Five Year Plan (1953–1957) the state began to nationalize at a rate faster than before. The previously tolerated bourgeois class was gradually being squeezed out, and most of China's private firms came under direct state ownership. At the same time there was a sharp decline in worker democracy in Chinese industry, as a strictly hierarchical pattern of management was put into place and rigid piece rates and quota systems were instituted.[11]

It is not difficult to work out why the CCP moved away from its earlier avowed principles toward the Five Year Plan approach to economic development. The model had worked in the Soviet Union, admittedly in different circumstances, and the Chinese had little experience in directing industrial development. There were some impressive results after the First Five Year Plan; for example, the output of heavy industry expanded by 300 percent, and light industry by 70 percent. The major problem, however, was that agriculture was not growing at a fast enough rate to support such a continued rate of accumulation. People in the countryside were, in relative terms, getting poorer while city dwellers were getting richer. The sharp growth in the urban population during these years also put an extra burden on the agricultural sector, and it was becoming difficult to see how the Second Five Year Plan, which would continue to emphasize capital-intensive heavy industry, would be financed.

In political terms this situation was unhealthy for the Chinese Communist party, which had risen to power with the help of the peasants. There was also a natural opposition in the CCP, voiced especially by Mao Zedong, to the level of bureaucratization and fundamental inegalitarianism inherent in Soviet-style economic development. In a well-known 1956 speech entitled "On the Ten Major Relationships," Mao Zedong expressed his growing concerns about the dangers of continuing along a path that would seriously widen the existing geographical imbalances between China's regions and between agriculture and industry.[12]

Collectivization

Some of the deviations from the Maoist principles of socialism that had occurred in the First Five Year Plan were addressed by the Great Leap Forward; in fact to a large extent the previous policies were reversed. The emphasis on heavy industry was to be balanced by the development of both light industry and agriculture. Rural industry and urban agriculture were to be emphasized as the twin policies to reduce the urban/rural dichotomy. Instead of developing industry at the expense of agriculture, the emphasis for the future was to be on labor, the one resource that China was well endowed with, especially in the countryside. Most notably, in geographical terms, there was to be a renewed emphasis on regional equality and local self-reliance, aided by a significant amount of decentralization of economic decision-making (to the local and regional levels). Provincial and municipal authorities were permitted to keep up to 20 percent of their profits to spend as they saw fit. The relative power of the factory workers was increased so that they were on a more equal footing with management (in terms of membership in the Party). Incentive systems were shifted more significantly over to the collective level, with workers being offered new reasons to work harder.

The effects of the Great Leap Forward on China's industry were not so disastrous as they were in the agricultural sector; in fact some major gains in industrial output were recorded in 1958. In terms of efficiency, however, the economy reached an all-time-low level, mainly as a result of the fanatical attempts to develop small-scale industry in rural areas.[13]

During this entire period the issue of decentralization became something of a political football in China. In the First Five Year Plan, the central government established mandatory targets for all aspects of industry, which were passed down in a dictatorial fashion to the enterprises. During the Great Leap this vertical structure was altered somewhat, and decision-makers at the local level were allowed greater independence in the realm of production. Provinces were allowed to plan industrial development on a territorial (horizontal) basis rather than being told what to do by the central government (vertical or functional coordination). After the Great Leap Forward the decision-making balance shifted back in favor of centralized economic planning, but during the Cultural Revolution years there was a tendency toward decentralization again, with the power of the central (vertical) command structure further damaged by the overall level of social and political chaos. In a significant break with the past, even huge firms in key sectors, such as the Anshan Steel Company, were turned over to provincial-level administration. The attempts to return decision-making to the local level at that time were sporadic and they were mainly politically driven—they did not represent a coherent strategy designed to bring about greater industrial efficiency through decentralization.

To summarize and simplify what was actually a very complex era: The political squabbles about what would be the best strategies for economic development had produced one major shift in policy: from the Soviet "line" (1953–1957) to the Maoist "line" (1958–1961) as well as a series of smaller but still significant shifts, which were either "rightward" (e.g., 1961–1965) or "leftward" (1966–1976). All of this caused major disruptions in the economy and, more important, in the political and social lives of the Chinese people.

Structural Defects in the Economic System

By the time the post-Mao leadership came to power there had already been several attempts to shift the responsibility for economic planning down to the local level. As the new leaders surveyed what had happened over the previous three decades, they probably experienced mixed emotions. Significant advances had been made, and industrial output had grown markedly (see Table 6.1), but this had been achieved by huge increases in the level of investment in fixed capital and by forgoing consumption. To develop China's industry it had always been necessary to devote a relatively high proportion of the GNP to investment funds (accumulation). In the Great Leap years, for example, investment was more than 40 percent of China's GNP, while consumption dropped to a rock-bottom (starvation) level. Even in the most chaotic years of the Cultural Revolution investment remained above the 20 percent level.[14]

To achieve an accumulation rate of this magnitude incomes had to be kept low, and people throughout China had very little money to spend on themselves and their families. In fact after Mao's death, Deng Xiaoping constantly reminded his critics that the workers in China's cities had not received a pay raise in the three decades of socialism. It was this cruel fact that made the comparison with Taiwan so difficult for the Chinese on the mainland to bear. There is no doubt that the CCP had advanced the cause of economic development in China, but it had been achieved at the expense of personal consumption. Another problem the new leadership faced in 1978 was the imbalance between different sectors of the economy, with agriculture and light industry still, in relative terms, playing second fiddle to heavy industry. Unemployment was also becoming an important concern, and it was recognized in 1978 that light industry could create far more jobs than heavy industry.[15]

Probably the most consistent concern at this time was *the chronically low level of efficiency in China's industry*. Although it had proved possible to expand production levels impressively by injecting huge amounts of investment capital, China's industry still needed to grow "intensively" as a result of technological improvement and innovation at the management level, as well as greater labor productivity.[16]

The major problem in this respect was that efficiency had never been the major goal of

Table 6.1 Industrial Output in China: 1952-1978

	1 Gross Value of Indust. Output	2 No. of Workers and Employees (per Year)	3 Fixed and Working Capital	4 Output per Worker[a]	5 Output per Unit of Capital[b]
1952[c]	100.0	100.0	100.0	100.0	100.0
1957	233.3	146.7	225.6	159.0	103.4
1965	510.1	242.7	705.2	210.4	67.9
1978	1,649.2	596.1	2,222.0	276.7	74.2
		Rates of Growth (% per Year)			
1952	18.5	8.0	17.7	9.7	0.7
1957	10.3	6.5	15.3	3.6	-5.1
1965	9.4	7.2	9.2	2.1	0.7
1978	11.4	7.1	12.7	4.0	-1.1

[a] Column 1 divided by column 2.
[b] Column 1 divided by column 3.
[c] 1952 = 100.

Source: Adapted from C. Riskin, 1987, *China's Political Economy: The Quest for Development Since 1949* (London: Oxford University Press), p. 264.

Chinese industry. Output quotas were set for a specific factory without any real consideration of the demand for the product in question. The result could be either stockpiling of unneeded goods or chronic shortages and lengthy delays. Quality control was rarely an important issue because the buyer had a contract with the state rather than with the factory, and this made it difficult to seek recourse if the goods were shoddy. The consideration of profit and loss in a socialist economy also took a backseat to other goals, such as the desire to create full employment. A factory in which many of the workers are standing around with nothing to do is obviously inefficient, but if unemployment is an especially sensitive local concern, there is little incentive to make such a factory more efficient by laying off the unnecessary workers.

It was clear to many economists within the CCP that enterprises needed to be shaken up and placed under "responsibility systems" similar to those that had been so successful in the rural areas. The managers of a factory, instead of being told what and how much to produce, ought to find their own materials and set their own output goals. Once these changes were established, it would not be long before others were suggested, such as

factory managers determining their own incentive systems, hiring and firing their own workers, and reinvesting their own profits.

The traditional explanation for the chronic inefficiency in China's industry during the Maoist period was *organizational*. Decision-making power at the enterprise level was largely in the hands of Party members. The enterprises themselves were still mostly controlled from "above," either at the central or regional level of government. China's factories, especially at the end of the 1970s, were excessively top-heavy with administrative and political cadres, most of whom were engaged in control and surveillance functions.[17] The prevalence of political appointments was the legacy of the long-standing desire of the CCP to maintain centralized control over the economy. What was needed urgently, the new leaders argued after Mao's death, was an attempt to make the economic sphere relatively independent from the political leadership, at all levels.

In addition to the political-control issue, Chinese industry was excessively overmanaged, with a complex and unyielding system of administration. Most enterprises belonged to two different sets of administrative hierarchies; one was the "line" organization (in which a local machine factory was under the auspices of one of the central industrial ministries, in this case, Machine Building); and the other was the "area" or "block" organization at the territorial level. It proved enormously difficult to coordinate the area and line proposals into one coherent plan for all regions and sectors of the economy. To complicate matters even further, there were several tiers to the regional administrative structure—at the provincial, county, and city levels. All of this produced a hopelessly complex chain of command. Enterprises had a very large number of different agencies and bureaus to respond to, at all levels of the administrative hierarchy. There were simply too many "chiefs" in the system, or in more familiar Chinese terms, factory managers had "too many mothers-in-law looking over their shoulders."[18]

There are many examples of the counterproductive effects of the byzantine administrative complexity of Chinese industry. In a Qingdao factory, for example, the managers received conflicting output targets. In 1982, the county included the factory in its annual plans and recommended an output level of Y 19 million; but the city Machine-Building Bureau set the output level for the same year at Y 13 million.[19]

The overmanaged administrative structure also contributed to overinvestment. Because capital goods were allocated through centralized plans, they were not costed to the individual enterprise, so there was little incentive for managers to limit their requests for raw materials. In fact, to cover for future uncertainties they were wise to request inputs far in excess of their current needs. The net effect was that in many parts of China there were vast stockpiles of some goods but chronic shortages of others. Central planning also produced the notorious "ratchet effect," which has a countradictory effect on overall enterprise productivity. In a situation in which next year's output targets are based on what was produced this year, it becomes more difficult every year to reach the established quota. The "smart" (but inefficient) solution chosen by many managers was to slow down production for the current year, to ensure a larger profit margin and greater bonuses for the workers the coming year.

REMAKING CHINA'S ECONOMY IN THE 1980s

It's as if a person who had carefully collected a box of marbles suddenly decided to spill them all out onto the middle of a wide street, where they could roll off in every direction. It's actually quite brave of the leadership. But it does make you wonder if they had any notion of how to control so many individuals all going their own different ways.[20]

As suggested by the epigraph, reforming China's urban industrial economy would prove to be considerably more difficult and less obviously successful than was the case for agriculture. The major problems were political in that the move toward an expanded use of market mechanisms represented a direct challenge to the bureaucrats who administered China's industry at all levels. When bureaucrats are faced with a new way of doing things, they are likely to react in a "highly 'feudalistic' and corrupt way that distorts and ultimately undermines the intent of the reform."[21]

This problem was exacerbated by the proliferation of administrators at both the line and the area levels, which had created myriad constituents who were unwilling to relinquish any of their power. Once the new reforms were in place, however, the initial resistance appears to have been replaced fairly quickly by widespread corruption, bureaucratic "squeeze," and bribery, as unscrupulous officials took advantage of the new reforms to line their own pockets.[22]

The traditional network of *guanxi*, the connections that open up the backdoors for people, had a new cash nexus superimposed onto it in the 1980s. With new opportunities to make and keep the profits from enterprises, many officials found themselves in an excellent position to "get rich" and "glorify" themselves.[23] Even leading cadres in the Chinese government have not been exempt from this sort of corruption, and rumors have circulated about top officials who managed to stash away their gains in foreign bank accounts. In her book *The New Chinese Revolution*, Lynn Pan told a story about a Japanese trader who actually preferred doing business with the Chinese before the reforms, in spite of all the old inefficiencies. In the 1980s, instead of being satisfied with "bribes" of pocket calculators or radios, Chinese businessmen were more likely to ask for computers or even cars when deals were being made.[24]

In the collective economy, enterprises bought and sold everything through official agents of the state, known as *caigouyuan*. Since the reforms the enterprises interact with each other in a predominantly market-like environment, which has generated a new subclass of speculative middlemen (*touji shangfan*), who arrange deals between buyers and sellers on a commission basis. A factory has to negotiate with, and if necessary bribe, the middlemen, a process usually referred to as *yanjiu yanjiu*, which implies wining and dining to extract the most favorable terms.[25] The major currency of the middleman, as it always has been, is his *guanxi*, the invisible web of connections through which business in China is transacted.

At a larger scale, the reform of China's economy has brought up the age-old problem of relationships between the center and the periphery. The reform process required some degree of decentralization of economic (and political) decision-making, but there is no evidence that the Communist party leaders were ready to relinquish their power. This problem is similar to the one parents face when they decide it is time to let their children be more independent. They cut some of the ties, but they are distressed to find that the children take advantage of their newfound freedoms. As China's leaders would quickly discover, economic reforms that were intended to allow the regions and localities to become more economically efficient often ended up being subverted by greedy and self-serving actions at the local level. After a few years of this, some of the Party leaders became naturally apprehensive about the wisdom of continuing with the reform experiments and began calling for retrenchments.

In addition to these difficulties with reform in the nonagricultural sector, it is evident that China's industry simply had far less experience with market mechanisms than the agricultural sector. Private plots and some private selling had always been a feature of the rural landscape, even in the heyday of collectivization, but urban industry had been pretty much dominated by the centralized control of prices and distribution mechanisms since the 1950s.

In spite of these difficulties, since 1978 there have been some major efforts to reform the nonagricultural economy. The thrust of the reforms has been in three major directions:

1. The first reform was the *decentralization* of economic decision-making. In a series of stages, greater autonomy was granted to regional authorities as well as to individual enterprises.

2. Next, *market principles* were introduced into the socialist command economy. Incentives were provided to individuals to work harder; and enterprises were encouraged to develop a new private sector in the economy. At a larger scale there were some major changes in the centralized system of distribution and, most important, in the area of price controls.

3. Finally, the reform focused on *regional specialization* strategies. The traditional Maoist emphasis on regional self-reliance and spatial egalitarianism took a backseat as regions and cities were gradually encouraged to expand on their areas of economic strength. The old idea of "balanced growth" gave way to the notion of "regional comparative advantage"— in other words, some regions, like some individuals and enterprises, were encouraged to "get rich" at a quicker rate than others. A further development after 1978 has been referred to as the Great Leap Westward, in which China began to reopen its doors to foreign trade, investments, and financing.[26] This evolved quickly with the development of a number of "free trade" cities, known as Special Economic Zones, in which foreign countries took advantage of tax and land concessions to set up industries that could benefit from China's cheap labor.

Decentralization: Regional and Enterprise Autonomy

Experiments with enterprise autonomy had started as early as 1978 in Sichuan Province, when some local industrial enterprises were granted "the eight rights," including the rights to retain part of their profits, to make their own investment decisions, to produce for outlets other than the state, and to sign contracts with foreign investors. In 1979 these experiments were extended to other provinces, and by 1980 more than 6,000 factories all across China had such rights.

In October 1984, the Party officially decided that the gains from the reforms thus far had been too timid and piecemeal, and a new resolution was announced.[27] Henceforth the government would be gradually easing itself out of the business of managing the industrial economy. The experiments with enterprise autonomy were to be extended to the entire country, amounting to an urban economic "revolution" similar to the one that had already occurred in the countryside.[28] Starting in 1985 all industrial enterprises were required to implement a "responsibility" system under the leadership of the plant manager. With the exception of the basic industries (mining, steel, energy), enterprises were expected to arrange their own supply of raw materials, set their own output targets, handle their own sales, and schedule their own investments.

Enterprises were also allowed to reward and motivate their workers however they wanted to, but it became clear that the state would no longer be willing to bail out enterprises that continually operated at a loss. Although this appeared to be a hollow threat in a socialist economy, some cities introduced bankruptcy laws, and in August 1986 the city of Shenyang announced China's first case of bankruptcy since 1949.[29] An instrument factory that had been operating at a loss was actually closed down and its labor force laid off with unemployment benefits. Although it is unlikely that such actions will become widespread, it served notice to China's enterprises that the new reforms would have some real teeth.

The magnitude of these changes is illustrated in Cheng Naishan's story about life in the reform-minded environment of Shanghai in the early 1980s. A young factory manager found himself torn between the old and the new ways. Inefficient workers had always been protected by the socialist guarantees of the "iron rice bowl" (the collective's guarantee that all individuals will be paid, either in food or wages, regardless of their productivity) that had persisted in Chinese industry for three decades. After some soul searching the manager decided that it was time to think purely in terms of efficiency: "There's a few illiterate old biddies and good-for-nothing slobs I'd like to get rid of. I've told the workers that if they did a good job and the factory made money, I could buy some apartments for them . . . we'll even pay to furnish their apartments. As for the ones who are still shiftless, regardless of how their private relations may be with me, I'll . . . cut them off."[30]

To retain some degree of government control over industry, and to continue with at least a modicum of state-level planning, many factories have been allowed to operate in a dual system. They would continue to have an "inside sector," in which production was closely guided by state quotas and controlled raw-material prices. In addition to this, enterprise managers would be encouraged to operate in an "outside sector," one that carried the freedoms (and risks) of the marketplace. After fulfilling their obligations to the state (in the form of taxes) they could make their own decisions about what else to produce, how to produce it, where to sell it, and at what price. With their profits they would also have the choice about how best to allocate the rewards. They could choose to invest in new capital, storage facilities, or services, or they could opt to boost the level of incentives for their workers.

Going along with these changes at the enterprise level, provinces and municipalities were also allowed greater authority over the revenues generated within their territory. Beginning in 1982 the provinces were allowed to keep up to 80 percent of their revenues generated through taxes on local businesses. Output and profit levels were generally rising as a result of the enterprise reforms, and this meant that some localities had more funds than ever before to invest in local projects. The net effect of this was that decision-making was effectively shifted away from the center to the periphery. The localities (provinces, counties, and cities) were encouraged to generate surplus or "extrabudgetary" funds by increasing taxes, which meant they were generating income that did not have to be returned to the central government. Most provinces, and a number of cities, were also allowed to enter into contracts with foreign countries and to keep a share of the resulting profits.

The reforms helped to boost industrial output and efficiency in China, but they have also been accompanied by the emergence (or reemergence) of defensive behaviors on behalf of the localities. Although they now have newly expanded powers and greater levels of funding, many localities are nervous about the declining role of central authority, and some of them have begun to implement strategies to insulate themselves from future shocks in the economy. It is not uncommon for localities to protect their self-interests by pushing their own products and refusing to allow the export of local goods or the import of goods from elsewhere. Others have encouraged the hoarding of some key goods and raw materials such as steel and cement. "Localities have used the hoarded supplies to construct new local enterprises, including small, local, duplicative, inefficient, outdated factories known in some quarters as 'local money trees.' "[31]

In recent years the Chinese press has carried many stories of local protectionism. For example, a township in Anhui Province imported cheap tractors from another province rather than buying the more expensive local tractors. In a retaliatory move, the county authorities responded by refusing to allocate diesel fuel, so the tractors lay idle.[32] The worst and most visible effects of local protectionism involve wasteful duplication of productive capacity, as each level of the administrative hierarchy (regional, county, and municipal) acts to protect its own interests. Barriers and blockades have been established to regulate local trading practices, and in some areas this has gone so far as the establishment of "toll gates" on public roads. There have even been stories of "highway robbery," as peasants have physically forced vehicles off the road, making them pay local taxes and "repair fees."[33]

Some local authorities have exercised tight control over the enterprises within their jurisdiction, effectively negating many of the benefits that could have accrued from the greater autonomy at the enterprise level. In addition, self-serving strategies have in some cases thwarted the flow of capital, commodities, and information among China's regions, thereby damaging the overall growth potential of the country. The result is that in spite of the greater local levels of efficiency stimulated by the reforms, the benefits to the economy as a whole have been mixed.

The national income grew significantly in the early 1980s, but the balance between the center and the periphery changed markedly. As some of the regional authorities got richer, the central government's revenues declined.[34]

The major problem was that only part of the economy had been "liberalized" by the reforms: Enterprises and regions had been allowed some degree of autonomy, but there was still central control over most prices and a centralized distribution and allocation system. For a factory to be able to expand its production significantly, it would need greater inputs of raw materials such as coal and energy; but with the state still largely in control of the pricing and distribution of such resources, it might prove very difficult for the enterprise to accumulate the raw materials it needed. This situation obviously led to frustration, and in many cases clever entrepreneurs managed to find semilegal ways of acquiring scarce resources, including what amounted to the theft of state assets. There were, for example, reports of the removal of railroad sleepers for fuel, and entire sections of railroad lines were purloined for steel supplies.[35]

In light of protectionism and corruption of this type, the central government began to question the wisdom of some of the reform policies and by the second half of the 1980s started to withdraw some of the regional autonomy, effectively recentralizing its economic decision-making powers. At the same time, however, there was also a contradictory move, as the state began to release its grip over the distribution system and its domination of commodity prices.

Marketization: The Shift from Socialism to Capitalism

It was necessary to introduce even more elements of a market economy to complement the experiments with enterprise and locality autonomy. The most visible aspect of these new developments was the *re-emergence of private enterprises* in China. This began as early as 1979, when many small businesses started to reappear in Chinese cities, the most common ones being restaurants, barbershops, photographers, tailors, and street vendors offering all kinds of goods and services (see Figures 6.1, 6.2, and 6.3). In 1981 there had been 1.13 million people working in such enterprises, but by 1983 there were 7.3 million, which amounted to almost 7 percent of the work force nationwide. By 1987 it was estimated that this figure had grown to a labor force of more than 20 million, working in

Figure 6.1 (top) The tailoring section of the street market outside the walls of Xibei University in Xian, where in 1986 visitors could have wool suits made to measure for about $20. Figure 6.2 (center) A balloon seller on the streets of Kunming, in Yunnan Province. Figure 6.3 (bottom) A barber working on the street in the county-seat town of Changan, south of Xian, in Shaanxi Province.

businesses whose turnover exceeded Y 76 billion.[36]

The promotion of an individual economy inspired some feelings of ambivalence in a country that so recently was committed to socialism.[37] Obviously the concept of private business is something closely associated with pre-Liberation China and with some of the despised "capitalist roader" tendencies. Even before the revolution there was a long-standing prejudice against self-employed businessmen in a country dominated by the values of Confucianism. The result was that private businessmen had a questionable political and social status. In Mao's China it had been dangerous to choose the road to private enterprise, and even in the more liberal, or pragmatic, climate of the 1980s there was still a marked preference to seek employment in the more secure realm of state-owned or collectively owned enterprises. As prosperous as the private sector has proved to be for many Chinese citizens, it does not offer the "iron rice bowl" type of security provided by the work units (see Chapter 12), either in terms of job security or welfare benefits. Another advantage of the state and collective work units is that they provide access to the Communist party, with all of the attendant privileges and avenues for social and political advancement.

These disadvantages notwithstanding, the post-Mao leadership in China actively encouraged the development of private enterprises. In a landmark resolution of 1984 the CCP made this clear: "We should promote [the] individual economy particularly in those economic fields mainly based on labor services and where decentralized operation is suitable . . . [and] we should . . . encourage . . . cooperative management and economic association among the state, collective and individual sectors of the economy."[38] The resolution relaxed constraints on what were permissible activities and encouraged individuals to overcome their fears of embarking on private careers. Contrary to the beliefs of most outsiders, the CCP leaders were arguing that such developments would help to strengthen rather than damage Chinese socialism: "It is our long-term policy and the need of socialist development to promote diversified economic forms and various methods of operation simultaneously."[39]

About 50 percent of all private businesses in 1987 were involved in trading, usually the buying and selling of food, clothes, or other goods. Restaurants, transportation, and miscellaneous services (including hotels) made up another 25 percent of the total.[40] There was also a significant growth in private industries during the 1980s, mostly turning out light manufactured goods and handicraft items (about 10 percent of the total in 1987). In 1985 the total value of industrial output in the private sector was approximately 1.8 percent of the nation's total, and the share had doubled by 1987, to 3.6 percent. The total number of privately owned enterprises has increased significantly in recent years, making major gains on both state and collective enterprises (Table 6.2).

It must have occurred to many individuals who began private enterprises that they were running the risk of being branded as "capitalist roaders" if the reform process should suddenly be reversed. In light of these fears it is interesting to speculate on the reasons for the rapid growth rate of private enterprises. The individual economy has helped to supplement the state and collective sectors by providing goods and services that would otherwise not be available. As most of the smaller private enterprises were established with relatively little capital, this represented a major gain to the state in terms of the circulation of capital needed to keep the economic-growth machine healthy. Private businesses also helped to generate surplus wealth that could be spent on goods or saved, thereby increasing the pool of investment funds. The result was that the net level of savings remained healthy in both urban and rural areas, in spite of inflation, throughout the 1980s. By 1987, bank deposits in cities and towns stood at Y 226 billion, an increase of 37 percent over a twelve-month period, and rural savings increased during the same period to Y 129 billion, an increase of more than 24 percent.[41] As these figures suggest, many Chinese people were reaping the benefits of the economic reforms, and at least some of the greater wealth was being made available for new investments.

As the private firms become larger and better established, they will also compete with enterprises in the state and collective sectors, which ought to result in greater efficiency

Table 6.2 The Increase of Privately Owned Industrial Enterprises and Percentage of Total Gross Output Value, 1985-1987

	1985		1986		1987	
	% of Total No.	% of Total Output Value	% of Total No.	% of Total Output Value	% of Total No.	% of Total Output Value
State enterprises	1.81	64.9	1.44	62.3	1.31	59.7
Collective enterprises	33.60	32.1	27.20	33.5	24.30	34.6
Private enterprises	64.60	1.8	71.30	2.8	74.30	3.6
In cities and towns	6.40	--	5.50	--	6.60	
In rural areas	58.20	--	65.80	--	67.70	

Source: Adapted from *China Statistical Yearbook 1988* (Beijing: State Statistical Bureau of the PRC, 1988), pp. 260, 287.

overall. Most important, from the government's point of view, however, is the role of the private sector in creating new jobs.[42] The massive threat of rural unemployment that is likely to be generated by the agricultural reforms calls for an expanded private enterprise sector in the small towns and cities all across the countryside—without which China will face the prospect of further increases in the rate of rural-to-urban migration.

The post-Mao leadership was also eager to see some reform in *the way goods were distributed* in China, with the introduction of market-oriented principles. The distribution system in the old command economy consisted of a centralized system of materials supply that allocated raw materials and capital to enterprises; a commercial network to handle retail and wholesale transactions; and a system of rural supply and marketing cooperatives to distribute industrial goods to the countryside and farm produce to the cities. From most accounts this system was often ineffective and cumbersome, and reformers had suggested several measures of deregulation.[43] Centralized allocation would be scrapped for many goods; private traders would be introduced into the system; and enterprises would be allowed to bypass the state channels to market a part of their output directly.

There was significant growth in private retail and wholesale markets in both cities and the countryside during the 1980s. In conjunction with the rapid expansion of collective and private service establishments such as restaurants, repair shops, and food stalls, these changes contributed to a major increase in the level of retail sales throughout China, and by 1984 collective and private units accounted for almost half of all such sales. As a result, employment in the service sector (e.g., retail, catering, and transportation) tripled between 1978 and 1983, and the majority of this growth was in the private sphere.[44]

The most difficult "marketization" reform to achieve in China, and by far the most controversial thus far, has involved the system of commodity exchange, in other words *the price system*. The problem in a command economy, according to the reformers, was that state control of prices reflected the planners' ideas of what the "exchange value" for particular goods should be, rather than an accurate assessment of the actual demand, or "use value." This resulted in many artificial and irrational prices (in purely economic terms). The price of steel, for example, was generally kept high and the price of coal low regardless of changes in market conditions, technology, or efficiency levels in the two industries. The reformers argued that until prices were decontrolled, it would not be possible to gauge the efficiency of enterprises. What was needed was a series of price reforms, in which prices would more accurately reflect changing market circumstances and regional variations, with local authorities given more autonomy to set price levels (although it was assumed that the state would continue to fix prices for strategic goods and consumer items such as food).

Price reform was seen as the key, the essential component that would make all of the other reforms "work." In actuality it has proved to be an extremely complex and difficult task to achieve. In the first place, if prices are to reflect market conditions accurately, they need to be realigned frequently, but China lacks the computer technology required to do this on a daily basis. With up to one million prices to be manipulated, and an infinite number of sectors in all corners of the country needing to be consulted, there is a simple physical problem involved.[45]

More important, however, is the political problem inherent in the old system of controlled prices. Each price that is controlled by the state creates a constituency that comes to see price control as an entitlement. If coal prices are not allowed to rise past a certain point, this acts as a subsidy to the users of coal; if food prices are kept low, this benefits millions of nonagricultural households in the cities. The experiments with decontrolling food prices resulted in sharp increases for many items and, not surprisingly, produced significant opposition in urban areas. To deal with this potentially explosive situation the government was forced to institute a series of very costly urban subsidies rather than return to the old price controls.[46]

It has been estimated that subsidies to counteract the harsh realities of price increases after decontrol have swallowed up about one-third of the state's budget since the reforms began. This suggests that the government has been "caught in a vice between price paralysis on the one side and escalating subsidies on the other."[47] The net effect was a period of uncertainty. At first it looked as though the leadership was willing to "tough out" the impacts of price reform in 1988 to make sure that the overall trajectory of economic reform was maintained. By that time about one-third of all agricultural and retail commodity prices were determined entirely by market forces, and in May the prices of four major food items were decontrolled, namely eggs, vegetables, sugar, and pork.[48]

The effects were dramatic. Within a matter of weeks food prices shot up from 30 to 60 percent. Chinese families found themselves paying out more than half of their incomes for food alone. In May, June, and July, the inflation rate reached 36 percent, three times higher than it was in the first three months of the year. This caused a panic among China's consumers. Millions of people rushed to the banks to withdraw their hard-earned savings; and others decided to spend what they had on consumer goods of any type, figuring that spending is better than saving during an inflationary period. On September 12, 1988, the government announced that it had had enough of price reforms for the time being. Controls reappeared on a nationwide scale and economic decision-making was recentralized to a level close to the pre-1979 situation. Deng Xiaoping is reported to have said, "We have been bold enough; now we need to take our steps in a more cautious way."[49]

Because of the vast difficulties involved and the opposition that was generated, price reform progressed very slowly, cautiously, and unevenly. All through the reform era there has been a tendency for market-type reforms to come and go in cycles. The first round of market loosenings occurred in 1979, but the negative effects resulted in a clampdown by 1981. The second wave of reforms begun in 1984 also had some disastrous effects, and the result was again a period of retrenchment. The process began with much-publicized complaints about the economic chaos and corruption that have been by-products of the economic reforms. It was argued that many enterprises had used the price decontrols as an excuse to gouge the public, with no increase in commodity quality. The resulting inflation meant that the reforms were eventually terminated. The unfortunate part of the cycle is that because individual aspirations remain high, markets are driven underground and there is a surge in the level of economic corruption and a new call for reforms—setting the process in motion all over again.[50]

Throughout 1988 the issue of price reform remained critical; in fact it was the linchpin of the entire reform movement. The government decided finally to cool its heels, especially in light of the other problems it was currently encountering: Unemployment was rising in the countryside, student protests were simmering in the cities, and minority unrest was sparking off at intervals in some of the Autonomous Regions.[51]

Regional Specialization: The Development of Comparative Advantage

One aspect of the economic reforms that would contrast particularly sharply with the spatially egalitarian policies of the Maoist period was the focus on a regional division of labor. Some parts of the country were to be encouraged to develop their economic strengths as fully as possible. The traditional emphasis in socialist regional development had been to encourage all regions to become "self-reliant," and serious efforts were made to reduce the gap in economic terms between the nation's richest and poorest regions (see Chapter 9).

After 1978 several key economic thinkers within the CCP started to consider some alternative strategies that would involve regional specialization. The traditionally strong coastal areas would continue to lead the way by focusing on high-technology growth; the more remote inland regions would concentrate on energy development, raw material extraction, or other local specialties.[52] In 1984 an official statement announced this new emphasis, implying that previous efforts to produce balanced regional growth had actually detracted from the nation's best interests: "The development of new and outlying backward regions on too large a scale will . . . retard the increase of the national income."[53]

A verbal commitment was made to China's neediest regions, but they must have felt increasingly insecure as they watched the gap growing between the rich and the poor parts of the country. The emphasis for economic development had clearly shifted toward regional specialization, and away from centralized support for the relatively deprived regions.

An important part of the new regional-development plans was a mandatory form of cooperation between the richer and the poorer regions of China. In the tradition of trickle-down economics, it was felt that by allowing the eastern coastal regions to "get rich first," the whole country would ultimately benefit. To make sure this process worked, there were to be trading arrangements, joint investment ventures, and technology transfers between regions—all of which amounted to core-periphery transfer relationships. In many cases these arrangements were not voluntary, and the officials in the richer areas were often unwilling to participate, preferring to build up their home economies rather than to risk faraway ventures.

Two sorts of regions were identified for the task of developing economic strengths. The first included six macroregions, each made up of several provinces; and the second was of a group of "key," or "central," cities. In 1984 about one-quarter of the nation's rural (in fact suburban) counties were "assigned" to the jurisdiction of nearby cities. In 1987, seventy-two cities were selected as experimental sites for further reforms in the area of enterprise management and new incentive schemes. According to one report, these strategies have been highly successful, with a one-year increase in the value of industrial output in the designated cities of 17.2 percent, far higher than the national average.[54]

Several other innovations occurred in these cities at the same time, including the establishment of wholesale markets for capital goods, funds, technology, and even labor. Some of the cities were also able to break down administrative barriers and improve on cross-departmental and transregional cooperation. In a number of ways, therefore, the continued success of the key cities is seen as crucial to the future development of other less fortunate cities and regions in China.

The underlying and usually unwritten principle behind the spatial reforms has been to establish jurisdictions for economic decision-making that are based on "natural" economic boundaries, rather than on administrative or political boundaries, as was the case in the past. Unfortunately, it appears that the reforms have resulted in more of the predictable rivalry and interregional squabbling that has continued to plague the reform process at all levels. There is evidence that local chauvinism and self-interest have continued to outweigh regional or national concerns. In the cities, for example, some cadres used their expanded powers over the newly annexed rural counties to further their own political and economic ends exclusively, and to some extent the cities have become the new "centers" bossing around and exploiting their "peripheries." Such developments run counter to the avowed goal of reducing the urban/rural dichotomy, and they also have serious consequences for the broader issue of regional equality in China—a topic we shall return to in Chapter 9.

Another group of cities, in fact a specific region of the country, has been targeted for rapid economic development, largely as a result of its coastal location. These are the much-publicized Special Economic Zones (SEZs), which were opened up as virtual free-trade cities, into which foreign investment was welcomed.[55] In 1979 four SEZs were opened up, with the express purpose of drawing in capital, stimulating exports, and gaining access to modern technology and management practices. All four cities are in the south of China: Shenzhen, just across the border from Hong Kong; Zhuhai, adjacent to the old Portuguese colony of Macao; and Shantou, are in Guangdong Province; and the fourth is Xiamen (formerly known as Amoy) in Fujian Province, across the strait from Taiwan.

From a purely geographical perspective it is obvious that these cities were not chosen at random. The Chinese want to encourage investment from their traditional Chinese (but temporarily estranged) outposts in Macao, Hong Kong, and Taiwan—perhaps as a way to smooth the path for their eventual political repatriation. In 1984 it was announced that fourteen coastal ports would also be designated as "open cities," with powers to bring in foreign investments (Figure 6.4).

The opening up of these new cities and regions can best be understood in the overall context of the larger economic reform movement. One of the major bottlenecks in the Chinese economy since the reforms began has been the scarcity of raw materials. Opening up the coastal areas to foreign capital was seen as a way to solve that problem by importing and processing raw materials from all over the world and then exporting the finished products.[56] The advantages to accrue from the development of foreign trade in China's coastal areas would be mainly in the transfer of experience and technology from foreign nations. This would (it was hoped) generate additional jobs to help soak up the surplus labor force in China's countryside. True to the spirit of regional comparative advantage, it was anticipated that the growth of economic activity in the coastal areas would help to generate surplus wealth that would subsequently provide a boost to the economies of China's peripheral and constantly lagging regions.

The parallel between the new zones and open cities and the nineteenth-century Treaty Ports is an obvious one, and to many Chinese people the concept of an "open door" to foreign capital is a painful reminder of the humiliation of foreign exploitation.[57] Although the economic power in the SEZs is now much more solidly in China's hands than was the case in the nineteenth century, the new policy still has an ominous ring to it, and critics have pointed out that it invites foreigners to launch further attacks on China's independence and self-reliance. This was also a blow to the few remaining Maoist radicals within China, who (assuming they still existed) would have argued that the open-door policy, in conjunction with the economic reforms, would have disastrous consequences for China. Some critics have suggested that the zones would essentially create "little Hong Kongs"—small-scale areas of foreign imperialism, where outside capital could legally exploit cheap Chinese labor.

The effect of the economic reforms, according to the critics, was that China's economy in the 1980s became prematurely exposed to the cut-throat world of international capitalism. "Foreign capital displaces and subordinates . . . important areas of Chinese industry. . . . The restoration of the market mechanism . . . in the context of the 'open-door' to foreign capital—is conducive to economic and social polarization, industrial concentration and a tendency toward the technological subordination of Chinese industry to foreign capital."[58]

In spite of these fears the SEZs were off to a flying start, especially Shenzhen, which grew from 20,000 in 1979 to more than 300,000 by 1984. In that time Y 1.9 billion was invested in capital construction projects in Shenzhen, and more than 2,500 contracts were signed with foreign investors. This early success led the Party leaders to think even more expansively, and they came to see the new open areas as the key to China's economic future. In 1984, for example, Zhao Ziyang (then premier) described their function as follows:

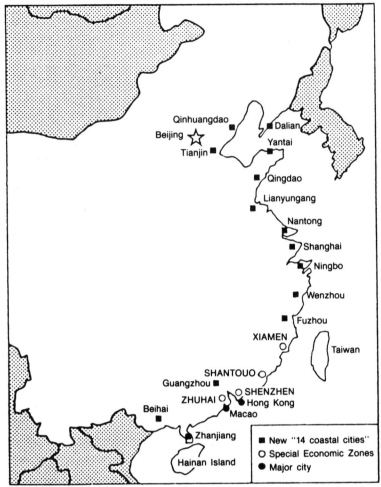

Figure 6.4 China's Special Economic Zones and "open cities." Source: Michael Osborne, 1986, China's Special Economic Zones *(Paris: Developmental Center of the O.E.C.D.), p. 185.*

The special economic zones . . . [and open cities] are the bridgeheads in our opening to the outside world, and they should play the role of spring-board. *On the one hand*, they should import advanced foreign technology, equipment, and management . . . absorb and digest them; apply them in innovations; and transfer them to the interior. *On the other hand*, they should send commodities produced in the coastal areas with foreign technology to the interior, and export the latter's raw materials and produce, with added value after processing . . . to the inter-national market.[59]

Enthusiasm for the SEZs, coupled with early reports of tremendous increases in em-ployment, salaries, and living conditions, was later tempered by some heavy criticisms. Shenzhen, for example, was intended to focus on the importation of "high tech" foreign capital to be used in the manufacture of goods for export. In fact, it appears that the bulk of the "foreign" investment has come from Hong Kong and that much of the money actually originated in the mainland. This meant, as the critics suggested, that the SEZs were being artificially supported by domestic "blood transfusions" that drained the rest of the country.[60] It seems that the zones were able to assemble goods using foreign parts, but they were far less effective in producing goods from scratch. Another problem was that most of the goods produced with foreign capital were being sold in the PRC, which was not one of the original goals of the SEZs. The effect of this was a sharp rise in imports, which soaked up much of China's supply of foreign-exchange resources without the expected rise in exports to rebuild that supply. As a result China's foreign-exchange reserves plummeted, dropping at one point in 1985 by one-third in just six months.[61] This inspired stringent measures to control foreign exchange, and in 1985 free-trading activities were sharply curtailed in all but four of the open cities.

The too-rapid pace of capital construction in the newly opened areas also threatened to widen the existing gap between the richer coastal regions and the poorer regions of the interior. Moreover, the old issue of "spiritual pollution" from the West was revived by the critics of the open-door policy. Not only had foreign capital been drawn into China, but a more insidious result was the encouragement of Western-style consumption habits that were considered to be wasteful, bourgeois in essence, and counterproductive to the nation's modernization drive. The critics suggested that the "open door" had in fact become a "backdoor" through which foreign corporations could enter China to exploit its huge markets and cheap supplies of labor.

The rapid population growth of the SEZs, especially Shenzhen, was not accompanied by a parallel growth in the level of service provision, and this was particularly the case in the areas of housing, health care, and utilities.[62] There was also an unfortunate political outcome that resulted from the opening of the SEZs, in that they became a highly prized destination for thousands of Chinese people who were unhappy with their lives in the PRC. It is reasonable to assume that many of the migrants to the coastal cities, in addition to wanting to "get rich," were also hoping to "escape" into the capitalist meccas of Hong Kong and Macao, and the SEZs were seen as a stopping-off point en route.

Some of the highly publicized scandals in the SEZs contributed to the mounting criticisms, and none was more serious than what happened on the island (later to be the province) of Hainan. The freedom to import foreign goods had been granted as part of the push to develop the island's weak economy. In actuality, the supply of scarce foreign exchange was used largely to import foreign cars and television sets cheaply and then resell them to eager customers in the mainland, for a healthy profit. This was used by the critics of the reform movement as an example of the sharp practices employed by localities to line their own pockets at the expense of the national economy. Criticisms of this sort produced some tightening up of the policies toward the SEZs and an attempt to get them to focus more on the production of goods for export (outside the PRC) than had previously been the case.

ASSESSING THE REFORMS

It might help to think of the Chinese economy as a water buffalo, which for decades was kept tethered. . . . The system brought fodder at regular intervals; the buffalo grew steadily. But the animal . . . was listless and dispirited; years of inactivity had robbed it of initiative. Why not loosen things, argued the reformers? Remove the stake and let the buffalo forage for itself. . . . After ten years, the buffalo has taken on some of the characteristics of a bull. . . . The economy rapidly discovered gaps in the fence. Excessive spending throughout the system, and the resulting breakout of inflation, were too alarming. Back to the tether.[63]

The industrial reforms in China have not been received with the kind of enthusiasm generated for the agricultural reforms. In part this is because it has proved more difficult to reform the urban industrial economy. At first the overall impact, in terms of industrial output at least, was not very impressive. Output grew at a slower rate between 1978 and 1982 than between 1965 and 1978 (7.0 percent versus 9.2 percent per year), but this was largely a result of the deliberate shift away from heavy industry, which was deemphasized relative to both light industry and agriculture. After 1982, light industry growth has managed to surpass that of heavy industry, and consequently total output value began to increase at a faster rate, averaging 10 percent per year between 1982 and 1985.[64]

The major goal of the reforms was to improve industrial efficiency, and although there is some evidence that labor productivity was higher after 1978 than before, there was still much room for improvement.[65] The major bone of contention among the Party leaders was that the other aspects of economic reform had proved so difficult to implement, especially the issue of price reform. The net effect was that relatively high rates of industrial growth had been achieved, but they have been accompanied by some very familiar problems, such as the wasteful use of raw materials, the duplication of product lines, and widespread charges of graft and corruption.

The reforms have certainly generated enough problems and conflicts to test very seriously the government's resolve to stay the course with its ambitious economic programs. Ironically, one of the most serious problems resulted from the oversuccess of the reforms, which by 1985 had helped to produce an "overheated" economy. Enterprises all over the country, in their rush to expand output, had launched into heavy capital-construction projects, producing a growth rate far higher than the economic planners had bargained for; in fact, China's economic growth during the 1980s was among the highest in the world (see Table 6.3). Much of the growth occurred in the village and township enterprises, which were largely outside the control of state planning and distribution. The net effect was that the reform plans had to be shelved temporarily; in 1983, 1986, and again in 1988, strict controls were placed on credit and the supply of money, which helped to slow down industrial growth to more manageable levels.

In spite of the belt-tightening activities, investments continued to grow rapidly throughout the 1980s, with vast amounts of public and private money going into building houses and developing the urban industrial infrastructure, activities not directly tied to raising productivity. Investments in fixed assets in the state sector grew by 25 percent in 1984 and 42 percent in 1985, but slowed down as a result of retrenchment measures to 15 percent in 1986. However, in the first half of 1987 the investment rate crept back up to 21 percent.[66]

The success of the agricultural and industrial reforms since 1978 meant that there were far greater levels of savings than ever before, and as a result, much more capital was available for investment purposes. However, as we have seen, the new profits kept by enterprises and the extra money available in people's pockets meant that spending went out of control,[67] and vast supplies of scarce foreign exchange were used up.[68]

The most worrisome and damaging impact of the reforms has been inflation. Because many goods were still in short supply, the expansion of industrial output, coupled with price decontrols, resulted in sharp price in-

Table 6.3 Growth of World Output (Industry and Agriculture) 1971-1988: China Compared with Other Groups of Countries (Percentage Change, per Year)

	1971-1980	1981-1986	Average per Year				
			1984	1985	1986	1987	1988
China	5.7	8.8	12.0	12.3	7.0	7.0	7.0
Worldwide	3.9	2.7	4.5	3.4	3.0	3.2	3.7
Developing countries	5.6	1.5	2.2	2.0	2.5	2.7	3.8
Developed market economies	3.1	2.2	4.7	2.9	2.4	2.6	3.0
In N. America	2.9	2.4	6.4	2.8	2.6	2.7	3.4
In W. Europe	2.9	1.5	2.4	2.3	2.4	2.4	2.4
Japan	4.7	3.6	5.1	4.5	2.5	2.6	3.0
Centrally planned economies (Europe)	5.2	3.3	3.8	3.6	4.3	4.1	4.5

Source: Adapted from United Nations, 1987, *World Economic Survey 1987: Current Trends and Policies in the World Economy* (New York: United Nations), p. 13, Table II.1.

creases in the 1980s. In 1980 there was a 7.5 percent inflation rate over the previous year. After that year, inflation slowed down, to average 2 percent per year until 1985, when it reached 11.5 percent after a new round of price decontrols. In 1987 the rate was 9.1 percent, and even the Chinese government was prepared for a significant rise in the rate in 1988 and 1989. The Economist Intelligence Unit (EIU) estimated that the inflation rate would easily reach 20 percent in 1988 and probably at least 25 percent in 1989.[69] The actual inflation statistics were almost as high as the EIU had predicted, with a 10 percent increase in retail prices from January to September 1988.[70] The prices of some food items went up at an even faster rate; for example, fresh vegetable prices increased by 30 percent and meat prices by 20 percent in 1987.[71]

It is important to put the problem of inflation into context. Based on the experience of numerous other socialist countries that have embarked on an ambitious program of economic reform, inflation was entirely predictable. It is in fact just one of many problems (including unemployment) to be expected when a command system switches over to a market-oriented system. Another familiar problem, and one that was first encountered as early as 1979, was the emergence of a budget deficit, as total state revenues failed to keep up with expenditures (see Table 6.4). This obviously came as a shock to a country used to balancing its budget or running a surplus. The major reason was the decline in revenues turned over to the Treasury by China's enterprises because the reform policies allowed them to keep a greater share of their profits. This resulted in a net loss to the state of Y 28.1 billion between 1978 and 1981, and the state's proportion of China's national income fell significantly during the early 1980s, from 34 percent before 1978 to 25 percent in 1984.[72]

As a result of the reforms the localities had begun to fund a larger share of total investments vis-à-vis the central government. In 1978, 66 percent of investments in state enterprises were centrally financed, but this had fallen to 38 percent by 1984. Although this decentralization was one of the goals of the planned reforms, it produced a rate of investment that was dangerously high when the localities launched into massive capital-investment projects, which increased from Y 22.5 billion in 1978, to Y 73.1 billion in 1984. Capital investment at this rate brought with it all sorts of other allocation problems. There were serious shortages of construction materials, which not only slowed the rate of new house building but also contributed to inflation. The investment boom also exposed the chronic bottlenecks in China's transportation system and its energy supplies—both of which were also starved of much-needed investment funds by the boom in industrial activity.[73]

Table 6.4 State Revenues and Expenditures, 1978-1987 (Billions of Current Yuan)

	Total Revenue	Total Expenditures	Net Surplus or Deficit	Total Borrowing	Net Deficit Including Borrowing
1978	112.11	111.10	+1.01	0.15	+0.86
1979	110.33	127.39	-17.06	3.64	-20.70
1980	108.52	121.27	-12.75	4.30	-17.05
1981	108.95	111.50	-2.55	7.31	-9.86
1982	112.40	115.33	-2.93	8.39	-11.32
1983	124.90	129.25	-4.35	7.94	-12.24
1984	146.50	157.50	-5.00	7.65	-12.65
1985	186.60	184.48	+2.16	8.99	-6.83
1986	226.03	233.08	-7.06	13.83	-20.89
1987	234.67	242.69	-8.03	16.59	-25.62

Source: Adapted from C. Riskin, 1987, *China's Political Economy: The Quest for Development Since 1949* (London: Oxford University Press), p. 362, Table 14.4, and *China Statistical Yearbook 1988* (Beijing: State Statistical Bureau of the PRC, 1988), p. 907.

Although some of these problems would have occurred in a fully planned economy, their appearance in China in the 1980s fueled the argument of the opponents to the reform process. The problems were made worse by the incremental and partial nature of the reforms, which had essentially evolved with small changes here and there, interspersed with periodic retrenchments. Reform in one realm, for example, the increase in enterprise autonomy, occurred before the price system had been fully reformed, and this effectively detracted from its overall success.

Clearly the most publicized negative effect of the reforms was the sharp practices, bordering on outright corruption, that accompanied the changes in the 1980s.[74] It is perhaps possible to justify the epidemic of corruption as a response to a cataclysmic change in operating procedures. Enterprise managers and government bureaucrats had worked for years in a centrally planned economy, and the shift toward market conditions propelled them rapidly into an entirely new environment. As one observer explained: "Where the entrepreneur is bold and adventuresome, the bureaucrat is obedient and staid. Where the former seeks to maximize gain, the latter tries to minimize loss."[75] When they entered the new and unfamiliar situation, such people were likely to go astray. "Thrust into a market environment, bureaucrats tend to behave not like capitalists, but like black marketeers, lining their pockets, stealing, and generally acting according to the rules of the market, but according to the street-smart, corrupt codes of the underground economy."[76]

It is difficult to determine to what extent the wave of economic crimes reported in the late 1980s was a result of the reforms and the economic chaos that came in their wake. It is possible, for example, that the actual level of corruption was not much higher than it had ever been in postrevolutionary China. It could be that crimes were much more likely to be reported, perhaps for reasons that were largely political[77] (see Chapter 14). The issue of corruption associated with the economic reforms has become a significant political and social concern in China, one that has fed directly into the hands of the opponents of reform and also those who would like to see some changes in the system of government in China (see Figure 6.5).

Figure 6.5 *Cartoon showing a criminal being led away for stealing a small bag of money while a well-placed cadre is squandering a bag of gold labeled "National Property—the blood and sweat of the people." The caption reads, "Graft is a crime; waste is unstopped." Source: R. Crozier, 1983, "The Thorny Flowers of 1979: Political Cartoons and Liberalization in China," in Bulletin of Concerned Asia Scholars (eds.), China from Mao to Deng: The Politics and Economics of Socialist Development (Armonk, N.Y.: M. E. Sharpe, Inc.), p. 35.*

At the same time another political problem has emerged from the threat the reforms have brought to the nation's cadres. In a market economy there is much less demand for bureaucrats to carry out planning, supervising, enforcing, and surveillance tasks. Not only are these jobs threatened by the reforms, but the prestige of the politicians and bureaucrats, so long based on political privilege, is also challenged in an economy increasingly dominated by hard cash, one where status is more likely to be related to wealth than to political position. Moreover, the reforms present a major threat to the ideological principles upon which a Marxist-Leninist state like China has been built. Marxism, especially in its Maoist guise, has strongly espoused such principles as full employment, egalitarianism, and the guarantee of secure food and housing. As we shall see at various points throughout this book, the costs associated with making these guarantees have been high, and the citizens of China have had to put up with chronic shortages of many consumer goods, low living standards, little job mobility, and drab surroundings.[78] The reforms of the 1980s offered a glimpse of changes for the better, but nevertheless the rewards did not come without some serious side effects, such as rising unemployment rates, higher food prices, and housing shortages.

It has also been clear that the gains in terms of wealth and consumption have not been spread evenly throughout the population. Although Chinese people had, on average, much more money to spend at the end of the 1980s than they did at the beginning, some degree of inequality had inevitably reappeared, effectively creating what one critic has described as "pockets of western consumption," and a "dual and divided structure of social consumption where a relatively small minority will have access to higher levels of consumption."[79] The reemergence of a wealthy subgroup raised the level of resentment among the have-nots, and it also encouraged extra demands for consumer durable goods. The production of such goods, to meet the new level of demand, threatened to detract further from the production of more "necessary" consumer goods such as basic housing, clothing, and food. The problem, as the Chinese leaders saw it, was that too much money was being spent on the "wrong" items, eating up resources that should be saved and used for more balanced economic growth. A study conducted by the Chinese Academy of Social Sciences in 1987 pointed out that too many Chinese families had been spending their newfound surpluses on "deviant" consumables, notably the so-called four new essentials: color TV sets, refrigerators, washing machines, and tape recorders—sales of which all increased by more than 50 percent between 1984 and 1986.[80] A similar trend could be detected in the production of consumer goods in China throughout the 1980s (see Table 6.5).

The rush to spend and consume among the newly rich threatens the essential classlessness of China's social structure. In the countryside and the city a new class of entrepreneurs is rapidly emerging—the new "rich" peasant households, the shopkeepers, the small business families, the brokers, and the venture capitalists. It is impossible to tell

how far this development will proceed before fundamental changes in China's political system are demanded by the newly enfranchised middle class or before the leadership decides to rein in the reform process and slow down such developments. This appears to be what has happened in 1990, after the tumultuous events of the previous year. The attempt made in 1989 to challenge the Leninist concept of Party domination over all aspects of life was soundly rejected, but as economic power and decision-making diffuses downward, the monopolist control by the center is increasingly likely to be challenged, calling into question how long the Communist party can survive the current pace of change in China. As the epigraph at the beginning of the section "Remaking China's Economy" (earlier in this chapter) suggested, the current situation is somewhat like rolling marbles down the middle of the street. No one can be certain where the marbles will end up. What is certain, however, is that the leaders of the CCP are still unwilling to follow the recent trends in the Soviet Union and Eastern Europe by allowing a sharing of political power.

THE DEMISE OF SOCIALISM?

In the middle of this tumultuous economic reform process, China's leaders steadfastly maintained that the reforms were not capitalist per se and that China was still deeply committed to socialism. In some public pronouncements the reforms were described as an essential part of the "primary" stage of socialism that China was then entering.[81] The trend toward mixed ownership of the means of production, with an increasing role for the private sector, was justified by the unique economic circumstances faced by China in the 1980s. Zhao Ziyang, who was at the time acting general secretary of the CCP, explained this in 1987, when he said that strict adherence in the past to "socialist" (in other words, Maoist) principles meant that attempts to introduce market forces were sharply criticized as "capitalist roader" tendencies. The effect of this, according to Zhao, was very damaging to China's economy and its political system, hindering the drive toward modernization. "Undue emphasis was placed on a single form of ownership [by the State], and a rigid economic structure took shape . . . this se-

Table 6.5 Output of Selected Major Industrial (Consumer) Products, China, 1979, 1983, 1987

	1979	1983	1987	1987 as a % of 1979
Chemical fibers (10,000 tons)	32.6	54.1	117.5	+360
Machine-made paper (10,000 tons)	493	661	1,141	+229
Synthetic detergents (10,000 tons)	32.4	67.7	119.2	+370
Bicycles (10,000)	1,009	2,758	4,117	+408
Wristwatches (10,000)	1,750	3,478	6,159	+349
Canned food (10,000 tons)	50.1	84.5	161.5	+322
Beer (10,000 tons)	52	163	540	+1,038
Cigarettes (10,000 cases)	1,303	1,938	2,881	+216

Source: China: Statistical Yearbook 1988 (Beijing: State Statistical Bureau of the PRC, 1988), p. 297.

riously hampered the development of the productive forces and of the socialist commodity economy."[82]

The economic reforms, in which market principles were added to the planned economy, were justified and defended in the light of the current situation.[83] According to Zhao, to achieve the Four Modernizations (of industry, agriculture, national defense, and science and technology) it was necessary for China to take some fairly bold steps away from the orthodox path. "To resolve the principal contradiction of the present stage we must vigorously expand the commodity economy, raise labour productivity . . . and, to this end, reform such aspects of the relations of production . . . as are incompatible with the growth of the productive forces."[84]

Although they accepted the need for economic reforms, and according to Zhao's published remarks, this involved some significant changes in the pattern of ownership, there was no consensus among the leaders that economic reforms should be accompanied by reforms of the political system or by a reduction in the centralized power of the CCP. Although little progress has yet been made in this direction, in spite of the massive outpouring of popular sentiment in the spring of 1989,[85] it appears that political reforms were being contemplated all through 1987 and 1988. The economist most closely as-

sociated with the "primary stage of socialism" theory espoused by Zhao Ziyang wrote in a Shanghai newspaper in 1987 that "no single person or organization can absolutely and completely represent . . . the interests of all people in society. The false impression of no conflict no longer exists. People's interests are no longer monolithic."[86]

Whether this sentiment reflected the views of a majority of the top brass within the Party will never be known. Even if it did, it seems clear that the events of 1989 moved far too quickly for the CCP. They may have been considering reforms at that time, but they were certainly not ready to have the details dictated to them by student demonstrators. The suppression of the student demonstrations in 1987 and 1989, and the hard line taken in Tibet, showed that any discussion about political reform in China was purely theoretical.

It has been difficult for the Party theoreticians to persuade many outsiders that the economic reforms that swept across China in the 1980s were in any realistic way a part of socialism. Responding to a speech about the "radiance" of the "great truth of Marxism," for example, Orville Schell noted that the only "radiance" he could detect on the streets of China in the late 1980s was that of people making money! As the reforms unfolded, Party officials and true believers in socialism were left to watch from the sidelines as they became increasingly irrelevant to the country's future. Schell argued that statements such as those quoted here from Zhao Ziyang were little more than futile attempts "to fit all the incongruities of the new situation into a convincing socialist framework."[87] In actual fact the Communists were probably not convincing anyone, but their fanaticism was perhaps understandable, as they tried desperately to hang onto the legacy of Marxism/Leninism/Mao Zedong Thought. For close to half a century this belief system had provided the "national essence" (*guocui*) of China. As Schell suggested, it is possible that the Party leaders were afraid that if China were to lose touch with this most recent incarnation of its *guocui*, especially after the pain and humiliation of the century before the revolution, the country would "once more become culturally and politically deracinated, and . . . [would] fall into ruin."[88]

CONCLUSION: WHAT DOES THE FUTURE HOLD IN STORE?

It is not easy to interpret the round of economic retrenchments of 1988 and 1989 without knowing how long they will last. However, it seems that for the time being the economic reforms have been put on hold, and of course the picture has been totally obfuscated by the dramatic happenings of June 1989. In 1985 Jurgen Domes outlined four scenarios for China's economic and political future, and with hindsight they now provide a useful framework with which to evaluate the later events.[89] The first scenario is a continuation of the market reforms and further openings to Western capital. This could be linked with major political changes and an eventual dismantling of the central control of the Communist party.[90] Of course, this option was soundly rejected in the summer of 1989.

The second scenario appears to be what was happening in late 1988 and early 1989, namely a continuation of some but not all aspects of the reforms, but with no basic changes in the political system to insert more democracy. Social tensions would continue to mount as earlier aspirations were blocked and there would be a growth in the "second economy," the area of economic corruption, which would result in a major crackdown on crime and calls for comprehensive reform of the criminal-justice system (see Chapter 14).

In spring 1989 when the student demonstrations began, the administration was not at all willing to discuss major changes in the political system to accompany the economic reforms. No decisions had been made to limit the power of the Party with a system of checks and balances or the development of alternative parties. The leaders, instead of contemplating such drastic measures, made efforts to placate the emerging tide of dissent by promising to make the Party "better" rather than changing it. In Zhao Ziyang's words, the goal was "to strengthen supervision to keep Party and government institutions clean and honest, which is vital to the reform movement."[91] Zhao was implying that there was a need for greater control over Party and government officials, as well as closer scrutiny in their selection, to help wipe out the crime and corruption that had become rampant in the 1980s. Another part of the campaign to cleanse the country of economic corruption involved an attempt to conduct regular checks on price rises and speculation, in order to protect consumers. In September 1987, thousands of "price supervision stations" were set up to check on the prices of consumer goods in the streets and marketplaces.[92] The government also announced in 1988 the establishment of "corruption report centers" all over China, to which individuals could make complaints about any corrupt practices they encountered. In the first two months, more than 12,000 cases were reported, half of them concerned with bribery and embezzlement— and the reporting is claimed to have resulted in the recovery of Y 10 million for the state treasury.[93]

The third and fourth scenarios outlined by Domes predicted a return either to the "Stalinist line" of the 1950s, with an emphasis on heavy industry (as in Czechoslovakia during the 1970s); or a shift back toward the "Maoist line," with a new drive toward greater collectivization and a reduction in market-based activities. Although both of these scenarios seem to be hopelessly out of step with recent developments in Europe, the problem with predicting the future in China is that no one can be sure about the next generation of leaders' commitment to the reform program.

If, as Domes suggested in 1985, the post-Deng leadership in the 1990s turns out to adopt a far less enthusiastic view of reform, there is a possibility of a return to either the Soviet or the Maoist scenarios.[94]

If one bears in mind that the Chinese economy changes quite rapidly and that the Chinese political system is unfathomable in nature, one can see that it would be foolish to rule out any possibilities. In October 1988, it was learned that Zhao Ziyang, the major spokesman for the economic reforms and the most enthusiastic advocate of further price decontrols, had retreated into the background, where he could no longer be blamed if things continued to "go wrong."[95] In light of Zhao's later demise during the demonstrations and after the crackdown of 1989, it appears that the decision to step down in 1988 was probably not his own. At the time of writing (September 1990), Zhao's whereabouts remained unknown.

Some Western economists recommended complete reform of the price system in the 1980s, accompanied by tight money controls to slow down spending and investment; but the more cautious Chinese leaders chose to leave the controls on certain food items such as grain, cotton, edible oils, and important industrial commodities such as steel and timber. Presumably they were hoping that by restricting credit they would be able to get the economy under control first, thereby creating enough breathing space to tackle the issue of total price reform at a later date. The problems with the economy in 1988 were obvious for all to see—spiraling inflation rates; the threat of massive rural unemployment; double-digit industrial growth rates; a credit explosion; and a boom in investment. It was unlikely that these trends could be reversed immediately, even with the best will of the government. Some Western academics were still optimistic about the future in late 1988, suggesting that the reforms would continue to create some "winners" and some "losers," hoping that in the long run things would come out right for China.[96] In retrospect, however, it is clear that the "growing pie" of economic wealth generated by the reforms was not being equitably reapportioned among the losers, and no significant attempts were being made to defuse political tensions. Such optimists could not possibly have predicted what happened on the streets of China's cities in 1989, nor would they have been able to predict the responses of the government. The high hopes of 1988 were seriously punctured by the events of 1989, leaving only the most died-in-the-wool optimists confident that the CCP could successfully regain any semblance of legitimacy.

As we review the many achievements of the economic reforms since Mao's death, we are reminded of Simon Leys's evaluation made toward the end of the Cultural Revolution in the early 1970s. Leys said then, "We must acknowledge the considerable material improvements in many areas of Chinese life since 1948."[97] This was still the case at the end of the 1980s, and no one could deny that, overall, the Chinese people were better off than they had been in 1978, when the new government ascended to power. In the political realm, however, it is remarkable how little has changed since Mao's time. In spite of more than a decade of embracing capitalism, the relationship between the people and the state in China has hardly been altered. After 1989 most observers would agree with Leys's initial assessment, even though it was made many years earlier: "It is a fantastic imposture to present the regime as socialist and revolutionary when in fact it is essentially totalitarian and feudal-bureaucratic."[98]

China's Population: Production, Reproduction, and the Role of the State

The bigger your family the bigger the fine . . . this boy of mine worked out at 1,300 [yuan]. . . . I paid cash on the nail. If I hadn't they'd have taken out the furniture.

—Big Sister Zheng[1]

INTRODUCTION

Big Sister Zheng lived in the mountains of eastern Sichuan Province. She had nine children in all, but her first, a boy, had died. The next seven were girls, and one of them had died also. The ninth time she was lucky: Heaven had sent her a son. In this chapter we shall attempt to explain why Zheng was so desperate to have a son; why it was so expensive to bring him into the world; and why the township cadres spent so much time trying to persuade her not to have another child. As soon as the word spread that she was pregnant, the local birth-control officials came around to talk her out of it, but she refused to listen. Eventually she had to go into hiding, and after her son was born it took her two years to pay off the money she had borrowed to pay for him. In spite of that she had no misgivings. As she said, "Having sons is what women come into the world for. What's the point of it all if you don't have a son?"[2]

A BRIEF HISTORICAL GEOGRAPHY OF CHINA'S POPULATION

It is possible to make only the roughest of estimates about the size and distribution of China's population during most of the past two thousand years. In addition to the numerous boundary changes, the sheer size of the country and the distances involved meant that the central government rarely had a precise estimate of how many people lived in each of the provinces. Reporting rates were inaccurate as a result of deliberate attempts to conceal births, either to avoid paying taxes or having to endure military service. From the estimates that are available, it appears that there may have been just less than 60 million people in the year A.D. 2 (during the Western Han Dynasty), but from that time on the estimates fluctuate widely.[3] For example, there was an estimated population of only 7.6 million in the Three Kingdoms period (A.D. 220–280), growing back to about 50 million by the year 742 (Tang Dynasty). Most scholars agree that China's population remained low, relative to its total land area, for the next several centuries, with an overall growth pattern similar to that in Europe.[4] Thus by the end of the fifteenth century China's population may have been less than 100 million, kept low by a combination of natural disasters, famines, and near constant warfare.

After 1750 a population explosion occurred in China, so that by the start of the twentieth century there were more than 426 million people, and by 1949, 549 million (see Figure 7.1). The tremendous growth of population during the Qing Dynasty has been partly attributed to the prolonged period of relative peace in China and partly to the introduction of new crops and the bringing of new lands into agricultural cultivation.[5]

By the 1980s China's population was more than 1 billion, which is over one-fifth of the world's total. In one year alone (1986) the population increased by 14 million, even after more than a decade of some of the most draconian birth-control policies the world has ever seen. In addition to the sheer size of the population, Chinese demographers and politicians in the late 1970s were worried about two other demographic facts of life. In the first place, the rapid growth during the 1950s, 1960s, and 1970s meant that by 1980 more than 50 percent of the population was younger than twenty-one years of age. This meant that about 10 million people would be eligible to get married each year, and even at a population growth rate of 12 per 1,000 (considerably lower than the world average of 17 in the middle 1980s), China's population would grow to more than 1.3 billion by the year 2000. The other major concern was that China's population had grown without any increases in the amount of cultivable land— in fact there was only half as much land per capita in 1979 as there was in 1949 (.10 hectares per person as opposed to .20 in 1949).[6] The declining land-to-people ratio in China has become one of the most threatening aspects to China's leaders, and it helps to account for the sharp reversal in agricultural

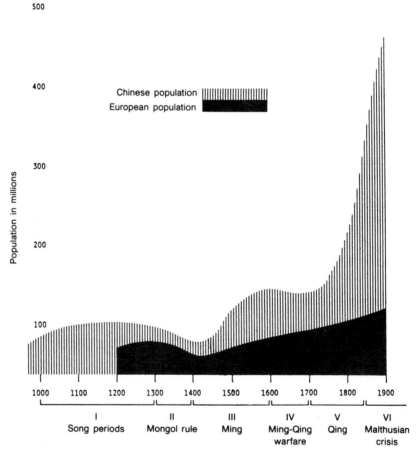

Figure 7.1 Graph comparing population growth in Europe and China over the centuries. Source: U.S. China People's Friendship Association, 1981, Teaching About China, No. 9 (Summer/Fall), p. 2; reprinted by permission.

policies since 1978 and the all-out attempt to increase agricultural productivity (see Chapter 5).

The land shortage is most critical in and around China's biggest cities. Beijing, for example, had a population of 2.03 million people in 1949, with 0.3 hectares per person on which to grow food, but by the early 1980s, Beijing had almost 9 million people and only 0.05 hectares of farmland per person.[7] The population growth meant that the per capita amount of land available to grow food in the city had been reduced sixfold.

The pressure placed on the land is not equal across the Chinese territory. The vast majority of China's population is concentrated in a few general areas, and in fact this has been the case for many centuries. These are areas that are relatively low lying and where there is sufficient rainfall and good enough soils to support intensive agriculture. There are major population concentrations in the North China Plain (Hebei, Shandong, and Henan provinces); the middle and lower Yangtze Valley area; the Pearl River delta area of the Xi (West) River Valley in south China; and the Sichuan basin (see Figure 7.2). Secondary population concentrations are evident in several other parts of south China, especially along the coast; the Songliao River basin in northeast China (the area that used to be called Manchuria); the Hexi corridor in Gansu Province; and the Wei River Valley in Shaanxi Province.

By contrast, in much of "Outer" China, for example, in Tibet, Inner Mongolia, Qinghai, Xinjiang, and Heilongjiang, population is distributed very sparsely—as a result of climate and topography. What is obvious from the population map is not so much that China has too many people but that it has too little cultivable land. Today, 90 percent of China's people live on about one-sixth of the total land area. As Keith Buchanan observed, "There are few areas in the world where gradients of population density are as steep as they are in China." The contrast between the empty and the filled lands is instantly noticeable "between the closely settled meticulously cultivated flatlands and the empty ravaged upland."[8] Buchanan also pointed out that these contrasts have essentially remained stable over the centuries. As the population of the most desirable land increased, the density rose, until

in some areas "500–600 people . . . were . . . living on an area equal to that of an American family farm supporting 5–6 people."[9]

Population pressures in such areas did not generally lead to a mass migration to the higher lands or to the unpopulated areas; rather, there was a spreading out into neighboring river basins. The effect was that the existing areas of the "good earth" would fill up, and as a result, the relative distribution of population has remained very static for hundreds of years.

FAMILY PLANNING IN THE NEW CHINA

In response to the growing threat of continued population growth, the new government in the PRC embarked on a series of campaigns to deal with the issue, but until the late 1970s the population policy remained essentially a *voluntary* one. It was obvious by that time, however, that something more drastic was required. In 1975 the average fertility rate (the number of live births per woman) was about 3.0. If that rate had continued, China's population would be 1.42 billion by the year 2000. Even if the fertility rate could be kept at the 1978 level of 2.3, the population would rise to 1.28 billion. This was a frightening prospect in a country so desperately short of land and resources, and to make matters worse, a "baby boom" was expected in the early 1980s as a result of high birthrates in the middle of the 1960s.[10] It was clear to population planners that a drastic reduction in family size was needed. In an attempt to reach zero population growth by the year 2000, a one-child per family policy was considered to be the only viable course of action (see Table 7.1).

Demographers were obviously aware of the difficulties in implementing such a policy in a country where there were 240 million women of childbearing age and where having a large family was the cultural norm. Mao Zedong, for example, only two decades earlier, had encouraged the expansion of China's population. He was not worried about China's having too many people because, as he said, "Every stomach comes with two hands attached."[11] The demographers also pointed out that if a one-child policy were adopted for

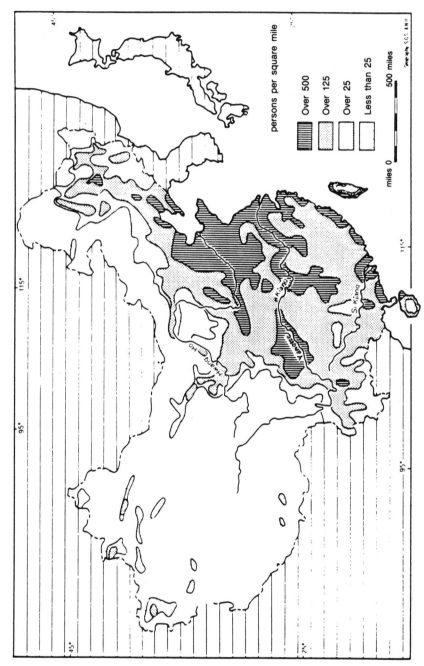

persons per square mile

Over 500

Over 125

Over 25

Less than 25

miles 0   500 miles

Figure 7.2 Map showing the distribution of population in China. Source: Adapted from The National Atlas of China 1976 (Beijing: Sciences Press), p. 119.

Table 7.1 China's Projected Population Increases Under the One-Child-Per-Couple Policy, 1985-2015

	Population Size (billions)	No. of Women of Child-bearing Age (millions)	Births (millions)	Deaths (millions)	Population Growth (per 1000)	Avg. Age of Population
1985	0.98	2.07	16.5	7.4	3.50	29.1
1990	1.02	2.79	10.2	7.0	3.02	31.7
1995	1.04	2.99	11.3	8.2	2.95	33.8
2000	1.05	3.00	10.8	8.9	1.87	35.9
2005	1.05	2.80	9.1	9.5	-0.39	38.0
2010	1.04	2.70	7.0	9.7	-2.63	40.5
2015	1.03	2.40	5.6	9.7	-4.06	43.2

Source: Adapted from *China ABC* (Beijing: New World Press, 1983), p. 48.

Figure 7.3 One of the many posters exhorting the people to have only one child and to consider that girl children are worth as much as boy children.

Figure 7.4 A child who is fat and overindulged—a predicted effect of the one-child policy. His warm outfit protects him from the chills of winter in Xian.

two decades, China's population structure would become grotesquely unbalanced, and each able-bodied person would have to support two parents and four grandparents. The prospects for a nationwide pension system did not (and still do not) look good, so it was not surprising that most people in the countryside felt it would never be possible for them to support a one-child policy (see Figures 7.3, 7.4, 7.5, and 7.6).

To sweeten the pill of this shocking new policy, financial incentives were made to couples with one child who would agree to sign a pledge promising to have no more children. In Beijing, for example, in 1979 it was announced that parents would receive a Y 5-per-month subsidy, preferential access to nurseries and kindergartens, priority in medical care, and the promise of favored treatment in the educational and employment spheres.

Figure 7.5 (above) The ideal Chinese offspring—a boy and a girl—now only a dream for most city dwellers. Figure 7.6 (right) Twins in a Chongqing storefront. Their parents outwitted the one-child policy.

The family would also receive additional housing space (or a larger plot of land in the countryside). If the family broke the pledge, it would have to return the subsidy, and if a third child was born the family would end up paying a fine that was about 10 percent of its annual income until the child was fourteen years old.[12]

There is no doubt that in statistical terms the one-child campaign has been successful. In the 1950s and 1960s, for example, the net growth of China's population (the difference between the birthrate and the death rate) was always in excess of 20 per 1,000; in fact even in 1971 it stood at 23.4 per 1,000. However, by 1978 the growth rate had been practically halved, to 12.1 per 1,000. The goal was to halve the growth rate again by 1985, to 5 per 1,000, and then reduce it to zero by the year 2000. The overall statistics show that between 1950 and 1982 the total fertility rate in China fell from 5.6 to 2.6 children per woman,[13] with an even greater decline in the cities.[14] Geographically the total fertility rate in China varies considerably, from a low in the east coast and northeastern provinces (e.g., Shanghai is the lowest at 1.32); increasing to the west and southwest, to reach highs of 4.36 in Guizhou Province and 4.12 in Ningxia Autonomous Region (AR) (see Figure 7.7).

By 1983, 56 percent of all births in China were first births, and only 19 percent were third births, which was a remarkable turnaround from the situation in 1970, when these statistics were 20 percent and 62 percent respectively.[15] Although the percentage of first births varies greatly across China, in many areas the figure is approaching that in more developed countries (e.g., in Taiwan it was 38 percent in 1982; and in the United States, 43 percent in 1981). All of this has been achieved in the face of an overwhelming desire expressed by Chinese families to have more than one child (see Table 7.2).

In light of the impressive statistics of the 1970s, the situation in the 1980s was disappointing to the demographers. By 1985 the net growth rate had fallen only to 11.2 per 1,000, and in 1986 it actually increased to 14.1, largely as a result of an increase in the birthrate from 17.8 per 1,000 in 1985 to 23.3 per 1,000 in 1987, and 21 per 1,000 in 1988.[16] These were worrying trends for China's family planners, and in this chapter we shall look

in some detail at the official response to them. It is important, however, to put the existing achievements into a broader historical and geographical context. The population statistics reveal that China has experienced its demographic transition in record time, in comparison to most other countries either in the distant or the near past. The normal phases of the demographic transition are a premodernization phase when both birthrates and death rates are high; a modernization phase in which death rates begin to fall but birthrates remain relatively high; and a postmodernization phase, in which both birthrates and death rates are low. The result is that natural population growth is extremely high in the first phase, moderately high in the second phase, and low in the final phase.

For most societies modernization precedes a significant fall in the birthrates, mainly because it takes many decades of education and improved living conditions before families are convinced it is in their best interests to limit their reproduction rate. In China, however, this has not been the case, and the birthrate fell very rapidly before modernization (for example, in 1953 it was 37 per 1,000, but it was 17.8 per 1,000 in 1985). If we compare China's demographic statistics in 1985 with those in other parts of the world (Table 7.3), we see that the birthrate is lower than the world average and is approaching that of the developed countries (although it is still not as low as Chinese demographers had hoped for). In comparison to other developing countries, however, China's birthrate is extremely low (21 as opposed to 35 per 1,000). China's death rate is actually slightly lower than that for the world's developed countries (7 per 1,000 as opposed to 9 per 1,000) and significantly lower than that in most of the developing countries (e.g., 17 in Bangladesh, 23 in Chad; and a Third World average of 12 per 1,000).

The reductions in death rates in China can largely be attributed to public health measures that represent part of the "medical revolution" since 1949 that helped to eliminate the pestilence that for so long cursed the Chinese landscape. The major diseases, such as malaria and schistosomiasis, were eliminated, and many of the others have been prevented, including dysentery, typhoid, and tuberculosis. Obviously a part of the success in this

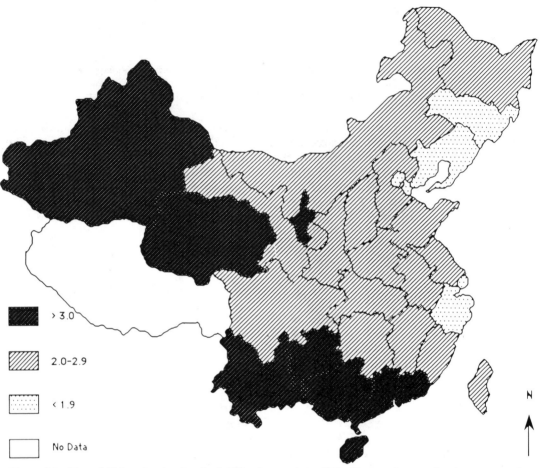

■	> 3.0
▨	2.0–2.9
⬚	< 1.9
☐	No Data

N

Figure 7.7 Map of China showing female fertility, by province, 1981. The provinces and autonomous regions in northwestern and southwestern China generally have the highest rates of fertility; those on the east coast and in the northeast have the lowest. Source: Redrawn from The Population Atlas of China *(Hong Kong: Oxford University Press, 1987).*

area can be attributed to an overall rise in the standard of living in the Chinese countryside. There have also been major campaigns to provide improved sanitation and better water supplies in both town and country; mass immunization programs; elimination of the "four pests" (mosquitoes, flies, rats, and sparrows); and large-scale training of rural medical personnel.[17]

As a result, the average Chinese person now lives much longer than was the case before Liberation and significantly longer than people in most developing countries (Table 7.3). Chinese parents can now expect their babies to survive beyond their first year, and the comparison with developing countries in terms of infant-mortality rates is startling (41 per 1,000 live births in China, compared with

135 in Bangladesh; 175 in Mali; and 96 in developing countries worldwide).

All these improvements in China—the raised living standards, more effective public health measures, longer life expectancy, and reduced infant mortality—have been welcomed in city and country alike, but from the perspective of the demographer they tended to create additional problems because they required a more intensive drive to reduce the birthrate.

THE POLITICS OF REPRODUCTION IN CHINA

When the Communists took over in China in 1949, demographers in the West were convinced that drastic measures were needed to

Table 7.2 Percent Distribution of Family Size Preferences and Mean Number of Children Preferred (Surveys in Selected Areas of China, 1980-1986)

| | Number of Children Preferred | | | | | Mean No. of Children |
	0	1	2	3	4+	
Rural Areas						
Jilin	0.0	15.5	77.8	4.3	2.4	1.93
Hunan	0.0	1.9	77.6	17.4	3.1	2.22
Guangdong	0.0	6.7	90.3	3.1	0.0	1.96
Shaanxi	0.0	22.0	74.0	4.0	0.0	1.82
Sichuan	0.0	16.1	80.8	3.1	0.0	1.88
Jiangsu	0.0	44.8	55.2	0.0	0.0	1.56
Shandong	0.0	27.7	72.3	0.0	0.0	1.72
Urban Areas						
Beijing	3.0	25.0	70.0	2.0	0.0	1.71
Wuhan	0.0	32.9	67.1	0.0	0.0	1.67
Jiangsu	1.6	46.7	51.7	0.0	0.0	1.50
Zhejiang	11.5	61.5	27.0	0.0	0.0	1.15
Sichuan	0.0	24.8	70.0	5.2	0.0	1.80
Shanghai	0.5	30.0	59.5	8.0	2.0	1.81
Suburbs						
Beijing	0.0	9.0	77.0	9.0	5.0	2.10
Tianjin	0.0	5.0	80.0	15.0	0.0	2.10
Shanghai	0.0	5.0	50.0	36.0	9.0	2.49

Source: Adapted from M. K. Whyte and S. Z. Gu, 1987, "Popular Response to China's Fertility Transition," *Population and Development Review* 13, No. 3 (September), p. 475, Table 3.

slow down the rate of growth of the population. Mao Zedong, however, was not convinced of this; in fact he tended to view such advice as "bourgeois" Malthusian propaganda. In what would later become one of his better known public pronouncements, Mao observed in 1949: "Of all things in the world, people are the most precious. Under the leadership of the Communist Party, as long as there are people, every kind of miracle can be performed. We believe that revolution can change everything, and that before long there will arise a new China with a big population and a great wealth of products, where life will be abundant and culture will flourish. All pessimistic views are utterly groundless."[18]

With this statement Mao effectively put a damper on the budding birth-control movement in China. After such an arduous struggle against the Japanese and then the extended civil war with the Nationalists, Mao felt that to implement birth-control policies would be a cruel and unusual punishment for the long-suffering Chinese people. He felt that it was unfair, in an egalitarian society, to punish the poor for having too many children. Birth control was, according to Mao, "a means of killing off the Chinese people without shedding blood."[19]

Mao believed that the Chinese masses were a major component of the productive forces, in fact the only component that was in a healthy condition after the long-drawn-out revolutionary struggle. For a few years, therefore, Mao's views were unchallenged, and in spite of much discussion about birth-control policies, the official party line was that China's population could continue to grow.

In 1956 the greatly revered premier, Zhou Enlai, publicly announced his support for the concept of planned parenthood, and the winds of change were in the air. Even Mao himself was heard to waver on the issue. In 1956, for example, he wrote: "We have this huge population. It is a good thing, but of course it also has difficulties. . . . Steps must therefore be taken to keep our population for a long time at a stable level, say, of 600 million. A wide campaign of explanation and proper help must be undertaken to achieve this aim."[20]

For the next two decades the Chinese government attempted to reduce population growth by a series of voluntary measures,

Table 7.3 China's Population--Comparisons with the Rest of the World, 1988

	Birthrate per 1,000	Death Rate per 1,000	Natural Increase % per yr.	Infant Mortality per 1,000 Live Births	Fertility (No. of children per Woman 15-49 yrs.)	Life Expec-tancy (yrs.)	Urban Pop. %	GNP Per Capita 1982 U.S. $
China	21	7	1.4	44.0	2.4	66	41	300
World	28	10	1.7	77.0	3.6	63	45	3,010
Developed	15	9	0.6	15.0	1.9	73	73	10,700
Less dev. (excl. China)	35	12	2.4	96.0	4.8	57	35	780
Sweden	12	11	0.1	5.90	1.8	77	83	13,170
Japan	11	6	0.5	5.20	1.7	78	77	12,850
U.S.	16	9	0.7	10.9	1.8	75	74	17,500
Canada	15	7	0.7	7.9	1.7	76	76	14,100
Australia	15	7	0.8	9.8	1.9	76	86	11,910
UK	13	12	0.2	9.5	1.8	75	91	8,920
New Zealand	16	8	0.8	10.8	2.0	74	84	7,110
Bangladesh	43	17	2.7	135.0	5.8	50	16	160
India	33	13	2.0	104.0	4.3	54	25	270
Haiti	41	13	2.8	117.0	5.7	54	25	330
Chad	43	23	2.0	143.0	5.3	39	27	100
Ethiopia	46	15	3.0	118.0	7.0	50	10	120
Mali	50	22	2.9	175.0	6.7	43	18	170

Source: Extracted from Population Reference Bureau, 1988, *World Population Data Sheet* (Washington, D.C.: Population Reference Bureau, Inc.).

including education campaigns and encouraging the use of contraception.[21] The goals of family planning at this time can be broadly described by the three words *wan* (late), *xi* (thin), and *shao* (fewer). The three words represented the hope that the Chinese people would defer childbirth by marrying later; spacing out their offspring in intervals of at least four years; and having fewer children overall.

Since his death, Mao has been criticized on many grounds, one of which was his reluctance to take a firmer stand on the issue of birth control. China's population had grown by more than 75 percent between 1949 and 1978, and it was clear to almost everyone that drastic measures were called for. At this time China had embarked on its much-heralded drive toward the Four Modernizations, the goal of which was to transform China into a powerful and modern socialist society by developing four sectors of the economy: agriculture, industry, science and technology, and national defense. The policies designed to bring about modernization emphasized the importance of production and the need to develop the skills and professional abilities of the Chinese labor force. There was to be an emphasis on the profitability of urban and rural enterprises, with a relatively lucrative system of material incentives designed to speed up production.

Ambitious planning to promote economic development was certainly not new in China, but for the first time the efforts to increase production were being linked to a vigorous effort to reduce the growth of the country's population. It was obvious to the Chinese government that a 1960s-style population increase would present a major barrier to the accumulation of the capital needed for the modernization drive. As a result, the government essentially redefined production to include both the production of material goods *and the reproduction of human beings.* The Chinese people were asked to "grasp these two kinds of production" and to help keep the population down as an integral part of developing the economy.

In announcing this new and unpopular development, the government looked for moral support in the writings of the major socialist theoreticians.[22] In the nineteenth century, Engels, for example, had written about the two-fold nature of production, suggesting that one of the unique strengths of a socialist system was the state's ability to include both production and reproduction within its planning domain. It was implicit in this new phase of population planning that the new leaders felt that Mao Zedong had not fully grasped the nature of the link between production and reproduction. Mao was, in other words, largely responsible for the too-rapid expansion of China's population.

To correct this situation specific targets were laid out in a series of Five Year Plans for both production and reproduction. The goals were to quadruple the gross value of industrial and agricultural production by the year 2000 and to keep the population down to about 1.2 billion by achieving zero population growth by the turn of the century. To do this it was essential to make major changes in China's population-control policies.

After extensive deliberations it was decided that regulations would be placed on the number of children each Chinese family was allowed to have. It was recommended that most families limit themselves to one child only. There was to be an almost total prohibition on a third child, but few consistent statements were made about the birth of a second child. In the cities, and for government officials, the slogans advocated "no second child," but in the countryside and for certain subgroups of the population the rule was "no more than two." No national standards were set for the official size of families, leaving such decisions to provincial and municipal authorities, who, it was argued, had the most accurate picture of what was required in their localities.

To give the new policy some "teeth," punitive economic sanctions were established for families who refused or otherwise failed to adhere to the local plans, and a variety of economic and noneconomic rewards were to be granted to families who pledged to have no more than one child.[23] Again it appears that the birth of a second child produced some ambivalence in official responses. The vast majority of penalties to date have been directed toward the families that have had three or more children, particularly if they happen to be political leaders, who are expected to set a good example to others.

For Westerners the most unpalatable part of the new policy was the increased amount of state intervention in the internal affairs of the family. In the 1950s and 1960s the government had hoped that people would voluntarily limit themselves; and in the 1970s this had evolved into a series of agreements made at the local level, in which the urban and rural collectives were allowed to negotiate birth quotas with their resident families. But by the end of the 1970s it had become clear to the Chinese leaders that family plans were too important to be left open for negotiation. This represented an almost unique attempt by the state to take control of individual family decision-making.

THE GEOGRAPHY OF REPRODUCTION IN CHINA

The new population policy has been one of the most unpopular and the most difficult to administer in the history of the People's Republic. It is something of a surprise, therefore, to survey the statistical success of the policy in its first few years. By 1985 the net growth rate of China's population had been halved compared with the rate for 1971. The declining fertility rate was mainly a result of the widespread adherence to the one-child policy—in fact by the early 1980s, 21 percent of the couples of childbearing age in China had only one child.

The Spatial Organization of Chinese Family Planning

To account for the extraordinary success in lowering the birthrate, we need look no further than China's political system and the spatial organization of administration that was introduced in the cities and the countryside in the 1950s. The government has, since the prerevolutionary days in Yenan, consistently supported mass campaigns in which people were required to participate. In the area of birth control this has greatly facilitated attempts to educate families both about the need to lower the birthrate and the means of achieving such an end. It has also been relatively easy in China, certainly much easier than in a more democratic political system, to enforce the new policies, even unpopular ones, and to impress upon the public the seriousness of noncompliance.

The new organizational structure that had been created in both the cities and the countryside helped greatly in the administration of the birth-control policies. Through the extensive and virtually all-embracing hierarchy of organizational units, educational propaganda about the wisdom of birth control was disseminated from the "top" all the way down to the street and the farm level. Moreover, the system facilitated the close surveillance of all individuals to make sure that they understood the reasons for the policy and to make sure they cooperated with it.

Using the spatial hierarchy, the Office of Family Planning of the State Council was able to transmit the policies of the state down to the lower levels for enforcement. In the rural communes and in the urban districts of the cities, all family-planning activity is coordinated by a family-planning committee that distributes contraceptives; organizes study groups to explain the need for family planning; sets out strategies to persuade or force compliance; and, as always, provides constant surveillance to monitor actual and potential deviations.

In the cities this work is performed either in the work unit (the *danwei*) or in the residents' committees, where detailed records are kept of all on the women of childbearing age. The norm is for face-to-face contact between families and trained medical and paramedical personnel. The advice provided by such people can be reinforced by neighborhood and work-unit leaders. In addition to all of this, there is constant pressure from fellow workers and neighbors to conform to the policy—not just because it will benefit China as a whole, but also because most people realize that noncompliance at the unit level will reflect badly on all of them. To outsiders, and probably to the Chinese people as well, the most objectionable part of the new policy has been the invasion of personal privacy.

Every woman of childbearing age is monitored by Family Planning representatives . . . her work or neighborhood unit . . . will have a dossier on her reproductive history, and will know what contraceptive method she is using. If a woman already has a child, it will not take many missed periods to set off an official reaction. Every kind of pressure, from interminable nagging to downright arm-twisting will be exerted.[24]

It was rumored that in the 1980s cadres in charge of birth-control matters were required to reinforce policies at any costs, in the knowledge that if the quota of births was exceeded, they would be the ones to suffer. This was especially important in the countryside, where the desire for extra children has always been greater than in the cities. Even such an incalcitrant as Big Sister Zheng in Sichuan, for example, felt sorry for the local Family Planning cadres. "They were just doing their job. . . . I hear the township fines the district party secretary and the Family Planning commissioner a lot of money if even one baby more than they're allowed gets born. . . . It has to come out of their own pockets! When they get fined at the end of each year they're in tears."[25]

Partly by efficiency and partly by intimidation, the spatial organization of Chinese society helps to spread the technology of birth control and to educate the people about why it is necessary. Most important, it provides a remarkably efficient way of implementing the new policies, particularly by making sure that people comply or if they do not, that they are fully aware of the consequences.

Rural and Urban Differentials in Birthrates

An official survey conducted in Jiangsu Province reported that 43 percent of the couples interviewed said they wanted to have only one child and 57 percent said they wanted no more than two children.[26] These statistics look a little suspect in a country where children are so highly treasured, but the evidence suggests that (in Jiangsu at least) the provincial government was able to coordinate production and reproduction plans very successfully in the 1980s. From 1981 to 1986 the population in the province grew slowly (averaging 0.83 percent per year), and 670,000 fewer babies were born than in the previous five-year period. Industrial and agricultural output was reported to be eighteen times higher than the population growth during this period, and according to official sources, this allowed the people of Jiangsu to experience some major improvements in their living standards.

Stories like this were coming in from many different parts of China, but in geographical terms the results of the new policies have been very mixed. The most marked variations have been between the countryside and the cities. The 1982 sample census estimated the birthrate in urban areas to be 14.5 per 1,000, compared to 22.4 in the rural areas. There has also been a marked discrepancy between individual cities. In two of China's largest cities, Shanghai and Chengdu, the growth rate had, by 1986, been brought down to the level required to set the entire country on the path toward zero population growth; but the growth rate in two other big cities, Beijing and Tianjin, was still twice as high as that.[27]

There is also some variability in the rural areas themselves. In contrast to the report from Jiangsu, a survey conducted in rural Hubei Province showed that only 5 percent of the families interviewed said they were willing to limit themselves to one child, whereas 51 percent said they wanted to have two, and 43 percent wanted three or more.[28] The percentage wanting to have at least three children appears to be a function of the degree of isolation and the physical hardships of the region in question. In the hilliest parts of southern Hubei, far from the cities, more than 70 percent of the families expressed a preference for three or more children. This reinforces the belief among many rural Chinese people that their best security for the future is to have as many children as possible, in the hope that at least some of them will be able to take care of them in their old age.

A number of plausible geographical hypotheses can be identified to explain the differences in the urban and rural population growth rates since the new policies have been in force. There is certainly greater access to family-planning clinics in the cities and a far lower perceived need for the additional labor supply provided by children. It seems, however, that most of the spatial variation is a result of differences in the way the one-child policy has been implemented. Reports from around the country demonstrate that there have been numerous legal exemptions from the one-child policy, allowing what amounts to second-child births "in conformity with the plan." These exemptions are granted at the provincial (or municipal) level and are intended to gear reproduction plans to local circumstances.

The most notable exemptions have been in China's Autonomous Regions, where many of the country's ethnic-minority people live.[29] In Ningxia Hui in northwest China, an area dominated by Muslims, minority families are allowed to have two children in the cities and three in the rural areas. The relaxation of the policy in the Autonomous Regions is part of the government's overall attempt to provide social and economic benefits to minority populations.[30]

In the provinces with a predominantly Han population, there have generally been fewer exemptions, but again the geographical differences have been considerable. In Guangdong Province, which is close to Hong Kong and generally considered to be one of the most Westernized parts of China, the population growth rate is still higher than the national average. This can be explained in part by the exemptions—couples have been allowed to have a second child in any of a number of circumstances:[31]

- If their first child is handicapped with a nongenetic disease and is unable to work as an able-bodied person
- If they are married for a second time and only one of them had a child by the former marriage, or if both had children that are being raised by their former spouses
- If they had adopted a child after one of them was incorrectly diagnosed as sterile
- If both of them were only children
- If either or both of them have worked for more than five consecutive years underground

Most people living in the rural areas of Guangdong were expected to observe the one-child rule, but if they wanted a second child they could apply to their local birth-control authorities. Permission was granted to couples who qualified in any of the first four categories *or if their first child was a girl.*

Preference for boys is evident all across China, but it is traditionally strongest in the rural areas.[32] In most cases the preference to have a son is inversely correlated with the usual indicators of modernization—hence it tends to be relatively low in the cities and among the better-educated families. The actual amount of son preference varies from place to place: For example, there is a slight preference for girl babies in Beijing, but in Jilin Province there is a 14 percent difference in favor of boys[33] (see Figure 7.8).

The major reason families prefer to have sons is *economic*—both to generate income and to provide security for the parents in their old age. Only a small percentage of China's peasants are entitled to a pension, and the traditional "five guarantees" of the welfare state (to cover the costs of food, clothing, fuel, burial, and raising children) are rarely adequate. Because of the tradition of exogamy in China, most women leave home to marry, so the consensus is that sons are more likely to be able to support their parents in the future. Hence only a son will satisfy many parents, and with the one-child policy, the birth of a daughter is often considered to be only a "small happiness." The sad truth is that under the one-child-per-family policy, simply by being born, "a daughter prevents

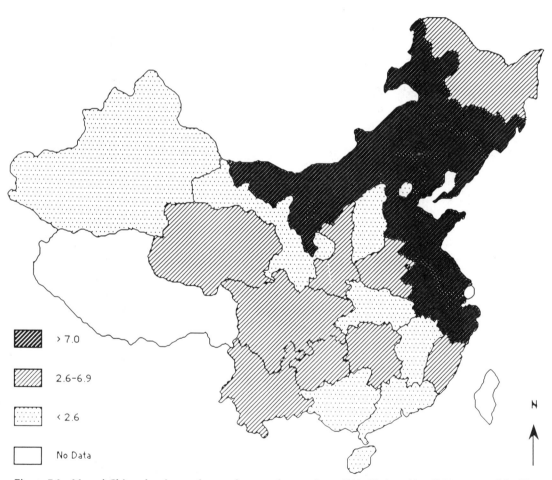

Figure 7.8 Map of China showing preference for sons, by province, 1982. Nationwide, 40.3 percent of families who already have a boy are willing to sign a one-child certificate, as against 34 percent of those with a girl, indicating an excess preference for boys of 6.3 percent. Source: Adapted from F. Arnold and Liu Zhaoxiang, 1986, "Sex Preference, Fertility, and Family Planning in China," Population and Development Review *12, No. 2, pp. 228–230.*

her parents from producing and thus acquiring something more precious than herself."[34]

The one-child policy has contributed to a return to the odious practice of female infanticide. Although the practice is officially illegal in China, the abnormally high male-to-female sex ratios among children in most parts of the country implies that local officials may be turning a blind eye. As much as the authorities would like to deny its existence, female infanticide is still in evidence in many parts of rural China. Some foreign journalists have taken particular delight in recounting tales; for example, in a piece entitled "The Best Baby is a Dead Baby," Tiziano Terzani reported a story from *China Youth News* in which a peasant from Shandong Province drowned his four-year-old daughter after being assured by a fortune-teller that his next child would be a boy.[35]

If couples are experiencing "true difficulties," they may be allowed to deviate from the one-child policy. As might be expected, the definition of what constitutes "difficulties" varies considerably from one place to another. In Shanxi Province a couple is allowed to have a second child if:

- The husband, after marriage, has settled in with the family of an only daughter
- The couple and their ancestors have been living for a long time in sparsely populated mountain villages remote from urban areas and transportation facilities
- Only one of the husband's three (or more) brothers is fertile
- Either the husband or wife has a first-degree deformity
- Either of them come from families that have had only one son for at least three generations in a row
- Both parties in the marriage are themselves only children.[36]

A final exemption is allowed if the husband (but not the wife?) is the only son of a revolutionary martyr. This is presumably considered to be a way of reproducing heroic genes for the struggle to modernize China.

An analysis of the exemptions in different parts of the country reveals that second children are generally allowed under two major categories, one of which is cultural, the other geographical or economic. The first set of exemptions exists to preserve the patrilineal family—for example, if the first child is a girl or if only one son in the family has been able to procreate. The second set of exemptions is intended to reduce gross spatial inequalities by giving special dispensations to underprivileged groups and deprived areas (which generally means minority areas and very remote rural counties).[37]

The Geography of Noncompliance

In spite of the legal loopholes, by far the majority of second and subsequent births have occurred "outside the plan," in other words, as a result of families' not complying with the one-child policy. Data from the 1982 One-per-Thousand Fertility Survey provide some evidence of the extent of noncompliance. A comparison of rural areas in four provinces shows that the percentage of families signing a one-child certificate varied from 24 percent to 76 percent, mainly as a result of differences in the intensity of the local campaigns.[38] Of the couples who signed the pledge, 6 percent reneged within a year, with a low of less than 1 percent in urban Beijing to a high of 18 percent in rural Henan Province. In general very few of the urban couples went on to have another child, but the violation rates in the rural areas varied from 11.3 percent in Henan to 26.8 percent in Hebei (see Table 7.4). In some areas there had been no instances of families breaking the pledge, whereas in others all of the eligible couples had gone on to have a second child.

To account for variations such as these, it would be necessary to look in detail at what is happening at the grass-roots level, in other words, in the counties, where national and provincial regulations are further modified to fit local conditions. A review of these local variations shows that fertility policies are generally designed to match local conditions, according to the level of economic development, existing population density, and the "carrying capacity" of the cultivable land.[39] In Emei County in Sichuan, for example, the following rules have been published:

- Larger urban areas—one child only
- Plains townships—one child only
- Hilly areas (500–1,000 meters above sea level)—two children if the first is a girl

Table 7.4 Percentage Distribution of Families with One-Child Certificates on July 1, 1981, Who Had a Second Child by July 1, 1982 (Hebei, Henan, Liaoning, and Sichuan Provinces)

	Hebei (41)	Henan (21)	Liaoning (16)	Sichuan (69)
Families with a second child				
0	56.1	76.1	12.5	39.1
1-9	2.4	9.5	12.5	13.0
10-19	4.9	0.0	25.0	10.1
20-29	4.9	0.0	18.8	11.6
30-39	0.0	0.0	12.5	15.9
40-49	7.3	0.0	6.3	4.3
50-59	4.9	0.0	0.0	1.4
60-69	4.9	0.0	0.0	2.9
70-79	4.8	4.8	0.0	1.4
80-89	2.4	0.0	6.3	0.0
90-100	7.3	9.6	0.0	0.0
Percent for province	26.8	11.3	18.5	14.7

Note: Total number of production units surveyed in parentheses.

Source: Adapted from R. Freedman, Xiao Zhenyu, Li Bohua, and W. Lavely, 1988, "Local Area Variations in Reproductive Behavior in the People's Republic of China, 1973-1982," *Population Studies* 42, No. 1 (March), p. 49, Table 8.

- Mountainous areas (1,000–2,000 meters above sea level)—two children permitted
- Ethnic-minority areas—no rules implemented.

In addition to the variability of rules, implementation methods vary considerably from one area to another. In some places gross mismanagement and excessively high-handed local cadres have alienated the local population; but in others educational campaigns, effective distribution of contraceptives, and the application of "scientific management" techniques have produced remarkable results.[40]

A Spatial Analysis of Contraception and Abortion Rates

Two of the most important indicators of the success of local programs to implement birth-control policies are the adoption of more flexible and "voluntary" methods of contraception and the prevalence of abortion. There has been a tendency in many parts of China for birth-control cadres to rely exclusively on the "safest" methods of contraception, namely sterilization and intrauterine devices (IUDs), because they are considered to be more effective, they require less education, and they are considerably less time consuming to administer. For the women involved, however, both of the "safe" methods have proved to be extremely unpopular, and the others have started to appear more frequently. In addition to the obvious evidence that IUDs are by no means universally effective in preventing pregnancy, one of the unanticipated consequences of the reliance on IUDs has been the flourishing business in their illegal removal, often with serious medical complications and health hazards involved. In one area of south China, for example, an entire network of IUD-removers was discovered in 1981, charging as much as Y 50 per operation.[41]

An analysis of contraception in China shows some significant geographical differences, both in the overall rate of use of all contraceptives and in the different methods being used (see Table 7.5). Among the general conclusions that are possible from these data are the following:

Table 7.5 Contraceptive Use Rates Among 15-49-Year-Old Women, by Region and Method in China, 1981 (in Percentages)

	Overall Use of Contraception	IUD	Sterilization Female	Sterilization Male	Pill	Condom
North China[a]	80	46.3	13.0	1.3	12.0	4.9
Northeast China[b]	87	47.0	29.3	0.9	4.5	4.2
Eastern China[c]	82	39.5	25.4	7.6	6.9	1.6
South China[d]	77	38.8	23.7	6.9	3.9	1.6
Southwest China[e]	75	37.1	9.0	22.2	3.1	1.5
Northwest China[f]	78	44.8	20.1	0.8	8.3	2.4
Beijing	85	20.8	11.3	1.4	29.5	14.3
Tianjin	82	29.4	10.6	2.1	21.4	13.9
Shanghai	84	23.9	22.7	3.8	23.1	7.9
Qinghai	54	21.5	7.8	0.1	20.4	1.7
Xinjiang	74	15.9	23.9	0.7	23.7	6.2
Guangxi	60	39.1	5.1	1.5	8.4	1.5
China	78	38.1	-	-	5.9	3.2

[a]Beijing, Tianjin, Hebei, Shanxi, Nei Mongol.
[b]Liaoning, Jilin, Heilongjiang.
[c]Shanghai, Jiangsu, Zhejiang, Anhui, Fujian, Jiangxi, Shandong
[d]Henan, Hubei, Hunan, Guangdong, Guangxi.
[e]Sichuan, Guizhou, Yunnan.
[f]Shaanxi, Gansu, Qinghai, Ningxia, Xinjiang.

Source: Adapted from D. L. Poston, Jr., 1986, "Patterns of Contraceptive Use in China," *Studies in Family Planning* 17, No. 5 (September), p. 222, Table 1.

- The use of contraception overall tends to be highest in the urban, industrial areas of China.
- In general IUDs are less prevalent in the urban, industrial parts of China (although they are also not popular among the predominantly Muslim minority groups in the northwestern provinces).
- Female sterilization follows a similar pattern to that of contraception use as a whole.
- Vasectomy rates are generally low in most areas, with the major exception of the big eastern cities and in Sichuan and Shandong provinces, where local programs have focused on this form of contraception.
- The use of birth-control pills and condoms is greatest in the urban areas, presumably because education levels are highest and more women work outside the home. In such areas the distribution system for "voluntary" contraceptives is more efficient than in most rural areas—which accounts for the

higher prevalence of IUDs in the countryside.[42]

Some of the factors that appear to be correlated with the overall use of contraceptive methods in China include ethnicity, geography (specifically the place of residence), education, and the sex of the first child.[43] The highest rate of contraception use is among the majority Han people (69 percent), with much lower (though variable) rates among the ethnic minorities (55 percent among the Wei nationality, 15 percent for Zhuang, 12 percent for Miao, but 79 percent for Manchu people). The average use of contraceptive methods varies directly with size of place; thus in rural farm villages the usage rate is 60 percent compared to 83 percent in towns and 87 percent in cities. Education appears to have a major influence on the usage rate of contraception; for example, the rate for illiterate families is 56 percent, increasing steadily by educational level to 88 percent for university graduates.

As might be expected, couples who already have a boy are generally more inclined to use contraceptives. In China as a whole there is a 6 percent difference—69.3 percent of one-child families with a boy use contraceptives, compared with 63.1 percent for families with a girl. The actual difference varies significantly from one province to another: For example, in Fujian the boy/girl differential for contraceptives usage is more than 12 percent (58.4 percent versus 46.2 percent); compared with 2.6 percent greater use for families with a girl in Beijing; and 0.8 percent greater use in Yunnan. The situation in Beijing and other large Chinese cities represents the more "Westernized," or "modernized," views of urban families, who realize there is little practical reason to cling to the traditional Chinese pattern of son preference. In Yunnan Province, however, the statistics suggest that among certain ethnic-minority groups (which are dominant in southwest China), there is little evidence of son preference, at least in terms of differences in contraceptive-usage rates.

Abortion is a controversial subject in China, as it is in other parts of the world. As more use is made of the voluntary and flexible forms of contraception, local authorities have tried to reduce the abortion rates, partly because of the physical and emotional trauma for the families involved, but also partly to reduce the overall costs. In Sichuan Province a low abortion rate is used as one of the standards to judge the effectiveness of local family-planning activities, but to achieve a low rate it has often been necessary to relax the one-child rule. For couples who wish to avoid either sterilization or abortion, contracts can be made allowing a second child but pledging not to have a third.[44]

At the other extreme, much has been made of the excessive use of abortion to help implement the one-child policy in China, and this has brought on the wrath of many foreign governments and right-to-life organizations, especially in the United States.[45] In 1986 the U.S. Agency for International Development (USAID) refused to contribute the $25 million Congress had approved for the United Nations Fund for Population Activities (UNFPA), because of USAID's belief that UNFPA had supported the program of coercive abortion and involuntary sterilization in China.[46]

In response to this, the Chinese authorities admitted that some coercion has occurred at the local level, partly in response to over-zealous attempts to meet the single-child quotas. Although birth-control planners deny vehemently that forced abortion is or has been the official policy, some very damaging stories have been reported of "abortion quotas," representing attempts to terminate all third and subsequent pregnancies.[47] Horrifying tales have also been leaked to the press; for example, in Huidong, in Guangdong Province, the public-security forces used armed guards to search out and publicly label the "delinquent" women, those who were pregnant but who refused to consider having abortions. These women were sent "directly to the hospital to undergo an abortion, the privileged ones by car, the others simply in chairs . . . in lorries surrounded by iron bars that were usually used to transport pigs."[48]

As always the issue of abortion remains one that is highly charged emotionally. A U.S. Congressional delegation to China in 1986 reported that such situations were not typical and that local officials were working hard to stamp out coercive tactics and were severely penalizing offenders.[49] The facts, unfortunately, do not help to clarify the situation. The 1982 fertility survey reported a national average rate of abortion at 21 percent of all births, which is actually much lower than the rate in the United States (43 percent) for the same years or in Bulgaria (98.5 percent), Sweden (36.5 percent), or Hungary (57 percent).[50] It seems reasonable, however, that the abortion rate measured in a self-reported survey will usually be undercounted. In contrast, "official" abortion rates, based on the data collected from the registration reports of local administrative bodies, are likely to overcount. The official abortion rate in China for 1981 was reported at 50 percent, rising to 75 percent in 1983, and falling again to 50 percent in 1984.[51]

In China, as we might expect from the earlier data on contraception, there are some major differences in the abortion rates from place to place. In the four provinces in which the fertility survey was conducted, abortion rates were significantly higher in cities than in the rural areas (with percentages ranging from 38 percent to 68 percent in the cities, and from 9 percent to 41 percent in rural areas).[52] Again, it is no surprise to find that existing family structure also influences abortion rates—thus for families who already had a daughter, the abortion rate was 22.8 percent, compared with 35.9 percent for families with a son.[53]

REPRODUCTION POLICY FOR THE FUTURE

In spite of the impressive achievements associated with the "fertility transition" in China, the rate of progress slowed down considerably in the late 1980s. In 1986 population growth increased for the first time since the implementation of the new policies, largely as a result of a rising birthrate.[54] This trend continued into 1987, when the growth rate rose to more than 15 per 1,000.[55]

This reversal is apparently a result of a larger-than-ever number of so-called baby boomers who were born in 1963 and 1964 when population growth was largely unchecked. By the middle 1980s the baby boomers were getting married and having children. This suggests that the all-time-low birthrates achieved in the early 1980s were in fact only partly a result of the one-child policies. An equally important component was the gap that occurred in the Chinese population pyramid in 1982. The famine that followed the disastrous Great Leap Forward in 1958–1960 was associated with an extremely high rate of infant mortality in the early 1960s. This meant that in the early 1980s there was a smaller than average cohort of women aged 20–24 (the cohort that accounts for more than half of all births). The consequence was an extremely low birthrate in 1983, 1984, and 1985. After the famine, the birthrate returned to normal (in 1962 and 1963), which meant that the cohort of women reaching marriageable age after 1985 was considerably larger than it had been in the 1983–1985 period. In 1987 this produced 1.2 million more babies than in 1986, helping to swell the population growth for 1987 to 15.9 million (compared to 14 million in 1986).

Another contributor to the rising birthrates after 1985 was the official relaxation of the one-child policy at the "central" level. In 1984 and again in 1986 the Party Central Committee issued documents that were intended to produce greater flexibility in the policy.[56]

Coercion was to be outlawed in favor of more systematic birth-control efforts (this would rule out crash programs based on quotas for either births or abortions). The reliance on inflexible methods of birth control (sterilization and IUDs) was to be switched over toward more voluntary methods, and educational propaganda was to replace the emphasis on economic sanctions and rewards that had previously been the mainstay of the one-child program. The policy changes indicate three major shifts in emphasis:

- Administrative improvements: to base policies on the "scientific" study of local conditions, and the introduction of more efficient styles of management
- Strategic improvements: a shift from focusing on changing peoples' ideas about having additional children to improving local socioeconomic conditions that will reduce the perceptions that having more children is an economic necessity
- Political improvements: a shift from the assumption that people can be ordered what to do, toward a greater reliance on persuasion and an understanding of geographical variations in social and cultural characteristics.[57]

The impact of these changes was felt almost immediately in the countryside. In many areas peasant families were allowed to have a second child, often with the stipulation that a certain length of time had elapsed since the birth of the first child. In spite of this shift the Party was at great pains to point out that the birth-control policy was far too important to be dismantled and that the relaxations did *not* herald any major changes, merely that it was time to improve the implementation of the policies.

These policy shifts may have already had some important effects: most notably a sharp drop in the number of official complaints made to family-planning agencies, a significant increase in the adoption of voluntary contraception methods, and an increase in the number of families wanting only one child even among those officially allowed to have two children.[58] This has been achieved by persuading families that having one child (or small families in general) will improve their chances for social mobility, help to provide them with greater levels of consumption, and give them more leisure time. The economic reforms have also contributed significantly to these aspirations, but in the current climate of uncertainty about both economic and political reforms, many families may be questioning the government's sincerity as well as its ability to guarantee prolonged economic well-being. People are being asked to limit the size of their families, which in cultural terms is a major sacrifice. If they subsequently discover that the advantages of smaller families are not forthcoming, the Party might have created an entirely new set of problems for itself in the future. "If people perceive that they are having to make sacrifices by bearing fewer children than they would prefer, and if they later discover that the rewards . . . do not materialize, then the grounds will have been prepared for disappointment and frustration."[59] There is no doubt that many of the people who complained about the government during the spring of 1989 were disappointed and frustrated. Things had not worked out the way they had hoped, and the Party was unable to convince them that the socialist utopia was just around the corner.

THE CONFLICT BETWEEN PRODUCTION AND REPRODUCTION

A particularly awkward problem for the CCP since the adoption of the one-child policy has been the apparent conflict between the population policy and the new economic reforms ushered in after the death of Mao Zedong. The population-growth rate had effectively been halved during the 1970s, but in 1986 there was an increase of 3.12 million births over 1985, about half of which were above the quota set by the state family-planning agencies. It was at this time that the pragmatic economic policies associated with Deng Xiaoping had started to take hold in both the rural and the urban areas. As we have seen in earlier chapters, the introduction of new responsibility systems has allowed much greater scope for individual families to raise their incomes by increasing productivity. In the low-technology environment that predominates in the Chinese countryside, both in industry and agriculture, one of the few ways this can be achieved is by increasing the labor supply. Many families still believe

that the only way to "get rich" is to have more hands in the fields and the factories.[60] A survey conducted in Danjiang County, Hubei Province, in 1986 demonstrated just how important this economic motive still is in China (see Table 7.6). Respondents were asked what they considered were the advantages of having more children. In the rural areas the dominant response was "to provide economic support in old age" (82 percent answered this way); the second most common response was "to increase the labor force" (48 percent).[61]

From the standpoint of individual families, therefore, the policies intended to encourage national production contradict the policies designed to limit the rate of reproduction. One of the major goals of the new agricultural responsibility system was a desire to solve the perennial problem of low productivity in many of the nation's collectives, by contracting out land to peasant households. As a result of the new rural policies, peasant incomes in many areas have increased significantly. The architects of the new responsibility system probably thought that as they became richer, Chinese families would stop thinking about having more children as a way of increasing their economic security for the future. What seems to have happened, however, is that although many families have been able to stop worrying about the future in economic terms, they still want to have children. In other words, the Chinese desire to have a large family is too deeply ingrained a cultural trait in the countryside to be changed significantly by economic circumstances. In fact, as they have become richer, many families seem to have decided that they could ignore the economic penalties with impunity, choosing to have as many children as they want (see Figure 7.9).

Although the contradiction between production and reproduction policies works itself out in many different ways, the following story from a poor corner of Sichuan Province may be a familiar one. In the village of Liujiasi the population had been declining steadily, partly as a result of the area's poverty and remoteness. Because the village was so poor, many of the young women had moved elsewhere to marry. The net effect was that the gender imbalance in the village was increasing, and many of the single men were unable to find wives. This was rapidly becoming a

Table 7.6 Percentage of Respondents Reporting Advantages of Having Children--Danjiang County, Hubei Province (1986 Survey Data)

	Rural Respondents (n=750)	Urban Respondents (n=350)
Economic advantages:		
To provide economic support in parents' old age	82	43
To increase the family's labor force	48	21
Family advantages:		
To preserve continuity of the family line	58	33
To add power to the kin group	22	11
Personal/parental advantages:		
To add to the bond between spouses	28	54
For enjoyment of the parents	28	89

Source: Adapted from M. K. Whyte and S. Z. Gu, 1987, "Popular Response to China's Fertility Transition," *Population and Development Review* 13, No. 3 (September), p. 484, Table 7.

"Don't be afraid, kids. Your dad has enough money to pay the fine." The sign says: A fine will be imposed for having extra children.
Chang Tiejun

Figure 7.9   Cartoon reflecting the ability of newly prosperous families to circumvent the one-child policy by paying the fines imposed for having additional children. Source: China Reconstructs 38, *No. 7 (July 1989), p. 31.*

village dominated by aging bachelors with few prospects for marriage, and as a result the local birthrate was extremely low.

When the new rural responsibility system was introduced some previously undreamed-of opportunities opened up for the village's beleaguered bachelors. The story of Yang Wenqing is a familiar one. He was forty-five years old and his marriage prospects were slim. He said: "I had four girlfriends, but none wanted to marry me. Ten years ago a girl showed interest in me. But when she found out that my cash income per day was only nine cents, she turned me down, saying that she was not prepared to live a half-starved life."[62]

Under the new system Yang was able to contract for a hectare of land on which he grew hybrid maize successfully. By trading this for regular maize at an inflated exchange rate, Yang became relatively prosperous, producing the equivalent of more than 3,000 kilograms of grain in a single harvest period. This newfound wealth made Yang much more "marriageable," and through a friend of a friend he was introduced to a woman ten years his junior. Today they are married and have a son, and if they continue to work hard they will be able to have more children. In similar situations all but one of the village's aging bachelors have subsequently been able to find wives. Obviously in this particular case the village was in urgent need of new blood, but if similar events are occurring all over the Chinese countryside, the success of the population-control policies will be further threatened.

The production responsibility system has been very popular among the Chinese peasants, in sharp contrast to the reproduction policies. In addition to taking the sting out of the economic sanctions associated with having a larger family, the responsibility system has begun to forge a new set of relationships between individual families and the larger collectives to which they have been tied. Now that a large part of the economic decision-making has reverted to the family unit, and with it the life-and-death issues related to the distribution of food, income, and resources, it has proved much more difficult for the collectives to administer unpopular policies authoritatively from the top down. Individual families have realized that

they like making their own decisions, and they naturally want to extend their newfound freedom into the area of birth control.

To help solve the contradiction between production and reproduction policies, new regulations have been emerging in some areas.[63] These will apparently link the distribution of contracted land and the setting of output quotas more closely to family size: Larger families will be assigned smaller plots of land and larger production quotas, and vice versa. This of course will prove to be administratively problematic in the future because to make the responsibility system work, it is necessary to guarantee a family a specific plot of land for a fixed number of years. If the family grows, it will be difficult to reduce the size of the plot without jeopardizing the intent of the new incentive system.

The most serious aspect of the contradiction between the production and the reproduction policies is that it will compound the implications of the structural change in China's population—namely the huge increase in the number of women who are at the peak of their reproductive capacity. If there is too much relaxation of birth controls at this time, China will have to face the prospect of major increases in population-growth rates, with all of the implications that will have for the modernization drive, or it will have to retreat to the tough birth-control measures that were so unpopular in the early 1980s.

The government remains firmly committed to the one-child policy and is unlikely to abandon it in the near future. The government is also strongly committed to the new production responsibility system and the opening up of domestic sideline activities for rural families. One solution to the contradiction between the two policies has been to allow families to hire labor as an alternative to having more children of their own.[64] The willingness to consider this as a solution indicates how determined the Chinese are when it comes to sticking with the one-child policy, because the very concept of hired labor runs counter to many of the principles on which the Chinese economic and social system is based.

In its latest public announcements the government has promised that if the people strictly adhere to a combination "one and two child policy" for the rest of this century, or at least until the 1960s baby boomers have passed through their marriageable years, then the policy will be gradually relaxed as the overall growth rate declines. This pronouncement accepts what is now obvious, that the long-cherished goal of 1.2 billion people and zero population growth by the year 2000 is not attainable.[65] What may have seemed like a very minor change in 1987—when the population target was altered from 1.2 billion to "about" 1.2 billion—in fact signified a major increase in the government's flexibility on the birth-control issue.[66]

Optimists hope that the predictions of some demographers will come true in China during the 1990s—that continued modernization will gradually reduce the desire of Chinese families to have children.[67] As long as China continues to develop its economy and emphasizes education, it should become easier with every passing year to encourage families to limit the number of children they have, without having to resort to drastic and unpopular measures. This would give the government considerably more breathing space and more time to think out realistic alternatives to the current policy.

The current policy is basically a "one-child only" plan with modifications, but there are in fact a number of viable alternative policies (see Table 7.7).[68] Based on the 1984 fertility rate (1.94), the existing policies could be expected to result in a total population in China of 1.24 billion by the year 2000 and 1.44 billion by 2025. Three of the alternative policies described in Table 7.7 (D, E, and F) would incorporate the desire of most Chinese people to have two children but would also, if implemented with effective "delaying" and "spacing" strategies, result in significantly lower total populations for the twenty-first century.

As a result of the current freeze in relations with the outside world, we can not be certain which way the government will turn during the 1990s, but recent official statements indicate that the hard line on birth control may have to be reinstated. For example, on April 4, 1989, the official population statistics were released. There were already more than 1.1 billion people in China.[69] The rate of addition to this total threatens to negate all the gains made in the drive toward economic modernization.

Table 7.7 Projected Population Size in 2000 and 2025, Under Current and Alternative Birth-Control Policies

	Total Fertility Rate, 1995-2000	Population Size (billions)	
		2000	2025
Current policy	1.94	1.24	1.44
One child only	1.00	1.09	1.16
Two children	1.76	1.21	1.34
Two children, with delays and spacing[a]	1.68	1.11	1.17
Two children, spaced[b]	1.72	1.17	1.27
Mixture of one- and two-child policies			
Cities (stop at one)	1.00	1.15	1.23
Rural areas (two and space)	1.72	--	--

[a]This is the so-called 27-4 option, with a minimum age at first childbearing of 27 and a 4-year spacing between the two children.
[b]No restrictions on the time of first birth, but a minimum age of 30 for the second birth, necessitating longer spacings of up to 8 or 10 years.

Source: Adapted from S. Greenhalgh and J. Bongaarts, 1987, "Fertility Policy in China: Future Options," Science 235, p. 1169, Tables 1 and 2.

The City in China

*The ambience of the Chinese city—the apparently gentle pace of life,
the throngs of bicycles, the village-like lanes and vegetable patches . . .
all contribute towards an anti-urban illusion to which Westerners seem
predisposed.*

—Richard Kirkby[1]

INTRODUCTION: THE CHINESE CITY IN HISTORY

Urbanization in China has occurred in three historical phases, and the impacts of the newer phases have been superimposed onto the legacies from earlier times. For nearly two thousand years there has been in China a national urban system consisting of a national capital, a small number of regional centers and provincial capitals, a network of county towns, and a vast number of villages and hamlets. In geographical terms this appeared to be a relatively "mature" urban system, in that there were cities of all different sizes in the urban hierarchy. By comparison, in most other countries the dominant pattern of urban development was a "primate" system, with one major city (or perhaps two) and hundreds of villages, and almost nothing of any consequence in between.[2]

In spite of the maturity of the urban system in ancient China, it was probably not a well-connected system. The county towns (*xians*) served as administrative outposts of the national capital, and to some extent they helped to hold together the vast territory of China by linking the countryside to the central government. Apart from this, however, there was not a great deal of spatial interaction between the different regions of the country. As we saw in Chapter 2, China had long been effectively subdivided into a small number of economic "macroregions," delimited primar-ily by geographical features such as river basins and mountain ranges.[3] In the center of some of these regions great market centers had emerged, but the pattern of spatial interaction tended to remain intra- rather than interregional. As a result of the vast distances involved and the difficulties associated with traveling across the country, the regions were generally poorly connected with each other.

By the nineteenth century this regionalized pattern of urbanization had been altered somewhat by improvements in transportation and industrial development, and in the latter part of the century the development of the so-called Treaty Ports produced even more significant changes in the urban system. In all, about a hundred cities were opened up to and partially colonized by Western nations. The influx of new technology, capital, and business know-how allowed the treaty-port cities to grow more rapidly than the others. Better transport links (along the rivers and the coasts) meant that these cities began to interact (trade) with each other more than they had in the past.

It is important not to overstress this point. China's urban system did not become fully integrated with the growth of the Treaty Ports—in fact, what happened was that a modern urban system was grafted onto the indigenous system that had been in place for centuries. In some respects the graft was incomplete, resulting in a dual urban system.[4] The new Treaty Ports were connected to each other and they also brought China into contact with the global economy, but this development was separate from and had relatively little effect on the old inland urban system. The inland regions remained geographically isolated and poorly integrated with the nation as a whole.

A third phase of urban development after 1949 brought still more changes to the Chinese urban system. In 1949 the cities were home to only about one-tenth of the total population. Except for the provincial capitals and the larger Treaty Ports, the cities had never really challenged the rural dominance of "feudal" China. We would expect a major increase in the level of urbanization as a result of the push toward economic development that occurred after 1949. This has been the case in most developing nations around the world, but the Chinese Communist party intervened to alter the normal course of events. By actively discouraging the growth of the largest cities and encouraging growth in medium-sized and small cities, China's urban planners were able to keep the overall rate of urbanization much lower than it might otherwise have been. At the same time, for a combination of strategic and economic reasons, the Communists also wanted to see some significant industrial growth in China's inland cities to counterbalance the concentration in the coastal areas.

In the First Five Year Plan, therefore, a policy of industrial deconcentration was announced, with the focus of development on a series of "cities of pivotal construction" in the interior regions of China, including Lanzhou, Xian, Wuhan, and Zhengzhou.[5] Although it was soon realized that China needed to continue to focus industrial growth on its traditionally strong coastal cities, the postrevolutionary pattern of urbanization was significantly influenced by Communist antiurban sentiments.

Chinese Antiurbanism

The theoretical underpinnings of socialism in the writings of Marx and Engels did not provide a totally coherent position on the issue of urbanization for the Chinese leadership after 1949. The huge disparity in wealth between the cities and the countryside was something that socialist theorists and practitioners alike were committed to eliminating, but, as we saw in Chapter 4, there was some apprehension among Soviet socialists about the wisdom of relying on the peasants to lead the Chinese revolution. It had also become clear to the CCP in the 1950s that to develop the countryside at the expense of the cities would be tantamount to committing political and economic suicide. Most of China's technology, industrial plant, and skilled labor was concentrated in the cities, and it was obvious to even the most diehard antiurbanists that national reconstruction would need to rely heavily on the economies of agglomeration made possible in the cities.[6]

In addition to this, Marxist ideology predicted that it would be in the cities, not the countryside, that the industrial proletariat would rise up to overthrow the capitalists. In other words, the Communists needed the cities to help create the right conditions for their revolution. Not surprisingly, therefore, there was some ambivalence among the CCP leaders toward cities and urban living. Some of them, most notably Mao Zedong, had a predominantly rural background, and the vast majority of the Party leaders had spent close to two decades living in exile in the Chinese countryside before reentering the cities in 1949. When the Communists finally took control of the cities, Mao Zedong and his associates were naturally apprehensive. "In the 1920s . . . [Mao] had turned his back on the cities and discovered revolutionary fires in the countryside. The fires had eventually spread across the lands of China until Mao stood once again facing the cities and once again fearful of them."[7]

Mao had a violently negative reaction to what he felt was the elitism of urban-led socialism, preferring to believe that China must focus on the spontaneous outpourings of the peasantry. The spatial manifestation of Mao's egalitarianism involved a desire to promote a self-reliant agriculture all across China and to direct settlement and industry away from the cities to the countryside. For Mao there was something entirely wholesome about the Chinese countryside: "Honesty, virtue, hard work, and plain living are to be found primarily among the peasants; it was their revolutionary vision which won the struggle, and which . . . [could] now create a new China."[8]

In Mao's opinion the countryside was untainted by the evils of Western capitalism that had been rampant in prerevolutionary China, especially in the Treaty Ports. The luxury-loving life-styles of Westerners and the Chinese bourgeois class were anathema to the new Communist elite. All that was corrupt and evil about city living was exhibited by the city of Shanghai, which was considered by Mao to epitomize Western-influenced decadence. To him and to the majority of the Party leaders, Shanghai demonstrated all of the nauseating features of urban capitalism: "Shanghai is a non-productive city. It is a parasitic city. It is a criminal city. It is a refugee city. It is the paradise of adventurers. In a word, Shanghai is a city where consumption is greater than production, indeed . . . where waste is greater than consumption."[9]

Although the writings of Mao Zedong suggest a virulent antiurbanist stance, some of the subsequent actions taken by the CCP belie such a simplistic viewpoint. In spite of the much-publicized efforts to hold down the growth of China's largest cities, urban growth continued after 1949, and for the first decade at least the revolution continued to be primarily industrial rather than rural in character. Investment in the industrial sector continued to outstrip that in agriculture, to such an extent that the growth in industrial output was seven times greater than that in agriculture in the first three decades of the People's Republic.[10]

In light of this evidence there is some cause to question the traditional assumption of antiurbanism among the elite of the CCP. Rather than an antiurbanism per se, it may be more accurate to think about a unique type of urbanism associated with Mao Zedong. Westerners cling to the appealing notion of Chinese antiurbanism, perhaps because we prefer to believe in the image of Chinese rustic wholesomeness. In reality the Chinese themselves probably find rural life dirty, hard, and unrewarding. It may seem attractive to us to think about life without cars, without the private ownership of homes, and without the peculiarly Western sense of individualism that is expressed in the suburban ideal of separate residences; but in fact the Chinese may not share our enthusiasm at all. As Kirkby noted, "If the Chinese are united in one thing, it is in a shared consciousness of struggle against the ravages of nature; it is an irony that we should choose to project onto such a people our own naive rusticism."[11]

Patterns of Urban Growth Since 1949

As noted earlier, in spite of the avowed antiurbanism in the CCP and the desire to reduce the urban/rural dichotomy, China's urban population continued to grow after 1949, and in fact it more than doubled between 1950 and 1960 (increasing from 62 to 130 million). This occurred in spite of reasonably vigorous policies to restrict rural-to-urban migration among the peasants and major efforts to increase opportunities for rural employment by creating more industrial jobs in the countryside. Throughout the 1950s sterner measures were implemented to discourage urban growth, including the physical "deportation" of some peasants who had illegally migrated to the cities.

The major economic goal of the Party during this (the "Stalinist") period was to maximize capital investment to speed up China's rate of industrialization. Consistent with this goal was a relative deemphasis on the provision of public services for city dwellers, including housing, roads, utilities, shops, and public transportation.[12] Critics of the CCP's policies in the cities have argued that this strategy was not so much based on the principle of egalitarianism as on a desire to build cities quickly and "on the cheap." The result was that China's city dwellers have been consistently shortchanged and life in the Chinese city has mostly been austere (Chapters 12 and 13). Shortages of everything and poor services have been the norm, but according to Party doctrine to suffer such privation was a virtue and a sacrifice for the good of socialism.[13]

The growth of China's cities during the period of the First Five Year Plan (1953–1957) resulted in some demographic changes that caused headaches for the socialist planners. Not only was there absolute growth; the cities also had to support a large population of "dependents," people who were unable to support themselves economically. The declining death rates and increasing birthrates during the 1950s meant that the dependent population (the old and the young) in China's fifteen largest cities represented 60 percent of their total population in 1957.[14] In addition to the financial burden associated with such development, the cities were becoming increasingly difficult to manage, and it was clear that new and more effective policies were needed to prevent excessive urban growth in the future.

Besides restrictions on rural-to-urban migration, and the emphasis on expanding rural industry, millions of city residents were involuntarily "sent down" to live in the countryside. In the 1960s these measures met with considerable success, at least in statistical terms, and the average annual rate of urban growth during the 1960s slowed down to about .75 million, compared with 3.4 million in the 1950s.[15]

Beginning in the 1960s and extending all through the 1970s, there was also a concerted effort to focus growth in cities other than the absolutely largest. Attempts were made to encourage the growth of medium-sized cities (those with populations from 200,000–500,000) and to promote the growth of smaller towns and cities. The success of these efforts can be seen in Table 8.1. The absolute numbers and relative shares increased for most categories of cities, but some major differences in growth rates are apparent. The largest cities (1 million plus) actually declined in their overall share of China's total urban population (from 39.3 percent to 36.5 percent), whereas the share in the medium-sized cities increased from 15.9 percent to 22.3 percent.

After a decade of very slow urban growth before 1975, China again experienced a rapid rate of urbanization in the late 1970s and throughout the 1980s. There were a number of contributing factors that appeared to account for this reversal:

- Many of the youth "sent down" during the Cultural Revolution returned to the cities.
- Delayed marriages among those youth resulted in higher birthrates (note that these youth were themselves part of the mid-1950s baby boom [see Chapter 7]).
- The relaxation of the state controls on urban residence allowed many rural residents to move to cities.
- There was a massive displacement of peasants, those made redundant by the agricultural reforms in the countryside (see Chapter 5).[16]

Although it is difficult at the present time to say exactly how far these developments will go, some experts have predicted that as a result of the agricultural reforms there may be as many as 200 million people who will move into China's cities in search of jobs and housing.[17] Between 1982 and 1983, for example, China's urban population increased by 14 percent, an urban explosion that followed three-and-a-half decades of relatively slow

Table 8.1 Urban Population by City Size in China, 1953 and 1979

	1953			1979		
	No. of Cities	Total Pop. (mill.)	% of Total	No. of Cities	Total Pop. (mill.)	% of Total
1,000,000+	9	17.5	39.3	15	33.9	36.5
500,000-999,999	16	9.4	21.1	28	20.6	22.1
200,000-499,999	28	7.1	15.9	68	20.8	22.3
100,000-199,999	40	5.9	13.5	72	10.1	10.8
50,000-99,999	71	4.6	10.3	147	7.6	8.2
Total		44.5			93.0	

Source: Adapted from R.J.R. Kirkby, 1985, *Urbanization in China: Town and Country in a Developing Economy*, 1949-2000 AD (New York: Columbia University Press), p. 150.

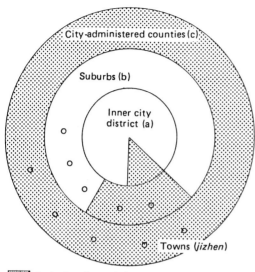

Figure 8.1 *Administrative division of urban areas, post-1983: The new city regions were divided into three sections: inner city districts, suburbs, and city-administered counties. All residents are counted as either agricultural or nonagricultural for the census. Source: R. Kojimo, 1987, Urbanization and Urban Problems in China (Tokyo: Institute of Developing Economies, Occasional Paper Series No. 22), p. 10; reprinted by permission.*

rates of urban growth (averaging 4.4 percent per year).[18]

Unfortunately, it is extremely difficult to assess exactly how much China's urban population is growing because of the frequent changes in the definition of the term *urban*. As we saw in Chapter 5, for example, at times in the past some cities were allowed to annex surrounding rural counties, thereby growing considerably in size overnight. This results in the uniquely Chinese situation in which the population of a city may actually be more than half rural. For example, in Nanjing, a city (*shi*) of the second order (after Beijing, Shanghai, and Tianjin), three rural counties have been annexed, adding 1.61 million people to the city's population, of whom only 100,000 are actually urban (see Figure 8.1). With an additional 420,000 rural residents living in the city's suburban districts, this means that almost 2 million of Nanjing's 3.74 million residents are essentially rural, although for legal purposes they are defined as residents of the city.[19]

The Chinese also have a fondness for creating new urban places. In 1976 there were only 189 cities, but by 1986 there were 300, and in 1987, 381. In 1984 the number of towns (*zhen*) was doubled, effectively increasing the urban population to more than 330 million, 31.9 percent of the total population, compared to 20.2 percent in 1981.[20] In 1987, according to the official State Statistical Bureau, the urban population stood at 503.6 million, which was 46.6 percent of the total (see Table 8.2).

In spite of these definitional changes, there is little doubt that China has recently witnessed a major population increase in its biggest cities. By 1986 there were thirty-eight "million-people cities," and forty-seven more with populations larger than a half million. This seriously threatened the "Chinese model" of urbanization, in which there was an emphasis on the development of small and medium-sized cities.

To try to soak up the surplus agricultural population the government has continued to champion the cause of the thousands of small rural towns all across the country, in an attempt to transform them into local centers of commerce, trade, and industry.[21] By the middle of the 1980s it looked as though these small towns had managed to double the number of manufacturing and processing jobs in small-scale rural enterprises, from 30 million in 1982 to 60 million in 1985.[22]

We can assume that this type of development, along with some of the traditional controls on rural-to-urban migration, have helped to keep the rate of China's largest cities to a level that was manageable. In the three decades since 1950 in-migration made up only about 30 percent of the total urban growth in China, which helped the Chinese to avoid the homelessness and mass urban squalor that has been typical of cities in Third World countries around the world.[23] The evidence suggests, however, that by the late 1980s China's cities were beginning to experience significantly higher rates of in-migration than at any other time since 1949, largely as a result of redundancies in the countryside. Before evaluating this most recent surge of urban growth and its consequences for urban planners, it is important to review the legacy that was left in China's cities after almost three decades of socialist city planning.

Table 8.2 China's Urban and Rural Population, 1978-1987

	Urban		% Increase in No. of Urban Residents from Previous Year	Rural	
	Pop. (mill.)	% of Total		Pop. (mill.)	% of Total
1978	172.45	17.9		790.14	82.1
1979	184.95	19.0	7.2	790.47	81.0
1980	191.40	19.4	3.5	795.65	80.6
1981	201.71	20.2	5.4	799.01	79.8
1982	211.30	20.8	4.8	804.59	79.2
1983	241.50	23.5	14.3	786.14	76.5
1984	331.36	31.9	37.2	707.40	68.1
1985	384.46	36.6	16.0	665.98	63.4
1986	441.03	41.4	14.7	624.26	48.6
1987	503.62	46.6	14.2	577.11	53.4

Source: *China Statistical Yearbook 1988* (Beijing: State Statistical Bureau of the PRC, 1988).

MAOIST CITY PLANNING

When the Communists marched victoriously into the Chinese cities in 1949 they faced the challenge of getting the country back on to its feet. In the short run it was clearly necessary for China to develop a strong economy and military to help it regain worldwide respect. China needed to "stand-up," both internationally and internally, by demonstrating to the world that it was finally a united country, an independent country, and one that could end forever the crushing poverty under which its people had labored for so long.[24]

In the longer term Mao Zedong predicted that the road to political and economic strength would be impeded by a series of contradictions, some of which could only be "correctly handled," rather than solved completely. One of the contradictions that most concerned Mao was that between the city and the countryside in China. The basic policy remained one in which significant attempts were made to reduce the dichotomy (in terms of wealth) between rural and urban workers, but as we have already seen, the actual policies implemented were refashioned at various times to meet changing circumstances, and they often deviated from the avowed goals. With the passage of time there were also changes in thinking about how best to handle the urban/rural contradiction. For purely pragmatic reasons, the early Soviet-style model of economic development heavily favored urban and industrial development over rural and agricultural development.

By the late 1950s this had given way to a pattern of development that improved the terms of trade for agriculture and that emphasized small-scale, decentralized development (see Chapter 4). This demonstrated that Mao's approach to the urban/rural issue was to be realistic rather than dogmatic—obviously it would have been a mistake to ignore China's cities in the push for development. Although Mao wanted to see the fundamental disparities between urban and rural life overcome in the first decade after the revolution, he was pragmatic enough to realize that both the city and the countryside had important contributions to make to China's development.

The compromise offered by Mao was to establish the communes, new economic entities that were not exclusively urban or rural, industrial or agricultural, but that contained elements of both. The communes are now largely defunct, but in the countryside the Maoist ideal of rural industrialization has survived even the changing leadership after his death. By the middle of the 1980s, rural collective industries made up nearly 80 percent of China's total industrial enterprises and provided 22 percent of the gross value of China's industrial output.[25] There is no doubt that this has contributed greatly to rural incomes and standards of living, thereby helping to narrow the gap between life in the city and the country.

At the other end of the scale, agriculture has been successfully brought into the Chinese city, a development that has helped to make cities self-sufficient in food production, but, more important, has also helped to bring peasants and workers together, effectively eroding the age-old dichotomy between them. "Peasants who work the land on the perimeter of the city live in the same urban neighborhoods as factory workers, intermingling with them at markets, political functions, cinemas, clinics and schools."[26]

Mao Zedong's solution to the urban/rural contradiction was to tease out what is best from both sides. He declined to make a clearcut choice between one thing and another, opting instead for a creative synthesis of the two. Mao was aware that the new Chinese society would be shaped by the strategies selected by the Party to tackle this and other contradictions that were emerging.

These contradictions came to a head in the city. The city, by definition, was the center of bourgeois activity, but it also contained remnants of the old "feudal" divisions between the rich and the poor as well as remnants of the imperialist domination of China. It was in the city, therefore, that the CCP now had to focus its attention. As Mao himself wrote in 1949: "The centre of gravity of the Party's work has shifted from the village to the city. . . . We must do our utmost to learn how to administer and build the cities . . . if we do not pay attention to these problems . . . we shall be unable to maintain our political power, we shall be unable to stand on our feet, we shall fail."[27]

When the Communists reentered the cities in 1949, as soon as the job of wiping out the opposition and pacifying any resistance had been completed, they faced the staggering task of recruiting and training the personnel needed to run all aspects of each city's administration: its finance, commerce, industry, transportation, and culture. Ezra Vogel described the situation in Guangzhou (Canton) when the Communists arrived in 1949, which was probably typical of what they encountered everywhere. "When the Communist troops entered Canton, they found the city in turmoil. . . . Some of the lower elements of society . . . were looting deserted homes and the

stores and gathering goods abandoned in the streets. Some remnants of the Kuomintang army . . . continued minor sabotage and sniping. . . . Inflation was rampant, the city was filled with transients, and both armies had sorely taxed the local food supply."[28]

In cities like Canton there were essentially two tasks: One was largely physical, the other social. In the first place it was necessary to take immediate action to respond to the problems they found. Everyone was exhorted to strive for "three years of recovery, then ten years of development."[29] Law and order had to be established, incomes had to be generated and taxes collected, and education and other collective services had to be provided.

To achieve these things, the necessary personnel had to be trained and organized. This required consolidating the existing Communist supporters and, more important, recruiting and training new ones. The leaders were convinced that all the correct solutions would eventually be found if they produced a high-quality core of officials (cadres). Like their Confucian predecessors, the Communists believed that the moral qualities of their cadres were all-important. The cadres would have to sacrifice their private interests for the public good and be able to form effective working relationships with the masses.

Unlike the Mandarins the new cadres were required to be egalitarian and activist. They would lead by example, demonstrating that they could resist the temptations of city life with all its comforts and "remain true to the ideal of asceticism, patriotism, and selfless service."[30] According to the Communists, the major difference between themselves and the vanquished Kuomintang was their moral superiority. The people had already made their choice; now it was up to the Communists to make good on their promises.

To examine some of the ways the CCP went about their task, we shall focus on three of the issues that the new urban elite considered to be most important. The first of these was the need to restructure the physical landscape of the city, to erase the legacies of "feudalism" and imperialism and replace them with symbols of the new socialist era. The second was to make China's cities economically self-sufficient, particularly in terms of food production. The third was to restore law and order to the Chinese city and to rebuild it in the image of the new socialist values of moral wholesomeness.

The Spatial Transformation of the Socialist City

In spatial and architectural terms many Chinese cities had inherited a "feudal" appearance, symbolizing the inequality that had persisted for centuries. City walls were used to separate town from country and leaders from masses. Distinct quarters of the city appeared, segregating different categories of the population according to their position in the social hierarchy. In many of the Treaty Ports an imperialist influence was superimposed onto this ancient pattern. In Shanghai, for example, the city had been divided up into international settlements by the colonists—and in time these areas developed a unique colonial appearance, sharply differentiating them from the ancient Chinese core of the city (see Figures 8.2 and 8.3).

In Shenyang (Mukden), which was the capital of the Japanese-held puppet state of Manchukuo, the imperial presence added an extra level of segregation to the city's land uses, as the comprador/bourgeoisie class was encouraged to build up the city's commerce and industry.[31] A new core area, built adjacent to the old Chinese walled city, was dominated by the Japanese and by foreign consuls; it was laid out along "Western" lines, with a gridiron road pattern, differentiating it sharply from the jumbled Chinese core area, with its familiar narrow, crooked streets.

Much of what they found in the cities in 1949 was abhorrent to the leaders of the CCP, who preferred to impose a much more centralized, highly standardized type of social organization. In social terms many of the Treaty Ports symbolized what the Communists detested about urban life. Cities were traditionally inhabited by the literati/intellectual class and were the focus for investment by the bourgeois class and rapacious foreign businessmen. As Fei Xiaotong pointed out, both of these urban types were considered by the Communists to be "parasites" on the "real" China.[32]

To transform the cities the CCP focused on three major goals from a larger set of socialist city planning objectives (see Table 8.3): (1) to stimulate industrial productivity; (2) to deliver collective services efficiently; and (3) to promote socioeconomic equality.[33] The priority given to each of these three goals has shifted over time, and of course the situations in each city were very different, but in general terms the objective was to produce a uniform and largely classless city, one in which there was minimal stratification of urban land uses. Streets were widened,

Figures 8.2 and 8.3   Two views of tourists mingling with locals along the narrow and crowded streets of Old Town in Shanghai, absorbing the high density and frantic pace of city life.

Table 8.3 Some Principles of Socialist City Planning

Emphasis on the city as a center for production rather than consumption and services
Parallel development of city and countryside
Controlled growth of the largest cities and the development of medium sized cities
Urban uniformity and classlessness (no land-use stratification)
Development of work and neighborhood units to help reduce commuting
Eradication of "feudal/imperial" symbols and replacement by symbols of revolutionary heroism
Building of political/administrative structures in city centers and key squares
Improvement of housing conditions to provide decent and safe accommodations for all residents

Source: Adapted from J. H. Bater, 1980, *The Soviet City: Ideal and Reality* (London: Edward Arnold),
pp. 27-40.

slum areas removed, public housing built, utilities installed.

In some cases the city centers were rebuilt to cater to the more egalitarian and political functions of a socialist state. This involved the opening up of formerly "forbidden areas," as in Beijing, and the destruction of temples, statues, and other relics of the "feudal" past.[34] The city was divided into self-contained and largely autonomous units at the ward and neighborhood level, and the concept of the work unit (*danwei*) was strengthened to reduce urban commuting and enhance the sense of local community (Table 8.3).

In the first two decades of the People's Republic the new socialist cities went through three major phases. The first was during the Soviet-inspired Five Year Plan (1953–1957), when the policies favored large-city development and emphasized heavy industry. Some "new industrial districts" were built to replace the old slum areas, as in Zhabei in Shanghai; and numerous "satellite towns" were created to act as industrial and residential counter-magnets at the urban fringe. The norm within all of these newly constructed areas was vast areas of uniform public housing, often built in drab five-story buildings (see Figures 8.4 and 8.5). In some of the city centers monumental Soviet-style buildings and vast revolutionary public concourses were constructed, as in Tiananmen Square in Beijing. New symbols of revolutionary heroism were erected to replace the "feudal" and colonial remnants.[35]

During the Great Leap Forward era (1958–1960) the Soviet influence on China's cities was formally denounced, and a second phase of "Chinese," or "Maoist," urban development was ushered in. The emphasis at that time was to narrow the so-called Three Great Differences: between mental and manual labor; between industry and agriculture; and between urban and rural standards of living.[36] This era brought a virtual end to most big-city construction projects and a new emphasis on urbanization in the countryside.[37]

A third phase of urban development, although on a very limited scale, occurred in the ultraegalitarian phase of the Cultural Revolution after 1966. The strong Maoist emphasis on self-reliance, self-sufficiency, and frugality—combined with the continued desire to reduce the urban/rural dichotomy—produced in a few locations a unique urban form that was a cross between a "rural style city and an urban style village."[38] The best-known example of this was the oil-field city of Daqing, in Heilongjiang Province, in northeast China. Daqing had no obvious city center; it intermixed oil fields and cultivated land; industrial facilities were dispersed across the urban landscape; and there was a mix of different-sized residential areas. Daqing essentially became the urban equivalent of Dazhai (see Chapter 5), acting as a model for Chinese urban development. "To symbolize the frugal spirit, earthen houses were built for the people. These embodied the utopian Chinese socialist city: high productivity, hard working spirit, and the integration of industry and agriculture. The principles of uniformity, standardization, and classlessness were all faithfully followed by the city planners."[39]

Creating Cities That Can Feed Themselves

In the decade immediately following Liberation, the CCP faced a serious conflict between two of its urban policies: on the one

Figure 8.5 Apartment buildings in downtown Kunming, Yunnan Province.

hand, the desire for all administrative units, including cities, to be agriculturally self-sufficient; and on the other hand, the attempt to transform the city into a production-dominated and essentially classless territory. Building the new urban-based factories and the necessary housing for industrial workers would obviously result in competition for valuable cultivable land at the urban fringe.

Making matters worse, the Soviet-style urban planning that was adopted in the 1950s was wasteful of urban space. Soviet-style

"giganticism" emphasized wide boulevards, huge buildings, large public parks, municipal stadiums, and massive public squares—all low-density land uses—which required the demolition of existing structures, especially housing—that is, higher-density land uses.[40] The resulting urban sprawl produced an inevitable conflict with the traditional market-gardening activities that are essential to a city's ability to feed itself. In the eight new "key point" cities identified for industrial development in the Chinese interior, for example, 5,160 hectares (12,900 acres) of vegetable fields were lost to city construction projects in 1953.[41]

At the national scale a crisis was brought on from the resulting steady decline in vegetable production, especially in the cities, which were forced to rely on more distant, and therefore less fresh and more expensive, sources of supply. This crisis stimulated a number of new policies devised to increase urban self-sufficiency.[42] It had traditionally been difficult to persuade Chinese farmers to grow vegetables because they were relatively capital intensive and provided low returns. Bank loans, subsidies, and other incentives were therefore provided to encourage greater vegetable production. Close to the urban areas new rural collectives were established in which agricultural activities were switched over from grain and livestock to vegetables.

Beginning in 1956 vegetable farmers were allowed to sell their produce at higher prices in free markets in the cities, and this in particular helped to increase the desirability of growing vegetables. This development, however, tended to conflict with other policies—for example, the farmers preferred to sell in the free markets, which meant they often had nothing left for the state vegetable corporations. In addition, there was a natural socialist hesitancy about fostering the growth of free markets during the 1950s, and in fact they were eventually abandoned, not to reappear until the late 1970s (see Chapter 5).

The ultimate solution to the urban self-sufficiency problem was considered to be the creation of "city regions" in 1958. These were large administrative units that were intended to integrate the city and the countryside and thereby allow a rational planning solution to the locational conflicts at the outskirts of the city between urban and agricultural land uses. At first fifty-eight new regions were allowed to annex surrounding (largely rural) counties, over which they would have control when it came to solving land-use conflicts. This new phase of urban/rural symbiosis gradually helped to facilitate large-scale conversions of land into vegetable cultivation as close as possible to the city center, thereby allowing the peasants to transport their produce easily into the urban markets.

Immediately adjacent to the built-up area, the communes were directed to focus the bulk of their energies on year-round vegetable production, and in many cities these areas were generally able to produce between 70 and 90 percent of the required vegetables. In a zone further out from the city center, vegetables were to be grown seasonally rather than year-round, which produced the familiar agricultural pattern in which there is a decreasing intensity of production: vegetable cultivation gradually giving way to other crops such as rice and cotton further away from the city (this is illustrated for Shanghai in Figure 8.6).[43]

Since 1958 the city-region concept has been applied to cities of all sizes, and in most cases it helped to formalize what had previously been a chaotic way of dealing with conflicts between urban and rural (central and peripheral) land uses. It should be noted, however, that the power of the cities to annex rural territory was often damaging to the independence of the rural communes, effectively subordinating them to the whims and desires of the industrialized urban cores. What this implies is that the solving of one of the contradictions between the city and the country in China inevitably allowed some new contradictions to emerge.

Restoring Order and Morality

The ethnocentricity and morality of the Chinese Communists meant that they were repelled by what they found in their cities, especially the Treaty Ports, after 1949. In architectural terms, as well as in their economic and social practices, the cities were redolent with foreign, bourgeois, and Kuomintang (Nationalist) influences. Shanghai, for example, was considered to be "a center of foreign and bourgeois culture. . . . Foreign-owned newspapers, American films, and schools where Chinese pupils were taught in foreign languages were all signs of cultural influences opposed by the Communists."[44]

Moreover, the coastal cities symbolized to the Communists the moral bankruptcy of the Western way of life and the dangers of allowing urbanization to proceed unchecked. The streets were littered with homeless beggars; crime and corruption were rampant; drug abuse was ubiquitous in certain districts. Shanghai, again acting as the symbol of Western decadence, was reported to have 30,000 prostitutes on its streets in 1949, a higher ratio per capita than even the "fleshpots" of Chicago, Berlin, and London.[45] As Edgar Snow observed, Shanghai was "a continuous freak circus with all manner of people performing almost every physical and social function in public: yelling, crushing throngs spilling through every kind of traffic . . . past 'honey-carts' filled with excrement . . . [and] past perfumed, exquisitely gowned, mid-thigh-exposed Chinese ladies."[46]

The shameless exploitation of women in Chinese cities was the result of a combination of different factors: (1) the obsession with sex and the desire for instant gratification among Westerners; (2) the traditional Confucian bias against women in China and the reluctance to provide education for girls; and (3) the simple fact that, partly because of their lack of education, Chinese women were virtually unemployable and therefore had very few

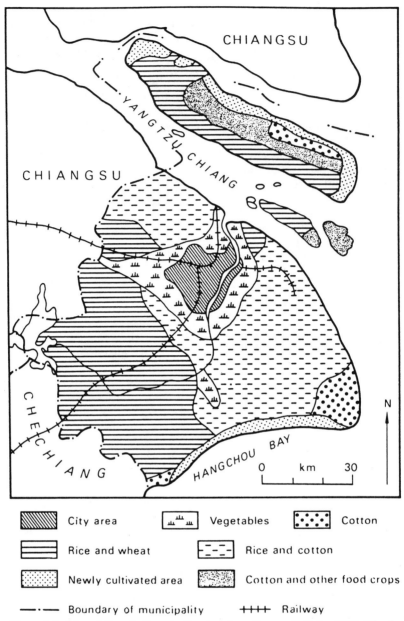

Figure 8.6 Map of Shanghai's agricultural regions. Source: C. P. Lo, 1980, "Shaping Socialist Chinese Cities: A Model of Form and Land Use," in N. Ginsburg and C. K. Leung (eds.), China: Urbanization and National Development *(Chicago: University of Chicago, Department of Geography Research Paper No. 146).*

options available to them outside the drudgery of home life and domestic service.

In *Chinese Lives*, the authors interviewed a woman who had been sold as a country girl to the local landlord before the revolution. A year later in a desperate search for a job, she signed on with a Shanghai labor contractor. On arriving at a plush house in the

city she was surprised when a woman looked her up and down and agreed to take her in.

She took out a cheongsam and a pair of embroidered slippers and told me to put them on.

"I can't get dressed up like that," I said. "I've come to do factory work."

"I've bought you," answered the woman with a strange smile. "There's no factory work here."

I had been sold into a brothel in a well-known red-light district. It was 1933 and I was fourteen.[47]

To reestablish order in the city and to purge it of this sort of degeneracy, the Communists attempted to legislate the immorality and crime out of existence, simply sweeping the streets clean. Brothels and opium dens were closed, and the prostitutes and addicts were rounded up for rehabilitation. This might not have been successful had it not been for the fact that it was supplemented by a policy of full employment. The new marriage laws prohibited overt discrimination against women; mass education for the first time meant that girls had the right to go to school on a regular basis; and the drive to push women into the labor force meant that new employment opportunities became available.

The intricate network of social control and surveillance at the neighborhood and work-unit levels helped to keep the streets clean of much of the former crime and corruption. Delinquents, good-for-nothings, and petty thieves were quickly ferreted out by resident-area guardians, so that "overnight these sons of old Shanghai became living symbols of the city's conversion from adventure to production."[48] In a relatively short time the Chinese city became a purposeful center of socialist production. The prostitutes had gone, the opium dens had disappeared; in fact the new cities were "squeaky clean." One observer reported, "You can no more find a singsong girl (or an opium pipe) in . . . [Shanghai] than in a Boy Scout Camp."[49]

The former prostitute interviewed in *Chinese Lives* was certainly grateful to the Communists for providing her with a new start in life. As she said, "The new society allowed us to be human beings for the first time."[50] In 1949 she had syphilis and was wasting away as a result of her opium addiction. She was sent to reform school and forcibly cured of her sickness and vices. Later on she managed to find a job, and in 1958 she married and settled down.

Completing the socialist transformation was the elimination of what the Communists considered to be the parasitic consumption characteristics of the old cities. In Nanjing, for example, the streets of the old part of the city were lined with wine shops and restaurants, where close to 100,000 people had once earned a living as waiters, servants, and lackeys to the official and moneyed elite. After Liberation, the Communists set out to put the people of the city to more useful work, following Mao Zedong's directive: "From the very first day we take over a city, we should direct our attention to restoring and developing its production."[51]

In Canton, after they had dealt with their political opponents, Kuomintang spies, and secret-society members, the Communists began to tackle the city's social problems—prostitution, gambling, opium addiction, and crime. People who committed such crimes were not treated as "counterrevolutionaries"; they were seen more as "feudal remnants" who could be reformed with the correct amount of socialist instruction. "All offenders . . . were carefully investigated and then suddenly rounded up. But instead of being executed . . . [like the political prisoners] they underwent a program of criticism, self-criticism, labor reform, and retraining. Before being released they were taught a trade and required to sign a statement guaranteeing that they would never again resort to a crime."[52]

For the first time in more than a century, public morality was restored and the people of Canton did not have to worry about walking on the streets at night. Human nature had not been altered, but tight surveillance and a strongly organized police force operating at the local level went a long way toward wiping out crime. In a symbolic gesture, on June 3, 1951, all the opium and opium-smoking paraphernalia in Canton were rounded up and burned in a huge bonfire. This was exactly 112 years after the Chinese burnt the opium they had confiscated from the British, an act that triggered the start of the Opium Wars (which ultimately resulted in the establishment of the Treaty Ports and the cession of Hong Kong to the British). The bonfire was accompanied by long patriotic speeches signifying the end to more than a century of oppression by chemicals and by foreigners. "In one stroke of political wizardry, local officials appealed to patriotism and promoted the eradication of vices. The obvious hero was the new government."[53]

Instead of being the locale of idle pastimes and decadent pursuits, the streets of the old Treaty Port cities were to be filled with a new breed of young and politically motivated workers who were willing and eager to be mobilized for the socialist future. As Vogel wrote, these were probably the most exciting times these youths had ever seen or were likely to see again. "Their idealism and optimism was at a peak, and they eagerly debated their views of the ideal society and how to realize that society. . . . As talented young individuals with a long future, they looked forward to great career opportunities. . . . They did not need or demand material rewards. . . . Their own sense of satisfaction, the respect of peers, the praise of superiors . . . were more than adequate."[54]

From a Western perspective the new puritanical city was probably a very dull place in which to live. Austerity came to be accepted as a feature of a progressive life-style. "Western fashions gave way to cotton clothing and the 'Lenin' suit . . . luxurious restaurants closed or converted to cater to a mass clientele, and the conspicuous consumption of automobiles, night life, and fine furnishings decreased."[55] On top of that, the constant surveillance and close social control brought a chilling vision of "big brotherism" to the Chinese city, and it would remain that way until the 1990s.

In keeping with the Maoist fetish for reducing the dichotomy between city and country, the new values to be inculcated into China's urban youth would be largely rural values. In 1958, for example, Miss Yao Fengchu became the model for revolutionary commitment in Shanghai. Her popularity was not a result of winning a talent show or a bourgeois beauty contest: She had won the All-City Pig-Feeding Championship. "She awoke each day at 4:30 A.M., to prepare several thousand catties of hog feed, fetch 60 to 70 buckets of water and wash the sties. Such an excellent worker could maintain almost 100 collectively owned hogs, plus three privately on the side. Few urban youths had Yao's rural competence, but many studied it."[56]

As we have seen in this brief overview of urban life after 1949, China's cities were largely rebuilt, reorganized, and substantially cleaned up in the post-Liberation era. The city was wrested from the bourgeois classes, from the intellectuals, the landlords, the money lenders, and from the foreign imperialists and given back to the Chinese. Most important, the city became the property of the working classes.

Gradually it was permeated with Maoist puritanism, and a heavy dose of rural values was instilled into all aspects of urban life.

After decades of Western exploitation and the subjugation of Chinese women, the city became the bastion of family values, plain living, and hard work. In the case of Shanghai, for example, it appeared that the city had been scrubbed clean and prepared for a new destiny. "Shanghai was being stripped for a new existence. Certainly what happened was the very negation of the city's 'raison d'etre' . . . [the message was that] vice will not breed here. Worlds will not meet here."[57]

CHINESE CITIES AND THE FOUR MODERNIZATIONS

With the new leadership safely ensconced by 1978, the CCP began to introduce a series of pragmatic reforms into all aspects of Chinese life, marking a virtual end to the utopian ideology of Mao Zedong. As we saw in previous chapters, the reforms in agriculture and industry produced some dramatic changes in the Chinese landscape. To some extent the new urban landscape has shifted back toward one that reflects much more of the trimmings of capitalism and colonialism than Mao would have liked to see.

We have also seen in the drive to "get rich" a marked tendency for land-use conflicts to reemerge at the urban fringe, as farmers have realized there are more profitable and prestigious ways both to earn a living and to spend their money—such as building new homes and starting up new enterprises on land that had previously been used to grow vegetables. There have also been ominous signs of the return of Western-style social problems to the Chinese city, and although the current situation is not nearly so bad as it was in the 1940s, there is definitely room for concern. All these trends suggest that the new economic reforms, along with some more specific changes in the approach to city planning, have contributed to the restructuring—some would say the dismantling—of the Maoist socialist city.[58]

The opening up of the new Special Economic Zones (SEZs) and the other coastal cities to foreign capital has seriously challenged some of the old principles of spatial equality that were touted by the Maoists. The resulting uneven spatial pattern of growth has been in sharp contrast to the traditionally "Chinese" model of slow urbanization, as some cities have been allowed and encouraged to grow as rapidly as possible.

Among outsiders, opinions are mixed about exactly how far this new trend will be allowed to go, and in fact China's urban planners still appear to be very much in favor of stressing small-town growth, rural industrialization, and the development of new towns and "satellites" to act as countermagnets to the biggest cities.[59] One observer even went as far as to suggest that the commitment to spatial egalitarianism was as strong in Deng's China as it was in Mao's, and that the Chinese "have faithfully upheld the Marxist ideology of bridging the gap between the proletariat in the country and the peasantry in the countryside."[60]

It is difficult to support such a statement in light of the dramatic increases in the urban population that occurred in China in the late 1980s, as millions of former rural residents streamed off the land in search of new jobs and new lives in the cities.[61] If this trend continues, China may begin to experience some dramatic reversals from the Maoist years, with the reemergence of urban problems that are all too familiar to Westerners, including unemployment, homelessness, and rising rates of crime and delinquency. As the new migrants arrive in the cities they may be shocked to find, for example, that as a result of the enterprise reforms, existing workers have been losing their jobs in the new efficiency drives. In the city of Qingdao 3,000 contract workers lost their jobs in 1988 and were forced to seek unemployment compensation.[62] No one can predict how far these challenges to the accepted principles of socialist theory will be allowed to continue, but they are no doubt causing a great deal of concern in the inner circles of the CCP.

The dilemma facing China's urban planners in the 1980s, and one that China shares with other poor countries in Asia and elsewhere, can be illustrated by the data in Table 8.4. As we saw in Chapter 7, China has already undergone the so-called fertility transition and now has a rate of population growth that is similar to that in developed countries. However, China's pattern of urbanization is still closer to that of other developing countries, in that until recently a relatively small per-

centage of the population was urbanized. What China has been experiencing, in common with other countries with a predominantly rural population, is a rapid increase in urbanization. The problem, however, as we have learned from similar situations around the world, is that the cities into which rural people begin to migrate are usually unable to provide enough manufacturing jobs for their new residents. China still has a relatively small percentage of its overall labor force engaged in manufacturing, as do the other poor Asian countries (Table 8.4), and there is danger that the rapid urbanization of China will be accompanied by rising rates of urban unemployment. Associated with urban unemployment will be the social problems associated with poverty that often dominate the landscape of large cities in the Third World. The management of this crisis as it evolves in the 1990s will present a serious test for the resolve of China's urban and economic planners.

Outsiders have noticed some important shifts in the approach to city planning in China during the Dengist era. In line with the new pragmatic economic reforms, it appears that planners are now allowing individual cities to develop according to their own specific characteristics, rather than attempting to force a uniformly socialist-style planning onto them. Thus we might expect to see some cities focusing on heavy industry, others on light industry, and still others looking mainly to services, commerce, and tourism—instead of all cities' becoming exclusively concerned with production activities. This implies that, consistent with the new approach to regional economic development that was outlined in Chapter 6, China's cities are now more likely than before to be allowed to concentrate on what they do best—an urban version of the comparative advantage principle. In Guangzhou (Canton), for example, the city plan called for "a socialist modern city with well-developed foreign trade and tourism, a center of scientific culture, with a balanced development of raw material . . . and farm produce processing, all built on a light industrial base."[63]

In the 1980s city planners reaffirmed this concept of urban diversity and added concerns about environmental degradation and the visual appearance of the city (see Chapter 10

Table 8.4 Population and Labor Force Statistics: Asian Developed and Developing Countries (1986 data)

	No. of Years Until Population Doubles	% of the Population Urban	% of Total Labor Force in Manufacturing
Bangladesh	26	13	9.8
India	31	23	11.1
Philippines	28	37	9.5
Pakistan	72	32	13.0
China (PRC)	72	32	16.7
Taiwan	47	67	32.5
Hong Kong	72	92	34.0
Singapore	64	100	25.0
South Korea	43	57	22.5
Japan	107	76	25.0

Source: Extracted from Far Eastern Review, 1988, *Asia 1987 Yearbook* (Hong Kong: Far Eastern Economic Review).

for a fuller discussion of the environmental issue). All cities are now required to submit "master plans" to the central government for approval, and then they are expected to follow the plans faithfully.[64] In the new era it is no longer considered to be "unproductive" to plan for the upgrading of city services such as transportation, housing, and recreation. Most surprisingly, urban beautification, a concept that not long ago would have clearly been branded as "bourgeois" and "decadent," has been promoted. What this suggests is a wholly new emphasis on "the individual character of the city, modernity, and the improved livelihood of the people . . . [rather than] the uniformity, frugality, and anti-consumerism objectives of the 1950s and 1960s."[65]

All this indicates a sharp reversal from the days of Maoist populism, in which most "experts" and technicians, including city planners, were considered to be suspect. In the 1980s the greater focus on living conditions within China's cities, on environmental protection, and on the need for carefully considered urban plans pointed to a rejuvenation of urban planning as a profession.

From the evidence that is currently available, it will not be easy for the planners to control the spatial structure of the contemporary Chinese city. As we saw in earlier chapters of this book, the forces unleashed by the shift toward market socialism are beginning to result in some significant alterations

in the use and value of urban land. What we are beginning to notice in China is a new "landscape of consumption" in the city, one that may bring back some of the painful memories of prerevolutionary inequality.[66] As some rural and urban folk fulfill their destinies and manage to "get rich," they will probably want to express their new monetary status in material terms. Until the present time the principles of socialist city planning have effectively militated against this sort of social and spatial stratification.[67] In the Chinese city, where residences are often tied to the workplace, no such obvious stratification had occurred by the middle of the 1980s, at least in terms of house size and the amount of living space per family. With the exception of small areas in the largest cities that were set aside for tourist development and luxury housing for overseas investors, there are few urban areas of extremely high land values dominated by real estate, banking, or other commercial functions. This is beginning to change now in some of China's most progressive cities and in the Special Economic Zone cities, especially Shenzen, where new precedents for China's urban landscapes are being established (see Figures 8.7 and 8.8).

One change in the Chinese city that is a direct result of the era of market-socialist reform is the growth of domestic (and to a lesser extent, foreign) tourism. The greater affluence and interest in traveling have re-

Figures 8.7 and 8.8   Advertisement from Chinese magazine Nexus: China in Focus, *illustrating new concern for comfort and luxury. The Beijing Binhe Garden Villas include "single-level ranch-style homes, two-story semidetached homes, and town homes in addition to low-rise apartment units." According to the ad, the units were to be available for long-term leasing in late 1989.*

sulted in the appearance of new hotels, restaurants, and even amusement parks. Housing for the newly rich peasants—who want to display their recently acquired wealth and status (see Chapter 13)—has been constructed.[68] This wealth and the obvious prestige that is associated with it will act to provide incentives to others who might want to tread a similar path. In many cities there are clearly visible reminders of the growing disparity of income in China, and in fact most parts of the urban landscape are now thoroughly pervaded by the symbols of cash, profits, and spending.[69]

Perhaps nowhere is the new urban landscape of consumption so clearly evident, and so much in contrast with the values of socialist China, Mao-style, as in Tiananmen Square. This is a vast public space, immediately outside the old Forbidden City. Mao Zedong and the CCP had made it clear that there would be no more forbidden cities in socialist China, and Tiananmen therefore has symbolic significance as a public meeting place adjacent to the traditional residence of the emperor. The square was the place chosen by Mao to declare the formation of the People's Republic of China in 1949, indicating that it represented the liberation of the Chinese from their oppressors—the imperialists, the Nationalists, and the landlords.

In the middle of the square thousands of people line up in all weather to tramp silently through the Mao Zedong mausoleum. If they keep going southwest after they have viewed the body, they will come to a Kentucky Fried Chicken restaurant that claims to be the largest of its kind in the world. This symbol of Western "spiritual pollution" would probably be enough to cause Mao to turn over in his coffin just across the square! (see Figure 8.9).

Tiananmen Square has become one of China's best-known landscapes. In 1990 it represented a mixed set of images, both to the Chinese people and to others around the world. It is the resting place for the body of

Mao Zedong, who led the Chinese people out of centuries of oppression and poverty, but it now also houses an artifact of the capitalist decadence he would have despised. It symbolized the release from oppression in 1949; so in 1989 it was the most obvious place for the students and other demonstrators to express their discontent. After what was witnessed in the square in 1989, it again came to symbolize repression and the centralization of Communist power—in fact the square became a "forbidden city" after martial law was enforced. Adjacent to the square are the headquarters of the CCP, and on June 4, 1989, the demonstrators discovered the full force of Communist power. The landscape of urban Beijing reflects the new era of wealth, consumption, tourism, and a range of Western influences. But when the tanks rolled into the square, it was powerfully evident that the new landscape did not reflect any significant political shifts. In fact, nothing had changed, in spite of all the changes.

Figure 8.9   Cartoon depicting Mao Zedong "turning over in his coffin" in reaction to the developments occurring in China in the 1980s. Source: G. Barmé and J. Minford (eds.), 1986, Seeds of Fire: Chinese Voices of Conscience *(Hong Kong: Far Eastern Economic Review, Ltd.), p. 190; reprinted by permission.*

Spatial Inequality and the Redistribution of Wealth in China

Notwithstanding Mao Zedong's peasant roots and the peasant origins of the Chinese Revolution, Mao's China did little to narrow the urban-rural gap.[1]

INTRODUCTION: SPATIAL EGALITARIANISM

The general tendency during the early phases of economic development in capitalist societies is for inequality to increase. As countries forge a path toward higher rates of industrialization and greater agricultural productivity, the distribution of income usually shifts in favor of the wealthy, and the better developed regions grow rapidly at the expense of those that are less developed.

As we have seen in previous chapters of this book, the economy that the Chinese Communist party inherited in 1949 was already riddled with inequality. The economic development policies of the CCP, especially in the post-1957 "Maoist" phase, were intended both to eliminate these divisions within Chinese society and to prevent their recurrence in the future. In geographical terms the CCP established two basic goals for economic development: (1) it should incorporate the entire country and avoid creating any further inequality at the regional or local level, or between the city and the countryside; and (2) it should be based on the principle of self-reliance, or self-sufficiency, building up economic capacity at both the local and the national levels to prevent further dependence on foreign nations.[2]

In his speeches and his writings Mao Zedong appeared to be deeply committed to egalitarianism, in the sense that he was in favor of redistributing wealth from the rich to the poor, at the personal as well as the geographical level.[3] In spite of this general commitment, the experimentation with different economic policies after 1949 meant that the socialist goal of spatial equality was *not* always at the forefront. The rural policies during the first decade, including land reform and the development of early cooperatives, were highly egalitarian, and they helped to bring about some major improvements in terms of income equality in the Chinese countryside. After land reform in 1952, for example, the poorest peasants (the bottom 20 percent of rural households) had a 12 percent share of the total income in China, compared to 6 percent in the 1930s.[4] At the same time, however, the Soviet-style concentration on industrial development and the relative deemphasis of agriculture during this era meant that most rural areas were lagging behind urban areas and were becoming poorer by comparison.

In the 1960s and during the Cultural Revolution, there was a stronger emphasis on economic decentralization, and the government realized that it was in the country's best interests to do whatever possible to foster development in the poorer peripheral regions of China. Of major concern at this time was the obvious imbalance between China's thriving eastern provinces and the more marginal provinces and autonomous regions in the northwest, west, and southwest of the country. The CCP considered this lopsidedness to be both dangerous in terms of national security and inequitable; and throughout the 1960s a number of informal spatial guidelines were established, effectively acting as the core of a regional policy for economic development. The central government was willing to intervene in regional development by investing in transportation, resource development, and industry in China's peripheral regions. One goal of these policies was to help bring about a more equitable spatial balance, both between the different regions of the country and between the nation's urban and rural areas.

After the death of Mao Zedong and the introduction of economic reforms, a more pragmatic attitude was adopted toward regional equality in China. As an implicit criticism of Mao, jibes were aimed at the naïveté and "excessive egalitarianism" of the recent past. Although the economic goal of the CCP was still to achieve common prosperity for the Chinese people, this did not necessarily imply *simultaneous* prosperity in all regions of the country. In the words of an official CCP source: "It is impossible to realize the goal of common prosperity for a large country such as China, with its billion people, *all at one go*. A time lag, and a difference in the rate of growth, is bound to exist."[5]

After a decade of economic reforms in the 1980s there is a strong case to be made that a "New" China has emerged, a China that is able to act independently, without the heavy-handed economic guidance typically provided in a socialist state by the central government. Arguably, however, this New China represents only a very small part of the total Chinese territory, and it is focused on the eastern provinces and the largest cities, including the old Treaty Ports and the new Special Economic Zones.

In comparison to the "Old" China in the country's hinterland, the New China has a much more rapid rate of industrial growth; prices are more likely to be determined on the free market; trade tends to be export oriented; and financing can usually be arranged by private lenders rather than by state-controlled banks (See Table 9.1). In a report in *Business Week*, for example, it was suggested that foreign investors, made nervous by the events of 1989, would be more likely than before to concentrate their activities in selected areas along the coast, where they have learned how to do business successfully with the entrepreneurs of the New China. The *Business Week* story went on to compare provinces in the Old and the New Chinas. In Guangdong, for example, close to capitalist Hong Kong and Macao, it was reported that "local officials thumb their noses at Beijing when they receive directives to slow down economic growth. . . . Some factories . . . raise money by selling shares in their company to their own employees. . . . Others raise investment money from rich farmer cooperatives, so that even when Beijing cuts off credit, private sector projects can proceed."[6]

In sharp contrast many of the inland provinces are stagnating in economic terms, and they have been forced to rely more and more on the state for investment funds. The severe austerity programs initiated in the late 1980s to curb the rapid inflation that was caused by the economic reforms have hit the state-owned sector with more force than the new cooperative and private enterprises, the bulk of which are located in the more prosperous regions of China.

Part of the problem, as we saw in Chapter 6, is that as a result of the economic reforms, cooperative and private enterprises are now able to keep a larger share of their profits, and investment funds are not being plowed back into the central government's coffers. This means that the rapid growth rates in certain industrial sectors and in selected provinces are *not* contributing to the total wealth of the nation, and to that extent the hoped-for trickle-down effect is not occurring. The *Business Week* report put this very bluntly: "At the most basic level, the New China is now starving the Old China for funds."[7] It would seem that after four decades of socialism, there are still two Chinas and that the gap between them is expanding.

It is generally assumed that during the Maoist era there was a fair amount of success in achieving spatial equality in China, both at the interregional level and at the urban/rural level. The corollary of this argument was that after Mao's death the emphasis on equality was relaxed, and the gap between the rich and the poor regions has been widening. In fact the situation is not as simple as this, and a case can be made (1) that the Maoist era was not nearly so egalitarian as either Mao had hoped or as earlier accounts

Table 9.1 An Impressionistic View of the "Old" and the "New" Chinas

	"Old" China	"New" China
Territory covered	All the inland provinces and autonomous regions	The eastern/coastal provinces
Share of total industrial output	56%	44%
Annual rate of industrial growth[a]	5.1%	24%
Prices and wages	Set mainly by Beijing	Determined largely at the local level
Management	CCP appointees	Entrepreneurs
Trade	Supplying mostly local and domestic markets	Largely export-oriented
Financing	State-controlled banks and central government invest-ment funds	Private (local) sources of funds; foreign invest-ments; Chinese funds routed through Hong Kong

[a]1980s.

Source: Adapted from *Business Week*, June 5, 1989, p. 38.

had indicated; and (2) that the post-Mao era has actually turned out to be considerably more egalitarian either than Deng had dared to hope for or than Mao and his supporters would have predicted.[8] In the following sections of this chapter we shall investigate some of the components of this complex issue, beginning with the issue of spatial equality at the regional and local levels.

SPATIAL (IN)EQUALITY

Most Western observers of the PRC between 1949 and 1978 were impressed by the emphasis on equality at all geographical levels. Although the Chinese were still poor by Western standards, there was very little evidence of abject poverty of the type one might find in countries such as India and Bangladesh. To some extent this level of equality was a function of the nature of the workplace in both the cities and the countryside. Until the advent of market socialism in the 1980s, most urban dwellers were employed by state or collective enterprises, where there was traditionally a strong element of egalitarianism in the wage and remuneration policies. The provision of nonmonetary fringe benefits and low-cost services (especially housing, health care, and education) helped to offset what income inequality existed in the urban workplace. In the countryside most of China's peasants at this time were not paid salaries or wages at all, and the result was that their incomes tended to be relatively equal within each production unit, although some significant variations did exist from one unit to another.[9]

The government's policy of restricting rural-to-urban migration also helped to foster equality by preventing the concentration of poor and deprived people in China's cities, again in sharp contrast to what occurs in most cities in developing countries.[10] Income inequality is also prevented in a number of other ways in China, for example, the low rate of ownership of housing and land and the deliberate attempts to hold down prices have militated against the development of a wealthy property-owning class. The policies that encouraged women to enter the labor force en masse, including the one-child population policy, have also contributed to greater equality in family incomes.[11]

In spite of the forces favoring income equality in China after 1949, significant amounts of inequality remained. Probably the most visible inequality was between residents in cities and in the countryside. In the 1950s, for example, the average ratio of per capita consumption between urban residents and peasants was 2.8 (Y 188 per year in the cities, compared to Y 73 in the countryside). In the 1960s the ratio was 2.5; and in the 1970s it was 2.6.[12] Part of this inequality was a result of the "scissors effect" of agricultural-pricing policies in China, which guaranteed city dwellers cheap food by keeping agricultural prices, and therefore rural incomes, artificially low. In addition to the monetary differentials in wealth, city dwellers generally had far greater access to services such as education, health care, recreation, and transportation— all of which tended to enhance the quality of life for China's city dwellers, effectively widening the urban/rural gap even further.

Because some of China's provinces are far more urbanized than others, the urban/rural differentials in wealth contributed to income inequality at the regional level in China. In 1979, for example, it was estimated that the ratio of the richest to the poorest regions (Shanghai versus Tibet) was 16:1, and the next-nearest poor relation to Tibet, Guizhou Province, had a per capita industrial-output level that was only 39 percent of the national average. In Shanghai, by comparison, the industrial-output level was more than five times higher than the national average.[13]

Even excluding the urban areas there were some major discrepancies in income levels among the regions of China by the end of the 1970s. Collective incomes per commune member varied from Y 139 in Jilin Province, in the northeast, to Y 56 in Guizhou and Y 68 in Gansu Province in 1979 (with 100 as the national average).[14] To a large extent these variations reflected geographical and ecological vicissitudes within the Chinese countryside: differences in climate, soil quality, topography, proximity to urban areas, and the availability of transportation, in addition to some obvious differences in administrative efficiency and management practices.[15]

In light of the socialist commitment to spatial equality, the size and persistence of these income discrepancies need to be explained. It is reasonable to suggest, for example, that there is a fatalistic acceptance of the traditional differences in physical endowment between the richer and poorer regions of China. The geographical variations are exacerbated by the distribution of China's ethnic minorities, the majority of whom live in the poorer regions of the countryside. The fatalism can be explained in part by Confucian paternalism, which would condone the continued dependence of localities (siblings) on the central government (parents), and the continued existence of inequalities between richer provinces (elder brothers or husbands) and poorer ones (sisters or wives).[16] The spatial inequality, in other words, is accepted as a fact of life, rather than something that must be eliminated. "A rich elder brother is expected to take care of poorer, younger brothers out of benevolence, but the latter are obligated to respect the oldest regardless of his behavior. Any demand to be equal would be regarded as a transgression."[17]

Interregional Comparisons

A review of the economic situation during the first three decades after 1949 suggests that at the interregional level a certain amount of spatial economic balance *was* achieved as a result of the government's willingness to sacrifice overall growth by enhancing the economies of China's peripheral regions. Measures of industrial and agricultural output, for example, show that regional inequality in China was reduced by the time of Mao's death. Between 1957 and 1979 the gap in industrial output between the most and the least developed provinces in China was reduced from 206 to 67 (see Table 9.2). This suggests that there was some convergence in the levels of industrialization among China's regions, with the most industrialized areas experiencing declining shares of the national total and the traditionally less industrial areas increasing their shares. At first glance, these data support the conclusion that under the Communists, China was able to reverse the

Table 9.2 Summary Measures of Spatial Inequality, 1957 to 1979

	Ratio Between Highest and Lowest Area	Absolute Difference Between Highest and Lowest Area (Yuan per Capita)	National Average Ouput (Yuan per Capita)
Industrial Output[a]			
1957	206.0	1,644	109
1965	93	2,213	192
1974	100	5,237	377
1979	67	5,161	473
Agricultural Output[a]			
1957	2.2	87	93
1979	2.2	128	163

[a]Gross value of output per capita.

Source: Adapted from C. Riskin, 1987, *China's Political Economy: The Quest for Development Since 1949* (London: Oxford University Press), p. 232.

general trend associated with economic development—in other words, a sustained rate of growth in GNP was accompanied by a *reduction* in regional inequality.[18]

A closer investigation, however, reveals much less cause for trumpeting the success of egalitarianism at the regional level in Mao's China. The first and most obvious problem is a methodological one, simply that a comparison of ratios from 1957 to 1979 is misleading because a small increase in output in a province that has very little industry represents a large percentage growth. The result is that in *relative* terms the gap between the most and the least industrial provinces declined; but in *absolute* terms the difference between the highest and lowest performing provinces actually increased during this period, from Y 1,644 per capita to Y 5,161.[19]

A second problem is that the data collected at the regional level (provinces, autonomous regions, and special municipalities) tell us little about urban/rural discrepancies or about intrarural inequality, much of which remained untouched. In fact, the official stress on local self-reliance and the tendency to focus on a very small number of highly successful localities for propaganda reasons have tended to widen existing inequalities at the local level.[20]

It is also clear that industrial output is not a very effective indicator of interregional equality because it is not necessarily closely correlated with differences in personal incomes. Wages were set nationally in China until the 1980s, and they did not vary significantly with labor productivity. In addition to this, only a small share of the profits earned by provincial and municipal enterprises stayed in the localities, most of it going to the central government. The net effect is that data describing differences in output levels may tell us very little about the actual differences in wealth among the regions.

Agricultural output is tied much more closely to local incomes and living standards, and the regional data give far less concern for optimism than is the case for industry. The *ratio* between the richest and poorest provinces in terms of agricultural output was the same in 1957 as it was in 1979 (2.2 in both years). In absolute terms the gap between the most and the least productive provinces increased from Y 87 in 1957 to Y 128 in 1979 (Table 9.2), and most of the provinces in the northwest and the southwest of China experienced a decline in agricultural output compared to the national average.[21]

Finally, no matter what was achieved at the regional level during the Maoist years, there is evidence that inequality increased after 1979, resulting in greater divergence between China's most and least productive provinces (see Table 9.3). Although in overall

Table 9.3 Industrial and Agricultural Output (1983, per Capita) and Growth Rates (1978-1983) by Provinces, Special Municipalities, and Autonomous Regions

	Industrial Output 1983 (per capita; Nat'l. Avg. = 100)	Agricultural Output 1983 (per capita; Nat'l. Avg. = 100)	Industrial Growth (% Output Increase 1978-1983)	Agricultural Growth (% Output Increase 1978-1983)
Beijing	446	103	77.7	43.8
Tianjin	483	103	71.8	47.8
Hebei	78	104	36.4	22.2
Shanxi	98	92	44.6	38.4
Inner Mongolia	64	94	37.5	41.1
Liaoning	237	108	46.5	33.1
Jilin	121	121	48.3	42.1
Heilongjiang	145	120	36.5	31.4
Shanghai	945	121	61.6	32.5
Jiangsu	154	148	54.2	77.9
Zhejiang	112	127	47.2	112.0
Anhui	53	90	47.4	53.6
Fujian	60	90	43.8	57.0
Jiangxi	52	94	62.5	33.6
Shandong	89	123	59.6	39.3
Henan	52	91	7.0	44.3
Hubei	108	103	26.0	91.8
Hunan	62	100	30.4	47.8
Guangdong	84	87	43.0	54.0
Guangxi	42	82	34.6	35.2
Sichuan	56	89	45.8	49.1
Guizhan	36	64	38.0	47.3
Yunnan	45	74	30.0	50.0
Shaanxi	73	77	28.4	32.5
Gansu	74	65	20.0	9.7
Qinghai	60	82	11.6	6.0
Ningxia	67	79	36.0	5.1
Xinjiang	67	109	52.8	60.8
China Total	100	100	46	46

Source: Adapted from P. Aguignier, 1988, "Regional Disparities Since 1978," in S. Feuchtwang, A. Hussain, and T. Pairault (eds.), *Transforming China's Economy in the Eighties*, Vol. 2: *Management, Industry and the Urban Economy* (Boulder, Colo.: Westview Press), pp. 101-102. Reprinted by permission.

terms, both industrial and agricultural productivity was high (averaging more than 9 percent growth per year in the early 1980s), as the most recent data illustrate, there were some major discrepancies at the regional level (see Figure 9.1). Agricultural output grew most rapidly in the traditionally productive areas in the Yangtze Valley and along the east coast (for example, Zhejiang Province reported 112 percent growth between 1978 and 1983; Hubei 92 percent; Jiangsu 78 percent; and Fujian 57 percent). In terms of industrial growth most of the provinces in the northwest and southwest of China grew at a much slower rate

than those in the eastern part of the country, and with the exception of Xinjiang's petroleum boom, industrial output in the peripheral regions has been stagnating, effectively widening the gap between the rich and the poor regions. In 1984, for example, Guizhou's per capita output was 46 percent of the nation's average. Although this was an increase for Guizhou from 39 percent in 1979, at the same time Shanghai's output increased to 654 percent of the national average (compared to 516 percent in 1979).

In spite of the efforts made to boost industrial growth in China's peripheral regions,

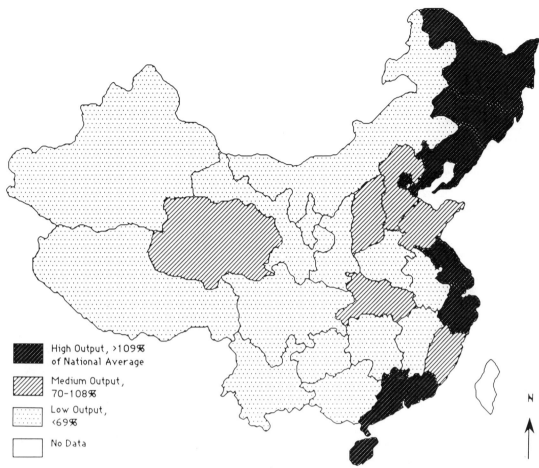

Figure 9.1   Industrial output, by province, 1987: The figures represent the value of gross output per capita for each province, expressed as a percentage of the national average for 1987. Source: China Statistical Yearbook, 1988 (Beijing: State Statistical Bureau of the PRC, 1988), p. 38.

industry remains heavily concentrated in certain provinces, mainly those in the northeast, along the east coast, and in the southeast of the country.[22] Furthermore, even within the most industrialized provinces, industry remains highly concentrated in the biggest cities and in the Special Economic Zones (see Figure 9.2).[23]

Interlocal Comparisons

Shifting down the focus of analysis to compare income levels between small units such as counties, villages, and production brigades (interlocal comparisons) reveals an even greater degree of spatial inequality in rural China. The ratio of the richest to the poorest brigades in the country in 1979 was 26:1 (compared

to about 2.5:1 for provinces), representing an absolute difference in per capita incomes of more than Y 1,000. These differences at the local level are primarily the result of long-standing geographical variations. In the years between 1977 and 1979, for example, 221 of China's 2,300 counties had average per capita incomes below Y 50, which represents some 88 million people who were essentially still living in poverty.[24] A spatial analysis of these counties reveals that they were clustered in three areas: the low-lying salty or sandy areas of the north China plain; the loess plateau in Gansu, Ningxia, Shaanxi, and Shanxi provinces; and the Yunnan-Guizhou plateau and the mountainous areas of northwest Guangxi Autonomous Region (see Figure 9.3). The pov-

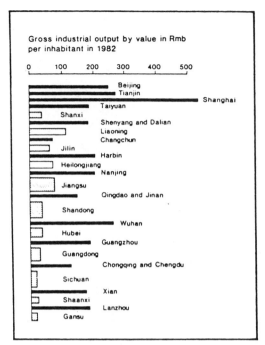

Gross industrial output by value in Rmb
per inhabitant in 1982

Figure 9.2   Graph showing provincial and urban gross industrial output and the dominance of the largest cities despite the attempts to decentralize industry. Source: J. P. Cole, 1987, "Regional Inequalities in the People's Republic of China," Tijdschrift voor Economische en Sociale Geografie 78, No. 3, p. 207; reprinted by permission.

erty in these regions is often rooted in long-standing ecological, demographic, or socioeconomic problems, although there are other explanations at the local level, such as unwillingness among the peasants to work in the collectives.[25] The wide geographical discrepancies in rural incomes were based largely on such factors as differential access to fertile land, the availability of water, and the proximity to urban markets and industrial inputs. It is no surprise, therefore, to find that the richest agricultural areas in China are in the "suburbs" of Shanghai, areas that are well endowed in all these ways.

In the face of the continued drive for equality in China, it is important to consider some of the other reasons that might account for the persistence of such wide levels of spatial inequality. It is reasonable to suggest that particular policies have at various times conflicted with and contradicted the goal of spatial inequality—for example, the restrictions on migration from country to city and the emphasis on local self-reliance—both of

which tended to block the natural redistribution of wealth and resources across space. In addition, the vastness of China and the relative lack of development of its transportation and communication systems may have resulted in a lack of awareness among some of the poorer localities of the extent of their impoverishment.[26] Contributing to this might be the lack of technical, managerial, and administrative skills in the poorest areas, which not only reinforces their poverty, but also militates against such areas' being able to fend for themselves in the political arena.

It is also important to reiterate that spatial variations in income across rural China appear to have been less important to the Maoists than discrepancies between urban and rural areas. The existence of the urban/rural dichotomy was a major contributor to the revolutionary struggle within China, and therefore it was an issue that was always closer to the heart of the CCP leadership than the issue of regional imbalance.[27] Equality, to the Maoists, was generally measured in terms of class or status, rather than income. Once the status distinctions between the elite (mental laborers) and the masses (manual laborers) was weakened or removed throughout China, for the Maoists the battle was largely won. Income differentials continued to exist, but they were not treated as significant compared to the problem of breaking down class barriers. Differences in income were considered to be relatively short-term problems that could be compensated for by the injection of non-cash "welfare" services or by campaigns designed to raise local levels of production.

Intralocal Comparisons

If we shift the focus downward one step further to look at the distribution of income among families within specific villages (intralocal variations) and among rural families across the whole of China, the picture becomes even less clear. In most of the detailed studies conducted in Chinese villages, significant income differences can be observed between households. For example, in a relatively prosperous production team in Wugong village (south Hebei Province) in 1977, the top 10 percent of households had mean per capita incomes of Y 427, while the bottom 10 percent had incomes averaging Y 107.[28] The major variable explaining this income inequality be-

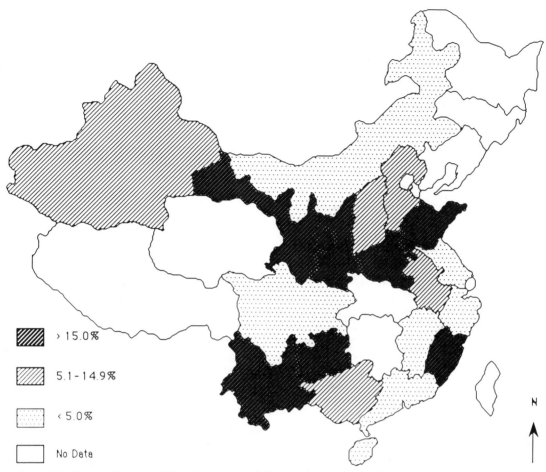

Figure 9.3 Poverty in rural China: Percentage of districts in province with per capita income below Y 50, 1977–1979 (average for China, 9.6 percent). Source: Adapted from E. B. Vermeer, 1982, "Income Differentials in Rural China," China Quarterly 89 (March), p. 25, Table f.

tween households was the size and composition of the families involved. The poorest families in Wugong had an average of 4.5 persons per household, typically including more children and retired parents than the richest households, which averaged 2.8 persons. The richest families were more likely to have children in the 15–28 year range, who were in the labor force and bringing home wages. In other words the major determinant of a family's income compared to its neighbors was its stage in the life cycle. The Chinese government does not appear to be overly worried about such inequality because it is considered to be a temporary situation. "A substantial portion of the inequality witnessed at any one point in time

is a transient inequality that will even out in the course of the life cycle as children become mature laborers earning good incomes."[29] Before the 1980s this type of transient inequality could be dealt with by the collective, which would step in to provide subsistence food for the poorer families. It follows that to some extent at least, income inequality in the Chinese countryside tends to vary over time, as each family passes through different stages in the life cycle.

The income data collected from numerous detailed studies conducted at the village level in China suggest that, overall, income inequality is relatively low, in the sense that incomes are fairly evenly distributed throughout the village population.[30] In a review of eight such studies, the gini coefficient, the traditional statistic for measuring inequality, ranged from a low of 0.16 to a high of 0.29.[31] A comparison of these results with those from villages in other poor countries around the world shows that the distribution of income in Chinese villages is very equal—for example, in a study of eighty-four villages in India, the average gini coefficient was 0.46.[32]

The primary reason for the equality in the Chinese countryside is the collective ownership of land, which provides the major source of income and food. As a result of land reform and the collectivization drive, intravillage inequality in China has been reduced significantly since the 1950s, and this pattern of relative equality continued until the 1980s.

If we look briefly at the distribution of personal incomes throughout the Chinese countryside, we see a slightly different picture, and China does not appear to exhibit significantly more equality than other Third World countries. By 1979 China had successfully restricted the wealth of the richest sectors of the rural population, but the poorest peasants in China were still not significantly better off than their counterparts in countries such as Bangladesh, India, or Pakistan, where the poorest 40 percent of the population have less than 20 percent of the country's total income (see Table 9.4).[33]

The conclusion that China did not have greater income equality than some of the other poor countries in Asia during the 1970s is supported by the gini coefficients (see Table 9.5). Once again, however, we need to remember that income alone provides only a partial picture of equality. In China the access to socialized medicine and education, and the availability of cheap food and housing, ensure that the majority of poor households have noncash benefits that probably make them considerably better off than their opposite numbers in many other developing countries.

As we saw in Chapter 5, the agricultural reforms in the post-Mao era brought relative prosperity to many poor households in the 1980s. Although some people feared this would result in larger gaps between rich and poor households, the evidence suggests otherwise. A Chinese survey conducted in 1984 shows that both the rich and the poor prospered between 1978 and 1983.[34] The percentage of "rich" families, those earning more than Y 400 per year, increased from less than 0.5 percent in 1978 to 23.5 percent in 1983; while the "poor" families, those earning less than 100 yuan in 1978, fell from 33.3 percent to less than 2 percent in 1983. For the Chinese countryside as a whole, income inequality was reduced in this period, as demonstrated by the gini coefficients (0.28 in 1978 and 0.22

Table 9.4 China's Overall Income Distribution in International Perspective

	% of Total Income Earned By:		
	Poorest 40%	Richest 40%	Gini Coefficient
China (1979)	18.4	22.5	0.33
Bangladesh (1973-74)	18.2	27.4	0.34
India (1975-76)	18.5	31.4	0.38
Pakistan (1970-71)	20.6	26.8	0.33
Sri Lanka (1969-70)	20.8	27.4	0.33
Indonesia (1976)	14.4	34.0	0.44
Malaysia (1973)	12.5	39.8	0.50
Philippines (1971)	14.2	38.5	0.47
Thailand (1975-76)	15.8	33.4	0.42
Yugoslavia (1978)	--	22.9	0.37

Source: C. Riskin, 1987, *China's Political Economy: The Quest for Development Since 1949* (London: Oxford University Press), Table 10.16, p. 250. Reprinted by permission.

Table 9.5 Distribution of Rural Households by per Capita Income (in Percentages)

	1978	1979	1980	1981	1982	1983	1984	1985	1986	1987
Income Group										
< Y 100	33.3	19.3	9.8	4.7	2.7	1.4	0.8	1.0	1.1	0.9
Y 100-149	31.7	24.2	24.7	14.4	8.1	6.2	8.8	3.4	3.2	2.4
Y 150-199	17.6	29.0	27.1	23.0	16.0	13.1	9.4	7.9	7.0	4.9
Y 200-299	15.0	20.4	25.3	34.8	37.0	32.9	29.2	25.6	21.8	17.5
Y 300-399	2.4[a]	5.0	8.6	14.4	20.8	11.6	24.5	24.0	21.7	21.3
Y 400-499	--	1.5	2.9	5.0	8.7	11.6	14.1	15.8	16.5	17.2
Y 500 +	--	0.6	1.6	3.2	6.7	11.9	18.2	22.3	28.7	35.7
Average income (yuan)	134	160	191	223	270	310	--	397	424	463
Gini coeff.	.28	.26	.25	.23	.22	.22	--	--	--	--

[a]The 2.4% includes all people with incomes over Y 300 in 1978.

Sources: Adapted from M. Selden, 1988, *The Political Economy of Chinese Socialism* (Armonk, N.Y.: M. E. Sharpe, Inc.), Table 5.6, p. 149, and *China Statistical Yearbook 1988* (Beijing: State Statistical Bureau of the PRC, 1988), p. 732.

in 1983 [see Table 9.5]). Thus it appears that the greater wealth generated in the Chinese countryside during the decade of reform has resulted in more rather than less equality between households.[35]

As this brief review implies, it is difficult to reach a simple conclusion on the issue of income inequality in China because the conclusions seem to vary depending on the·level of analysis. Perhaps the only conclusion that can be drawn simply is that "China's poor emerged from the Maoist era significantly better off than the poor in most other developing countries."[36] From the available data it is possible to suggest that (1) personal incomes in China are more equally distributed throughout the urban and the rural populations than is the case in most other poor countries, and (2) the economic reforms appear to have resulted in less inequality in personal incomes in the countryside, as the overall income share of the poorest families has increased during the 1980s.

In geographical terms, however, as we shall see later in this chapter, inequality has been increasing throughout the 1980s. Poverty persists in many pockets throughout rural China, and without the former guarantees of state aid to struggling localities, spatial inequality seems likely to increase in the 1990s.

URBAN/RURAL INEQUALITY

Mao Zedong's desire to reduce and possibly eliminate the discrepancy between life in China's cities and life in the countryside inspired a number of drastic measures. There was a virtual freeze on urban wages to prevent urban/rural inequalities from increasing further; millions of urban educated youths were forcibly "rusticated" (sent down); and severe limitations were placed on rural-to-urban migration. The encouragement of industrial development in the countryside, and deliberate efforts to enhance the social and physical infrastructure in China's countless rural villages, were intended to prevent some of the traditional patterns of spatial inequality that are commonplace in impoverished countries.[37]

Paradoxically, it appears that the gap between the cities and the countryside actually *widened* during the Maoist era and has been *narrowed* as a result of the post-Mao agricultural reforms.[38] Although the Party leaders were making a lot of noise about reducing the urban/rural gap in China, much of what occurred was restricted to political and ideological posturing. During the 1950s, for example, industry and the cities were heavily favored over agriculture. For a brief period following the Great Leap Forward debacle, capital investment in agriculture was boosted, but after the recovery in the early 1960s, agricultural investment dropped back to its formerly low level.[39] In other words, in spite of the Maoist rhetoric, investment funds were not shifted over toward the countryside in any major way. The result was that rural incomes and per capita levels of consumption continued to fall further behind those in the urban sector (Table 9.6); in fact the ratio between urban and rural incomes had opened up considerably by 1979, with estimates ranging anywhere from 25:1 to 6:1.[40]

During this period rural residents were also deprived of the opportunities to supplement their meager incomes by developing sideline activities, growing commercial cash crops, or selling their farm surpluses in the open markets. At the time these activities were considered to be inherently antisocialist and the majority of agricultural activity was directed toward grain production ("taking grain as the key"), in the interests of local and national self-sufficiency. The result was that in almost all walks of life, China's rural areas lagged further behind the cities: health status, nutrition, education, life expectancy, overall living standards, and the enjoyment of the so-called luxury consumer items.[41]

The statistics imply a serious discrepancy between the official pronouncements on the issue of urban/rural inequality and what actually took place. Mao Zedong's "mobiliza-tional collectivism" ended up with the rural poor being increasingly disadvantaged in relation to their counterparts in the cities. In sharp contrast to this gloomy picture, after the first few years of the agricultural reforms, China's peasants began to experience a major gain in incomes.[42] Data provided by the official State Statistical Bureau show an increase in average rural incomes by 1985 to Y 463 per year, compared to Y 134 in 1978. This helped rural residents to buy some of the "luxury" consumer items they had wanted for so long (see Table 9.7). The gains from the economic reforms are undeniable, and as one observer has concluded, "The stimulus of the household contract system, in conjunction with the rejuvenation of the market and rural sideline and industrial production and a substantial boost in state agricultural purchasing prices, have generated the first sustained growth spurt in the rural economy since collectivization."[43]

Life in the cities changed much less than life in the countryside in the 1980s, and the opportunities for such dramatic increases in incomes and consumption were not the same. With the exception of the SEZs, urban workers were not able to increase their salaries significantly. As we saw in Chapter 6, most of the efforts to reform China's urban enterprises have only been partially successful. By comparison, the spectacular gains made in the countryside—in terms of productivity and income—helped to narrow the gap between China's cities and the countryside, after a three-decade-long trend in the other direction.

Table 9.6 Consumption (per Capita) of Agricultural and Nonagricultural Population, 1952-1979

| | | Per Capita Consumption[a] | | Ratio of Consumption: |
	National Average	Agricultural Population	Nonagricultural Population	Agric. to Nonagric. Populations
1952	100.0	100.0	100.0	1:2.4
1957	122.9	117.1	126.3	1:2.6
1965	126.4	116.0	136.5	1:2.4
1975	156.9	143.1	181.1	1:2.6
1979	184.9	165.2	214.5	1:2.7

[a]1952 = Y 100.

Source: *China Statistical Yearbook 1988* (Beijing: State Statistical Bureau of the PRC), p. 711.

Table 9.7   Rural and Urban Ownership of Selected Consumer Durables (1978, 1982, and 1987)

	No. Owned per 100 Persons (Whole of China)			Ratio of Urban to Rural per Capita Ownership		
	1978	1982	1987	1978	1982	1987
Sewing machines	3.5	6.6	11.0	3.6	3.1	1.8
Wristwatches	8.5	18.8	42.8	7.3	5.5	1.5
Bicycles	7.7	13.1	27.1	5.4	4.1	1.3
Radios	7.8	18.2	24.1	4.0	2.2	1.9
Television sets	0.3	2.7	10.7	13.0	10.2	2.7

Sources: Adapted from P. B. Trescott, 1985, "Incentive Versus Equality: What Does China's Recent Experience Show?" *World Development* 13, No. 2, p. 210, Table 3, and also *China Statistical Yearbook 1988* (Beijing: State Statistical Bureau of the PRC, 1988), p. 718.

Although this was a welcome departure, it is important to note that the reduction of the urban/rural disparity was possible only after a significant dismantling of earlier socialist principles and at the risk of contradicting some policies that were important parts of China's modernization drive. For example, the potential profits to be earned in sideline enterprises and rural industries have encouraged many peasant families to allow their children to drop out of school and enter the labor force as soon as possible, thereby rejecting the nationwide call to emphasize higher education.

In addition, as we saw in Chapter 7, the reforms in the countryside have also encouraged many families to ignore the birth-control policies in their thirst for extra family income. Perhaps the most threatening aspect of the agricultural boom, however, is the cutback that has occurred in investments in agricultural infrastructure,[44] a trend that has been accelerated by the demise of the collectives. Nobody, including the state, seems to be very interested in investing in agriculture anymore, and the enormous infrastructural gains made during the collectivization years— the terracing, the irrigation networks, and the economies of large-scale farming—are now seriously jeopardized by the rush to privatize the countryside. It is also clear that whereas overall income inequality may have been reduced, *spatial inequality* has increased, particularly between the coastal and the inland regions of China, and at a smaller scale between the traditionally fertile and productive

areas in the countryside and the infertile and marginal areas.[45]

THE SPATIAL IMPLICATIONS OF PRIVATIZATION IN THE CHINESE COUNTRYSIDE

Although most people in the countryside were ultimately enthusiastic about the agricultural reforms, many local cadres in the production teams and the communes were initially opposed to the reforms because they were afraid of losing their jobs and their political power. Although this did occur to some extent, many cadres were soon able to parlay their *guanxi* into successful enterprises and sidelines, effectively reinforcing their local status. Since the reforms began, one of the most important tasks of the local cadres has been to help individuals find jobs in industry and to encourage the start-up of collective enterprises, which are intended to boost overall family incomes.[46] Opposition also came, probably naturally, from hard-line Maoists and other "leftists," who argued that the HRS could result in new levels of economic disparity if those who "got rich" began to leave the others too far behind. Although there was some convergence between urban and rural areas in terms of consumption levels, as we have seen, rural poverty still exists in many parts of China, and the gap between the richest and the poorest families in many villages has widened.[47] The reappearance of inequality in the countryside has been greeted with some ambivalence, but it is a trend that has been directly encouraged by specific policy changes. Beginning in 1984, for example, individual households were allowed to transfer their land contracts to other households. Some families had developed their land more efficiently than others and were soon in a position to acquire larger shares of the means of production, mainly land and machinery. In some areas a relatively small number of peasant households have proved themselves quite capable of producing all the food required in their communities.[48] The corollary of this situation is that the households who sell or contract their land to others will be left with nothing to sell but their labor power, which is allowable under the new laws.

The fear that inequality between households, villages, and whole regions will increase is exacerbated by the withdrawal of the central government from the business of supporting inefficient rural producers. There are no longer any guarantees that either the state or the collectives will step in with funds to counteract inequalities, for example, by subsidizing infrastructure projects in depressed regions. Without support from the state, the nation's poorer areas will find it increasingly difficult to generate enough wealth to invest in local agriculture. The consequence is that such areas will be unable to support their dependent populations, and they may gradually slip even further behind the more prosperous regions. The old guarantees that used to help insulate the poor regions, such as the state's regional-equalization payments, the "iron rice bowl" security of the collective work-point system, and the centralized distribution system with controlled prices, have now largely been dismantled.

At the present time it is difficult to be precise about the effect of the agricultural reforms on income disparity in China. The available data are quite confusing because there were actually far fewer "poor" families in the mid-1980s than there were in the late 1970s (5–10 percent in 1984, compared to 32 percent in 1978). At the same time the "richer" families are now richer than ever, which indicates that the gap between them and the "poorer" families has widened.[49] There are stories from Guizhou Province and other remote regions of China about the reappearance of itinerant beggars and a new class of rural poor eking out a living on thin soils, with no access to markets, and without the *guanxi* or the skills needed to succeed within the HRS.[50]

The reforms have also had the effect of pushing many of the poorer peasants off the land and into the status of hired laborers in sideline enterprises and rural industries, and this trend will probably increase as land becomes more concentrated in the hands of a relatively small number of rich peasant households. The quick successes associated with the HRS made it clear that the Chinese countryside before 1978 was extremely inefficient, and the increases in output since then with a smaller labor force imply that there was a massive amount of disguised overemployment on the land. The people no longer needed on the land now have some choices open to them. They can enter rural industries, and some of them can move into the cities. It remains to be seen, however, if these escape valves will be able to cope with the surplus rural population that is predicted over the next few years. Economists in China have estimated that the proportion of the labor force working in agriculture will continue to plummet, from 80 percent in 1984 to about 30 percent by the year 2000.[51]

The relatively rapid adoption of the HRS resulted in some important changes in the pattern of land use in the Chinese countryside. Increased productivity in grain-growing areas and the lure of greater profits to be earned from cash crops such as cotton, tobacco, and silk mean that the area sown with grain has fallen in the 1980s. Between 1979 and 1982, for example, there was a reduction of 7 million hectares (−6 percent), while cash-crop cultivated land increased by 4 million hectares in the same three years. In economic terms this could be seen as a healthy response to market forces because it produced a more efficient usage of land and brought with it the salutary effects of regional "comparative advantages." However, it was also a trend that disturbed state agricultural planners, who wanted to have greater control over what was to be planted. In some areas the land-use changes have threatened local food supplies because suburban farmers have been abandoning vegetables for more lucrative crops. The result in certain cities has been serious shortages of vegetables, which has been especially damaging during the long winter months in the north of China.[52] In the new private economy the production of relatively low-return crops such as rice and grain has given way to fruits and cash crops such as rapeseed (for oils) and cotton. One recent effect of this has been an increase in grain imports, which reached a record 16 million tons in 1987. In addition to threatening China's avowed goal of food self-sufficiency, this produced an unwelcome drain on the country's reserves of foreign exchange and a further deterioration in the balance of payments.

The mushrooming of rural industry and commerce has also presented a threat to the future of Chinese agriculture. The growth rates have been astounding, greater than 40 percent per year between 1984 and 1986, and in 1987 for the first time the output value of rural enterprises exceeded that of agriculture. All the market signals point to a prolonged decline in the agricultural sector for the simple reason that the incomes paid and the profits to be gained are far greater for everyone in industry and commerce. In addition to the obvious threat of food shortages in the near future, valuable land will be taken out of agricultural use and switched over to factories, houses, and roads.

It is important to point out that not all of the land-use changes are necessarily negative. For example, the concentration of land in the hands of prosperous peasants can allow greater technical efficiency in the countryside, the use of larger-scale equipment, and the financing of ambitious irrigation projects. These advantages notwithstanding, the emergence of rich peasant households, the subletting of land from one household to another, and the reappearance of a market for land in rural China are disturbing trends in a society that had so recently been embroiled in a bitter struggle to collectivize the ownership of the means of production in the countryside.[53]

The HRS has also resulted in some major, though possibly temporary, problems of distribution. In material terms rural rates of production for almost all commodities have expanded, but management skills, transportation, and refrigeration capacity have not advanced nearly to the same extent. The result is that in many parts of the countryside food is stockpiled and often left to rot, while in other areas people are going hungry. To avoid such disasters the marketing cooperatives need

to be developed to match the new production capacities. Other problems have emerged in an economy that is partly planned and partly free-enterprise based: For example, there have been shortages of inputs for agriculture, and the lack of construction materials has created serious bottlenecks for the rural industrial economy. There is also evidence that some rural consumers have been unable to spend all of their newly acquired earnings because many goods remain in chronically short supply.[54] This is a peculiar irony for those people who only recently became wealthy enough to enjoy their little taste of prosperity.

Another feature that is disturbing to many people in the countryside is the high level of insecurity and anxiety that has resulted from the dismantling of the "iron rice bowl." With market forces intervening and inflation reaching record levels, the pressures on individual households have been increasing. At the same time the state is steadily retreating from the area of agricultural investment. The result is that many peasants have been scrambling to spend as much of their newfound wealth as they can, on whatever they can find, whether it be expensive vacations, new houses, weddings, or consumer durables such as television sets and washing machines. What is needed, however, in the face of declining rates of state and collective investments, is for households and rural enterprises to use their surplus wealth to fund agricultural investments.

CONCLUSION: THE NEW CAPITALIST LANDSCAPE?

As a result of the agricultural reforms, the communes have all but disappeared, and most of their old functions have been returned to the townships. Decision-making is therefore far more decentralized than it was in the collective years, and the individual households have come to value their newfound freedoms. It is not likely that they will want to surrender these freedoms easily, nor will they ever again be so willing to listen passively to state and collective exhortations. The new production arrangements could dramatically alter the patterns of spatial interaction among China's peasants, as well as their traditional ties to the land and to their villages. In the enterprises and economic associations of the

1980s individuals were no longer tied to their ancient roots. As households and collectives diversified into new pursuits, many of them began to experience, perhaps for the first time, a variety of freedoms: to go anywhere they want to go; do what they want to do; and spend what they want to spend. The new contracts and associations being entered into were cooperative ventures, as they were in the past, but they were very different from those of the collective era. "The kind of cooperation that is emerging . . . is a cooperation between individuals who are more independent and more able to realize their individual capacities. It is no longer assumed that communal interests and . . . obligations are self-evident, like some 'general will.' The only 'social contract' is the one being worked out on paper after being debated in countless negotiations among those whose interests are at stake."[55]

What this means for the future is unpredictable, but it is likely that the new economic arrangements will be fundamentally different from those that evolved in the collective era. As decision-making is decentralized, new political constituencies and centers of power will emerge, based largely on economic wealth. These groups may be able and willing to challenge the administrative framework that has been established in the countryside. The old collective structures of the communes, brigades, and teams are being replaced by new types of peasant organizations for production and marketing purposes. Similarly, the traditional instruments of bureaucratic control over the ownership of land and the distribution of food will not only be obsolete; they may even obstruct progress if the cadres involved are unwilling to relinquish their authority. The old bureaucratic methods will need to be reformed to meet the demands of the new market forces. The emerging class of powerful merchants and rich producers has already changed the nature of the linkages between town and country in China, and it is not unreasonable to expect them sooner or later to challenge the existing power structure by demanding a greater share of the political leadership in the countryside.

The emergence of free markets in both the city and the countryside is also producing some major alterations in the patterns of spatial interaction (trade) in China. Many of the new wholesale markets, for example, are beginning to serve much larger areas; in fact some of them are acting as regional rather than local trading centers. As the new rules allow long-distance trading, the "export" to and the "import" of goods from other parts of China is becoming commonplace. In Chongqing, for example, in 1984, one such market handled goods from eleven other provinces and autonomous regions as far afield as Shandong and Xinjiang.[56] Sichuan oranges, dispatched from Chongqing, were being sold in Shanghai and Jinan; pears were coming in all the way from Anhui; and bananas from Yunnan. Market managers have branch offices in provinces and cities all around the country, expanding their role considerably beyond the original one of food wholesaling. Shenyang, for example, is beginning to serve as a center for collecting and reshipping products into and out of northeastern China from all over the country. One immediately noticeable impact of this is the appearance of exotic southern foods in the street markets in the middle of winter.

It also seems likely that as these regional-trading functions develop, some of the wholesale and retail markets in rural areas will begin to act as the nuclei for significant urban growth, further blurring the traditional urban/rural dichotomy in China. As the markets attract processing factories, service industries, and commercial facilities, they will increasingly be able to grow in size by "siphoning off" a large portion of the population that is being made redundant by the agricultural reforms. In Hunan Province, for example, six of the thirty rural market villages in one county had grown in this way to such an extent that they applied to be reclassified as towns in 1983. This process, if it continues in other parts of the country, could set in motion a rural revolution based on the urbanization of existing market centers. This illustrates not only how one set of reforms can help to bring about pressure for further reforms, but also how one set of policies can conflict with those in another area. The agricultural reforms will both *push* former peasants off the land and *pull* them toward the new market centers. As the growing market centers seek to acquire urban status, they will continue to attract more people from the countryside. In the 1980s the new migrants have been freer to move off the land than ever before since the 1950s, but they do not necessarily acquire permanent residence cards in the towns to which they are drawn, nor are they assured of state grain rations. It appears, therefore, that if the new towns in the countryside are to continue to grow, it will be necessary to loosen the traditional restrictions on household mobility even further. This could open up the floodgates of migration into all of China's largest cities, a process that may be accompanied by a rising prevalence of the social problems that China's urban planners have tried so hard to avoid since 1949.

Politics and the Physical Environment

Chinese society resembles some of the scenery in China. At a little distance it appears fair and attractive. Upon a nearer approach, however, there is invariably much that is shabby and repulsive, and the air is full of odors which are not fragrant.

—A. H. Smith[1]

INTRODUCTION: ENVIRONMENTAL AMBIVALENCE IN CHINA'S HISTORY

It is clear that some things have hardly changed at all since the missionary Arthur Smith surveyed the Chinese landscape almost a century ago. Then, as now, what we know about the Chinese love for their land seems at odds with their obvious contempt for it on a day-to-day basis. There are at least two distinct ways to interpret such contempt. In the first place it is conceivable that the Chinese landscape is simply an expression of "work in progress," representing the adjustments between people and their physical surroundings. What we see at any time is, therefore, only a temporary situation, and evidence of despoliation and environmental degradation represents only a short-term imbalance as people attempt to carve out homes and lives for themselves on the land. In this sense, "every landscape is . . . basically a blend of man and nature. Man may make mistakes, damage nature and therefore himself, but in the long run man learns and nature heals. Thus even when a landscape seems to display some maladjustment, it is only a phase in man, the domesticate, working toward symbiosis, a process he has been engaged in for a million years."[2]

This notion of "landscape as habitat" helps to explain why the Chinese people over the centuries have so persistently sought to refashion their environment. To shelter and feed themselves under the severe constraints dictated by topography and climate, they have launched countless assaults on their landscape. The surface of the earth has been modified in many different ways, from backyard terracing all the way to entire floodplain reconstruction. At any point the result, to the outsider, may be a landscape that looks messy and unsettled.

This has never been more the case than in the late 1980s. Visitors to China were overwhelmed by the rate of construction in the cities and the countryside. To some extent this was a result of the feverish pace of economic reform, but as the travel-writer Paul Theroux suggested, the Chinese have always had a penchant for fixing up and mending their environment. During the austerity of the Maoist era, this provided a low-cost alternative to new construction. The result has been a "second-hand" environment, a patchwork that, as Theroux noted, is "familiar to anyone who has looked under the hood of an old Chinese bus, or closely scrutinized the welds in a Chinese steam locomotive, or watched a Chinese street tailor or cobbler at work."[3]

This sort of "pride in poverty" was written off by many as old-fashioned and unnecessary during the more affluent Dengist era of the

175

1980s. Everything had to be new, and by the late 1980s the most lasting impression to the outsider was of a landscape under construction, which is difficult to reconcile with the idea of "landscape as habitat." To us it appears that the Chinese view the landscape not so much as their home but as an "artifact," something that has to be constructed anew from the ground upward. What we see, therefore, is not a refashioning of nature to produce adjustments but a fundamental alteration of nature. In his travels across the countryside Theroux concluded that the Chinese have always had a fierce desire to recreate the landscape, often literally tearing it down and rebuilding it. The result was that during the 1950s and 1960s entire provinces were turned into vegetable gardens, usually with little consideration for the long-term environmental impacts. It is difficult for Westerners to appreciate how people could be so cruel to the land they love, the land they have been willing to die for. One answer, as Theroux pointed out, was the force of numbers. The Chinese simply outnumbered their environment: "[They] had moved mountains, diverted rivers, wiped out the animals, eliminated the wilderness; they had subdued nature and had it screaming for mercy. If there were enough of you it was really very easy to dig up a whole continent and plant cabbages."[4]

Since the revolution in 1949, much of the landscape alteration has been politically motivated, reflecting the underlying philosophies of Maoist socialism. In the countryside, land reform and collectivization produced an entirely new rural landscape. In the cities, the goal of egalitarianism produced landscapes that are monotonic and featureless. The fervor to wipe out regional and historical differences and to produce uniformly Han Chinese environments has, in places like Tibet and Xinjiang, resulted in some egregious destruction of priceless religious artifacts.

As these examples suggest, the landscape history of China reveals evidence of ambivalence toward the environment. On the one hand we know that the Chinese elite have traditionally revered nature, as expressed in their landscape art and their love for all things natural. Gradually a fear of nature during the Han Dynasty was replaced by an appreciation of the serenity and charms offered by the natural world. This was expressed by the Tang poet Li Po, who described for his skeptical readers the benefits of communing with nature:

> If you were to ask me why I dwell among green
>   mountains,
> I should laugh silently; my soul is serene.
> The peach blossom follows the moving water;
> There is another heaven and earth beyond the
>   world of man.[5]

In spite of this reverence among the literati, encroachment on the landscape produced irreparable damage. The demand for ink among the bureaucrats and intellectuals resulted in the burning of vast portions of the ancient pine forests in northern China. As the population grew, farmers further encroached upon the forests and waters of China, "turning lakes, ponds, and marshes into cultivated fields."[6] The growth of industry, especially ironworks, and the need for firewood in the cities created a huge demand for timber, and it appears that the rapid deforestation of much of the landscape began as early as the Northern Sung period (A.D. 960–1279). To counteract such tendencies, there were some sporadic attempts to protect the environment. For example, during the Tang Dynasty, "the government increasingly recognized the value of forests and laws were promulgated against arson, against the unreasonable burning of fields, and against making fires alongside public roads."[7]

At the individual level, sensitivity to the environment and the appreciation of nature were reflected in Chinese works of art, including poetry, painting, and gardening. It appears that there were at least two interrelated elements in such works: One was the desire for solitude and the simplicity of a pastoral life; the other was a less tangible desire to escape from the crowds into a magical environment of peace and contentment (see Figures 10.1 and 10.2). The rich were able to create such places for themselves in their elaborate gardens, and even the poorer poets and artists could retire to their cottages surrounded by a few trees and perhaps a pool. Although some parks and gardens were opened to the public, often on the grounds of Buddhist or Taoist temples, for the vast majority of China's peasants there was no way to escape from the humdrum pace of everyday life. They had neither the time nor

Figure 10.1   A moon gate in one of Suzhou's many urban gardens provides a rare glimpse of China's tranquil past.

the opportunity to appreciate the aesthetic qualities of the landscape.

SOCIALISM AND THE ENVIRONMENT

In most other countries, a landscape feature was a grove of trees, or a meadow, or even a desert; so you immediately associated the maple tree with Canada, the oak with England, the birch with the Soviet Union. . . . But no such thing comes to mind in China, where the most common and obvious feature of a landscape was a person—or usually many people. Every time I stared at a landscape there was a person in it staring back at me.[8]

Over the centuries there had always been a conflict between environmental ideals and the harsh practical realities of housing, feeding, warming, and clothing a huge population. Whenever it was necessary, the environment had to be subordinated to the requirements of everyday life. After the revolution in 1949 the conflict between ideals and reality was

effectively solved by the dictates of socialist ideology. The concerns for "beautification" and the traditional appreciation of landscape for its own sake were interpreted as bourgeois values. The proper use of the environment was above all else to "serve the people," implying the masses rather than a relatively small group of privileged artists and intellectuals. The environment, therefore, was above all else a resource that could be used to create value. A tree was seen not so much as something to look at, or even as an essential component of the delicate ecological balance, but as the source of timber for homes, fires, and factories (see Figure 10.3).

In the countryside the Maoist exhortation to "take grain as the key link" resulted in the exclusive production of wheat or rice in the interests of local self-reliance, often in areas totally unsuited to such intensive cultivation. The effects in many areas were disastrous. In some of the northern provinces, entire areas of grassland were destroyed in the futile efforts to grow wheat. This is what

Figure 10.2   Huang Shan (Yellow Mountain) in the early morning: Every day thousands of Chinese make the long journey to the top to see the sunset, and most of them stay overnight to watch the sun rise over the mountain.

happened in Ningxia, where the author Zhang Xianliang served his time in a labor camp. He eventually learned to love his adopted homeland, but he mourned its demise at the hands of socialist agriculture. "Man and nature together had been flogged with whips here . . . the result . . . was to create barren land, on whose alkaline surface not a blade of grass would grow. A light spring breeze came blowing in from the banks of the Yellow River. When it reached this place, it suddenly stopped to a whimper, deploring the ruin of what once were grassy plains. This is what had become of my land."[9]

Anecdotal evidence of this type has been combined with scientific observations to suggest that Chinese socialism has had disastrous consequences for the environment. As we saw in Chapter 2, the modern version of the ancient folktale about the old man who moved the mountain symbolized Mao's belief that the Chinese people could (and should) remake the landscape to serve their needs. Whatever damage was inflicted on the land could be justified by the demands of society at large. In addition, without any private ownership of land and environmental resources, there was no one (in the form of individuals or activist groups) to represent the interests of the environment. Collective land, in other words, belongs to everyone—therefore it belongs to no one, and there is no one to speak up when it is mistreated.

The obvious retorts to arguments such as this come in two basic forms. In the first place, as the industrial revolution demonstrated in both Europe and North America, capitalist development can match socialist development blow for blow in terms of its ability to destroy the environment systematically.

may 1981

Unemployed woodpeckers

Figure 10.3 Unemployed woodpeckers: a comment on environmental degradation in China. Source: M. Haigh and D. Elsom, 1987, "An Environmental Snapshot of South China," China Now, No. 122, p. 26; reprinted by permission.

There is evidence from all over the world that the ecological plunder associated with atmospheric pollution, rain forest encroachment, and oil spills is as likely to occur in capitalist as in socialist societies.

A second retort is more specific to China's recent era of economic reforms, in which the principles of "market socialism" have been introduced with potentially disastrous effects on the environment. Some critics have suggested that the shift back to the individual ownership of land and resources, and the lure of material incentives, have already resulted in environmental degradation at a rate that was unprecedented during the three decades of the collective economy. William Hinton has observed the changes in the rural economy over the last four decades, and he has been a sharp critic of the agricultural reforms. One dimension of his argument is environmental: "It is doubtful if in history there has ever been such a massive, wholesale attack on the environment as is occurring in China now. . . . By atomizing landholding and making each family responsible for its own profits and losses, this regime has vir-

tually guaranteed such destruction. Neither regulation nor exhortation will stop it."[10]

Behind Hinton's rhetoric are three possible lines of reasoning: (1) To a large extent environmental degradation is a function of the level of economic activity, and with the economy expanding at the rate it did during the 1980s, the environment was under attack on all sides. (2) Pollution and a lack of concern for the environment are considered to be the result of the amoral behavior associated with the individual desire to "get rich" in the environment of market socialism, which is now relatively unfettered by central planning or the decrees of the government. (3) The critics argue that the government is in cahoots with industry, prosperous households, and foreign investors to push forward the economy as rapidly as possible, without any serious consideration for the effects on the environment.[11]

Arguments such as these indicate that the relationship between politics and environmental degradation is a complex one and that it is impossible to state definitively that one political system results in significantly more damage to the environment than another. We have seen that critics of the new regime in China, people like William Hinton, warned about the environmental impacts of privatization in the countryside. Others, like Vaclav Smil, argued that doctrinaire socialism and the Communist party's approach to environmental issues have been disastrous for the country. Smil talked about some of the "towering inconsistencies" and the "pervasive mismanagement" that have brought about environmental degradation at a level unprecedented in recent history and that have helped to produce *The Bad Earth*, which is the title of his book. "On the one hand, there is the waste of much heavy labor, investment, and scarce materials (iron, cement) for massive reclamation of land from waters that could yield valuable protein, regulate water supplies, and moderate local climate; on the other hand, there is the cultivation of rice or wheat in the newly reclaimed land with often very low yields."[12]

As these two opposing views suggest, opinions about the influence of politics on the physical environment are, as with almost everything else in China, subject to bias and misinformation. What is beyond doubt, however, is that China now faces an environmental crisis of staggering proportions, both in the countryside and in the cities.

China's Countryside Since the Revolution

Visitors to China's rural areas are invariably shocked to see the impact of economic development and population growth on the landscape. Perhaps the most stunning of these impacts is the *loss* of valuable resources: particularly, forests that have been converted to grain fields; soils that have been blown or washed away; lakes that have been drained for croplands; and fields that have been transformed into brick works, houses, or factories (Figure 10.3). In many areas there is no longer any evidence of wildlife. A British team traveling recently through Yunnan Province reported that "birds were absent, even from the reserves, and signs of mammal life were scarce compared with similar environments elsewhere."[13]

Environmental damage as widespread as that reported in many areas of China is probably the result of a number of overlapping factors. Specific economic policies have turned out to be both unrealistic and devastating to the landscape. For example, the massive production drives during the Great Leap Forward resulted in the decimation of much of China's forestland, with insufficient plans for replacement planting.[14] This is an example of careless exploitation that was probably unintentional, but other policies appear to have been deliberately damaging to the environment. The Maoist policy of "planting crops in the middle of lakes and on the top of mountains," for example, dictated a fetish for reclaiming lakes and ponds to grow grain. The result—a serious loss of surface water—flew in the face of logic, given the agricultural and ecological benefits of lakes and ponds, and the (often) minimal gains in terms of food output.[15]

The absence or chaotic nature of local and regional planning tended to exacerbate this problem, for example, when the building of reservoirs at one point along a river's course choked off the supply of water to downstream lakes. This happened in Anxin County in Hebei Province, when the Baiyang Lake dried up during the dry summer of 1987. An estimated 120,000 people had eked out a living from the produce of the lake, which was

about 360 square kilometers: "At its peak, there were 12,000 boats coming and going on the lake, and they netted 9,000 tons of fish . . . 10,000 ducks laid eggs weighing 1.5 million kilograms, and 75,000 tons of reeds were harvested. . . . Now nothing is left. . . . Many former fishermen have turned to other trades. . . . So far emigrants number over 3,000."[16]

Deliberate attempts to conserve timber resources and to renew the nation's forestlands have been threatened by other policies with contradictory goals. For example, the rigid monopoly exerted by the state over timber production has, according to one report, resulted in "gross inefficiencies in the wood-using bureaucracies, appalling waste and low profits per employee."[17] As part of the process of economic reform, the price of timber, which had been pegged at an artificially low level, was eventually allowed to fluctuate. In some areas this resulted in timber being overcut, with serious impacts on the rate of forest depletion. In this case the reform measures that were intended to speed up commodity exchange in the marketplace have had disastrous local consequences on the environment.

Contributing to this planned and unplanned exploitation were the plundering activities of the peasants themselves, who were most often acting out of sheer desperation. It has been estimated, for example, that wood represents about 38 percent of the energy sources in rural China, with another 41 percent coming from stalks and other plant matter (see Table 10.1). The decline in the amount of wood that resulted from deforestation meant that many families in the countryside were chronically short of fuel for heating and cooking. As they had done in the past, the peasants had to take matters into their own hands: "In desperation, people uprooted or chopped down vegetation, depriving the soil of organic nutrients and tilth, and plundered historical landmarks and other structures for wood."[18]

China's Forests: Problems and Solutions

The forestry issue illustrates the multidimensional nature of China's environmental problems and the problems associated with the search for effective solutions. The data provide a reasonably clear picture of what

Table 10.1 Energy Sources for Daily Life in Rural China, 1979

	Volume[a]	Standard Coal Equivalent[a]	Standard Coal Equivalent[a] (% of Total)
Coal	39,300	28,070	10.3
Fuelwood	181,600	103,770	38.1
Plant Stalks	231,800	112,590	41.3
Animal Dung	9,400	4,030	1.5
Methane Gas	703,760	500	0.2
Other	48,000	23,310	8.6
Total	1,213,860	272,270	100.0

[a]1,000 tons.

Source: Adapted from L. Ross, 1988, *Environmental Policy in China* (Bloomington: Indiana University Press), p. 26, Table 1.

happened to China's forests in the first three decades of the PRC. In the three most heavily forested provinces (Heilongjiang, Sichuan, and Yunnan), more than 16 million hectares of forest were lost, representing about 25 percent of the nation's total. In one prefecture of Sichuan Province alone there was a 68 percent loss, and the average loss was in excess of 30 percent. The net effect in Sichuan was that by 1980 only 12 of the provinces' 139 counties had more than 30 percent forest cover, and 105 had less than 10 percent.[19] The effect of forest depletion at this rate means that China lags far behind the world's average in terms of per capita forest cover, with 0.12 hectares per person, compared to 1.1 hectares worldwide.[20]

This has resulted in a serious shortage of timber for both industrial and domestic purposes in China, and the per capita consumption of timber, at 0.05 cubic meters, is considerably below the world's average of 0.65 cubic meters and less than one-thirtieth of the consumption in the United States.[21] There is not enough timber to meet the needs of the paper, construction, mining, and railway industries in China, and this shortfall has produced a bottleneck for economic development during the modernization period. Delays in supplies also jeopardize some of the government's reform plans—most notably in the construction of new houses; and in the schools and universities a desperate shortage of writing paper and books has seriously

inhibited the progress of China's education system.

Perhaps an even more serious consequence of deforestation is the long-term ecological effects of the loss of forestlands. It is common knowledge that "deforestation increases water runoff and aggravates erosion. Soil loss can affect farming in the source areas, but far worse is the heightened danger of flooding in lowland areas because heavy sediment loads aggrade streambeds and clog natural drainage channels."[22] In addition to their scenic value and their ability to moderate temperature extremes, trees and the cover of organic material on the forest floor help to hold water, thereby preventing runoff and soil erosion. A major concern in recent years has been in the Yangtze River basin, where deforestation has accelerated the cycle in which soil is eroded and washed into the river, contributing to flooding downstream. It has been calculated that if all the barren hills in the Yangtze basin were reforested, in addition to preventing future flood damage, an extra 20–30 billion cubic meters of water could be saved, which is twice the capacity of China's largest reservoir.[23]

Benefiting from the help of experienced forestry researchers around the world, China has in recent years launched some impressive campaigns to slow down the rate of deforestation. On the demand side of the equation, extensive efforts have been made to encourage greater conservation of timber products in factories and homes. On the supply side there has been a significant increase in the level of investment in forestry activities, including attempts to manage the growth of young forests more effectively and ambitious efforts to reforest large areas using areal seeding and faster-growing trees. Policies have been implemented to prohibit unauthorized tree felling and to close all black markets for timber, but in statistical terms none of these efforts have met with much obvious success. The problem, as Smil insisted, lies in the graft and corruption that is encouraged by the climate of austerity typical during the thirty years of collective socialism: "As long as the need for lumber or fuel wood remains acute, as long as quick cash can be made on the sale of wood . . . false permits and certificates will be issued, payoffs will be accepted, and the black market will continue to thrive."[24]

The search for solutions to the forestry problem provides a useful illustration of a far more general policy debate in post-Mao China, namely the conflict between the reformers and the conservatives within the CCP leadership. The trend toward economic reform in both the cities and the countryside spread to China's forestlands after 1978 in an effort to unleash greater peasant production rates. Consistent with the introduction of market-oriented forces in agriculture and industry, bold moves were also made to privatize China's forestry industry, effectively extending the idea of private plots to woodlots and establishing a production responsibility system for timber.

After 1978, in an attempt to speed up the rate of afforestation, households were allowed to cultivate their own "private" plots of forest. Certificates of possession were granted to small parcels of land, varying from 1 to 10 mu (15 mu = 1 hectare), which were later to be increased in size. The power of the collective was reduced, and in 1984 the right of inheritance to the plots was granted. By 1985, 50 million households held over 50 million hectares. Most of the land was mountainous or wasteland, but it represented approximately one-third of all China's forestable territory.[25]

The other major source of privatization was the development of household responsibility systems for forests owned by the state or by collectives. Either the contracts, as in the case of agriculture, were task-specific (for example, peasants were required to deliver seedlings, plant trees, or protect forests), or, more usually, an entire area was assigned to a household or a group of households for management. The collective provided the site, the seedlings, and the other inputs, and the contractors provided all the labor and made all the management decisions. The collective retained ownership of the land and had to approve all logging and planting plans, but the households kept most of the profits, as well as the incidental by-products, such as firewood. By 1986 over 40 million hectares had been contracted in this way. As was the case in agriculture, household contracting for forestland was never specifically planned, but it became extraordinarily popular among the peasantry.

As might be expected, privatization was viewed with suspicion by the more conservative elements within the Party leadership, and a wave of deforestation in 1979 was blamed on the reforms. The critics argued that the loosening of controls resulted in sharply escalating prices for timber, which encouraged producers, eager to profit from the boom, to overlog their land without consideration for the ecological consequences. In spite of this opposition, however, and a series of measures intended to slow down the rate of privatization, the reform movement continued to gather momentum throughout the 1980s.

Just as this new approach was getting off the ground, a new campaign was launched in late 1981 to speed up the rate of afforestation. This was known as the Obligatory Tree Planting program (OTP), in which all physically able-bodied citizens were required to take part in massive tree-planting activities. The program was launched with great fanfare, rather in the spirit of the old Maoist campaigns, but with the major difference that this program was backed up by law rather than relying on group pressures, as had usually been the case in the past. There was the threat of legal sanctions to people who did not comply and the promise of economic rewards to those who did. A campaign of this type was something of an anachronism in the climate of pragmatism and economic reform that prevailed during the Dengist era. The idea was originally attributed to Deng

Xiaoping's farsightedness, but it was also seen as a low-cost option for responding to the ever-present threat of flooding in China's major river basins, especially the Yangtze.[26]

It is also possible to interpret the campaign as part of a much larger attempt by the CCP to tackle the general malaise within society, especially the breakdown of social order and the spread of "capitalist" tendencies associated with the new reform era. Planting trees was a simple and cheap strategy that would benefit both the environment and society as a whole, and it could also contribute to China's modernization by providing more timber. More important, it would help to boost the nation's sagging morale. Deng and others in the leadership were interested in reviving some of the spirit of Maoist-style communism, but without the old and detested tactics of severe criticism and punishment that had characterized so many of the earlier campaigns. The advantage of the OTP campaign was that "tree planting without pay could help to create a Communist ethic of service to the people, build patriotism and collectivism, combine theory and intellectual awareness with practice and physical labor, and inculcate a spirit of arduous struggle rather than passive dependence on government funds."[27]

In other words, OTP was much more than a program to plant trees and produce a greener China. It can be interpreted as part of the ongoing struggle within the leadership, representing a backlash among the conservative elements to the "spiritual pollution" associated with the economic reform movement. It represented an attempt to "do something" rather than "do nothing" about some very serious environmental problems, but it was in fact much too simplistic a solution to the problems of soil erosion, desertification, and flood control. The OTP was little more than an attempt to "paper over the cracks" of the deforestation problem. It was a superficial, high-publicity program that few people could object to in principle but that actually left the root of the problems untouched.

In statistical terms, the first few years of OTP were marked by relatively minor gains in the total area of forests in China, and although more than 500 million people may have participated in the program, most of the effort was concentrated among mass organizations such as the Communist Youth League (CYL) and the People's Liberation Army (PLA), arguably the sectors of the population that were already well indoctrinated with the Party's ideology. One of the major problems was that although massive effort and great fanfare have been devoted to the planting of trees, this burst of activity was often not followed up by sound management and long-term care. As one observer concluded, "Since the cultivators have no material interest in tree survival, the tendency is to follow a brief flurry of activity in the spring by inaction, frequently leading to plantation failure."[28]

In comparison to the modest achievements of the OTP program, the shift to a private forest economy, supported by the pragmatists within the post-Mao leadership, has been highly successful. The private sector, represented by both individual households and voluntary production cooperatives, seemed to be providing the best solution to China's forestry problem.[29] New areas were being brought into production, and a profit-oriented forestry industry promised to induce more active conservation and less overlogging. In spite of the early optimism, the long-term success of the reforms will require continued support by the state to the burgeoning private forestry sector. Funds for capital investment must be forthcoming; guarantees of food (grain) supplies will be needed in areas reverting to timber production; higher prices must be possible and freer markets for timber opened up; and protection must be provided against local governments that threaten to drain off the profits of the new forest entrepreneurs.

The most important guarantee for the new foresters will be the hardest one to make in the current political climate in China, namely, continued policy stability. In a business with such a lengthy time lag as forestry, the private producers need to be reasonably certain that the existing policies will not suddenly change, resulting in the confiscation of their newly acquired property rights, the closing down of free markets, and a return to controlled timber prices. As we saw in 1989, some of the major supporters of the private economy subsequently came under extreme censorship and criticism for their stance on the entire issue of reform, most notably Hu Yaobang (who died just before the 1989 democracy demonstrations) and Zhao Ziyang. With the conservatives fully in control again, it is difficult to know what the 1990s hold in store for China's forestlands and for the economic reforms in general.

China's Cities: The Externality Effects of Production

Most travelers to China come back with horror stories about how noisy, cramped, and generally uncomfortable the cities are. Although there is no real way of comparing over time, it is thought that life in the modern Chinese city must be similar to life in industrial Europe in the nineteenth and early twentieth centuries. Colin Thubron found that the Yangtze River city of Chongqing, in Sichuan Province, had "mushroomed into an industrial Gehenna of six million."[30] It had been the Nationalist capital during the Japanese occupation, but Thubron was convinced that a Japanese pilot trying to fly over the city today would be asphyxiated by the smog (see Figures 10.4 and 10.5). The effect on the local people, even at ground level, was devastating: "They plodded their hill-streets in wan fatigue . . . [as] a suffocated sun was being rolled across the sky on waves of chimney smoke. Ash appeared from nowhere out of the air."[31]

In Shanghai, one of the world's most crowded cities—its density is five times higher than Paris and three times higher than Tokyo and Beijing—the most immediate problem appears to be the sheer mass of humanity, which Thubron likened to an enveloping body of water. "Shanghai lay drowned in the ocean of its populace. Through its humid evening, they resembled a whole landscape on the move. They marched eight abreast along the pavements. They broke over every street and square, flooded the shops, poured along the waterfronts, swarmed into the lanes."[32]

The environmental problems in such cities are enormous. Between 1949 and 1980, industry in Beijing expanded its acreage 120 times, and the city produced 2 million tons of steel and 10 billion kilowatt hours of coal-fired electricity. Shanghai was home to one-eighth of China's industry and only one-hundredth of its population. More than 7,000 factories were built, many of them in residential neighborhoods throughout the city. The most obvious impact of this concentration of industry is air pollution. In just one small area of Shanghai, for example, "more than 50 hazardous materials plants are interspersed with some 2,000 residences, where dust fallout surpasses the standard by three to eight times, where levels of sulfur dioxide . . . hydrogen sulfide . . . and hydrochloric acid are tens or even hundreds of times above the standard, and where three-fifths of the local high school students have chronic rhinitis and one-third suffer from chronic pharyngitis."[33]

The severity of pollution in Chinese cities is influenced by three sets of factors: (1) the absolute volume of the pollutants discharged or emitted into the air or the water; (2) the properties of the pollutants themselves; and (3) the ability of the local environment to absorb them. Because of the strong push to convert China's cities into centers of production rather than hubs of services or consumption, there was an enormous buildup of pollutants in a relatively short time.[34] To some extent the pollution problem currently facing China's cities is common to all countries that are pursuing extensive modernization plans. The quicker the buildup of factories, the greater the risk of extensive industrial pollution. One important difference, however, is the nature of the pollutants in China, where the major sources of energy are high-sulfur coals and other fuels of poor quality. In the low-technology environment of China's industry, there have been few attempts to reduce emission rates (until recently at least). Only rarely were economic incentives offered to enterprises that became more efficient energy users, and few penalties have been imposed upon the polluters.

An issue that is not as obvious to outsiders as air pollution is the problem of water in the Chinese city, particularly the availability of water and its potability. In the north of China the supply of water has become crucial in certain cities in recent years. In Beijing, for example, there is a critical balance between the supply of water and the demand for it. The skyrocketing population, growing from about two million in 1949 to more than nine million by 1980, and the rapid rate of industrial development meant that even with constant efforts to build new reservoirs and sink new wells, demand has continued to outstrip supply.

The local climate and the region's physical geography have worsened the water-supply problem. Although Beijing has a significant

Figure 10.4 (top) Looking north from the Small Wild Goose Pagoda toward the center of Xian, with Shaanxi Provincial People's Stadium in the background. Figure 10.5 (bottom) Looking north from the Small Wild Goose Pagoda toward the center of Xian, with Shaanxi Provincial People's Stadium barely visible because of the pollution, particularly noticeable during the winter months, when low-grade coal is used as household-heating fuel.

amount of rainfall (626 millimeters per year, amounting to about 10.5 billion cubic meters of rain), most of it falls in the summer months, which means that as much as 75 percent is lost to evapotranspiration. In addition, there are extreme variations in the amount of rainfall from one year to the next: In some years there may be six times more rain than the year before. Unlike other large cities in China, there are no major rivers in the area, only a number of small streams with variable and unreliable flows. As a result, the majority of Beijing's water lies underground, in shallow aquifers, and more than 80 new storage reservoirs have been built in the region since 1949.

The delicate balance between supply and demand can be illustrated by the overall statistics. In 1980 Beijing used 4.67 billion cubic meters of water, an amount that could not be met from existing supplies, which stood at 4.5 billion cubic meters, in dry years falling as low as 3.5 billion.[35] The consequence has been that, even in the wet years, Beijing has less water than it needs, which results in the depletion of the aquifers and a lowering of the water table.[36]

This problem will be exacerbated if the demand for water rises, as it seems most likely to do during an extensive modernization drive. In the early 1980s, the majority of Beijing's water was used by agriculture and industry, with only .28 million cubic meters used by households. This level of demand will probably increase significantly as larger houses are built, with multiple bathrooms equipped with showers and bathtubs, and as automatic dishwashers are installed. As the population increases and as people come to expect and demand more water, Beijing's water problems will multiply into crisis proportions.[37] Conservative forecasts for the whole of China, based on proposed rates of economic growth, suggest that by the year 2000 water consumption will increase by about 50 percent to more that 700 cubic kilometers (see Table 10.2). This includes an estimate for industrial water usage rising three times faster than agricultural use and domestic use doubling.

The other side of the water issue in Beijing is concerned with quality rather than quantity. As a result of the emphasis on heavy industry within the city limits, toxic material dumped into the cities streams has ultimately found its way into the drinking water.[38] In addition, the lack of sewage treatment facilities in most of China's cities means that the local rivers often become open sewers. In Beijing it is estimated that 1.8 million tons of raw untreated sewage is generated each day, but the city's sewers can only carry about one-third of the total, and (in 1980) there were only two sewage-treatment plants. Obviously, potable drinking water in Beijing, and in other cities, is difficult to find, and even boiled water remains hazardous. In Shanghai, the daily discharge of polluted water is more than 5 million tons, but only 200,000 tons are treated. Vaclav Smil estimated that 4 million cubic meters of unprocessed sewage are dumped into the Huangpu River each day, which makes it one of the world's largest toilets.[39]

Environmental Consciousness in China

As depressing as all of this may sound, some attempts have been made to raise environmental consciousness in urban China. New environmental protection laws have been implemented to punish polluters, and in 1987, Y 3.6 billion was spent on pollution treatment in China (see Table 10.3). The problem is that in many cases it is impossible for enterprises to meet environmental standards for emission and discharge without investing in expensive new equipment. Here again we are witnessing one of the many contradictions in China's multifaceted modernization drive. The desire for cleaner air and water requires environmental standards that could seriously threaten the push toward greater levels of production. It has become clear that to safeguard the environment it will be necessary to combine strategies rather than to concentrate on just one. What might prove successful, for example, is a mixed set of policies, combining more effective planning for environmental protection at the state, collective, and ministry levels with market-oriented strategies at the enterprise level. Factories and farms need to be coerced into recycling more of their waste water; fees for excessive usage have to be collected; and some major improvements in the management of water resources is needed at the enterprise level.

In the suburban agricultural areas of China's cities there is tremendous potential for water conservancy. It has been estimated that con-

Table 10.2 China's Water Consumption by Sector (1978) and Forecasts for 2000 (cubic kilometers)

	1978	2000 (Projected)	Average Annual Growth Rate (%)
Agriculture	419.5	529.3-595.3	1.2-1.8
Industry	52.3	108.7-136.5	3.7-4.9
Urban Domestic	4.9	11.0	4.1
Total	476.7	648.0-743.0	1.54-2.24

Source: Adapted from A. J. Jowett, 1986, "China's Water Crisis: The Case of Tianjin," *Geographical Journal* 152, Pt. 1 (March), p. 14, Table 2.

Table 10.3 Spending on Pollution Treatment and Number of New Treatment Projects Started by Enterprises and Institutions, 1987

	Total Pollution	Waste Water	Waste Gas	Waste Residue (Solid waste)	Noise	Other
Yuan spent	3.59 bill.	1.50 bill.	1.24 bill.	398 mill.	110 mill.	278 mill.
New projects[a]	25,652	6,545	12,106	1,605	3,731	--

[a]Started and completed in 1987.

Source: *China Statistical Yearbook 1988* (Beijing: State Statistical Bureau of the PRC, 1988), p. 773.

version of existing surface (channel) irrigation to sprinkling or drip methods could save more than half the water currently in use. The reuse of water in urban enterprises remains chronically low, and increasing it from the current rate of 20–30 percent reuse to 60–70 percent would save an estimated 400 million cubic meters per year in Beijing alone, which would be about 40 percent of the total water used by industry in the city. By the end of the 1980s progress in this direction was reported, although much remains to be done. Conservation activities were being combined both with industrial-location policies designed to restrict the establishment of heavily polluting land uses within China's cities and with a greater emphasis on the introduction of light industry, which is generally less likely to be a source of pollution.

As we saw in the case of forestry, the search for solutions to the urban water problem has proceeded along more than one front.

Approximately equal emphasis has been placed on the need for continued planning at the state and collective levels, and the gradual introduction of market-oriented principles into the business of producing, distributing, and consuming water resources. In light of the chronic shortage of water in many of China's northern cities, there has been a tendency to favor water conservation strategies over the much more costly and potentially ecologically disruptive construction projects to increase the city's water supplies.[40] In a series of conferences held in the early 1980s to discuss the issue of urban water usage, there was general agreement on the need to solve the "big water pitcher" problem, the equivalent of the "iron rice bowl"—the symbol of socialist inefficiency. The "big water pitcher" implies that water is a free resource, an attitude that generates little concern for efficiency or conservation.[41]

To many critics the cause of most of the urban water problems in post-Mao China has been the low cost of water, estimated to average less than 1 percent of industrial-production costs and usually a negligible proportion of household costs. At both the household and the enterprise level, so the argument goes, consumers would use much less water and be more willing to recycle if they were being charged an economic price for what they were using. In one study, for example, a flat rate resulted in a usage rate of 8.5 tons per person per month, compared to a usage of 2.4 tons when water was priced at the level of its production cost.[42]

By the middle of the 1980s a variety of market-oriented principles had been instituted. In Shanghai, for example, where excessive groundwater withdrawals had produced surface subsidence and extensive structural damage, instructions went out to regulate the drilling of new wells in sensitive areas. In 1982 volume-based charges replaced flat rates, and consumption norms were established for economic enterprises, with financial penalties levied on violators. Industrial users were required to recycle water wherever possible, and by the mid-1980s there was a slight decrease in groundwater withdrawals, with a rise in the water table. Households were to be served by individual water meters, instead of the old system in which the work unit footed the bill for all its employees.[43]

By 1985 the market-oriented strategies had become the orthodox solution to the urban water problem; a new set of regulations stressed that "water must be regarded as a commodity rather than as a gift of nature."[44] Water rates were recalculated to include the cost of delivery, management expenses, maintenance, and depreciation charges, as well as a margin of profit for the production companies.

Naturally the commodification of water is a controversial topic in China.[45] To bring about significant changes in demand and usage behavior, rates will have to be raised to levels that will probably be politically unacceptable. The supply of cheap water is one of the ways urban governments can redistribute wealth in the city. Poor families and small enterprises struggling to survive have come to rely on cheap water as a socialist entitlement, one they will not relish giving up.[46] Charging the market rate for water will put all sorts of pressure on households and enterprises alike. In the spirit of the reform era the new measures will ultimately benefit the efficient producers, the ones who are able to use less and recycle more. It is not yet clear what will happen to the less efficient producers and to the poorer households, which have come to rely on heavily subsidized water.

THE POLITICS OF
ENVIRONMENTALISM IN CHINA

There is no evidence that the early socialist theoreticians spent a great deal of time thinking about the topic of environmental degradation, but if they had, we can assume that they would have considered pollution to be one of the negative by-products of greed within the capitalist economy. In the face of environmental threats, the centralized planning system characteristic of many socialist societies should allow the government to act in the best interests of society as a whole rather than pander to special interests or to certain classes within the population. In other words, in a socialist society there ought to be a higher level of environmental quality than in a capitalist society and a greater ability and willingness to respond to environmental threats.

The experience in China since 1949, as well as in the Soviet Union and the socialist states in Eastern Europe, suggests that this is not the case.[47] In China, as in most socialist societies, there has been an almost fanatical concern with industrial and agricultural production. During the big-push phases there was a tendency for environmental concerns to take a backseat and for physical resources to be thought of purely as inputs to the production process, with little or no concern given to their long-term survival or replenishment. In addition, according to critics like Vaclav Smil, the widespread inefficiency, waste, mismanagement, corruption, and laziness often associated with socialist command economies have contributed in a negative way to a cavalier attitude toward environmental concerns.

From an ideological perspective, in a poor country committed to egalitarianism, a concern with environmental issues may have been interpreted as an irrelevance, perhaps even part of the "spiritual pollution" threatening to drift into China from the West (somewhat like the moral equivalent of acid rain!). In the country's struggle to modernize itself, concern for environmental aesthetics, for clean air, or for potable water was relegated to a position of low priority—it was a luxury that China simply could not afford. Westerners have learned the hard way that this is a very shortsighted view, and by the late 1970s the Chinese were beginning to see this clearly for themselves.

China was not involved in the environmentalist movement that swept the Western world in the 1960s and early 1970s, largely because of its self-imposed isolation and its mistrust of such Western "bourgeois" values. Few of the major industrial projects started either during the "Soviet" era of economic development in the 1950s or later in the 1960s had shown any concern for the externality or spillover effects on the environment. The main, and in fact the only, priority during these phases, was economic development.

As China returned to the world community in the latter part of the 1970s, and as the magnitude of its own looming environmental crisis became increasingly apparent, researchers began to think and write about their concerns, and "the environment" gradually became a political issue. During the early 1970s a number of pilot projects were introduced; for example, an emission-control project in Shanghai was funded, and a water-quality-improvement project began in Beijing's Guanting Reservoir.[48]

After China had fully reopened itself to the West in the late 1970s, it was immediately obvious to outsiders that the physical environment had suffered greatly on behalf of economic development. In the cities in particular, years of infrastructural neglect and fanatical concentration on production resulted in a decayed environment. In Shanghai, Westerners found that the city "had been run into the ground, its housing dilapidated, its waters befouled, its traffic a torment, and its resources milked to the point of exhaustion."[49] At first the new concern for the environment was restricted, as might be expected in a Leninist society, to the need to ensure that environmental concerns were built into centralized planning agendas, all the time taking great care to avoid doing anything to inhibit economic growth. In 1974 an Environmental Protection Office was established in the central government and in the provinces, but its status as an office rather than a ministry or a bureau indicated its advisory capacity and its tenuous position at that time. The government was distracted by bitter infighting at the leadership level (as it always seems to be), with the Gang of Four enforcing the primacy of "leftist" (Maoist) politics, in which discussion of a topic as "bourgeois" as environmental policy could only be framed within the broader confines of class conflict.

After the demise of the "Gang," environmental issues returned to the political agenda in a more comprehensive way, and in 1979 a statute on environmental protection was drafted, establishing the basis for future governmental action.[50] The law required environmental-impact assessments for all new construction projects; paved the way for a new environmental bureaucracy; set out the rudiments of sanction, reward, and enforcement procedures; and established a schedule of effluent charges and fines for excessive discharge of pollutants.[51]

Even after the legislation, however, the major problem was one of enforcement. Without any real "teeth," the environmental protection office, although it had been promoted to a bureau of the Ministry of Urban and Rural Construction (and Environmental Protection), was still perceived as a peripheral agency. In 1984 this situation changed somewhat when an Environmental Protection Commission was established to coordinate all environmental activities, with Li Peng (the future premier) as its chairman. Later the same year, the commission became a state bureau, finally sloughing off its parental ministry.

In spite of the commission's pronouncements on pollution, it still had no formal authority, and more important, no influence over agency budgets. Although it still functioned in a largely persuasive role, the commission appeared to be receiving strong moral and vocal support from the Party leadership. This was especially the case during the retrenchment phases in the 1980s, when efforts were made to slow down the construction boom initiated by the economic reforms (see Chapter 6). In a roundabout way stricter environmental controls were helping to enforce the policies designed to cool down the overheated economy, therefore also contributing to attempts to control inflation and budget deficits. For this reason the new environmental laws were likely to be supported by the more conservative elements within the Party leadership, even though the actual environmental concerns were secondary. The irony of this situation was that "environmental protection, which first blossomed in a period of liberalization, remained a priority item in . . . a more budget-conscious and politically conservative phase."[52]

By the middle of the 1980s environmentalists within the leadership had won an important moral victory. In the past it was made clear that environmental policies must not interrupt economic progress in any way. Now that situation had been reversed, and it was clear that the economy would not be allowed to expand without due consideration for environmental impacts. Although funding for environmental protection came from localities and enterprises rather than directly from the central government, the greater level of commitment was beginning to be manifested in financial terms. In 1980 environmental-protection expenditures totaled Y 1.8 billion, but by 1985 this had increased to Y 5.4 billion, representing 0.5 percent of the country's total output value, a figure that was expected to have increased to more than 1 percent by 1990.[53]

CONCLUSION: IS THERE A FUTURE FOR "THE BAD EARTH"?

In spite of the major steps that have already been taken, it is difficult to project a rosy future for environmental protection in China during the 1990s. Over the past four decades, China has witnessed a wide variety of approaches to policy implementation in all areas, including environmental issues. To outsiders these different strategies look like a hodgepodge, but in fact it is possible to identify three different ways of implementing policies.[54]

1. *A bureaucratic-authoritative mode of implementation*—which involves a set of imperative plans or commands that are communicated "downward" from the central government through the bureaucracies. This

mode of implementation was most closely associated with the so-called Soviet era of the 1950s.
2. *A campaign-exhortation mode of implementation*—which relies on the widespread mobilization of some or all of the population by the government or by a collective entity. Campaigns often have an underlying goal of developing the political consciousness of the masses, as was clearly the case during the Great Leap and the Cultural Revolution eras.[55]
3. *A market-exchange mode of implementation*—which relies largely on the incentive system made possible in the free market and the desire to benefit in material terms. This mode of implementation also relies largely on self-interest, with a relatively minor role played by planning and governmental coordination. It therefore represents a sharp deviation from the practices of the other two modes of policy implementation, and intervention from "above" is considered to be secondary or irrelevant.

As we have seen in this chapter, environmental policies in China since 1949 have involved a combination of all three modes of implementation. In general, with the passage of time there has been a shift from the first, to the second, and increasingly in the 1980s, to the third mode. Occasionally, however, the clock has been put back, with a temporary return to an earlier mode, as was the case with the Obligatory Tree Planting program in 1981.[56]

Support for the new environmental laws throughout the 1980s could be interpreted as part of a general pattern of liberalization in all walks of life—including the respectability afforded to intellectuals, scientists, city planners, and environmental researchers.[57] We can only surmise that after the purges of 1989 the new status afforded to intellectuals and scientists in China is once again in jeopardy.[58] Although Mao Zedong has been pretty much in disgrace, the purges suggested that China was entering yet another era in which political "redness" was preferred to "expertness." After the events of summer 1989, it will be a long time before many people assert themselves again, on any issue at all.

Prior to 1989, the regime had been somewhat tolerant of popular outbursts of dissent.

Pollution from factories, for example, had become a major source of local discontent in China's cities, often leading to plant shutdowns, letters to newspaper editors, and even neighborhood protests. In some instances the government supported such protests, if it helped to gain important leverage over recalcitrant local agencies and their officials. Although this could hardly be called a break in the political repression in China, it seemed after 1989 that even this small window of light was closed. In the years to come, both the clampdown on popular dissent and the succession crisis will make it unlikely that any great leaps forward will be made in the area of environmental protection.

This depressing conclusion reinforces the belief that a society is more likely to adopt major policy reforms such as environmental protection if it has an "open" political system, in the sense of being receptive to new ideas, both from the outside and from within its own ranks.[59] In addition, the new policy is far more likely to be implemented if the system of government is "conflict oriented" rather than "consensus driven"—the characterization of a one-party system. From this observation it is possible to construct a two-by-two matrix to represent China's responses to the problem of environmental degradation during the past four decades, and also to compare what has happened in other societies. As illustrated in Figure 10.6, under a "closed-consensual" situation such as the pre-Gorbachev Soviet Union and post-1989 China, a country is not open to external political influence or in fact to any new ideas, and little change can be anticipated. In the post-Mao era, but prior to 1989, China could be placed in the "open-consensual" category, implying that during the 1980s the country was quite receptive to ideas from abroad about how to solve its environmental crisis and also that a diversity of views about how to solve the problems was tolerated. Presumably the door that was closed in 1989 will open again sooner or later, but it is useless to predict when that might be. In the meantime, most people will be too frightened to act or even to think independently—on environmental or any other issues.

OPENNESS TO EXTERNAL AND
INTERNAL INFLUENCES

		Open	Closed
TYPE OF POLITICAL SYSTEM	Conflictual	United States	Cultural Revolution China
	Consensual	Pre-1989 China Gorbachev's USSR	Pre-Gorbachev USSR Maoist China (pre-Cultural Revolution)

Figure 10.6 A matrix of potential policy outcomes. Source: Adapted from L. Ross, 1988, Environmental Policy in China (Bloomington: Indiana University Press), pp. 148–149, Figure 2.

PART THREE

The Geography of Everyday Life in China

CHAPTER ELEVEN

Women's Place
in the New China

*In Socialist China, we have always advocated that husband and wife help
each other and work towards a democratic and harmonious way of life
within the family. It is necessary to promote communist morality and oppose
rash decisions in marriage.*

—Wu Xinya[1]

INTRODUCTION: WOMEN
AND SOCIALISM

Mao Zedong was repelled by the Confucian traditions that had continued the servitude of women in China over the centuries. Even before he joined the Communist party he had been outraged about the suicide of a young woman in his home province. She had been betrothed by her parents to a much older man—a rich antique dealer she detested. On the day of the wedding, the woman cut her throat just as she was being put into the bridal chair to be carried to her husband's home. Mao was deeply affected by the incident, and he referred to the bridal sedan chair as a "prisoner's cart," a vehicle that took a young woman away from her own home and planted her in someone else's, usually to live the rest of her life in silent despair. Mao felt that China's young people should have the courage to oppose arranged marriages: "As soon as a person drops out of his mother's belly, it is said that his marriage is settled [but] . . . we must . . . destroy all superstitions regarding marriage, of which the most important is the destruction of belief in 'predestined marriage.' "[2]

In his later years Mao's championing of the cause of women was contradicted by some of his actions: He was married several times; he had a reputation as a womanizer; and he abandoned his longtime revolutionary partner in Yenan for the urbane charms of a younger woman.[3] In spite of this, his prerevolutionary sentiments were clearly in favor of equality for Chinese women. He ridiculed the traditional double standard in Chinese society that excluded women from inheriting property and from all important positions, yet still required them to behave with the utmost propriety. Writing from the perspective of women, he also denounced the Chinese tradition of concubinage: "Shameless, villainous men make us their playthings and force us to prostitute ourselves to them indefinitely. Devils, who destroy the freedom of love! Devils, who destroy the sanctity of love! They keep us surrounded all day long, but this 'chastity' is confined to us women! Everywhere there are shrines to virtuous women, but where are the shrines for chaste boys?"[4]

Although Mao was probably ahead of his time with his ideas about how women should be treated in China, there was some precedent for his views in the socialist literature of Engels and Marx that he was just beginning to read. It was assumed that marriage and mate selection in capitalist societies were strongly influenced by concerns for material wealth, status, and political power. In a socialist society, therefore, Mao hoped to see a decline in the functional basis of marriage and a move toward partnerships based on love and personal attraction. As we shall see in this chapter, after four decades of Chinese socialism there is little evidence that this has been the case. During the Cultural Revolution for example, the political acceptability of one's proposed mate was the single most important factor. Divorce and separation for political reasons were commonplace, as were marriages for political convenience, many of which were later dissolved. Rather than following the dictates of the heart, a young couple wishing to marry had to satisfy the Party that they were suitable candidates for marriage. The letter asking for permission might have read as follows:

> The farm-worker Zhang Youglin, male, age thirty-nine, marital status: never before married, and the farm-worker Huang Xianglu, female, age thirty-one, marital status, divorced, hereby apply to get married. Both parties . . . guarantee that after marriage they will continue to remake themselves, will receive supervision and re-education under the leadership of the Party Branch and the Lower Middle Farming Class, and will do their best to aid in the construction of a socialist society.[5]

In the 1980s a couple who wanted to get married would have found such a humble request ludicrously outdated. In the new era of materialism, wealth and possessions had once again become the major criteria in the marriage game, and those who were unable to make an attractive offer might find themselves "on the shelf." One of Zhang and Sang's respondents in *Chinese Lives* faced just such a prospect: "My biggest headache is finding a wife. My job's nothing great. Even with bonuses and extras the best is a little over seventy yuan a month . . . the girls I go for wouldn't give me a second glance . . . if I had 3,000 yuan I could buy a colour TV, a sofa and a fridge, and they'd all be after me."[6]

Engels and Marx, and Mao after them, had expected that complete equality for women would gradually come about in a socialist society under a number of conditions. The first was the abolition of private property and wealth as the basis for status differentiation and dependency relationships between men and women. The second was a gradual shift in the direction of full and equally paid status for women within the labor force; and the third was the public provision of the domestic services that are usually the sole responsibility of women, such as cooking, cleaning, and child care. As we shall see in this chapter there has been progress in all these directions since 1949, but the reports thus far have been disappointing to Chinese women; the progress has also been disappointing from the perspective of socialist theory.

THE CONFUCIAN HERITAGE: BEING A PROPER CHINESE WOMAN

The liberation of women from the centuries of Confucian-based oppression was one of the major platforms of the intellectual revolution that began in China in the second decade of the twentieth century.[7] The subjugation of women provided the young radicals of the May Fourth Movement with a powerful symbol of everything they loathed about Confucianism. The "woman problem" (*funu wenti*) became one of the most emotionally charged issues of the time, and in fact it has even been suggested that the feminist issue "radicalized many of the future Chinese Communist leaders before their conversion to Marxism-Leninism."[8]

Although few could argue that the position of women in China has not improved significantly since 1949, it is clear that the May Fourth goal of full equality for women has not been achieved. The facts speak reasonably clearly on this issue, particularly if we focus on three of the themes that are most amenable to measurement, namely, educational achievements, status in the labor force, and participation in politics.

School

The gap between the amount of education received by men and by women in China has declined significantly throughout the twentieth century. Among a sample of Hong Kong expatriates, for example, for those who began school before 1918 the male/female difference in the length of schooling was more than six years, but for those who started school after 1958, the difference was less than half a year.[9] However, it is important to qualify this observation. In the first place, although schooling opportunities for Chinese women appear to be greater than they are in other developing countries in Asia, they still fall below those in the countries China would like to be compared with, the European socialist states and the capitalist societies of Europe and North America (see Table 11.1). The proportion of China's women in tertiary education is lower than it is in most other countries, including the poorest Asian nations such as India and Bangladesh. It is apparent that there is still far from equal access for women to universities and other institutions of higher learning in China. In 1986, for example, only one-quarter of all students in Chinese universities and colleges were women, although the percentage appears to have risen slightly in the following years.

At the other end of the academic ladder, the evidence is even worse. In a study of 416 adults aged between eighteen and thirty-nine, for example, Margery Wolf reported that the illiteracy rate was eleven times higher for women than for men (22 percent versus 2 percent), and only 45 percent of the women in her study reached middle school, compared to 68 percent of the men.[10] As expected, the illiteracy rates were much higher among older people—75 percent for the women and 21 percent for the men; and only 7 percent of the women over forty years old had reached middle school. Wolf's data also indicated the existence of a wide gap between urban and rural areas in terms of educational opportunities, and the differences were even greater for girls than for boys. What this suggested is that although girls in the countryside today have greater access to schooling than ever

before, their parents are far less likely to allow them to stay in school. One of Wolf's respondents in the countryside told her why this is the case: "With no self-consciousness at all, he explained that girls were simply better at other things, such as cooking and feeding pigs, so their parents preferred to keep them at home. Besides, he said, they marry into other families so people are reluctant to waste too much money educating them."[11]

Work

In absolute terms women have fared much better in the labor force, to the extent that for younger women there is almost equal participation with men. Again older women, who are less likely to have received training and education in the past, are not as well represented in the labor force (see Table 11.2). In total women constitute 48 percent of the labor force in China, a figure that is significantly higher than that in other poor Asian countries (28 percent), in capitalist countries (33 percent), and even in other socialist states (44 percent).[12]

Labor force participation rates of this magnitude for women obviously represent greater opportunities, but working outside the home is an economic necessity rather than a matter of choice for many women. The result is that most Chinese women now find themselves laboring under the double burden of working and running a household.[13] In addition, the evidence shows that urban Chinese women are more concentrated in lower paying jobs than men, and in jobs that are generally low

Table 11.1 Comparative Data on Female Enrollments in Schools at Different Levels, late 1970s (in Percentages)

	Primary	Secondary	Tertiary
China	45	41	24
9 European socialist states	48	48	41
19 European/ American capitalist states	49	44	34
15 Asian Developing states	46	39	29

Source: M. K. Whyte and W. L. Parish, 1984, *Urban Life in Contemporary China* (Chicago: University of Chicago Press), p. 200, Table 21. Reprinted by permission.

Table 11.2 Proportion of Urban Men and Women Employed, by Age (in Percentages)

Age	Women	Men
10-19	21	19
20-29	93	93
30-39	94	97
40-49	89	98
50-59	73	99
60-64	20	38

Source: M. K. Whyte and W. L. Parish, 1984, *Urban Life in Contemporary China* (Chicago: University of Chicago Press), p. 200, Table 22. Reprinted by permission.

in status, with fewer fringe benefits and considerably less opportunity for upward mobility.[14] Among the Hong Kong emigrés, women earned, on average, 77 percent of what the men earned, although that varied by age, with younger women generally earning more. In Wolf's sample (within the PRC), the women earned 72 percent of the men's wages, averaging Y 546 per year.[15] It is difficult to compare these statistics with information from other countries, but it appears that compared with men, Chinese women are probably no worse off than their counterparts elsewhere.[16]

Politics

In the world of politics it is not uncommon nowadays to find women at all levels of the hierarchy in China, but with some notable exceptions, few women reach high positions. This situation is not atypical of other socialist countries: For example, 11 percent of the members of the CCP Central Committee in the late 1970s were women, compared with an average of 9 percent in European socialist states.[17] As in the world of work in general, Chinese women in political jobs tend to be unevenly clustered at the bottom of the hierarchy. They have a virtual monopoly on the administrative posts in street-level organizations, heading residents' and neighborhood committees, important but often intensely unpopular and poorly paid work.

On balance, therefore, there is no strong support for the Engels-Marx theory that greater participation in the labor force will ultimately result in complete equality for women. As a number of feminist scholars have suggested in recent years, the CCP, after its radical

beginnings, has dragged its heels on the issue of gender equality. The Party has used labor force statistics to create the impression that giant steps have been taken on the gender issue, but in fact relatively little has been done to improve the position of women in Chinese society. In spite of its radical feminist roots in the 1920s, the CCP became fairly conservative on women's issues in the 1930s and has remained that way ever since. The usual explanation for this is that the Party did not want to do anything that would damage its support in the countryside. That support was strongest among the rural patriarchs who dominated village life throughout China.[18] The result was that although some of the worst aspects of Confucian suppression of women were abolished (such as concubinage and bound feet), the Communists never launched any frontal attacks on the structure of patriarchal authority in the rural areas. Therefore, even after the revolution in 1949, the two major stanchions of local authority structure—patrilocal marriages and the entrenched division of labor—have never been substantially challenged.[19]

As some of the evidence discussed here illustrates, women in China have made significant gains, but they have done so in the position of "subordinate daughters" rather than as "equal sisters of fraternal Communist men."[20] Chinese women have managed to achieve at least as much if not more than women elsewhere in the world—greater labor force participation, better access to education, and less occupational segregation. In spite of these gains in a country that has been dominated for so long by traditions of male superiority, the revolution that promised women

Figure 11.1 Cartoon depicting the stereotypical view of women in China and endorsing the idea that women are better off with a male partner. Source: China Now, No. 130 (May), p. 23; reprinted by permission.

patriarchal biases. Women are still defined as a commodity in China, and this is illustrated by the official response to the upsurge of female infanticide after the imposition of the one-child policies. The official newspaper *China Youth News* reported that "if female infanticide is not stopped quickly, in twenty years a serious social problem may arise."[22] It was clear from the report that the problem was not that baby girls were being murdered but that in the future there would not be enough women around to be wives. Once again we are reminded that Chinese women over the centuries have been defined, and have come to define themselves, by their relationships. They are first and foremost wives, or mothers, or daughters.

The Chinese revolution has broken its promise to women. The more optimistic feminists like Margery Wolf suggested that the gender revolution has only been "postponed," and that the path toward liberation can once again be cleared. She said, "Revolutions are made, not delivered in a package; women must make their own revolution."[23] As we shall see, however, it is difficult to imagine how this can be the case, particularly in light of some of the economic reform policies that have worked, inadvertently or otherwise, to close the door to women's liberation even further. As Wolf herself pointed out, in the 1980s a Chinese woman was still expected to be "the good wife and devoted mother," a role she has been playing for centuries.[24]

MARRIAGE AND THE FAMILY IN CHINA

In feudal China, the patriarchal family system went hand in hand with arranged marriages, male chauvinism and indifference to women's wants and feelings.[25]

Marriage and the family were important concerns of the Chinese government after the 1949 revolution.[26] One of the earliest pieces of legislation was the Marriage Law of 1950, which abolished arranged marriages; restricted payments for brides as well as much of the ritual and ceremony associated with marriages; prohibited concubinage, foot binding, and child marriages; and provided greater access to divorce. "In effect the . . . Law not only put an end to the feudal marriage code

so much has actually delivered them very little (see Figure 11.1). Even if the Chinese had been able to bring about total income equality between men and women, female subordination, especially in the countryside, would not have been changed significantly. The reason for this is that the subjugation of women in the Chinese village rests on ancient principles of kinship organization and family formation. Even after four decades of socialism, there is no evidence that patriarchy is losing its grip in the countryside. It is still the case that "in China a woman's life is . . . determined by her relationship to a man, be he father or husband, not by her own efforts or failures."[21]

The leaders of the Communist party may have genuinely wanted to relieve women of this patriarchal burden, but they have been unable to do so largely because of their own but also encouraged marriages founded on mutual affection."[27] Three decades later the new Marriage Law of 1981 retained the basic spirit of the earlier law, while extending some of its provisions. Later marriages were to be officially encouraged; men and women were supposed to enjoy equal status in the home; both partners were to share the responsibility of caring for their parents and their children; and divorce was to be granted in cases of "complete alienation" even if only one party felt it was necessary.[28] It is useful to review the progress that was made in some of these areas during the four decades since the revolution and, more specifically, during the 1980s.

Matchmaking and Mate Selection

As a general rule, the age at which people marry rises as a country modernizes, and for this reason it is no surprise to find that since 1980 Chinese couples have been marrying later.[29] Government pressure to delay marriage as a form of birth control, exerted through work units and residents' committees, has contributed to this trend. There are other practical reasons for marrying later in contemporary China: Low wages make it difficult for many people to save; there is a chronic shortage of housing for young families; and more young people than ever before are participating in higher education.

The new laws were intended to sweep away the tradition of arranged marriages, replacing them with marriages based on free choice and true feelings of affection between the partners.[30] The evidence suggests that movement in these directions has been very gradual. In the 1950s and 1960s, for example, many marriages were still "partly arranged" through the mediating work of go-betweens. Among the Hong Kong emigrés, 44 percent of the couples in post-1958 marriages had been introduced by others, usually their parents.[31] Although marriages in China are still not the result of an entirely free culture of "dating," surveys conducted in China's largest cities show that with the passage of time, courtship patterns have changed in a number of ways (see Table 11.3):

- The proportion of couples introduced by relatives has fallen considerably but still represents more than one in five of all marriages.

- The proportion of couples introduced by friends or colleagues has increased significantly, to about one-half in some cases.
- About one-third of the couples became acquainted as a result of their own efforts.

Even in the cities, however, it is still difficult for young Chinese people to find the opportunities to meet others. There are relatively few places where young people can go to do their courting, and in spite of the recent changes in attitude, there is still a strong sentiment that young people, especially women, should not "play the field" too much. "Pairing up" and dating on a regular basis is often interpreted as a permanent relationship and one that will generally end with marriage (see Figures 11.2 and 11.3).[32] The dominance of the work unit in Chinese urban life has prevented many young people from having an active social life. The units tend to be isolated, requiring that people both live and work in a specific area, thus limiting their opportunities for meeting people apart from those they work with. The result is that a lot of public matchmaking still occurs, with meetings arranged by friends, fellow workers, and family members.

The major difference today is that there is no longer any compulsion involved in the matchmaking. Nevertheless, it is clear that considerable pressure is exerted on many young people to make a "good" marriage choice or to move quickly while they are still young—a consideration usually more important for women than men. The pressure this can put on young people is illustrated in the story "Phoenix Eyes" by Chen Jiangong. The hero's mother is desperate to find a match for her son. He is a miner who works underground, and in a largely sex-segregated workplace he is obviously unlikely to meet girls of his own age. The girls he does meet are usually unwilling to consider anyone with so lowly a job. The son, Xiaoliang, has developed an inferiority complex after several abortive attempts to meet suitable girls. He is tired of the constant matchmaking and he refuses to take it seriously, which only makes matters worse. On one occasion, Xiaoliang's grandmother arranges for a beautiful girl (Phoenix Eyes—"double eyelids, delicate skin") to visit the boy's home, but by this time he has convinced himself that no self-respecting

Table 11.3 How Partners Met, pre- and post-1949 (Beijing, Shanghai, and Chengdu)

	\% of Total Who													
	Had Arranged Marriages			Were Introduced by Relatives			Were Introduced by Friends			Made Acquaintance on Own			Total No.		
	B	S	C	B	S	C	B	S	C	B	S	C	B	S	C
Pre-1949	35.3	34.6	18.9	32.3	26.6	34.3	23.7	18.4	43.3	4.3	20.0	3.6	232	289	111
Post-1949	4.1	3.8	1.1	17.1	22.6	20.9	56.8	37.8	47.1	21.5	34.8	30.9	387	500	278

Source: Adapted from Wu Benxue, 1987, "The Urban Family in Flux," in *New Trends in Chinese Marriages and the Family* (Beijing: Women of China), pp. 28-29.

woman would consider him a good prospect for marriage. As he says to the matchmaker who brings Phoenix Eyes to his home: "It's very kind of you to take the trouble to come all this way, and I'm sorry to disappoint you. I'll tell you what: you find me a girl so ugly even her grandmother can't bring herself to love her and I'll consider the matter settled. The girl you have picked out is not for me. She is reserved for section chiefs, party secretaries, or their sons."[33]

Xiaoliang's barbed comment contains more than a kernel of truth, and in spite of the stated aims of the Marriage Laws, there is evidence that mate selection in China is still governed by instrumentalist considerations, especially wealth, security, and status. In the materialistic 1980s this has become increasingly the case, and there is widespread evidence that prospective brides are able to "raise their price," often demanding a range of electrical goods and furniture from their spouse. The advice given to young women is still the same as it always was: "If it is 30 yuan [his salary], don't consider it; if 50 yuan, examine his appearance; and if 100 yuan, run after him."[34] The only difference is that today the stakes are much higher—the principle has not changed at all.

In spite of the overwhelming evidence pointing toward an increasingly functional basis for mate selection, there is some evidence pointing in the other direction. The results of a survey conducted in Chengdu in 1983 show that young Chinese people are now likely to be "looking for qualities that en-

courage mutual affection" in their prospective mates[35] (see Table 11.4). Money and status, according to this survey, were no longer important considerations, especially compared to considerations of character and moral qualities. There is still a difference between men and women in the characteristics they consider to be important in their spouse. A woman is likely to be more concerned with the personality of her husband; whereas a man is more interested in the physical appearance of his wife as well as her cooking and housekeeping skills.[36]

These conclusions indicate a major change in marriage behavior, but we need to bear in mind the discrepancy between the survey data (what young people say they are looking for) and the empirical evidence of greater materialism in modern marriages.[37] As with much of the research conducted in the social sciences, there are many other studies that can provide contradictory data. It is clear, however, that the major criteria for mate selection have changed dramatically in China since 1949. An in-depth study of ninety-eight Shanghai couples married at different eras during the four decades of the PRC showed evidence of this. Women married during the Cultural Revolution reported that their ideal mate would be selected along rational and highly politicized lines:

- He should be of a "higher" political status than she.
- He should have "good" connections.

Figure 11.2 A couple in a Canton park: Some years ago such a scene would have been extremely rare.

- He should be from a worker, peasant, or government official's family.[38]

In Mao's China, the break with the traditions of the past was most poignantly demonstrated by the wedding itself. This is nicely illustrated in Wang Meng's story "Anecdotes of Chairman Maimaiti," which is about a rural couple who are to be married. They asked a local cadre to describe what a truly socialist wedding would be like. The answer surprised them:

> It means reciting Mao's quotations; it means listening to speeches by leading Party officials . . . it means that the bride and bridegroom make three bows to the portrait of Chairman Mao, one bow to all the officials present, and one last bow to each other. It means no dowry and no bridal gifts; and newly-weds give each other gifts of the precious red book [Mao's quotations], the precious portrait [of Mao], a

hoe, a sickle, and a dung raker. It means no fun and games; the bridegroom must go water the fields on his wedding night, opening up and sealing off irrigation channels, and the bride must make forty wooden sign boards in red and yellow carrying inscriptions of the quotations.[39]

All of this probably seemed foolishly anachronistic to young people thinking about getting married in the more materialistic 1980s. The women in the Shanghai study made it quite clear what they were looking for when they thought about their partner. Ideally, he should be one of the following: clever and clearly skillful in his work; a capable young factory director, manager, or administrator; or a young scientist or technologist.

Sex, Love, and the Revolution

It is interesting to speculate whether these changes have been accompanied by changes

Figure 11.3 Two young soldiers relaxing together in Banpo village, Shaanxi Province: Expressions of affection between two young people of the same sex were until recently far more common than between young men and women.

in the more intimate aspects of the relationships between men and women in China. We might expect to find that with increasing Westernization, young people in China are becoming more sexually active before marriage and that a greater proportion of marriages are based on Western notions of "romantic love" than has traditionally been the case. It seems likely, however, that the instrumentalist underpinnings to matchmaking in China, whether performed by family members or official agencies, has produced a somewhat blasé attitude toward marriage among young people. In difficult times one should "make do" with a suitable match, rather than wait for the perfect love. Obviously not all young people are happy about this prospect. Wenwen, the leading character in Wang Anyi's story "And the Rain Patters On," for example, has a very "acceptable" boy introduced to her by a friend. He has a university education

and extremely good prospects, but Wenwen simply does not love him. She is repelled by the whole business of matchmaking because it reduces love and marriage to the status of a contest. "Both parties come to the starting line and at the sound of a starting gun they are off and running: meet-get-to-know-each-other-marriage."[40] Wenwen is hoping desperately for a dashing young prince to come and sweep her off her feet. "In her heart love was like an unpainted canvas, a soundless song. This was the purest of beauty, a boundless beauty, a beauty she could not be without."[41]

Much of the evidence about the nature of personal relationships in China remains very sketchy. A number of Western observers have noted a tendency toward greater openness about sex and a greater degree of what the Chinese still refer to as "promiscuity," but it would be unwise to leap to any conclusions

Table 11.4 Criteria for Choosing a Spouse (Chengdu Survey Data, 1983)

	Men's First Choice (No.)	Women's First Choice (No.)	% of First Choices (No.)
Sincerity, kindness, honesty, and integrity	160	220	61.1
Similar character and interests	41	44	13.6
Diligence and ambition	21	31	8.3
Stature and physical appearance	30	10	6.4
Extensive knowledge, promising future	6	25	4.9
Good housekeeping skills; kind, gentle disposition	22	0	3.5
Prestigious occupation and high status	1	3	0.6
High salary or wealthy family	4	0	0.6
Others[a]	3	3	0.9

[a]Examples included financial help from relatives overseas; Party membership; official job; extensive connections.

Source: Adapted from Wu Benxue, 1987, *New Trends in Chinese Marriage and the Family* (Beijing: Women of China, 1987), pp. 32-33.

about Chinese standards of morality: "For all these hints of debauchery . . . the Chinese remain a straitlaced people. An open-air dance . . . in Chengdu had a notice at the entrance forbidding couples to dance cheek-to-cheek."[42] Lynn Pan spoke with a Chinese gynecologist who reported that in his experience the vast majority of young people in China still have only a dim notion of sex. Pan concluded that even in the late 1980s, "premarital sex is not allowed . . . when it happens [it] is vehemently denounced as immorality."[43]

The popularity of explicit portrayals of sex in some recent books and films can be interpreted as evidence of changing views on moral issues in China, although some of the more explicit works, such as Zhang Xianliang's *Half of Man Is Woman* and Yu Luojin's *A Chinese Winter's Tale*, are difficult to obtain in China and are probably still officially banned by the government. It is possible that in the era of repression after the events of 1989 and the criticism of all sources of "spiritual pollution" from the West, there will be a re-

surgence of censorship in the world of literature and art in China.

In a survey of 997 Beijing families conducted in 1985, there was some evidence of more liberal or Westernized views on sex. Fewer than two-thirds of the respondents said they were opposed to premarital sex, compared to four-fifths in 1982, and only one in five of the respondents aged under thirty considered marital fidelity to be important.[44] These sorts of findings are interpreted with considerable dismay by the authorities. Sexual "promiscuity" and the erosion of traditional moral values are interpreted as further symptoms of the creeping "spiritual pollution" from Hong Kong and the West.

Divorce and Morality in the New China

The liberalization of the divorce law in China was considered to be a crucial part of the overall effort to improve the quality of women's lives. It represented an acceptance that the long-term suffering of women who were stuck in unhappy and loveless marriages did not have to be perpetuated. In spite of this, public opinions on divorce in China have changed very slowly, and divorced women are still likely to be treated with contempt. Divorce is seen as a last resort, frowned on, and discouraged, and most couples are required to seek extensive mediation before taking such a step.

The experiences of divorced and widowed women have been the theme of a new strand of literature being produced by Chinese women writers in the 1980s. One of the best known of these women, Zhang Jie, has documented the humiliation and constant haranguing that women living alone are still exposed to within their neighborhoods.[45] Within the family, the pressure on divorcées and widows may be even stronger. In Zhang Xian's story "The Widow," the woman in question is expected to remain faithful to her deceased husband and to give up any rights to happiness in the future. She recalls an ancient tale about the "coins of chastity" that describes the behavior expected of her by her grown-up children:

> In order to overcome her feelings of emptiness and loneliness, a widow tossed a hundred coins onto the floor every night, then turned out the light and groped around on the floor picking them up one by one. By the time they were all back in her purse she was finally tired enough to go to bed and fall asleep. And that's how she spent her nights right up till the day she died, letting a hundred coins, shiny from being rubbed countless times, stand as proof of her bitterly attained virtue. She died with a clear conscience and a sense of pride.[46]

The new laws and the changing times have produced two distinct "waves" in the pattern of divorces in China since 1949. Immediately after the 1950 law, thousands and perhaps millions of divorces were granted to women who had married under the old patriarchal, oppressive system. Afterwards, the divorce rate dropped back to its normal rate, much lower than that in most Western countries. In the 1980s, especially after the 1981 law was passed, divorces began to rise again.[47] The traditionally conservative response to such a trend among the Chinese leadership is to assume it is caused by the importation of "bourgeois" practices from the West.

Part of the rise in the divorce rate after 1981 was the result of reapplications from couples who had previously been denied a divorce. In addition, many couples applied for the dissolution of marriages that were politically desirable during the 1960s and 1970s, but in which the partners were basically incompatible. Under the new law such marriages could be dissolved much more easily than in the past. The changing attitude to divorce in China in the 1980s might also have been reflecting some of the changes in the economic system. "It is not surprising that relations between people are . . . changing, as all seek to maximize the benefits according to themselves personally through this shift in development strategy. In the sphere of divorce this can manifest itself in selfish or mercenary behavior."[48]

In the 1980s individuals were allowed and even encouraged to follow their own chosen paths in the economic sphere, and it could be that divorce is also being seen as an entitlement. However, over and above what the law stated about the grounds for divorce from a strictly legal perspective, society in general and the courts in particular were still biased by the double standard of morality that persisted in China. In the past it was easy for a court to define "immoral behavior" because the norms were clearly stated in political terms—divorce was seen as a "bourgeois" act that threatened the viability of the socialist family.[49] In the 1980s the definitions tended to be more liberal, but with the law being not nearly so clear-cut as it had been, the door was open for considerable antidivorce sentiment. It is reasonable to assume that the political crackdown in the summer of 1989 might also have brought with it a new wave of moral repression, which would put the clock back even further on the issue of women's liberation in China.

The Chinese Family in the 1990s

Family life in China has changed considerably since 1949. Modern families tend to be smaller as a result of the new birth-control policies as well as the general evolutionary trends typical in a society that is modernizing and urbanizing rapidly. In China, as in the rest of the world, the "conjugal" family is gradually replacing the "extended" family, particularly in the cities. The Chinese claim with some pride that, in spite of these trends, there is very little evidence of the breakdown of family life that is so apparent in both the Third World and in the underclass ghettoes of cities in many developed countries (especially the United States). To some extent this is a result of the deliberate urban and regional policies that have been implemented in China since 1949 (see Chapters 8 and 9). It may also have something to do with Chinese culture itself, in which the patriarchal kinship system and the almost fanatical desire to maintain close family ties have helped to keep the Chinese family together through times of major political upheaval and economic austerity. The sociodemographic characteristics of the Chinese city provide a sharp contrast from what is typical in the cities of most other poor nations around the world: the breakdown of family solidarity, early sex and marriage, promiscuity and prostitution, and the prevalence of female-headed households. In China the norm is for the traditional family to remain intact; sex and marriage are delayed; illegitimacy rates are low; and men still dominate family life.[50]

Family life is an issue about which Chinese women probably have mixed emotions. The strength of the traditional Chinese family, and the continued male dominance in all spheres of life, have helped to maintain social cohesiveness in the Chinese city as well as in the countryside, which is surely a positive development. However, at the same time the aspirations of Chinese women have effectively been stifled. Countless numbers of Chinese women are still trapped in unhappy marriages from which, for cultural reasons, they have very little chance of escaping. The density at which most urban families live; the lack of the labor-saving devices in the home that have come to be standard equipment elsewhere; and the pressures of promoting their children's welfare in an overcrowded and overcompetitive educational system—all add to the strains placed on women, for whom work at home begins only after a full day in the factory or at the office.

There has not been as much change in the Chinese family as most people might have predicted (or expected) in 1949. From the perspective of men therefore (and the Chinese government) this is probably perceived as a positive outcome, but for Chinese women and feminists around the world it is a bitter disappointment. The changes that have occurred are best described as "evolutionary" rather than "revolutionary," and the influence of socialism and the new Marriage Laws has been minimal. What holds the Chinese family together is an unwritten set of ancient cultural traditions that have been left largely intact after forty years under the Communists.

There is one way, however, in which socialism has made a contribution to family life, albeit a negative contribution. The modern Chinese family, especially the urban family, has had to be strong and resourceful in the face of the privations of life in Communist China. Family members cling to each other tenaciously in an effort to cope with the austerity of the socialist city and the oppression of the Chinese bureaucracy. For many people the state has become the enemy, a fact that has made it increasingly important for them to maintain their kinship and family ties as a way of surviving.

In the 1990s Chinese families will have to stick together, not so much because they want to, but because they need to in the face of continued austerity and the renewed threat of repression. The situation is very far removed from the romantic view of socialist family life that Marx and Mao had hoped for. The Chinese family today is still intact because it has to be: "Families may not provide a peaceful haven or a warm nest of human feelings for their members, but they are still the primary resources urbanites turn to for the cooperative efforts needed to cope with urban life."[51] The government has allowed and even encouraged this sort of family cohesiveness because, in most cases, it has served the Party's purposes. At other times, however, the government has acted swiftly and ruthlessly to break down the connectedness between family members. This has proved to be particularly useful for isolating "counterrevolutionary elements," and it was no doubt being used to round up the dissidents who were still on the run in 1990. The author Zhang Xianliang, himself a dissident during the Cultural Revolution, pointed out that this is by no means a new tactic. The long tentacles of the Party have always worked hard to tear apart the ancient bonds between Chinese people. Zhang wrote: "I consider that to be the greatest crime they have perpetrated. They've destroyed a sense of trust among men. Instead of building good intentions and a readiness to help one another, they've made men into wild animals."[52]

CONCLUSION: GENDER AND THE REFORM MOVEMENT

If a certain proportion of women were to return home [instead of working] things would be very different. Wives would have enough energy to make their families happy. . . . Husbands freed from household worries, would be able to devote all their energies to their work and study . . . very quickly there would be a highly-efficient, trained, disciplined and active work force. Our children would benefit from more maternal care . . . and there would be less delinquency.[53]

As this statement suggests, not everyone is happy about the near-full employment experienced by women in China. Some of the standard arguments for women staying at home were reiterated in the statement, but another argument had come to the forefront by the middle of the 1980s. The economic reform movement in both the cities and the countryside was based primarily on a desire to make the Chinese economy more efficient. It was evident that everywhere in China there was extensive overemployment. People were going out to work in the fields and the factories, but many of them simply did not have enough to do.[54]

In the new climate of greater economic efficiency, one predictable response has been a resurgence of discrimination against women in the workplace. Another has been for women to take themselves out of the work force voluntarily. "Returning home" has become a controversial issue: From the feminist perspective, it is a clear step backward, a return to the old subordination of women to men. "If women relinquish their right to employment, it amounts to giving up their rights to possessions and to their fair share of the wealth produced by a socialist economy. It means denying themselves the protection of socialist law and forsaking economic independence and autonomy."[55] From another perspective, however, "returning home" signals an end to the crippling "double burden" placed on the Chinese woman. As a rural woman observed: "When we finally got home at night [from the fields] men could throw themselves down on the brick bed, but we

had to cook, look after our old people and children, wash, mend, feed the chickens and pigs. Now things are much better, the men earn more. And someone is really needed at home. We're glad to come back to an easier life."[56]

The increase in rural prosperity in the 1950s has raised this issue in rural areas all over China. When a village experiences economic success, the absolute need for women to go out to work is reduced. The land is now being farmed by the most efficient households; new village enterprises provide relatively high paying jobs for male family members; and household "sidelines" have helped to boost family incomes. The effect of this has been a further challenge to the independence of rural women.

We have seen at various points throughout this book that a number of the government's policies implemented during the 1980s threatened some of the long-term aspirations of the Chinese people. Nowhere is this more true than in the area of women's issues. The family-planning policy, for example, is generally considered to be beneficial to women because it helps to free them from the onerous responsibilities associated with large families. However, the attempts to enforce compliance with the one-child policy have, as we saw in Chapter 7, had some odious consequences for women.

The birth-control policy also acted to strengthen the already dominant pattern of son preference in China, particularly among rural families. In other words, if only one child is allowed, most people want that child to be a boy. This feeling has been reinforced by the household responsibility system in the countryside. Sons promise greater labor power, and they can bring in extra workers to the family when they marry and have children. Daughters usually have to leave home to marry, depleting the family's labor force, and as a result they are unable to contribute to the future welfare and security of their parents.[57] The result is a further deterioration in the woman's position in the family. Baby girls are poorly treated (assuming they are allowed to survive). Wives are beaten and harshly criticized for their failure to deliver sons; their personal lives are subject to intensive surveillance and scrutiny; and in many cases they are forced to terminate pregnancies.

This raises a very important issue—can the Chinese government reduce this overwhelming preference for sons, a preference that is threatening to derail the one-child policy? At the present time, the government is simply trying to wipe out the resistance to the policy, rather than making any fundamental changes to bring about full gender equality. Only a few very feeble arguments have been put forward in favor of matrilocal marriages to replace the ancient custom of female exogamy. The current leaders consider such structural changes in rural society to be unnecessary. They deplore the continued existence of such degradations as wife beating and infanticide, but they prefer to believe that such practices are the result of "feudal remnants" and mistakes made by previous party leaders, especially Mao Zedong. What this suggests is that if the one-child policy is to remain in place, it may in the long run force the CCP to return to the agenda of women's liberation in China, to carry out finally the goals of the May Fourth Movement. At the present time, however, the position of China's rural woman is desperate. They continue to "carry the hoe outdoors, handle the pot indoors, and take a back seat in a meeting."[58] In addition they have to deal with the humiliating consequences of a birth-control policy sharply at odds with the dictates of a patriarchal system that appears to be as dominant as it has ever been.

The economic reforms may act to reinforce the subordinate position of women in both the countryside and the cities. In the collective economy women earned work-points as individuals; therefore they had their own sources of income, which gave them a modicum of independence from their husbands. Under the HRS, the household as a unit contracts with the collective or the production team, and invariably the contract is negotiated by the husband. "Now instead of reporting to the team leader for job assignments . . . a woman will be under the supervision of the male head of household. He will decide when she works, what she does, and whether she can take time off."[59] In the collective economy the women of the household had some control over the sideline activities, such as chickens, pigs, and the private plot. Although the income from such activities was not theirs alone, they had the power to organize and regulate such activities. By comparison, individual family enterprises are mostly male controlled,

and women are little more than hired hands—a phenomenon that could be disastrous for them. Not only are they losing their decision-making powers, but in the new cooperative and private economy, they are also likely to lose their individual paychecks, as well as health-care benefits and pensions.[60]

In all these areas, the independence of women in the family has been undercut. This has reinforced the traditionally low status of women that results from their position within the household as temporary adult strangers living in their husbands' homes. The Chinese press carries many stories about the great riches being earned by some women in sideline activities all over the country, but it is important to remember that in many cases rural women are laboring under sweatshop conditions: "Much sideline production is monotonous, isolated, undercapitalized, and, even by Chinese standards, poorly remunerated."[61]

The prosperity that has resulted from the economic reforms, in both rural and urban China, has further eroded the women's movement in China, in what amounts to a shift from "feminism" to "femininity." As a result of greater purchasing power, more openness, and higher levels of contact with the West, many contemporary Chinese women appear to have lost any real interest in either working or studying. They are choosing instead to focus most of their energies on their appearance: on clothes, makeup, and hairstyles (see Figures 11.4, 11.5, and 11.6). Associated with this is the increasing use of the female face and body in advertisements and posters, something commonplace in the West and in Hong Kong, but extremely rare in China until recently. Although this appears to be a superficial change, it may in fact reflect a more fundamental shift in attitudes. "The revival of feminine interests, set against the awareness of fewer educational and employment opportunities and the official stress on women's domestic role, has strengthened the traditional female vision of a desirable personal future: not one's . . . [personal] socio-economic advancement but marriage to a man who is on the pathway to success. . . . Indeed a higher education might be positively detrimental to a young woman's marriage prospects."[62]

There is also some evidence that traditional patterns of patriarchal kinship are being strengthened by the HRS. The private plots of

Figure 11.4 (left) Women and modernization in China: A smiling woman in men's work clothes on a propaganda poster of the early 1970s. Figure 11.5 (below) The more fashion-conscious and consumerist 1980s are reflected in an advertisement for women's clothes.

Figure 11.6 In the 1980s the shift from "feminism" to "femininity" was accompanied by the use of fashionable and attractive young women in advertisements. This picture accompanied an ad for a Beijing travel agency.

the newly contracting households tend to be in small, scattered strips, and cooperation within the village is needed to manage crop rotation, irrigation, and pest control. This has produced a greater degree of mutual aid than might have been expected, but much of it tends to be along kinship lines, thereby strengthening the male-based lineage associated with village life in the countryside, a development that is not likely to further women's interests.[63]

The newly found wealth of the household in many parts of rural China could have benefited women greatly as a result of the inheritance law that became effective in 1985.[64] As a result of rising incomes, the possessions of many families are now more extensive— houses are larger, and families can build up their supply of capital, including land. The new law appeared to promise women an equal share of this greater wealth, but as it turns out a woman who survives her spouse has to share the inheritance with her children and his parents. The greater the role played by such family members in the family economy, the greater will be their claim to the inheritance. This means that the children who supported their own parents would be well rewarded, and in China these are most often sons. In addition, women's rights to the household's means of production are lost if they leave their spouse through divorce. Clearly this works to discourage divorce even more than is normally the case in rural China.

Women in general will continue to benefit in financial terms from the rural reforms, but their status within the family has been seriously jeopardized. The examples described here illustrate the contradictory impact of policies in different spheres and the apparent failure to consider the ramifications of new policies at the stage of implementation.[65] When the household economy allowed both greater prosperity and greater independence from the collective authorities, the response was a rise in the birthrates, as we noted in Chapter 7. In this case the introduction of a "pronatalist" economic policy occurred at almost exactly the same time as the introduction of an "antinatalist" birth-control policy. The new population policy brought out into the open some of the more egregious forms of discrimination against women, especially in rural China. In that sense women benefited from the policy, but the conflict with the new economic reforms has threatened the success of the one-child policy and also negated the benefits to modern women of having smaller families. At the same time the government, and the male hierarchy at all levels of administration (even down to the villages), assumed an unprecedented increase of social control over the lives and reproductive actions of individual women.[66]

The Delivery of Urban Services

What does it matter if it is difficult for me to make a telephone call. When I shall die, my son will try. When he shall die, my grandson will continue to try.

—Tiziano Terzani[1]

INTRODUCTION: COLLECTIVE CONSUMPTION AND GOVERNMENT LEGITIMACY

Until relatively recently, even in the most market-oriented societies, responsibility for the provision of basic urban services lay almost entirely with the government. It was assumed that without direct intervention from the state there could be no guarantee that health care, education, services for the elderly, and the whole range of urban support services, such as public transportation, roads, parks, and utilities, would be provided.[2] Because of the scale of the operations involved, the importance of the services provided, and the need to keep the costs as low as possible, the general consensus was that the private sector either could not be trusted to provide such services equitably or would not be interested in doing so. As a result, a sizable portion of collective-service provision, for better or worse, became the responsibility of the state.

In recent years we have witnessed the erosion of the arguments favoring public-service provision in many capitalist societies. The "commodification" of the services involved and the "privatization" of their delivery have now become standard practice.[3] In noncapitalist societies, however, the role of the state in the provision of public services has remained dominant, especially in the absence of any viable alternatives. This situation is beginning to change slowly. In China the examples provided from overseas and the ongoing experiment with economic reforms in the 1980s have helped to generate some lively debates about privatization. As we shall see in this chapter, progress along the private path has thus far been limited, and as with all of the reforms in China, the shadow of the political crisis in 1989 casts even further doubt on such developments.

The standard argument in socialist societies was that the legitimacy of the government was largely dependent on its ability to ensure an equitable distribution of goods and services to its people. In other words it was essential for the Communist party "to devise a system of distribution that would enable even poorer families to get reliable access to the food, housing, schooling, health care, and other resources needed for a decent life."[4]

When the Communists first reentered the cities in 1949, one of their priorities was to restore them to some semblance of order. Food had to be put on the table regularly; the people had to have decent and safe housing; and access to education and medical services had to be assured. After several decades of struggle, the majority of Chinese people had cast their lot with the CCP, and it was important for the local Party organizations to prove to them they had made the

213

correct choice. In Canton, for example, the Communists took over a city that was in tremendous disarray after the departure of the Nationalists (see Chapter 8).[5]

The immediate task of the Communists was to win the cooperation of the local residents. On a day-to-day basis the goal was simply "to keep the schools in session, the factories in operation ... [and] the government offices open."[6] To ensure that goods and services were equally available to *all* of the people, the CCP followed a course that would gradually result in the abolition of market forces in the cities, replacing them with a system of centralized allocation.

At this point the Chinese government encountered a true dilemma. The national defense of China and the reconstruction of its war-ravaged economy dictated an emphasis on "production first," in both the cities and the countryside. To that extent, the provision of goods and services for consumption would have a lower priority, at least in the short run. The CCP was walking a tightrope, because the decision to delay present consumption and service provision ran the risk of widespread dissent.

It was in the cities that the CCP felt it most urgent to effect the transformation over to production. Canton was a prime example. The city was seen by the Communists as a hotbed of "bourgeois" corruption that needed to be swept clean. Mao Zedong had warned the Chinese people that they should expect a lengthy struggle, and many of them were prepared to make some sacrifices. By the time of his death, however (nearly three decades later), the credibility of such a request had been sorely stretched. Consumption of essentials, such as food and clothing, and service delivery had been neglected for more than twenty-five years. In spite of the determined efforts to increase the supply of basic urban utilities (see Table 12.1), there were shortages of almost everything that would help to ease the flow of daily life: consumer goods, housing, transportation, libraries, cinemas, and parks. In most cases the quality of what was available was questionable and access to it was tortuous. There was food but the quantity and quality were variable; there were buses, but they were decrepit, crowded, and dangerous; there was housing, but it was cramped, poorly designed, and often impossible to obtain.

Even making a telephone call could become an ordeal, as the epigraph for this chapter suggests. An old man, after trying unsuccessfully to make a phone call at several phone booths in his neighborhood, eventually admitted defeat. Philosophically, he recalled the ancient folktale, "Old Fool Who Moved the Mountain," which implies that everything comes to him who waits, but very slowly! Anyone who has ever tried to make a telephone call in China will appreciate the irony and the humor in this situation.

Fox Butterfield, a *New York Times* reporter, has gathered an amusing collection of anecdotes describing the difficulties of everyday living in the Chinese city. A newlywed couple discovered some of the trials and tribulations that would never occur to Westerners:

> Buying furniture, taking a bath, finding a house— require all the connections, luck, and artifices that [the] Chinese can muster ... to purchase three of the most essential items, a double bed, a folding dinner table, and a dresser cabinet, you had to have a special ration coupon issued only to newly married couples. To prevent cheating, you also had to present your marriage certificate, which the furniture shop stamped on the back. Even so, it took a six-month wait to get a bed.[7]

It comes as no surprise to find that many city dwellers have resigned themselves either to the black market or to a permanent use of the *guanxi* network to acquire the goods and services they need. "In this environment many began to lose faith in the distribution system and to feel that one had to pursue special angles to get your needs met. One had to cultivate special ties with gatekeepers guarding access to various goods and services or with truck drivers or others who were able to go around the barriers in the system."[8]

The long-term consequences of such activities were serious. Time and energy were needed to keep attuned to the underground economy, and this effort acted as a drain on the productive work that was supposed to be the focus of life in a socialist society. Naturally people became cynical about the long-term benefits of socialism because in order to survive, it was necessary to bend the law. In circumstances such as these, it was difficult to blame the people for thinking only of their own needs rather than of the overall good of society.

Table 12.1 The Provision of Basic Urban Utilities (1957, 1978, and 1987)

	1957	1978	1987
Population with access to tap water (%)	57.0	81.0	87.0
Buses (per 10,000 population)	1.0	3.3	4.6
Sewer pipes (kms per 10,000 population)	1.4	2.5	3.6
Population with access to natural gas (%)	1.5	13.9	32.6
Parks and green areas (hectares per 10,000 population)	4.3	10.6	21.6

Source: *China Statistical Yearbook 1988* (Beijing: State Statistical Bureau of the PRC, 1988), p. 751.

The inadequacies of the distribution system also had an indirect influence on patterns of social interaction. Sometimes this meant putting up with obnoxious people because they were well connected. One family in a Cheng Naishan story, "No. 2 and No. 4 of Shanghai," had a tiresome uncle and they would rather have nothing to do with him. The problem was that the uncle had extraordinarily good *guanxi*, and if they were to live well they simply could not manage without him. "This in-law . . . was a real nuisance, yet the painful truth was that . . . [he] was indispensable. From big things like plane and boat tickets to little things like movie tickets or a TV purchase coupon, not to mention arranging hotel dinner parties or even getting a taxi, without Ahwei none of this was possible. So Ahwei . . . made himself completely at home. . . . He even addressed the family . . . with glib intimacy."[9]

In spite of the apparent knack the Chinese have for coping with all manner of adversity, it is not surprising that, in 1978, after three decades of deprivation, many city dwellers were ready to demand some changes. It is generally assumed that the new regime headed by Deng Xiaoping correctly perceived this level of discontent after Mao's death and promised the long-suffering Chinese access to the stuff of their dreams. "Deng and his practical-minded colleagues understood better than Mao that centuries of living with scarcity had bred a strong strain of materialism . . . a craving only intensified by the shortages of recent years."[10]

As we have seen in earlier chapters, the new economic reforms quickly brought some relief to the long-suffering city dwellers in the 1980s, but life in the city remained tedious and trying. All this was made worse by the drabness of the urban landscape in China. To outsiders in particular, the Chinese city is an exceptionally grim place. On one of his many journeys through the countryside, Paul Theroux expressed his contempt in no uncertain terms. Arriving by train in Changsha, near Mao's birthplace, in Hunan Province, Theroux must have been pining for his native Boston: "The words 'a Chinese city' had acquired a peculiar horror for me, like 'Russian toilet,' or 'Turkish prison.' In the cold rain of winter, with the cracked and sooty apartment houses, the muddy streets, the skinny trees and dark brown sky, Chinese cities are at their very worst."[11]

It is much more important, however, to determine how the Chinese people themselves feel about the quality of life in their cities. In 1989 most Western journalists reported that discontent with life in the cities had contributed to the demonstrations by students and workers. In spite of the benefits of reform, life in the city for many people had deteriorated, especially for those who had drifted in from the countryside in search of work.[12]

QUALITY OF LIFE IN THE CHINESE CITY

Although it is difficult to make valid assessments of something as subjective as the quality of life, there have been two broad approaches to the topic within the social sciences. The first approach uses "objective" data to measure the availability of facilities and services that are thought to contribute to one's overall quality of life.[13] For example, if we compare city A with city B we may find that city A has far more schools, hospitals, and parks per capita. We can assume that for most people city A is a better place to live than city B. Obviously there are many dangers inherent in such a simplistic method of assessment, but it provides a rough guide for comparing the relative "livability" of different places. Data of this type can be useful for testing the general assumption that Chinese people prefer to live in larger rather than smaller cities. There is evidence from all around the world that the majority of people, if they are free to choose, would prefer to live in larger rather than smaller cities.

This issue can be boiled down into two questions: first, do larger cities offer greater access to urban services than smaller cities? and second, does that greater access result in higher levels of satisfaction for their residents? The first question is easier to answer than the second. If we focus on the variables that are traditionally thought to influence quality of life in the city, we see that with a couple of exceptions ("living space" and "cinemas/ theaters") there is a roughly linear relationship between city size and the per capita availability of urban services (see Table 12.2). If we are correct in assuming that a greater availability of such services contributes positively to urban "livability," then we have some indication that life may be more acceptable in China's larger cities than it is in the smaller cities.[14] Clearly this would help to explain why so many Chinese people express a preference for living in larger cities and of course why those cities have continued to grow rapidly in spite of the persistent attempts made by the government to restrict their size.[15]

To answer the second question it is necessary to explore the other major branch of quality of life studies, those involving "subjective" assessments of the satisfaction or dissatisfaction associated with urban living. To tap this source of information in China, we still have to rely heavily on journalistic accounts and individualized case studies. A useful source of data in recent years has been the publication of personal narratives, in which ordinary people tell the stories of their lives to Chinese or Western scholars. These books have provided some revealing snapshots of everyday life in China.[16]

As one might expect, the more the Chinese learn about life outside China, not only in the West but also in other Chinese communities such as Taiwan, Hong Kong, and Singapore, the more they come to realize the extent of their deprivation. One woman complained that the daily routine of her life in China was "just too hard." The search for what Westerners would consider the most mundane of services is an ongoing nightmare in the Chinese city. To illustrate her point she talked about what happens when a Chinese woman becomes pregnant. "Although you get free medical care you have to worry about finding a good doctor . . . after the baby is born, you have to look for nutritious foods. . . . Even ordering milk is difficult, because you need a hospital certificate. . . . After that you have to find a babysitter you can trust . . . [then] a good nursery. Most nurseries will only take fifty children, and usually there are 400 people who want to get their babies in."[17]

The legal response to shortages has been an elaborate network of rationing, but the Byzantine complexity of the rationing schemes often serves only to frustrate people even further. Coupons are needed for almost everything; if you lose your coupons, you could go hungry. If you need a new light bulb you may have to turn in the broken one to the authorities to get a new one. "Each bulb bears a serial number—those used in factories are different from those intended for home uses, and those sold in Peking are marked with a different sequence from those in other places. That way, you can't cheat and bring in a light bulb from anyplace but your home. If your bulb is stolen, you have to get a letter from the police before you can replace it."[18]

Another source of information about the quality of life in the Chinese city has been the short stories and novels that have proliferated in the post-Mao era. Much of this literature is set in contemporary urban China. In contrast to the unrealistically patriotic literature that was commonplace during the earlier years of the PRC, many of the new authors felt much freer in the 1980s to describe the details of their everyday lives—the houses they live in, the places where they work, and the harrowing details of trying to make ends meet.

Table 12.2 Indicators of Quality of Life in Chinese Cities, 1984

	China Avg.	2 mill.+	1-2 mill.	.5-1 mill.	200,000-500,000	< 200,000
			No. of Services per 10,000 People			
			City Size			
Books in public libraries	0.91	1.63	1.65	1.07	0.65	0.35
Clinics/ hospitals	3.94	5.30	4.21	4.65	3.76	2.79
Hospital beds	46.00	49.30	55.90	57.90	46.50	33.90
Doctors	34.80	49.20	46.10	41.40	30.90	22.00
Medical personnel	83.10	112.90	109.70	102.80	74.80	52.60
Cinemas/ theaters	0.19	0.13	0.13	0.19	0.21	0.23
Telephones per 1,000 persons	1.58	2.96	2.24	1.76	1.24	0.73
Public buses	2.20	4.93	3.66	2.44	1.40	0.65
Paved roads (kms per capita)	1.76	2.14	2.64	2.11	1.66	1.12
Sewage lines (kms)	1.54	2.37	2.54	1.86	1.34	0.72
Green space (m^2 per capita)	0.23	1.88	3.21	0.40	0.25	0.07
Living space (m^2 per capita)	4.89	4.84	4.95	4.89	4.86	4.97

Note: Per 10,000 population unless otherwise specified.

Source: Adapted from PRC State Statistical Bureau, 1985, *China: Urban Statistics* (London: Longman Group, Ltd.).

To get a feel for what everyday life might be like for the Chinese city dweller, many foreigners like to go for a ride on a bus. For some of them the jostling, the dirt, the noise, and the intense discomfort of bus travel provides a culturally rewarding experience, something they can describe in great detail to their friends at home. As a tourist it can be fun to be cheek by jowl with so many others for a short time, but on a daily basis, through winter and summer, with neither heating nor air-conditioning, the experience is probably less than enchanting. There can be no doubt in anyone's mind that most people would prefer to slip into the warmth, privacy, and security of their own car and drive themselves to work, if that were possible (see Figures 12.1 and 12.2). One of the new authors, Cheng Naishan, described the traffic scene in Shanghai, a city that is (in)famous for its crowded buses:

> The scene at the bus stop boggled the mind. Throngs of people clustered into several long, disorderly lines. . . . At long last a tandem bus came along, and people started swarming aboard in a confused mass. . . . 'Push! Push! Push!,' urged a woman in front of him [the hero]. Obviously schooled in the art of squeezing into Shanghai's crowded buses, the woman was snaking her way aboard with marvelous bodily contortion, when she let out a painful, 'Ouch!' as someone . . . accidentally jabbed her in the cheek with the sharp tip of his umbrella.[19]

These disparate sources of information all present a picture of acute dissatisfaction with

Figure 12.1 *A bicycle storage area in Canton where workers park their bicycles before taking the ferry across the Pearl River to their jobs.*

Figure 12.2 *Bicyclist transporting goods, an integral part of the haulage system in the intraurban economy.*

the way things are in the Chinese city. One worker reported, for example, that dealing with life from one day to the next was like planning out a battle strategy. "One family member goes out to buy rice, another coal, another vegetables, another meat."[20] By the end of the week they are all too jaded, physically and mentally, to enjoy their one day off. With a fine sense of irony this person asked how, after getting through such a week, "can we possibly have the strength to think of the four modernizations or carry them out" on the weekends?[21]

A common response to the extraordinary difficulties of everyday life in China is to become passively resigned to adversity. A worker riding on a crowded train expressed an air of helplessness when he said: "Life's like this train. If the station it gets to is Beidaihe [a popular seaside resort] you can have a great time. But if the station's just a hall in the desert with nothing to eat, nothing to drink and nobody around it's still your station. We didn't lay the track and we can't choose where to stop."[22]

Straddling the objective and the subjective approaches to the quality of life issue are some recent attempts to conduct survey research in China. Although such studies have been common in the West for many years, they came into fashion in China only in the late 1980s. It is difficult to know exactly how reliable are conclusions based on survey data, and this is particularly a problem with most of the Chinese studies, where the survey methods are not described in any detail. It is also difficult to know how to deal with the political bias because most official publications are unlikely to criticize urban governments by reporting that city dwellers are dissatisfied with local-services provision.

Numerous surveys have been conducted to determine how urban residents feel about their lives in general and specifically whether their lives have improved as a result of the recent reforms. The general consensus has been that people are supportive of the reforms but feel that change has been too slow in coming. A popular complaint was the inadequate and corrupt responses of middle-level officials (cadres) and bureaucrats to the changes. All of these are very "safe" responses, and (probably not coincidentally) they also reflect the government's concerns.[23] Longitudinal surveys conducted among urban families show that greater wealth has allowed higher levels of consumption and savings as well as an overall improvement in living standards.[24] Again it is difficult to assess how representative such conclusions are, and there is little or no information on the respondents' subjective evaluations of their lives.

One of the potential uses of such survey research is to influence municipal policy in the areas of service provision. In the city of Tianjin, for example, 1,000 families have been surveyed at random every year since 1983. The city government has pledged to respond to the issues that appear to be perennial problems. In 1983, for example, 680 of the families asked for better access to gas for cooking. This became a priority item, and by 1985, 680,000 families (70 percent of the city's total) were cooking with gas. In 1986 there was extensive criticism of Tianjin's state vegetable stores and those collectively run, and the response was to allow private enterprise a larger share of the business.[25]

SOME NEW TRENDS IN THE CHINESE CITY

Life in the Chinese city since 1949 has not been easy, and many people came to think of the urban reforms in the 1980s as a panacea. In many ways they were, but there were also some unexpected and often unwelcome results of city growth and higher levels of affluence.

Transient Workers

The new wealth experienced by some city dwellers resulted in a greater demand for leisure and recreational activities. Others, with families to support, required just the opposite. To make ends meet they needed to have someone at home, either to look after the children or to do chores, while they were out at work. In both cases this resulted in a greater demand for domestic helpers or "maids" (baomu or ayi—a combination babysitter and housemaid). This has come as a shock to many in a society where only a few years ago hiring someone to work for you was frowned upon. The trend coincided with the influx of young people into the cities from the countryside as a result of the agricultural reforms.[26] To some extent, therefore, this match between demand and supply was fortuitous—well-off city dwellers could find the help they needed, and transients found ways to support themselves in the city. Before long the whole process became institutionalized, and people could respond to advertisements in their local newspapers for maids—producing what amounted to a free market in cheap (and probably exploited) casual labor.

In a similar way, the urban boom of the 1980s attracted huge numbers of itinerant carpenters, bricklayers, and construction workers to the cities.[27] As the countryside continues to push out more and more of these surplus workers, the cities will have difficulty finding suitable homes and jobs for them and providing them with services. For these people, the quality of life in the city will be marginal. They will work, if they work at all, for low wages with no benefits; they will be culturally isolated and lonely; and they will probably end up living in squalor.

This is illustrated by the story of the "cobbler girls" in Beijing, of whom most have come from Zhejiang Province. They are attracted by the lure of the big city, but they usually find out very quickly that the streets are not paved with gold.[28] The story of one young woman who left her home in Zhejiang illustrates the problems. She is twenty years old and in search of a way to make a living. She arrived in Beijing with her suitcase and a stitching machine, but with no *guanxi* she found she could not get a permit to operate in the city. She was forced to set up shop in a drab suburb at the edge of town, making less than Y 150 a month, half of which went to covering her expenses. She lived with three other cobbler girls in a small dirt shack rented from a farmer. She knew ten other girls from her village (population of 1,000) who were also working as cobblers in Beijing, all of them with similar dreams. Her life was, by anyone's account, one of gloom and squalor, but she planned to stick it out until she had saved enough to go back to Zhejiang to get married.

In the coastal cities of south China the problem of migrant workers in search of urban employment is much worse than it is elsewhere. In Guangzhou (Canton), for example, the city's mayor has called for all migrants to be "forcibly put aboard trains" and sent back to their home provinces.[29] As this suggests there is clearly another side to the rising wealth in the countryside and the cities. The potential impact of large numbers of unemployed peasants in the cities, with no official food coupons and without urban registration cards, has become a nightmare for local city officials.

Transportation Dilemmas

The trappings of prosperity are highly sought after, but the other side of the picture needs to be considered. As we saw in Chapter 6, one major consequence of the economic reforms was the soaring rate of inflation, especially of food prices. The government's response was to hand out cash subsidies to many city residents, a policy that helped to divert the crisis but crippled the economy.[30] Another feature associated with a bustling economy and rising incomes has been a tremendous increase in motor vehicles on the roads, with some consequences familiar to Westerners. Because motor vehicle usage was so low until recently, the rate of increase in

the middle 1980s was dramatic—amounting to 16 percent more vehicles each year in Beijing and 20 percent in Guangzhou.[31] Although the total vehicular traffic on China's city streets is still low by international standards, the number of vehicles has grown at a far faster rate than the mileage of urban roads on which they can travel. It was estimated that the annual growth rate for bicycles and cars has been on the order of 10 percent per year since 1949, but the growth rate in road mileage has been 5 percent. The result is that large cities in China, in comparison to others around the world, have a very small proportion of their total land area devoted to roads.[32]

The most frightening aspect of this rate of growth is that it will continue, especially in light of the low level of private car ownership in China. As incomes rise, the Chinese will probably be quick to realize the enormous personal benefits to be gained by having their own cars. Plans call for an increase in production of domestic cars from 20,000 in 1987 to 159,000 by 1995; but the majority of vehicles are, and will continue to be, imported. The traditionally low level of spending on roads means that all these new vehicles will be jammed together with the growing armada of bicycles, buses, and commercial vehicles. There has been a frenzy of road construction in many of the larger cities in recent years, and plans have been made to build subways in some cities (currently they are in existence only in Beijing and Tianjin).

As the cities become increasingly congested, the buses, as the only viable method of traveling long distances, become more crowded and less punctual than ever. In 1983, for example, average travel-to-work times for the inner city and suburbs of Beijing were 44 minutes and 66 minutes; by 1986 these had increased to 60 and 90 minutes respectively.[33] In 1985 the death toll from road-traffic accidents in China rose by almost 20 percent from the previous year, claiming 12,043 lives, more than the number of deaths resulting from crime in China.[34] The major problem is the lack of space for all the new vehicles on roads that were not designed for motor-vehicle traffic. Although the congestion is part of the problem (in terms of noise and air pollution), it actually helps to keep down the death and injury rates by ensuring that traffic continues to move slowly. One estimate is that the average traffic speed in Chinese cities is now below 16 kph, compared to 24 in the 1960s.[35]

A sure sign that times are changing is the shortage of parking spaces in some city-center areas. Along the 15 kilometers of Shanghai's main shopping street, Nanjing Road, there is nowhere at all to park (see Figure 12.3). It is difficult to imagine what China's cities would look like if car ownership were to rise significantly from the current level, which is less than 1 percent. Major efforts have been made to reduce the demand for private transportation, for example, by planning for workers to be closer to their companies or by encouraging enterprises and offices to relocate outside the city centers. Once again we see evidence of a contradiction between different arms of government policy. The natural consequences of rising personal wealth are the demand for more travel and a greater level of private car ownership, but this will conflict sharply with the broader goals of Chinese city planning and the continued efforts to limit the rate of urban growth.[36]

Solid Waste and Mountains of Garbage

One final and unwelcome side effect of the new prosperity and population growth in China's cities is the problem of solid waste and garbage. In Shanghai and Beijing, for example, in the inner city alone there are between 5,000 and 6,000 tons of household garbage and trash to be disposed of each day, which amounts to about 2 million tons per year in each city.[37] As per capita incomes rise, so do the consumption of luxury items and the use of prepackaged goods, all of which generate extra waste.

The time, energy, and resources needed to deal with garbage in a city of 10 million people are enormous. In Beijing, for example, the sanitation bureau has 2,466 vehicles, including 466 refuse trucks and 55 sprinkler vehicles; but even so, less than 35 percent of the job is done by machines.[38] As any visitor to a Chinese city will attest, the streets are swept clean meticulously every day, sometimes several times a day. The sight of middle-aged and elderly women thrashing away at the sidewalks with handmade brooms is common all across the country. Rather than cleaning the streets, the action strips them bare and renders them desertlike and dusty. Most Westerners conclude that the goal is not to keep the city clean, simply to keep the sweepers busy. As Paul Theroux said, "Sweeping doesn't freshen a city. It gives it a disconcerting

Figure 12.3 Nanjing Road in Shanghai: The city's most famous shopping area and busiest street. People get around either by bus or on foot; no space is allocated for parking.

baldness. The effect is of a place that has been trampled."[39]

The combination of population growth and an increase in the per capita amount of garbage generated has placed a considerable strain on the available dumping sites, the majority of which are located in the predominantly agricultural suburbs. With each passing year the city's garbage trucks have to travel farther and farther out to find suitable sites. The long-distance travel into the heart of the suburban agricultural districts represents an obvious traffic and health hazard, as does the search for new sites. There is currently a proposal to construct three new mountains out of garbage on the outskirts of Beijing, but the city's sanitation bureau is facing stiff opposition from farmers who object to dumping in their vicinity. In the past farmers had welcomed human waste (night soil) as a cheap source of fertilizer, but now they prefer chemicals because they are more effective and cleaner.

THE SPATIAL ORGANIZATION OF URBAN-SERVICE DELIVERY

Most services available to city dwellers in China have traditionally been provided either by their work unit (the *danwei*) or by the local neighborhood organizations. *Danwei*s vary considerably in size and the comprehensiveness of the services they provide. They are primarily associated with urban factories and state-controlled enterprises, and because of the fringe benefits they offer, especially housing, attachment to a *danwei* has usually been highly valued. The largest work units are actively involved in almost all aspects of their member's lives.

> [They] may run nurseries, clinics, canteens, and recreational facilities; they convene employees to hear government decrees and for political study; they organize campaigns for birth control . . . they approve marriages and divorces and mediate disputes; they hold meetings to discuss crimes and misbehavior . . . by their members; they distribute rations and carry out cleanliness campaigns; they supervise untrustworthy employees and organize patrols to guard the area; and they may employ family members of employees in . . . small workshops or vegetable farms.[40]

To the average Westerner who is used to going home from work to complete independence at home, the all-embraciveness of the *danwei* would be difficult to stomach. Nevertheless, the advantages are substantial. Not only are crucial services provided—housing, utilities, health care, nurseries, primary schools, and stores—the *danwei* also provides some identity and a sense of community within the alienating context of urban life. The *danwei* is also the major point of contact between the people and the state in China. The dictates of the state, for example production drives or birth-control policies, are interpreted at the *danwei* level, a factor that helps to reduce the anonymity of the Chinese bureaucratic machine. Rather than responding to the state per se, a person responds to his or her work unit, presumably a more human (and humane) level for interaction.

The *danwei* provides a tightly knit social grouping, fostering cohesive patterns of social interaction. In spite of these benefits and the considerable advantage of reduced commuting time (as a result of living and working at the same location), a life spent almost entirely within a walled compound, with a gate for exit and entry, is extremely restrictive. The *danwei* is similar in some ways to the binding of a woman's feet in prerevolutionary China: It keeps people at home, where they can be kept under close scrutiny; and it restricts their interaction with the outside world. Thus although the *danwei* may well provide a stable and secure community, it is also a dangerously parochial community. Within the walls surveillance is constant. The guard at the gate keeps a record of everyone's comings and goings, as well as full information on who comes to visit.[41]

The "big brotherism" of life in the *danwei* reached a head during the Cultural Revolution, when the work unit was often the scene for the humiliating struggle sessions, in which politically "suspect" workers were interrogated and often tortured. Anne Thurston assembled many individual accounts of inhumanity almost beyond belief during the Cultural Revolution in her book *Enemies of the People*.[42] The personnel department of the *danwei*, whether it was a factory or an office, kept a detailed dossier on everybody in its employ. The dossiers could be used as evidence against almost anyone, at any time.

In the universities, which were well known to the CCP as the home of "stinking intellectuals" and as hotbeds of "counterrevolutionary" thought, the struggle sessions often became grotesque public spectacles. Attendance was encouraged by the local Party officials, but the events actually became quite popular with students and workers, who often appeared to treat them as a form of spectator sport. When asked why people appeared to enjoy such appalling brutality, one of Thurston's respondents suggested that it was part of the Chinese character to be drawn to excitement (renao), a commodity that was usually in extremely short supply in the Chinese city. Everyday life for the vast majority was excruciatingly boring, with routine events punctuated only by tedious delays and frustrating ineptitude in all areas of service provision. For all but the top cadres the possibility of a little rest and recreation, for example at the seaside, was a distant dream. After the rigors of work and managing family life, there was precious little time or energy left over for socializing outside the unit. As macabre as it may seem, a public argument on the street, a traffic accident, or even the torture session of a fellow worker helped to provide some much-needed entertainment.

In the 1980s city dwellers began to experience greater independence from the work unit. In the new era of urban economic reforms, the growth of smaller collective and private enterprises has been rapidly breaking the monopoly of the danweis, with the effect that more people are having to make their own living arrangements and organize services for themselves.

One indicator of the desire to live in the city is the prized status of the urban residence card. Although the new employment patterns generated by the economic reforms are beginning to alter the picture somewhat, a residence card still brings with it the promise of employment, housing, medicine, and entertainment—usually at rock-bottom prices.[43] In these difficult times the level of subsidy provided to city dwellers acts as a strong magnet for people who have been made redundant in the countryside. The desire to move to the city is constrained by the need to have a residency card, and this presents a familiar Catch-22 situation. Country folk want to move to the city to "get rich" or at least to make a decent living, but before they can do so they have to be rich enough to obtain a residence permit. In spite of the difficulties involved, thousands of peasants have begged, borrowed, and perhaps even stolen enough to acquire the prized cards; and thousands more have simply slipped into the cities without them.[44] As a result the cities have had to shoulder an increasingly heavy burden to provide the services and subsidies required by the expanding urban population. It has been estimated that for every extra 10,000 migrants to the city of Shanghai, there is an exponential increase in the cost of providing additional services. The costs are already sky-high: Y 3.5 million each year for infrastructure, including roads, buses, and utilities; Y 6.4 million for new housing; Y 1.2 million in food subsidies; and Y 2.3 million for education and health care.[45]

In spite of the obvious oversaturation of the urban-service-delivery systems, the desire to obtain a residence card for those without one and the determination of those who have them to hold onto them mean that very few people leave the cities voluntarily. The city has in fact become "an overloaded machine with an influx but no exodus at all."[46] To obtain a valid residence card, some people are willing to pay almost any price.[47] A doctor living in an urban work unit in Henan Province had tried for years to acquire residence cards for his wife and three children. In the new materialist economy he discovered that the cards could be bought easily, so he borrowed from the factory and used all his savings. He was broke, but he had no regrets. "Although I've lost my family fortune, I feel very happy at heart, for I'll have bequeathed to my three children a most precious legacy— the urban residency booklet."[48]

In a short story about life in the post-economic-reform environment of urban Shanghai, Cheng Naishan illustrated the powerful effect the residency card can have on human relationships in the city. One of the characters in the story had been exiled to faraway Xinjiang during the Cultural Revolution, mainly because of his "bourgeois" background as the son of a wealthy tailor. Although he had served his sentence, he was not allowed to return home until his wife "pulled strings" for him, based on her own urban residency. This was an unhappy marriage, and his wife never tired of reminding him how she had saved him from the nether reaches of frontier life in Outer China. Every time they argued she would bring the issue up again:

> "Don't forget, if it hadn't been for me, you'd never have been able to get back to Shanghai." That fact was ever present in Zijeh's mind . . . though he loved his wife not the least bit, he still had to endure her and fulfill his spousal responsibilities . . . he'd used his wife's Shanghai residency to extricate himself from his predicament [his exile in Xinjiang]. But to have [her] torture him with that contribution night and day . . . was more than he could endure.[49]

For those lucky enough to hold urban residency cards there is a hierarchy of neighborhood organizations responsible for delivering a wide range of urban services. This is especially important for people who are not connected to a specific work unit, but in fact there is a considerable amount of overlap between what is provided by the neighborhood and the *danweis*. As we saw in Chapter 2, the neighborhood committees function at different levels. On the one hand they administer national-level plans for economic and social development; but on the other hand, they also carry out a great number of routine functions within the neighborhood: mediating disputes, implementing hygiene campaigns, and punishing minor acts of delinquency.

In many ways the local organizations provide examples of state socialism at its best. Through the local structures help can be provided to families in financial need; old people are cared for; teenagers are counseled; and friendship networks and supports are available. At the other extreme the neighborhood surveillance system is an example of socialism at its worst. "The neighborhood committees may be turned into organs of petty harassment against any persons or family not thought to be going along enthusiastically enough."[50]

The most important functions of the neighborhood organizations are related to the maintenance of order and local cohesiveness, expressed largely through the security (police) committees and the mediation committees. In a fine piece of socialist understatement, a *Beijing Review* reporter observed how the local security forces have helped to implement the

new emphasis on law and order in China, by "explaining the newly enacted laws to the local populace so that everyone knows their content."[51] Most of the people who fail to understand the explanations will be apprehended by the tightly knit surveillance system that is made up of an unknown number of watchful eyes and well-trained ears.[52]

In addition to the police function, however, there is a strong emphasis on prevention at the neighborhood level, and efforts are made to mediate personal disputes before they escalate. In 1980, the mediation committees in Beijing reputedly handled more than 43,000 cases of civil disputes, which was five times more than the number of cases dealt with by the district people's courts. Whether this activity is interpreted by the residents as "busybodying" or as a real contribution to local problem solving is impossible to determine. The majority of official reports, not surprisingly, still speak about the work of the committees in glowing terms. As always, the major goal of neighborhood committee work remains political. "They [committee members] are often able to solve problems in a practical and sensible way. They are liked and trusted and so can act as competent assistants to the people's government, helping to improve community life and cementing ties between the government and the people."[53]

From a Western perspective, deeply colored by the desire for privacy and independence, it has been assumed that most Chinese city dwellers are tired of being watched continually and having so many other people interfering in their affairs. It would seem quite natural that after all the campaigns during the first three decades after 1949, people would simply want to be left alone to live their lives as they choose. Perhaps this is a part of what the Chinese people meant when they talked vaguely about "democracy" and "freedom," as they did intermittently from the late 1970s until the traumatic events of 1989.

It is interesting to speculate on what the people would do with their freedom if they ever experienced it. Some of them have difficulty adjusting to life elsewhere. One thing they find very odd is not having anyone around telling them what to do. A defector from the Chinese Embassy in the United States in the mid-1960s explained this dilemma: "Everyone keeps asking me what I *want* to do. I do not *know* what I want to do because I have never been expected to consider the matter."[54]

It is probably safe to conclude that the urban Chinese harbor ambivalent feelings toward their neighborhood-level service providers. Some of the local activities are clearly beneficial: For example, the constant surveillance allows committee members to monitor family dynamics extremely closely, which provides information that can be used to intervene in egregious cases of wife beating and child abuse. In such instances the costs of gathering the information are high, but the benefits are considerable.[55]

Offsetting such potentially positive services, the neighborhood committees have been actively engaged in administering and enforcing unpopular policies, a role that can only help to heap scorn upon them. As we saw in Chapter 7, the "one-child only" policy has been one of the most unpopular in the four decades of the PRC, but a large part of the success in implementing the policy in urban areas must go to the neighborhood committees. In addition to the provision of contraceptives and the availability of birth-control clinics, it is at the residents' committee level that the core of the propaganda work is conducted.

Elisabeth Croll has studied the operation of birth-control policies in urban Beijing, at the neighborhood level. (See Figure 12.4 for an illustration of the organization of local family-planning agencies.) In one residents' committee, for example, there were 735 households, and 408 women of child-bearing age.[56] Within the neighborhood a 6-person "leading group" was responsible for family-planning issues. This group trained 113 "propagand-

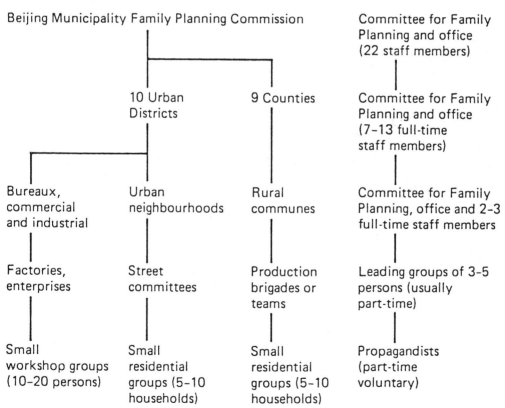

Municipal administration   *Family-planning administration*

Beijing Municipality Family Planning Commission			Committee for Family Planning and office (22 staff members)
	10 Urban Districts	9 Counties	Committee for Family Planning and office (7–13 full-time staff members)
Bureaux, commercial and industrial	Urban neighbourhoods	Rural communes	Committee for Family Planning, office and 2–3 full-time staff members
Factories, enterprises	Street committees	Production brigades or teams	Leading groups of 3–5 persons (usually part-time)
Small workshop groups (10–20 persons)	Small residential groups (5–10 households)	Small residential groups (5–10 households)	Propagandists (part-time voluntary)

Figure 12.4 The spatial organization of birth control in Beijing. Source: E. Croll, 1985, "The Single-Child Family in Beijing: A First-Hand Report," in E. Croll, D. Davin, and P. Kane (eds.), China's One-Child Family Policy *(London: Macmillan), p. 197; reprinted by permission.*

ists" who would visit each household to "explain" the ramifications of the new policies. In 1983 they reported a 100 percent success rate in "persuading" couples to sign a one-child certificate.

The story of one of these propagandists, an elderly woman, herself the mother of two children, is illuminating. She kept a detailed record of all the relevant facts on the women to whom she was assigned, including the method of contraception being used and the date they were officially permitted to become pregnant. She checked the regularity of the women's monthly cycles and any changes in their contraceptive plans. As Croll said, "Anything out of the ordinary will be reported to the health station."[57] The whole system is based on regular contacts and face-to-face interaction. "Since [the] propagandist . . . resides so near to the women for whom she is responsible, she is in frequent informal doorstep contact with them."[58] As this suggests, even the most unpopular policy has a human face at the grass-roots level, without which it could not possibly be effective.

Food and the Comforts of Home in the Chinese City

In shallow bins among the fish stalls, yellow-headed tortoises scrambled over one another's backs . . . strings of frogs dangled for sale in pendants of pulsing gullets and legs. . . . The vendors . . . weighed and dismembered them as if they were vegetables. Throats were cut and limbs amputated at a casual stroke.

—Colin Thubron[1]

INTRODUCTION

In this chapter our attention turns to the pleasures (or otherwise) of home life in urban China. We shall consider two areas of urban provision that have been crucial to the lives of millions of China's city dwellers as well as to the legitimacy of the Chinese government. The first of these involves food, something about which the Chinese are passionate, if not obsessed (see Figure 13.1). The second issue deals with housing and the comforts of home life in China, such as they are. This is an area that had been sorely neglected until the 1980s, by which time the only solution appeared to be a drastic reversal of policy and ideology.

PUTTING FOOD ON THE TABLE EVERY DAY

In a country that already has more city dwellers than any other in the world, with more streaming in every day from the countryside, it is difficult to see how the Chinese will ever be able to produce enough to feed them all. The hopelessly slow transportation system and the virtual absence of large-scale refrigeration raise the question of the distribution of food to the cities. How is it possible to guarantee the availability of fresh and wholesome food for more than 300 million urban residents on a daily basis? The answer to the *production* question lies in the unique spatial relationship that has been forged between the city and the countryside in China and the development of an intensive agricultural belt within the city limits. To answer the *distribution* question we need to consider the typically complex, but generally successful, spatial organization of agricultural marketing in the city.

Production: Growing the Food

One of the most important agricultural goals for the Chinese government in the Maoist era was for all regions, including the cities, to provide for their own food needs. In large part this was achieved, and the legacy of local self-sufficiency continued into the 1980s, although there were some important geographical variations depending on climate, time of year, and local conditions. The staple Chinese diet consists of grain (rice, wheat, corn, or millet) with vegetables—supplemented with small amounts of protein from meat, eggs, fish, soybeans (tofu), or peanuts. With the national government's emphasis on grain production, the major problem at the urban level has been the need for all cities

227

Figure 13.1   Mutton soup (yang ro pa), a local delicacy in Xian: It is eaten with crumbled bread and topped with whole cloves of garlic.

to be self-sufficient in vegetable production. The result, as all tourists to China can attest, is that highly intensive vegetable growing is common all across the urban landscape, sometimes even within walking distance of the city center.[2]

The number of city dwellers actually working as farmers and the amount of urban land devoted to agriculture vary considerably, but in the early 1980s an average of 20 percent of the residents of China's largest cities were defined as agricultural residents; 17 percent of all urban land was devoted to food production; and 60 percent of the cities' total vegetables were grown within the city limits[3] (Table 13.1).

Local vegetable self-sufficiency makes excellent economic sense in a country with so few roads, such congested train networks, and virtually no capacity to store and refrigerate perishable foodstuffs. Growing food within the city reduces the overall cost and increases the chances of the food arriving fresh. It also makes good ecological sense

because the cities, for historical reasons, are usually located in fertile areas with good soils and with adequate access to water supplies for irrigation.[4] In addition the city has been able to provide valuable soil nutrients, in the form of both animal (pig) manure and human waste (night soil) that could be carted out to the fields on a regular basis.

Local self-sufficiency is also practical because there are relatively few areas in which China could realistically produce specialized cash crops for export to compete with other parts of the world, such as the Mediterranean or California. The one possible exception would be certain parts of south China, but these are most valuable as triple-cropped, high-yielding, rice-growing areas.

Urban food self-sufficiency simplifies the agricultural planning process. By juxtaposing production and consumption within a few miles of each other, it is possible to move food to the market on a daily basis using a gamut of premodern forms of transportation, ranging from foot (and back), to bicycle, to

Table 13.1 Urban Agriculture, Selected Cities in China, 1982

	Total Popu-lation (mill.)	% Agri-cultural Residents	Total Land Area (km²)	% Culti-vated	Vegetable Production	
					Amount (000,000 kgs)	% of City's Total Consumption
Shenyang	5.1	25	8,515	43	1,195	91
Xian	2.9	26	2,441	44	432	87
Chengdu	4.0	43	3,801	36	423	69
Beijing	9.2	14	16,807	14	2,083	58
Jinan	3.4	21	4,875	1	161	31
Chongqing	6.5	27	9,848	12	1,052	35
Average for 17 largest cities	--	20	--	17	--	60
Average for next 31 cities (> 500,000)	--	39	--	--	--	--

Note: Dashes indicate dates unavailable.

Source: Adapted from E. M. Bjorklund, 1987, "Olericulture and Urban Development in China," *Tijdschrift voor Economische en Sociale Geografie* 78, No. 1, p. 5, Table 1.

horse-drawn cart, and all the way up to flatbed trucks and pickups. The Chinese city in the early morning provides a spectacular sight, as thousands of short trips are made in all sorts of vehicles, carrying everything from livestock to fruit from the agricultural suburbs into the city markets.

The Chinese "suburb," as a result, looks very different from its North American counterpart. New housing at the edge of the city tends to consist of large apartment buildings rather than single-family homes, and the rest of the land is devoted to intensive agriculture. Just a few miles out of Beijing, for example, Colin Thubron noticed the sharp difference between city and suburb in China: "Between fields of maize and sorghum plodded chestnut horses, and bullock-carts carrying sweet corn and stones. Some peasants trudged beside miniature tractors. Others were bent under harness, men and women together, pulling their ploughs like oxen over the earth. The torpid tempo of the city had stilled into rural quiet."[5]

In addition to making sense geographically, economically, and organizationally, food self-sufficiency has had an important political function in China because it contributed to

the Maoist ideal of minimizing the urban/rural dichotomy. For centuries cities had been the eager consumers of what was produced in rural areas but remained aloof from the countryside. The city was invariably the locus of individual and family wealth, and it usually offered considerably more economic, social, and cultural diversity. The city has always offered the prospect of a better life to the Chinese peasants and has tempted them to leave the land permanently.

The traditional conflict between city and country is exacerbated as urbanization advances and agricultural land is swallowed up by urban uses. To slow down this inexorable process the suburbs have become a *contact zone* between rural and urban life. The effect is to reduce the income gap between city and country residents, which helps to slow down the rate of rural-to-urban migration. The attempts made since 1949 to reinforce urban self-sufficiency have contributed to this overall goal by helping to keep food prices relatively low, which was one of the most important considerations of the new government. In addition, efforts have been made to enable urban-fringe residents to earn higher incomes from vegetable farming so that they would not be enticed to leave for the city.[6] Urban/rural linkages were further strengthened in the 1980s when local vegetable production stimulated the development of sideline activities in the suburbs, including food-processing factories and the manufacture of fertilizer and other agricultural inputs. New jobs were created in the suburbs and peasant families could expand their incomes, enabling them to travel into the cities to shop for urban goods. In this way, China has been partially successful at slowing down the depletion of the rural economy, a phenomenon that has been common in developing countries around the world.

As we saw in Chapter 8, the functional relationship between cities and their rural peripheries has been strengthened by official changes in the spatial organization of territory. In most parts of the country the prefectures have been abolished, and vast portions of rural China have been shared out among the cities.[7] Thus, for administrative purposes, the rural counties that surround cities are now formally attached to those cities, in a policy euphemistically referred to as "the city managing the country."[8] One of the major goals of this policy was to increase the spatial interaction in both directions, while at the same time adding symbolically to the disappearance of urban and rural differences. Although still formally designated "urban" or "rural" according to occupation, almost everyone now within the newly delimited city regions is defined as a city dweller, whether he or she works in a downtown bank or spends her days up to her knees in a field of cabbages.[9]

The spatial pattern of land uses at the urban/rural interface might look like that envisioned by Johann Von Thünen in the latter part of the nineteenth century. Close to the urban core, land use would be primarily urban, in other words a mix of residential, commercial, and industrial; but even within the official urban core, intensive vegetable production would be interspersed, gradually increasing in proportion until it dominated the land-use pattern at the urban fringe. Further out, vegetables give way to less intensive agricultural production, usually grain or fiber crops such as cotton and oil-bearing plants.

In a hypothetical land-use model of the Chinese city region, the interface between urban land uses and vegetable cultivation has

important implications for the labor force (see Figure 13.2). Agricultural workers would be dominant in the outer suburbs and in the largely rural counties; and urban workers would predominate in the urban districts of the inner city. There would also be opportunities for workers to switch between urban and agricultural jobs. This would provide employment opportunities for part-time workers and for agricultural workers who would otherwise be idle after harvest periods and during times of slack production. In this way the traditional city/country dichotomy would be reduced. Workers could move into or out of the urban employment sector (and vice versa) as their needs and local circumstances dictated. The whole process would be extended as land uses became increasingly intermingled, for example, as food-processing plants emerged inside the city or as new factories were built in the largely rural suburbs.

The model implies that land uses at the urban fringe would be in a constant state of flux. Closest to the city, as urban land uses pushed outward, land would be lost to vegetable production. To maintain local self-sufficiency this land would have to be replaced, which means that further out, land previously devoted to grains might be transferred over to intensive vegetable production. As we saw in Chapters 5 and 6, the HRS and other agricultural reforms have resulted in a complex set of land-use changes at the urban fringe as households and small cooperatives have been switching over their activities to produce whatever they think will be most profitable. From the distant perspective of Maoist self-sufficiency, there is a real danger that the geographical haphazardness produced by free-market decision-making could threaten local food supplies, for example, if too many households, and therefore *too much land*, shift to nonfood cultivation or sideline activities. Also, with their newfound wealth, peasant families might want to use suburban land to build new houses or to develop new rural enterprises, further reducing the supply of valuable cultivable land.

Distribution: Getting the Food onto the Table

As a result of the agricultural reforms, the distribution system for urban food has changed dramatically in recent years. During the so-

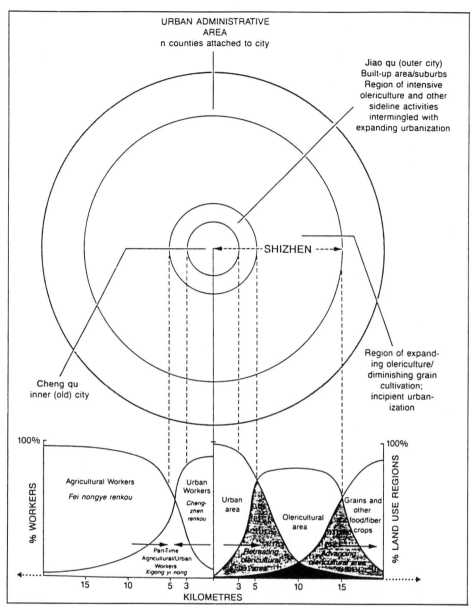

Figure 13.2   The spatial pattern of land uses and employment in a Chinese city: Traditional urban land uses compete with agricultural land uses at the urban fringe. Source: E. M. Bjorklund, 1987, "Olericulture and Urban Development in China," Tijdschrift voor Economische en Sociale Geografie 78, No. 1, p. 8; reprinted by permission.

cialist heyday, the city administration attempted to coordinate the supply of food with the demand for it—providing an infrastructure that enabled producers and consumers to be connected. In Shanghai, for example, vegetable distribution was coordinated by the Municipal Vegetable Company, which drew up a master plan for each type of vegetable.[10] The company negotiated with the production

brigades in the outlying communes, and a company agent would be in charge of weighing, grading, and valuing the produce. In Shanghai there were 24 "linking stations" at the edge of the city, each one receiving vegetables from a number of brigades. The stations then distributed the food wholesale to the closest of 146 "marketing clusters" that were located in neighborhoods all around the city. Each of these subsequently supplied a large number of submarkets. In the early years these were mostly state and collective stores and shops in work units; but in the 1980s they included an increasing number of "free" retail street markets and stalls. In the collective era the plan for vegetable distribution at the local level was to have one food outlet for every 300–400 households. The goal of a system such as this, reproduced with variations in all of China's cities, was to guarantee that food would arrive fresh every day in markets that were no more than a ten-minute walk for any city resident. Fresh food was usually delivered at night, after 8 P.M., often with the carriers staying overnight in a makeshift bunkhouse.[11]

In the 1980s, according to the available sources, urban food supplies were considerably more plentiful, the food fresher, and there was more choice from the consumer's perspective. This can be accounted for in a number of ways. "Free" wholesale markets started to appear in some cities to compete with the state markets, and their numbers grew rapidly, from around 300 in 1984 to more than 7,000 by the middle of 1986.[12] Some of these handle all foodstuffs, but others deal only with specialized products such as fruit, poultry, or wood. It appears that free wholesale markets supplied between 45 and 60 percent of the total volume of vegetables handled by the state wholesale markets; 30 to 50 percent of the pork, poultry, and eggs; and 60 to 70 percent of the fruit; with a total transaction value in 1984 of Y 196.9 million.[13]

At the retail end, the urban food-distribution system has been revolutionized in recent years by the appearance of the "free" markets on the city streets, where peasants sell their surpluses at whatever prices they can get. In general, the prices are higher in the free markets than elsewhere, but most shoppers seem willing to pay the extra to have a greater variety of products and fresher food. In 1980 the free markets still played only a minor role in the urban economy; thus in fifty Shanghai markets the average spent per person in 1980 was only Y 4.23; and only Y 2.04 in seventy-three free markets in Beijing.[14] In subsequent years this situation changed drastically; in fact the total value of sales in urban free markets increased from Y 12 million in 1980 to Y 181 million in 1985.[15]

Once the HRS allowed the sale of above-quota food and the government decontrolled food prices, there was a powerful incentive for farmers to grow as much as they could and to sell it wherever they could get the best price. In Xian, for example, potatoes driven several hundred miles from villages in northern Shaanxi Province could fetch more than twice the price they could locally, making the long trip worthwhile. Although this sounds like normal business practice to Westerners, after three decades of command socialism in China, it was something of a revelation for farmers to have the freedom to haul their produce over long distances in search of profits.

As we saw in Chapter 5, the agricultural reforms have resulted in greater levels of specialization, higher farm incomes, and more varied, interesting, and nutritious diets for the Chinese.[16] As these benefits became apparent, free markets were hastily erected in rural and urban areas all over the country. By 1979 there were more than 2,000 urban free markets and by 1983 more than 4,000. Further legislation in 1983 and 1984 sanctioned even more trade for the free markets, no longer restricting them to agricultural goods, and by 1985 they numbered more than 8,000. It has been estimated that urban free markets handled three-quarters of all farm products and one-third of all "sideline" goods in 1985, and in terms of value this approached 50 percent of all agricultural sales.[17] This implies that an increasing amount of specialized (high-value) agricultural products, such as live animals and fish, as well as industrial products, were being sold in the street markets, often replacing lower-value vegetables.

The free markets have helped to expand the level of spatial interaction between city and countryside even further—in that the markets in the cities sell a large proportion of the produce from the countryside and vice versa. By 1984, some highly specialized free markets had emerged, for example, those dealing in second-hand agricultural machinery, scrap metal, clothing, and even traditional medicines.[18] Street markets were no longer simply places where surplus food was sold. "They were being transformed into a sophisticated network of urban-rural exchange."[19]

In many ways this new development represents the reemergence of something very similar to the traditional periodic markets that existed in China during the late imperial era.[20] Some of the larger markets operate on a five- or ten-day cycle, serving an area up to one day's travel time. They provide an outlet for a combination of trade, services, and cultural activities. In addition, they have a regional distribution function: Goods are sold and resold by itinerant traders (traditionally known in China as *keshang*). It has been estimated that 70–90 percent of all goods sold in big-city free markets in the mid-1980s were items being resold after purchase elsewhere.[21]

It is important to point out that not everybody "gets rich" as a result of the street markets and the new outlets for enterprise that they have made possible. Work on the streets involves long hours and is often tedious and unprofitable. There are none of the fringe benefits associated with attachment to a work unit. A flower seller at a street market in Nanjing, for example, made her life sound anything but glamorous. "I buy the flowers from the country folk who sell them . . . from four in the morning. I bring them home, string them up and sell them in pairs. Every day I buy 200—that costs six yuan. If I sell them all I can make four yuan profit. Out of that I pay sixty cents . . . for my pitch. Sometimes . . . I can't get rid of them, like today. I've got dozens left, and by tomorrow they won't be smelling as good."[22]

HOW WELL FED ARE THE CHINESE?

Most visitors are fascinated by Chinese eating habits and the apparent love affair the Chinese have with their food. Greetings between people are often predicated by questions about food—"have you eaten yet?" replaces "hello" or "how are you?" Colin Thubron was convinced that for the Chinese food has become a "national panacea and obsession."[23] The population is counted not as the number of people per se, but the number of mouths to be fed (*kuo*). As Lynn Pan exclaimed, "No people on earth, save perhaps the French, are as preoccupied with food as the Chinese, for whom it has always been the first pleasure of life."[24]

Perhaps it was the centuries of eating at a near-subsistence level that helped Chinese chefs to develop all of the nuances of their trade, but it is obvious that even the cleverest chefs can not sharpen their skills unless food is plentiful. From this perspective Chinese socialism must be judged harshly, because during the first three decades the promise of the revolution did not materialize.[25] The consensus view among Western scholars has been that China's agricultural performance remained sluggish until the end of the 1970s.[26] It is important to point out that in comparison to other Third World countries, China's agricultural output in the 1950s, 1960s, and 1970s was impressive, and with the exception of the disastrous years immediately after the Great Leap Forward, there was relatively little starvation in China after 1949.[27] Nevertheless, the available data show that food-energy and protein availability per capita in China did not surpass the average level for the 1952–1958 period until after 1978 (see Table 13.2). After the years of austerity in the postrevolutionary era, the vast majority of Chinese chefs (outside the major tourist hotels) were rusty. When new restaurants started opening in China in the 1980s, many of them had to send their old chefs to Hong Kong to be retrained.[28]

The reforms provided a major boost to the production of food, and at the same time a vast array of new enterprises sprang up as sidelines in rural areas. The Chinese appeared to be eating well—or at least it seemed that way from the frenzy of activity in the food stalls and restaurants throughout the country in the 1980s. There was evidence that shopping once again was a pleasure in China, and the newly reopened street markets have become the center of Chinese social life. People went to the markets to shop, to eat, and to visit with their friends.[29]

Trips to the food markets also became a spectator sport for Western visitors to China. In Guangzhou, everybody's favorite place to be horrified, the tourists are told that the locals will eat anything with legs except tables and everything that flies except airplanes! As the epigraph at the beginning of this chapter demonstrates, Colin Thubron was able to entertain and disgust himself at the same time as he walked through the marketplaces watching the scenes of dismemberment.

The dismal picture painted by the statistics on food consumption up to 1978 appeared to have been changed in the 1980s. This is indicated in Table 13.3, and much of this

Table 13.2 Estimated Daily per Capita Nutritional Adequacy, 1950-1982 (Selected Years)

	Energy Availability		Protein Availability	
	Kilocalories	% of Req.	Grams	% of Req.
1950	1,742	84.2	48.5	122.8
1952	2,083	100.2	57.8	145.9
1958	2,248	106.7	58.0	145.0
1960	1,578	74.6	41.4	103.1
1965	2,021	94.5	52.8	130.5
1970	2,192	101.6	56.2	137.6
1975	2,266	103.4	57.9	138.8
1977	2,233	100.8	56.4	133.0
1978	2,413	108.3	60.4	141.4
1979	2,592	115.8	67.0	155.7
1980	2,473	109.8	63.7	147.0
1981	2,511	110.9	65.1	148.9
1982	2,725	119.8	69.7	158.5
1952-58 average	2,170	103.7	58.8	147.6
1960-1977 average	2,047	94.9	53.2	130.0
1978-1982 average	2,543	112.9	65.2	150.3

Source: A. Piazza, 1986, *Food Consumption and Nutritional Status in the PRC* (Boulder, Colo.: Westview Press), p. 92, Table 4.8. Reprinted by permission.

Table 13.3 Rural and Urban Consumption of Grains and Meat, per Capita (in Kilograms)

	Grain		Meat	
	Rural	Urban	Rural	Urban
1952	195	250	5.16	8.00
1957	205	225	4.77	7.92
1977	220	210	5.75	15.90
1983	260	196	9.97	19.86

Source: C. Aubert, 1988, "China's Food Take-Off?" in S. Feuchtwang, A. Hussain, and T. Pairault (eds.), *Transforming China's Economy in the Eighties*, Vol. 1: *The Rural Sector, Welfare and Employment* (Boulder, Colo.: Westview Press), p. 121. Reprinted by permission.

improvement can be attributed to the agricultural reforms.[30] The most dramatic changes appear to be in the countryside. The consumption gap between the cities and the countryside had widened by 1978, but the most recent data show that not only has this trend ended, but in fact it has been reversed. By 1983 people in China's rural areas consumed considerably more grain per capita than those in the cities. In part this reflected the desire of urban dwellers to vary their diets by eating more meat, which diverted a considerable amount of grain in the direction of animal fodder. In spite of this trend, however, in the 1980s the rate of increase of meat eating in the countryside was faster than in the cities; in fact between 1978 and 1987 China's peasants more than doubled their per capita consumption of meat (see Table 13.4). These statistics describe what amounts to a "food takeoff" since 1978, which has made possible "a new abundance in the peasant

Table 13.4 Changes in per Capita Consumption Among Chinese Peasants, 1978-1987 (Selected Foodstuffs)

	1978 (kg)	1987 (kg)	1987 as % of 1978
Grain	248.00	259.00	104.4
Vegetables	142.00	130.00	91.5
Oils	1.96	4.69	293.3
Meat	5.76	11.65	202.3
Eggs	0.80	2.25	281.3
Sugar	0.73	1.70	232.9
Liquor	1.22	5.48	449.2

Source: *China Statistical Yearbook 1988* (Beijing: State Statistical Bureau of the PRC, 1988), p. 735.

intake."[31] By international standards an acceptable level of food consumption per capita has been reached in China, averaging 2,400 calories per day in the rural areas and 2,200 in the cities.[32]

In addition to their greater consumption levels, by the end of the 1980s China's peasants were more mobile than they had ever been in the previous four decades, in both geographical and occupational terms. They had greater opportunities to move off the land into the cities, but they could also move into more profitable activities. The result, in addition to higher incomes in the countryside, was a significant increase in the productivity of the agricultural labor force, from a base level of 100 in 1952 to 155 in 1988.[33]

There is some real evidence then, that the risky business of "breaking the iron rice-bowl,"[34] although eliminating the security associated with the collective production and distribution of food, has helped to bring about some major gains in China. There are, however, some worrisome side effects of the food takeoff. It is evident, for example, that the vicissitudes of the market have already started to produce serious problems, the worst of which has been an inflation in food prices. Without the security blanket of collectivism, there is a natural fear of bad harvests caused by variations in the weather. Prolonged droughts in the summer of 1986, for example, extending until the spring of 1987 in north China, seriously damaged the winter wheat crops.[35] As noted in Chapter 9, another fear at about the same time was that the peasants, in their desire to grow more profitable crops, would move away from grain production to

such an extent that output would drop to a dangerously low level, which is exactly what has happened since 1985.[36]

Perhaps an even more serious issue, however, is the regional disparity in food intake that occurred (or was reinforced) during the reform era. Although there have been great leaps forward on a national scale, some parts of China have remained persistently poor, and the gap between the poor and the rich regions is threatening to widen each year. In the early 1980s, for example, the gap between the highest and the lowest provinces in terms of daily caloric intake was considerable (3,084 calories per person in Heliongjiang, versus 1,577 in nearby Inner Mongolia, and 1,631 in Guizhou). This geographic variability is illustrated in Figure 13.3. In 1980 indices of caloric intake (with a mean of 100 for the whole of China) ranged from below 80 to above 110.[37] Similarly the index of food-energy availability in 1982 ranged from 118.5 in Jilin Province to 84.7 in Guizhou; and the amount of food protein per day ranged from 75.2 grams in Beijing to 44.8 grams in Guangxi AR (the average for the country was 58.3 grams). It is abundantly clear, therefore, that certain parts of China did not benefit from the reforms as much as others, and some are once again in danger of experiencing chronic poverty.[38] As noted earlier, the major fear in these regions is that without efforts by the state or the collectives to correct such imbalances, the problem of regional disparities could deteriorate.[39]

The effect of the regional variations in nutritional status is also evident in the pattern of mortality rates in China. At the national

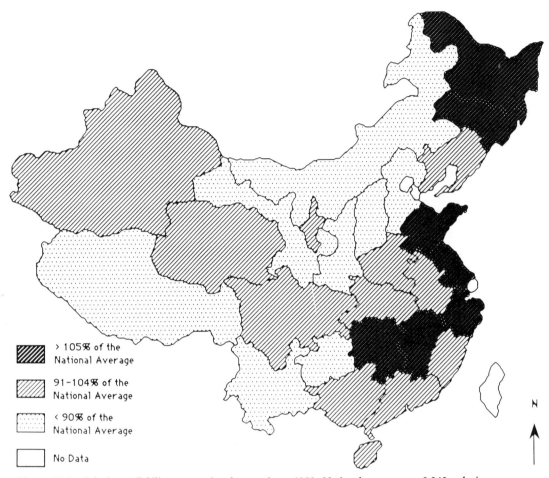

> 105% of the
National Average

91–104% of the
National Average

< 90% of the
National Average

No Data

N

Figure 13.3 Caloric availability per capita, by province, 1980: National average = 2,243 calories per person per day. Source: Adapted from A. Piazza, 1986, Food Consumption and Nutritional Status in the PRC *(Boulder, Colo.: Westview Press), Table 5.2.*

level the mortality rate, which is a useful indicator of nutritional status, fell from 25.8 per 1,000 in 1953 to 7.9 in 1982. In geographical terms, however, there are some sharp variations in the mortality rate across the country, from the highs in the western and southwestern provinces (where the rates averaged 8.5), to the lows in the industrial northeastern provinces (where the rates averaged less than 5.0).[40]

One of the major advantages of the Household Responsibility System was that it stimulated the overall productivity of China's farmland, by allowing households to exploit their local geographical advantages. For example, in Jiangsu Province—which has good soils, transportation links, and a favorable

climate—the benefits of the new ownership system quickly became apparent. In one small area near Suzhou more than 900 hectares of land were contracted out to 260 households in 1985. The farms ranged in size from 3 to 30 hectares, whereas the average size of farms in the area was about 1 hectare at the time.[41] Within a year the average income on the larger farms was about half as much again as it was on the smaller operations, presumably as a result of greater efficiency in both production and distribution.

This is a record that has been reproduced all over China, but nevertheless, some regions have fallen further behind in relative terms. As we saw in Chapter 9, the official statistics reveal that at least 10 percent of China's population is still trapped in poverty, a figure that is unacceptably high for a society committed to human equality.[42]

HOUSING (AND HOMELESSNESS) SINCE THE REVOLUTION

Those with power (government officers), those with money (merchants and traders), those with materials (distributors of production goods), and those with connections get to live in large places, while people with little power and workers in small enterprises . . . have to live in cramped housing. . . . In Beijing, while the average living area is 3.6 square meters per capita, employees of the government . . . enjoy an average of over 7 square meters.[43]

Since 1949 there has been far less emphasis on personal consumption in China than in most Western societies. This has been especially evident in the area of housing and the comfort-providing contents of the home.[44] The Communist party after 1949 deliberately steered a course away from personal consumption. This was partly a way to ensure rapid development of the productive forces, but it was also intended to denigrate the "decadent" consumption habits typical of the West and of the old treaty-port cities along China's eastern seaboard.[45] In Mao Zedong's China, private home ownership was not officially encouraged and facilitated in the way it was in most capitalist societies.[46]

In the austerity of the first decades after the revolution and the all-out drive toward national reconstruction, the deemphasis of private home ownership in China was a valuable way to conserve scarce resources. A low rate of private home ownership also facilitated the social-control functions that were considered to be necessary in a totalitarian state. In China, as in most countries with one-party systems of government, there has been an almost fanatical concern with security, law and order, and compliance with Party policy (see Chapter 14). To maintain order in the city, it was necessary for the Party to establish a hierarchical system of organization, one that made sure the policies of the central government could be administered effectively at the local level. The lowest tier in this hierarchy operated on the streets and in the courtyards, where locally appointed resident-officials could keep a close watch on the comings and goings of everyone within their domain. Unlike an American family, an urban Chinese family was rarely able to use the home to close itself off from the outside world. Neighborhood-security officials considered homes within their jurisdiction to be in the public rather than the private domain, and they could enter those homes on any pretext.[47]

As a result of the ever-present surveillance it is likely that most Chinese city dwellers have never been able to think of their home as being exclusively "theirs": It was something they rented from the state, from which they could be moved at any time if others' needs were greater, and over which they had little individual control. In Mao's China, therefore, the role of the home as the bulwark against the state was virtually nonexistent. There was no effective way the Chinese people could insulate themselves from the pervasive web of Party control.

By Western standards of evaluation the home in post-Liberation urban China was certainly not a castle. Although there was some private home ownership, until the 1980s the home itself was rarely considered to be a major source of investment, and equally rarely was it a showplace for personal-consumption preferences. The socialist city was intended to be a place that would not exclude the poor; in fact the goal was to provide cheap and affordable housing for *all* of its residents. The cities that the Chinese Communists entered in 1949 had been devastated by more than two decades of foreign invasion and civil war. Part of the contract the Communists had with Chinese people was to provide adequate jobs, enough food, and satisfactory homes for everyone to live in. Life would continue to be austere, but there was to be no starvation and no homelessness. Even the poorest people would have their material needs provided for by the "iron rice bowl."

Moreover, the new Chinese city was a spartan environment, not a place of beauty. The Communists hoped to build cities that would contribute usefully to China's modernization, rather than to provide an arena for what they considered to be the wasteful and decadent practices of privatized consumption. For most ordinary Chinese people this sort of socialist city proved to be functional but probably unlovable (see Figures 13.4, 13.5, and 13.6). It is difficult to compare standards of living from one country to another, but there can be little doubt that the average Chinese home is far less spacious and more sparsely furnished than its equivalent in most Western capitalist countries.[48] In addition it was common for Chinese families to have to share what Westerners consider to be basic facilities, and many had to double up, often providing permanent homes for their newly married sons and daughters-in-law.

The Emergence of a Housing Crisis in Urban China

By the end of 1970s the post-Mao leadership had begun to think seriously about the need for major overhauls in China's housing policy. There was a reasonably high level of dissatisfaction with the overall quality of life in the Chinese city, but it was still rare for individual citizens to criticize the government's policies openly. In a strictly controlled regime with a history of people being seriously punished for airing dissenting views,

there had been very little official opposition. As we shall see in Chapter 15, this situation changed briefly in late 1978 and early 1979. At that time long-standing public resentment bubbled up to the surface in a new literature of dissent, some of which was highly critical of the government's policies for the provision of urban services. One poet, signing himself only as a "revolutionary citizen," was bold enough to point out some of the glaring inequalities in the way different sectors of the population were housed in socialist China:

There's a housing shortage in Beijing,
But in Zhongnanhai new buildings are built.
When Chairman Mao and Premier Zhou were
  still alive,
Was there that kind of extravagant spending?
Sites of culture and history are completely
  demolished,
Really it is not just absurd but gross!
There's a forest of building cranes which daily
  revolve,
And the lorries come and the seasons go,
Still half the city's construction force is employed
  here

Figure 13.4 Cave dwellings near Xian. More than 35 million people still live in caves in China.

Figure 13.5 High-rise apartment buildings in north Beijing.

Figure 13.6 Old-style apartment buildings in downtown Shanghai.

239

If local authorities thus break the view, they
  should be severely punished,
For when those above behave unworthily, those
  below will do the same.
Premier Zhou's attitude to the masses should
  be copied
Rather than Qin Shihuang's when he built the
  Afang palace.
Think carefully Vice-Chairman Wang
We lesser mortals only live in two square metres
  each.[49]

As the poem suggested, in spite of the
Maoist aspirations for a classless city, there
were well-known inequalities in the housing-
allocation system that had made many people
quietly resentful for years. The poet also talked
about the furious new construction that was
occurring in Zhongnanhai, the Communist
party headquarters, which tended to increase
the resentment of the ordinary people. What
evidence there is suggests that government
officials and other well-placed individuals were
often much better housed than the majority.
In the middle 1950s, for example, a survey
showed that "class" differences were reflected
in significantly greater amounts of living space
for Party officials and white-collar workers.[50]
The low cost of public housing in China
was considered to be necessary as a subsidy
in the presence of low wages and the relative
absence of consumer goods. In fact the subsidies themselves contributed to inequality,
because the low cost of housing meant that
the better-paid workers had more money left
over to spend on food and consumer goods.
When some families started to "get rich" as
a result of the economic reforms in the 1980s,
the magnitude of this subsidy was effectively
increased.[51] The newly rich were able to spend
more on the commodities they felt they had
been deprived of for so long.
At the interurban scale there were also
some significant variations in the standard of
housing. The country's largest cities were
usually the most crowded. In Shanghai, for
example, almost one-fifth of the five million
inner-city inhabitants were encountering severe housing problems by the end of the
1970s, and they were living at an average
density of less than two square meters of
floor space per person, about the space taken
up by a twin bed.[52]
China's urban housing stock was in a poor
state of repair. Years of neglect and the shortage of building materials resulted in a hodgepodge of dilapidation, with many of the older
structures crumbling, patched up, and dangerous.[53] In the back streets of Shanghai and
Beijing, and in fact in all Chinese cities,
ancient, decrepit buildings coexisted with a
jumble of newly built structures.
As bad as it was in 1978, the housing
situation would have been a lot worse had
it not been for persistent efforts throughout
the previous two decades to slow down the
growth of the largest cities. The effect of these
policies was to reduce the pressure on the
urban infrastructure, especially housing.[54]
There had also been a major drive to expand
the industrial base of the countryside, which
increased the supply of local jobs and thereby
reduced the rate of rural out-migration. In
addition, millions of youths were forcibly
"sent down" from the biggest cities to work
(indefinitely) in the countryside. This reduced
the existing urban population in absolute
terms and also resulted in a lower demand
for new homes in the future.
The statistics themselves can tell only part
of the story of what life was actually like in
the crowded environment of the Chinese city.
Most homes had access to kitchen, toilet, and
bathing facilities, but the sharing that was
commonplace was a constant source of frustration and conflict.[55] The public control of
housing and the bureaucratic method of allocation also resulted in widespread claims
of slowness, ineptitude, and corruption. The
housing stock varied significantly, both in
quantity and quality, from one work unit to
another. People who were not connected to
a specific unit were placed on the interminable
waiting lists of the city housing bureaus.[56]
By the end of the 1970s, after three decades
of relatively austere state socialism, the urban
housing situation had reached crisis proportions. Although in comparison with other poor
nations the Chinese were relatively well
housed, the country's leaders by that time
preferred to compare China with the world's
developed countries. From that perspective
the housing situation in China's cities was
deplorable, and even official Party sources
were in agreement. In 1980, for example, the
People's Daily newspaper estimated that 20
percent of urban residents were "slum dwellers."[57] The final ignominy came with the
realization that socialist China had not even

been able to improve on the housing situation that existed in 1949. As a result of general population growth, by the late 1970s the absolute amount of living space per person in China's cities had actually fallen *below the 1949 level* (3.6 square meters as opposed to 4.5), and in the largest cities the average was considerably lower than that.

Finding Someone to Blame for the Crisis

After 1978 the new leadership was eager to lay some of the blame for the housing crisis on Mao and the recently vanquished Gang of Four. One of the contributing causes, the leaders argued, was the "excessive" egalitarianism in Maoist philosophy that resulted in a desire to provide everyone with equal access to extremely cheap housing. With rents pegged at an artificially low level, there were few opportunities to increase the supply of housing because virtually no revenue was being generated. In most cases the revenue collected from rentals did not even come close to the repair bills, so ongoing maintenance and new construction were continually falling behind demand levels.[58] The shortage of funds for housing construction became especially serious during the push for industrial expansion that began in the late 1970s.

Maoist egalitarianism contributed to a persistent tendency to shortchange the Chinese public in the area of housing, particularly in comparison to other collective-consumption services such as education and health care. This tendency has been observed in the Soviet Union as well as in various Eastern European socialist countries.[59] The norm in such countries, as in China, is for permanently inadequate housing—questionable structures that are poorly equipped and constantly in need of repair. It is difficult to avoid the conclusion that the "comforts of home," so cherished in capitalist societies, are usually considered too bourgeois for socialist countries. During the Cultural Revolution, when widespread attacks were made on all facets of inequality, the most vulnerable areas were housing and bourgeois possessions such as books, art collections, and furniture; all these became popular targets for the Red Guards' truncheons.[60]

The housing crisis at the end of the 1970s was also interpreted as the result of Maoist investment priorities. The push to develop the productive forces rather than allow higher

levels of consumption and service provision meant that the amount of investment in the "nonproductive" categories had always been extremely low, especially during the Second Five Year Plan at the end of the 1950s (see Table 13.5).[61] The housing portion of this investment fell to as low as 4 percent during the early (and most radical) years of the Cultural Revolution (1966–1976).

HOUSING REFORM IN THE DENGIST ERA

The post-Mao leadership made a determined effort to change investment priorities, which had resulted in the chronic neglect of all aspects of the urban infrastructure, especially housing (Table 13.5). The plan for the seven-year period beginning in 1979 called for a housing construction boom that would generate more living space than had been built in the previous thirty years combined (a total of 550 million square meters).[62] This effectively required tripling the portion of the total investment funds allocated to housing, from less than 7 percent in 1977 to 22 percent in 1984. In physical terms it represented an astonishing increase in the amount of new floor space built, from 28.3 to 100 million square meters.[63]

It was clear that a plan as ambitious as this would overstretch the economy, which was already struggling by the end of the 1970s. An all-out attempt to solve the housing crisis thus not only represented a serious pragmatic problem, it also required a major ideological shift in the direction of an increasingly market-oriented economy. To generate the revenue surplus needed as investment funds for new housing construction, it would be necessary to allow individuals and enterprises to expand their incomes, both in the countryside and in the cities. This would boost the level of savings and thereby the supply of credit. It would also be necessary to allow people to move freely off the land and into the cities, to help supply the vast labor force needed to construct the new housing. It would be necessary to liberalize the state's monopoly over commodity distribution and decontrol the rigid price system to facilitate the huge increases in building materials that would be needed. What all of this suggests is that the proposed expansion in housing

Table 13.5 "Nonproductive" Investment, Housing Investment, and Floor Space Produced in China, 1950-1985

	% Investment		Urban Housing Floor Space (mill. m²)
	Nonproductive	Housing	
1950-1952	34.0	10.6	4.5
First Five Yr. Plan (1953-57)	33.0	9.1	18.9
Second Five Yr. Plan (1958-62)	14.6	4.1	22.0
1963-1965	20.6	6.9	14.2
Third Five Yr. Plan (1966-70)	16.2	4.0	10.8
Fourth Five Yr. Plan (1971-78)	17.5	5.7	25.2
Fifth Five Yr. Plan (1976-80)	26.1	11.8	47.0
1976	18.8	6.1	24.2
1977	20.6	6.9	28.3
1978	20.9	7.8	33.5
1979	30.3	14.8	62.6
1980	35.7	20.0	82.3
1981	43.0	25.1	79.0
1982	45.5	25.4	90.2
1983	41.7	21.1	82.5
1984	42.0	22.0	100.0
1985	40.0	21.0	90.0

Source: Adapted from R.J.R. Kirkby, 1988, "Urban Housing Policy After Mao," in S. Feuchtwang, A. Hussain, and T. Pairault (eds.), *Transforming China's Economy in the Eighties*, Vol. 1: *The Rural Sector, Welfare and Employment* (Boulder, Colo.: Westview Press), p. 233.

construction was an integral part of the overall restructuring and "marketization" of the Chinese economy that began in earnest after 1978 and continued throughout the 1980s (see Chapters 5 and 6).[64]

The housing crisis at the end of the 1970s was associated with the overall austerity of Mao's China. Mao had convinced himself (but not all the CCP leaders) that China's people should not anticipate any major improvements in their living standards in the near future. It was Mao's belief that the struggle aspect of the revolution had not ended in 1949 and that it would in fact continue until the last remnants of the old bourgeois society had been permanently exorcised.[65] Consistent with this belief was Mao's assertion that self-sacrifice was required of the Chinese people. Instead of aspiring to the consumption standards of the West, he felt they should accept the need for frugality, hard work, and the ascetic life-styles of a new socialist order. In

the home this translated to the rejection of luxury and comfort and the tolerance of extremely basic living quarters. It is unlikely that this revolutionary commitment is still widespread in the beginning of the 1990s (in fact some Western scholars argued that it was never widespread, except in propaganda documents; see Chapter 4).

To construct new housing at the level specified in the plan, it was necessary for the Chinese to build high-rises, which had already been excoriated and often abandoned in the West on social grounds. There has also been strong criticism within China of the overall low quality of much of the new construction, the lack of landscaping, and the inadequate provision of ancillary facilities such as shopping and social services.[66] In Beijing many of the residents in the new high-rise towers found themselves without basic utilities such as elevators, water, heating, and sewage disposal—the result of a shortage of key building supplies and an overeager construction rate by some work units, many of which ran out of money before the basic services had been installed. An official survey conducted in 1985 showed that more than 3.2 million urban families were still living in "nonhousing" spaces such as corridors, closets, and offices; 13 percent of families had less than four square meters per person, which was half of the newly announced standard for the future; and 10.5 percent were living in one room only.[67]

The progress made in the construction of new housing since 1978 was effectively canceled out by the growth rate of Chinese cities. Thus even though the urban building boom continued through the 1980s, the population expansion ensured that the average amount of floor space per person in China's cities increased only marginally, from 5.2 square meters in 1977 to 6.3 in 1982. The official estimate of the families considered to be living in "poor housing" had stayed the same since 1978, at about 20 percent of the total, but as a result of the population growth in China's cities, the actual number of families involved in 1982 had increased from 6–7 million to about 11 million. By 1987 the average amount of floor space per person in China's cities varied from 6.0 to 7.2 square meters, usually with less space available in the larger cities. The vast exodus from the countryside to the cities during the 1980s is now threatening to produce some of the housing shortages so common in other countries, notably the United Kingdom and the United States. Unemployed peasants have been reported "squatting" in Chinese cities all across the country, sleeping in the streets and any available spaces they can find. At the present time there is very little information on the extent of actual "homelessness" in China, but unless some extremely effective prohibitions are placed on rural out-migration, it is difficult to see how China's already overstretched cities will be able to house the influx.[68]

COMMODIFIED HOUSING: THE ULTIMATE SOLUTION?

In spite of the virtual revolution in investment priorities, it had been possible only to ease minimally the housing crisis by the early 1980s, and some of the key thinkers within the CCP had already started to prepare the ground for a radical shift in housing policies. The preferred solution to the housing crisis required a headlong confrontation with the ideology that had inspired Maoist social and economic policies. It had already been considered necessary to introduce market-oriented principles into the economy as a whole. This helped to generate the investment funds to build new houses, but at the same time it acted to stimulate the level of effective demand among the Chinese for more and better housing. It was clear to many that similar principles needed to be injected into the housing market itself.

The solution that was proposed was to move toward the commodification of housing—which meant a greater emphasis than ever before on private home ownership; the acceptance of a "user pays" concept of housing rent; and the introduction of market principles into the business of housing construction.[69] In the tradition of previous five-year and longer-term plans, the government set a goal of housing all of its citizens by the year 2000, with an average of 8 square meters per person. In the middle of the 1980s the average monthly rent for a two-room apartment was less than Y 4 (just over U.S. $1), but the cost of new construction averaged between Y 300 and Y 500 per square meter of floor space. Obviously, to have even the slightest hope of reaching the established target, the state and its collective units would have to start charging much more for housing. It was hoped that this would allow cities and enterprises to speed up the rate of housing construction, as rental revenues began to approximate construction costs.

Experiments began in various cities in the middle of the 1980s, with house buyers paying up to one-third of the total costs. To date these experiments have been immensely successful, with the demand almost constantly outstripping the supply, especially as family and individual resources have continued to rise at an unprecedented rate in some parts of the country. An experiment conducted in the city of Yantai in 1987 was recommended as the basis of a new reform plan for China's urban housing in 1988. The proposal involved a sharp increase in the level of rents for housing, up to Y 1.56 per square meter per month. This meant that any families who wanted more space could be accommodated as long as they were able to pay for it. For example, a family in Yantai with 60 square meters had to pay Y 25 per month, which was more than 10 percent of its salary, about three times the proportion it had been paying. To ease the transition to this "user pays" system, the government started to issue housing-allowance vouchers, amounting to as much as 25 percent of the family's income, which could only be used for rent. The vouchers meant that most of the families who could tolerate living in small houses, or who were too poor to consider moving, were not seriously affected by the new higher level of rents.[70]

Among the leaders of the CCP, it was obviously not a simple or a unanimous decision to move toward a commodification of housing. Even raising housing prices to the level of the total value of the labor embodied in the construction process proved to be controversial. There was a natural hesitancy among many of the old-timers in the Party, as well as among the relatively few people who still harbored ideas of Maoist radicalism. After three decades of almost constant propaganda and mass movements to continue the class struggle, the faithful were hesitant about producing a new class of small-property owners in the cities, although the class was already well developed in the countryside. Nevertheless, the movement continued throughout the 1980s, and by 1987 official survey data published by the State Statistical Bureau showed a significant improvement in the urban housing situation, when compared with the data for the early 1980s (see Table 13.6). Unfortunately there are no details about how or where the sample was compiled or about how some of the categories were defined. In spite of the fact that we have reason to be suspicious of these statistics, it is interesting to note that in 1987 a considerable proportion of China's city dwellers were still living in what were officially defined as "crowded" or "insufficient" quarters.

Although the debate was finally settled in favor of commodification, ambivalence about the whole process slowed it down to a far more moderate level than had at first been envisioned. The sale of housing continued to expand in the late 1980s, but prices did not increase dramatically. Because of the sharp rise in prices in most consumer items that had accompanied the economic reforms, it was prudent of the government to prevent house prices from rising too rapidly. As the Chinese have already learned, the public outcry that results from inflation can lead to calls for retrenchment and a slowing down of the entire reform process.

In theory at least, the success of the economic reform movement called for a much more ambitious rate of housing commodification just as the government was beginning to slow down the process. The reforms resulted in higher family incomes all through the 1980s, so that even with the new higher rents, the proportion of the average family income spent on housing actually decreased, from 2.3 percent in 1979 to 1.5 percent in 1983, and again to 1.2 percent in 1985.[71]

CONCLUSION: HOUSING AND THE CHINESE PERESTROIKA

The steps taken to commodify urban housing in China can be interpreted as just one component of the larger set of economic reforms, resulting from major ideological shifts in thinking within the CCP. The danger inherent in such reforms was always that they would generate demands for even further ideological shifts. The newfound wealth and the highly prized possession of land, housing, and capital will continue to produce wider disparities between the different elements within Chinese society, and it is possible that the new "gentry" will soon demand political powers to match their wealth.

Many Westerners viewed what was happening in China in the 1980s as a triumph for capitalism over socialism. Certainly advertisements of the type that began to appear in some of China's glossy magazines represented a radical break with the past (see Figures 8.7 and 8.8). As the events of spring 1989 demonstrated, however, in political terms the triumph was far from complete. Whatever happened in the economic sphere, China remained solidly committed to its one-party system of government. As Lynn Pan observed in 1988, "China may have abandoned Stalin . . . she may have abandoned Marx, but by the one remaining measure, Lenin's, China will continue to be a communist state, where the true power lies in a single party organized

Table 13.6 Housing Conditions: Urban, Rural, and Inadequate, 1981-1987

	1981	1985	1987
Rural areas			
Average living space per capita (m^2)	9.40	14.70	16.00
Average no. of rooms per family	4.06	5.11	5.36
Urban areas			
Average living space per capita (m^2)	5.2	7.46	8.47
Average no. of rooms per family	NA	2.24	2.39
Inadequate housing			
Urban households without housing			
(% of total in each year)	3.22	1.50	0.48
Crowded households	24.6	12.5	7.9
Inconvenient households	9.7	8.7	7.6
< 6 m^2 per person	31.3	19.4	19.1
6-8 m^2 per person	17.7	22.6	22.2

Source: *China Statistical Yearbook 1988* (Beijing: State Statistical Bureau of the PRC, 1988), p. 746. Based on survey data (definitions not provided).

in the Leninist image, headed by a self-selecting group of men who make decisions for the vast majority of the people."[72]

After the vicious response to the widespread outburst of dissatisfaction in 1989, it is painfully obvious that the current leaders of the CCP are not yet ready to give up their power, even at the risk of losing their legitimacy. In fact, it seems entirely plausible that in the 1990s we might see a slowing down of the market-oriented reforms, as the leaders attempt to reduce the risk of further demands for political reform. It is intriguing to speculate about the role of the market solution to the housing crisis, along with the other economic reforms, in the destabilization of the existing system of government in China at the end of the 1980s. By attempting to respond to the people's call for a greater share of the nation's wealth, the government may have unwittingly contributed to the tumultuous events of 1989. It remains to be seen how it will manage the delicate process of building back the people's confidence in the 1990s.

Crime and Punishment in a Revolutionary Society

"You must be careful when you buy children's books," I quickly told my husband. "Don't buy any that have too many pictures of Chairman Mao." "Don't worry," he answered with an understanding smile. "My colleagues have already warned me that it's best not to buy comic books . . . [with] pictures of Chairman Mao on almost every other page. Children have caused a lot of trouble by spoiling the Chairman's pictures when they color the books."

—Chen Jo-Hsi[1]

INTRODUCTION

In this chapter and in Chapter 15, we turn our attention to the maintenance of law and order in China. As the discussion in both chapters will demonstrate, the issues of crime and human rights cannot be separated in China because the definition of what is a "crime" and the treatment of "criminals" are largely based on political considerations. In the West, by contrast, such matters are determined primarily by the "rule of law." As we shall see, in spite of some effort (and much rhetoric) in this direction in China in the 1980s, little progress has yet been made.

This chapter begins with a very brief review of the history of social-control practices in China over the centuries, focusing on the situation in postrevolutionary times. The major purpose here is to highlight some of the fundamental differences between the Chinese system of criminal justice and those in the United States and other Western democracies. To illustrate how law and order is maintained, and at what price in human (and humane) terms, we investigate some of the grass-roots policing and mediation activities in the Chinese city. The chapter closes with a consideration of some trends that suggest a con-

vergence between China and the West, in terms of both the overall rates of crime and the structure of the criminal justice systems.

SOCIAL CONTROL IN POSTREVOLUTIONARY CHINA

As we saw in the previous chapters, the state's performance in the provision of services in China since 1949 leaves much to be desired. The story from one city to another is a familiar one. Services are basic at best, shoddy and dangerous at worst. There are constant shortages, delays, and frequent opportunities for graft and corruption. In one area of service provision, however, the state has spared no expense and left nothing to chance. This is *the police function of the state*—the provision of services to control the actions and perhaps even the thoughts of the Chinese people.

It is useful to begin again with the situation in Canton in 1949 to see how the Communists went about normalizing life in their part of war-ravaged China. According to Ezra Vogel the resumption of law and order was a priority at that time.[2] The most urgent threat perceived by the Communists was the continued presence of "counterrevolutionaries," which in that case meant soldiers of the recently surrendered Kuomintang (KMT) army who had not fled to Taiwan. Rather than trying to kill off their enemies immediately, the Communists went about their task stealthily. For years the Communists had been actively engaged in sabotage and disruption, but now it was their turn to put an end to such activities. Ironically, the tactics they employed were borrowed largely from the KMT itself: They attempted to control all available weapons; they required all KMT members to register with public-security officials; they put pressure on citizens to report all known members and associates of the KMT; and they employed counteragents (spies) to infiltrate KMT hiding places. In a strategy that would become one of the hallmarks of the Communists in later years, they also set about restricting human movements; in this case the most important action was to close off the border between Guangdong Province and Hong Kong.

From an initial kid-glove approach the Communists quickly shifted to a harder stance. They had guaranteed clemency to all people who registered as spies and KMT sympathizers, but they were sufficiently worried about the security risk to countermand their own promises by arresting and executing men who had been promised leniency. This was not interpreted by the Communists as a breach of faith; it simply meant that circumstances had changed, necessitating a new strategy. Such an interpretation portended behavior that would become commonplace during the next four decades—saying one thing, then doing another. It seemed that denying something would happen virtually guaranteed its happening. As Paul Theroux observed, only partly tongue-in-cheek, we should "never believe anything . . . [about the actions of the Chinese government] until it has been officially denied."[3]

Ezra Vogel estimated that after an immense roundup, during a ten-month period beginning in October 1950, the Communists executed more than 28,000 of their enemies, that is, 1 out of every 1,000 people in the province of Guangdong. To explain the need for such brutal measures, mass rallies and exhibitions were staged and radio programs were aired. Running the risk of alienating the citizens of Canton before they had embarked upon the process of rebuilding the city, the Communists had learned a very important lesson. "By killing the most serious opposition and intimidating the rest in a well-organized campaign, the Communists produced more fear than love, but their campaign was the vehicle for establishing a greater sense of public security throughout the province than the people had ever previously known in their lives."[4]

In these early activities the Communists revealed much about the strategies they would continue to employ in their attempts to restore and maintain order. People from all walks of life were labeled, sometimes almost indiscriminately, as "fascists," "feudal remnants," "counterrevolutionaries," and "imperialists." These were people who had opposed the new government in some way. To discredit them, the entire artillery of the propaganda machinery was mobilized.

The overall success of the CCP in bringing about order can be attributed to disciplined organization, careful planning, and the cultivation of mass support from "the people." Although all of this was backed up by the continuous threat of force, the CCP realized from very early on that its best strategy was to be patient and selective. As Vogel described the situation: "They first built up their own organizational support and struck at a few key targets *while assuring others they had nothing to fear.* By careful selection of targets they removed potential rivals for power and influence and obtained a modicum of compliance from others, thus consolidating their own control."[5]

What happened in Canton illustrates that complete social control was achieved by a combination of strategies, one in which the violence associated with totalitarian regimes was complemented by more subtle forms of persuasion and socialization.[6] The suppression of "counterrevolutionaries" would have been a hollow victory without equal success in the attempt to "reform" the city's intellectuals— which meant getting them to shift their focus away from bourgeois thoughts, books, and art forms and toward more acceptable socialist pursuits such as production and economic development.

As sinister as the concept of "thought reform" may be to anyone who enjoys the intellectual freedoms of the West, it was (and it remains) an important issue for the Communists. They sought nothing less than "the elimination of ancient patterns of thought and the immediate replacement of these . . . by a body of beliefs appropriate to their conception of a modern Communist nation."[7] Before going on with the discussion of law and order in post-1949 China, it will be useful to examine, if only briefly, what some of these "ancient patterns of thought" actually involved.

CRIME, JUSTICE, AND THE RULE OF LAW IN CHINA

China has a long history of codified law and legal development, beginning with the Qin Dynasty in 221 B.C. Over the centuries the state established a set of formal controls over the behavior of individuals (known as *fa*), but these were complemented by a set of rules of proper conduct (known as *li*, or ritual—see Chapter 3). *Li* was based on the Confucian moralist tradition, in which it was hoped that individuals could be educated or persuaded to behave virtuously.[8] For serious crimes the formal control system was invoked; but for the management of everyday life, the informal mechanisms dictated by *li* were considered to be not only more natural but also more effective. Confucius himself is reported to have said, "If the people are guided by laws and regulated by punishment, they will try to avoid the punishment but have no sense of shame; if they are guided by virtue and regulated by 'li' they will have the sense of shame and become good."[9]

In contrast to the formal aspects of social control, the informal system was considered to be preventive and proactive, but as a result a much wider range of behaviors came under the umbrella of public scrutiny than would normally be tolerated in most Western societies.[10] Since the founding of the PRC in 1949 there have been some important developments in the Chinese criminal justice system. The Communist conception of justice is based on the Marxist-Leninist notion that law emanates from and is intended to serve the class that is dominant in society. In China this is the worker and peasant class, and crime is interpreted as an expression of hostility toward that class.[11] It follows that in Communist justice, the spheres of political and legal activities have always been closely related. To establish a hierarchy of guilt, in other words to discriminate between noncriminals (the "people") and criminals (the "enemy"), the criteria used in China have typically been based on political value judgments. The inherently political nature of many of the categories of defined crimes in China is evident from the listing provided in Table 14.1. As we shall see in Chapter 15, the continuation of this practice in the 1980s resulted in some criticism from the international human rights community long before the Tiananmen Square incident.

Mao Zedong distinguished between two types of "contradictions" that resulted in wrongdoing and that called for different solutions. "Antagonistic" contradictions occurred between the people and the state (for example, "counterrevolutionary" activity; see Table 14.1). Such actions were to be dealt with through the formal control system, and they generally elicited serious punishment. "Nonantagonistic" contradictions occurred solely among the people, and in all but the most extreme cases they called for responses from the informal social-control system, including dispute mediation, education, and persuasion.[12]

As a general rule, Mao favored informal methods of social control, and he shared with many other CCP members a fundamental distrust of law and lawyers. For the Communists, legal formality was considered too "mechanistic"—they wanted a system with more flexibility to facilitate the requirements of revolutionary change. The implications of this are ominous. In the first place Party officials (cadres) rather than lawyers were selected to operate the criminal justice system. This of course opened up the possibility of corruption and left most of the decision-making in the hands of individuals.

The second consequence of the Communists' view of justice was that in the name of the revolution, sanctions of all types could be inflicted upon a wide range of people who were defined as "enemies of the people."[13] As Amnesty International reported, China probably has more offenses currently punishable by death than any other country in the world, a chilling fact that was brought home sharply in the televised accounts of the postdemonstration crackdown activities in the summer of 1989.[14]

Table 14.1 China's Published Crime Statistics, 1986 Data

Classification of Offense	Arrests (No. Persons)	Prosecutions (No. Cases)
Counterrevolutionary acts	620	368
Endangering public security	10,801	10,304
Undermining economic order	7,965	5,647
Infringing personal rights	75,958	67,304
Property violations	217,692	143,273
Disrupting social administration	34,353	22,070
Disruption of marriage and family	1,014	1,170
Dereliction of duty	6,066	5,862
Other offenses[a]	1,074	1,221
Total	355,603	257,219

[a]Offenses determined by analogy to similar offenses that are illegal.

Source: *China Law Yearbook* (Beijing: Law Publishing House, 1988), p. 883. Reprinted in *Far Eastern Economic Review* 139, No. 12 (March 24, 1988), p. 81.

In the 1980s the area of criminal law came under intensive scrutiny in China. This can be interpreted in part as an attempt to restore the "rule of law" after the horrors of the Cultural Revolution, during which gross miscarriages of justice and widespread purging activities were commonplace. The Chinese recognized, in principle at least, that in addition to protecting the interests of society by suppressing crime, the law must provide a bulwark against tyranny by the state. To achieve this it is necessary to stipulate clearly the rights and duties of citizens and the state by constitutional *principles* and to define the formal legal *processes* whereby these principles are adhered to.

In spite of the apparent wishes of legal reformers, and some progress, the Chinese system of justice still differs sharply from that in most Western countries. As a result, a criminal defendant in the PRC is at a considerable, and by Western standards an unacceptable, disadvantage in several ways.[15] First, the Chinese reject the principle that a person is innocent until proven guilty—hence the suspect is usually referred to as "the offender" (*renfan*). The disadvantages of such a system are obvious in comparison to one in which the burden of proof rests with the prosecution, which has to furnish clear evidence of guilt, and in which the accused is supposed to be given the benefit of the doubt.

Second, the Chinese deny the accused person access to legal assistance until the trial. This means there may be as little time as three days to prepare the case. Perhaps even more important, the lawyer is not really expected to contest the charges by recommending a plea of "not guilty." The lawyer is still seen as an agent of the state, who functions largely to make a plea for leniency for the "guilty" party.[16] It is no great surprise to discover that a much higher proportion of arrests in China, compared with the United States, result in prosecutions (Table 14.1).

Third, the Chinese judiciary does not always function independently of the Party; in fact there are many cases in which the verdict is reached *before* the trial (*xian pan hou shen*, "verdict first, trial second"). Fourth, the Chinese reserve the right to detain some offenders for lengthy periods without a trial, with the punishment administered solely by the local security officials (the police) and no right of appeal.[17]

There is evidence that all these situations were being keenly debated in China at the end of the 1980s and that reforms might be imminent. The fact remains, however, that the entire system currently falls far short of internationally agreed upon standards of judicial procedure. Some progress was made, but as the events of 1989 clearly demonstrated, the continuing struggle between the Party and the "rule of law" is still being decided by the dictates of political expediency.

GEOGRAPHY AND SOCIAL CONTROL

Perhaps partly as a result of the deterrent effect of the draconian system of criminal justice, the rate of crime in China is much lower than it is in most other parts of the world.[18] Naturally the CCP would prefer outsiders to believe that the prevalence of crime has been reduced significantly by the replacement of materialistic motives with communistic and socially responsible behavior. The Chinese can not deny that social control has been achieved through external means, in the shape of deterrence and the fear of punishment; but they would also be quick to point out that a great deal of internal social control has been achieved through the development of a collective social conscience that makes criminal behavior less likely to occur.

Somewhere between these two poles of the crime-reduction argument is the rather simplistic view that the administrative structures put in place after 1949 have helped to keep down the rate of crime in the PRC.[19] As we noted in earlier chapters, the spatial organization of everyday life in China, particularly in the cities, was more than anything else an attempt to achieve order—which meant compliance with the law. Contributions to this effort have been made in two major ways: There has been the implementation of what can be referred to as "passive control structures," mechanisms that directly or indirectly work to reduce the rate of crime; and there are "active control structures," deliberate attempts to change individual thoughts and behaviors on the issue of crime.[20] A few examples in each category will suffice to illustrate what is implied here. In comparison to its counterpart in the United States, the Chinese city has far fewer danger spots where crimes are likely to be committed. The bars, clubs, parking lots, and empty alleyways of the U.S. city do not exist in such profusion in China. There are also fewer breeding grounds for the development of criminal subcultures, a phenomenon that has typically been associated with slum enclaves and high-

rise housing projects in the U.S. city. Until about the end of the 1970s the development of criminal subcultures within the Chinese city was effectively inhibited in a number of ways:

- Rural in-migration of underprivileged peasants was tightly controlled.
- The paucity of job and residential mobility aided in fostering local cohesiveness, mutual helping, and a strong presence of neighborhood-watch-type local surveillance.
- Many of the discontented youth and "undesirable elements" were "sent down" to the countryside, thereby eliminating them and their potential influence on others.

Several other characteristics of Chinese urban life can be considered, from a Western perspective, to be "healthy," in the sense that they keep down crime rates. There is a very low incidence of problem drinking, alcoholism, and drug abuse; a virtual absence of handguns; a low rate of divorce and marital instability; a very limited autonomous youth culture; a strong sense of intergenerational family cohesiveness; very little ethnic or racial tension (at least at the intracity level); generally low rates of unemployment (a situation that seems to have changed very rapidly in the last years of the 1980s); and a high degree of citizen involvement in both surveillance and mediation functions. The result has been that the Chinese city since 1949 has for the most part been a safe and orderly place in which to live, and the prevalence of crime has been extraordinarily low by international standards.

The organization of urban life in China helps to keep down the occurrence of crime. In addition, deliberate efforts are made in the work units and neighborhoods to provide mediation and policing services at the local level. This work is combined with propaganda campaigns intended to foster conformist behavior, devise ongoing strategies to deal with the problem of crime, and streamline local surveillance and "busybodying" activities.

Both the passive and the active control structures have led, in theory at least, to a city in which there are no "dead corners." There are very few parts of the city that are unpatrolled or unsurveyed. When the new neighborhood structures were first established in the 1950s, the goal was to create an environment in which criminals were unwelcome and where if they showed their faces, they would be chased away. "We should create an atmosphere in which the black sheep [criminals] find themselves like rats scurrying across the street with everyone yelling 'kill them, kill them' so that they can find no market and no hiding place."[21]

From the late 1970s to the late 1980s, there were some interruptions in this idyllic picture of the low-crime Chinese city. One contributing event was the illegal return of some of the millions of youths who had been "sent down" to the countryside. Many of these youths arrived in the cities illegally, with no jobs, no residence cards, and their education disrupted. They were often bitter and resentful of the system that had exiled them, and it has been suggested that many among this population of illegally returning youth were forced into criminal activities such as engaging in private businesses (which were illegal until the late 1970s), picking pockets, gambling, and black-marketing. The consensus is that as a group they "had no real stake or responsibility in the city. They saw themselves as living by their wits outside of the system, and they were not easy to shame into repentance and good behavior."[22]

In the middle-to-late 1980s the vast influx of unemployed peasants from the countryside further strained the social-control capacities of China's cities. As we saw in earlier chapters, the Chinese city, with a limited number of jobs to go around and with services already stretched to bursting point, will face a crisis in the not-too-distant future. On the basis of their research with Hong King emigrés, Whyte and Parish characterized this crisis as one in which city dwellers, especially youth, have very few legitimate opportunities available to them.[23]

As a result of the post–Cultural Revolution return migrations, the 1980s influx of rural-to-urban migrants, and the already overloaded education system, many young people in China's cities simply cannot look to the future with much optimism. "Urban youths no longer . . . [were able] to see clear strategies for planning their futures, and had neither predictable rewards for good behavior presented to them, nor certain penalties for getting in

trouble. . . . This . . . dismantling . . . of the urban opportunity structure was sufficient to offset the solidarity and sanction mechanisms fostering urban orderliness."[24]

MODERNIZATION AND THE "CRIME WAVE"

If the Whyte and Parish hypothesis is correct, we would expect to find an upsurge in the level of crime in the Chinese city in the 1980s. Given that crime statistics in any country are notoriously unreliable and difficult to interpret, a combination of the official data in China and some of the stories carried in the major newspapers provides evidence of certain patterns that have emerged over the last three decades. The data are summarized in Table 14.2, and they suggest that the prevalence of "serious crime" was at its highest in 1949, immediately following the disorder of the civil war.[25] From that time until the Cultural Revolution, crime levels were exceptionally low, effectively halved from the 1949 level. There are no data at all for the Cultural Revolution period (1966–1976), partly because the country was in chaos most of the time; in any case, the suspension of normal judicial procedures would render such data virtually meaningless.[26]

By the late 1970s the crime rate had increased to approximately 6.5 per 10,000 in the population, and a dramatic increase was observed in the first years of the 1980s, to somewhere in excess of 8 and perhaps as high as 10 per 10,000. The increases have been corroborated by academic studies conducted by outsiders, as well as by after-the-fact reports in the official Chinese press.[27] Although the causes of this increase, if indeed it represents a true increase, are probably extremely complex, the data support the Whyte and Parish hypothesis. The major issues highlighted in the media were juvenile crime, serious and violent crimes, and economic crimes.[28]

The appearance of a "crime wave" in the early 1980s resulted in a major "crackdown," after which the crime rate was reported to have been cut by about 35 percent.[29] In spite of the continuing hard line on crime during this period, the rates started to rise again after 1984 and appeared to have reached about

Table 14.2 "Crime Waves" in the People's Republic of China

	Rate of "Serious Crime"[a] (per 10,000 Pop.)
1949	9.3[b]
1952	4.2[b]
1950-1965	4.5[b]
1966-1976	--
1977-1979	6.5[b]
1980-1982	8-10[c]
1984	7.3[d]
1985	7.0[d]
1986	7.7[d]

[a]"Serious crime" is the sum of the rates for homicide, assault, robbery, and rape.
[b]*Source*: Estimates from M. K. Whyte and W. L. Parish, 1984, *Urban Life in Contemporary China* (Chicago: University of Chicago Press), p. 249.
[c]*Source*: The high estimate is from *China Law Yearbook 1987* (Beijing: Law Publishing House, 1988). The low estimate is from *China Daily*, April 7, 1987.
[d]*Source*: *China Law Yearbook 1987* (Beijing: Law Publishing House, 1988).

7.7 per 10,000 by 1986 (Table 14.2). The official statistics had not been released by early 1990, but it was known that the crime rate continued to move upward in both 1987 and 1988.[30] By the end of the decade, therefore, the crime rate in China was lower than at the beginning of the decade, but it was still much higher than in the 1950s and 1960s.

If we accept these statistics at their face value, there is evidence that the crime rate in China has fluctuated in a "wavelike" pattern during the four decades after Liberation. It seems likely, however, that the statistics released by the government will reflect the current political agenda, rather than the actual "facts."[31] An announcement that crime rates have increased, therefore, may be completely unrelated to the actual prevalence of crime. The purpose of such a fabrication may be to elicit support for an all-out war on crime, which appears to be what happened in 1983 and again in 1988 (see Figure 14.1). Similarly, to demonstrate that the crackdown efforts have been successful, the crime statistics can, at a later date, be manipulated in the other direction. As cynical as this might sound, it fits with the obvious evidence that the Chinese

Figure 14.1 *Cartoon showing two high-level policemen discussing strategies for cracking down even further, in an attempt to reduce the rate of crime, which rose steadily throughout the 1980s. Source: Far Eastern Economic Review, November 3, 1988, p. 23; reprinted by permission.*

government is willing to distort the facts and rewrite the news to suit its own goals.[32] There is another side to this story, however, in that by acknowledging that it has a growing problem with crime, China's leaders have to accept publicly, both to the Chinese and to outsiders, that the crime-free socialist society they promised has eluded them.[33]

CHINESE CRIMINAL JUSTICE: A CONVERGENCE WITH THE WEST?

Accompanying the major increases in crime rates in the 1980s has been considerable evidence that the role of the law in China is being increased, presumably in an attempt to define a new and more stable relationship between law and politics. A number of important new pieces of legislation dealing with substantive and procedural laws in both criminal and civil realms have been passed since 1979.[34] Major constitutional change has also occurred, with new constitutions introduced in 1978 and 1982.[35] In recent publications more than 300 new laws and regulations have been reported, a dramatic escalation since the Maoist era, in which China functioned virtually without any written laws.[36]

It would appear from these reports that the informal or "revolutionary" model of deviance control that predominated during the Maoist era is in the process of being replaced by the "procedural," or "jural," model that is familiar in the West—in other words, one that is based on written rules and bureaucratic management.[37] In the sort of headline that is very familiar in the West, it was reported that the National People's Congress Standing Committee stressed the overriding importance of "law and public order" during its nineteenth session in 1987.[38]

Another development that has been highlighted is the increasing professionalization of the social-control apparatus in China. In the middle of the 1970s China, a country with almost 1 billion people, had functioned with only about 3,500 lawyers. During the Cultural Revolution legal practice as recognized in the West had virtually disappeared and political cadres essentially had taken over all legal functions. In contrast, by the end of 1986 the number of full- and part-time lawyers was reported to be 40,000 and was predicted to reach 100,000 by 1990. Extensive programs of legal training and education have been instituted, and there are plans to expand the staffing of the judicial system at all levels, including public-security officials, the courts, and prosecutors.[39]

Again, there is more than one way to interpret these developments. Although in China the law is available as a resource in fighting wrongdoing, politics still dictates when legal procedures rather than more informal administrative procedures will be used. For example, in spite of what the new constitution says, administrative sanctions available to the police can include incarcerations of up to three years without trial.[40] Although the 1982 constitution stipulates that the Supreme People's Court is empowered to review death sentences, recent history, especially the events of 1989, showed that at certain times the review process is suspended and speedy sentencing imposed.[41] This suggests that the shift from the revolutionary to the jural model of justice may be a shift in name only, and in fact the jural court that sentenced dissidents in the 1980s was similar in most respects to the revolutionary court that sentenced dissidents both before and during the Cultural Revolution.[42]

How then are we to interpret the mounting evidence of increasing crime rates in China and the movement away from the traditional emphasis on informal methods of social control to more formalized methods? These trends suggest that China is slowly catching up with the West, both in its pattern of crime and in its responses to crime—this is the "convergence" hypothesis. There are a number of ways to interpret the evidence, and we need to remember that what we think we are seeing may not actually be what is happening at all. As always in China the pervasive influence of culture and politics lies just below the surface.

A Criminological Interpretation

Much of Western criminological theory predicts that rising crime rates will accompany (or follow) major periods of economic and social change.[43] During such times values and priorities change rapidly, and opportunities (especially in terms of wealth, employment, education, and living standards) cannot keep pace with rising expectations.[44] In these circumstances traditional (informal) forms of social control are expected to lose their efficacy, and formal criminal-justice institutions have to be expanded to cater to the rising level of deviance. According to the criminologists, this is basically what has occurred in most Western societies, and the pattern is now belatedly being reproduced in China.[45]

The major problem with this interpretation is that it assumes that the informal methods are being replaced by formal methods of social control. In fact we have no evidence that the informal methods are being used any less than they ever have been. It could simply be that the publicity given to the new legal reforms and the other aspects of the "formal" control system have diverted attention away from the informal structures, which may actually be functioning in pretty much the same way that they always have.[46]

A Modernization Interpretation

Another criticism of the criminological "convergence" hypothesis is that it tends to disconnect crime from its economic and political context and to underestimate the role of the state.[47] In China there can be no such simple separation. The events of the 1980s, especially those of 1989, suggest that changes in crime patterns and efforts at crime control are probably only incidentally related, rather than causally connected, as the criminological hypothesis suggests.

An alternative interpretation considers the impact of the large-scale push to achieve the Four Modernizations, which has been so central in post-Mao China.[48] It is reasonable to assume that the development of a more formalized system of justice would help to instill confidence within the world economy by demonstrating that the current situation is stable. In comparison to the chaotic years of the past, such stability would be interpreted by China's trading partners as a considerable advantage. "The Chinese leadership views the reform of China's legal system as an integral part of its modernization effort. Establishing a 'rule of law' is recognized as important to China's international standing as well as to its further economic development and modernization."[49]

The tremendous political upheavals that occurred during the past three decades in China, particularly during the Cultural Revolution (1966–1976), created a crisis of confidence both at home and abroad. In the Maoist years, struggle was seen as an inevitable feature of progressive change, but when the "moderates" regained control in 1978, continuing internal political conflicts were seen as barriers to economic growth. By the middle of the 1980s it appeared that the international confidence sought by China's leaders had been achieved. Unfortunately, the second wave of the Democracy Movement events after 1986 and the demonstrations illustrated that the old revolutionary justice system was as strong as ever.

A Political Interpretation

As is the case with just about everything else that happens in China, the recent changes in the system of justice are intimately tied up with politics. The constitutions drafted in the 1970s and 1980s appeared to extend the rights of individual citizens, but there can be no doubt in anyone's mind that the real objective of the newly drafted provisions was "to serve as a means of authorizing limited political participation as dictated and controlled by the Party."[50] In other words, the needs of the state and the desire for law and order would continue to take precedence over the consideration of individual rights. It is clear that the criminal justice system in China, in spite of recent developments, is still not an independent entity.[51] Although it may seem preposterous to Western observers, the increase in the crime rates and the newfound emphasis on the need for strong "law and order" responses may represent little more than the desperate efforts of the Communists to maintain the one-party system of government and to crush any attempts to alter the status quo.

A Misinterpretation:
Have We Misread the Signs?

The events of 1989 suggested that the shift toward a Westernized jural model of criminal justice in China may in fact be little more than a symbolic act, and what we have interpreted as a sign of real progress may have been a smoke screen. In spite of the recent developments, the new laws, the growing army of lawyers, and the constitutional amendments can and will be overridden at any time in the interests of maintaining the existing political system. In addition, far from being replaced by a formal system of criminal justice, the traditional informal social-control mechanisms have actually been strengthened during the 1980s and brought increasingly under the aegis of the state.[52] In other words, most of the unique features of informal social control are still in place, but they have now been augmented and "institutionalized"—

which suggests that the Party is no longer prepared to leave the responsibility for such practices to the people themselves.

Two significant examples of this are the developments in *legal education* for the masses and in the ancient practice of *dispute mediation*. Education has been at the center of the efforts to control deviance in China throughout the four decades of Communist rule and has been the most visible aspect of preventive crime control. Such education relies on the traditional notion that human beings can behave well if they are provided with the appropriate leadership and the correct training. The education they receive is provided within the context of mass involvement in decision-making, which is generally referred to as the "mass line,"[53] a concept that has remained solidly in place since the prerevolutionary days in Yenan. The natural infrastructure of small-group solidarity at the level of family and community in China, and the organizational structures within the work units and neighborhoods, have been utilized by the state to launch mass-education campaigns.[54]

In recent years this mechanism has been used successfully to provide detailed education and discussion about the new laws and regulations that have been implemented. China's five-year drive to publicize the law began in earnest in 1986 with small-group discussions at the neighborhood level, augmented by an intense media-publicity campaign. The purpose of this campaign was to make "law a household word in China."[55] Since that time the press has been blitzed periodically with stories describing how "legal education surges ahead . . . and . . . helps change daily life."[56]

Although military and political officials have priority in receiving legal education, everyone has been involved, from schoolchildren to prisoners, in a variety of settings.[57] The purpose of this education, according to Vice Premier Qiao Shi, was to ensure not only that laws are obeyed but also that the "people become fully aware of their rights and interests as masters of . . . [their] country."[58] It was expected that mass legal education would ultimately help to combat the wave of corruption and abuses of power that seemed to have dominated local affairs in the reform era of the 1980s. Deng Xiaoping, for example, predicted that as a result of their education people will become knowledgeable enough to resist injustice whenever they encounter it.[59]

Another feature of traditional social control has been mediation, which is based on a long-standing preference for the avoidance of formal criminal procedures and penalties in situations of social conflict—according to an old saying, "the Chinese people would rather put their head in a tiger's mouth than go to court." Resorting to services provided by known intermediaries has historically been favored over the involvement of outsiders (such as the courts), who have been viewed with suspicion and deemed to lack the tradition of fairness and impartiality essential to an acceptable outcome. As we saw in Chapter 12, mediation work since the early 1950s has been incorporated as an official function of the neighborhood and work-unit organizations.

The work of the mediation committees involves the settlement of disputes and minor infractions through the use of peer pressure, the development of a social consensus about the appropriate solution, and community follow-up. Extravagant claims have been made about the potential success of mediation efforts in China. There is a consensus that about 80 percent of criminal cases can be avoided if mediation occurs. The ratio of cases mediated to cases adjudicated in court is thought to be about 10:1, although there is no formal requirement to submit to mediation. Official sources report that in 1985 more than 7 million disputes were mediated in China, and this prevented between 60,000 and 80,000 homicides and suicides (see Table 14.3).[60]

Mediation is an aspect of traditional deviance control that has proved very attractive to Western observers.[61] Former U.S. Chief Justice Warren Burger, for example, publicly praised the Chinese system of mediation, and perhaps partly in response to the outside interest, mediation work in China has been revitalized since 1978.[62] Mediation committees are now becoming part of legal-service bureaus, which include other traditional functions such as receiving and responding to complaints about local officials. Although this has to be interpreted as a positive step, it is also possible that this sort of professionalization will jeopardize precisely those aspects of mediation that are the most flexible and responsive to local concerns.

Table 14.3 Disputes Resolved by Mediation in China, 1985

Type of Dispute	Number	% of Total
Marriage	1,222,836	16.8
Inheritance	262,408	3.6
Support	404,356	5.5
Estate	1,107,453	15.2
Debt	333,102	4.6
Workplace related	725,889	9.9
Damage	535,584	7.3
Family	1,044,849	14.3
Neighbors	875,576	12.0
Others	793,996	10.8
Total resolved	7,307,049	

Source: *China Law Yearbook, 1987* (Beijing: Law Publishing House, 1988).

One aspect of the informal social-control mechanisms extant in China that is definitely not envied in the West is the *public exposure of wrongdoers*. The purpose, we must presume, is to remind members of the public that crime does not pay. At the extreme end of this behavior is the barbaric practice of parading criminals through the streets at gunpoint, with their heads shaved and bowed. Loudspeakers warn the crowds to avoid making the same mistakes as the criminals. Public executions, although now reportedly illegal in China, still occur.[63]

In addition to these blatant practices, there are many other ways in which the public is expected and required to pay attention to the judicial process. Well-publicized trials, involving both media exposure and public appearances of the criminals, are still important mechanisms of education in China.[64] Public participation in trials through the practice of lay assessment and public commentary is frequently reported in the media. Posters describing individual criminals and their sentences and newspaper stories recounting how people went astray and, more important, their subsequent reform are common fare.[65] This public approach to wrongdoing and wrong-doers is in sharp contrast with the Western emphasis on privacy and the maintenance of human dignity.

Chinese history is filled with morality tales, and many of the expressions in current use in the Chinese language contain references to the expected standards for moral behavior. In contemporary times this is still a concern, as witnessed by the frequent exposure of public officials whose behavior is judged to lack morality.[66] According to the Confucian tradition of *li*, the self-evident goodness of leaders has always been an important force in maintaining social stability and acceptance of the social order.[67] In contrast to the Western concept of division of powers to restrain the abuses of office, the Chinese have put far more emphasis on housecleaning from the inside, relying on the traditional belief in the value of education (about the law and the current ideology), and the benefits of persuasion (through exposure and self-criticism). The public is constantly barraged with propaganda about the benefits of the new legal-education programs. The education process is meant to be ongoing, even for legal officials.

CONCLUSION: IS EAST MEETING WEST?

In an orientation lecture for members of the Communist party, officials were exhorted to "make themselves specialists in the understanding of the law, experts at implementing the law, and models of acting according to law." It was hoped that as a result they would become "selfless, upright and unyielding judicial warriors," able to fulfill their mission of service and correction in the greater society.[68] This kind of message illustrates that the law will continue to serve the interests of the state and the Party for the foreseeable future in China. It also demonstrates one of the fundamental differences between China and the West, in terms of what is expected from the people in their service to the state. Differences of this magnitude prevent us from making cross-cultural comparisons and predictions based on Western assumptions. John King Fairbank suggested that in the area of crime and justice it is probably a mistake to think about China either as a "backward case" or as a "latecomer" to modernization. As he said, and as the tragedy of Tiananmen Square indicated, we will probably have to accept that China is still a "deviant other culture," one that will continue to follow its own tortuous path into the future.[69]

What we would have liked to interpret as a switch over to Western methods of criminal justice and an adherence to the rule of law may not have been anything of the sort. It is apparent that instead of formal methods of social control replacing informal methods, China has simply added the new methods to the old. As a result, the total amount of social control in China has been increased and the rights of ordinary citizens have been jeopardized even further.[70] This became apparent to millions of television viewers around the world in 1989, when they watched in horror as the Party used its considerable resources to "round up" the leading "counterrevolutionaries." It is a fitting conclusion for this book, therefore, to consider the momentous events of 1989 and to discuss some of the more abstract concepts of justice involved in the issue of human rights.

Human Rights and the Crime of Dissent in China

If the Chinese People don't stand up and speak, if they don't move to the front line of struggle themselves, then one billion people will no longer have the right to live on the globe. We will have been the most stupid, good for nothing, weak, despicable race on earth. . . . We've been played with . . . used like guinea pigs in an experiment—we've been cheated and tricked. Can it be that when the experiment has utterly failed and we are on the verge of death, we don't even have the guts to shout out, "It hurts"? People who are so numb they can't even yell "It hurts" are people who are really better off dead.

—Zhang Xianliang[1]

INTRODUCTION: THE BEIJING SPRING OF 1978–1979

In a society where people have been sent to labor camps for life because they disagreed with the government, where wives have been forced to denounce husbands because of their political beliefs, and where criminals have been marched out and shot in front of live audiences, there is no doubt that ordinary human rights have been denied. This has consistently been the case for the people of China.[2] To illustrate this shameful aspect of everyday life in contemporary China, this chapter opens with an exploration of the Chinese Democracy Movement, from its beginnings in 1978 to its apparent destruction in 1989.

Much has been made since the late 1970s of China's campaign to achieve the Four Modernizations. There were all-out efforts to modernize China on four fronts: agriculture, industry, military, and science and technology. But for many people both inside and outside China, the achievements of the Four Modernizations were worthless unless a "Fifth Modernization" could be attained, that is,

unless Chinese society could be restructured to base it on democratic principles and the free exercise of human rights.[3] One of the most outspoken critics of the government in the 1970s was a young electrician from Anhui Province, Wei Jingsheng. Wei wrote in 1978: "The leaders of our nation must be informed that we want to take our destiny into our own hands. We want no more gods and emperors. No more saviours of any kind. We want to be masters of our own country. . . . Democracy, freedom and happiness are the only gods of modernization. Without this fifth modernization, the four others are nothing more than a new-fangled lie."[4]

In his new magazine of literary and political criticism entitled *Tansuo* ("Exploration"), Wei attempted to exercise his rights by speaking his mind freely. In theory his right to do so was protected by the Chinese constitution of 1978; but in 1979 he was arrested, tried, and convicted in the Beijing Municipal Court. His crime was recorded as "leaking state secrets" and carrying out "counterrevolutionary" agitation.[5] Wei had, according to the court, written many "reactionary" articles that were explicitly intended to incite the overthrow of the existing government. He was sentenced to fifteen years in prison, most of which has thus far been spent in solitary confinement.

The treatment of Wei Jingsheng sounded what the Communist party hoped would be the official death knell of the emerging Democracy Movement in China. Beginning in November 1978 a number of "big-character posters" appeared on a wall near Xidan in central Beijing. "Democracy Wall," as it became known, was soon the official meeting place of the new movement. Thousands of posters, containing news, poems and stories, cartoons, political manifestos, and calls for political reform appeared on the wall. The authors of the posters, people like Wei, soon branched out into pamphlets and magazines.

By early 1979 the new Deng Xiaoping government decided the movement had gone too far. The posters and the gatherings were prohibited; the leaders of the movement were jailed and turned into nonpersons. The Democracy Movement had been referred to as the beginning of a new era of political freedom in Communist China. As a Beijing worker wrote in a poem called "Dawn" in December 1978:

> China is the native place of Mao Zedong Thought.
> Let's go forward hand in hand,
> March forward towards the bright new dawning.
> The early morning sunlight chases the fog away,
> On "Democracy Wall"
> The People have shown their strength.[6]

The mere existence of the movement was seen as evidence of a distinct relaxation of the apparent freeze on individual liberties in Communist China, and for this reason the period was referred to as the "Beijing Spring." As it turned out, the spring proved to be only a very brief thaw, but as the events of the 1980s, and especially 1989, illustrated, the Democracy Movement refused to die in 1979. It went underground and it was forced out of mainland China into Hong Kong, Taiwan, and the international community of emigrés, as some of the more outspoken critics joined the ranks of the Chinese diaspora. Democracy Wall itself had been dismantled, but what it stood for would not be forgotten. To the demonstrators in Tiananmen Square in 1989, the words of the poet Ling Bing in 1978 would appear to be prophetic:

> Farewell—Democracy Wall
> What can I say to you?
> A few more days
> And maybe I'll be sitting
> Beneath a window, behind bars,
> And people will stare, hard as ice,
> Will cross-examine me,
> Will not understand
> That you and I are one
> But I believe
> That you will never vanish,
> Will never die
> Remember,
> While humanity lives,
> You will never die.[7]

THE CONCEPT OF FREE SPEECH IN COMMUNIST CHINA

Democracy Wall was founded when Chinese dissidents felt a real thawing in the climate of opinion on the issue of free speech and human rights. After the death of Mao and the purging of the Gang of Four, such radical departures from normal practices seemed to be acceptable. The government, under Deng Xiaoping, decided in 1978 to reverse its decision on the public demonstrations that had occurred in Beijing in April 1976. On April 5 a huge crowd had gathered in Tiananmen Square ostensibly to pay homage to their beloved premier, Zhou Enlai, who had died three months earlier.[8] In fact most of the assembled crowd had intended to protest against the oppressive rule of the Communist party and the especially odious events that had been commonplace in China since the start of the Cultural Revolution in 1966.

The demonstration quickly got out of control and the full power of the security forces was unleashed on the masses. As in June 1989, it was difficult to determine exactly what happened in the square. It appeared that many people were killed or wounded for refusing to leave the area; others were arrested, some to be executed later. One of the staff members at the British Embassy in Beijing recalled the scene:

> Suddenly at 9:35 [P.M.] all the lights in the square were switched on, making it almost as bright as day, and loudspeakers blared a military song. Thousands of men with Workers Militia armbands and staves marched out of the Imperial City (adjacent to the Square). . . . They

began to clear the Square, surrounding one section at a time. They blocked the exits to prevent escape. Staves rose and fell. Bodies slumped to the ground. Men screamed in agony. Blood stained the paving stones. Young men drew pocket knives to defend themselves, to no avail. Hundreds, at least, were marched or dragged to the Imperial City, and thence to prison.[9]

The CCP had not experienced such a serious challenge to its legitimacy since 1949. It was a symbolic act of defiance, in what turned out to be Mao Zedong's last year and the end of his era as the supreme ruler of China. In 1978, however, Deng Xiaoping was beginning to launch a subtle campaign to de-emphasize the significance of Mao (see Chapter 4). As the prologue to what many hoped would be a much more democratic era, Deng announced that the Tiananmen incident had in fact been an expression of popular will. Its leaders were not only to be rehabilitated, but they were designated as heroes and martyrs.

This reversal of policy gave the dissenters new hope and once again protestors returned to the streets to express their opinions. This is how the Democracy Movement began, and it was often referred to as the April Fifth Movement in memory of the original Tiananmen demonstration. As one of the posters on Democracy Wall explained, "The banner of the April Fifth Movement was that of socialist China against dictatorship, a demand for fundamental human rights and democracy. . . . [It] is an awakening of the Chinese people who have been kept in the dark and ignorant."[10]

It appears that there *is* free speech in China, and there *is* a right to dissent; but that right can be exercised only at certain times and in certain places (see Figure 15.1). In 1978 and 1979, for a few months, and again briefly in 1989, the Chinese people were allowed, even encouraged, to speak out freely. As the epigraph to this chapter suggested, one of the problems for potential dissenters in China has traditionally been the unwillingness of many people to speak out about their oppression. One important reason for this unwillingness was the memory of an earlier pronouncement to do so that had been rescinded, with disastrous consequences for those involved. In 1956 a campaign was launched to

Figure 15.1 Cartoon depicting cadre (top frame) asking, "What democracy? What I say goes!" with dissident (lower frame) saying, "What I say goes, only then is it democracy." The casual clothing of the latter reflects Western influences. Both are portrayed as authoritarian. Source: R. Crozier, 1983, "The Thorny Flowers of 1979: Political Cartoons and Liberalization in China," in Bulletin of Concerned Asia Scholars (eds.), China from Mao to Deng: The Politics and Economics of Socialist Development (Armonk, N.Y.: M. E. Sharpe, Inc.), p. 38.

"Let a Hundred Flowers Bloom, a Hundred Schools of Thought Contend." The government appeared to be sincere in asking the people to be critical of the regime, but in the following years this decision was reversed, and the critics were branded as "rightists." Some were expelled from the Party, many were "sent down" from the cities to the countryside as a punishment or subjected to mass criticism and required to undergo a thorough self-criticism.[11]

How can outsiders interpret these periods of brief thaw in the traditional hard line on free speech in China? A first possibility is to think of them as thoroughly Machiavellian. In other words, a government that is obsessed with minimizing opposition can use such tactics to draw its critics out into the open. Once they have exposed themselves the government can deal with them, either by "reeducation" or by removing them from the scene. One of Ann Thurston's respondents in *Enemies of the People* told her that "such encouragement . . . was a ruse, like coaxing a snake out of its hole only to lop it in two."[12]

Obviously, the more frequently this sort of thing happens, the less willing the people become to exercise their right to free speech, even when they are encouraged to do so. After the events of 1989, for example, it will be a long time before many people will feel free to voice their opinions. By almost any definition, of course, free speech under the ground rules dictated in both 1956 and 1978 is not really free speech by Western standards. As it turned out, the invitation was little more than a license for people to commit political suicide—they were given enough rope, and they chose to hang themselves.

A variant on this interpretation would be to see the government's acceptance of a limited era of "free speech" as an attempt to "smoke out" the "counterrevolutionary" elements within the leadership. In 1989, for example, former Premier Zhao Ziyang was severely criticized for supporting or appearing to sympathize with the dissenters—later he was even accused of hatching or contributing to a plot to overthrow the leadership.[13]

A second interpretation of the Chinese government's record on the issue of free speech is possible. In the many pronouncements made over the years by political leaders, there has usually been some emphasis placed on the need to improve China's record in the area of human rights. As early as 1940, for example, Mao Zedong stated that "the freedoms of speech, of the press, of assembly, of association, of political conviction, of religious belief, and of persons are the most important freedoms for the people."[14]

The spirit of this sentiment has been expressed in the several attempts the government has made over the years to incorporate international standards of human rights into the constitutions of the PRC. This may or may not have been considered desirable by the Party leaders, but it was perhaps seen as necessary to improve China's record in this area in the eyes of the international community, particularly the countries with which China wants to be trading and investment partners. Thus in every constitution written since 1949, there has been an explicit recognition of the rights of Chinese citizens to speak out freely.[15] After 1989 it should be clear to everyone that this is not the case. We can interpret this situation as either the failure of will (in other words, a lack of courage to carry out what is intended in the constitution) or, more likely, as an example of the not-too-subtle instrumentality of the Party leadership in seeking international approval.

A third interpretation is possible, however, one that involves a culturally unique definition of what the constitution actually means in China. Instead of being a cherished document that guarantees the fundamental civil rights of citizens (as would be the case in the West), in China a constitution is an instrument of propaganda, a way of making a rather vague statement about the regime's goals for the future.

A close look at the way "crimes" of dissent have been dealt with in China in the past few decades suggests that citizens are free to express themselves as long as what they say or write does not contradict the major principles on which the Chinese state is governed. For example, during the "Hundred Flowers" era, the people were encouraged to "bloom and contend," but as it later turned out, those who exercised their right to challenge the Party were not considered to be "the people" at all—they were branded as "traitors," "counterrevolutionaries," or "rightists."[16] In one celebrated case, Lin Xiling, a People's University law student, was sentenced to fifteen years in prison in 1957.[17] Lin was a vociferous critic of the CCP, and her complaint was that China was undemocratic and essentially lawless. Tragically, her own case proved that she was correct—she had overstepped the limit of acceptable behavior. She was judged to have challenged the rule of the Party, divulged state secrets, and contradicted the "dictatorship of the proletariat."[18]

Twenty years later the case of Wei Jingsheng proved that in spite of several new constitutions, very little had changed in China. Wei's case demonstrated that although an individual has the right to speak out freely, he or she in fact only has the right to *support* the major principles adhered to by the state.

As the court put it at the time: "Freedom of speech of the individual must be based on the four principles of insisting on the socialist road, the dictatorship of the proletariat, the leadership of the party, and Marxism-Leninism-Mao Zedong Thought."[19]

This implies that a citizen's "duties" outweigh his or her "rights." Lin and Wei were within their rights when they spoke out, but it was decided that what they said far surpassed what could be tolerated without being defined as a "crime." In their cases, as in many others, constitutional rights were subordinated to political expediency.[20]

In spite of Deng Xiaoping's promises to institute a system of procedural justice (a "rule of law") in China, as we saw in Chapter 14, the most recent constitutions have hardly changed anything. Although citizens are permitted to express their views on all issues, there are numerous and major qualifications. As the constitution of 1982 states, "the exercise by citizens of . . . their freedoms and rights may not infringe upon the interests of the state, of society, and of the collective."[21]

It appears, therefore, that the old Maoist system of "revolutionary" justice still has the upper hand, even in Deng's China. As is always the case in China, politics comes before everything, even the law. The law as *we* know it, and the "rule of law," recognize no exceptions—before the law all citizens are equal. But what pervades in China is still a form of *socialist legality:* There is a written law, but superimposed onto this are rules for applying the law. It appears that these rules "can vary with the category of people, with the interests of the Party . . . with the Party directive operating at any given moment or the ideological campaign running at the time, *or simply with circumstances.*"[22]

What this meant in effect was that at any time, Party discipline and dictates could supersede judicial procedures. The people, in other words, would never know exactly what their rights were until after the fact. Those bold enough to want to find out would do so at their own peril.[23]

THE CHINESE GULAG

The desks in the schools had shelves, not drawers, just a top and a bottom. They made me put my head inside . . . and then they began beating on

the outside. . . . It only frightens you. It doesn't really hurt you. They tried not to kill people when they wanted a fake confession. But when they were hitting me like that, I peed. Involuntarily. My physical response was out of my control . . . it wasn't so much the pain as that I couldn't control my own physical response. That humiliated me.
—Ann Thurston[24]

In addition to the well-publicized cases, those of Lin Xiling and Wei Jingsheng, there are probably tens of thousands of individuals throughout China serving sentences in labor camps and penal institutions—the Gulag—for crimes of dissent. In the camps those people are to be "cured" of their mistakes, and translating literally from the Chinese term used to describe the process, this meant "reeducation through labor."[25] More serious offenders of both a civil and political nature, such as "counterrevolutionaries," are sent to be "remolded" (often in the same camps) or, more specifically, to experience "reform through labor."

It is not clear exactly what a "remolded" person would be like, although we get some idea from Zhang Xianliang's masterful account in his book *Half of Man Is Woman.* Zhang, who was considered to be a "counterrevolutionary" element, had been prohibited from writing anything other than weekly "thought reports" and self-criticism. As he said, the goal was to cleanse him of his counterrevolutionary tendencies: "Perhaps this was the purpose of my 'reform'—like skinning the pelt off an animal, I had to be scraped free of culture. Although the person being skinned undeniably suffered, to the hunter it was only a natural and necessary procedure."[26]

In practice there is no clear-cut legal definition distinguishing the two categories of "remolding," and much is left to the discretion of the police, the Party, and the courts. As this suggests, the law in China is extremely vague, so that citizens can never be sure exactly what will be defined as a "counterrevolutionary act." In the latest constitution, for example, it is defined very loosely as "any act of endangering the PRC committed with the purpose of overthrowing the political powers of the dictatorship of the proletariat and the socialist system."[27]

To Westerners the major problem with such a category as "counterrevolutionary" is that the nature of the "revolution" has changed considerably over the last four decades, at least in the minds of the Party leaders and in their policies. As these definitions change, so do the definitions of what constitutes a counterrevolutionary act. For example, as we saw in Chapter 5, the private ownership of land was considered to be a "crime" during the Cultural Revolution years, but by the late 1980s it had become common practice. This reflects the fundamentally transient nature of a term such as *counterrevolutionary* and its blatantly political, rather than legal, basis.

The change in a definition is just one of the countless examples of the subservience of China's law, and the entire criminal justice system, to politics—in spite of the pious statements that have been made about the need for law to be universal and above politics. In 1984, for example, Peng Zhen (then the leader of China's "parliament," the National People's Congress) stated, "We must gradually make the transition from relying on policy in managing affairs to establishing and strengthening the legal system and relying not only on policy but also on law."[28] As we might expect, for pragmatic reasons Peng would need to change his tune several times during the 1980s, and in 1985 he stated that the law must, after all, be based on the goals and policies of the Party. In 1989 it was obvious to the whole world that policy and politics could overstep the law at will.

Another offense that is frequently invoked is covered by the term *breaking state secrets*, although no one is sure what the term actually means. In addition to the categories stipulated in the constitution, there is an Orwellian catch-all category, defining as a *state secret* "all other state affairs which should be kept secret."[29] There is also still extant in China a principle of "crime by analogy," which means that although an action may not actually be prohibited by law, it can be defined as a "crime" if it is analogous to other crimes considered to be criminal by the Party.[30]

Thus it appears that the Chinese people cannot predict exactly what will be judged to be a political "crime." The law can be applied, or bent, or ignored at will, depending on what particular campaign is currently in vogue or which clique is in control of the Party. It is not surprising, therefore, that the Chinese people and outsiders alike have only the vaguest of ideas about how many people are inside the Chinese Gulag. It seems likely that the ones we hear about, the most illustrious victims—the ones featured by Amnesty International and other agents of the international human rights community—may represent only the tip of the iceberg. The writer who uses the pen name Simon Leys, for example, in his book *The Burning Forest*, urged us not to forget "the immense crowd of humble, anonymous people who were subjected to mass arrests . . . or who are suffering individual persecution all over China. They are imprisoned, condemned to hard labour, or even executed merely for having expressed unorthodox opinions."[31]

Until the widely publicized events of 1989, few people in the West had been prepared to believe such a statement. For Leys, however, even before those events, China should have been excommunicated from the civilized world until the issue of human rights was dealt with in a satisfactory fashion. Although many people would have made such a statement after what they saw in 1989, it is remarkable how few sanctions against China were actually imposed in the subsequent months, and how quickly other governments have been willing to resume normal relationships with the Chinese government.

We have equally meager details about what life is like inside the labor camps, although the secrecy surrounding the camps can lead us only to assume the worst. The first-hand reports usually come from the lucky few who have been released and are willing to talk about their experiences. Yu Luojin, for example, is now living in Germany, and she told her story without fear of recrimination, in *A Chinese Winter's Tale*. She pointed out the functional nature of the camps, in that their major purpose is to rehabilitate "criminals" through "reform" or "reeducation." As Yu pointed out, to get their old jobs back after they return to civilian life, many of the inmates have to go through the humiliating ritual of kowtowing to their superiors, who are often the same people who had initially persecuted them. It follows that the only people allowed back from the camps into the outside world are the compliant ones, the ones who either were willing to be rehabilitated or could be relied on not to talk too much. In this sense Yu was suggesting that until the traditional pattern of compliance is challenged, the Chinese people will continue to be trampled upon by the dictates of the Party, with disastrous consequences. "If . . . we refuse to speak honestly, if we force ourselves to enjoy our punishment, if we insist that this country of ours, which is capable at any time of wantonly killing its own people, must be obeyed like a mother, then, I think, a second Cultural Revolution is on its way."[32]

From the accounts that have been published, we can piece together a partial picture of life in the camps. In the first place there is evidence that many of the long-term internees in the camps are permitted to live reasonably regular lives, notwithstanding the fact that they have been exiled, often to isolated and forsaken parts of China. Zhang Xianliang's largely autobiographical account of his term in a camp in Ningxia Autonomous Republic, for example, indicated that his life, although heavily regulated, was not unlike that of many free peasants in the vicinity. He tended animals, he had a small plot of his own, and he and his new wife (who was a fellow-prisoner) were permitted to set up their own home. As Zhang pointed out, life inside the camps had a certain logic to it that was rarely found on the outside: "A labour camp is a kind of independent kingdom, set up with all the necessary occupations of life. . . . The principle of using a man's skills to the utmost is practiced like a religion. If a doctor enters . . . he is soon Chief Internist, treating patients."[33] On the outside, especially during the Cultural Revolution, life was not so rational. The doctor, if he had been branded as part of the "stinking ninth" category of intellectuals, might well have spent his time cleaning out the toilets.

It is a sad commentary on postrevolutionary China, especially during the Cultural Revolution, that the only place where life was not turned on its head was in the labor camps. As a political prisoner, Zhang found that he usually got a better deal in the camp than he had outside. "On the Outside, a person of dubious political leanings is shunned. He is an outcast who cannot be trusted. Those who have committed some moral offense . . . are merely considered unfortunate . . . [but] on the Inside [in a labour camp] it is . . . the political prisoner who is trusted. 'Criminals' or moral degenerates receive very different treatment."[34]

A second observation about life in the labor camps has to do with the extraordinary system adopted by the CCP to label its political enemies and the consequences of some of the labels. If your parents, or even your grandparents, were landlords, you could be branded as a "landlord element," even if you had been dirt poor since birth. Once you were "hatted" in this way and sent off for punishment, it was extremely difficult to have the decision reversed.[35] Zhang Xianliang told the story of a woman he met in the camp who had been falsely labeled a "landlord element" by the chairman of her production brigade, after rejecting his sexual advances. Although she had long since served her sentence, she spent years trying to have her "hat" removed, only to discover that her judge was the same person who had originally branded her, in the meantime elevated to the position of Party secretary of her commune.[36]

What little we know about life in the camps paints a chilling picture. Wei Jingsheng, for example, has described the infamous Qin Cheng political prison (known locally as Q1), just north of Beijing and near the Great Wall. From such reports, as well as the fragments collected by Amnesty International researchers and the stories from former prisoners such as Yu Luojin and Bao Ruowang (Jean Pasqualini),[37] we have a picture of inhumane treatment, a drastic lack of space, and hopelessly inadequate diets. The most sinister aspect of the whole system, however, is the degree to which the camps and prisons are totally isolated from the mainstream of Chinese life, even when they are geographically adjacent to cities, as is the case with Q1. In that infamous prison, for example, there is absolutely no contact with the outside world. "Only former prisoners, their families and close friends ever know or talk about it. The prison is run by Section 5 of the Ministry of Public Security, and it is even kept a secret from the regular prison forces."[38]

There is apparently very little attempt made to send political prisoners to facilities close to their homes. In fact, in the early years after Liberation, most of the counterrevolutionaries and "rightists" were sent to camps in the far northeast of China, the area that became known to most prisoners as the "Chinese Siberia" or the "Great Northern Wilderness" because of its harsh climate and sparse population. According to Amnesty International, there are more than one hundred state farms in the northeast of China alone, most of which are penal institutions of one type of another.[39] Other reports suggest that most of the Gulag's facilities are in the country's border regions, such as Inner Mongolia, Xinjiang, Tibet, and particularly, Qinghai Province.

By physically removing the political prisoners or by shipping them off to totally isolated places, the Chinese Gulag manages to keep the problem of political dissenters out of the public's sight. It is impossible to know whether this also keeps the issue off the public's mind. It seems reasonable that even before the much-publicized events of 1989, the ever-pervasive infrastructure of surveillance and the ubiquity of security mechanisms kept the issue of dissidence constantly in the thoughts of the Chinese people. Presumably, people know when someone has disappeared, even if they do not know exactly where the person has been taken or what has become of him.

CONCLUSION: HUMAN RIGHTS IN THE 1990s

The long tentacles of the Public Security Bureau, the constant fear of reprisals to dissidents, and the haunting but distant specter of the Gulag: All these contributed to repressing the Democracy Movement during the first part of the 1980s. At the end of 1986 and the beginning of 1987, however, the future looked a little brighter, and there was a forerunner to the events of 1989 with the emergence of political activity on a number of university campuses throughout China. This represented a renewed although altered form of agitation for democracy in China.[40]

In more than a dozen cities students took to the streets calling for democracy and greater freedoms, producing some of the largest public demonstrations in China for almost a decade. They wanted to see a loosening of Party control over politics and a greater degree of popular participation in decision-making. For several years the Party leaders had been discussing the possibility of political reform to accompany the widespread economic reforms, but what the students were demanding was too much, too soon. The Party's response was

to blame the student demonstrations on the "spiritual pollution" that was the work of a few intellectuals who wanted China to Westernize too rapidly. In an interview with *Beijing Review*, for example, the vice-minister of the State Education Commission, He Dong-chang, wrote that although some students had valid grievances against their universities, "on the whole, the agitation reflected the influence of bourgeois liberalization that had appeared in the last few years. To advocate bourgeois liberalization is to write off the socialist system and replace it with the capitalist system, with the purpose of opposing the Communist Party Leadership."[41] Precisely what is meant by the often-used term *bourgeois liberalization* is anyone's guess, and in fact it is usually left deliberately vague to cover the activities of anyone advocating change inconsistent with the best interests of the Party.

One of the major perpetrators of bourgeois liberalizations was Fang Lizhi, who would become an international celebrity in 1989 when, as one of the principal "counterrevolutionaries," he was granted asylum in the U.S. Embassy in Beijing in June. In spite of continued pressure from the Chinese, Fang remained in the embassy until spring 1990, when he was allowed to take up a university post in England. Fang was the former deputy president of the China University of Science and Technology. He had always been a vigorous champion of academic freedom and he supported some of the student's demands for greater political involvement in 1986 and 1987. He felt that the time had come for the Chinese people to demand greater freedoms, but he recognized that this would not be an easy task. Fang's speeches, although not intended to be deliberately inflammatory, were supportive of the student movement. He had in fact warned that the people would have to fight for any freedoms they were to receive. As he said, "Democracy is not a favor bestowed from above. It should be won by . . . [the] people's efforts."[42] According to the Party leaders, the speeches Fang gave contributed greatly to the level of agitation among the students, and a vicious public attack on him was launched in the official Party newspapers. Eventually he was thoroughly discredited and removed from his position at the university.

The response to the events during the winter months of 1986 and 1987 caused another of the remarkable "turnarounds" in official PRC policy. In all respects 1986 was the peak year of liberalization in China. The *People's Daily*, for example, had made a strong case in mid-November 1986 for greater levels of public debate on all issues of importance, but by February 1987 the newspaper was demanding that all debates must take place under the guidance of the Party. As in past campaigns, the official organs of propaganda depicted one or two individuals, in this case Fang and the popular Premier Hu Yaobang, as the scapegoats and the embodiment of the evil.[43] In addition, the Party imposed strict new regulations on public gatherings, effectively outlawing any further spontaneous demonstrations.[44] Without arousing too much attention around the world, the government had been able to keep a lid on the Democracy Movement, which had reemerged in China, criticizing and vaguely challenging the system of one-party government.

In hindsight we know that the Democracy Movement had not been crushed in 1987; it was simply dormant, and the prediction made by one of the leaders of the movement, shortly before his arrest in 1979, proved to be remarkably prescient:

The cry "we want democracy not dictatorship" has now subsided throughout the vast land of China. Our ancient and immense motherland is still struggling in a mire of poverty and ignorance. But look! The rulers who created this poverty and ignorance are already panicking. They rely on their "invincible" dictatorship of blood and iron, and yet a few little sheets of paper and a few lines of writing, a few shots and they're frightened out of their wits. . . . For the moment they use their swords to cut the throats of others; but remember, this is not the first time during the past 30 years! This generation of China's youth will not remain silent, they will not give up, they will not surrender! In the face of violence, let there be no doubt that we shall grit our teeth and join hands, unite once more, and for the sake of our nation and our motherland, for the sake of truth and for the sake of the future we shall explore new roads, overthrow tyranny, and establish a new society.[45]

After 1987, order was temporarily restored to the campuses, but two important questions remained. First, it was never completely clear what the students of 1986 (or for that matter their counterparts in 1989 or their predecessors in 1978) actually meant when they requested more "democracy." The students wanted more representation and a freer press, but there was no consensus on what was the new political system they were advocating.[46] Some outsiders have agreed with the Party leadership that China was probably not ready for a democratic political system in the 1980s. Political pluralism has never really been tried in China, so there is very little in the way of experience to guide the way.[47]

Another question that emerged in 1987 was answered clearly in 1989: What did the future hold for reform in the general area of individual freedoms? Even after the student demonstrations were halted, it seemed likely in 1987 that if the economic reforms continued at their current pace, then it would not be too long before corresponding demands for legal reforms and greater human rights were addressed.

As it turned out, the mass demonstrations in 1989 forced the government's hand, and a much more cynical and repressive course of action was taken, bringing on a storm of international criticism that would seriously threaten China's plans for economic development and modernization (see "Appendix: Two Months That Shocked the World—A Chronology"). Ironically, instead of the economic reforms leading to political reforms, as had been predicted, a political event (the mass demonstrations) ended up threatening the future of the economic reforms. As a result of the crackdowns in 1989, China's economic reforms were seriously jeopardized by the withdrawal of foreign support and probably also by a tightening of the individual economic freedoms that had been allowed during the reform era.

The crackdown brought back strong images of the Cultural Revolution, involving a reign of terror and a return to the traditional system of "revolutionary justice," rather than the continued shift toward the rule of law that had been predicted in the early 1980s. Suspects were rounded up, there were trials and executions, and many people simply disappeared. What happened in Beijing in 1989 was not all that different from what had happened in Canton in 1949 when the Communists were attempting to round up and wipe out the "counterrevolutionary" elements. Fewer people lost their lives in 1989, but in terms of human rights, four decades of progress had apparently come to nothing.

China observers around the world, and the Chinese people themselves, had hoped to see political reforms following economic reforms. The alternative, the repressive course of action that could be the one pursued throughout the early 1990s, was almost unthinkable at the beginning of 1989. There was a third option, but even that now looks unlikely. If the economic and political situation had remained stable, the leaders might have had enough time to experiment with a series of legal reforms that could blend some of the principles of a Western rule of law with the unique features of traditional Chinese culture—a sort of "political science with Chinese characteristics."[48] The whole of this agenda has now been shelved, and it is impossible to tell when it might resurface. Only a fool would now try to predict what will happen next. If nothing else, the Chinese have proven to the world once again that they are still an unknown quantity.

In Chapter 14 the conclusion reached was that it was probably misguided to try to interpret legal events in China from our own perspective or based on what we would like to think is happening. In 1988 most China watchers were quietly confident that everything was moving smoothly toward further economic reforms and that political reform was simply a matter of time. These predictions helped us to grapple mentally with some of the difficult economic and political problems that were facing China. The economy was in a shambles, and corruption was rampant; but the major concerns were about the future. As Frank Ching asked in his article "Red Star Over Hong Kong," what will happen to the five million Hong Kong Chinese when the British hand the "colony" back to the PRC in 1997?[49] Most people were expecting a peaceful and amicable transition, even though it was clear that the holders of Hong Kong's fabulous wealth were planning to move it elsewhere before the dreaded date arrived.

Perhaps more significant in emotional terms, what did the future hold in store for the relationship between the PRC and Taiwan? The economic trends on the mainland, especially in the "New China" (see Chapter 9), suggested that there was a rapid process of convergence between China and its offshore territories. The year 1997 was beginning to be less threatening to the money-minded citizens of Hong Kong. It was also beginning to look as though the Taiwan problem could be dealt with, and there was even talk in some quarters about the possibility of reunification. Conflicts were being worked out; both sides were talking to each other; families were being repatriated—progress was being made on both sides of the water.

The events of June 1989 put an end to all this. The goodwill and the optimism that had been so carefully nurtured were crushed like the bodies in Tiananmen Square. The people who had set themselves up as China experts were dumbfounded.[50] It appeared that there was far less unity within the Party leadership than outsiders had been led to believe. When a strong, unified, and sensible response to the demonstrations was needed, it was not forthcoming. What we witnessed instead was evidence of the infighting that had been common throughout the Cultural Revolution years.

It also appears that very few outsiders correctly gauged the resolve of either the young demonstrators in Beijing or of the elderly Party leaders. The students proved that they were ready to take Zhang Xianliang's advice, and plenty of them were willing to die to defend their beliefs. The Party leaders for their part proved that they were willing to "spill some blood" to protect the power they had spent their entire lives building up.

From the outside the stubbornness and rigidity of the Party leadership seemed distressingly obvious. The Communists appear to have failed to grasp what everyone else around the world was starting to take for granted—simply that the modernization of China's technology and the opening up of its economy were bound to bring about demands for political and cultural change. It also appears that everyone, with the possible exception of the students, underestimated the importance of the global revolution in communications. The student leaders, even in comparison to 1986 and 1987, knew that everything they did and said had an almost instantaneous audience all around the world. The visibility of the whole process also added to our complete shock at the harshness of the crackdown, which occurred at a time when the outside world was watching very closely.

It seems that the China experts had it all wrong, or rather they had built up their hopes much more than was warranted by the evidence. The monumental changes associated with the leadership of Deng Xiaoping have been described throughout this book—the Special Economic Zones, the agricultural reforms, the glittering tourist hotels, the emergence of stock markets, the new housing market, and the real estate transactions. It appears, however, that the changes had hardly had any effect on the way things were done in China. As we saw in earlier chapters, there have been some political changes as a result of the economic reforms in China in the 1980s. One of the most dramatic of these has been the decollectivization in the countryside and the increasing independence of the peasants from the oppression of the local cadres (and, by association, the state). However, as Edward Friedman has pointed out, these changes are far from complete because China remains a solidly Leninist state, and the dictates of the ruling elite are still all-powerful.[51] When the tanks rolled into Beijing we were rudely reminded that, beneath the surface, everything in China was just as it had always been (see Figure 15.2). Instead of helping us to come to terms with what had happened, the Party offered its grossly distorted version of the events, which became known as the "big lie."[52]

How can we pretend to understand such a desperate attempt to save face and the flagrant disregard for the values we consider to be so important? Perhaps the only fitting way to end is with a quotation from Deng Xiaoping himself. The 1980s was Deng's decade. Most Westerners were convinced that his economic reforms would be followed by political reforms. We now know that this was not to be. Four days after the crackdown in Tiananmen Square Deng stood before the commanders of the martial law troops and praised them for their work in suppressing the attempted "counterrevolution." He told them:

The people's army is truly a Great Wall of iron and steel . . . no matter how heavy the losses we suffer . . . this army of ours is forever . . . under the leadership of the Party, forever the defender of socialism, forever the defender of the public interest, and they are the most beloved of the people. . . . At the same time,

we should never forget how cruel our enemies are. For them we should not have one iota of forgiveness.[53]

APPENDIX: TWO MONTHS THAT SHOCKED THE WORLD— A CHRONOLOGY (APRIL–JUNE 1990)

April 15: Former Chinese Communist party (CCP) leader Hu Yaobang dies. He was popular with China's students and had been deposed because of his "support" for the demonstrations in 1986–1987.[54]

April 16–18: An estimated 6,000 students march to Tiananmen Square in Beijing demanding more freedom of speech; protesting corruption in the government; and mourning the death of Hu Yaobang. Students begin a sit-in in front of the Great Hall of the People in Tiananmen Square.

April 19: Students move the sit-in to the front of Zhongnanhai, headquarters of the Chinese Communist party. Some students attempt to break into the compound.

April 21–22: About 100,000 gather in Tiananmen, defying a government ban announcing that the square will be closed during the memorial service for Hu Yaobang. Thousands camp out in the square overnight. After the services, three students are allowed to present a petition to the government, but no officials arrive to receive them. The demonstrations spread to Shanghai, Xian, and Changsha. Some "lawless" elements are arrested.

April 23: A newly formed independent students' union is created in Beijing and calls for a boycott of all classes.

April 25: In the absence of Zhao Ziyang, Deng Xiaoping calls a secret Politburo meeting to denounce the student activities and to threaten the use of force if necessary.

April 26–May 3: Ideological warfare continues in the press. Student leaders are denounced in a People's Daily editorial as a "bunch of troublemakers" and "conspirators"; the movement is referred to as "counterrevolutionary." In Shanghai, the editor of the World Economic Herald is fired for writing an article sympathetic to Hu Yaobang. Students make further demands.

April 27–May 2: About 500,000 students break the police barricades and march to the square, in defiance of the People's Daily editorial. The government agrees to speak with student representatives, but it is later revealed that the students were selected by the official students' union, not the newly formed Autonomous Association, and therefore they were not considered to be acceptable. Students present the government with an ultimatum—unless there is dialogue, they will take to the streets again.

Cartoonist's Comment

Figure 15.2   June 4, 1989. Source: Miami Herald, June 6, 1989. Copyright © 1989, the Miami Herald, reprinted by permission.

May 3: The ultimatum is ignored and the Autonomous Association of Beijing Universities is declared illegal.

May 4: About 20,000 students march to Tiananmen Square, accompanied by some 200 journalists demanding that Chinese newspapers "tell the truth" about what is happening. Demonstrations in Beijing, Hangzhou, and Shanghai draw large crowds and attract international attention.

May 12: Students begin a hunger strike in Tiananmen Square. Estimates of those involved vary from 500 to 2,000. The initial turnout is low, but other students join in later. The hunger strike achieves its objective of gaining attention worldwide for the demonstrations, even detracting from the upcoming visit of Mikhail Gorbachev.

May 15: Gorbachev arrives in Beijing, but hunger strikers and demonstrators disrupt the scheduled events: The disruptions are captured by media from around the world. The Chinese government is humiliated in full view of the Soviet delegation and the world's media.

May 17: The so-called May 17 Declaration is signed by a number of China's leading intellectuals, attacking Deng Xiaoping and calling him the "last emperor without a title." Zhao Ziyang promises the students there will be no reprisals if they retreat now. Demonstrations in support of the hunger strikers spread to other cities: Taiyuan, Harbin, Zhengzhou, Liaoning, Chengdu, Lanzhou, Changchun, and Hefei. A hunger strike begins in Shanghai. An estimated 1 million people, including ordinary citizens and workers, march in Beijing in support of the students. Reports suggest that some PLA members joined in or sympathized with the marchers.

May 18: Prime Minister Li Peng meets with student leaders in a tense confrontation that is televised. The students are defiant, telling Li that he has "come too late."

May 19: Li Peng makes some strong warnings about bringing in troops, as demonstrations spread to many other cities across China. Li's response is in part to negate the moderate tones of Zhao Ziyang, who had been meeting with the hunger strikers.

Li accuses a "handful of people with ulterior motives" of taking advantage of the hunger strike to create turmoil.

May 20: Troops are ordered into some parts of Beijing. Martial law is officially announced, and restrictions are placed on foreign news coverage. Thousands of Beijing residents erect barriers to prevent troops from reaching the demonstrators in Tiananmen Square. Troops settle in the outskirts of Beijing.

May 21–22: Some members of the Standing Committee of the National People's Congress appeal to the congress to try to get martial law lifted and to remove Li Peng. This move was reportedly supported by Zhao Ziyang.

May 24: In further ideological warfare, it is reported that several of China's provinces are expressing their support for the government and for Li Peng's hard line on the demonstrations. This is countered by further mass demonstrations in Beijing, with an estimated 1 million people—workers and ordinary citizens—joining the students, calling for Li's resignation, and openly defying martial law.

May 25: With a reported 100,000-plus troops surrounding the city, Li declares that his government is in control of the situation, suppressing rumors of splits between the People's Liberation Army and the government.

May 27: The official press continues to boast of the widespread support for Li Peng and the government in the provinces and focuses on "an extremely small number" of individuals who are thought to be plotting a political conspiracy.

May 30: The students who have voted to stay on in the square erect a statue—the "Goddess of Democracy," which attracts more students to join or rejoin in the demonstrations.

June 2: Unarmed troops try to march into Tiananmen Square but are driven back by thousands of citizens. Three people die in an accident involving a police vehicle. Carrying the dead bodies, angry citizens vow to demonstrate in the streets the next day.

June 3: A violent confrontation begins as thousands of soldiers again march on the square. Dozens of protestors are reportedly beaten by troops before they retreat.

June 4: Troops and tanks return to the square in the early hours of the morning, opening fire on crowds of demonstrators and destroying barricades. Unknown numbers of people are shot down or crushed by tanks on the streets. The events are viewed with cries of outrage around the world, but relatively few countries impose serious sanctions on China.

June 6–8: A wide-ranging "crackdown" is announced on students, workers, and other "counterrevolutionaries" who have been involved in the demonstrations. New martial law orders are announced, and student leaders are urged to surrender. Citizens are exhorted to inform on student and worker activists. Troops enter university districts in northwest Beijing to impose night-time curfews.

June 10: Crackdown activities are escalated; the government announces the arrest of 400 students and workers active in the demonstrations. Government leaders claim that the events were caused by "counterrevolutionary thugs and hooligans," who will be punished. Rumors of purging among government leaders who were "sympathetic" to student demands, especially Zhao Ziyang.

June 14: Efforts to round up key student leaders are accelerated, with photographs on national television and "wanted" notices placed in public places. Key dissidents Fang Lizhi and his wife, Li Shuxian, take refuge in the U.S. Embassy, which results in a long-term diplomatic stalemate between the United States and China (resolved in spring 1990 when they were allowed to leave for England).

June 15: China orders the expulsion of Beijing-based American news reporters, including one working for the Voice of America, for their violations of the censorship restrictions after martial law was declared and for sympathizing and meeting with "illegal" student organizations.

June 16: After televised trials, three young workers are sentenced to death for their role in demonstrations in Shanghai in which a passenger train was set on fire. Roundups and arrests of student leaders continue.

June 17: Another eight workers are given the death sentence for their role in the demonstrations, again following brief but well-publicized trials. Announcements indicate, unofficially, that arrests total more than 1,000. Those sentenced to death are accused of specific acts of violence during the crackdown on June 4.

June 25: Zhao Ziyang is officially ousted from his position of Party general secretary and is blamed for the spread of "bourgeois ideology" throughout the country. Leaders call for continued purging of "liberals" and "intellectuals" at all levels, in the Party and in society at large.

Conclusion:
China in the 1990s

The real malaise of Beijing . . . [is] its domination by an ideology so all-pervading, so arbitrary . . . so inconstant . . . [it] can change the way the nation thinks from one year to another. Today *it is liberal and welcoming, Chinese tradition is honored, people are free to wear what they like, consort with foreigners if they will, sell their ducks in a free market and even build themselves houses with the profits.* Yesterday *it was puritanically narrow, the revolutionary condition was permanent, aliens were devils, Mao caps and floppy trousers were* de rigueur. *. . . And tomorrow, when another generation succeeds to domination, everything may be different again, and all the values so painstakingly absorbed into the public consciousness may have to be ripped out of mind once more.*

—Jan Morris[1]

In Chapter 1 the major goals of this book were described as follows: first, to provide an introduction to the contemporary lives and landscapes of the Chinese people; second, to introduce a small number of geographical concepts that can be used to describe and interpret the events that have been occurring in present-day China; third, to introduce the reader to the economic reforms that swept through urban and rural China during the 1980s; and fourth, to evaluate the extent to which the reforms had significantly altered the lives of the Chinese people by the end of the 1980s.

THE POWER OF GEOGRAPHY
IN CONTEMPORARY CHINA

Part 1 of the book makes the case for looking at contemporary China through the eyes, or rather the concepts, of a geographer. In spite of the plea for geography, it is essential to be sensitive to the overwhelming significance of culture and politics in China. As we have seen throughout the book, it is the differences between the Chinese and ourselves, rather than the similarities, that continue to stand out; and these differences are never so apparent as they are in the realms of culture and politics. This is driven home to us in issues as seemingly minor as the food preferences of the Chinese (Chapters 5 and 13) and as major as the differences between "us" and "them" on the issue of human rights (Chapters 14 and 15).

Notwithstanding that reservation, Chapter 2 introduced a small set of geographical concepts that were used throughout the text to illustrate the relevance of geography:

- Spatial interaction and the role of distance
- The two-way relationships between human beings and the physical environment
- The importance of place for human activity and sentiment
- The spatial organization of urban and rural structures
- The demarcation of territory into regions

It is neither necessary nor appropriate to evaluate all the instances in which these concepts appeared in the text (see Table 2.1). It is useful, however, in drawing this book to a conclusion, to illustrate some of the ways in which the concepts are relevant to everyday lives and landscapes in China. The basic argument is that geographical concepts can provide a useful intellectual structure for looking at contemporary China; or, conversely, that the study of contemporary China offers an exciting vehicle by which to introduce the relevance of modern geography.

Distance and Spatial Interaction

At various points throughout the book the enduring significance of distance and spatial interaction in contemporary China has been illustrated. In much of the rest of the world a marked "shrinkage" of territory has accompanied the communications revolution. Until the end of the 1980s this shrinkage hardly touched large parts of China, where patterns of interaction remained almost as constrained by distance as they have been for centuries.

The issue of politics has also contributed to determining the pattern of spatial interaction in postrevolutionary China. The Chinese government has deliberately intervened to alter much of what would otherwise have been "normal" patterns of movement and migration between the countryside and the city. Ironically, it appears from what happened in China's cities during the 1980s that the effects of forcibly removing people from one place to another, and of interrupting the normal channels of migration, tend to be relatively short-lived. Many of the peasants who are restrained eventually end up moving into the cities, and the majority of the urban dwellers who want to return are able to find a way back. This suggests that the manipulation of spatial interaction is at best a temporary measure, one that is ultimately doomed to fail. It is a testament to the remarkable persistence and patience of the Chinese people that an overwhelming desire to live in the city has effectively canceled out the draconian efforts to restrict human migration during the Maoist era. As the British geographer Richard Kirkby noted, although the preference for urban living is similar in China to that elsewhere, the response of the government illustrates another of the fundamental differences between ourselves and the Chinese.[2]

The Human-Environment Interface

Throughout the four decades of the People's Republic of China there has been an escalation of the long-drawn-out struggle between the Chinese people and their environment. Critics of the regime have argued that the furious pace of economic development since 1949 and the communal ownership of land and physical resources combined to produce an unprecedented rate of environmental degradation in China. The empirical evidence examined in Chapter 10 supports such an argument. Environmentalists from around the world have been horrified by the alarming rate of destruction of forestlands and wildlife in China and the poisoning of the air and water. It now seems, however, that an almost equally high rate of environmental damage occurred during the "market socialist" era after the death of Mao Zedong. In other words it would appear that the key to the crucial issue of the human-environment interface in China may not be the political system per se, but the obsession with economic growth, a pursuit that has been a feature of both the collectivization and the decollectivization eras in China's recent development history.

There is some evidence that environmental awareness was beginning to be significant in the 1980s. It was still not clear to what extent the government was willing to sacrifice economic growth in the interests of the environment, but as with virtually all other aspects of life in contemporary China, the future of the environment will probably be determined by politics. As we saw in Chapter 10, in the late 1980s the shift toward a greater level of environmental awareness could be interpreted as a strategy used by the opponents of the economic reforms to slow down the trends they considered to be politically dangerous.

It is also likely that a concern with the environment may be one of the casualties in the post-Tiananmen era. To some of the hardliners the environmental movement was one of the many examples of "Western" and "bourgeois" influences sweeping through China in the 1980s, and as a result it may be one of the first to be abandoned. This would represent another sign that the country is heading back in the direction of what has been referred to as "communist fundamentalism."[3] It is also a cruel irony that the new environmental consciousness in China was emerging just as Westernization and modernization were also on a rapidly upward trajectory. Vehicle ownership has been increasing; the packaging of foodstuffs is becoming the norm; and the Chinese are beginning to mimic the "throwaway" culture of the West. All of these trends indicate greater environmental problems for the Chinese in the near future.

The Importance of Place

From all accounts the characteristic attachment to place in China was strengthened in the postrevolutionary era, both in the cities and in the countryside. Although we would normally expect the process of development to result in a weakening of traditional ties to localities, in China after 1949 the opposite appears to have been the case. In spite of the liberating principles of the Chinese revolution, the cooperatives, and later the communes, actually worked to increase the bondage of the peasants to the land. In "feudal" China the peasants had been extremely poor, but they were never serfs. They could walk off their land to seek work, and throughout history there is evidence that many of them chose this path whenever conditions in the countryside became intolerable. As American journalists like Graham Peck and Jack Belden reported, the prerevolutionary countryside was often overrun by hobos, medicine men, tinkers, and small-time traders.

After land reform and the early cooperative movement (see Chapter 5) every peasant was firmly tied to the land, and it became much more difficult to opt for a life on the road. The peasants were secure as long as the crops grew well, but in the bad years, for example after the disastrous Great Leap Forward, they all suffered together. When times were hard they could not leave the land because they had nowhere else to go. Their bondage was confirmed with the formation of the State Grain Company in 1954. The state bought and sold all the grain, and it established a rationing system that split the Chinese population into two groups. In the cities people received ration books that were linked to urban residency, which meant they were not allowed to move away from their assigned places. In the countryside the peasants did not have access to grain–ration books, which meant they could not live in the cities. Unless

they could somehow secure urban-residence permits, they were tied to their production brigades as the only source of food. As William Hinton pointed out, "Without a ration book one could not buy grain and therefore one could not survive away from home for very long."[4] This policy was extremely effective in slowing down urban growth, especially during the 1960s and 1970s, and as a result it helped to reduce the problem of urban unemployment and the social problems associated with poverty and homelessness (Chapter 8).

Forced residence in a specific location was a harsh sentence to impose on the beleaguered peasantry. Because the peasants had no viable options, their problems could be ignored by a cynical and self-satisfied middle tier of officials. The residence-card situation gave the commune administration complete control over the rural population, control that the elites of the past, especially the landlords, had never quite been able to achieve. The process of decollectivization and the introduction of the household responsibility system (HRS) in the 1980s brought some change to the Chinese countryside, but very little has actually changed in terms of the relationships between the peasants and the Party officials. It would appear that in spite of the rhetoric of Chinese socialism, many Communist party officials still have a fundamental contempt for the peasants that is essentially "feudal" in character. In this sense the reforms introduced in the countryside (see Chapter 5) represent a serious challenge to the cadre class in China because they have helped to create a peasantry that is wealthier and much more independent than had ever been the case in the past. As Hinton remarked, the cadres would have much preferred things to stay as they were. "As long as the peasants are down there endlessly laboring with their hoes, the official in his office feels secure. 'Why should we do anything to rock the boat?' "[5]

Spatial Organization

Many outsiders have remarked on the enormity of the administrative tasks in a country as large and as technologically underdeveloped as China. How is it possible for the Chinese to collect taxes, maintain law and order, and make sure that everyone is fed? How does the government operate to satisfy the needs of so many people over such vast expanses of territory? One answer to this question is that it does not. At the local level, as we have seen, there is evidence of considerable inefficiency; in fact there are many trials and tribulations for the average Chinese citizens as they go about their everyday tasks. Seen from the macrolevel, however, the evidence indicates that for the most part the system has "worked."

One explanation of how things get done in both the city and the countryside in China credits the all-encompassing pattern of spatial organization that was instituted at the local level by the Communists after 1949. As we saw in Chapter 5 (dealing with agriculture), and also in Chapters 12 and 13 (dealing with urban-service provision), the enormously complex business of food distribution and the execution of a vast assortment of campaigns, some of which were highly unpopular, have been facilitated by the spatial organization of administrative territory in urban and rural areas. This has made possible the enormous number of face-to-face interactions that are required with so many people, and it has also helped in the local administration of complex policies mandated at the national and regional levels.

The spatial structures also provide the mechanisms for close surveillance, which effectively reduces the chances for individual acts of noncompliance and deviance from the norms. Not surprisingly the pervasiveness of the administrative structures has also proved to be a mixed blessing for the Chinese people because the state has been able to use those structures to infiltrate and dominate the everyday lives of the Chinese people. Most Western social scientists share the opinion that the Chinese people have reacted extremely negatively to this domination. In a discussion of the peasant reactions to collectivization in the Chinese countryside, for example, political scientist Edward Friedman launched a vitriolic attack on collectivization and the tyranny of Party rule in Communist China, drawing an analogy with religious fundamentalism rather than utopian socialism. "The language of communist fundamentalism and the policies it legitimated are more in line with the telos of Ayatollah Ruhollah Khomeini than with the human solidarity and harmony envisaged by Peter Kropotkin."[6]

Regions and Regionalization

One of the most significant results of the economic reforms in the Chinese countryside in the 1980s has been the effective redrawing of regional boundaries and a new regionalization along largely economic rather than political or administrative lines. At the local level this has been underscored by the demise of the communes as the administrative units in the Chinese countryside, accompanied by the rise of local and regional marketing cooperatives organized predominantly by economic considerations. As we saw in Chapter 9, the emphasis on economic comparative advantage has allowed China's more favored regions, especially those in the eastern and southeastern provinces, to grow at rates greatly in excess of those in less favored regions. This has resulted in a widening of regional disparities in China, negating to some extent the spatial egalitarianism of the Maoist era. The economic advantages of the region referred to in Chapter 9 as the "New" China have been accentuated in the 1980s, and the "Old" China of the interior has been left even further behind. Nowhere has this new development been more marked than in Guangdong Province, especially the city of Guangzhou (Canton) and the Pearl River delta. By the end of the 1980s this region had achieved a rate of economic development as well as a technological capability that is the closest China has yet been able to come to the performance level of its neighbors in East Asia—the newly industrializing countries (NICs).

ECONOMIC REFORM: CHINA IN ITS EAST ASIAN CONTEXT

The vast majority of this book has been concerned, in one way or another, with the impacts of the economic reforms on the lives of the Chinese people and the landscapes they inhabit. The success of the reforms has been mixed, especially in geographical terms, and there is a real concern today about the reemergence of spatial inequality. It is important to point out that even in the Maoist era inequality was by no means eradicated (see Chapter 9), but the danger in the expansionary 1980s was that the gap between

China's richest and poorest regions would widen unacceptably.

In addition to the spatial inequality issue, it was also evident that the Chinese economy had not "taken off" in quite the way that had been expected. In absolute terms production in China grew massively throughout the 1980s, but it was evident that the per worker and per machine levels of productivity remained chronically low, particularly in comparison to the levels attained in the East Asian NICs. There was also evidence that the negative side effects of the economic reforms were tearing away at the fabric of Chinese society in the late 1980s. As we have seen at various points throughout this book, the most damaging of these were the issues of *corruption* in the government at all levels; high rates of *inflation*, particularly for foodstuffs; and a new concern about *unemployment* and poverty among China's once secure labor force. In spite of the dangers involved in trying to explain events in contemporary China, it is eminently reasonable to assume that there was a connection between the pervasive level of discontent and the uprisings in 1989.[7]

Probably the most humiliating aspect of the reform era to the Chinese government was that even after the leadership abandoned most of the hard-won gains of the collectivist period, the economy remained very far behind the other countries in the region. In evaluating the overall successes and failures of the reform movement, it is useful to compare the PRC experience in the 1980s with that of China's neighbors in East Asia. In his recent study of Guangdong Province, Ezra Vogel pointed out that although there are some obvious differences between them, the NICs, and particularly Japan, South Korea, and Taiwan, shared a number of characteristics that contributed toward their economic development.[8] Most notable among these:

- An ability to borrow and apply technology from the developed nations
- An ability to maintain close contact with and receive major economic support from an advanced economic power (usually the United States, as well as Japan in the case of South Korea and Taiwan)
- A powerful national drive to succeed in the global economy

- A stable and authoritarian system of government that was willing to combine strong central guidance with a high level of private initiative
- An emphasis on "import substitution," in which previously imported goods are produced domestically, and the rapid development of manufactured goods for export in markets all over the world
- A willingness to invest significantly in human resources, especially in the areas of education and job training
- An apparent willingness to work hard and forgo consumption in the early stages of development

The PRC shared some of these advantages for development, particularly the Confucian work ethic (see Chapter 3); the strong and stable government (Chapter 4); and the willingness to forgo consumption in the interests of long-term economic growth (although it should be pointed out that this was probably not a voluntary willingness on the part of the Chinese people). However, some of the features of state socialism have seriously inhibited the prospects of China's becoming the "next Japan," or even the "next Taiwan." Even in Guangdong Province there were a number of obstacles that Vogel identified: "a bloated, poorly trained bureaucracy, a rigid system of planning, and no experience in guiding a market economy. Its intellectuals were disaffected, its workforce poorly disciplined . . . [and the economy was] subject to far more political and economic constraints."[9]

By the time China began to experiment with market socialism at the end of the 1970s, the world was fairly well saturated with manufactured goods from cheap-labor countries. This meant that China did not have the same access to the enormously profitable markets that Hong Kong, Taiwan, and the other NICs had been able to exploit in the two previous decades and that were so important in their economic "miracles." In spite of this Guangdong was relatively successful in launching its economic "takeoff" and in achieving what amounted to an explosive rate of economic growth by the middle of the 1980s. What had made this possible in Guangdong, and presumably what is required if the rest of China is to follow suit, was a significant break with the stultifying traditions associated with state socialism. As we saw in Chapter 6, some of these changes were made in the 1980s, but by the end of the decade the government decided it was essential, for economic and political reasons, to slow down the pace of the economic reforms.

Guangdong's economic success was not an accident; in fact the reforms described in Chapters 5 and 6 were carried out more comprehensively and more ambitiously there than almost anywhere else in China. There was a relatively swift and painless transition to a commodity economy and a much lower rate of involvement of the government in economic decision-making. Perhaps the single greatest asset that Guangdong has had all through the reform era, however, has been *the advantage of geography.* Proximity to Hong Kong allowed the new entrepreneurs in Guangdong Province to seek out economic support and the transfer of technology from their highly successful cousins in the colony. Hong Kong also provided a powerful example to the people and the political leaders of Guangdong, by encouraging them to push hard for material success and to end the three-decade-long period of socialist austerity. "By flaunting the benefits of their economic progress, Hong Kong made people in Guangdong acutely dissatisfied with their state of backwardness, mobilizing them to pursue what their brethren across the border had achieved."[10]

Closeness to capitalist Hong Kong has been a mixed blessing from the perspective of the Chinese government. In 1997 the British will return Hong Kong to the Chinese, and the obvious gap in wealth between the residents of the mainland and those in the fabulously successful colony will become painfully obvious. Hong Kong in 1989 had a higher gross national product than the whole of Guangdong Province, with less than one-tenth of the population. The return of Hong Kong represents an exciting prospect, but also a clear danger. "It was one thing for the people of Guangdong to hear that people somewhere in the world had access to . . . [material] possession[s], and quite another to learn that their own friends and relatives, less than a hundred miles away had them."[11]

Guangdong's economic takeoff in the 1980s has shown the way for the rest of China, but it will represent a serious threat to the government in the more austere 1990s. The major problem is that the desire for economic progress cannot be easily switched off at will. After the dangerous level of "overheating" in the Chinese economy that was apparent by 1988, some drastic retrenchment measures were introduced (Chapter 6). This was partly to achieve a more balanced rate of economic growth and partly to defuse the almost inevitable call for political reform that was beginning to accompany greater economic freedoms. After the opening up of the economy in the early 1980s, the Chinese people experienced some prosperity and a little taste of the freedom that can accompany greater wealth. After a decade in which the badly damaged legitimacy of the government had been partially restored by economic progress, the decision to turn back the clock was a momentous one, one that may ultimately seal the fate of the current regime by opening up a new torrent of dissatisfaction and protest.

THE LAST WORDS: WAITING FOR RABBITS TO BUMP INTO TREES

After everything that happened in China during the 1980s, and particularly in 1989, many China scholars are uncharacteristically reticent. They find themselves in an awkward predicament. They can make predictions about what is likely to happen in China in the near future, only to be proven wrong by the latest in an extraordinary turn of events; or they can sit tight-lipped, waiting to see what will happen next. There is an ancient Chinese folktale that is appropriate in this situation. The simple-minded youngest son of a poor peasant family was sent out into the wilderness to forage for food. At the end of a fruitless day he sat down to rest. A rabbit flashed by, and in a panic it crashed into a nearby tree, knocking itself unconscious. The youth brought the rabbit home and the family feasted, convinced that their fortunes had changed (and that their son was not as dim-witted as they had thought). The next day the parents again sent the boy out in search of food. He still knew nothing about trapping wildlife, so he returned to the scene of his earlier triumph, sat down, and waited for another rabbit to bump into the tree.

When dealing with contemporary China, Western academics often find themselves waiting for rabbits to bump into trees. We have to resort to the unhappily gray areas of guesswork and hunches. Failing that, there is little else to do but wait to see what happens next. It is difficult to evaluate the official data released by the government, and practically impossible to decipher, or to believe, the public pronouncements made in the regular media channels. As suggested in Chapter 1, social scientists are usually uncomfortable with the easy and sweeping generalizations of travel writers and journalists. Not only are they considered to be "unscientific," they also require that we rely too heavily on our own intuitions. From a cognitive (rather than a philosophical) perspective, successful intuition involves leaping to correct conclusions in the absence of what would normally be required as sufficient empirical evidence. Using our intuition to predict what will happen in China in the 1990s is a particularly hit-and-miss activity. This was brought home dramatically by the events of 1989, the course and outcome of which were predicted very inaccurately by most China watchers.

It is slightly easier to interpret the past than to predict the future. A review of the 1980s suggests that there are two major ways to characterize the flow of events in contemporary China. The first emphasizes the rate of change that occurred in Chinese society, and from this perspective the 1980s can be viewed as a series of dramatic, often cataclysmic *policy reversals*. In just about every chapter of this book extraordinary changes in the way things were done in China were examined. These reversals have resulted in new patterns of everyday life for the Chinese people and, to a lesser extent, in changes in the character of the places where they live and work. Many of these changes occurred very rapidly. No sooner was a new program launched than it was swept up and carried along.

Besides being marked by speed, many of these changes occurred in pendulum fashion, as Jan Morris suggested in the epigraph to this chapter. The trends of one decade were dramatically reversed in the next decade. Often the changes were much quicker than that, occurring in a matter of one or two years, or months, or sometimes even days. Deng Xiaoping was twice purged from the Communist party, but he was able to bounce back

successfully after 1978. Once he was back at the top he remained in power for more than a decade, earning himself the nickname of the "comeback comrade." Western perceptions of Deng also changed during the 1980s, almost as violently as the swings in his career. In the mid-1980s he was selected as *Time* magazine's "Man of the Year," mainly because he was associated with China's shift toward capitalism. Tragically for all concerned, by the end of the decade many Western journalists were describing Deng as a senile fascist.

After the chaos of the Cultural Revolution, the Chinese people hoped they had seen the last of the inhumane tactics that were used to sweep away political enemies. During the 1980s the gradual relaxation of such tactics and a marked tendency toward more liberal practices were evident. By the end of the decade, however, and particularly after the Tiananmen demonstrations, it was clear that some of the old practices had been brought back into regular use. After having learned about the inhumanities that occurred in the Cultural Revolution, Chinese people and Westerners alike were horrified to see a return of the purges, the self-criticisms, the mobilization campaigns, and the public excoriation sessions.

There is even evidence that some of the model citizens of the Maoist era have come back into fashion in 1990, largely in response to Party propaganda. Lei Feng, for example, was a young worker whose ascetic life-style and dedication to Communist principles and morality were upheld as the norms to which all Chinese people should aspire. During the 1980s most of China's young people would have scoffed at Lei Feng, who was a ridiculous anachronism in the era of Hong Kong–inspired materialism. It remains to be seen how the Party will be able to convince the Chinese people to eschew the new goals of freedom and wealth and return to the high road of Communist morality, Lei Feng style. The task has been made doubly difficult by the disastrous events that befell Communist parties around the world in 1989 and 1990.

Equally pervasive as we survey the happenings in China during the 1980s was the prevalence of serious *contradictions* that resulted from the implementation of fundamentally opposing policies. In the Chinese countryside, for example, the goals and impacts of the agricultural reforms clashed with several of the other modernization policies in Deng's China. As we saw in Chapter 7, the conflict between the agricultural production policy inherent in the new household responsibility systems (HRS) and the reproduction policies designed to lower the birthrate was detrimental to the objectives of both policies. As sideline activities have opened up, and as jobs in rural enterprises became more easily available, many parents in rural China realized that their future earning potential could be increased considerably by having more children.

The agricultural reforms also made it extremely difficult for China's city planners to go about their business in a logical fashion (see Chapter 8). The greater agricultural efficiency on the land meant that the surplus rural population grew rapidly in the 1980s, and many of the people displaced from the land have moved (or would like to move) into the cities. As this happens it will be increasingly difficult for the cities to avoid the problems associated with rapid urbanization and to provide the services needed to support a growing population of poor and dependent people.

The increasing rate of crime and corruption (see Chapters 6 and 14) is one of the most serious threats to the legitimacy of the current regime, and it too can be interpreted as a side effect of the economic reforms in the 1980s. Western and Chinese criminologists agree that the higher crime rates might be attributable to the new level of material concern and the avariciousness that have accompanied the reforms. As the drive to "get rich" took hold firmly in the 1980s, the economy took a great step forward, but at the same time embezzlement, tax evasion, theft, and large-scale corruption became everyday media events.

The new wealth also threatens to upset what had become well known around the world as the "Chinese model" of urbanization, in which the prevalence of social problems has been kept at a relatively low level, at least in comparison to cities in the West, and particularly the United States. As a result of the agricultural reforms it is likely that the growing "reserve army" of unemployed (and perhaps unemployable) peasants will want to leave the land and seek work elsewhere. The newly dispossessed will look enviously at the precedent set by the families that have become "rich" and longingly at those lucky enough to be able to live in the cities. It remains to be seen what consequences these unfulfilled aspirations will have for patterns of crime and other social problems in contemporary urban China (see Chapters 8, 9, and 13).

As we look back at the 1980s the fundamental impression is one of rapid change and frequent contradictions. However, in many ways the changes have been superficial. It is reasonable to hypothesize that outsiders have focused on the shadows rather than the substance, to use Simon Leys's terminology (see Preface). The evidence may have fooled us into thinking that major changes were afoot and that the pace of change would continue to accelerate. After the sobering events of 1989, it now appears that in the most important areas of life very little of significance has changed in China. This was well illustrated in China's largest cities, where by the end of the 1980s a new landscape of capitalism (or "market socialism") appeared to have succeeded the austerity of the Maoist city (Chapters 8 and 9). There had been a tremendous increase in the level of vehicular traffic; new hotels had been built for Chinese and foreign tourists; restaurants and shops appeared to cater to the newly wealthy; and billboards and advertisements for all manner of consumer goods sprang up like mushrooms. It was clear, however, as the Party acted swiftly to wipe out the challenge to its authority in June 1989, that there had not been any fundamental political change in China.

In fact it is in the areas of culture and politics that the least amount of real change has occurred in contemporary China. The old Confucian values may have faded somewhat, but they have certainly not withered away. There is still ample evidence in China of the cultural legacies that have dominated lives and landscapes for centuries. This is particularly true for women, especially in the heavily male-dominated countryside. It is also still obvious that the norm for most Chinese people, both in the cities and the countryside, is to be told what to do by the Party. After four decades of socialism and freedom from the landlords, there is still evidence of widespread passivity and acceptance of one's station in life, a cultural trait that is usually associated with Confucian values in China and other traditional Asian societies. As we saw in Chapter 3 there is some empirical evidence of greater levels of individuality in China today, associated with the new materialism and increased exposure to the norms of the West, but it is important not to overemphasize this. In the aftermath of the Tiananmen Square incident, for example, we saw that the Chinese family was still of critical importance, mainly because it is virtually the only source of protection for the individual from the pervasive reach of the state.

A detailed look at the Chinese economy also reveals that in spite of the enormous successes reported in parts of the "New" China, there is still plenty of evidence of themes that have been persistent in China for centuries. Among the most obvious of these is the fundamental disparity between the wealth of the cities and the countryside, and between the richer regions of the eastern and southeastern provinces and the interior of the country. As has always been the case, there are still pockets of crushing poverty in rural China, and as some of the better endowed areas "get richer," the gap between the two extremes will widen.

One of the most dramatic changes in the economic landscape during the 1980s was the emergence and rapid growth of a private and semiprivate sector, both in the countryside and in the cities. In the wake of the serious economic problems in 1988 and the political problems in 1989, however, the government has shut down many of the new construction projects and seriously tightened up on the flow of credit, in an attempt to restrict the level of consumer demand and to slow down the rate of inflation. Rural industries were one of the major success stories in the reform period (Chapter 5), and they provided a vital escape valve for the millions of former peasants who were being made redundant by the agricultural reforms. At their peak in 1988, rural factories employed one-quarter of the labor force in the countryside (about ninety-four million people), and they produced almost 30 percent of the nation's industrial output.[12] In the round of retrenchments that began in the late 1980s, however, scarce raw materials and energy sources were being siphoned away from the relatively small rural private enterprises to larger state enterprises.

It is predicted that as a result many of the new factories will soon be faced with some unenviable choices: to shift over their activities into processing farm products, to become accessories to urban state enterprises, or to declare bankruptcy. In 1989 more than eight million workers in rural firms were made redundant.[13] The only realistic option for many of them was to return to work on the land, where they were not really needed.

The future looks grim, and the real tragedy is that the retrenchments represent a crushing blow to the long-suffering Chinese people, after what looked like being a period of sustained prosperity in the 1980s. The swing of the pendulum back in the direction of state-controlled enterprises, if it turns out to be sustained, seems as if it will waste potential. At the beginning of the 1980s it was argued that the reform movement threatened to abandon the gains of three decades of socialism, by dismantling the collectives to make way for the new landscape of materialism, privatization, and commodification. Less than ten years later it looked as though another major reversal was under way, and the entire economic infrastructure might once again be unraveled, thrusting China back into the past and wiping out most of the gains that had been made. Although it is unlikely that the entire reform program will be terminated, the pace of change has been seriously curtailed, and the air of optimism has been sharply deflated.

Outsiders, and probably more than a few Chinese people, can be forgiven for becoming apathetic and cynical. Today's heroes might be tomorrow's criminals, so the only safe response is to keep quiet and fall into line. Astonishingly, what happened in 1989 in Beijing and in many other cities around the country suggests that the Chinese people have not yet given up hope. In the post-Tiananmen era the round of retrenchments that had already begun in 1988 has been reinforced, and China is facing the sort of austerity that the people had to live with throughout the Maoist years. They have again been asked to tighten their belts, in return for which the government promised that things would improve, sometime in the not-too-distant future. It is difficult to see how this new round of deprivations can be swallowed by the ordinary people, who know that many Communist party officials are enjoying far better circumstances and have heard about the widespread corruption in the highest echelons of the government. The people have their belts as tight as they can be. They are waiting for evidence of belt-tightening among the Party leaders.

The events of 1989 represented to the Chinese government a uniquely threatening combination of students and workers. Although the government considers its actions successful, the brutality of the crackdown has given all future popular rebellions in China an incredibly powerful symbol around which to rally. It is important to remember that it was actually the ordinary citizens, rather than the students, who bore the brunt of the massacre and the subsequent police actions in 1989[14] (see Chapter 15). This suggests that the workers, and perhaps even the peasants, may play an important role in any future demonstrations. Many Western evaluators believe that the key to the future may well lie in the activities of a disaffected elite within the Party. If this represents the necessary condition for political reform in China, the sufficient condition could be the actions of the ordinary citizens: on the streets; in the workplace; and even in the countryside. From this perspective the current retrenchments and the threat of a prolonged economic downturn are dangerous trends because, as Walder noted, "any future economic stagnation will once again make this group [the workers] available for political mobilization. In a situation of heightened political repression, through slowdowns and isolated walkouts, workers will have more effective means of political leverage than students and intellectuals."[15] The prospect of further economic austerity could, therefore, represent political dynamite for the Party, because a rebellion by the workers and the peasants would be a much more serious threat than could ever be presented by the students.

Feng Shui: The Ancient Chinese Art of Placement

It is important to point out that a concern with the environment in China is certainly not a new phenomenon, and as we have seen in so many areas of life in China, human/environmental relationships have been significantly affected by enduring cultural practices. For centuries there has been a special relationship between the Chinese people and their social landscapes—the places they have called home. This concern has been expressed in the enormous and intricate lengths to which the Chinese will go to "placate" the land, and it is evident in the ageless practices of *feng shui*. *Feng shui*, which literally refers to wind and water, is a term used to describe the forces that are believed to be responsible for determining health, prosperity, good luck, and longevity.

Feng shui evolved over the centuries from the simple observations that people are affected, for better or worse, by their surroundings. The layout of a village had to be planned with great care, as did the placement of a grave and the location of a well. It was crucial to consider the local topography and the course and flow of the local streams before making any important geographical or environmental decisions.[1] *Feng shui* practitioners, some of whom are referred to as "geomancers," have acted over the years as consultants to advise on the positioning of human settlements and activities to make sure they can harmonize with the environment. The goal of the geomancer is to make possible a rearrangement of the *qi* (cosmic forces, or currents), which emanate both from people and from the atmosphere. *Qi* has been described as "the vital force that breathes life into animals and vegetation, inflates the earth to form mountains, and carries water through the earth's ducts."[2] It is the essence of life, a powerful force that flows through the animate and inanimate worlds. Atmospheric *qi* encompasses air, steam, gas, water, and the weather; human *qi* includes breath and energy—it is similar perhaps to what we have come to recognize as a person's "aura." *Qi* is a motivating force, and without it people will not

be healthy or prosperous. According to the legacy of *feng shui*, without *qi* trees will not blossom and rivers will not flow.[3]

It is important for people to be responsive to and aware of other people's *qi*, but it is equally important that they be sensitive to the *qi* of their environment. The *feng shui* expert attempts to direct a strong current of positive *qi* to a person and, if possible, to divert or prevent the flowing of harmful *qi*. In premodern times any changes that were made to the land required the blessing of the *feng shui* experts. Like a combination of architects and doctors, they advised on where to build. In this sense they were early planners and environmentalists because to violate the earth was considered to be heresy. In spite of this it is evident that at many times over the centuries, and in almost all parts of China, the advice of the *feng shui* practitioners was not always followed. Throughout the seventeenth, eighteenth, and nineteenth centuries, for example, the Chinese people persisted in lumbering in China's delicate forestlands in the north, decimating them, and leaving many parts of north China desertified by the twentieth century. This process, as we saw in Chapter 10, has been accelerated in the postrevolutionary era.

The Communists have exhorted the Chinese people to abandon their "feudal" practices and beliefs, including *feng shui*. In spite of the evidence that modernization has been accompanied by less adherence to such ancient cultural customs, it is interesting to note that even in Hong Kong, the ultimately modern Asian city, *feng shui* is still practiced by Chinese and British alike. In her book about Hong Kong, for example, Jan Morris described how the Bank of Hong Kong and Shanghai brought in a geomancer to consult on the design and layout of the city's most spectacular new skyscraper in the early 1980s. He was delighted with the site selection because the glittering tower was to be built in one of the best *feng shui* sites in the colony—with its back to the mountains, facing the sea. He also recommended a slight repositioning of the building's elevators, to which the owners were receptive, in spite of the need to change the architect's plans.

It is hard to know whether the owners of that new skyscraper, when they agreed to shift the escalators, really believed it would be beneficial, or whether they simply wanted to keep their employees happy; but some expatriates certainly employ a geomancer to approve the siting, the architecture or even the furnishings of their new house, "just in case"—for they have caught from the Chinese the cheerful if fatalistic attitude that it is worth appeasing all gods, in case one of them exists.[4]

A New Language
of Dissent in China

Since the days of the Yenan base area in Shaanxi Province, the Chinese Communist party has generated what amounts to a new language of revolution. Because of the importance of propaganda at each stage of the revolution, the terminology involved assumed a significance probably much greater than it deserved. During the 1950s and 1960s almost everything Mao Zedong said or wrote was considered to be an imperial decree. It is obvious that Mao realized the importance of language, which accounts for the hundreds of slogans and catchphrases that came to be synonymous with specific campaigns, for example the "three antis"; "land reform"; the "Hundred Flowers Campaign"; and the "sending down" policies. It is difficult for translators to come up with suitable terms to convey the exact meaning of the terminology associated with the Chinese revolution, but in an attempt to start a new language of dissent, the translators of Yu Luojin's book *A Chinese Winter's Tale* have provided a glossary of terms. As they pointed out, this language is as strange to us as George Orwell's was in his book *1984*. This should not be surprising, however, because as they say, "the strangeness of this language itself says a great deal about the strangeness of the society that formed it."[1] It is their hope, in translating what they believe to be a landmark work in the literature of Chinese dissidence, that the new language will catch on—in the same way that the language of the revolution caught on and inspired a nation. They wrote, "It is words that incite people to action: it is slogans uttered by the men on top and echoed by the propaganda machine that start what is often described in the Communist process as the 'tidal waves' or the 'conflagration that reaches the sky.'"[2]

The weight of slogans has been demonstrated in revolutions around the world: in France, in the Soviet Union, and in China. To reinforce the importance of words and to illustrate the new language, it is useful to consider some of the terms.

Proledic. Proledic is a single word used to describe a most baffling term that has been used throughout this book, especially in Chapter 15, namely the "dictatorship of the proletariat." In Marxist theory, the proletariat is assumed to have a leading role over the bourgeoisie and all exploiting classes. In actual practice though, the Communist party, acting as the "vanguard of the proletariat," can and usually does commandeer the entire state apparatus, including the Ministries of Public and State Security; the police; the network of prisons and labor camps; and even the army. More important, however, proledic has a pervasive influence over the whole of everyday life in China because it operates through the interlocking webs of work-unit and neighborhood-level government, and it makes use of the constant surveillance and the detailed dossiers that help to maintain absolute control over the lives of individuals. Proledic is supposed to be a process—a transitional stage, one that will not necessarily be required as the communist utopia is realized and the need for continuing the class struggle disappears. In actual fact, however, the proledic has become stronger and stronger and is no longer even remotely connected to the people or their interests.

Urblings. Urblings is a quaint term used to describe the millions of educated youth who were "sent down" from the cities to the countryside during the 1960s and 1970s. The experience, for many of them, was disastrous. They were separated from their families and most often were resented by the peasants in their new homes. Some of the urblings managed to return home after the death of Mao, but many of them experienced serious readjustment problems, and some have been associated with the so-called problem youth, and the youth "waiting for jobs," which is a cruel euphemism for the unemployed in China's cities. It is this group that is most closely associated with the original Democracy Movement in the late 1970s as well as with the new breed of authors, poets, filmmakers, and artists who rose to the forefront in the period immediately after the Cultural Revolution.

Sodality. Sodality is a translation of the Chinese word *renqing*, which means something like "human feelings," but is in fact used to describe the entire network of favors and obligations surrounding Chinese relationships. The term seems to be more widely used, however: The British author and composer Anthony Burgess mentioned it frequently in his autobiography.[3] This is an interesting coincidence because Burgess, like George Orwell, was interested in the future, and in his book *A Clockwork Orange* he painted an equally chilling picture of it, complete with his own version of Orwellian future-speak.

N O T E S

■ ═══════════════════════════════════ ■

CHAPTER 1

1. C. Thubron, 1987, *Behind the Wall: A Journey Through China* (London: Heinemann), p. 88.

2. M. Selden, 1988, *The Political Economy of Chinese Socialism* (Armonk, N.Y.: M. E. Sharpe), p. 144.

3. J. K. Fairbank, 1987, *The Great Chinese Revolution: 1800–1985* (New York: Harper and Row), p. 7.

4. Ibid., p. 7.

CHAPTER 2

1. Zhang Xianliang, 1988, "Shorbloc: A Driver's Story," pp. 117–151 in Zhu Hong (trans.), *The Chinese Western: Short Fiction from Today's China* (New York: Available Press), quote from p. 118.

2. C. Blunden and M. Elvin, 1983, *Cultural Atlas of China* (New York: Facts on File, Inc.).

3. This is one of the numerous sayings that became commonplace in China during the centuries of imperial rule over far-flung provinces.

4. See some of the stories in Hong Zhu (translator), 1988, *The Chinese Western: Short Fiction From Today's China* (New York: Available Press).

5. This explanation is provided by N. C. Doo, 1987, "Phrase and Fable," *China Now*, No. 120 (Spring), p. 20.

6. Quoted from an editorial in the Young Communist League's official newspaper, *China Youth Daily*; reprinted in T. P. Bernstein, 1977, *Up to the Mountains and Down to the Villages: The Transfer of Youth From Urban to Rural China* (New Haven: Yale University Press), p. 56.

7. For vivid accounts of the experiences of "sent down" youths in the Chinese countryside, see for example: Liang Heng and J. Shapiro, 1984, *Son of the Revolution* (New York: Vintage Books); and also Lo Fulang, 1989, *Morning Breeze: A True Story of Chinese Cultural Revolution* (San Francisco: China Books and Periodicals, Inc.). In some cities, for example, Shanghai, government decrees dictated that if families had more than one educated child, at least one of them would have to be sent down.

This resulted in some excruciating decisions. Some families believed that if they lacked the necessary connections, a failure to volunteer early would result in their children's being sent off to outlandishly remote places such as Xinjiang, Tibet, or Inner Mongolia—places that for most urban Chinese people were "foreign countries." There is also some evidence that certain classes of educated youths (or their parents) were willing to act in a fully "revolutionary red" way, by volunteering to go off to such remote places, regardless of their education levels or their class backgrounds. These and other situations are beautifully described in Wang Anyi's (1988) book *Lapse of Time* (San Francisco: China Books and Periodicals).

8. See, for example, J. K. Fairbank, 1987, *The Great Chinese Revolution: 1800–1985* (New York: Harper and Row). For perhaps the finest treatment of the relationship between the Chinese people and their land, see K. Buchanan, 1970, *The Transformation of the Chinese Earth: Aspects of the Evaluation of the Chinese Earth from Earliest Times to Mao Tse-tung* (London: G. Bell and Sons).

9. C. O. Sauer, 1963, *Land and Life* (Berkeley: University of California Press), pp. 159–160.

10. G. B. Cressey, 1955, *Land of Five Hundred Million: A Geography of China* (New York: McGraw Hill), p. 1.

11. J. Morris, 1988, *Hong Kong* (New York: Random House), p. 8.

12. Y. F. Tuan, 1969, *China* (Chicago: Aldine Publishing Co.), p. 6.

13. R. Murphey, 1976, "Man and Nature in China," *Modern Asian Studies* 1 (October), pp. 313–33.

14. Of course in China, perhaps more so than in most other countries, the environment has also "won a few" over the centuries, particularly the droughts in northern China and the floods in South China.

15. M. J. Coye, J. Livingston, and J. Highland (eds.), 1984, *China: Yesterday and Today* (3rd ed.) (Toronto: Bantam Books), p. 289.

16. M. S. Samuels, 1978, "Individual and Landscape: Thoughts on China and the Tao of Mao," pp. 283–96 in D. Ley and M. S. Samuels (eds.), *Humanistic Geography: Prospects and Problems* (Chicago: Maaroufa Press).

17. Ibid.

18. Cressey, op. cit., p. 3.

19. E. Relph, 1976, *Place and Placelessness* (London: Pion), p. 43.

20. J. Belden, 1949, *China Shakes the World* (New York: Monthly Review Press), p. 129.

21. A. H. Smith, 1899, *Village Life in China: A Study in Sociology* (New York: Fleming H. Revell, Co.), p. 262.

22. G. W. Skinner, 1977, "Introduction: Urban Social Structures in Ch'ing China," pp. 522–53 in G. W. Skinner (ed.), *The City in Late Imperial China* (Stanford, Calif.: Stanford University Press), p. 539.

23. Skinner referred to these itinerants as "sojourners." See ibid., pp. 545–46.

24. Y. Shiba, 1977, "Ningpo and Its Hinterland," pp. 391–440 in Skinner, op. cit.

25. Ibid., p. 438.

26. Zhang Xinxin and Sang Ye, 1987, *Chinese Lives: An Oral History of Contemporary China* (New York: Pantheon Books), p. 124.

27. Smith, op. cit., p. 319.

28. M. C. Yang, 1945, *A Chinese Village: Taitou, Shantung Province* (New York: Columbia University Press), p. 200.

29. Morris, op. cit., p. 134.

30. See Hou Ren-Zhi, 1986, "Evolution of the City Plan of Beijing," *Third World Planning Review* 8, No. 1, pp. 5–17.

31. T. Terzani, 1986, *Behind the Forbidden Door: Travels in China* (London: Allen and Unwin), p. 57.

32. Ibid., p. 25.

33. C. Thubron, 1987, *Behind the Wall: A Journey Through China* (London: Heinemann), p. 294.

34. Skinner, op. cit.

35. Ibid., see esp. pp. 3–31 and 211–249.

36. In recent years Skinner's idea of the "macroregions" has not withstood the rigors of empirical analysis; in fact it has been seriously challenged. See, for example, B. Sands and R. H. Meyers, 1986, "The Spatial Approach to Chinese History," *Journal of Asian Studies* 45, No. 4 (August), pp. 721–43. For another view on the evolution of administrative regions in China, see J.B.R. Whitney, 1970, *China: Area Administration and Nation Building* (Chicago: University of Chicago, Department of Geography Research Paper No. 123).

37. See Blunden and Elvin, op. cit.

38. For a more detailed discussion of this, see C. W. Pannell and L.J.C. Ma, 1983, *China: The Geography of Development and Modernization* (London: V. H. Winston).

39. In the mid-1980s most of the prefectures were abolished and many rural counties adjacent to cities were annexed for administrative purposes. This issue is discussed in more detail in Chapter 12. See also L.J.C. Ma and Cui Conghuo, 1987, "Administrative Changes and Urban Population in China," *Annals of the Association of American Geographers* 77, No. 3 (September), pp. 373–95.

40. For a further discussion of the original structure and purpose of the neighborhood organizations, see J. A. Cohen, 1968, *Criminal Process in the Peoples' Republic of China, 1949-1963: An Introduction* (Cambridge: Harvard University Press), esp. pp. 106–112.

41. See F. Schurmann, 1968, *Ideology and Organization in Communist China* (Berkeley: University of California Press).

42. For details, see Cohen, op. cit., pp. 106–113.

43. For an illustration of the services provided at the neighborhood level in one Beijing district, see Luo Fu, 1980, "City Dwellers and the Neighborhood Committee," *Beijing Review*, No. 44 (November 3), pp. 19–25.

44. It is this local level of record-keeping and surveillance that makes it extremely difficult for anyone "on the run" to remain at large from the government—as the dissident students in Beijing found after the crackdown in 1989.

45. Zhang Jie, 1986, "The Ark," pp. 113–202 in *Love Must Not Be Forgotten* (San Francisco: China Books and Periodicals), quote from pp. 122–23.

46. Terzani, op. cit., p. 53.

47. Ibid.

48. Ibid, p. 53.

CHAPTER 3

1. Quoted in L. E. Stover, 1974, *The Cultural Ecology of Chinese Civilization: Peasants and Elites in the Last of the Agrarian States* (New York: Pica Press), p. 258.

2. F. Mote, 1971, *Intellectual Foundations of China* (New York: Alfred A. Knopf), pp. 51–52.

3. Stover, op. cit., p. 246.

4. Mote, op. cit., p. 39.

5. From *The Analects*, 7/18, quoted in ibid., p. 37.

6. This is an adaptation of a well-known saying usually attributed to the Confucian scholar, Mencius. See Lin Yutang, 1966, *The Wisdom of Confucius* (New York: Random House).

7. M. H. Bond and Hwang Kwang-Kuo, 1986, "The Social Psychology of the Chinese People," pp. 213–66 in M. H. Bond (ed.), *The Psychology of the Chinese People* (Hong Kong: Oxford University Press), p. 216.

8. Lin, op. cit., p. 20.

9. Mote, op. cit., p. 47.

10. R. J. Smith, 1983, *China's Cultural Heritage: The Ch'ing Dynasty, 1644–1912* (Boulder, Colo.: Westview Press), p. 114.

11. Ibid. To define *li* in specific social situations, three Confucian classics on ritual were produced: The *I-li, Chou-li,* and *Li-chi.* These texts described

in minute detail how a Confucian gentleman should behave.

12. Stover, op. cit., p. 267.

13. Ibid., p. 247.

14. Quote attributed to Sun Longji, 1983, from *The Deep Structure of Chinese Culture* (Hong Kong: Yishan Publishing Co.). Quoted in G. Barmé and J. Minford, 1986, *Seeds of Fire: Chinese Voices of Conscience* (Hong Kong: Far Eastern Review, Ltd.), p. 34.

15. A.Y.C. King and M. H. Bond, 1985, "The Confucian Paradigm of Man: A Sociological Review," pp. 29–45 in Tseng Wen-Shing and D.Y.H. Wu (eds.), *Chinese Culture and Mental Health* (Orlando, Fla.: Academic Press), quote from p. 29.

16. Sun, op. cit., quoted in Barmé and Minford, op. cit., p. 31.

17. J. Legge (translator), 1960, *The Chinese Classics* (reprint, 5 vol.) (Hong Kong: University of Hong Kong Press), p. 359.

18. Smith, op. cit.

19. L. Pan, 1988, *The New Chinese Revolution* (Chicago: Contemporary Books), p. 68.

20. This issue is taken up in greater detail in Chapter 15.

21. B. Hooper, 1985, *Youth in China* (London: Penguin Books).

22. Ibid., esp. Chap. 11, "Falling in Love with Love," pp. 175–188.

23. Yu Luojin, 1986, *A Chinese Winter's Tale* (Hong Kong: Renditions Paperbacks), p. 106.

24. Ibid., p. 106.

25. C. Thubron, 1987, *Behind the Wall: A Journey Through China* (London: Heinemann), pp. 182–83.

26. Ibid., pp. 183–84. According to most Chinese and outside observers, premarital sex is rare in China and is associated with great shame, partly because sexual independence is seen as a rebellion against the group and the family. Sun Longji even goes as far as suggesting that the suppression of normal sexual drives results in them being "rechannelled" into oral fixations, such as spitting, passing wind in public, and littering—all of which are childlike and dependent behaviors. See Barmé and Minford, op. cit.

27. Stover, op. cit.

28. Ibid.

29. See Bond and Hwang, op. cit., for a detailed discussion of "face" and its implications in Chinese society.

30. J. K. Fairbank, 1967, "The Nature of Chinese Society," pp. 35–66 in F. Schurmann and O. Schell (eds.), *Imperial China: The Decline of the Last Dynasty and the Origins of Modern China—The 18th and 19th Centuries* (New York: Vintage Books), p. 55.

31. Ibid. (emphasis added).

32. Mote, op. cit., p. 41.

33. O. Schell, 1979, "Private Life in a Public Culture," pp. 23–36 in R. Terrill (ed.), *The China*
Difference (New York: Harper Colophon Books), quote from p. 29.

34. Ibid., pp. 29–30.

35. Pan, op. cit., p. 141.

36. See, for example, A. Kleinman and Lin Tsung-Yi, 1981, *Normal and Abnormal Behavior in Chinese Culture* (Dordrecht, Holland: D. Reidel Publishing Co.); Tseng and Wu, op. cit.; and Bond, op. cit.

37. G. C. Chu, 1985, "The Emergence of the New Chinese Culture," pp. 15–28 in Tseng and Wu, op. cit.

38. Soong Wei-Tsuen and Soong Ko-Ping, 1981, "Sex Differences in School Adjustment in Taiwan," pp. 157–168 in Kleinman and Lin, op. cit.; F.M.C. Cheung, 1986, "Psychopathology Among Chinese People," pp. 171–212 in Bond, op. cit.; and D.H.F. Ho, 1986, "Chinese Patterns of Socialization: A Critical Review," pp. 1–37 in Bond, op. cit.

39. Yang Kuo-Shu, 1986, "Chinese Personality and Its Change," pp. 106–170 in Bond, op. cit.

40. D.Y.H. Wu and Tseng Wen-Shing, 1985, "Introduction: The Characteristics of Chinese Culture," pp. 3–13 in Tseng and Wu, op. cit.

41. D. C. McClelland, 1963, "Motivational Patterns in South-East Asia, With Special Reference to the Chinese Case," *Social Issues* 19, No. 1, pp. 6–19.

42. G. Hofstede, 1980, *Culture's Consequences: International Differences in Work-Related Values* (Beverly Hills, Calif.: Sage Publications). Additional work by Hofstede is discussed in his "Dimensions of National Cultures in Fifty Countries and Three Regions," pp. 335–355 in J. B. Deregowski, S. Dziurawiec, and R. C. Annis (eds.), 1983, *Expectations in Cross Cultural Psychology* (Lisse, Netherlands: Swets and Zeitlinger B.V.).

43. Follow-up studies conducted in the PRC have basically reproduced these findings for residents of the mainland. See Yang, op. cit.

44. The Chinese Culture Connection, 1987, "Chinese Values and the Search for Culture Free Dimensions of Culture," *Journal of Cross-Cultural Psychology* 18, No. 2 (June), pp. 143–164.

45. G. Hicks and S. G. Redding, 1983, "The Story of the East Asian Economic Miracle: II. The Cultural Connection," *Euro-Asian Business Review* 2 (February), pp. 18–22.

46. H. Kahn, 1979, *World Economic Development: 1979 and Beyond* (London: Croom Helm), p. 122.

47. For examples of such studies, see the collection of articles in H. M. Proshansky, W. Ittelson, and L. G. Rivlin, 1970, *Environmental Psychology: An Introduction* (Englewood Cliffs, N.J.: Prentice-Hall).

48. This should not, of course, be taken to mean that the Chinese necessarily like such practices, just as they probably do not like to live in crowded cities. Evidence from novels and from the more explicit outpourings from the Democracy

Movement suggest that the Chinese, like people everywhere else in the world, loathe the invasion of privacy they have to endure. See, for examples, some of the selections in Barmé and Minford, op. cit.

49. The author, for example, recalls trying to take a picture of a statue of Buddha in a cave in Yenan. Chinese onlookers kept insisting that the photograph should have a human being in the foreground; in fact one woman physically picked up one of my children and sat her on a ledge next to the statue!

50. Thubron, op. cit., p. 63.

51. A number of scholars interested in this issue have attempted to outline cultural/ecological models for this purpose. See, for an example, M. H. Fried, 1969, *The Fabric of Chinese Society: A Study of Social Life of a Chinese County Seat* (New York: Octagon Books). See also the chapters in Bond, op. cit., and Stover, op. cit.

52. Yang, op. cit.

53. Ibid., p. 153.

54. As is the case with just about everything else in China, the events of 1989 now make such statements more questionable than ever. The increasing isolation that China has been experiencing after the crushing of the Democracy Movement; the severance of political and economic ties with the outside world; and the limitations on tourism could all work to slow down the convergence trend in social and personality traits, with Chinese characteristics becoming more solidly unique than ever before.

55. J. W. Lewis (ed.), 1971, *The City in Communist China* (Stanford, Calif.: Stanford University Press).

56. E. Vogel, 1965, "From Friendship to Comradeship," *China Quarterly* 21 (January), pp. 46–60.

57. M. K. Whyte and W. L. Parish, 1984, *Urban Life in Contemporary China* (Chicago: University of Chicago Press).

58. Ibid., p. 340.

59. Zhang Xianliang, 1988, *Half of Man Is Woman* (New York: W. W. Norton and Co.), p. 266.

60. Yue Daiyun and C. Wakeman, 1985, *To the Storm: The Odyssey of a Revolutionary Chinese Woman* (Berkeley: University of California Press), pp. 31–32.

61. Zhang Jie, 1986, "The Ark," pp. 113–201 in *Love Must Not Be Forgotten* (San Francisco: China Books and Periodicals), quote from pp. 170–71.

62. A. F. Thurston, 1988, *Enemies of the People: The Ordeal of the Intellectuals in China's Great Cultural Revolution* (Cambridge, Mass.: Harvard University Press), p. 58.

63. Pan, op. cit., p. 135.

64. Gao Yuan, 1987, *Born Red: A Chronicle of the Cultural Revolution* (Stanford, Calif.: Stanford University Press).

65. Thurston, op. cit., p. 58.

66. Pan, op. cit., p. 175.

67. O. Schell, 1984, *To Get Rich Is Glorious: China in the Eighties* (New York: Pantheon Books).

68. T. B. Gold, 1985, "After Comradeship: Personal Relations in China Since the Cultural Revolution," *China Quarterly*, No. 104 (December), pp. 657–675, quote from p. 671.

69. W. H. Hinton, 1989, "A Response to Hugh Deane," *Monthly Review* 40, No. 10 (March), pp. 10–35, quote from p. 18.

70. Ibid., p. 19.

71. Gold, op. cit., noted that brides today are likely to ask for much more than just the traditional "three things that go round" (watches, bicycles, and sewing machines) and are now expecting anything with "legs" (furniture), everything with *ji* (machinery, tape recorders, televisions, and refrigerators), and everything with *ya* (duck down, as in bedclothes). See also Pan, op. cit., p. 146. (U.S. $1 equaled approximately Y 3.8 at the time.)

72. Pan, op. cit., p. 140.

73. Gold, op. cit., p. 671. According to Gold, the expression commonly used for "a bit of prosperity," to which many Chinese now aspire, is an ancient Confucian term *xiao kang.*

74. Pan, op. cit., p. 175. A survey recently conducted among Chinese college students confirms some of the trends referred to here. The values traditionally associated with China, such as having a great concern for others and a reverence for the elderly, appear to be in decline, whereas values China shares with the West, such as the desire to work hard to get ahead and the importance of money, are increasing. See Zhao Wen, 1989, "New Times, New Values: Changes in Social Ethics," *Nexus: China in Focus*, Summer, p. 30.

75. A. F. Thurston, 1985, "Victims of China's Cultural Revolution: The Invisible Wounds, Part 1," *Pacific Affairs* 57, No. 2, pp. 599–620; quote from p. 619.

76. This is a quote from T. Terzani, 1986, *Behind the Forbidden Door: Travels in Unknown China* (London: Allen and Unwin), p. 20. Terzani was an exceedingly bitter reporter on contemporary China, and he was finally expelled from the country for his extremely negative views on the current regime and its policies.

CHAPTER 4

1. A Shandong peasant saying, quoted in T. Terzani, 1986, *Behind the Forbidden Door: Travels in Unknown China* (London: Allen and Unwin), p. 128.

2. P. Theroux, 1988, *Riding the Iron Rooster: By Train Through China* (New York: Ivy Books), p. 378.

3. G. Peck, 1967, *Two Kinds of Time: Life in Provincial China During the Crucial Years 1940–1941* (Boston: Houghton-Mifflin Co.).

4. Ibid., p. 91.

5. Bo Yang, 1986, *The Ugly Chinaman*. Quoted on p. 172 in G. Barmé and J. Minford (eds.), *Seeds of Fire: Chinese Voices of Conscience* (Hong Kong: Far Eastern Economic Review, Ltd.)

6. It is interesting to note that even in the midst of the student demonstrations in spring 1989, Western journalists were able to find and interview many students who, in spite of their actions, praised the Party and realized its significance. See, for example, "Students Praised in China," *Times Union* (Albany, N.Y.), May 9, 1989, p. 21.

7. J. Baum, 1986, "Party Membership: Youth Takes Hard Look," *Christian Science Monitor*, March 10.

8. Ibid.

9. R. Delfs, 1988, "In Search of a Socialist Theory," *Far Eastern Economic Review* 138, No. 41 (October 8), pp. 50–51.

10. This was one of the major areas of complaint being voiced in spring 1989. See, for example, E. Salem, 1988, "Barons and Bandits, a Law Unto Themselves," *Far Eastern Economic Review* 139, No. 44 (October 27).

11. Jiang Zilong, 1985, "The Diary of a Factory Clerk," pp. 332–359 in Ke Yunlu and Zhang Xianliang (eds.), *Prize Winning Stories from China 1980–1981* (Beijing: Foreign Languages Press). For a scholarly discussion of the importance and the role of politics in the Chinese workplace, see A. G. Walder, 1986, *Communist Neo-Traditionalism: Work and Authority in Chinese Industry* (Berkeley: University of California Press).

12. This is very well illustrated in some of the anecdotes reported by Lynn Pan in her 1988 book, *The New Chinese Revolution* (Chicago: Contemporary Books), see esp. Chap. 10.

13. See "Deng Xiaoping Leads a Far-Reaching, Audacious but Risky Second Revolution," *Time*, January 6, 1986, pp. 24–40, quote from p. 24.

14. D. Wilson, 1979, *The People's Emperor: Mao, A Biography of Mao Tse-tung* (New York: Lee Publishing Group).

15. K. Marx, 1935, *Class Struggles in France* (London: Lawrence and Wishart), p. 173.

16. L. Bianco, 1971, *Origins of the Chinese Revolution, 1915–1944* (Stanford, Calif.: Stanford University Press), p. 74. For a further discussion of Stalin's brutality toward the Kulaks (and others) see R. Medvedev, 1989, *Let History Judge* (New York: Columbia University Press).

17. H. Feis, 1953, *The China Tangle* (Princeton, N.J.: Princeton University Press), p. 140.

18. Bianco, op. cit., p. 59.

19. For details of this event, see ibid. and also J. K. Fairbank, 1987, *The Great Chinese Revolution, 1800–1985* (New York: Harper and Row), esp. Chap. 12, "The Nationalist Revolution and the First KMT-CCP United Front," pp. 204–216.

20. Mao Zedong, 1927, "Report on an Investigation of the Peasant Movement in Hunan" (March). Reprinted in *Selected Readings From the Works of Mao Tse-tung* (Beijing: Foreign Languages Press, 1971), pp. 23–39, quote from p. 24.

21. The best exposition of this argument was provided by Chalmers A. Johnson in his 1962 book, *Peasant Nationalism and Communist Power: The Emergence of Revolutionary China, 1937–1945* (Stanford, Calif.: Stanford University Press).

22. See, for example, M. Meisner, 1979, "Marxism and Chinese Values," pp. 99–116 in R. Terrill (ed.), *The China Difference: A Portrait of Life Inside the Country of One Billion* (New York: Colophon Books), quote from pp. 101–02.

23. For an excellent account of why this was the case, see M. Blecher, 1986, *China: Politics, Economics and Society: Iconoclasm and Innovation in a Revolutionary Socialist Country* (London: Frances Pinter Pub.). Blecher argued that the landed elite continued to dominate the economic landscape at this time, in addition to which much of the industry remained in the hands of the Western capitalists and was concentrated in the east coast Treaty Ports.

24. R. H. Tawney, 1932, *Land and Labour in China* (Boston: Beacon Press), pp. 73–77.

25. J. G. Gurley, 1976, *China's Economy and the Maoist Strategy* (New York: Monthly Review Press), p. 232.

26. Peck, op. cit., p. 23.

27. Ibid.

28. K. Buchanan, 1970, *The Transformation of the Chinese Earth* (London: G. Bell and Sons), quote from pp. 35–36.

29. Meisner, op. cit., p. 105.

30. Ibid., p. 108.

31. Ibid., p. 103.

32. The term *feudal* is used in quotation marks to signify prerevolutionary China, but that is in fact a misnomer. Most historians use "feudal" to describe the serf and manor system characteristic of medieval Europe. In China the peasants were not serfs or slaves, but in fact they were so closely tied to the land that they were little better than serfs. "Feudal," therefore, herein loosely describes a society in which a ruling class owned most of the land and lived off the surplus produced on that land by the peasants, who were actually a "propertied proletariat" (Tawney, op. cit., p. 73).

33. Meisner, op. cit., p. 107.

34. This is essentially what was meant by the phrase "better red than expert," which is often associated with Mao and Mao Zedong Thought. See, for example, Blecher, op. cit.

35. See J. K. Fairbank, 1967, "The Nature of Chinese Society," pp. 34–66 in F. Schurmann and O. Schell (eds.), *Imperial China: The Decline of the Last Dynasty and the Origins of Modern China—The 18th and 19th Centuries* (New York: Vintage Books). Even in this belief, however, Confucius did not

suggest that ethical and moral behavior should be practiced because it could produce a better world—simply because it was in man's nature to behave that way.

36. T. B. Gold, 1985, "After Comradeship: Personal Relations in China Since the Cultural Revolution," *The China Quarterly*, No. 104 (December), pp. 657–675, quote from p. 674.

37. See Blecher, op. cit., pp. 190–92.

38. See C. Riskin, 1987, *China's Political Economy: The Quest for Development Since 1949* (London: Oxford University Press).

39. See Blecher, op. cit.

40. The term *forces of production* usually refers to the means of production or the factors of production, in other words, the land, technology, tools, raw materials, and capital that are used to produce goods and services. Obviously, in China in 1949, the only part of this that was in mass supply was the vast labor force, hence the importance of efforts to improve the value of labor through education, training and, above all, attempts to increase revolutionary consciousness. The term *relations of production* refers to the relationship between people in the process of production. As we saw earlier, most of the means of production (especially the land and the capital) was in the hands of an elite group of landlords and moneylenders, with the mass of the peasants essentially working at a subsistence level to support this group. Thus the relations of production effectively define the class system in a society, which is usually translated into wealth and well-being that can be handed down to later generations, thereby "reproducing" the present system of class relationships into the future. See Gurley, op. cit., and also V. D. Lippit, 1987, *The Economic Development of China* (Armonk, N.Y.: M. E. Sharpe, Inc.), esp. Chaps. 1 and 4, pp. 3–34 and 78–102.

41. See W. Hinton, 1984, *Shenfan: The Continuing Revolution in a Chinese Village* (New York: Vintage Books), see pp. 63–67.

42. Bianco, op. cit., p. 190.

43. Gurley, op. cit.

44. This is the concept of "continuous revolution," which is generally associated with Mao Zedong Thought. See, for example, L. Dittmer, 1987, *China's Continuous Revolution: The Post-Liberation Epoch, 1949–1981* (Berkeley: University of California Press).

45. Although as Blecher, op. cit., suggested, more realistic evidence available much later would place this estimate at closer to 15 percent growth per year.

46. V. Shue, 1980, *Peasant China in Transition: The Dynamics of Development Towards Socialism, 1949–1956* (Berkeley: University of California Press).

47. See, for example, A. G. Walder, 1986, *Communist Neo-Traditionalism: Work and Authority in Chinese Industry* (Berkeley: University of California

Press). See esp. Chap. 6, "Maoist Asceticism," pp. 190–221.

48. Mao Zedong, 1977, *Selected Works*, Vol. 5 (Beijing: Foreign Languages Press), p. 134.

49. This era is generally referred to as the "Yenan period," after the style of politics and mass mobilization campaigns developed in the Communist-base area that was centered in rural northern Shaanxi Province. For details, see M. Selden, 1971, *The Yenan Way in Revolutionary China* (Cambridge, Mass.: Harvard University Press).

50. See Blecher, op. cit., esp. Chap. 2, pp. 42–92; and also Gurley, op. cit., Chap. 5, pp. 236–263.

51. An excellent introduction to the chaotic situation that prevailed during the Cultural Revolution is provided by W. A. Joseph, 1987, in the Foreword to Gao Yuan's book, *Born Red: A Chronicle of the Cultural Revolution* (Stanford, Calif.: Stanford University Press). The period is also discussed by P. Van Ness and S. Raichur, 1983, "Dilemmas of Socialist Development: An Analysis of Strategic Lines in China, 1949–1981," pp. 77–89 in Bulletin of Concerned Asia Scholars (eds.), *China from Mao to Deng: The Politics and Economics of Socialist Development* (Armonk, N.Y.: M. E. Sharpe, Inc.).

52. See Van Ness and Raichur, op. cit., p. 82.

53. See R. Delfs, 1987, "Now the Right Turns," *Far Eastern Economic Review*, January 8, pp. 8–9.

54. This phrase is usually associated with Deng Xiaoping, but is here taken from Zhao Ziyang, 1987, "The Primary Stage of Socialism," pp. 20–24 in *The 13th Party Congress and China's Reforms* (Beijing: Beijing Review Press). Presumably, after Zhao had fallen from grace and been discredited by his supposed complicity with the student demonstrators in 1989, his words and his sentiment on economic and political reforms were "reinterpreted."

55. Ibid., pp. 23–24.

56. The events in Beijing during April, May, and June 1989 dominated the world's media headlines for many weeks. Much was written on the background of the demonstrations, and there was extensive coverage of the events up until the imposition of martial law in May and the crackdown and purging that began in early June. From the massive number of newspaper and magazine articles that were generated, a representative sampling includes: S. WuDunn, 1989, "Hu's Death Stirs Up Political Unrest," *New York Times*, April 16, p. 1; the Nicholas D. Kristoff obituary of Hu Yaobang, *New York Times*, April 16, p. 38; and the article by W. R. Doerner, 1989, "Come Out, Come Out: Mourning for a Fallen Leader Erupts into Defiant Demands for Political Change," *Time*, May 1, pp. 24–25. These articles describe the outpouring of student emotions when former CCP Chief Hu died in April 1989. Hu had been ousted from the Party in 1987, supposedly for supporting the students in

the earlier demonstrations during the winter of 1986–1987. Another symbolic figurehead, and now perhaps China's most famous dissident, is Fang Lizhi, who was also pinpointed by the Party as an instigator of the demonstrations in 1986–1987 and again in 1989. The buildup to the May and June activities in Tiananmen Square, and Fang's importance in the minds of both the Party and the students, have been nicely described by O. Schell, 1989, "An Act of Defiance," *New York Times Magazine*, April 16, pp. 27–30 and 43. One of the best reviews of the entire buildup, attempting to account for the students' discontent, was provided by N. D. Kristoff, 1989, "China Erupts: The Reasons Why," *New York Times Magazine*, June 4, pp. 26–29 and 85–90. Later in 1989 and early in 1990 a series of books began to hit the presses, mostly written by journalists. Among the better of these are S. Simmie and B. Nixon, 1989, *Tiananmen Square* (Seattle: University of Washington Press); Yi Mu and M. V. Thompson, 1989, *Crisis at Tiananmen: Reform and Reality in Modern China* (San Francisco: China Books and Periodicals); and also M. Fathers and A. Higgins, 1989, *Tiananmen: The Rape of Peking* (London: The Independent). Some important information is also available in the recent report of Amnesty International, 1989, *People's Republic of China: Preliminary Findings on Killings of Unarmed Civilians, Arbitrary Arrests and Summary Executions Since June 3, 1989*, October, New York.

57. After such a sweeping statement we should remember that there have been periods of starvation in the postrevolutionary era, most notably the "three disastrous years" following the Great Leap Forward in 1958. It is also clear that most evaluations of food output levels and incomes are based on nationally aggregated statistics and that there are still considerable pockets of poverty in many areas throughout China. See E. B. Vermeer, 1982, "Income Differentials in Rural China," *China Quarterly*, No. 89 (March), pp. 1–33. On the "three disastrous years," see A. J. Jowett, 1989, "Mao's Man-Made Famine," *Geographical Magazine* 61, No. 4, pp. 16–19; and also A. J. Jowett, 1987, "Famine in the People's Republic of China," Department of Geography, University of Glasgow, Occasional Paper Series, No. 21.

58. Extending the comparison to the global level, the evidence also suggests that in the 1970s and especially in the 1980s, in terms of absolute growth rates, the gross national product (GNP) was higher than in most other countries of the world; see B. J. Reynolds, 1989, "The Chinese Economy in 1988," pp. 27–48 in A. J. Kane (ed.), *China Briefing, 1989* (Boulder, Colo.: Westview Press).

59. P. Theroux, 1988, *Riding the Iron Rooster: By Train Through China* (New York: Ivy Books), p. 340.

60. For a discussion of this process, see Blecher, op. cit., pp. 91–92.

61. See M. Chossudovsky, 1986, *Towards Capitalist Restoration: Chinese Socialism After Mao* (Hong Kong: Macmillan).

62. Chinese Communist Party, 1981, *Resolution on Certain Questions in the History of Our Party, 1949–1981. Authoritative Assessment of Mao Zedong, The Cultural Revolution, Achievements of the People's Republic* (Beijing: Foreign Languages Press), p. 46.

63. Ibid.

64. Deng Xiaoping, 1984, *Selected Works* (Beijing: Foreign Languages Press), p. 202. The apparent ability of China's political leaders, and in fact of most Chinese people, to "bury the hatchet" has surprised Western observers. The widespread return to the workplace of many individuals who had been criticized by some of their fellow workers, then tried and exiled, and who worked alongside the same people after serving their sentences seems remarkable to us. This situation is brilliantly interpreted in Dai Houying's 1987 novel, *Stones of the Wall* (London: Sceptre Books). In his book about life in the prison camps, Zhang Xianliang (1988) recalled how Deng Xiaoping was supposed to have gone rowing on the lake adjacent to the CCP headquarters with some the very same people who had been involved in his public criticism and removal from office. See Zhang, op. cit., pp. 97–98.

65. Chossudovsky, op. cit., p. 19.

66. Deng Xiaoping, quoted in Sun Xiacun, 1981, "Seeking the Truth from Facts," *China Reconstructs* 30, No. 11 (November).

67. This is the view of Chossudovsky, op. cit. However, given the extremely widespread purging that occurred in 1989, it is possible that what took place in the early 1980s was similar. The obvious difference was that the eyes and the media of the outside world were not focused on China at that time.

68. "Deng Xiaoping on Mao Zedong," *Beijing Review*, September 8, 1986, pp. 14–15.

69. Jing Wei, 1986, "Mao Zedong Still Fresh in Memory," *Beijing Review*, September 8, pp. 15–18.

70. R. J. Thompson, 1988, "Reassessing Personality Cults: The Cases of Stalin and Mao," *Studies in Comparative Communism* 21, No. 1 (Spring), pp. 99–128.

71. T. P. Bernstein, 1985, "How Stalinist Was Mao's China?" *Problems of Communism* 34, No. 2 (March/April), pp. 118–125.

72. M. Selden and V. D. Lippitt (eds.), 1982, *The Transition to Socialism in China* (Armonk, N.Y.: M. E. Sharpe, Inc.).

73. Bernstein, op. cit., p. 119.

74. A. G. Walder, 1987, "Actually Existing Maoism," *Australian Journal of Chinese Affairs*, No. 18 (July), pp. 155–166.

75. Ibid., p. 156.

76. See, for example, Chossudovsky, op. cit., and Bernstein, op. cit.

77. E. Friedman, 1987, "The Flaws and Failures of Mao Zedong's Communist Fundamentalism," *Australian Journal of Chinese Affairs*, No. 18 (July), pp. 147–154, quote from p. 148.

78. Naturally, all of this documentation and the charges that had been made appeared to be vindicated by the events of 1989.

79. R. Delfs, 1988, "Helmsman's Lost Bearings," *Far Eastern Economic Review* 139, No. 44 (October 27), pp. 36–38, quote from p. 36. Again, however, we have reports that many of the student leaders in the 1989 demonstrations had publicly expressed their basic loyalty toward and support of the Party. They simply wanted to see changes and some reasonable progress being made toward giving the people more say in government. This view is reiterated in a story about Wuer Kaixi, one of the leaders of the 1989 demonstrations and currently one of the most wanted "counterrevolutionary" elements in China. See "Portrait of a 'Hooligan,' " *Time*, June 26, 1989, p. 35. In spite of these reports, however, many Western journalists wrote that according to their observations, the vast majority of the people on the streets actively loathed the Party and everything it stood for. See, for example, Kristoff, op. cit. (*China Erupts*).

80. Delfs, 1988, op. cit., p. 37.

81. Hinton, op. cit., p. 49.

82. Delfs, 1988, op. cit., p. 37.

83. Kristoff, op. cit. (*China Erupts*).

CHAPTER 5

1. See W. Hinton, 1984, *Shenfan: The Continuing Revolution in a Chinese Village* (New York: Vintage Books), p. 80.

2. Ibid., p. 78. See also C. L. Salter, 1977, "Dazhai Beyond Dazhai: Some Unsuspected Lessons for the USA from a Chinese Campaign," *China Geographer*, No. 7, pp. 59–66.

3. C. W. Pannell and L.J.C. Ma, 1983, *China: The Geography of Development and Modernization* (London: V. H. Winston).

4. V. Smil, 1984, *The Bad Earth: Environmental Degradation in China* (Armonk, N.Y.: M. E. Sharpe, Inc.).

5. By comparison, the United States, with only a quarter as many people, has half again as much cultivable land (156 million hectares).

6. By 1984 a new record-high level of 405 million tons was reached, partly because of the new agricultural reforms since 1978. However, the production of grain fell in the next year (1985) to 379 million tons, as a result of adverse weather conditions and a reduction in the amount of land cultivated—and partly because many farmers decided to spend their surplus not on more production but on consumption goods. In Shanxi Province, for example, farmers' spending on consumption goods increased by 5.4 percent in 1986, but investment for production fell by 11.2 percent. See *China Daily*, February 28, 1987.

7. C. Aubert, 1988, "China's Food Take-Off?" pp. 101–136 in S. Feuchtwang, A. Hussain, and T. Pairault (eds.), *Transforming China's Economy in the Eighties*, Vol. 1: *The Rural Sector, Welfare and Employment* (Boulder, Colo.: Westview Press), quote from p. 107.

8. A. Piazza, 1986, *Food Consumption and Nutritional Status in the PRC* (Boulder, Colo.: Westview Press).

9. In 1957 the per capita net income in the countryside was Y 72.9. By 1978 it was Y 133.6, and by 1987 it was Y 462.6. *China Statistical Yearbook 1988* (Beijing: State Statistical Bureau of the PRC, 1988), p. 732.

10. A. P. Liu, 1986, *How China Is Ruled* (Englewood Cliffs, N.J.: Prentice-Hall).

11. For a scathing critique of the Maoist drive toward large-scale collectivization, see M. Selden, 1988, *Chinese Political Economy* (Armonk, N.Y.: M. E. Sharpe).

12. For examples of this argument, see "Whither China's Agricultural Reforms: An Interview with William Hinton," *Contemporary Marxism* 12–13 (Spring 1986), pp. 137–143; and P. Howard, 1986, "Some Comments on China's Controversial Rural Economic Reforms," *Contemporary Marxism* 12–13 (Spring), pp. 163–201. Perhaps the most polemically negative critique of the agricultural reforms has been provided by M. Chossudovsky, 1986, *Towards Capitalist Restoration? Chinese Socialism After Mao* (London: Macmillan), p. 25.

13. M. Blecher, 1986, *China: Politics, Economics and Society: Iconoclasm and Innovation in a Revolutionary Socialist Country* (London: Frances Pinter Pub.), p. 45. In spite of the obvious advantages there were two major problems associated with the process of land reform. In the first place, the poorest peasants, many of whom were given land, were often the worst farmers, in addition to which they were usually too poor to invest in the small amounts of land they were granted. Second, many of the relatively small number of well-off farmers who managed to hold on to their land lost all interest in doing well, for fear of political reprisals. See Blecher, op. cit., pp. 43–49.

14. Hinton, op. cit., p. 65.

15. Ibid.

16. Ibid., p. 71.

17. Ibid., p. 72.

18. Mao's concerns are expressed in Mao Zedong, 1977, *Selected Works*, Vol. 5 (Beijing: Foreign Languages Press), p. 206. In spite of the push toward collectivization, class differences, at least in monetary (income) terms, remained significant, and this reinforced Mao's argument. For example, Vivienne Shue (1980) showed that a group of "rich" peasants living within her study area earned a combined

family income that was twice the average (in 1954)—Y 861 compared to Y 421. The average for the families in cooperatives was Y 466, and for "poor" peasants the average was Y 272. It is interesting to note that the incomes of "former landlords" was only Y 286 at that time. See V. Shue, 1980, *Peasant China in Transition: The Dynamics of Development Toward Socialism, 1949–1956* (Berkeley: University of California Press), p. 283.

19. Hinton, op. cit.

20. Ibid., p. 133.

21. Liu, op. cit., p. 198.

22. Hinton, op. cit., p. 128.

23. Blecher, op. cit.

24. Ibid., p. 71.

25. Aubert, op. cit.

26. William Hinton (op. cit.) also explained another problem that began with the cooperatives, and worsened with the communes, namely the bondage of the peasants to the land. In "feudal" China the peasants had been dirt poor, but they were not actually serfs. They were bound to the land, but only by debt, not by contract. They could and did walk off their land to seek work whenever it seemed to be available. Pre-Liberation China was in fact a land of itinerant hoboes, but after about 1953 every peasant was firmly tied to the land in the collectives. The ration-book policy, which made it impossible for peasants to buy food away from home, has effectively kept down the rate of rural-to-urban migration, thereby helping to control the size of China's cities, and as a result it has contributed to the reduction of urban unemployment and the associated social problems. But it was also a very harsh sentence to serve on the peasants. According to Hinton, it is precisely because they had no viable options that the peasants' problems could be ignored by a cynical and self-satisfied middle tier of officials. Thus, the peasants were kept on the land, and to stay alive they had to work hard. As the old Chinese proverb says, "When the peasants are content the empire is stable" (T. Terzani, 1986, *Behind the Forbidden Door: Travels in China* [London: Allen and Unwin], p. 104). In 1960, after the Great Leap Forward, however, it was clear that all was not well on the Chinese land. As Hinton said, this situation actually gave the administration complete control over the rural population, which was something the old elites had always wanted but could never actually achieve. Elsewhere Hinton (in "Whither China's Agricultural Reforms") expanded this idea and brought it forward into the 1980s. He argued that there is still a basic contempt for the peasants among China's bureaucratic elite, the cadres, which suggests an effective return to the old Mandarin mentality. In this sense both the "green revolution" (the increasing industrialization of agriculture) and the new household responsibility system (in which some peasants could "get rich" again) would rep-

resent a serious challenge to the cadre class: "As long as the peasants are down there endlessly laboring with their hoes, the official in his office feels secure. Why should we do anything to rock the boat?" See "Whither China's Agricultural Reforms," p. 142.

27. Howard, op. cit.

28. Liu, op. cit.

29. A. Watson, 1983, "Agriculture Looks for 'Shoes That Fit': The Production Responsibility System and Its Implications," *World Development* 11, No. 8, pp. 705–730, quote from p. 706. In fact it has been suggested that the original intent of the reforms was not nearly so radical as things actually turned out. Elizabeth Croll, for example, argued that the individual household economy was never intended to expand on the scale that ultimately occurred. According to Croll, the production team was expected to continue to be in control of the bulk of production activities in the countryside. See E. Croll, 1988, "The New Peasant Economy in China," pp. 77–100 in Feuchtwang, Hussain, and Pairault, op. cit.

30. Peasants were required to sell their mandated quota at the fixed (lower) price, but after that they could dispose of what was left to the highest bidder. In the years after 1979 further price increases were allowed, and the price increases for farm goods were: 7.1 percent in 1980; 5.9 percent in 1981; 2.2 percent in 1982; 4.4 percent in 1983, and 4.0 percent in 1984 (see C. Riskin, 1987, *China's Political Economy: The Quest for Development Since 1949* [London: Oxford University Press], p. 285). Since then food price increases have been even higher, in fact the rate of inflation has become a major problem, holding back further aspects of the reform program.

31. It is worthwhile pointing out here that the agricultural reforms did not really represent a planned sequence of reforms (see Watson, op. cit.). To a large extent the Party and the government were passive reactors to the dynamic economic pressures and the enthusiasm for the reforms at the local level. Thus the new contracting system resulted in greater production levels, which contributed to the growth of free markets in many areas. This then challenged the state's monopoly over prices and distribution networks, so in time changes were also made in those directions. The whole process, according to Croll (op. cit.), took on a momentum of its own, and it soon outpaced the aspirations of even the most optimistic planners within the Party.

32. For details see Riskin, op. cit., and Croll, op. cit. Croll has pointed out that the HRS needs to be put into its historical context. The household peasant economy had always been an important element in the Chinese countryside. Even during the heyday of collectivization, the household was expected to remain as the fourth tier in the rural production system, subservient to the communes,

brigades, and teams, but still an important element. In a similar way, there had always been opportunities for sideline activities in the countryside. In 1978, before the reforms were started, 5.7 percent of all arable land in China was allocated to private plots; by 1980 this had increased to 7.1 percent; and in 1981, a provision was made for this portion to increase to 15 percent. Jonathon Unger has also suggested that the shift over to the HRS was probably not as much of a voluntary process as the Chinese press (and the government) would like the rest of the world to believe. In his survey of 28 villages, for example, the shift had been mandated from above in 26 of them, and it is certainly not true to say that all villages were equally enthusiastic about the reforms. Unger also pointed out that the *baogan daohu* system was originally intended only for the very poorest areas, but the early successes resulted in a very rapid spread to villages of all types. Again, according to Unger, the entire reform process was probably not a well-thought-out master plan for a newly efficient system of agriculture—it was partly the result of planning, but mostly a piecemeal process that spread in an almost contagious fashion after the early successes. See J. Unger, 1985–1986, "The Decollectivization of the Chinese Countryside: A Survey of Twenty-Eight Villages," *Pacific Affairs* 58, No. 4, pp. 585–606.

33. Chossudovsky, op. cit., p. 50. Croll (op. cit.) has shown that the families who were most likely to "get rich" were generally the largest ones, those with access to the greatest supplies of labor. In her study area, for example, Croll reported that 31 percent of the richest families had more than six members; whereas only 8 percent had one to two members.

34. O. Schell, 1984, *To Get Rich Is Glorious: China in the Eighties* (New York: Pantheon Books).

35. Zhang Xinxin and Sang Ye, 1987, *Chinese Lives: An Oral History of Contemporary China* (New York: Pantheon Books), p. 12.

36. See, for example, W. Hinton, 1988, "Dazhai Revisited," *China Now*, No. 126, pp. 23–27.

37. See, for example, S. Wittwer, Yu Youtai, Sun Han, and Wang Lianzheng, 1987, *Feeding a Billion: Frontiers of Chinese Agriculture* (East Lansing: Michigan State University Press); and also Howard, op. cit. Probably the most significant impact of the HRS has been the creation of a new "balance of power" between the individual households (the private economy) and the villages (the collective economy). The village now has, in most cases, a subordinate role in the production process, and its role is pretty much restricted to that of servicing the private economy, through the provision of technology, capital, transportation, and so on (in addition to the welfare function). There was a certain amount of contagiousness in this transformation, in that the individual households found that they liked their new-found independence, and they naturally wanted to extend it to other areas of their lives, most notably into the area of birth control (see Chapter 7). Unger commented on this new independence at the household level, noting that it extended into both the political and the economic realm: "Before, brigade and team cadres had had the authority . . . to bring pressures to bear against ordinary peasants; now the system . . . would entirely eliminate the cadres' daily supervision and, by pulling the land and other resources out of their control, would severely curtail their powers over the peasants. Under the collectives, the peasantry had been required to devote most of their days to raising low-priced grain on the collective fields; now many peasants foresaw that, by controlling the use of their own time, they would be able to put their spare hours into endeavors that paid better" (Unger, op. cit., pp. 592–593). One of Unger's respondents said, "We felt like birds freed from a cage" (p. 593).

38. Gu Hua, 1985, *Pagoda Ridge and Other Stories* (Beijing: Panda Books), p. 113.

39. Riskin, op. cit., p. 291, Table 12.1; and p. 292, Table 12.2. This of course was one of the major benefits of the HRS, in that it allowed a relaxation of the very restrictive Maoist focus on growing grain everywhere ("taking grain as the key link"). By contrast, in the reform era the emphasis has been on the "all-round development of agriculture" (Croll, op. cit., p. 81). The essence of the new policy was to allow a basic free-for-all, in which each family (and presumably therefore each area) would specialize in whatever it could produce most efficiently. Agricultural output slowed down a little after the mid-1980s—in fact the rate of growth in output was 14.4 percent each year between 1980 and 1984, slowing to 10.9 percent after that, and reaching a new low level in 1988 of only 3 percent growth. More seriously, the production of three major crops declined in 1988: grain by 2.2 percent, cotton by 1.1 percent, and edible oil seeds, so important in Chinese cooking, by 13.3 percent. There are a number of reasons for these statistics, the most significant being the apparent lack of interest many farmers have in growing crops for which the sale price (still set by the government) remains fairly low. They are choosing to move into crops that fetch higher prices or out of agriculture altogether, either into sideline activities or, more likely, into rural industries where the wages are considerably higher. See B. L. Reynolds, 1989, "The Chinese Economy in 1988," pp. 27–48 in A. J. Kane (ed.), *China Briefing, 1989* (Boulder, Colo.: Westview Press).

40. The consumption of edible oils grew by 14 percent per year and meat output by 9 percent. See Riskin, op. cit.

41. Ibid., p. 292—note that a significant proportion, up to a fifth, of this increase is the result of agricultural price increases.

42. D. Perkins and S. Yusuf, 1984, *Rural Development in China* (Baltimore: Johns Hopkins University Press).

43. It is important to point out that a large part of the per capita reduction in sales between the years 1978 and 1984 was a result of the increase in the urban population—much of which resulted from the annexation of rural counties in the nation's biggest cities. See Chapter 8 for further discussion of this issue.

44. Howard, op. cit., p. 181.

45. T. G. Rawski, 1979, *Economic Growth and Employment in China* (New York: Oxford University Press), pp. 119–121.

46. Reynolds, op. cit., pointed out that the output for rural workers in China increased by a staggering 250 percent between 1978 and 1987. Most of this, however, can be accounted for by growth in village and township enterprises, as an estimated 85 million people were absorbed into rural industries. Rural enterprises increased their share of the nation's total output from 5 percent to 21 percent in those nine years (p. 37). Nevertheless, agricultural output increased significantly during that period; for example, grain production increased by 43 percent overall and cotton by 93 percent (see p. 35).

47. Unger, op. cit., pp. 592–593.

CHAPTER 6

1. A slogan from *Gongren Ribao* (Workers daily), 1980, quoted in A. Clayre, 1986, *The Heart of the Dragon* (Boston: Houghton Mifflin Co.), p. 166.

2. See J. Domes, 1985, *The Government and Politics of the PRC: A Time of Transition* (Boulder, Colo.: Westview Press), esp. Chap. 12, "Economic Development," pp. 195–210.

3. For a description of the Taiwan "miracle," see R. G. Sutter, 1988, *Taiwan: Entering the 21st Century* (New York: University Press of America); T. B. Gold, 1986, *State and Society and the Taiwan Miracle* (Armonk, N.Y.: M.E. Sharpe); and the special issue of the *China Quarterly*, No. 94 (October 1984), entitled "Taiwan Briefing."

4. According to Ezra Vogel, the term "socialist transformation" refers to the "transfer of economic ownership from private to public hands." See E. F. Vogel, 1969, *Canton Under Communism: Programs and Politics in a Provincial Capital,1949–1968* (Cambridge, Mass.: Harvard University Press), p. 125.

5. Ibid., p. 132.

6. T. Cannon and A. Jenkins, 1986, "Freeing the Market Forces," *Geographical Magazine* 58, No. 11, pp. 566–571. See also M. Blecher, 1986, *China: Politics, Economics and Society: Iconoclasm and Innovation in a Revolutionary Socialist Country* (London: Frances Pinter Pub.), p. 509.

7. M. Chossudovsky, 1986, *Towards Capitalist Restoration: Chinese Socialism After Mao* (Hong Kong: Macmillan), see Chap. 4.

8. The campaigns are described in detail by Vogel, op. cit., esp. Chap. 4, pp. 125–180; and also by J. Gardner, "The Wu-Fan Campaign in Shanghai: A Study in the Consolidation of Urban Control," pp. 477–539 in A. D. Barnett (ed.), 1972, *Chinese Communist Politics in Action* (Seattle: University of Washington Press).

9. Vogel, op. cit., Chap. 4.

10. V. Shue, 1980, *Peasant China in Transition: The Dynamics of Development Towards Socialism, 1949–1956* (Berkeley: University of California Press).

11. This process is described by Vogel, op. cit., see esp. pp. 173–180.

12. Mao Zedong, 1977, *Selected Works*, Vol. 5 (Beijing: Foreign Languages Press), see pp. 284–307.

13. Blecher, op. cit., pp. 73–74.

14. Ibid. In 1959, for example, the accumulation rate was 43.8 percent and it was 39.6 percent in 1960. The rate averaged around 33 percent in the early 1970s and 31 percent in the early 1980s. In 1987 it was 34.7 percent. See *China Statistical Yearbook 1988* (Beijing: State Statistical Bureau of the PRC), p. 50.

15. A survey conducted by the Chinese Ministry of Light Industry in 1980 showed that a 10,000 yuan investment would create only 94 jobs on average in heavy industry, 257 in light industry, and 800 in handicraft "sidelines." See F. Gipouloux, "Industrial Restructuring and Autonomy of Enterprises in China: Is Reform Possible?" pp. 107–117 in S. Feuchtwang, A. Hussain, and T. Pairault (eds.), 1988, *Transforming China's Economy in the Eighties*, Vol. 2: *Management, Industry and the Urban Economy* (Boulder, Colo.: Westview Press). The different emphasis on heavy as opposed to light industry reflects some important changes in economic philosophy. For example, in 1952, 65 percent of total output value in China came from heavy industry; but this had been reversed by 1982, when the figure was only 47 percent. By 1987 the balance was almost equal, 48 percent heavy and 52 percent light industry. See *China Statistical Yearbook 1988*, p. 37.

16. This issue is discussed by L. Pan, 1988, *The New Chinese Revolution* (Chicago: Contemporary Books), p. 50. As the statistics in Table 6.1 illustrate, there was a significant increase in the value of industrial output between 1952 and 1978 (a more than 16-fold increase). But this was achieved mainly by a massive (x 22) increase in the investment of fixed capital, rather than a more efficient usage of inputs. The statistics also suggest that the increase in labor productivity (nearly 3-fold) was also achieved in this way, and in fact the level of output per unit of capital declined steadily between 1957

and 1978. Part of the explanation for this lies in the structural imbalance in Chinese industry toward heavy industry, but part stems from "deficiencies in the system of economic organization, planning and management that are rather deep-rooted." See C. Riskin, 1987, *China's Political Economy: The Quest for Development Since 1949* (Oxford, UK: Oxford University Press), p. 265.

17. Gipouloux, op. cit., p. 114. Probably the best account of authority relationships in Chinese industry has been provided by A. G. Walder, 1986, *Communist Neo-Traditionalism: Work and Authority in Chinese Industry* (Berkeley: University of California Press).

18. Pan, op. cit., p. 52.

19. Ibid.

20. A quote from a Western diplomat in Beijing, reported by O. Schell, 1984, *To Get Rich Is Glorious: China in the Eighties* (New York: Pantheon), p. 27.

21. J. S. Prybyla, 1986, "China's Economic Experiments: From Mao to Market," *Problems of Communism* 35, No. 1 (Jan./Feb.), pp. 21–38.

22. Pan, op. cit., pp. 219–241. It is interesting to note that a large part of the criticisms leveled at the government during the waves of student demonstrations in 1986, 1987, and 1989 has focused on the extent of corruption in China, especially among high-level Party officials. See for example: O. Schell, 1989, "An Act of Defiance," *New York Times Magazine*, April 16, pp. 27 and 43, and S. WuDunn, 1989, "Hu's Death Stirs Political Unrest," *New York Times*, April 15.

23. Schell, 1984, op. cit.

24. Pan, op. cit., p. 223.

25. Schell, 1984, p. 84. Schell noted that there is actually a double entendre involved in the term *yanjiu yanjiu*, "to make a study of a situation," which also means "wine and cigarettes"!

26. This phrase was used by Jurgen Domes, 1985, *The Government and Politics of the PRC: A Time of Transition* (Boulder, Colo.: Westview Press), pp. 197–202.

27. Chinese Communist Party, 1984, *Decision of the Central Committee of the Communist Party of China on Reform of the Economic Structure* (Beijing: Foreign Languages Press).

28. Riskin, op. cit., p. 342. For a discussion of this "revolution," see *Time*, "China: Deng Xiaoping Leads a Far-Reaching Audacious But Risky Second Revolution," January 6, 1986, pp. 24–40.

29. "Chinese Experiments with Allowing Enterprises to Go Belly Up," *Christian Science Monitor*, August 8, 1986. See also Da Chen, 1988, "Labour Combination System Practiced in Qingdao," *Nexus: China in Focus*, Winter, pp. 29–31.

30. See Cheng Naishan, 1989, "No. 2 and No. 4 of Shanghai," pp. 1–116 in Cheng Naishan, *The Piano Tuner* (San Francisco: China Books and Periodicals).

31. D. J. Solinger, 1987, "Uncertain Paternalism: Tensions in Recent Regional Restructuring in China," *International Regional Science Review* 11, No. 1, pp. 23–42, quote from p. 32.

32. Pan, op. cit., p. 60.

33. W. Zafonelli, "A Brief Outline of China's Second Economy," pp. 138–155 in Feuchtwang, Hussain, and Pairault, op. cit., terms quoted from pp. 148 and 149.

34. Solinger, op. cit., p. 40.

35. Zafonelli, op. cit., p. 149.

36. Gong Shiqi, 1988, "Economic Features of the Primary Stage of Socialism," *Beijing Review*, No. 7 (February 15–28), pp. 18–20.

37. L. Herschkovitz, 1985, "The Fruits of Ambivalence: China's Urban Individual Economy," *Pacific Affairs* 58, No. 3 (Fall), pp. 427–450.

38. "Decision on Reforms of Economic Structure," *China Daily*, October 23, 1984, pp. 9–12, quote from p. 11.

39. Ibid.

40. "Peddling the Private Road," *Far Eastern Economic Review*, October 8, 1987, pp. 106–08.

41. Economist Intelligence Unit, 1988, *China and North Korea: Country Report*, Analysis of Economic and Political Trends Every Quarter, No. 3 (London: The Economist Intelligence Unit, Ltd.), pp. 24–25.

42. J. P. Emerson, 1983, "Urban School-Leavers and Unemployment in China," *China Quarterly* 93 (January), pp. 1–16.

43. Riskin, op. cit., esp. Chaps. 11 and 14.

44. Ibid., p. 359.

45. Ibid., pp. 347–348.

46. "Let Them Eat Cash: China Tries to Scrap Food-Price Controls," *Far Eastern Economic Review*, May 26, 1988, pp. 72–73.

47. G. White, 1988, "Evolving Relations Between State and Markets in the Reform of China's Urban-Industrial Economy," pp. 7–25 in Feuchtwang, Hussain, and Pairault, op. cit., quote from p. 23.

48. "A Hunt for Economic Steroids," *Far Eastern Economic Review*, October 20, 1988, pp. 100–101. According to Bruce Reynolds, by September 1988, "the five-year plan to decontrol prices was dead . . . the government imposed direct administrative quotas and controls over the spending of all state units (and collective and township enterprises as well). New bank lending was simply frozen" (p. 45). See B. L. Reynolds, 1989, "The Chinese Economy in 1988," pp. 27–48 in A. J. Kane (ed.), 1989, *China Briefing, 1989* (Boulder, Colo.: Westview Press).

49. "Toughing Out Price Reforms," *Far Eastern Economic Review*, July 21, 1988, pp. 19–20. There are some rather ludicrous stories about the panic buying that occurred during 1988. One man in Wuhan went out and stocked up on salt, enough for ten years! The sales of refrigerators and other "luxury" items shot up by close to 100 percent compared to 1987.

50. This process is described by White, op. cit., p. 22.

51. "Toughing Out Price Reforms." Reynolds, op. cit., gave three major reasons for the failure of the price reforms: first, the rate of inflation killed off the enthusiasm among both the public and the government, although as Reynolds argued, this was entirely predictable given the rate of growth in China's productive capacity during the 1980s; second, China's workers, long starved of material benefits, pushed very hard for pay raises, and were often successful, with the costs being shifted on to the prices of finished goods and services; and third, it appears that the Chinese government made some serious mistakes—by announcing the price decontrols before they happened, which resulted in panic spending—and by not allowing the interest rate for savings to rise with the inflation rate, which would have reduced the rate of panic withdrawals. See pp. 45–46.

52. Solinger, op. cit. See also Riskin, op. cit., Chap. 9, pp. 201–222.

53. Foreign Broadcast Information Service, February 8, 1984, p. k20 (quoted in Solinger, op. cit., p. 29).

54. Ge Wu, 1988, "Urban Reform Experiment Goes In Depth," Beijing Review 31, No. 12 (March 21–27), p. 7.

55. For a detailed discussion of China's Special Economic Zones, see Chossudovsky, op. cit., esp. Chaps. 7, 8, and 9, pp. 132–190.

56. Rong Ye, 1988, "Foreign Economic Cooperation in the Coastal Areas," China Reconstructs 37, No. 9 (Sept.), pp. 8–10. Although few people in the PRC leadership would be willing to admit it, the phenomenal success of Taiwan on the world trade markets probably provided an important model and a powerful incentive to the CCP's plans for modernization; see Sutter, op. cit.

57. J. Fewsmith, 1986, "Special Economic Zones in the PRC," Problems of Communism 35, No. 6 (Nov./Dec.), pp. 78–85.

58. Chossudovsky, op. cit., p. 131.

59. Zhao Ziyang, Foreign Broadcast Information Services, 1984, Daily Report: China, December 26, pp. k1–3 (quoted in Fewsmith, op. cit., p. 79) (emphasis added).

60. Pan, op. cit., p. 122.

61. Huan Guocang, 1986, "China's Opening to the World," Problems of Communism 35, No. 6 (Nov./Dec.), pp. 59–77.

62. D. R. Phillips and A.G.O. Yeh, 1987, "The Provision of Housing and Social Services in China's Special Economic Zones," Environment and Planning C: Government and Policy 5, pp. 447–468.

63. Reynolds, op. cit., pp. 46–47.

64. Riskin, op. cit., p. 369, Table 14.8. This growth rate has continued; for example, 1987 output statistics show that light industry grew by 18.6 percent in 1986, and heavy industry by 16.7 percent

(see China Statistical Yearbook 1988, p. 267). This of course is a mixed blessing, because growth rates of these proportions have inevitably led to some very serious problems usually associated with an "overheated" economy, most notably, inflation. The growth rate in China's GDP was higher during the first six years of the 1980s than it was in any other country in the world—averaging 10.5 percent per year, compared to South Korea's 8.2 percent and Japan's 3.7 percent. Reynolds, op. cit., suggested that it was only growth of this magnitude that enabled China to cope with its devastatingly high rate of inflation in 1987 and 1988, when the figure was close to 20 percent. It is also important to point out that industrial growth in China in the 1980s was not geographically even. Growth rates in the eastern provinces far outstripped those in the interior provinces (see Chapter 9). In addition, state-run enterprises were relatively sluggish, growing at an average of 8 percent per year, compared to a 21 percent growth rate for township and village enterprises in the countryside.

65. Riskin, op. cit., pp. 368–371.

66. Far Eastern Economic Review, 1988, Asia Yearbook: 1988 (Hong Kong: Review Publications Co.), p. 120. Investments in fixed assets in 1987 were up by 16 percent over 1986: see China: Statistical Yearbook 1988, p. 499.

67. "China's Spending Frenzy," Far Eastern Economic Review 141, August 4, 1988, p. 48.

68. To purchase foreign-made goods, such as Japanese radios, tape recorders, and motorcycles, Chinese people must use what is known as "foreign exchange certificates" (FEC, or waiweichuan). They are not allowed to use the "people's money" (RMB, or renminbi). Because of the attractiveness of FEC, and its relative scarcity, a black market has developed in which Chinese people (illegally) do everything they can to increase their holdings—hence the near-constant demands made on tourists to "change money" as they wander through the streets of China's cities.

69. Economist Intelligence Unit, op. cit., p. 4.

70. Gao Shangquan, 1989, "China's Economy After 10 Years of Reform," China Reconstructs 38, No. 1 (January), pp. 13–16.

71. Guo Zhongyi, 1988, "Combatting Price Rices," China Reconstructs 37, No. 5 (May), pp. 8–10. Reynolds, op. cit., reported an inflation rate of 18.5 percent in China during 1988, and for the first three months of 1989 the figure stood at 27 percent, meaning that the direst predictions of the Economist Intelligence Unit had pretty much been vindicated. It is important to remember that in a socialist country, the effect of inflation may work to redistribute wealth, effectively negating much of the egalitarianism inherent in social policies, and destroying the attempts to hold income differentials down to a minimum. For the CCP, inflation also has a symbolic significance, in that the hyperin-

flation of the late 1940s helped to topple the Kuomintang government, making the Communist takeover possible. As we witnessed in 1989, many of the demonstrators in urban China, as well as many outside commentators, cited the rate of inflation as one of the major irritants and a significant contributor to the growing level of dissatisfaction with the government. This has been very well described in M. Fathers and A. Higgins, 1989, *Tiananmen: The Rape of Peking* (London: The Independent).

72. Riskin, op. cit., p. 362.

73. Ibid., p. 365.

74. See, for examples, O. Schell, 1988, *Discos and Democracy: China in the Throes of Reform* (New York: Pantheon); and P. B. Prime, "Low Expectations, High Growth: The Economy and Reform in 1987," pp. 19–30 in A. J. Kane (ed.), 1988, *China Briefing, 1988* (Boulder, Colo.: Westview Press).

75. Prybyla, op. cit., p. 37.

76. Ibid., pp. 37–38.

77. Zafonelli, op. cit. See aslo M. Findlay and T.C.W. Chiu, 1989, "Sugar-Coated Bullets: Corruption and the New Economic Order in China," *Contemporary Crises* 13, No. 2 (June), pp. 145–162.

78. M. K. Whyte and W. L. Parish, 1984, *Urban Life in Contemporary China*. (Chicago: University of Chicago Press).

79. Chossudovsky, op. cit., quotations from pp. 124 and 126.

80. "China's Spending Frenzy," *Far Eastern Economic Review* 141 (August 4, 1988), p. 48. The term *deviant* here refers to the belief that consumption of these sorts of consumer durables should probably not be occurring at this early stage of China's modernization drive. As the statistics show, the ownership of these items increased significantly during the 1980s. For example, ownership of TV sets increased by more than 3,000 percent between 1978 and 1987, from 0.3 to 10.7 per 100 persons; radio ownership increased by 309 percent; tape recorders by 3,250 percent; and bicycles by 139 percent. See *China: Statistical Yearbook 1988*, p. 709.

81. Gong, op. cit.; see also M. Yudkin, 1986, *Making Good: Private Business in Socialist China* (Beijing: Foreign Languages Press).

82. Zhao Ziyang, 1987, "The Primary Stage of Socialism," pp. 20–25 in *The 13th Party Congress and China's Reforms* (Beijing: Beijing Review Press), p. 24.

83. Qian Jiaju, 1988, "The Primary Stage of Socialism," *China Reconstructs* 37, No. 3 (March), pp. 15–18.

84. Zhao, 1987, op. cit., pp. 24–25. With a statement like this, it is easy to see that Zhao would be in trouble within the Party long before he was accused of siding with the student demonstrators in 1989. It seems likely that his thinking on the economic issue was too far ahead of the events, and he was treated as the scapegoat when things began to go wrong, as they did in 1988.

85. The massive student demonstrations in April and May 1989 received front-page and prime-time television coverage around the world. In spite of repeated calls for greater freedom of speech, freedom of the press, and freedom to travel, few visible signs of compromise by the CCP were in evidence. See for example, "Chinese Students March, Break Police Barricades," *Schenectady Gazette*, April 28, 1989.

86. This quote was attributed to Su Shaozhi. See "Ideological Inconsistencies: Attacks on Reforms Force Leadership to Redefine Socialism," *Far Eastern Economic Review* 138 (October 8, 1987), pp. 50–52. After a statement such as this, one can only wonder what was the fate of Su after the crackdown of 1989, because he appeared to be saying pretty much the same as most of the student demonstrators were saying.

87. Schell, 1984, op. cit., p. 105.

88. Ibid., p. 107.

89. Domes, op. cit.

90. When Party officials speak about this, they invariably uphold the necessity for China to continue supporting the "four basic principles" of socialism, which are usually listed as: dictatorship of the proletariat, leadership of the Party, following the socialist road, and Marxism/Leninism/Mao Zedong Thought. There as yet appears to be no signs that the four principles will be abandoned (*Far Eastern Economic Review* 138, No. 41 [October 8, 1987], pp. 51–52).

91. "The Perils of Trying to Roll History Out of the Way," *Economist*, July 9, 1988, pp. 15–16.

92. Guo Zhongyi, 1988, "Price Reform and People's Lives," *China Reconstructs* 37, No. 1 (January), pp. 30–32.

93. "Public Supervision over Corruption" (Editorial) *China Reconstructs* 37 (1988), p. 5.

94. Domes, op. cit., pp. 207–208.

95. "It's Going Wrong in China Too," *Economist*, October 1, 1988.

96. See Reynolds, op. cit.

97. S. Leys [Pierre Ryckmans, pseud.], 1978, *Chinese Shadows* (London: Penguin Books), p. xi.

98. Ibid., p. 98.

CHAPTER 7

1. Zhang Xinxin and Sang Ye, 1987, *Chinese Lives: An Oral History of Contemporary China* (New York: Pantheon Books), p. 131.

2. Ibid., p. 132.

3. Shou Jinghua, 1979, "Interview with a Specialist on Population," *Beijing Review* 22, No. 46, pp. 20–21.

4. C. W. Pannell and L.J.C. Ma, 1983, *China: The Geography of Development and Modernization* (London: V. H. Winston).

5. P. Woodruff, 1981, "A Historical Survey of Population in China," pp. 1–8 in *Teaching About China* (Washington, D.C.: U.S.-China Peoples Friendship Association), No. 9 (Summer/Fall).

6. E. J. Croll, 1984, "The Single-Child Family: The First Five Years," pp. 125–139 in N. Maxwell and B. McFarlane (eds.), *China's Changed Road to Development* (Oxford: Pergamon Press). In some provinces there is even less cultivable land per person; for example, in Zhejiang the figure is closer to 0.05 hectares per person. In recent years the loss of arable land has averaged 7 million mu (15 mu = 1 hectare) per year, while the population has been growing by more than 15 million each year. Grain output, although growing steadily until 1984, has been matched by the growth of population, so that in 1987 China's per capita grain availability was only 63 kilograms more than in 1952, and in many provinces the per capita share of grain has actually fallen. See Zhing Qing, 1989, "1.1 Billion and Rising: The Population Problem Still Dominates China's Future," *Nexus: China in Focus*, Summer, pp. 4–6.

7. V. Smil, 1984, *The Bad Earth: Environmental Degradation in China* (Armonk, N.Y.: M.E. Sharpe, Inc.), p. 70.

8. K. Buchanan, 1970, *The Transformation of the Chinese Earth* (London: G. Bell and Sons), p. 26.

9. Ibid., p. 28.

10. *China ABC* (Beijing: New World Press, 1983).

11. L. Pan, 1988, *The New Chinese Revolution* (Chicago: Contemporary Books), p. 152.

12. E. J. Croll, 1985, "The Single-Child Family in Beijing: A First-Hand Report," pp. 190–232 in E. J. Croll, D. Davin, and P. Kane (eds.), *China's One Child Family Policy* (London: Macmillan).

13. A. J. Coale and Chen Shenli, 1987, *Basic Data on Fertility in the Provinces of China, 1940–1982* (Honolulu: East-West Center).

14. Shen Yimin, 1987, "Selected Findings From Recent Fertility Surveys in Three Regions of China," *International Family Planning Perspectives* 12, No. 3 (September), pp. 80–85.

15. R. Freedman, Xiao Zhenyu, Li Bohua, and W. Lavely, 1988, "Local Area Variations in Reproductive Behavior in the People's Republic of China, 1973–1982," *Population Studies* 42, No. 1 (March), pp. 39–57.

16. *China Daily*, April 18, 1987. This increase in birthrate will be interpreted in greater detail later in this chapter. The statistics here are from Guo Xiao, 1989, "The Population Threat," *Nexus: China in Focus*, Summer, pp. 2–3.

17. R. Sidel and V. W. Sidel, 1982, *The Health of China* (Boston: Beacon Press).

18. Mao Zedong, 1956, *Mao Tse-tung: Selected Works*, Vol. 4 (1941–1945) (New York: International Publications), p. 454.

19. H. Y. Tien, 1973, *China's Population Struggle: Demographic Decisions of the People's Republic, 1949–1969* (Columbus: Ohio State University Press), p. 179.

20. Mao Zedong, 1960, *On the Correct Handling of Contradictions Among the People* (Beijing, Foreign Languages Press), pp. 46–47.

21. Croll, 1984, op. cit.

22. Ibid.

23. Croll, 1985, op. cit.

24. Pan, op. cit., p. 153.

25. Zhang and Sang, op. cit., p. 132. To press home the importance of continuing the fight to lower the birthrate, the government has continually bombarded the people of China with masses of data about the drastic consequences of allowing things to go on unchecked. There is of course a lot of information available, and the government does not need to exaggerate the seriousness of the situation. For example, the cost of raising a child in a Chinese city averages Y 18,740, 64 percent of which is borne by the state (compared to Y 6,695 in the countryside). The babies born each year consume about 20 percent of the country's increase in national income, e.g., 49 percent of the increased grain harvest; 46 percent of the increased meat production. Some economists have predicted that with a population of "only" 1.2 billion in the year 2000 (which will now be surpassed easily), every increase of 10 million babies will lower the per capita share of the national income by Y 10. In the middle to late 1980s there were at least 15 million babies born every year. See Guo Xiao, op. cit.

26. *China Daily*, March 25, 1986.

27. *China Daily*, March 14, 1987. In 1986 the birthrate in China's cities averaged 17.4 per 1,000, compared to 21.9 for the rural areas. The variations from the highest to the lowest areas were from 15.3 per 1,000 in Shanghai (highly urbanized), to 27.3 per 1,000 in Xinjiang (mostly rural). See *China Statistical Yearbook 1988* (Beijing: State Statistical Bureau of the PRC), pp. 76–77.

28. Croll, 1984, op. cit.

29. L. Bianco, 1985, "Family Planning Programs and Fertility Decline in Taiwan and Mainland China: A Comparison," *Issues and Studies* 21, No. 11.

30. *China Daily*, May 6, 1986.

31. *China Daily*, May 21, 1986.

32. B. Robey, 1985, "Sons and Daughters in China," *Asian and Pacific Census Forum* (East-West Center) 12, No. 2 (November), pp. 1–5.

33. F. Arnold and Liu Zhaoxiang, 1986, "Sex Preference, Fertility, and Family Planning in China," *Population and Development Review* 12, No. 2, pp. 229–230; son preference is quantified as the per-

centage difference between couples with sons who have signed the one-child pledge and couples with daughters who have signed.

34. L. Bianco and Hua Chang-ming, 1988, "Implementation and Resistance: The Single-Child Family Policy," pp. 147–168 in S. Feuchtwang, A. Hussain, and T. Pairault (eds.), *Transforming China's Economy in the Eighties*, Vol. 1: *The Rural Sector, Welfare and Employment* (Boulder, Colo.: Westview Press), quote from p. 156.

35. T. Terzani, 1986, *Behind the Forbidden Door: Travels in China.* (London: Allen and Unwin), pp. 194–195. As always seems to be the case in Chinese morality tales, even the true ones, there is a tragic ending, because the baby turned out to be a girl. In general the Chinese government has kept fairly quiet on the issue of female infanticide, although it regularly reminds people that it is an odious and "feudal" practice that is illegal. In official publications the extraordinarily high ratio of male to female babies born is explained in a much less sinister way. According to one source, for example, many families in rural areas simply do not report the births of girl babies to the authorities. See Zhing, op. cit., pp. 4–6.

36. D. Davin, 1985, "The Implementation of the Single-Child Family Policy in the Chinese Countryside," pp. 37–65 in E. Croll (ed.), *China's One Child Policy* (Hong Kong: Macmillan).

37. S. Greenhalgh, 1986, "Shifts in China's Population Policy, 1984–1986: Views from the Central, Provincial and Local Levels," *Population and Development Review* 12, No. 3 (September), pp. 491–515.

38. Freedman et al., op. cit., p. 48; the four provinces were Hebei, Henan, Liaoning, and Sichuan.

39. Greenhalgh, op. cit.

40. Bianco and Hua, op. cit.

41. Ibid., pp. 154–155. The evidence shows that China accounts for 70 percent of all IUD users in the world; see A. J. Coale, 1984, *Rapid Population Change in China, 1952–1982* (Washington, D.C.: National Academy Press). In comparison to the United States, for example, 35 percent of Chinese women, compared to 5 percent in the United States, use IUDs; although the sterilization rates, for women (not men) are about the same (18 percent). Overall, the contraception rate among Chinese women (69 percent) is very similar to that in other countries, e.g., the United States (68 percent), Canada (73 percent), Taiwan (65 percent), and Hong Kong (72 percent); see D. L. Poston, Jr., 1986, "Patterns of Contraceptive Use in China," *Studies in Family Planning* 17, No. 5 (September), pp. 217–227. Apart from the use of IUDs, the major area of differences are in the low usage of birth-control pills, condoms, and diaphragms in China (Poston, 1986, pp. 220–221). The recent evidence suggests that in China there is a 9.8 percent failure rate with IUDs. Because

of the prevalence of IUDs a failure rate of 1 percent will produce an estimated 1 million extra pregnancies. See Zhing, op. cit., pp. 4–6.

42. Poston, op. cit.

43. Arnold and Liu, op. cit.

44. Greenhalgh, op. cit.

45. Terzani, op. cit.

46. *China Daily*, March 16, 1987.

47. Arnold and Liu, op. cit.

48. Bianco and Hua, op. cit., pp. 151–152.

49. *China Daily*, January 28, 1987.

50. C. Tietze, 1981, *Induced Abortion: A World Review* (New York: Population Council).

51. Freedman et al., op. cit., p. 47.

52. Ibid., p. 46, Table 6.

53. Arnold and Liu, op. cit., p. 241. The assumption here is that couples who already have a boy are more likely to be persuaded to abort "out of plan" pregnancies than couples who have a girl.

54. *China Daily*, April 18, 1987.

55. *Times Union* (Albany, N.Y.), April 15, 1989.

56. E. Salem, 1987, "Procreating for Profit: China's Population Growth Threatens Economic Reforms," *Far Eastern Economic Review* 136, No. 26 (June 25), pp. 56–57.

57. Greenhalgh, op. cit. Note, however, the difficulty involved with trying to predict what the future might bring in China. By early 1989, for example, a new push in the direction of further controls of the birthrate appeared imminent, and the population problem was being described as "out of control" (see *Times Union*, April 15, 1989, p. 1).

58. Greenhalgh, op. cit.

59. M. K. Whyte and S. Z. Gu, 1987, "Popular Response to China's Fertility Transition," *Population and Development Review* 13, No. 3 (September), pp. 471–493.

60. M. Selden, 1985, "Income Inequality and the State," pp. 193–218 in W. L. Parish (ed.), *Chinese Rural Development: The Great Transformation* (Armonk, N.Y.: M. E. Sharpe). Selden showed convincingly that the best predictor of which families become "rich" is family size; in other words, more children means more production, which means higher incomes.

61. Whyte and Gu, op. cit., p. 484.

62. Yuan Zhangfu, 1987, "Family Planning in a Sichuan Village," *China Reconstructs* 36, No. 2 (February), pp. 25–27.

63. Bianco and Hua, op. cit., p. 151.

64. Croll, 1984, op. cit.

65. In actual fact, the 1.2 billion figure had almost been reached by April 1989, and the government has been putting out some very strongly worded propaganda about the importance of staying with (or close) to the original goals of the population policy. See, for example: Deng Shulin, 1989, "Sounding the Alarm on Population Growth,"

China Reconstructs 38, No. 7 (July), pp. 30–33; and Zhing, op. cit.

66. Greenhalgh, op. cit.

67. M. Wolf, 1985, *Revolution Postponed: Women in Contemporary China* (Stanford, Calif.: Stanford University Press).

68. S. Greenhalgh and J. Bongaarts, 1987, "Fertility Policy in China: Future Options," *Science* 235 (March 6), pp. 1167–1172.

69. Deng, op. cit., p. 30. A new and largely unanticipated nightmare for Chinese family planners is the problem of the "floating populations" that have fled to the cities in the wake of the agricultural reforms. There may be as many as 180 million surplus workers in the countryside, and some reports claim that an estimated 50 million of them have taken up unofficial residence in the cities. Because this population is attached neither to work nor to residence units, it is very difficult for family planners to institute birth-control strategies among them, and the average number of children per family is consequently far higher than the government regulations allow. See Zhing, op. cit., and also Deng, op. cit. Another major problem is the illegal trading in "second-child birth certificates," costing anywhere from Y 800 to Y 2,000.

CHAPTER 8

1. R.J.R. Kirkby, 1985, *Urbanization in China: Town and Country in a Developing Economy, 1949–2000 AD* (New York: Columbia University Press), p. 18.

2. For more detailed discussions of the history of Chinese urbanization, see C. M. Nelson, 1988, "Urban Planning in Pre-industrial China," *U.S. China Review* 12, No. 2 (Summer), pp. 17–21; and C. W. Pannell and L.J.C. Ma, 1983, *China: The Geography of Development and Modernization* (London: V. H. Winston). Although not directly relevant in the present context, the reader is encouraged to consult the scholarly works of Paul Wheatley, who has written what is probably the most authoritative history of the city in ancient China. See P. Wheatley, 1971, *Pivot of the Four Quarters: A Preliminary Enquiry into the Origins and Character of the Ancient Chinese City* (Chicago: Aldine Pub. Co.).

3. G. W. Skinner, 1977, "Introduction: Urban Development in Imperial China," pp. 3–32 in G. W. Skinner (ed.), *The City in Late Imperial China* (Stanford, Calif.: Stanford University Press).

4. R. Murphey, 1980, *The Fading of the Maoist Vision: City and Country in China's Development* (New York: Methuen).

5. K. Buchanan, 1970, *The Transformation of the Chinese Earth* (London: G. Bell and Sons), p. 233.

6. Murphey, op. cit.

7. J. G. Gurley, 1976, *China's Economy and the Maoist Strategy* (New York: Monthly Review Press), p. 81.

8. Murphey, op. cit., p. 35.

9. R. Gaulton, 1981, "Political Mobilization in Shanghai: 1949–1951," pp. 35–65 in C. Howe (ed.), *Shanghai: Revolution and Development in an Asian Metropolis* (Cambridge, UK: Cambridge University Press), p. 46.

10. This observation was made by Kirkby, op. cit. Kirkby estimated that industrial output in China grew twenty-one times between 1952 and 1982 compared to a threefold growth in agricultural output.

11. Ibid., p. 18.

12. Ibid., p. 19.

13. This point was elaborated by M. K. Whyte and W. L. Parish, 1984, *Urban Life in Contemporary China* (Chicago: University of Chicago Press). It is important to point out that we have no evidence to indicate whether this norm was shared by the majority of the urban population or was simply a piece of Communist fiction.

14. Kirkby, op. cit., described a survey conducted in 1957 that showed that the dependent population in these fifteen cities increased by 70 percent between 1953 and 1956; during that time productive employment increased by only 28 percent and service employment increased by 5 percent.

15. Chen Pi-chao, 1972, "Overurbanization, Rustication of Urban-Educated Youths, and the Politics of Rural Transformation," *Comparative Politics* 4, No. 1 (April), pp. 381–386. Chinese cities continued to grow until 1959, after which they declined both in relative and in absolute terms. See C. P. Cell, 1979, "Deurbanization in China: The Urban-Rural Contradiction," *Bulletin of Concerned Asia Scholars* 11, No. 1, pp. 62–72. This trend and in fact the relatively slow rate of urbanization during the entire history of the PRC since 1949 suggest a pattern of "underurbanization" in China—a situation in which the actual rate of urbanization remains significantly below the expected rate. In general this is found to be the case in most of the world's socialist nations. See Ran Maoxing and B.J.L. Berry, 1989, "Underurbanization Policies Assessed: China, 1949–1986," *Urban Geography* 10, No. 2, pp. 111–120.

16. Kirkby, op. cit., esp. Chap. 7, pp. 180–200.

17. C. Riskin, 1987, *China's Political Economy: The Quest For Development Since 1949* (Oxford: Oxford University Press).

18. C. P. Lo, 1987, "Socialist Ideology and Urban Strategies in China," *Urban Geography* 8, No. 5 (Sept./Oct.), pp. 440–458.

19. Kirkby, op. cit., pp. 93–99.

20. L.J.C. Ma, 1986, "Chinese Cities: A Research Agenda," *Urban Geography* 7, pp. 279–290. According to the Chinese State Statistical Bureau, in 1987 there were 381 cities, and 632 out of the

total number of 1986 counties were directly under the administration of cities.

21. D. Zweig, 1987, "From Village to City: Reforming Urban-Rural Relations in China," *International Regional Science Review* 11, No. 11, pp. 43–58.

22. R.J.R. Kirkby, "China Goes to Town," *Geographical Magazine* 58, No. 10 (October), pp. 508–511, quote from p. 510.

23. Whyte and Parish, op. cit.

24. Gurley, op. cit.

25. M. Blecher, 1986, *China: Politics, Economics and Society* (London: Frances Pinter).

26. Ibid., p. 162.

27. Mao Zedong, 1956, *Mao Tse-tung: Selected Works*, Vol. 4 (1941–1945) (New York: International Publications), pp. 363–364.

28. E. F. Vogel, 1969, *Canton Under Communism: Program and Politics in a Provincial Capital, 1949–1968* (Cambridge, Mass.: Harvard University Press), p. 46.

29. Ibid., p. 51.

30. Ibid., p. 44.

31. C. P. Lo, C. W. Pannell, and R. Welch, 1977, "Land Use Changes and City Planning in Shenyang and Canton," *Geographical Review* 67, No. 3 (July), pp. 268–283.

32. Fei Xiaotong, 1953, *China's Gentry: Essays in Rural-Urban Relations* (Chicago: University of Chicago Press). In addition to the intraurban patterns of inequality, the CCP also inherited an extremely uneven pattern of economic development at the regional level, with the urbanized and "Westernized" coastal areas sharply differentiated from the largely rural and premodern interior. This issue will be raised in more detail in Chapter 9.

33. W. T. Rowe, 1984, "Urban Policy in China," *Problems of Communism* 33, No. 6 (Nov./Dec.), pp. 75–80.

34. This rather sad chapter of socialist city planning, in which the Chinese destroyed much of their urban heritage, has been well documented, both by Chinese urban scholars and by foreign observers. For different views, see Hou Ren-Zhi, 1986, "Evolution of the City Plan of Beijing," *Third World Planning Review* 8, No. 1, pp. 5–17; and T. Terzani, 1986, "Death by a Thousand Cuts: The Destruction of Old Peking," pp. 22–59 in T. Terzani, *Behind the Forbidden Door: Travels in China* (London: Allen and Unwin). The land use of the ancient Chinese city often followed religious and geomantic considerations. There was a preoccupation with both nature's dominance over "man" and the Confucian belief in the merits of order, symmetry, and heirarchy. The Communists rejected this in favor of a more pragmatic approach to planning, in which "man" was to conquer nature. See Nelson, op. cit.

35. For a detailed discussion of the rebuilding of Beijing, see Zhang Jinggan, 1989, "Beijing: Yesterday, Today, and Tomorrow," pp. 207–225 in F. J. Costa, A. K. Durr, L.J.C. Ma, and A. G. Noble (eds.), *Urbanization in Asia: Spatial Dimensions and Policy Issues* (Honolulu: University of Hawaii Press).

36. Rowe, op. cit., p. 77.

37. The experiment with and failure of the urban communes is discussed by J. Salaff, 1971, "Urban Residential Communities in the Wake of the Cultural Revolution," pp. 289–324 in J. W. Lewis (ed.), *The City in Communist China* (Stanford, Calif.: Stanford University Press).

38. Lo, op. cit., p. 446.

39. Ibid.

40. Fung Ka-iu, 1980, "Suburban Agricultural Land Use Since 1949," pp. 156–184 in C. K. Leung and N. Ginsburg (eds.), *China: Urbanization and National Development* (Chicago: University of Chicago, Department of Geography Research Paper No. 196). Fung estimated that in 1956 alone, for example, 2.48 million square meters of housing were demolished in 175 cities.

41. Fung, for example, indicated that in Harbin between 1954 and 1956, the population increased from 1.21 million to 1.47 million, but the land available for growing vegetables fell from 4,980 to 2,662 hectares during the same period.

42. It is important to point out that the goal of urban self-sufficiency represented much more than simple Maoist egalitarian dogma. In addition to the obvious geographical advantages, growing vegetables within the city made good ecological sense, in that it helped to provide labor and technology from the cities, as well as using local sources of fertilizer, including night soil and ash from domestic fires. In organizational terms the propinquity of production and consumption also made things much easier. Most important, however, self-sufficiency would help to lower China's dependency on imported food, and it would help to establish the independence of the interior cities from the traditionally dominant cities on the east coast. In economic terms local self-sufficiency helped the government to hold down food prices, which was essential in its quest for legitimacy in the first decade after Liberation. Urban self-sufficiency, because it helped maintain peasant incomes and smooth out fluctuations in the demand for agricultural labor throughout the year, also helped keep down the rate of unemployment and the inevitable urban unrest it could bring. For further details on the self-sufficiency concept, see G. W. Skinner, 1978, "Vegetable Supply and Marketing in Chinese Cities," *China Quarterly* 76 (December), pp. 733–793.

43. Skinner (ibid.) has shown that in spite (or perhaps because) of the intensity of agricultural production in the inner production zone, relatively little of the actually available land in this zone is devoted to agriculture—16 percent in Shanghai and 28 percent in Canton. He also noted that the size/width of the zone required to make a city

self-sufficient is a function of spatial variations in productivity and, of course, city size. Assuming an annual vegetable yield of 60 tons per hectare and the use of an average of 20 percent of the available land, Skinner estimated that the vegetable zone would need to be close to 10 kilometers wide for a city of 6 million people, but only 2.8 kilometers wide for a city of .5 million.

44. Gaulton, op. cit., p. 40.

45. R. Terrill, 1975, *Flowers On An Iron Tree: Five Cities in China* (Boston: Little, Brown and Co.), p. 47.

46. L. W. Snow, 1981, *Edgar Snow's China: A Personal Account of the Chinese Revolution Compiled from the Writings of Edgar Snow* (New York: Random House), p. 21.

47. Zhang Xinxin and Sang Ye, 1987, *Chinese Lives: An Oral History of Contemporary China* (New York: Pantheon Books); see "Her Past," pp. 31–38; quote from p. 32.

48. Terrill, op. cit., pp. 82–83.

49. Ibid., p. 85.

50. Zhang and Sang, op. cit., p. 37.

51. "The New Conquers the Old in Nanking," *China Reconstructs* 22, No. 3 (March 1973), pp. 21–26.

52. Vogel, op. cit., p. 65.

53. Ibid., pp. 65–66.

54. Ibid., p. 56.

55. Gaulton, op. cit., p. 61.

56. L. T. White III, 1981, "Shanghai-Suburb Relations: 1949–1966," pp. 241–268 in Howe, op. cit., pp. 254–55.

57. Pan Ling, *Old Shanghai: Gangsters in Paradise* (Hong Kong: Heinemann, Asia), p. 236.

58. This is essentially the thesis put forward by Murphey in op. cit., although in the late 1970s it was still impossible to predict the impact of the reforms that had just begun. The view from the middle and late 1980s appeared to vindicate many of Murphey's suspicions. See, for example, R. Cherrington, 1987, "Bulldozing into the Future," *China Now* 120, pp. 26–27; L.J.C. Ma and A. G. Noble, 1986, "Chinese Cities: A Research Agenda," *Urban Geography* 7, No. 4, pp. 279–290; and M. Selden, 1988, "City Versus Countryside? The Social Consequences of Development Choices in China," pp. 153–180 in M. Selden, *The Political Consequence of Chinese Socialism* (Armonk, N.Y.: M. E. Sharpe, Inc.).

59. For samples of this work, see L. Hoa, 1984, "Rural Industrialization and Stress on Small Towns," *Third World Planning Review* 6, No. 1 (November), pp. 27–36; K. C. Tan, 1986, "Small Towns in Chinese Urbanization," *Geographical Review* 76, No. 2 (April), pp. 265–275; and A.G.O. Yeh and H. Q. Yuan, 1987, "Satellite Town Development in China: Problems and Prospects," *Tijdschrift voor Economische en Sociale Geografie* 78, No. 3, pp. 190–200.

60. Lo, op. cit., p. 444.

61. This process has been described by Ye Shunzan, 1989, "Urban Development Trends in China," pp. 75–92 in Costa et al., op. cit.

62. Sun Yuantao, 1988, "Shock Wave of Unemployment in Qingdao City," *Nexus: China in Focus*, Winter, pp. 27–28.

63. D. D. Buck, 1984, "Changes in Chinese Urban Planning Since 1976," *Third World Planning Review* 6, No. 1 (February), pp. 5–26, quote on p. 19.

64. Ibid., pp. 18–20.

65. Lo, op. cit., p. 449.

66. This argument has probably been made most forcefully by M. Chossudovsky, 1986, *Towards Capitalist Restoration? Chinese Socialism After Mao* (Hong Kong: Macmillan).

67. I. Szelenyi, 1983, *Urban Inequality Under State Socialism* (London: Oxford University Press).

68. C. W. Pannell, 1989, "Employment Structure and the Chinese Urban Economy," pp. 285–308 in Costa et al., op. cit.

69. O. Schell, 1988, *Discos and Democracy: China in the Throes of Reform* (New York: Pantheon), p. 125.

CHAPTER 9

1. D. Zweig, 1987, "From Village to City: Reforming Urban-Rural Relations in China," *International Regional Science Review* 11, No. 1, pp. 43–58, quote from p. 43.

2. According to Carl Riskin, Mao's principles for economic development were "self-reliance" and "egalitarianism" (see Chapter 9, pp. 201–222). Self-reliance included the following characteristics: (1) the full utilization of domestic resources, including labor and skills; (2) the rejection of indiscriminate imitation of foreign methods in favor of developing indigenous technology; (3) reliance on domestic rather than foreign sources of finance; and (4) the establishment of a comprehensive industrial system. As Riskin pointed out, the goal of "self-reliance" was sometimes contradictory to the goal of "egalitarianism," for example, when a specific rural area industrialized, it often tended to produce wider income disparities between localities (p. 201). See C. Riskin, 1987, *China's Political Economy: The Quest For Development Since 1949* (New York: Oxford University Press), esp. Chap. 10, "Late Maoism, II: Egalitarianism," pp. 223–253.

3. The majority of this chapter refers to inequality and redistribution in terms of income and consumption in China. Obviously, for a country where material wealth and possessions have been restricted, it is also possible to think of inequality in terms of occupation, prestige, status, and of course between men and women; these other measures of inequality are not necessarily consistent

with income and consumption. We should also note that in China there are numerous benefits provided to both urban and rural workers in the form of state-provided services, including education and health care, as well as subsized food, housing, transportation, and utilities. In this sense a focus on income alone as a measure of inequality is not sufficient because the noncash benefits in a socialist society contribute significantly to higher standards of living, in spite of low income levels. From Mao's speeches we are aware of his avowed efforts to eliminate inequalities—or what he referred to as the "three great differences" (see ibid., pp. 201–202 and 223.). These were differences between the city and the countryside, between urban workers and rural peasants, and between mental (intellectual) and manual labor.

4. C. Roll, 1980, *The Distribution of Rural Incomes in China: A Comparison of the 1930's and 1950's* (New York: Guilford), p. 76.

5. Huan Xiang, 1985, "On Reform of Chinese Economic Structure," *Beijing Review* 28 (May 20), pp. 15–19 (emphasis added).

6. "China Begins a New Long March," *Business Week*, June 5, 1989, pp. 38–46.

7. Ibid., p. 40.

8. See M. K. Whyte, 1986, "Social Trends in China: The Triumph of Inequality," pp. 103–123 in A. Doak Barnett and R. N. Clough (eds.), *Modernizing China: Post-Mao Reform and Development* (Boulder, Colo.: Westview Press).

9. P. B. Trescott, 1985, "Incentive Versus Equality: What Does China's Recent Experience Show?" *World Development* 13, No. 2, pp. 205–217.

10. It is important to observe, however, that population controls have different, and sometimes contradictory, effects. The prevention of out-migration from rural areas may help to retain skilled labor, as well as the more energetic and creative (and younger) segment of the population. However, the same policies prevent people from moving from poorer (rural) areas, to richer (urban) areas, which may have the opposite effect of reinforcing spatial inequalities by keeping the poor trapped in their home localities. See M. Selden, 1988, *The Political Economy of Chinese Socialism* (Armonk, N.Y.: M. E. Sharpe, Inc.); esp. Chap. 5, "Income Inequality and the State in Rural China," pp. 129–152.

11. Ibid., pp. 131–37. Ironically, the same policies that allowed some families to earn more and thereby reduce income inequality have also been the major source of income inequality during the last decade, as Selden (op. cit.) has observed. The major difference between rich and poor families is the size of the family and the ratio of able-bodied workers to dependents.

12. See Trescott, op. cit., p. 207, Table 2.

13. T. R. Lakshmanan and Hua Chang-i, 1987, "Regional Disparities in China," *International Regional Science Review* 11, No. 1, pp. 97–104.

14. Riskin, op. cit., p. 230, Table 10.2.

15. It is important to point out here that in addition to the spatial sources of inequality in China, there are significant sources of inequality between individuals, for example, between the crippling workload of peasants laboring in the rice fields or porters carrying heavy loads up mountainsides, and the relatively cushy life of many office workers. Gender inequality, as we shall see in Chapter 11, is also still evident in China, as are some of the vast discrepancies in power and status that are generally associated with Party membership. See Trescott, op. cit., pp. 207–09.

16. This analogy is drawn effectively by D. J. Solinger, 1987, "Uncertain Paternalism: Tensions in Recent Regional Restructuring in China," *International Regional Science Review* 11, No. 1, pp. 23–42.

17. Lakshmanan and Hua, op. cit., p. 100.

18. See Selden, op. cit., p. 141.

19. Riskin, op. cit., p. 231.

20. Selden (op. cit.) also argued that in spite of its commitment to spatial egalitarianism, the Chinese government after 1949 rejected a number of very obvious ways to redistribute wealth between localities, most notably progressive taxation and direct subsidies to poor rural regions. As he noted, in fact, "China's tax policies have been consistently regressive, stimulating rapidly developing units while acting as a brake on the economic performance of those who lag behind" (p. 142). In addition, there has been no development of nationwide social security or national health systems that would help to reduce inequality. Selden also noted that "in siphoning off much . . . [rural] accumulation to accelerate industrial growth . . . [and] curbing such important sources of rural income as . . . sidelines, handicrafts, and marketing, the state has maintained a series of policies that favored the cities to the detriment of the countryside" (p. 143).

21. Riskin, op. cit., p. 229 and p. 230, Table 10.2. For example, agricultural output per capita in 1957 in Qinghai Province was Y 119, but it fell to Y 92 in 1979; and in Guizhou Province it fell from Y 102 to Y 64 in the same period. This lack of agricultural productivity is closely correlated to lower personal incomes. As Riskin demonstrated, farm incomes per capita in the most productive province (Jilin) resulted in incomes that were 2.5 times higher than those in the least productive province (Guizhou) in 1979 (p. 229).

22. J. P. Cole, 1987, "Regional Inequalities in the People's Republic of China," *Tijdschrift voor Economische en Sociale Geografie* 78, No. 3, pp. 201–13.

23. Ibid., p. 207, Figure 2.

24. E. B. Vermeer, 1982, "Income Differentials in Rural China," *China Quarterly* 89 (March), pp. 1–33. As Vermeer pointed out, Y 50 (about U.S.

$35.00 in 1979 terms) has been in use for some time as the norm for state relief—essentially acting as a indicator of poverty for China. It is important to note, however, that the number of "poverty stricken" areas in rural China decreased significantly in the late 1970s, from 515 in 1977, to 381 in 1978, and 283 in 1979 (221 of the total had been below the poverty level in each of the three years). Vermeer described some of the events and policies that have helped to reduce the number of poverty-stricken districts. In some cases it was favorable weather conditions allowing bumper harvests; in others it was the greater efficiency made possible by the advent of the new household responsibility system (pp. 28–30).

25. Ibid., p. 28. Vermeer also reported a tendency in many backward and isolated areas of China to underreport incomes and earnings, resulting perhaps in some artificial estimates of rural poverty. William Hinton has also pointed out that the new household responsibility system was more likely to be successful in raising agricultural productivity in areas that had not wholeheartedly taken to collectivization, in other words, those areas where "capitalist tendencies" had persisted. See "Whither China's Agricultural Reforms: An Interview with William Hinton," *Contemporary Marxism* 12-13 (Spring 1986), pp. 137–143.

26. See Riskin, op. cit., p. 236. Riskin pointed out that because there was very little inequality *within* individual villages, the peasants in poor areas were less likely to perceive the existence of great inequality within the countryside. Obviously this was to change very drastically with the economic reforms in the countryside after 1980 (see Chapter 5), when visible symbols of wealth started to appear.

27. Ibid.

28. Selden, op. cit., p. 134.

29. Ibid., pp. 136–37.

30. The gini coefficient is a useful measure of inequality, ranging from 0.0 for a perfectly even distribution of income to 1.0 for a totally uneven distribution. The lower the coefficient, the closer the spread of income throughout the population—thus if the poorest 10% of the families earned much less than 10% of the village's total income, and if the richest 10% earned much more than 10% of the total income, the gini coefficient would be high. The closer each group of the population comes to earning its proportionate share of the total income, the lower will be the gini coefficient.

31. Selden, op. cit., p. 139, Table 5.3.

32. Ibid., p. 138. Selden's conclusion here is supported by that of Riskin, op. cit., who, using the World Bank's data, argued that "rural income inequality in China is significantly less than in other South Asian countries" (p. 234).

33. Riskin, op. cit., showed that there was a remarkable amount of income equality in China's cities in the earlier 1980s, with a gini coefficient of 0.16, compared to coefficients in excess of .40 in most of the other poor Asian nations (p. 249, Table 10.5). This is largely explained by the restrictions on rural-to-urban migration in many Third World cities, which has occurred in other countries, causing an influx of very poor rural people in the cities, thereby increasing inequality. In China, where the rural poor have not been able to enter the cities in large numbers, there has been less evidence of the ghettoization and shantytown development typical in most poor countries.

34. See Selden, op. cit., pp. 148–49 and Table 5.6.

35. It would be unwise to put too much stock in this conclusion, for a number of reasons. In the first place, we need to await the results of studies conducted throughout the 1980s to determine whether the equality-inducing effects of the agricultural reforms have persisted. Second, as Selden himself noted in his 1988 book, the economic gains in the countryside have certainly not been reaped equally. Some localities and even whole regions have tended to slip further and further behind. See, for example, W. Hinton, 1989, "A Response to Hugh Deane," *Monthly Review* 40, No. 10 (March), pp. 10–35. Third, other studies have presented data that challenge those reported by Selden. Trescott, op. cit., for example, showed that the proportion of low-income earners in the rural sector actually *increased* between 1978 and 1983, even considering the "low" category to be Y 200 in 1983 instead of the Y 100 level in 1978. Trescott concluded that there has been a *slight* increase in rural inequality in the Chinese countryside since 1978, although he also believed that the inequality would be reduced as a result of the greater innovation and competition unleashed by the new economic reforms (p. 211). Also, as mobility increases, and as nonfarm enterprises develop, we ought to see some of the poorer regions and villages catching up with the richer ones. In 1990, it remained to be seen whether this prediction would become a reality.

36. Riskin, op. cit., p. 250.

37. Wu Chung-Tong and D. F. Ip, 1980, "Structural Transformation and Spatial Equity," pp. 56–88 in C. K. Leung and N. Ginsburg (eds.), *China: Urbanization and National Development* (Chicago: University of Chicago, Department of Geography Research Paper No. 196).

38. D. Zweig, 1987, "From Village to City: Reforming Urban-Rural Relations in China," *International Regional Science Review* 11, No. 1, pp. 43–58.

39. See Riskin, op. cit., p. 238.

40. These various estimates are provided in Selden, op. cit., p. 162. The higher estimates were obtained by considering the effect of the massive subsidies on food in China's cities. There is a general consensus within the literature that the

gap between urban and rural incomes probably doubled between 1952 to 1979, partly as a result of the food, housing, and other subsidies offered to city dwellers, but also as a result of absolute gains in urban residents' incomes and the lack of investment and low productivity in the agricultural sector.

41. See ibid., pp. 169–170.

42. More important, according to Selden, than the absolute increases in rural incomes, was the change at the two poles, in other words, the reduction in the number of poor households and the expansion in the rich households; see ibid., pp. 170–71. An official survey conducted in 1985 also showed that for a sample of urban and rural households, the average annual growth in incomes was 15% in the rural areas, compared to 8% in urban areas (1978–1984). Rural consumption during the same period grew by an average of 13% each year, compared to 7% for urban households. Although rural incomes tripled, incomes in state enterprises, which are mainly urban based, increased by less than 100%. However, in spite of these relative gains, it is important to point out that the absolute per capita gap between urban and rural workers increased between 1978 and 1984, from Y 488 to Y 751 (ibid., p. 175).

43. Ibid.

44. According to Selden, the government cut back the level of agricultural investment in an attempt to avoid alienating urban workers, who were seeing the advantages of the countryside stacking up against them—and also in fear of a politically explosive situation in which workers and intellectuals might unite to demand political reforms, along the lines of the Solidarity movement in Poland (ibid., p. 180).

45. Selden has shown, for example, that the per capita output value of industry and agriculture combined was Y 669 greater in the eastern provinces in 1981, but this figure increased to Y 1,018 by 1985 (ibid., p. 172).

46. P. Howard, 1986, "Some Comments on China's Controversial Rural Economic Reforms," *Contemporary Marxism* 12-13 (Spring), pp. 163–201.

47. Vermeer, op. cit.; see also P. Augignier, 1988, "Regional Disparities Since 1978," pp. 93–106 in S. Feuchtwang, A. Hussain, and T. Pairault (eds.), *Transforming China's Economy in the Eighties*, Vol. 2: *Management, Industry and the Urban Economy* (Boulder, Colo.: Westview Press).

48. Howard, op. cit., p. 174.

49. Selden, op. cit.

50. Riskin, op. cit.

51. Economist Intelligence Unit, 1988, *China, North Korea: Country Report*, Analysis of Economic and Political Trends Every Quarter, No. 3 (London: The Economist Intelligence Unit, Ltd).

52. See Riskin, op. cit., p. 300.

53. "More Land to Those Who Till It," *Economist*, December 12, 1987, pp. 32–33; see also M. Blecher, 1986, *China: Politics, Economics and Society* (London: Frances Pinter Pub.), p. 183.

54. See L. Pan, 1988, *The New Chinese Revolution* (Chicago: Contemporary Books). The lack of consumer goods has contributed to the huge increases in savings that has occurred in the Chinese countryside, from Y 5.6 billion in 1974 to Y 47 billion in 1984, and an exponential increase since that time (see Howard, op. cit., and Economist Intelligence Unit, op. cit.).

55. Howard, op. cit., p. 198.

56. A. Watson, 1988, "The Reform of Agricultural Marketing in China Since 1878," *China Quarterly*, No. 113 (March), pp. 1–28; see p. 21.

CHAPTER 10

1. A. H. Smith, 1894, *Chinese Characteristics* (New York: Fleming H. Revell Co.), p. 194.

2. D. W. Meinig, 1976, "The Beholding Eye: Ten Versions of the Same Scene," *Landscape Architecture*, January, pp. 47–54.

3. P. Theroux, 1988, *Riding the Iron Rooster: By Train Through China* (New York: Ivy Books), p. 129.

4. Ibid., pp. 231–32.

5. Li Po, 1960, *The White Pony*, trans. R. Payne (New York: Mentor Books), quote in Yi Fu Tuan, 1969, *China: The World's Landscapes* (Chicago: Aldine), p. 100.

6. Tuan, op. cit., p. 128.

7. Ibid., p. 100.

8. Theroux, op. cit., p. 172.

9. Zhang Xianliang, 1988, *Half of Man Is Woman* (New York: W. W. Norton), p. 271.

10. In the 1980s the strongest case against Maoist socialism and its utter disregard for the environment was made by V. Smil, 1984, *The Bad Earth: Environmental Degradation in China* (Armonk, N.Y.: M. E. Sharpe). Smil believed that the return to market socialism offered the only ray of hope for the Chinese environment, in sharp contrast to the ideas expressed by William Hinton. See W. H. Hinton, 1989, "A Response to Hugh Deane," *Monthly Review* 40, No. 10 (March), pp. 10–35. The price of progress has been recorded by teams of outsiders visiting China; see, for example, D. Elsom and M. Haigh, 1986, "Progress and Pollution," *Geographical Magazine* 58, No. 12, pp. 640–45. In addition to the impact of industrial development on the Chinese landscape, another major dimension of environmental degradation, associated with the opening up of China, has been the impact on the landscape of tourism. In Tibet, for example, the evidence that foreigners are interested in Buddhism, temples, minority people, and remote scenery prompted a major phase of hotel development in Lhasa. The irony of this is that the ancient religious landscape

that even Maoism could not wipe out is now threatened by tourism! In 1985 the modern Lhasa Hotel opened, and in the following year the Holiday Inn chain opened up a new Y 100 million hotel. A special hillside is planned to allow tourists to view by telescope the "sky burial" rituals, the age-old practice of dismembering the dead and feeding them to the vultures to hasten their reincarnation. As Lynn Pan observed, "The authorities have not grasped how corrupting tourism can be. . . . Economics has overtaken politics, and as buildings go up and more scenic areas open, it is difficult to avoid the conclusion that Tibetan culture, which has survived the worst that Maoism and force could do to stamp it out, has been left to be killed by tourism" (p. 281). See L. Pan, 1988, *The New Chinese Revolution* (Chicago: Contemporary Books).

11. In the face of such arguments, some critics have suggested that the rate and the level of environmental degradation in China has been reduced since 1978, partly as a result of new laws to exert compliance from potential polluters. The general line from the critics of the Maoist era is that the Chinese economy has become considerably more efficient as a result of the reforms and that this has had positive environmental results. A major impact, for example, has been felt from the system of charging polluters a fee, in an attempt to make them realize the potential social costs of their behavior. For a discussion of this argument; see L. Ross, 1988, *Environmental Policy in China* (Bloomington: Indiana University Press), esp. Chap. 4, "Pollution Control," pp. 131–175.

12. Smil, op. cit., p. 66. It is important to point out that although urban pollution receives the most publicity in China, we should not forget the widespread damage being inflicted in the countryside, especially with the major drive to bring industry into rural areas. See, for example, "Pollution Threatens Rural Environment," *China Daily*, December 19, 1986.

13. M. Haigh and D. Elsom, 1987, "An Environmental Snapshot of South China," *China Now*, No. 122, pp. 24–26. The loss of cultivable land has become a major concern. By 1985 there was less than half the amount of land per person in China that there was in 1949, approximately 0.09 hectares. The loss continued: From 1983 to 1985 an average of 757,000 hectares were lost per year; and a further 620,000 hectares were lost in 1986. See "Not Enough Land," *China Daily*, March 27, 1987. In response the state has introduced quotas for nonagricultural construction on cultivable land and is considering legislation to curb the loss. See, for example, "Law Needed to Save Farmland," *China Daily*, April 11, 1987. Cultivable land is lost to forestation, animal husbandry, urban and enterprise construction—but the most worrying aspect is the illegal occupation of cultivable land by nonagricultural land uses. In a survey of ten prov-

inces in 1986, inspectors discovered 1.84 million cases of illegal farmland use, involving more than 173,000 hectares. In Hubei Province alone, 8,700 illegal buildings were dismantled over a three-year period to restore 653 hectares of land, and the illegal tenants were fined a total of Y 1.1 million. See "Illegal Use of Farmland Led to Loss in Output," *China Daily*, February 21, 1987.

14. L. Ross, 1987, "Obligatory Tree Planting: The Role of Campaigns in Policy Implementation in Post-Mao China," pp. 225–252 in D. M. Lampton (ed.), *Policy Implementation in Post-Mao China* (Berkeley: University of California Press). Vaclav Smil (op. cit.) presented data to show that the decimation actually began before the Great Leap; for example, 1.33 million hectares of forest were cut down between 1950 and 1957, during which time only 18 percent was regenerated (p. 15).

15. Smil, op. cit., p. 63. The major loss, in agricultural terms, was in the fish harvests, representing a valuable source of protein. Smil estimated, for example, that Shanghai had lost 30 percent of its fish breeding areas by 1979, and that 3,000 hectares of fish ponds were turned into fields. The province of Hubei, "the province of a thousand lakes" now has fewer than 400 lakes larger than 66.6 hectares, and the provinces' total lake water surface area fell by 75% between 1949 and 1979 (p. 63).

16. Huang Ching, 1987, "A Way of Life Runs Dry," *China Daily*, June 1, p. 3.

17. D. Richardson and E. Salem, 1987, "A Policy in the Ashes: Poor Management, Not Fire, Is Destroying China's Forests," *Far Eastern Economic Review*, June 4, pp. 63–64; see also "Forest Fire in Heilongjiang" (editorial comment), *China Now*, No. 122, p. 4. Other examples of contradictory policies are legion, for example, in the business of planting trees. Peasants took part in tree-planting campaigns at intervals, only later to be told to cut down the trees to fuel the "backyard furnaces" during the Great Leap Forward. One peasant recalled having to cut down his beloved orchard during a campaign to rid the countryside of such "capitalist" tendencies as growing fruit to sell privately: "We had our little orchard—160 square meters . . . I planted vines and grafted peaches . . . real darlings, all red and with a little twist at the end. . . . But when the 'four cleanups' business came along in 1964 I had to cut them all down . . . I cried my eyes out and couldn't go near that end of the village for two weeks" (p. 121). Interview of Zhang Yuxi, a peasant in Xuecheng County, Shandong, in Zhang Xinxin and Sang Ye, 1987, *Chinese Lives: An Oral History of Contemporary China* (New York: Pantheon Books), p. 121.

18. Smil, op. cit., p. 16.

19. Ibid., p. 19.

20. In 1983 China actually ranked 120th out of 160 countries in terms of per capita forest cover, with 115 million hectares, amounting to about 12% of the country's total surface area (compared to an average of 22% worldwide). By comparison, the United States averages about 1.5 hectares per person, with a total coverage of about 32%. See Ross, 1988, op. cit., esp. Chap. 2, "Forestry Policy," pp. 25–85. As Smil (op. cit.) has pointed out, China's forest cover is low even in comparison with other poor countries where deforestation has been rampant. For example, in Brazil, there were approximately 4.0 hectares per person, with a forest cover of 40% (p. 12).

21. Ross, 1988, op. cit., p. 26.

22. Ibid., p. 27. Ross noted that the Yellow River, generally referred to as "China's Sorrow" because of its history of flooding, is probably the muddiest river in the world, as a result of soil erosion aided by deforestation. The sediment load and its annual erosion rate are approximately ten times greater than the most heavily silted stream in the United States (p. 27).

23. Smil, op. cit., p. 27. This estimate is based on the assumption that each hectare of forest is able to retain 300 cubic meters of water. The removal of tree cover therefore reduces water-retention capabilities and increases the likelihood of major natural disasters. In 1981 there was a warning of what was to come in the Yangtze basin when torrential summer rains helped to flood homes, fields, and factories in 135 counties, affecting nearly 12 million people (p. 28). In spite of the intellectual attraction of this argument, Ross, 1987, op. cit., questioned the validity of the hypothesis, suggesting that there was no hard evidence that reforesting could significantly ease the flooding potential in the Yangtze basin.

24. Smil, op. cit., p. 31.

25. See Ross, 1988, op. cit., p. 70. The actual amount of wasteland allocated as private plots varied significantly from one area to another. The reformer Hu Yaobang, then Party general secretary, advocated private plots covering 15–20 percent of the wasteland, a larger amount than was allocated for agriculture (p. 70).

26. It is interesting to note that although the publicity campaign suggested that the fear of future flooding in the Yangtze Valley stimulated the adoption of OTP, the program was actually focused largely on China's urban areas rather than the remote rural areas where it was probably needed much more. Ross (ibid.) has suggested that this was because of OTP's ideological advantages and its attractiveness as a program to motivate urban youth, in addition to Premier Hu Yaobang's commitment to market rather than campaign/command strategies in the rural areas. In other words, as Ross observed, "in a curious fashion, problems involving rural ecology and urban youth had become joined in a solution well suited to neither" (p. 235).

27. Ibid., p. 234. It is important to point out that the OTP program was supplemented by numerous regional efforts at reforestation throughout the country. See, for example, the efforts to prevent desertification in the lowest reaches of the Yellow River in western Shandong Province: Zheng Fang-kun, 1986, "Making the Desert Bloom," *Beijing Review*, No. 50 (December 15), pp. 19–21.

28. Ross, 1988, op. cit., p. 68.

29. Privatization of forestry, including the adoption of responsibility systems, was approved in 1984. As was the case in agriculture, in 1985, reforms were introduced in the pricing and distribution systems for timber. The reforms enhanced private forestry and speeded up participation in afforestation, which increased by 25 percent in 1983 and by another 10 percent in 1984. Individual households were responsible for 38% of the afforestation in 1984 and more than 50% in 1985 (ibid., pp. 74–77).

30. C. Thubron, 1987, *Behind the Wall: A Journey Through China* (London: Heinemann), p. 239.

31. Ibid.

32. Ibid., p. 138.

33. Smil, op. cit., p. 165. Ross (1988, op. cit.) estimated that there were more than 42 million tons of residuals discharged into the atmosphere in China in 1981, including 18 million tons of sulfur dioxide, which is almost as great as the output of the United States, which has an industrial production rate nearly six times greater than China's (p. 134). Not surprisingly, the incidence rates of lung cancer, respiratory diseases, and poisoning have recorded major leaps in recent years.

34. The push to establish industry in or close to China's cities since 1949 has produced a unique ratio of industrial to other land uses and jobs. As we shall see in Chapter 12, there has been an uneven development of local services, with housing, transportation, and recreation traditionally receiving a lower priority than industry. In employment terms this manifested itself in a small (and declining) ratio of industrial to service workers. For example, in Beijing there were 100 residents for every 5.6 service workers in 1949; but by 1980 this had been reduced to 3.6 service workers. See Smil, op. cit., pp. 153–167.

35. L.J.C. Ma and Liu Changming, 1984, "Water Resources Development and Its Environmental Impact on Beijing," pp. 101–116 in C. Pannell and C. L. Salter (eds.), *China Geographer, No. 12: The Environment* (Boulder, Colo.: Westview Press). Ma and Liu estimated that of the normal 4.5 billion cubic meters, 2 billion come from surface sources (the reservoirs) and 2.5 billion from groundwater.

36. Smil, op. cit., estimated that in 1979 Beijing's water supply was 140 million cubic meters below what was needed and that as a result the water

table had already fallen to 20 meters below the normal level. Deep cones of depression have appeared, especially in the heavily industrialized suburbs where there are too many wells (p. 157). The crisis had reached a head by 1987, when it was estimated that 200 cities throughout China were facing a shortage of water, approaching a total of 10 million tons a day, resulting in economic losses of Y 20 billion. The problem, as expressed by Song Xutong, section chief of the Ministry of Urban and Rural Construction and Environmental Protection, was that "water consumption in urban areas increases at an average annual rate of 10%, but construction of water supply projects remains at 6 to 8% growth." See "200 Cities Affected by Water Shortages," *China Daily*, March 17, 1987. Citizens all over the country were being exhorted to conserve water. See, for example, "Water Savings Help," *China Daily*, April 11, 1987.

37. To illustrate the potential increase in demand for domestic water in China as modernization proceeds, it is interesting to compare daily-usage rates in Chinese cities with those elsewhere. Residential use averages about 140 liters per person per day in Beijing, higher than the overall urban average in China of 120 liters, but far less than the overall usage in U.S. cities (Ross, 1988, op. cit., p. 90). The average use in China's new "luxury" apartment buildings is 300 liters per day, but in the big tourist hotels it is as high as 2000 liters per day (Ma and Liu, op. cit., p. 107). Obviously the impact of major increases in the demand for water will be felt very soon. Similar problems are being experienced in other northern Chinese cities; see for example, A. J. Jowett, 1986, "China's Water Crisis: The Case of Tianjin," *Geographical Journal* 152, Pt. 1 (March), pp. 9–18.

38. The Hai River in Tianjin apparently carries mercury concentrations that are seventeen times above the generally allowed amount, and in Jilin the concentrations reach 2–20 milligrams per liter of water, more than five times higher than those at the infamous Minimata Bay site in Japan (international drinking-water standards specify no more than 0.001 milligrams per liter). See V. Smil, 1987, "Rivers of Waste," *China Business Review*, July/August, pp. 18–20. A shocking story but one that has become familiar in recent years involves the Nanzhang River in Shanxi Province, into which a chemical factory poured 18 tons of highly poisonous ammonium hydrogen carbonate, killing fish and making a total of 15,400 people ill as a result of drinking the river's water. The accident resulted in a Y 30,000 fine for the factory. See "Poisoned River Makes 15,400 People Sick," *China Daily*, March 23, 1987.

39. Smil, 1987, op. cit., stated that "the most frequent pollutants endangering both ground and surface water supplies are oil products, phenolic compounds, cyanide, arsenic, heavy metals (lead,

chromium, cadmium, mercury), chlorinated hydrocarbons, nitrates, and sulfates (p. 18). In Guilin, many of the famous cormorants that used to catch up to 5 kilograms of fish each day on the Li River, have died (p. 18). In Beijing, the dumping of untreated oil waste in the Ba River has caused fires on more than one occasion (p. 19).

40. Ross, 1988, op. cit., p. 127, is confident that strategies based on market-oriented principles such as water commodification will, in the long run, prove to be much more effective in solving China's water shortage. For example, it is estimated that increasing the irrigation efficiency of north China's farmers by only 20 percent would generate as much water as promised by the hugely expensive and potentially damaging engineering schemes to transport water from the South of China (the Yangtze basin) to the North. See Liu Changming and L.J.C. Ma, 1983, "Interbasin Water Transfer in China," *Geographical Review* 73, No. 3 (July), pp. 253–270. An extensive debate was conducted throughout the early 1980s on the advisability and feasibility of huge new construction projects intended to create new water supplies, as well as on smoothing the flow of specific rivers. The most heated issue is concerned with the so-called Three Gorges Dam on the Yangtze River at Gezhouba. Although it has been billed as the "Impossible Dam," the Chinese have taken great pains to convince themselves, and the outside world, that the project is feasible. See, for example, Han Baocheng, 1986, "Three Gorges Project: Is it Feasible?" *Beijing Review*, No. 29 (July 21), pp. 16–20, and "The Benefits of the Three Gorges Project," *Beijing Review*, No. 30 (July 28), pp. 22–25. Outside evaluators of the project remained skeptical and unconvinced. See P. M. Fearnside, 1988, "China's Three Gorges Dam: 'Fatal' Project or Step Toward Modernization?" *World Development* 16, No. 5, pp. 615–30; and also B. Boxer, 1988, "China's Three Gorges Dam: Questions and Prospects," *China Quarterly*, No. 113 (March), pp. 94–108.

41. Ross, 1988, op. cit., p. 111.

42. Ma and Liu, op. cit., p. 114.

43. Ibid., pp. 111–12.

44. Ibid., p. 112.

45. D. M. Lampton, 1986, "Water Politics and Economic Change in China," pp. 387–406 in *China's Economy Looks Toward the Year 2000*, Vol. 1: *The Four Modernizations*, Selected papers submitted to the U.S. Congress, May 21 (Washington, D.C.: U.S. Government Printing Office).

46. D. M. Lampton, 1983, "Water Politics," *China Business Review*, July/August, pp. 10–17.

47. See, for example, C. W. Pannell and L.J.C. Ma, 1983, *China: The Geography of Development and Modernization* (London: V. H. Winston), pp. 7–8. For evidence of environmental pollution and policy in the Soviet Union, see T. Gustafson, 1981, *Reform in Soviet Politics: Lessons of Recent Policies on Land*

and Water (Cambridge, UK: Cambridge University Press).

48. Ross, 1988, op. cit., p. 137.

49. Pan, op. cit., p. 62.

50. Ross, 1988, op. cit., pp. 139–140.

51. L. Ross and M. A. Silk, 1985, "Post-Mao China and Environmental Protection: The Effects of Legal and Politico-Economic Reform," *UCLA Pacific Basin Law Journal* 4, No. 1–2 (Spring-Fall), pp. 63–89.

52. Ross, 1988, op. cit., pp. 142–43.

53. Ibid., p. 144. An example of the workings of environmental policy is provided by the efforts made to reduce pollution by steel factories. The Ministry of Metallurgical Industry has been conducting research and planning for its new plants to adopt advanced antipollution devices. The ministry will allocate 10 percent of the total investment in new blast furnaces to environmental protection. The ministry also reported that the amount of recycled water in steel plants has been rising yearly, reaching 79 percent by 1987. See "Steel Makers Bid for Less Pollution," *China Daily*, February 7, 1987. The overall achievements in the area of environmental protection have been described by Qu Geping, director of the State Environmental Protection Bureau. See his article "Urban Environmental Protection Well Under Way," *Beijing Review*, No. 2 (January 12, 1987), pp. 20–21. For a description of some of the attempts being made to pursue, arrest, and fine polluters, see Chaozhong Chen and Wang Geng, 1987, "Luoyang Arrests the 'Yellow Dragon,'" *Beijing Review*, No. 2 (January 12), pp. 22–23.

54. See Ross, 1988, op. cit., esp. Chap. 1, "Strategies for Implementation," pp. 1–24.

55. C. P. Cell, 1977, *Revolution at Work: Mobilizational Campaigns in China* (New York: Academic Press).

56. The campaign-like drive to plant trees continued throughout the 1980s. An announcement was made in 1987 describing a new program to plant 11.2 million trees in Beijing. Statistics from 324 cities showed that since the OTP program began, 89 cities have 20 percent or more of their open land covered with trees—an increase from 37 cities with that much in 1983. See "Volunteers Will Plant 11.2m. Trees in Beijing," *China Daily*, March 10, 1987. This renewed campaign resulted in a number of editorials and the appearance of Deng Xiaoping, eighty-two years old, at a "tree-planting" party in the capital that involved 1.4 million volunteers. Since 1981 over 5 billion trees were planted. See "Deng Joins Volunteers in 'Green' Campaign," *China Daily*, April 6, 1987.

57. D. D. Buck, 1986, "Changes in Chinese Urban Planning Since 1976," *Third World Planning Review* 6, No. 1, pp. 5–26.

58. As the purges continued throughout the summer of 1989, the news from China slowed to a trickle, but what there was confirmed the impression that intellectuals were increasingly feeling the weight of the new era of oppression. In August, for example, two of the country's leading social scientists at the Chinese Academy of Social Sciences in Beijing were ousted from the Party, and warrants were issued for their arrest. One of them, Yan Jiaqi, had reportedly escaped from China; the other, Bao Zunxin, had disappeared from sight completely after being arrested. See "China Expels Two Social Scientists From Party For Opposing Li Peng," *Schenectady Gazette*, August 10, 1989, p. 47.

59. L. J. Lundquist, 1980, *The Hare and the Tortoise: Clean Air Policies in the United States and Sweden* (Ann Arbor: University of Michigan Press).

CHAPTER 11

1. Wu Xinyu, 1980, "Explanatory Notes on the Marriage Law" (Excerpts—given at the Third Session of the Fifth National People's Congress, September 2). Reprinted in *New Trends in Chinese Marriage and the Family* (Beijing: Women of China, 1987), p. 17.

2. Quoted in D. Wilson, 1979, *The People's Emperor: Mao, A Biography of Mao Tse-tung* (New York: Lee Publishers Group, Inc.), p. 75.

3. For a discussion of Mao and his views about and behavior toward women, see R. Terrill, 1984, *The White-Boned Demon: A Biography of Madame Mao Zedong* (New York: William Morrow and Co.).

4. Quoted in Wilson, op. cit., p. 74.

5. Zhang Xianliang, 1988, *Half of Man Is Woman* (New York: W. W. Norton and Co.), p. 125.

6. Zhang Xinxin and Sang Ye, 1987, *Chinese Lives: An Oral History of Contemporary China* (New York: Pantheon Books), p. 138.

7. S. W. O'Sullivan, 1985, "Traditionalizing China's Modern Women," *Problems of Communism* 34, No. 6 (Nov./Dec.), pp. 58–69.

8. J. Stacey, 1983, *Patriarchy and Socialist Revolution in China* (Berkeley: University of California Press). This would of course also include Mao Zedong.

9. M. K. Whyte and W. L. Parish, 1984, *Urban Life in Contemporary China* (Chicago: University of Chicago Press), p. 198.

10. M. Wolf, 1985, *Revolution Postponed: Women in Contemporary China* (Stanford, Calif.: Stanford University Press), pp. 124–125. National data for 1987 showed that 26.8% of China's population over 12 years old were either illiterate or semiliterate; for females this figure was 38.1%, for males 15.8%. See *China Statistical Yearbook 1988* (Beijing: State Statistical Bureau of the PRC), p. 91. The statistics on women in college are from the same source, p. 793 (1988). Although women represent about 50% or more of the student population in low-status teachers' colleges, they form only 16.5% of

the students at the nation's top technological institution, Qinghua University in Beijing. Of 72 students sent from the China University for Science and Technology to the United States to study for PhDs, only 3 were women. Of China's first group of PhDs in 1983, only 1 (out of 18) was a woman. See B. Hooper, 1985, *Youth in China* (London: Penguin Books).

11. Wolf, op. cit., p. 128. It is important to point out that in China, the cost of educating a child includes the money needed to buy books and pay fees as well as the loss of potential income to the family. As we saw in Chapter 9, there is a marked fear that the economic reforms in the countryside will work to discourage parents from keeping their children, especially their daughters, at school. The tradition of "patrilocal exogamous" marriage customs, whereby girls go to live with their husbands' parents, has been continually supported by the Chinese government, both before and after 1949. This was one way of stabilizing local communities and rural family life, but it also helped to garner support for the Communists among the largely patriarchal structure of village life in the countryside. The tradition of girls moving away to marry perpetuated the rural habit of denying education to girls, thereby reducing their overall opportunities. This has been described in detail by K. A. Johnston, 1983, *Women, The Family and Peasant Revolution in China* (Chicago: University of Chicago Press). Johnston argued that the tradition of exporting girls supported "male supremacist attitudes, which favor sons over daughters, . . . community power structures which . . . discriminate against women and exclude women from public authority, and . . . family practices which continue to assign subordinate traditional roles and obligations to women" (p. 216).

12. Whyte and Parish, op. cit., p. 202, Table 23. For China as a whole, based on the 1% sample survey conducted in 1987, 69.2% of women over the age of 15 were currently in the labor force. See *China Statistical Yearbook 1988*, p. 92.

13. It is obvious that the public provision of child care, cooking, cleaning, and other household services has *not* emerged to liberate women from the drudgery of housework. Women in rural areas, for example, spend an average of 3.5 hours each day simply buying and preparing food. See E. Croll, 1983, *Chinese Women Since Mao* (Armonk, N.Y.: M. E. Sharpe, Inc.), p. 61. As Whyte and Parish, op. cit., showed, there is no evidence to suggest that Chinese men (husbands) are any more likely than men in other countries around the world to share the "burden" of housework with their wives (p. 217).

14. Whyte and Parish's data showed a fairly high inverse correlation between jobs with high status and high salaries and the proportion of the labor force that is female. In the top four occupations

in terms of salary (and presumably status), college professors, engineers and technicians, doctors, and government administrators, between 22% and 39% of the labor force were women (early 1980s data); percentages of women in the bottom four occupations were as follows: preschool teachers (100%), nursemaids and servants (93%), temporary workers (75%), and street cleaners (86%). See Whyte and Parish, op. cit., p. 204, Table 24. In addition, the jobs many women find are more likely to be in collective or private enterprises than in state enterprises. This has serious implications for women because these jobs are less likely to carry the collective benefits provided in the state sector, such as health care, insurance coverage, retirement benefits, and so on.

15. Wolf, op. cit, p. 66.

16. Whyte and Parish, op. cit., suggested that the average women's wage in capitalist countries ranges from 50 to 80% of men's wages; and in socialist countries it ranges from 63 to 84% (p. 207).

17. The official media made available in the English language are fond of printing stories about women who have done well in traditionally male strongholds; see for example the story about Wan Shaofen, who is Party secretary for Jiangxi Province: "Party's Woman at the Top," *China Daily*, March 3, 1987; and the story about a well-known woman pilot, Xue Wenshu: "Xue's 3000 Hours Aloft," *China Daily*, March 11, 1987. For an entire story written about successful women, see Tan Manni, 1987, "Vast Sky, Heavy Wings," *China Reconstructs*, March 1987, pp. 13–18.

18. Stacey, op. cit.

19. For a discussion of this, see O'Sullivan, op. cit.

20. Stacey believed that the CCP could only keep its support base among the vastly patriarchal countryside by keeping its promise not to alter the status quo in any significant way. She suggested that during the Great Leap Forward the CCP violated this unwritten pact with the male-dominated villagers by pushing forward too rapidly with antipatriarchal policies—particularly the socialization of domestic work and the concept of family production units. According to Stacey, opposition to these policies at the village level was one of the major causes of the disasters following the Great Leap (pp. 212–213). In spite of the strength of patriarchal traditions in the countryside, there are some historical examples in which women have temporarily been able to break free. In the silk factories of Guangdong Province, for example, the largely female workforce in the late nineteenth century offered some serious resistance to local (and Chinese) customs. Among their strategies were to refuse to join their husband's family after marriage and to pledge themselves to celibacy by binding themselves on their wedding night. After

two nights they were allowed to return home to live as spinsters. See A. Y. So, 1986, *The South China Silk District: Local Historical Transformation and World System Theory* (Albany: State University of New York Press), esp. pp. 123–131.

21. Stacey, op. cit., p. 256. Hooper has suggested that the absence of a strong women's movement in China is a result of the weakness of the Women's Federation, which was intended to look after women's interests, but which actually does little more than parrot the government's line on women's issues. Basically the CCP believes that male-female inequality is not a gender issue at all but a class issue, and as class differences are eliminated, so will gender differences. As a result the government condemns independent feminist organizations as "women's rights movements of the bourgeoisie." See Hooper, op. cit., p. 111.

22. Wolf, op. cit., p. 261. The contributors to a book of personal stories related by Chinese women in 1988 reinforced this depressing conclusion. The 1982 census in China showed that 70 percent of illiterate or barely literate Chinese were female, and the gap appears to be increasing. Although girls are told to study hard at school, many articles in the press promote "scientific conclusions that boys are superior to girls intellectually." Three out of five couples in the countryside still meet through matchmakers, and the phenomenon of childhood betrothals is reappearing. These reports demonstrated that many of the oppressive and patriarchal aspects of traditional Chinese family life have not only survived, but have taken on modern, respectable forms. See E. Honig and G. Hershatter, 1988, *Personal Voices: Chinese Women in the 1980's* (Stanford, Calif.: Stanford University Press).

23. Wolf, op. cit., p. 271.

24. Ibid., p. 261.

25. Lei Jieqiang, 1987, Preface, *New Trends in Chinese Marriages and the Family* (Beijing: Women of China), p. i.

26. See Wolf, op. cit.

27. Lei, op. cit.

28. R. Sidel and V. W. Sidel, 1982, *The Health of China* (Boston: Beacon Press), see Chap. 6, "The Family and Child Care: The First Collective," pp. 125–149.

29. Whyte and Parish, op. cit., reported that among their 831 married respondents from Hong Kong (emigrés from the PRC), the average age of those married before 1949 was 22.6 for the men and 19.6 for the women; the ages for those married in the 1970s were 28.5 for the men and 24.4 for the women. See p. 113, Table 19. The general explanation for the rising age of marriage as countries develop involves the increase in school enrollments, which delays earning capacity; a greater desire among young people to travel and experience independent single life; and the increasing demand

for labor in the industrializing countryside. In a survey conducted by the Chinese Academy of Social Sciences in 1982 among 5,057 urban families, the proportion of women married before they were 17 dropped very sharply, from 27–30 percent before 1949, to 1–4 percent after 1949. See Wu Benxue, 1987, "The Urban Family in Flux," pp. 23–36 in *New Trends in Chinese Marriages and the Family*, p. 26.

30. For example, Article 4 of the 1981 Marriage Law states: "Marriage must be based on the complete willingness of the two parties. Neither party shall use compulsion and no third party is allowed to interfere." See Marriage Law of the People's Republic of China, Reprinted in *New Trends in Chinese Marriages and the Family*, pp. 3–14.

31. Whyte and Parish, op. cit., p. 119. This may not vary much from other countries in the world, of course, because it is not at all uncommon for people to be introduced by a third party. In this case, however, there is a well-established custom of matchmaking in China, and "introductions are usually meant to lead to marriage." Data from a survey in rural Anhui Province in 1979 demonstrated that not much had changed in the way courtship was structured in the Chinese countryside. Of more than 15,000 marriages, 10% had been arranged by parents without consent; 75% had been arranged with consent; and only 15% were arranged totally independently by the couple in question. Another survey also showed that most rural weddings, in spite of the intention of the new laws, were still extremely expensive affairs. In rural Hebei Province it was costing a man Y 3,000 on average to furnish the new home, and another Y 1,000 to pay for the wedding. The average rural income in the province at that time was Y 50 per month. See Sidel and Sidel, op. cit., p. 130. A report in the official *Beijing Daily* newspaper in 1987 reported a threefold increase in wedding expenses over the previous three years. A survey of 55 newlyweds showed that an average of nearly Y 6,000 ($1,600) was spent on weddings in 1986, more than half of which covered the purchase of sofas, televisions, refrigerators, and other household items. The paper's editorial comment criticized this trend as evidence of "feudal" behavior: "taking into consideration the present level of income and spending power of most people, it is nothing else but extravagance to spend thousands of yuan on weddings." See "Wedding Expenses Triple in 3 Years," *China Daily*, February 11, 1987.

32. There is also still a very strong feeling that couples should remain chaste until they marry. This is partly the result of circumstance, of course, with relatively few private places where young people can be alone together: there are no cars, no "drive-ins," and very few bars and "discos." A worldwide survey conducted in 1988, for example, shows that in China chastity among future

mates is considered to be more important than anywhere else in the world, with the possible exception of Iran. On a scale of 0–3, with 3 meaning "indispensable," Chinese respondents scored 2.5 (men) and 2.6 (women); compared to 0.9 and 0.5 in the United States. See A. Sachs, 1989, "The Delights of the Mating Game," *Time*, May 1, pp. 66–67.

33. Chen Jiangong, 1985, "Phoenix Eyes," pp. 162–185 in Ke Yunlu, Zhang Xianliang, and others, *Prize Winning Stories from China, 1980–1981*, English text ed. W. C. Chau (Beijing: Foreign Language Press), p. 167. It is important to consider the growing use of matchmaking agencies, which have sprung up in almost all cities in China in recent years. One such agency in Shanghai uses videotape, costing Y 13, in which women agree to have themselves photographed, so that prospective matches can be made with suitable men. This reflects the obvious sexism in mate choice, as no videotape service is available for women to view men. It also reflects the reality of marriage demographics in Shanghai, where there are more women looking for spouses than there are men available. See "Singles Use Video Tapes to Get Mate," *China Daily*, December 3, 1987. The article noted that 100 marriage agencies have been established since 1980 in Shanghai, and an estimated 120,000 singles were having difficulty finding a spouse.

34. Whyte and Parish, op. cit., p. 127. See also T. B. Gold, 1985, "After Comradeship: Personal Relations in China Since the Cultural Revolution," *China Quarterly*, No. 104 (December), pp. 657–675. Gold described some of the anecdotal evidence of the increasingly large "dowries" being exacted in the 1980s.

35. Wu Benxue, op. cit, p. 31.

36. Similar results were reported by Whyte and Parish's Hong Kong respondents, but with some important differences. The women were in general far less concerned than the men with "good looks"— for them the most important variables were (1) their spouse's income potential; (2) his class label and political record; (3) his family income, housing situation, and family connection; (4) his urban (rather than rural) registration; (5) his overseas connections (especially important to Hong Kongers); (6) a pleasing personality; and (7) good looks (pp. 127–128). For men, however, "good looks" were ranked second most important overall.

37. See Gold, op. cit.

38. Dong Xijian, 1987, "Changing Conceptions of the Ideal Mate," pp. 60–66 in *New Trends in Chinese Marriages and the Family*; see pp. 63 and 65.

39. Wang Meng, 1988, "Anecdotes of Chairman Maimaiti," pp. 152–163 in Zhu Hong (trans.), *The Chinese Western: Short Fiction from Today's China* (New York: Available Press).

40. Wang Anyi, 1988, "And the Rain Patters On," pp. 25–38 in *Lapse of Time* (San Francisco: China Books and Periodicals), p. 27. The CCP has attempted at various times, as ludicrous as it may seem to Westerners, to define "love" in socialist terms and has even denounced "bourgeois" love as individualistic and overly self-centered. As Hooper, op. cit., has noted, one of the pronouncements read as follows: "Socialist love . . . should not be based on strange feelings in one's heart or flights of passion, but on common political attitudes and interests. . . . And personal feelings must always be subordinated to the development of socialist new China, even if this meant separation from the man or woman one loved" (p. 176).

41. Wang Anyi, op. cit., p. 27.

42. L. Pan, 1988, *The New Chinese Revolution* (Chicago: Contemporary Books), p. 177. When asked whether China's prim attitude toward sex is a remnant of "feudal" tendencies, one student answered, "No. . . . It is a socialist attitude. Dissolute behavior between the sexes is a phenomenon of capitalist society." Quoted in Hooper, op. cit., p. 183, from Zhang Xian's story, "The Corner Forsaken By Love," in H. F. Siu and Z. Stern (eds.), 1983, *Mao's Harvest: Voices from China's New Generation* (New York: Oxford University Press).

43. Pan, op. cit., p. 176. Pan did note, however, that there was journalistic evidence of higher rates of illegitimate births, sexual offenses, rape, and even prostitution in China's cities.

44. Sha Yin, 1987, "A Survey on Marriage and the Family in Beijing," pp. 106–119 in *New Trends in Chinese Marriages and the Family*; see pp. 118–119.

45. Zhang Jie's story "Love Must Not Be Forgotten" dealt with the nearly taboo topic of marital infidelity, although in this story the couple in question had never even held hands. The issue of loveless marriages, arranged by parents in the prerevolutionary era, came to a head after the new marriage law because couples were then free to get divorced. In another story, "The Ark," Zhang described the constant surveillance and oppression experienced by three divorced women who lived together and were constantly accused by vicious neighbors of immoral behavior. See pp. 113–202 in *Love Must Not Be Forgotten* (San Francisco: China Books and Periodicals, 1986). According to Lynn Pan, in spite of the new law allowing divorce, the official disapproval resulted in less than half of the petitions ending up with a divorce. The rest of the couples were talked into to a settlement of some sort, usually as the result of mediation (op. cit., p. 183). For an interesting perspective on divorce in China and a look at the way the divorce court handles cases that come before it, see T. K. Haraven, 1987, "Divorce, Chinese Style," *Atlantic Monthly*, April, pp. 70–76. See also K. S. Kerpen,

1987, "Divorce and Custody in China," *U.S. China Review* 11, No. 4 (July-August), pp. 5–8.

46. Zhang Xian, 1987, "The Widow," *China Now*, No. 122 (Autumn), pp. 31–35, quote on p. 33.

47. Pan, op. cit., pp. 182–183.

48. R. Conroy, 1987, "Patterns of Divorce in China," *Australian Journal of Chinese Affairs*, No. 17 (January), pp. 53–75. Conroy estimated that the divorce rate in China in the late 1970s and 1980s was on the vicinity of 3–4 percent; the estimate in the United States is close to 50 percent.

49. Ibid., p. 73.

50. Whyte and Parish, op. cit., pp. 191–194.

51. Ibid., p. 194.

52. Zhang Xianliang, op. cit., p. 267.

53. Ma Lizhen, 1989, "Women: The Debate on Jobs vs. Homemaking," *China Reconstructs* 38, No. 3, pp. 66–68; quote from p. 68 (a letter written to the author, by Jian Shufan, a woman).

54. Ma estimated that 20 million employees, 60 percent of them women, have paid jobs but little work to do (ibid., p. 67).

55. Ibid., p. 68. Efforts to make enterprises more efficient are also currently working against women because officials are simply choosing not to hire women in key positions. See O'Sullivan, op. cit., p. 65.

56. Ma, op. cit., p. 68.

57. The HRS threatens the population policy in a number of ways. The amount of land allocated to each family is determined by family size, which encourages parents to "go against the plan." In addition local cadres have been neglecting their birth-control duties to take care of their own plots in an attempt to reap some of the benefits of the economic reforms. The HRS also diminishes the pool of local welfare funds, which means less funds are available locally to pay the rewards to compliant (one-child) families. It is also much more difficult to extract penalties from deviant families under HRS, in comparison to the old work-point system— because it is difficult to determine incomes that are earned largely outside the collective unit. For a discussion of these issues, see T. Whyte, 1987, "Implementing the One-Child Population Program in Rural China: National Goals and Local Politics," pp. 284–317 in D. M. Lampton (ed.), *Policy Implementation in Post-Mao China* (Berkeley: University of California Press), esp. pp. 308–309. There is some evidence that the successful implementation of the HRS is associated with greater son preference. For example, the male-to-female survival rate for children appears to be highest in those parts of China that have implemented the HRS most completely, for example, in Anhui Province, where the male-to-female infant ratio is 111:100. See O'Sullivan, op. cit., pp. 67–68.

58. O'Sullivan, op. cit., p. 69.

59. Wolf, op. cit., pp. 268–269. The hidden impacts of this new situation could be enormous.

Young women (daughters) will be less able to go out to meet people, which threatens to increase the parental role in the area of matchmaking. The safety rules of the workplace may be abandoned in the home, and women could be seriously overworked with no one to report their husbands to. Urban and rural women alike are also much more likely nowadays to work at home, in the rapidly growing "putting out" system, in which they contract with local enterprises or cooperatives to work at home. This could result in women becoming increasingly isolated from the wider community and more subject to family (male) authority, in addition to the threat of working under "sweatshop" conditions, with no adequate fringe benefits and the normal protections of the state workplace.

60. D. Davin, 1988, "The Implications of Contract Agriculture for the Employment and Status of Chinese Peasant Women," pp. 137–146 in S. Feuchtwang, A. Hussain, and T. Pairault (eds.), *Transforming China's Economy in the Eighties*, Vol. 1: *The Rural Sector, Welfare and Employment* (Boulder, Colo.: Westview Press), p. 140.

61. Ibid., p. 140.

62. A survey conducted in 1983 found that only 28 percent of the current male university students wanted their wives to be university graduates, compared to 80 percent of the women in universities who wanted their husbands to be university graduates. See Hooper, op. cit., p. 109.

63. M. Palmer, 1988, "China's New Inheritance Law: Some Preliminary Observations," pp. 169–197 in Feuchtwang, Hussain, and Pairault, op. cit.

64. See Whyte, op. cit.

65. Davin, op. cit., p. 146.

66. It is putting it mildly to suggest that the concatenation of these two policies is "an extraordinary example of the failure to make connections."

CHAPTER 12

1. Quoted (from an issue of *Youth Daily*) in T. Terzani, 1986, *Behind the Forbidden Door: Travels in China* (London: Allen and Unwin), p. 52.

2. S. Pinch, 1985, *Cities and Services: The Geography of Collective Consumption* (London: Routledge and Kegan Paul).

3. J. LeGrand and J. Robinson, 1984, *Privatization and the Welfare State* (London: Allen and Unwin).

4. M. K. Whyte and W. L. Parish, 1984, *Urban Life in Contemporary China* (Chicago: University of Chicago Press), p. 57.

5. E. F. Vogel, 1969, *Canton Under Communism: Programs and Politics in a Provincial Capital, 1949–1968* (Cambridge, Mass.: Harvard University Press), p. 46.

6. Ibid., p. 44.

7. F. Butterfield, 1983, *China: Alive in the Bitter Sea* (Toronto: Bantam Books), p. 108.

8. Whyte and Parish, op. cit., p. 102.

9. Cheng Naishan, 1989, "No. 2 and No. 4 of Shanghai," pp. 1–116 in *The Piano Tuner* (San Francisco: China Books and Periodicals), p. 84.

10. Butterfield, op. cit., p. 102.

11. P. Theroux, 1988, *Riding the Iron Rooster: By Train Through China* (New York: Ivy Books), p. 275.

12. An editorial in *China Now*, for example, which was published in London before the 1989 demonstrations, predicted some of the later events. The major problem appeared to be the grimness of the economic picture throughout 1988, exacerbated by skyrocketing inflation rates and energy shortages. The editorial reported on several calls for Zhao Ziyang to resign, presumably for his role in creating the economic crisis. The influx of unemployed peasants, for example, 2.5 million of them in Guangdong coastal cities alone, seriously stretched the employment and service capabilities of many cities. Rising crime rates have been reported, as well as new record levels of unemployment. See "Sinofile," *China Now*, No. 129 (Summer 1989), pp. 3–5.

13. For a discussion of quality of life studies, see P. Knox, 1988, *Urban Social Geography: An Introduction* (London: Wiley).

14. These data were gathered from State Statistical Bureau of the PRC; see *China: Urban Statistics, 1985* (London: Longman Group, Ltd.). The data presented here do not of course necessarily mean that the people in the largest cities have better access to such services or that they make use of or appreciate them any more than residents of smaller cities. We also have no indication of the quality of the services in question—it could be, for example, that the greater level of usage in larger cities may result in lower quality or slower access (e.g., longer lines, worse roads, buses in worse condition, etc.). It is also impossible to locate comparable statistics for rural areas, but in general it is assumed that many of the services and facilities in question are likely to be less available than they are in cities. See, for example, R.J.R. Kirkby, 1985, *Urbanization in China: Town and Country in a Developing Economy, 1949–2000* AD (New York: Columbia University Press).

15. For a discussion of recent urban population trends, see S. S. Goldstein, 1985, *Urbanization in China: New Insights From the 1982 Census*, Papers of the East-West Population Institute, No. 93, July (Honolulu: University of Hawaii).

16. Among the best examples are Zhang Xinxin and Sang Ye, 1987, *Chinese Lives: An Oral History of Contemporary China* (New York: Pantheon Books); and E. Honig and G. Hershatter, 1988, *Personal Voices: Chinese Women in the 1980's* (Stanford, Calif.: Stanford University Press).

17. S. Peck (ed.), 1985, *Halls of Jade, Walls of Stone: Women in China Today* (New York: Franklin Watts), p. 266.

18. Cheng, op. cit., p. 55.

19. It has been estimated that in China the ratio of people to buses is on the order of 2,640:1, compared to a worldwide average of around 1,000:1; see R. Kojimo, 1987, *Urbanization and Urban Problems in China* (Tokyo: Institute of Developing Economies, Occasional Paper Series No. 22). The major problem with the bus situation in most of China's large cities is the decrepit state of the buses themselves. The estimated depreciation time for buses in China is twenty-seven years, which is about five times longer than in Japan and the United States. The low fares, offered as a government subsidy, hardly even contribute to operating expenses. The quotation is from Cheng Naishan's story "No. 2 and No. 4 of Shanghai," in op. cit.

20. Whyte and Parish, op. cit., p. 99.

21. Ibid.

22. Zhang and Sang, op. cit., p. 156.

23. Li Ping, 1987, "Opinion Poll: How People Feel About Urban Reform," *China Reconstructs*, January, pp. 55–57.

24. Sheng Huochu and Liu Hongfa, 1986, "Resurvey of Workers' Living Standards in Tianjin," *China Reconstructs*, December, pp. 29–32.

25. "Polls Help to Improve Tianjin," *China Daily*, January 8, 1987.

26. "Maids and Families Helped," *China Daily*, June 15, 1987; see also "Beijing Families in Search for More 'Official' House Help," *China Daily*, February 17, 1987.

27. "Builders' Life on the Move," *China Daily*, January 12, 1987. The lives of itinerant construction workers are extremely hard. They usually work long hours, moving wherever they have to, and often they live on the building sites in small crude houses that are no better than shacks. Those with families have particular problems without residence cards, and their children are often poorly treated in the local schools. Other groups of itinerant workers include tailors, many of them from Jiangsu Province, who are drawn into cities all over China, but especially in the north. See "Tailor's Life Suits Jiangsu Native," *China Daily*, January 13, 1987.

28. "Zhejiang Girl Cobblers," *China Daily*, February 17, 1987.

29. "Sinofile," *China Now*, op cit., p. 5.

30. "Let Them Eat Cash: China Tries to Scrap Food-Price Controls," *Far Eastern Economic Review*, May 26, 1988, pp. 72–73. The inflation of food prices throughout 1985 and 1986 continued into 1987. Vegetable prices, for example, increased by more than 25% in the summer months and by more than 50% in the winter months. Poultry and egg prices increased at an average of 20% in 1987, and the urban retail price index rose by 10%. The trend continued into 1988, and in the first quarter

food prices rose by 24%, with vegetable prices going up by more than 50%.

31. T. M. Cheung, 1988, "Road Works Ahead: Traffic Congestion Is Choking China's Cities," *Far Eastern Economic Review* 141, No. 27 (July 7), p. 79. The demand for travel among the Chinese, and particularly among tourists, with such antiquated road systems, slow and decrepit buses, and a virtual absence of urban trains, has meant a bonanza for taxis in China's cities. See, for example, "Guangzhou's 6,000 Taxis Hustle for Fares," *China Daily*, March 7, 1987. Orville Schell estimated that there were 14,000 cabs in Beijing, 3,000 more than in New York City. See O. Schell, 1988, *Discos and Democracy: China in the Throes of Reform* (New York: Pantheon Books), p. 65.

32. It was estimated that Beijing's vehicles have expanded 100 times since 1949, and Shanghai's 13-fold, compared to a 12- and 5-fold increase in the total road mileage in each city. See Cheung, op. cit., p. 79.

33. "Traffic Rethink Needed," *China Daily*, March 31, 1987.

34. Guo Zhangshi, 1986, "Road Death Toll Rises 20 Percent in 1985," *China Daily*, April 8. The rising rates have been blamed on growing populations, including the influx of rural migrants; streets that are too narrow; too many bicycles; poor driving habits; and a shortage of "road traffic controllers."

35. "Vehicle Increase Causes More Accidents," *China Daily*, April 10, 1987.

36. Schell, op. cit., p. 66. The appearance of fleets of Japanese taxis (commonplace on the streets of Guangzhou) and even Mercedes and Cadillac limousines aimed at the high end of the tourist market has symbolized the end of a chapter in China's recent history. In the not-too-distant past virtually the only cars on the streets of Beijing were the chunky old Red Flag limousines that were domestically made and had the Chinese characters for "Red Flag" written in Mao's own hand affixed to their rear trunks!

37. Hu Sigang, 1986, "City Bids to Fight Garbage Problem," *China Daily*, December 11.

38. Shen Ji and Si Jiuye, 1986, "Making Mountains Out of Rubbish," *China Daily*, April 24.

39. Theroux, op. cit., p. 389. The Beijing Sanitation Bureau pays Y 2,500 for one mu of land to dump garbage on (one-fifteenth of a hectare). In 1985 the bureau spent Y 150,000 for land for its dumps. Obviously the loss of arable land in the suburbs is a major concern, as is the pollution of local air and water sources. These problems have prompted a considerable amount of research into viable options to dumping, including incineration, biodegradation, and irradiation treatment. The problem is that 50 percent of China's waste tends to be inorganic and is therefore very difficult to dispose of. The only solution appears to be the landfill method, which will cost an estimated Y

300 million, a staggering amount in comparison to the bureau's current budget of Y 40 million—already one-third of the city's total maintenance expenses (see Shen and Si, op. cit.).

40. Whyte and Parish, op. cit., p. 25.

41. E. M. Bjorklund, 1986, "The Danwei: Socio-Spatial Characteristics of Work Units in China's Urban Society," *Economic Geography* 62, No. 1 (January), pp. 19–29.

42. A. F. Thurston, 1988, *Enemies of the People: The Ordeal of the Intellectuals in China's Great Cultural Revolution* (Cambridge, Mass.: Harvard University Press), see pp. 124–125.

43. For purposes of maintaining public support, most charges for urban services have remained extremely low. Bus fares in Shanghai, for example, have now been 4, 7, and 10 fen for several decades (10 fen = 0.1 yuan, 3.8 yuan [recently raised to 4.7 yuan] = U.S. $1). Tickets to urban parks, zoos, museums, and galleries cost next to nothing, a few fen (but usually several yuan for "foreigners"). It has been estimated that what is collected at the gates of such entertainment facilities does not cover even 1 percent of the wages for the workers involved. See Tian Binjxin, 1988, "A Tragicomedy Concerning Residence Cards," *Nexus: China in Focus*, Winter, pp. 24–26.

44. For a detailed discussion of the significance of urban residence cards, see L. T. White, 1977, "Deviance, Modernization, Rations, and Household Registers in Urban China," pp. 151–171 in A. A. Wilson, S. L. Greenblatt, and R. W. Wilson (eds.), *Deviance and Social Control in Chinese Society* (New York: Praeger).

45. To meet the needs of the "floating population" of Guangzhou (those without residency cards, estimated at 880,000 in 1988), an investment increase estimated to be between Y 4.4 and Y 6.2 billion is needed, along with a daily increase of 440,000 kilowatts of electricity, 270,000 tons of tap water, and 1,000 tons of grain and vegetables. See Tian, op. cit., p. 26.

46. Ibid.

47. As we noted in Chapter 8, however, ongoing attempts are being made to encourage both enterprises and people to move to medium-sized and smaller cities, where urban services are cheaper to provide and less in demand. Of course, as we saw earlier, such services also tend to be less plentiful in smaller cities. The irony of this situation is that in spite of their great desire to obtain residency cards, both urban and rural dwellers alike realize the mixed blessing the cards represent. The card ties a family down to a specific city, making any voluntary movement, for example, to seek a new job or to get married, extremely difficult. Nevertheless, most city residents realize they must acquire a card and hold onto it at all costs. The only exceptions are some of the new breed of peasants involved in commodity production in the country-

side, who are free to go where they please in search of profitable work. Included in this category are the itinerant "tribes" of construction workers, cobblers, housemaids, and tailors that have sprung up in most cities across China. See ibid.

48. Ibid., p. 24.

49. Cheng, op. cit., p. 46.

50. D. Bonavia, 1989, *The Chinese* (rev. ed.) (London: Penguin), p. 24.

51. Luo Fu, 1980, "City Dwellers and the Neighborhood Committee," *Beijing Review*, No. 44 (November 3), pp. 19–25, quote from p. 20.

52. According to a *China Daily* report, Beijing neighborhood committees provided 13,600 "clues," which led to the solution of 1,500 criminal cases in 1986. Interestingly, however, the same article noted that more than half of the committees had never reported any criminal cases, implying the importance of prevention and mediation activities. See "Committees Play Vital Roles in Urban Areas," *China Daily*, March 13, 1987.

53. Luo, op. cit., p. 21.

54. Quoted in B. Hooper, 1985, *Youth in China* (London: Penguin), p. 141.

55. It is one thing to have such information of course, but it is not known to what extent it is used to intervene on behalf of unfortunate family members. The evidence is widespread that spouse abuse remains at an unacceptably high level in China. See Whyte and Parish, op. cit., Chap. 7, pp. 195–228. Some of the benefits of neighborhood committee work in this area are illustrated by the results of surveys conducted in specific locations. See, for example, "Neighborhood Findings," *China Daily*, March 10, 1987.

56. E. Croll, 1985, "The Single-Child Family in Beijing: A First-Hand Report," pp. 190–232 in E. Croll, D. Davin, and P. Kane (eds.), *China's One Child Family Policy* (London: Macmillan).

57. Ibid., p. 209.

58. Ibid.

CHAPTER 13

1. C. Thubron, 1987, *Behind the Wall: A Journey Through China* (London: Heinemann), p. 191.

2. S. Wittwer, Yu Yontai, Sun Hau, and Wang Lianzheng, 1987, *Feeding a Billion: Frontiers of Chinese Agriculture* (East Lansing: Michigan State University Press).

3. E. M. Bjorklund, 1987, "Olericulture and Urban Development in China," *Tijdschrift voor Economische en Sociale Geografie* 78, No. 1, pp. 2–15. The data from which Table 13.1 is constructed show that the percentage of "agricultural residents" tends to be much higher in China's "smaller" cities. For example, for the 31 cities larger than 500,000, the average is 39%, ranging from 5% in Urumqi to 71% in Zibo. See p. 5.

4. See G. W. Skinner, 1978, "Vegetable Supply and Marketing in Chinese Cities," *China Quarterly*, No. 76 (December), pp. 733–793.

5. Thubron, op. cit., pp. 62–63. As we saw in earlier chapters, however, on balance the average incomes earned in the countryside did not keep pace with those in the city. The only way, therefore, to reduce rural-to-urban migration was to prohibit it—mainly by limiting the availability of food rationing cards and urban registration cards.

6. R.J.R. Kirkby, 1985, *Urbanization in China: Town and Country in a Developing Economy, 1949–2000 AD* (New York: Columbia University Press).

7. Bjorklund, op. cit., p. 12.

8. The interactions could involve food moving from the periphery to the core, and reverse flows, for example, technology and machinery moving from the city to the countryside. See Wu Chung-Tong and D. F. Ip, 1980, "Structural Transformation and Spatial Equity," pp. 56–88 in C. K. Leung and N. Ginsburg (eds.), *China: Urbanization and National Development* (Chicago: University of Chicago, Department of Geography Research Paper No. 196).

9. E. Croll, 1983, *The Family Rice Bowl: Food and Domestic Economy in China* (Geneva: United Nations Research Institute for Social Development).

10. See J. H. Hawkins, 1982, "Shanghai: An Exploratory Report on Food for the City," *Geo Journal*, suppl. issue, No. 41, pp. 83–98.

11. In a Chongqing street market, for example, the author came across an entire open dormitory area, undercover, where transporters and sellers from the surrounding countryside sleep for the night on rollaway beds or tables, rising early the next morning to sell their wares.

12. A. Watson, 1988, "The Reform of Agricultural Marketing in China Since 1978," *China Quarterly*, No. 113 (March), pp. 1–28.

13. Ibid., pp. 20–21.

14. Croll, op. cit., pp. 228–231.

15. Watson, op. cit., p. 12.

16. Between 1978 and 1986 the annual per capita expenditure on food in China almost doubled, from Y 147 to Y 274. Consumption of all foodstuffs rose, but major increases were observed in the amount of protein eaten. For example, meat consumption rose from 8.1 to 16.1 kilograms per capita per year; milk consumption tripled from 1.0 kgs to 3.0; eggs from 2.0 to 5.3 kgs; and fish from 3.5 to 5.4 kgs. The amount of fruit consumed doubled, from 6.8 to 12.5 kgs. There is a growing concern about the health consequences of these trends; for example, the Chinese are now eating far more fat than they have in the past (in addition to the meat, oil consumption increased from 1.6 to 5.2 kgs per person); and sugar consumption almost doubled. See Mei Fung, 1989, "Changing the National Diet Structure," *China Reconstructs* 38, No. 3 (March), pp. 44–46.

17. Watson, op. cit. p. 14.

18. Ibid., p. 17.

19. Ibid.

20. G. W. Skinner (ed.), 1977, *The City in Late Imperial China* (Stanford, Calif.: Stanford University Press).

21. Watson, op. cit., p. 16.

22. See "Selling Flowers," pp. 261–64 in Zhang Xinxin and Sang Ye, 1987, *Chinese Lives: An Oral History of Contemporary China* (New York: Pantheon Books).

23. Thubron, op. cit., p. 133.

24. L. Pan, 1988, *The New Chinese Revolution* (Chicago: Contemporary Books), p. 113.

25. N. R. Lardy, 1983, *Agriculture in China's Modern Economic Development* (Cambridge, UK: Cambridge University Press).

26. K. R. Walker, 1984, *Food Grain Procurement and Consumption in China* (Cambridge: Cambridge University Press); A. Piazza, 1986, *Food Consumption and Nutritional Status in the PRC* (Boulder, Colo.: Westview Press); and Croll, op. cit.

27. B. Stone, 1986, "Chinese Socialism's Record on Food and Agriculture," *Problems of Communism* 35, No. 5 (Sept./Oct.), pp. 63–72. Of course this statement ignores or at least underestimates the evidence that from 10 to 20 million peasants may have died in the Chinese countryside as a result of starvation and undernutrition after the Great Leap Forward in the early 1960s. For a discussion of this issue, see M. Selden, 1988, *The Political Economy of Chinese Socialism* (Armonk, N.Y.: M. E. Sharpe), esp. Chaps. 1 and 3.

28. Pan, op. cit., p. 116.

29. Croll, op. cit.

30. C. Aubert, 1988, "China's Food Take-Off?" pp. 101–136 in S. Feuchtwang, A. Hussain, and T. Pairault (eds.), *Transforming China's Economy in the Eighties*, Vol. 1: *The Rural Sector, Welfare and Employment* (Boulder, Colo.: Westview Press).

31. Ibid., p. 121.

32. Ibid.

33. Ibid., p. 131, Table 4.18.

34. P. Howard, 1988, *Breaking the Iron Rice-Bowl: Prospects for Socialism in China's Countryside* (Armonk, N.Y.: M. E. Sharpe).

35. "Prolonged Drought Hits Spring Crops, Impedes Transport," *China Daily*, March 21, 1987, p. 1.

36. See "It's Been a Better Year for Grain," *China Daily*, December 16, 1986, p. 4; see also B. L. Reynolds, 1989, "The Chinese Economy in 1988," pp. 27–48 in A. J. Kane (ed.), *China Briefing, 1989* (Boulder, Colo.: Westview Press).

37. Piazza, op. cit.

38. E. B. Vermeer, 1982, "Income Differentials in Rural China," *China Quarterly*, No. 89 (March), pp. 1–33.

39. A. Hussain and S. Feuchtwang, 1988, "The People's Livelihood and the Incidence of Poverty," pp. 36–76 in Feuchtwang, Hussain, and Pairault, op. cit., p. 41.

40. Ibid., p. 63, Table 2.4.

41. "Merging of Farms Raises Efficiency," *China Daily*, December 18, 1986, p. 3.

42. Hussain and Feuchtwang, op. cit., p. 63.

43. This is a direct quotation from Lin Zhiqun, in R. Kojimo, 1987, *Urbanization and Urban Problems in China* (Tokyo: Institute of Developing Economies, Occasional Paper Series No. 22), p. 38.

44. D. R. Phillips and A.G.O. Yeh, 1987, "The Provision of Housing and Social Services in China's Special Economic Zones," *Environment and Planning C: Government and Policy* 5, pp. 447–468. It is useful to remember that there are still an estimated 35 million Chinese people living in caves, ranging from the luxurious to the squalid. See, for example, "Living in a Cave Has Its Own Charm," *China Daily*, August 19, 1987. In many cases cave dwellers reckon that their homes are larger than the average city dwellers' homes and easier to keep warm in the winter and cool in the summer.

45. R. Murphey, 1980, *The Fading of the Maoist Vision: City and Country in China's Development* (New York: Methuen).

46. The housing that was owned privately was usually old and generally a remnant from before Liberation. Much of it has been passed from parents to children and it does not generally enter into a commodity-like housing market. Kirkby indicated that the average monthly rental for private housing varied between .10 and .14 of a yuan per square meter of floor space, compared to 0.08 to 0.12 for houses owned by municipal housing bureaus, and less than 0.08 yuan per month for houses owned by production units and enterprises. It is important for Westerners to avoid the trap of assuming that the lack of luxury or apparent comfort in the Chinese home necessarily assumes a lack of attachment to or affection for the home. For most outsiders the typical "room" that is home to many Chinese people appears to be cramped, hopelessly ill equipped, and relatively unadorned by such luxuries as carpets or wallpaper. Many young families with only one room have to cook in the hallways or on the balconies and share toilets and even water faucets. By Western standards such homes would be intolerable, but it is clear that real attachments can develop even to the most basic spaces. See R.J.R. Kirkby, 1988, "Urban Housing Policy After Mao," pp. 227–244 in Feuchtwang, Hussain, and Pairault, op. cit.

47. T. Terzani, 1986, *Behind the Forbidden Door: Travels in China* (London: Allen and Unwin), p. 53.

48. Whyte and Parish, op. cit.

49. D.S.G. Goodman, 1981, *Beijing Street Voices: The Poetry and Politics of China's Democracy Movement* (London: Marion Boyars), p. 94. According to Goodman the main target of this poem was

Wang Dongxing, vice chairman of the Chinese Communist party at that time, and the person in charge of the Administrative Offices in Zhongnanhai—the Politburo and State Council headquarters—where the nation's leaders were reportedly living comfortably and in spacious surroundings. This of course was the source of the poet's discontent, in that it symbolized the corruption and inequality in contemporary China. Qin Shihuang, China's first emperor, was justifiably considered to be a tyrant, the creator of the first totalitarian state. We can assume that the poet implied an analogy here with Mao Zedong, who was often referred to as the "people's emperor." See D. Wilson, 1979, *The People's Emperor: A Biography of Mao Zedong* (New York: Lee Publishing Co.).

50. Kirkby, 1988, op. cit. Although these sorts of differences were persistent, there is little evidence that class variations in housing standards in China had any spatial pattern to them, as they typically might in a North American city, with high quality and more spacious housing in the suburbs and poverty in the city centers. In the socialist cities of Eastern Europe, housing inequalities have also been persistent, and although there is a spatial pattern to such inequality, it is generally not as simply observable as it usually is in capitalist cities. In the Chinese city, by comparison, housing inequality was more likely to occur at the microscale, and in the confines of each individual work unit, for example, where the top administrators and party officials lived. In recent years there had also been a boom in private-housing construction, especially in the small towns and rural counties administratively attached to the larger cities, as a result of new levels of affluence among peasants and "specialized households." Many peasants have built themselves relatively luxurious homes that now stand as examples of conspicious consumption for others to see and admire. See, for example, O. Schell, 1984, *To Get Rich Is Glorious: China in the Eighties* (New York: Pantheon Books). There is also some evidence of housing inequality emerging as a result of recent government experiments with providing housing for sale in various cities. In Changzhou, for example, there is a three-tier development of new housing; the first offers relatively luxurious and spacious apartments and detached units, averaging more than 100 square meters per person, and usually only affordable by "overseas Chinese" from Taiwan or Hong Kong. The other two tiers of housing, still relatively spacious, are intended for newly wealthy families. See "Apartments for Sale in Changzhou," *China Daily*, February 2, 1987. A similar hierarchical structure also has been developed in Shanghai. See "Shanghai Savers Buy Homes," *China Daily*, May 19, 1986.

51. C. Riskin, 1987, *China's Political Economy: The Quest for Development Since 1949* (Oxford: Oxford University Press).

52. Kirkby, 1988, op. cit. p. 230. See also Kojimo, op. cit., esp. Chap. 3, "Urban Housing."

53. Kirkby suggested that the level of neglect actually resulted in the loss of a huge amount of floor space between 1949 and 1980. Although 675 million square meters were built, the total housing stock increased only by 469 million square meters (Kirkby, 1988, op. cit., p. 230). Very little housing was demolished to make room for new construction, and Kirkby argued that as much as 150 million square meters was lost due to the neglect of simple repairs.

54. C. P. Lo, 1987, "Socialist Ideology and Urban Strategies in China," *Urban Geography* 8, No. 5 (Sept.-Oct.), pp. 440–458.

55. "Housing Policy Changes Pushed," *China Daily*, June 30, 1987.

56. One innovative and logical solution to the chronic housing shortage in China's largest cities has been a system of housing exchanges. This began informally but soon blossomed into a semiofficial and computerized service. The usual reason for wanting to exchange was to avoid a lengthy journey to work, a chronic problem in the absence of rapid transit systems in China's hugely overcrowded cities. See "Beijing Fair Busy With House-Swappers," *China Daily*, August 22, 1986; and also "Exchanging Homes is Popular in Beijing," *China Daily*, February 28, 1987.

57. Whyte and Parish, op. cit., p. 78.

58. "Too Low Rents Cause Housing Shortage," *China Daily*, March 21, 1987.

59. For examples from Eastern European countries, see I. Szelenyi, 1983, *Urban Inequality Under State Socialism* (London: Oxford University Press). Housing and housing policies in the Soviet Union were well described by G. Littlejohn, 1984, *A Sociology of the Soviet Union* (London: Macmillan), by J. H. Bater, 1980, *The Soviet City* (Beverly Hills, Calif.: Sage Publications), and by V. George and N. Manning, 1980, *Socialism, Social Welfare and the Soviet Union* (London: Routledge and Kegan Paul).

60. Among the most terrifying of the accounts, all of which were provided from actual interviews, are available in Anne Thurston, 1988, *Enemies of the People: The Ordeal of the Intellectuals in China's Great Cultural Revolution* (Cambridge, Mass.: Harvard University Press). In recent years many accounts have been written in short story and novel formats by Chinese people who lived through the Cultural Revolution. See, for example, Gao Yuan, 1987, *Born Red: A Chronicle of the Cultural Revolution* (Stanford, Calif.: Stanford University Press); Liang Heng and J. Shapiro, 1984, *Son of the Revolution* (New York: Vintage Books); and Lo Fulang, 1989, *Morning Breeze: A True Story of China's Cultural Revolution* (San Francisco: China Books and Pe-

riodicals). As we see in *Lapse of Time*, a story beautifully told by Wang Anyi, during the Cultural Revolution "rich" families were often under constant scrutiny from the Red Guards. The family in Wang's story had had all of their expensive possessions commandeered and placed in storage in the ground floor of their house. At irregular intervals, totally unannounced, groups of Red Guards would back lorries up to the front door and cart off varying amounts of the family's belongings. The family, too terrified to respond, was totally passive in the face of what amounted to theft of their possessions. One day the rest of their belongings were moved out and a poor (working-class) family was moved in—effectively to live as squatters, but with the sanction of the local Party and the Red Guards. See Wang Anyi, 1989, *Lapse of Time* (San Francisco: China Books and Periodicals).

61. This generally refers to investments in the area of urban utilities, education, social services, cultural facilities, recreation, transportation, and housing. In the national construction period during the early 1950s, investment in these areas was relatively high. See J. Domes, 1985, *The Government and Politics of the PRC: A Time of Transition* (Boulder, Colo.: Westview Press).

62. "How to End the Shortage of Housing," *China Daily*, March 6, 1987.

63. Kirkby, 1988, op. cit.

64. See Riskin, op. cit., and also M. Chossudovsky, 1986, *Towards Capitalist Restoration: Chinese Socialism After Mao* (Hong Kong: Macmillan).

65. This is the Maoist concept of the "permanent" or "continuing" revolution. See L. Dittmer, 1987, *China's Continuing Revolution: The Post-Liberation Epoch, 1949–1981* (Berkeley: University of California Press).

66. See Phillips and Yeh, op. cit.; L.J.C. Ma, 1981, "Urban Housing Supply in the People's Republic of China," pp. 222–259 in L.J.C. Ma and E. W. Hanten (eds.), *Urban Development in Modern China* (Boulder, Colo.: Westview Press). See also R.J.R. Kirkby, 1987, "Housing the Masses," *China Now*, No. 120, pp. 28–30.

67. "New Housing Criticized by Residents," *China Daily*, March 13, 1987. The survey results and the proposed housing reform plans were discussed by Liu Hong, 1989, "Housing Construction and Reform," *China Reconstructs* 38, No. 8 (August), pp. 8–11; see also Mou Zhentou, 1989, "Housing Reform in Yantai," *China Reconstructs*, No. 8 (August), pp. 12–13.

68. For evidence of the rising prevalence of unemployment and homelessness in some of China's cities, see Sun Yuntao, 1988, "Shock Wave of Unemployment in Qingdao City," *Nexus: China in Focus*, Winter, pp. 27–28. In a 1989 editorial, *China Now* reported that the official newspaper *Economic Daily* considered the rural surplus/redundant population to be China's most serious problem for the 1990s and estimated that by the year 2000 there could be as many as 260 million surplus laborers in China. See "Sinofile" by Angela Knox, 1989, *China Now*, No. 129 (Summer), p. 5.

69. Official statements about this move have been made by Xiao Tong, 1987, "Moving Toward Home Ownership," *China Reconstructs* 36, No. 7 (July), pp. 39–40; and also by Ye Rutang, 1987, "Providing Shelter for a Billion People," *China Reconstructs* 36, No. 7 (July), pp. 33–39.

70. Riskin, op. cit. On average the state charged 0.1 yuan per square meter of built housing, whereas the actual housing cost, accounting for depreciation, repairs, maintenance, and management, was 0.38 yuan. This amounted to an annual state subsidy (or a loss) of 3.5 billion yuan. See Kirkby, 1988, op. cit., p. 234. The budget deficits (which continued in subsequent years but not at quite such high levels) were largely attributed to the new economic reform measures. There had been a significant decline in state revenues as a result of the decision to allow individual enterprises and localities to keep a larger portion of their own profits. In addition, as part of the agricultural reforms, the state had started to decontrol food prices, which meant the government was paying far more for food than it had been in the recent past. The success of China's new Special Economic Zones had also produced a sizable increase in foreign imports, which had helped to drain the country's scarce reserves of foreign exchange (see Chapter 6). In light of the mounting budget problems, the commodification of housing, in addition to catering to the absolute need for additional housing in China and providing a viable outlet for consumption among the newly wealthy, had actually become a financial necessity by 1980. In 1979 China experienced, for the first time since 1949, a significant budget deficit, amounting to Y 17 billion. For details of the Yantai experiments see Mou Zhentou, op. cit.

71. "Housing Policy Changes Pushed," *China Daily*, June 30, 1987.

72. Pan, op. cit., p. 8.

CHAPTER 14

1. Chen Jo-Hsi, 1978, "Chairman Mao Is a Rotten Egg," pp. 37–66 in Chen Jo-Hsi, *The Execution of Mayor Yin and Other Stories From the Great Proletarian Revolution* (Bloomington: Indiana University Press), quote from p. 59.

2. E. Vogel, 1969, *Canton Under Communism: Programs and Politics in a Provincial Capital* (Cambridge, Mass.: Harvard University Press), see esp. Chap. 2, "Local Urban Control: Takeover and Consolidation, 1949–1952," pp. 41–90.

3. P. Theroux, 1988, *Riding the Iron Rooster: By Train Through China* (New York: Ivy Books), p. 273.

4. Vogel, op. cit., p. 64.

5. Ibid., p. 89 (emphasis added).

6. Achieving social control can be defined narrowly as the process by which people come to (or are made to) comply with (obey) the law; in other words, it centers around crime. A wider definition would be more useful in this context—for example, achieving social control is a situation in which individuals come to accept the common concepts and codes of a society. In the PRC after 1949 this involved getting the maximum number of people to accept the new regime, to work for it, study for it, live and (perhaps) die for it. For a more detailed discussion of the concept of social control, see C. J. Smith, 1988, *Public Problems: The Management of Urban Distress* (New York: Guilford Press).

7. Vogel, op. cit., p. 83. In most discussions of social control, reference is made to *internal* as opposed to *external* means of achieving the desired goals. Internal social control involves socialization, a process in which individuals simply "do the right" thing, based on conscience and internalized rules and values, much of which comes from family, kin, and community role models. This type of social control obviously overlaps considerably with external sources of social control, which are imposed on individuals either by family and kin (informal social controls) or by the various agencies of the state (external). For a more detailed discussion, see M. K. Whyte and W. L. Parish, 1984, *Urban Life in Contemporary China* (Chicago: University of Chicago Press), esp. Chap. 8, "Crime and Social Control," pp. 231–273.

8. V. H. Li, 1978, *Law Without Lawyers: A Comparative View of Law in China and the United States* (Boulder, Colo.: Westview Press).

9. S. C. Leng and H. Chiu, 1985, *Criminal Justice in Post-Mao China: Analysis and Documents* (Albany: State University of New York Press), p. 8. This quote is attributed to Confucius himself. The opposing positions of the Legalist and the Confucian schools of thought illustrate the different views on "external" as opposed to "internal" sources of social control. For example, "when punishments are heavy, people dare not transgress, and therefore there will be no punishments" (Hou Fei-tzu, the Legalist School). Confucius, on the other hand, would prefer people to be led by virtue: "Lead people by regulations, keep them in order by punishments, and they will flee from you and lose all self-respect. But lead them by virtue and keep them in order by established morality, and they will keep their self-respect and come to you" (Analects, Book II [3]). See R. Baum, 1986, "Modernization and Legal Reform in Post-Mao China: The Rebirth of Socialist Legality," *Studies in Comparative Communism* 19, No. 2 (Summer), pp. 69–103, quotes from p. 71.

10. D. G. Rojek, 1985, "The Criminal Process in the People's Republic of China," *Justice Quarterly* 2, No. 1 (March), pp. 117–125.

11. R. Munro, 1989, "Party, Politics, and Interference in the Law," *China Now*, No. 129 (Summer), pp. 22–23. It has been a constant source of fascination for outsiders to listen to Chinese socialists trying to explain why there are any crimes at all in a Marxist society! The traditional answer is that China has not yet reached the final stage of communism. Socialism is an intermediate stage, and there are still some "remnants" of the old society, such as economic repression, alienation associated with class oppression, and so on. In recent years a number of other theories have been generated by Chinese observers as well as outsiders. Most of these are connected in some way to the new economic forces that have been unleashed in the reform movement, and the consequent reemergence of polarity and inequality, which tend to raise expectations too quickly for the society to respond. For a more detailed discussion of some of these theories, the reader is directed to Whyte and Parish, op. cit.

12. Baum, op. cit., pp. 70–103. In practice Mao recognized the difficulties involved with making clear-cut distinctions between these two categories, but the behavior of the so-called bad-class elements (landlords, capitalists, intellectuals, et al.) was characterized as antagonistic by definition—reinforcing the class-based foundation of the criminal justice system. See Leng and Chiu, op. cit., for further details. The original doctrine of Mao Zedong's, specifying these two contradictions in 1957, actually became sacrosanct and was used during the lawless years of the Cultural Revolution as a simple yardstick for administering popular (or, by Western standards, "kangaroo-court") justice.

13. The abuse of the law and the application of sanction to innocent people, whose only crime has been to disagree with the government, has been well reported by Westerners in journalistic, humanistic, and legalistic accounts. Examples of each approach are F. Butterfield, 1983, *China: Alive in the Bitter Sea* (New York: Bantam Books); G. Barmé and J. Minford (eds.), 1986, *Seeds of Fire: Chinese Voices of Conscience* (Hong Kong: Far Eastern Economic Review, Ltd.); and Amnesty International, 1984, *China: Violations of Human Rights: Prisoners of Conscience and the Death Penalty in the PRC* (London: Amnesty International Publications). In spite of such publications as these, for a variety of reasons, mostly economic and political, human rights abuse in China remained a very low-key issue on the international scene through most of the 1980s. By comparison, the Soviet Union has received far greater condemnation for its abuses of human rights. In part the problem may have been a lack of information. China, at least until 1989, had not had a Solzhenitsyn or a Sakharov

to publicize the more egregious aspects of criminal justice in that country (even though many dissenters are in fact imprisoned in Chinese labor camps). Although all of that changed dramatically in 1989, it is apparent that many countries, particularly the United States, still favor a kid-glove approach to China on this issue. There was plenty of rage and disbelief but relatively little was done to apply effective sanctions. See N. D. Kristoff, 1989, "Relations With US Seem Badly Hurt by Crushing of Democracy Protests," *New York Times*, June 11, p. 16. The apparent tolerance of China displayed by the current U.S. government was sharply criticized by a recent publication of Asia Watch, an organization based in New York. See Asia Watch, 1990, *Punishment Season: Human Rights in China After Martial Law* (New York: The Asia Watch Committee).

14. The statistics are obviously difficult to gather, with the number of executions since the crackdown on crime in 1983 estimated to be anywhere between 10 and 30,000. See J. Fleming, 1989, "To Warn a Hundred," *China Now*, No. 129 (Summer), pp. 16–19; see also Asia Watch, op. cit. The cold facts about the offenses punishable by execution, and the methods used, were illustrated to the world in June and July 1989, in addition to the purge of "liberals," "intellectuals," and "counterrevolutionaries." See S. WeDunn, 1989, "Chinese Arrest 400 in Beijing Amid Fears of a Wide Purge; Roundups On in Other Cities," *New York Times*, June 11, pp. 1, 16; N. D. Kristoff, 1989, "China Sentences 8 Workers to Die; Sharply Attacks US Interference," *New York Times*, June 18, pp. 1, 13; and also N. D. Kristoff, 1989, "Unleashing the Dark Methods of the Cultural Revolution," *New York Times*, June 18.

15. See Munro, "Criminal Justice and the Rule of Law," pp. 8–10.

16. Some justice bureaus actually stipulate that a lawyer who wants to put forward a "not guilty" defense must obtain permission from the local Party organization. Obviously, this situation provides no legal safeguards to the accused in the event of judicial errors, wrongful accusation, or miscarriages of justice, such as the elicitation of confessions using torture. See ibid., p. 10, and Amnesty International, 1987, *Report on Torture and Ill-Treatment of Prisoners in China* (London: Amnesty International Publications).

17. This is mainly used in thousands of cases of "minor" offenses of a "counterrevolutionary" nature, or disruptions of social order, where criminal sanction is not considered necessary. The official term for such punishment is "reeducation through labor," which will be discussed in more detail in Chapter 15.

18. See Whyte and Parish, op. cit., pp. 246–261.

19. In other words the reduction in the level of crime has been the result of specific activities that have either prevented opportunities for crimes to occur or have militated against the concentration of large "subcultures" of criminally inclined people. Although this is in itself an impressive achievement, it is not really a result of the switchover to socialism per se, in the sense of "producing" a new type of person (the "new communist man") who is inherently less likely to commit crimes.

20. This conceptualization is based on a discussion by R.J.R. Kirkby, 1985, *Urbanization in China: Town and Country in a Developing Economy, 1949–2000* AD (New York: Columbia University Press).

21. Whyte and Parish, op. cit., p. 247. This raises the now familiar theme of "defensible space," which is part of a broader area of study known as "environmental criminology." The defensible space idea implies that crime rates can be lowered if there are fewer open and unwatched spaces, such as parks, empty lots, parking garages, and hallways. The solution, according to this theory, is to redesign urban and residential spaces to eliminate or reduce the amount of "nondefensible" space. The obvious counter to the theory is that criminals will simply shift their activities elsewhere, implying that the solution is little more than a cosmetic activity that does little to deal with the root causes of crime. See, for example, O. Newman, 1972, *Defensible Space* (New York: Macmillan); and for a review of the different components of environmental criminology, see P. J. Brantingham and P. L. Brantingham (eds.), 1981, *Environmental Criminology* (Beverly Hills, Calif.: Sage Publications).

22. Whyte and Parish, op. cit., p. 257.

23. Ibid., p. 234.

24. Ibid., p. 258. It is essential to note that the 1980s also offered many people in China, both urban and rural, a dream of or at least a hope for a new future, one that would involve a certain amount of prosperity they had been denied in the past. The new population trends need to be considered, therefore, within the context of rising aspirations nationwide, which strengthens Whyte and Parish's "blocked opportunities" hypothesis.

25. In the United States "serious crimes" are the so-called index crimes, including murder, rape, robbery, and arson. It is not known if the Chinese also use the same definitions. It is impossible to determine how the statistics used here have been calculated, or what crimes they include. See ibid., pp. 248–250, for a detailed discussion of Chinese crime statistics, what they might mean, and how they should be interpreted. From the statistics themselves, it would appear that crime in China is as much as 15 times lower than in the average U.S. city. In their survey work, Whyte and Parish (p. 249) reported that among their respondents 8% reported that serious crimes had been committed

against family members in the past year; and 18% said there were crimes in their neighborhoods. These were statistics for Canton (Guangzhou). The equivalent figures for Detroit were 22% and 49%, respectively.

26. During the Cultural Revolution there were totally new definitions of "deviance" and "crime," mostly along political (class) lines. In addition, by earlier and later standards of evaluation, as well as from an international and Western perspective, much of the behavior of the so-called social-control agents, including the local cadres, Party members, the police, and especially the fanatical Red Guards, was itself "deviant" behavior that would have been a criminal offense in more normal times. For a discussion of some of the tumultuous events, see Gao Yuan, 1987, *Born Red: A Chronicle of the Cultural Revolution* (Stanford, Calif.: Stanford University Press), particularly the Foreword by William A. Joseph, pp. ix–xxx.

27. See, for example, Leng and Chiu, op. cit.; "Why the Crime Rate Is Declining," *Beijing Review* 26, No. 27 (1983), pp. 4–6; "Success in Preventing Crime," *Beijing Review* 28, No. 50 (1985), p. 21; and "Meeting Over Youth Crimes," *China Daily*, April 28, 1987, p. 3.

28. R. Wingrove, 1989, "Robbing the Revolution," *China Now*, No. 129 (Summer), pp. 11–13. See also L. Pan, 1988, *The New Chinese Revolution* (Chicago: Contemporary Books), esp. Chap. 10, "Wrongdoers," pp. 219–242. For example, the peak age of criminal involvement had dropped from 16 in the 1950s to 14 in the 1980s (see Leng and Chiu, op. cit., p. 142), and 70% of the people held in custody were under 25 years old; see "Juvenile Delinquency Increases," *China News Analysis*, July 15, 1987, p. 5. The rise in juvenile and economic crimes are of special concern to the CCP because the successful "remolding" and socialization of youth, and protection of the economy, are considered to be among the most important prerequisites for the continuation of the socialist order. See J. P. Brady, 1983, "People's Republic of China," pp. 107–141 in E. H. Johnson (ed.), *International Handbook of Contemporary Developments in Criminology*, Vol. 2 (Westport, Conn.: Greenwood Press).

29. "Nation's Three Year Crackdown Cuts Crime Rate by 35%," *China Daily*, December 20, 1986, p. 1. The crackdown involved a massive execution drive, with several thousand people executed after very brief trials during a short time period. See J. Fleming, 1989, "To Warn a Hundred," *China Now*, No. 129 (Summer), pp. 16–18.

30. These statistics have been reproduced in a report prepared by a "visiting scholar" to the State University of New York at Albany from the PRC (1990). In the circumstances, it is best not to identify this person any further, but from his official position within the government, there is reason to believe that the reports are fundamentally accurate. See

also Guo Zhongshi, 1987, "Chief Judge Points to Obvious Drop in Violent Crimes," *China Daily*, April 7, p. 3; "Crackdown on Crime," *Far Eastern Economic Review* 141, No. 44 (November 3, 1988), pp. 23–25. This report noted that serious crimes in the first six months of 1988 were up by 34.8% over the previous year, in spite of continuing hard-line policies to hand out very heavy punishments, including widespread use of the death penalty even for economic crimes.

31. L. L. Tifft, 1985, "Reflections on Capital Punishment and the 'Campaign Against Crime' in the PRC," *Justice Quarterly* 2, No. 1 (March), pp. 127–137. See also S. Rosen, 1987, "China in 1986: A Year of Consolidation," *Asian Survey* 27 (January), pp. 35–55.

32. This was dramatically obvious to the entire world when, in the aftermath of the 1989 crackdown on the Democracy Movement, the official government line was startlingly different from what had been seen and reported by journalists from all around the world. See, for example, "Statement Calls for 'Quelling the Riot,'" *China Daily*, June 6, 1989, p. 1. As the official line stated the case, "In the course of the action [to quell the riot] the PLA martial law units tried their best to avoid bloodshed, but some casualties nevertheless occurred, mostly involving military personnel." The demonstrations were described as a "shocking counterrevolutionary riot instigated by a handful of people with ulterior motives."

33. However, the increasing crime rate in the 1980s could be blamed on "spiritual pollution" from the West, which represented an important contribution to ongoing campaign strategies.

34. See Baum, op. cit., and Leng and Chiu, op. cit.

35. A. J. Nathan, L. Henkin, and R. R. Edwards, 1986, *Human Rights in Contemporary China* (New York: Columbia University Press); see also M. A. Silk, 1985, "The Crime of Dissent in China," *Problems of Communism* 34, No. 4, pp. 61–68.

36. See "Making Law a Household Word in China," *Beijing Review* 28, No. 3 (1985), pp. 26–27.

37. See S. C. Leng, 1977, "The Role of Law in the PRC as Reflecting Mao Tse-Tung's Influence," *Journal of Criminal Law and Criminology*, September, pp. 356–57. See also E. H. Johnson, 1986, "Politics, Power and Prevention: The PRC Case," *Journal of Criminal Justice* 14, pp. 449–457.

38. *China Daily*, January 23, 1987, p. 1.

39. Wang Gangyi, 1987, "Reform Revives Role of Lawyers," *China Daily*, March 18, p. 4. For data providing recent historical comparisons on the number of lawyers in China, see Li, op. cit. It is important to stress again here, however, that in China the term *lawyer* does not mean what it means in the West. Although there are some moves to train an independent profession of lawyers, they

remain closely identified with the political system and therefore not truly independent from the political process.

40. See Liu Qing, 1982–1983, "Liu Qing's Prison Memoirs," *Chinese Sociology and Anthropology* 15 (Fall/Winter), pp. 3–181.

41. See Nathan, Henkin, and Edwards, op. cit., p. 64.

42. Silk, op. cit.

43. Whyte and Parish, op. cit., esp. pp. 269–273.

44. See Hooper, op. cit., esp. Chap. 6, "Waiting for Employment," pp. 77–94; Chap. 8, "The Misfits," pp. 113–132; and Chap. 9, "Temptations from the West," pp. 133–158.

45. This hypothesis and its adaptation to Marxist societies in general was explained by P. Hollander, 1982, "Research on Marxist Societies: The Relationship Between Theory and Practice," *Annual Review of Sociology* 8, pp. 319–351. In part this argument is based on Donald Black's thesis that the amount of law in a society varies inversely with the other (informal) sources of social control that are available. See R. M. Regoli, A. W. Miracle, and E. D. Poole, 1984, "Law and Social Control in China: An Application of Black's Thesis," *Criminal Justice Review* 9, No. 2, pp. 1–7.

46. See Hollander, op. cit.

47. R. F. Meier, 1982, "Perspectives on the Concept of Social Control," *Annual Review of Sociology* 8, pp. 35–55.

48. Leng and Chiu, op. cit.

49. Silk, op. cit., p. 61. To illustrate the importance of political and legal stability to China's trading partners, it is interesting to recall the recommendations of then U.S. Attorney General Edward Meese at a joint China-U.S. trade conference in 1987. Meese was attempting to describe the features of a legal system for China that would best secure international cooperation, and he stressed the need for consistency, stability, and predictability. See "Law Is the Cornerstone of Progress," *China Daily*, August 22, 1987. Although there were few immediate signs of joint ventures and business contacts being withdrawn from China in the summer of 1989, only time will tell what the long-term effects will be. The short-term effects were considerable, as tourists, conventions, journalists, and academics canceled their plans to visit and travel in China in the summer of 1989.

50. Silk, op. cit., p. 64.

51. Deng Xiaoping had spoken in 1987 on the need for greater judicial independence, although the events of 1989 rendered such remarks irrelevant. See An Ziguo, 1987, " 'Cultural Revolution' Not To Be Repeated," *Beijing Review* 30, No. 35, pp. 4–5.

52. This of course means that the "informal" systems of social control are no longer "informal" processes but are actually fairly well-regulated processes. Because they do not correspond to our own experiences, many Westerners assume that these informal practices will wither away, but in fact they may simply slip out of the limelight in an era of major legal reforms.

53. See Brady, op. cit.

54. For a discussion of this during the Cultural Revolution emphasizing the situation in urban China, see J. W. Salaff, 1971, "Urban Residential Communities in the Wake of the Cultural Revolution," pp. 289–431 in J. W. Lewis (ed.), *The City in Communist China* (Stanford, Calif.: Stanford University Press).

55. "Making Law a Household Word in China," op. cit.

56. Li Ning, 1985, "Legal Education Surges Ahead," *Beijing Review* 28, No. 18, pp. 22–25; and "Law Helps to Change Daily Life," *China Daily*, May 9, 1987, p. 3.

57. Zhu Ling, 1986, "Penal Study Drive Aims to Tackle Youth Crime," *China Daily*, February 27, p. 1.

58. "Law Drive Vital," *China Daily*, December 23, 1986, p. 3.

59. An Ziguo, op. cit.

60. The data are collected from the *China Law Yearbook, 1987* (Beijing: Law Publishing House, 1988). See also S. Tailong and P. Gagnon, 1986, "Mediation Committees Are Revitalized," *China Daily*, December 31, p. 4.

61. G. I. Felkenes, 1986, "Criminal Justice in the PRC: A System of Contradictions," *Judicature* 68, No. 6, pp. 344–352.

62. See Leng and Chiu, op. cit.

63. Amnesty International, 1984, op. cit.

64. D. Fogel, 1979, "Criminal Justice in China," pp. 59–84 in C. Alexander and S. Alexander (eds.), *China View* (Washington, D.C.: National Association of Social Workers).

65. Zhi Ling, 1987, "Ex-Thief Becomes Model of Honesty," *China Daily*, January 14, p. 6.

66. Exposure of public officials for a variety of wrongdoings has been one of the most frequently debated criminal-justice issues addressed in recent years. There has been a focus on economic crimes and the susceptibility of officials to being corrupted, with a secondary emphasis on issues of moral turpitude. See Pan, op. cit., esp. pp. 219–242; and D. Bonavia, 1988, *The Chinese: A Portrait* (rev. ed.) (London: Penguin Books), esp. Chap. 10, "Laws, Lawmakers, and Lawbreakers," pp. 149–169. See also "Growing Problems With the Abuse of Power," *Far Eastern Economic Review* 139, No. 12 (March 22, 1988), pp. 81–82.

67. See V. H. Li, op. cit.

68. Brady, op. cit., p. 68.

69. J. K. Fairbank, 1979, "Self-Expression in China," pp. 81–89 in R. Terrill (ed.), *The China Difference* (New York: Harper and Row).

70. Asia Watch, 1990, *Punishment Season: Human Rights in China After Martial Law* (New York: Asia Watch Committee).

CHAPTER 15

1. Zhang Xianliang, 1988, *Half of Man Is Woman* (New York: W. W. Norton and Co.), p. 264.

2. V. H. Li, 1979, "Human Rights in a Chinese Context," pp. 219–236 in R. Terrill (ed.), *The China Difference: A Portrait of Life Inside the Country of One Billion* (New York: Harper Colophon Books). For a devastating report on the current human rights situation in China, see the recent report: Amnesty International, August 1989, *People's Republic of China: Preliminary Findings on Killings of Unarmed Civilians, Arbitrary Arrests, and Summary Executions, June 3, 1989* (New York: Amnesty International); and also Asia Watch, 1990, *Punishment Season: Human Rights in China After Martial Law* (New York: Asia Watch Committee).

3. J. D. Seymour (ed.), 1980, *The Fifth Modernization: China's Human Rights Movement, 1978–1979* (New York: Human Rights Publishing Group). See also R. Barnett, 1989, "The Missing Modernization," *China Now*, No. 129 (Summer), pp. 24–26. For a devastating report on the current human rights situation in China, see Amnesty International's report on the Tiananmen massacre (August 1989).

4. Quoted in G. Barmé and J. Minford (eds.), 1986, *Seeds of Fire: Chinese Voices of Conscience* (Hong Kong: Far Eastern Economic Review, Ltd.), p. 277.

5. M. A. Silk, 1985, "The Crime of Dissent in China," *Problems of Communism* 34, No. 4, pp. 61–68.

6. From *April 5th Forum*, No. 2, p. 3 (December 7, 1978). Reprinted in D.S.G. Goodman, 1981, *Beijing Street Voices: The Poetry and Politics of China's Democracy Movement* (London: Marion Boyars), p. 69.

7. Barmé and Minford, op. cit., p. 272.

8. R. Garside, 1981, *Coming Alive: China After Mao* (New York: Mentor Books).

9. Ibid., pp. 122–23.

10. Ibid., p. 223.

11. M. Blecher, 1986, *China: Politics, Economics and Society* (London: Frances Pinter Pub.).

12. A. Thurston, 1988, *Enemies of the People: The Ordeal of the Intellectuals in China's Great Cultural Revolution* (Cambridge, Mass.: Harvard University Press).

13. N. D. Kristoff, 1989, "A Look at the Men Who Would Be Deng," *New York Times*, June 18. All through the summer of 1989 and into the fall, the Chinese government kept up its campaign against anyone who might have been a sympathizer of the Democracy Movement, or who contributed in any way to the odious and insidious process of "spiritual pollution." In early September, for example, Wang Meng, a former author and at the time minister of culture, was dismissed and replaced by He Jingzhi, who was described as "a Maoist poet." Wang's dismissal appears to be based on his tolerance of a new brand of literature and artistic expression in China during the 1980s. See John Gittings, 1989, "Beijing Steps up Pressure on Liberals," *Guardian* (UK), Sept. 5, p. 10.

14. Mao Zedong, 1956, *Mao Tse-tung: Selected Works*, Vol. 4: *1941–1945* (New York: International Publications).

15. S. C. Leng and H. Chiu, 1985, *Criminal Justice in Post-Mao China: Analysis and Documents* (Albany: State University of New York Press).

16. Silk, op. cit.

17. Lin Xiling, 1984, *A Statement of Views for 'Emperor' Deng Xiaoping's Perusal* (Hong Kong: Guangjiao Jing Chubanshe).

18. Silk, op. cit., pp. 63–64.

19. Ibid., p. 66.

20. Amnesty International, 1984, *China: Violations of Human Rights: Prisoners of Conscience and the Death Penalty in the PRC* (London: Amnesty International Publications).

21. *Constitution of the People's Republic of China* (Oxford: Pergamon Press, 1982), p. 39.

22. Silk, op. cit., p. 66.

23. It is also clear to most Westerners who are used to living in more democratic societies that the law is generally a very conservative force, tending to maintain the status quo. Not surprisingly, it has very little relevance to people who want to carry out radical social change, as is case with the revolutionary CCP. In such cases the "laws of the state" (*quofa*) naturally take a back seat to the needs of "Party policy" (*zhengce*). As one commentator observed, "policies could always be adopted, then reshaped at a later date, or even dropped altogether. . . . But laws, being more permanent and universal . . . tended to restrict the Party's freedom of action." See R. Munro, 1989, "Criminal Justice and the Rule of Law," *China Now*, No. 129 (Summer), p. 22 (emphasis added).

24. Thurston, op. cit., p. 122.

25. Yu Luojin, 1986, *A Chinese Winter's Tale* (Hong Kong: Renditions Paperbacks), p. 188.

26. Zhang Xianliang, op. cit., p. 238.

27. Silk, op. cit., p. 65.

28. Munro, "Party, Politics, and Interference in the Law," p. 22.

29. Leng and Chiu, op. cit., quote from the Appendix.

30. Silk, op. cit., p. 67.

31. S. Leys, 1985, *The Burning Forest* (New York: Holt, Rinehart and Winston), p. 64. The name "Leys" has been used as a pen name, for obvious reasons, to ensure that the author could continue to travel incognito to China, unlike some of the

other foreigners who have been expelled for their uncomplimentary views about contemporary China.

32. Quoted in John Minford, 1986, Introduction, in Yu Luojin, op. cit., p. xv.

33. Zhang Xianliang, op. cit., p. 6.

34. Ibid.

35. The expression to be "hatted" originally referred to the practice of putting tall dunce caps on "criminals" and forcing them to parade through the streets telling people about their crimes. In a larger sense, the term came to imply the loss of all civil rights (though usually without a trial) and becoming an outcast in society. "Hatted" people usually were assigned to the most menial tasks and were paid the lowest salaries. Their families were ostracized, and often the children were not allowed to go to school. Husbands or wives were often pressured into seeking a divorce. See Zhang Xianliang, op. cit., p. 84.

36. Ibid., pp. 84–85.

37. J. Pasqualini (Bao Ruowang) and Rudolph Cheminski, 1976, *Prisoner of Mao* (Harmondsworth, UK: Penguin). In one section of his book, Pasqualini told about an experiment to save food in the labor camp he was sent to. It involved stretching out the dough used to make dumplings with a tasteless paper compound called "food substitute." After only a few days of eating this the prisoners were seized with constipation because the paper absorbed all of the moisture in their digestive systems. "By Christmas Day the whole farm was in agony from . . . one of the most serious cases of mass constipation in history. . . . Men were bent double with cramps. Even soapy water enemas did hardly any good. . . . I had to stick my finger up my anus and dig it out, in dry lumps, like sawdust" (pp. 72–73).

38. Barmé and Minford, op. cit., p. 280.

39. Ibid., p. 327.

40. "Student Upheaval: What's It All About?" *Beijing Review*, No. 8, February 23, 1987, pp. 17–21. For an outsider's point of view on the student demonstrations see "Talking Out of School: Widening Student Grievance Touches Political Leadership," *Far Eastern Economic Review* 140, No. 24, p. 18; and R. Thomson, 1987, "Peking Students Secure Release of Detained Protestors," *Financial Times* (London), February 2, p. 1.

41. "Campus Unrest: Result of 'Liberalization,'" *Beijing Review*, No. 8 (February 23, 1987), pp. 14–16, quote from p. 14.

42. C. DuRand, 1987, "Party Slams the Brakes on Political Reform," *Guardian* (UK), February 4, p. 14.

43. Paul Theroux has observed that this appears to be a peculiarly Chinese trait—pinning the lion's share of the blame for political fiascoes on just one or two people, effectively absolving everyone else from responsibility. This was, according to Theroux, a useful way of dealing with the collective guilt in the aftermath of the Cultural Revolution: "The entire horror show, the whole ten years of it . . . had been the work of four skinny demons: the Gang of Four. No Red Guard was ever held personally responsible for any act of terror." P. Theroux, 1988, *Riding the Iron Rooster: By Train Through China* (New York: Ivy Books), p. 109. Anyone who has read about some of the depravities committed in the name of Mao's Cultural Revolution will find this extremely difficult to comprehend. See, for example, Thurston, op. cit.

44. "Beijing Issues New Rules on Public Meetings," *China Daily*, December 27, 1986, p. 1.

45. Quoted in Goodman, op. cit., p. 142.

46. A statement that was attributed to one of the leaders of the student demonstrations in 1989 was "we don't know what democracy is, but we know we want it." See N. D. Kristoff, 1989, "China Erupts . . . The Reasons Why," *New York Times Magazine*, June 4, pp. 26–29; 85–90.

47. L. Pan, 1988, *The New Chinese Revolution* (Chicago: Contemporary Books), pp. 189–190.

48. Ibid., p. 191.

49. F. Ching, 1989, "Red Star Over Hong Kong," *World Policy Journal* 6, No. 4 (Fall), pp. 657–666.

50. See for example M. Oksenberg, 1989, "Confession of a China Watcher: Why No One Predicted the Bloodbath in Beijing," *Newsweek*, June 19, p. 30.

51. E. Friedman, 1989, "Decollectivization and Democratization in China," *Problems in Communism* 38, No. 5 (Sept./Oct.), pp. 103–107.

52. Among the better of the (already voluminous) books written about the Tiananmen incident, its causes and the aftermath, see Liu Binyan (with Ruan Ming and Xu Gang), 1989, *"Tell the World": What Happened in China and Why* (New York: Pantheon Books); M. Fathers and A. Higgins, 1989, *Tiananmen: The Rape of Peking* (London: The Independent); Yi Mu and M. V. Thompson, 1989, *Crisis at Tiananmen: Reform and Reality in Modern China* (San Francisco: China Books and Periodicals); and Chu-yuan Cheng, 1990, *Behind the Tiananmen Massacre* (Boulder, Colo.: Westview Press). A number of academic journals have also published symposia on the issues; see, for example: *World Policy Journal* 6 (Fall 1989), with articles by Huan Guocang, Dorothy Solinger, David Zweig, June Teufel Dreyer, Frank Ching, and Marie Gottschalk; also *Problems in Communism* 38, No. 5 (Sept./Oct. 1989), with articles by: Lowell Dittmer, Andrew Nathan, Andrew Walder, and June Teufel Dreyer.

53. Deng Xiaoping, in a speech delivered to commanders above the corps level of the martial law enforcement troops, June 9, 1989, Beijing, reprinted in *U.S. China Review* 12, No. 2 (Fall 1989), p. 6 (emphasis added).

54. Sources include: various *New York Times* articles; *Times-Union* (Albany, N.Y.) articles; *San Francisco Examiner* articles; *China Now*, No. 130,

pp. 3–5; *Newsweek,* June 19, 1989, pp. 14–30; *Time,* June 26, 1989, pp. 32–35. See also Liu Binyan, op. cit.; and Yi Mu and M. V. Thompson, 1989, *Crisis at Tiananmen: Reform and Reality in Modern China* (San Francisco: China Books and Periodicals).

CHAPTER 16

1. J. Morris, 1984, "Very Strange Feeling: A Chinese Journey," pp. 152–171 in *Journeys* (New York: Oxford University Press), quote from p. 167 (emphasis added).

2. R.J.R. Kirkby, 1985, *Urbanization in China: Town and Country in a Developing Economy 1949–2000 AD* (New York: Columbia University Press).

3. E. Friedman, 1989, "Decollectivization and Democratization in China," *Problems of Communism* 38, No. 5 (Sept./Oct.), pp. 103–107.

4. W. Hinton, 1984, *Shenfan: The Continuing Revolution in a Chinese Village* (New York: Vintage Books), p. 107.

5. "Whither China's Agricultural Reforms: An Interview with William Hinton," *Contemporary Marxism* 12-13 (Spring 1986), pp. 137–143, quote from p. 142.

6. Friedman, op. cit., quote from p. 104.

7. Since the events of 1989 this has been the topic of a number of books and journal articles, some of which have been referred to in other chapters of this book. Among the most persuasive of the arguments include: D. J. Solinger, 1989, "Capitalist Measures with Chinese Characteristics," *Problems of Communism* 38, No. 1 (Jan./Feb.), pp. 19–33; A. J. Nathan, 1989, "Chinese Democracy in 1989: Continuity and Change," *Problems of Communism* 38, No. 5 (Sept./Oct.), pp. 17–29; and also D. Zweig, 1989, "Peasants and Politics," *World Policy Journal* 6, No. 4 (Fall), pp. 633–646.

8. E. F. Vogel, 1989, *One Step Ahead in China: Guangdong Under Reform* (Cambridge, Mass: Harvard University Press). Another interesting perspective on the relationships between China and its East Asian neighbors, with a largely political rather than economic thrust, was provided in G. Segal, 1989, "East Asia: The New Balances of Power," *World Policy Journal* 5, No. 4 (Fall), pp. 731–758.

9. Vogel, op. cit., p. 434.

10. Ibid., p. 437.

11. Ibid., p. 74. For an illuminating discussion of the proposal to transfer Hong Kong back to China in 1997, and the problems associated with the process in the wake of the Tiananmen massacre, see F. Ching, 1989, "Red Star Over Hong Kong," *World Policy Journal* 6, No. 4 (Fall), pp. 657–666.

12. "Tighter Belts, Changing Moods," *U.S. News & World Report,* March 12, 1990, pp. 48–49.

13. "Economic Woes Sink China's Morale," *Guardian* (UK), January 24, 1990, p. 2.

14. A. G. Walder, 1989, "The Political Sociology of the Beijing Upheaval of 1989," *Problems of Communism* 38, No. 5 (Sept./Oct.), pp. 30–40. David Zweig, op. cit., also argued that the Chinese peasants, although not as involved in the uprisings of 1989, are anything but passive in the face of contemporary events. According to Zweig, "At no time since the great famine of the early 1960s has the potential for rural instability been greater. . . . The recent return to power in Beijing of aging conservatives, many of whom were the architects of the unpopular and unproductive agricultural policies of earlier decades, makes widespread rural unrest and violence more likely in China in the near future" (p. 633).

15. Walder, op. cit., p. 40.

APPENDIX 1

1. The importance of seeking out the help of geomancers in choosing a location for a well is beautifully illustrated in Zheng Yi's novel *Old Well* (San Francisco: China Books and Periodicals, 1989). The story, which has also been made into a film (*Lao Jing*), is set in the brutally poor countryside of North China. It describes the centuries-old struggle of the people in a small village to find enough water to ensure their survival.

2. S. Rossbach, 1983, *Feng Shui: The Chinese Art of Placement* (New York: E. P. Dutton), p. 21.

3. Ibid.

4. J. Morris, 1988, *Hong Kong* (New York: Random House), p. 132.

APPENDIX 2

1. Yu Luojin, 1986, *A Chinese Winter's Tale: Autobiographical Fragment,* trans. Rachel May and Zhu Zhiyu (Hong Kong: Renditions Paperbacks), p. 173.

2. Ibid., p. 174.

3. A. Burgess, 1987, *Little Wilson and Big God* (London: Heinemann).

S E L E C T E D
B I B L I O G R A P H Y

Some of the works that inspired and informed me as I wrote this book were referred to in the Preface. In addition I would like to highlight just a few of the key references that students should find useful in their explorations of China and things Chinese. For complete references, of course, readers should consult the notes.

INTRODUCTIONS TO CONTEMPORARY CHINA

Travel Books

Morris, Jan. 1989. *Hong Kong*. New York: Random House.
Theroux, P. 1988. *Riding the Iron Rooster: By Train Through China*. New York: Ivy Books.
Thubron, C. 1987. *Behind the Wall: A Journey Through China*. London: Heinemann.

Journalistic Books

Bonavia, D. 1989. *The Chinese* (rev. ed.). London: Penguin.
Butterfield, F. 1983. *China: Alive in the Bitter Sea*. Toronto: Bantam Books.
Pan, L. 1988. *The New Chinese Revolution*. Chicago: Contemporary Books.
Schell, O. 1988. *Discos and Democracy: China in the Throes of Reform*. New York: Pantheon.
Terzani, T. 1986. *Behind the Forbidden Door: Travels in China*. London: Allen and Unwin.

Academic Books

Coye, M. J., Livingston, J., and Highland, J. (eds.). 1984. *China: Yesterday and Today* (3rd ed.). Toronto: Bantam Books.
Terrill, R. (ed.). 1979. *The China Difference*. New York: Harper Colophon Books.

INTRODUCTIONS TO CHINESE CULTURE

Bond, M. H. (ed.). 1986. *The Psychology of the Chinese People*. Hong Kong: Oxford University Press.
Clayre, A. 1986. *The Heart of the Dragon*. Boston: Houghton Mifflin Co.
Gold, T. B. 1985. "After Comradeship: Personal Relations in China Since the Cultural Revolution." *China Quarterly*, No. 104 (December): 657–675.
Mote, F. 1971. *Intellectual Foundations of China*. New York: Alfred A. Knopf.

CHINESE HISTORY

General Histories

Blunden, C., and Elvin, M. 1983. *Cultural Atlas of China*. New York: Facts on File, Inc.
Fairbank, J. K. 1987. *The Great Chinese Revolution: 1800–1985*. New York: Harper and Row.

Histories of the Chinese Revolution, 1949

Bianco, L. 1971. *Origins of the Chinese Revolution, 1915–1944*. Stanford, Calif.: Stanford University Press.
Johnson, C. A. 1962. *Peasant Nationalism and Communist Power: The Emergence of Revolutionary China, 1937–1945*. Stanford, Calif.: Stanford University Press.
Peck, G. 1967. *Two Kinds of Time: Life in Provincial China During the Crucial Years 1940–1941*. Boston: Houghton Mifflin Co.
Selden, M. 1971. *The Yenan Way in Revolutionary China*. Cambridge, Mass.: Harvard University Press.
Vogel, E. F. 1969. *Canton Under Communism: Programs and Politics in a Provincial Capital, 1949–1968*. Cambridge, Mass.: Harvard University Press.

The Cultural Revolution

Gao Yuan. 1987. *Born Red: A Chronicle of the Cultural Revolution.* Stanford, Calif.: Stanford University Press.

Thurston, A. F. 1988. *Enemies of the People: The Ordeal of the Intellectuals in China's Great Cultural Revolution.* Cambridge, Mass.: Harvard University Press.

Yu Luojin. 1986. *A Chinese Winter's Tale.* Hong Kong: Renditions Paperbacks.

Zhang Xianliang. 1988. *Half of Man Is Woman.* New York: W. W. Norton and Co.

The Socialist Transformation of China

Gurley, J. G. 1976. *China's Economy and the Maoist Strategy.* New York: Monthly Review Press.

Hinton, W. 1984. *Shenfan: The Continuing Revolution in a Chinese Village.* New York: Vintage Books.

Selden, M., and Lippitt, V. D. (eds.). 1982. *The Transition to Socialism in China.* Armonk, N.Y.: M. E. Sharpe, Inc.

Shue, V. 1980. *Peasant China in Transition: The Dynamics of Development Toward Socialism, 1949–1956.* Berkeley: University of California Press.

INTRODUCTIONS TO POLITICS AND POLITICAL ECONOMY, POST-1949

Politics

Domes, J. 1985. *The Government and Politics of the PRC: A Time of Transition.* Boulder, Colo.: Westview Press.

Liu, A. P. 1986. *How China Is Ruled.* Englewood Cliffs, N.J.: Prentice-Hall.

Walder, A. G. 1986. *Communist Neo-Traditionalism: Work and Authority in Chinese Industry.* Berkeley: University of California Press.

———. 1987. "Actually Existing Maoism." *Australian Journal of Chinese Affairs*, No. 18 (July): 155–166.

Political Economy

Blecher, M. 1986. *China: Politics, Economics and Society: Iconoclasm and Innovation in a Revolutionary Socialist Country.* London: Frances Pinter Pub.

Lippit, V. D. 1987. *The Economic Development of China.* Armonk, N.Y.: M. E. Sharpe, Inc.

Riskin, C. 1987. *China's Political Economy: The Quest for Development Since 1949.* London: Oxford University Press.

Selden, M. 1988. *The Political Economy of Chinese Socialism.* Armonk, N.Y.: M. E. Sharpe.

Van Ness, P., and Raichur, S. 1983. "Dilemma of Socialist Development: An Analysis of Strategic Lines in China, 1949–1981." Pp. 77–89 in the *Bulletin of Concerned Asia Scholars* (eds.). *China from Mao to Deng: The Politics and Economics of Socialist Development.* Armonk, N.Y.: M. E. Sharpe, Inc.

CHINA'S GEOGRAPHY: AN INTRODUCTION

Introductory Surveys

Buchanan, K. 1970. *The Transformation of the Chinese Earth: Aspects of the Evaluation of the Chinese Earth from Earliest Times to Mao Tse-tung.* London: G. Bell and Sons.

Cannon, T., and Jenkins, A. 1990. *The Geography of China.* London: Routledge.

Pannell, C. W., and Ma, L.J.C. 1983. *China: The Geography of Development and Modernization.* London: V. H. Winston.

Atlases

Atlas of China. 1990. Chicago: Rand McNally.

The Contemporary Atlas of China. 1988. Boston: Houghton-Mifflin Co.

Agriculture and Food

Croll, E. 1988. "The New Peasant Economy in China." Pp. 77–100 in S. Feuchtwang, A. Hussain, and T. Pairault (eds.). *Transforming China's Economy in the Eighties.* Vol. 1: *The Rural Sector, Welfare and Employment.* Boulder, Colo.: Westview Press.

Perkins, D., and Yusuf, S. 1984. *Rural Development in China.* Baltimore: Johns Hopkins University Press.

Piazza, A. 1986. *Food Consumption and Nutritional Status in the PRC.* Boulder, Colo.: Westview Press.

Skinner, G. W. 1978. "Vegetable Supply and Marketing in Chinese Cities." *China Quarterly* 76 (December): 733–793.

Unger, J. 1985–1986. "The Decollectivization of the Chinese Countryside: A Survey of 28 Villages." *Pacific Affairs* 58, No. 4: 585–606.

Watson, A. 1983. "Agriculture Looks for 'Shoes That Fit': The Production Responsibility System and Its Implications." *World Development* 11, No. 8: 705–730.

Cities, Urbanization, and Planning

Fei Xiaotong. 1953. *China's Gentry: Essays in Rural-Urban Relations.* Chicago, Ill.: University of Chicago Press.

Goldstein, S. 1985. *Urbanization in China: New Insights From the 1982 Census.* Papers of the East-West Population Institute, No. 93 (July). Honolulu: University of Hawaii.

Hou Ren-Zhi. 1986. "Evolution of the City Plan of Beijing." *Third World Planning Review* 8, No. 1: 5–17.

Kirkby, R.J.R. 1985. *Urbanization in China: Town and Country in a Developing Economy, 1949–2000 AD.* New York: Columbia University Press.

Kojimo R. 1987. *Urbanization and Urban Problems in China.* Tokyo: Institute of Developing Economies, Occasional Paper Series No. 22.

Leung, C. K., and Ginsburg, N. (eds.). 1980. *China: Urbanization and National Development.* Chicago: University of Chicago, Dept. of Geography Research Paper No. 196.

Lewis, J. W. 1971. *The City in Communist China.* Stanford, Calif.: Stanford University Press.

Lo, C. P. 1987. "Socialist Ideology and Urban Strategies in China." *Urban Geography* 8, No. 5 (Sep./Oct.): 440–458.

Lo, C. P., Pannell, C. W., and Welch, R. 1977. "Land Use Changes and City Planning in Shenyang and Canton." *Geographical Review* 67, No. 3 (July): 268–283.

Ma, L.J.C. 1986. "Chinese Cities: A Research Agenda." *Urban Geography* 7: 279–290.

Murphey, R. 1980. *The Fading of the Maoist Vision: City and Country in China's Development.* New York: Methuen.

Nelson, C. M. 1988. "Urban Planning in Preindustrial China." *U.S. China Review* 12, No. 2 (Summer): 17–21.

Rowe, W. T. 1984. "Urban Policy in China." *Problems of Communism* 33, No. 6 (Nov./Dec.): 75–80.

Skinner, G. W. (ed.). 1977. *The City in Late Imperial China.* Stanford, Calif.: Stanford University Press.

Regional Development and Inequality

Aguignier, P. 1988. "Regional Disparities Since 1978." Pp. 93–106 in S. Feuchtwang, A. Hussain, and T. Pairault (eds.). *Transforming China's Economy in the Eighties.* Vol. 2: *Management, Industry and the Urban Economy.* Boulder, Colo.: Westview Press.

Kirkby, Richard, and Cannon, Terry. 1989. Introduction, *China's Regional Development.* Ed. D.S.G. Goodman. London: Routledge.

Lakshmanan, T. R., and Hua Chang-i. 1987. "Regional Disparities in China." *International Regional Science Review* 11, No. 1: 97–104.

Lyons, T. P. 1987. *Economic Integration and Planning in Maoist China.* New York: Columbia University Press.

Selden, M. 1985. "Income Inequality and the State." Pp. 193–218 in W. L. Parish (ed.). *Chinese Rural Development: The Great Transformation.* Armonk, N.Y.: M. E. Sharpe.

Trescott, P. B. 1985. "Incentive Versus Equality: What Does China's Recent Experience Show?" *World Development* 13, No. 2: 205–217.

Vermeer, E. B. 1982. "Income Differentials in Rural China." *China Quarterly* 89 (March): 1–33.

Whyte, M. K. "Social Trends in China: The Triumph of Inequality." Pp. 103–123 in A. Doak Barnett and R. N. Clough (eds.). *Modernizing China: Post-Mao Reform and Development.* Boulder, Colo.: Westview Press.

Environmental Issues

Jowett, A. J. 1986. "China's Water Crisis: The Case of Tianjin." *Geographical Journal* 152, Pt. 1 (March): 9–18.

Lampton, D. M. 1986. "Water Politics and Economic Change in China." Pp. 387–406 in *China's Economy Looks Toward the Year 2000. Vol. 1: The Four Modernizations.* Selected papers submitted to the U.S. Congress. May 21. Washington, D.C.: U.S. Government Printing Office.

Ma, L.J.C., and Liu Changming. 1984. "Water Resources Development and Its Environmental Impact on Beijing." Pp. 101–116 in C. Pannell and C. L. Salter (eds.). *China Geographer, No. 12: The Environment.* Boulder, Colo.: Westview Press.

Ross, L. 1987. "Obligatory Tree Planting: The Role of Campaigns in Policy Implementation in Post-Mao China." Pp. 225–252 in D. M. Lampton (ed.). *Policy Implementation in Post-Mao China.* Berkeley: University of California Press.

———. 1988. *Environmental Policy in China.* Bloomington: Indiana University Press.

Smil, V. 1984. *The Bad Earth: Environmental Degradation in China.* Armonk, N.Y.: M. E. Sharpe.

THE POST-MAO REFORM ERA

The Agricultural Reforms

Feuchtwang, S., Hussain, A., and Pairault, T. (eds.). 1988. *Transforming China's Economy in the Eighties.* Vol. 1: *The Rural Sector, Welfare and Employment.* Boulder, Colo.: Westview Press.

Howard, P. 1988. *Breaking the Iron Rice Bowl: Prospects for Socialism in China's Countryside.* Armonk, N.Y.: M. E. Sharpe.

The Urban Reforms

Chossudovsky, M. 1986. *Towards Capitalist Restoration: Chinese Socialism After Mao.* Hong Kong: Macmillan.

Prybyla, J. S. 1986. "China's Economic Experiments: From Mao to Market." *Problems of Communism* 35, No. 1 (Jan./Feb.): 21–38.

Reynolds, B. J. 1989. "The Chinese Economy in 1988." Pp. 27–48 in A. J. Kane (ed.). *China Briefing, 1989.* Boulder, Colo.: Westview Press.

General Studies

Schell, O. 1984. *To Get Rich Is Glorious: China in the 80's*. New York: Pantheon Books.

Vogel, E. F. 1989. *One Step Ahead in China: Guangdong Under Reform*. Cambridge, Mass.: Harvard University Press.

HUMAN RIGHTS IN CHINA

An Introduction

Barmé, G., and Minford, J. 1986. *Seeds of Fire: Chinese Voices of Conscience*. Hong Kong: Far Eastern Review, Ltd.

Leys, S. [Pierre Ryckmans, pseud.]. 1978. *Chinese Shadows*. London: Penguin Books.

———. 1985. *The Burning Forest*. New York: Holt, Rinehart and Winston.

Li, V. 1979. "Human Rights in a Chinese Context." Pp. 219–236 in R. Terrill (ed.). *The China Difference: A Portrait of Life Inside the Country of One Billion*. New York: Harper Colophon Books.

Nathan, A. J., Henkin, L., and Edwards, R. R. 1986. *Human Rights in Contemporary China*. New York: Columbia University Press.

Silk, M. A. 1985. "The Crime of Dissent in China." *Problems of Communism* 34, No. 4: 61–68.

Yu Luojin. 1986. *A Chinese Winter's Tale: Autobiographical Fragment*. Trans. Rachel May and Zhu Zhiyu. Hong Kong: Renditions Paperbacks.

The Democracy Movement and Tiananmen Square

Amnesty International. 1989. *People's Republic of China: Preliminary Findings on Killings of Unarmed Civilians, Arbitrary Arrests and Summary Executions Since June 3, 1989*. August. New York: Amnesty International.

Asia Watch. 1990. *Punishment Season: Human Rights in China After Martial Law*. New York: Asia Watch Committee.

Cheng, Chu-yuan. 1990. *Behind the Tiananmen Massacre*. Boulder, Colo.: Westview Press.

Fathers, M., and Higgins, A. 1989. *Tiananmen: The Rape of Peking*. London: The Independent.

Liu Binyan (with Ruan Ming and Xu Gang). 1989. *"Tell the World": What Happened in China and Why*. New York: Pantheon Books.

Nathan, A. J. 1989. "Chinese Democracy in 1989: Continuity and Change." *Problems of Communism* 38, No 5 (Sept./Oct.): 17–29.

Simmie, S., and Nixon, B. 1989. *Tiananmen Square*. Seattle: University of Washington Press.

Solinger, D. J. 1989. "Capitalist Measures with Chinese Characteristics." *Problems of Communism* 38, No. 1 (Jan./Feb.): 19–33.

Yi Mu and Thompson, M. V. 1989. *Crisis at Tiananmen: Reform and Reality in Modern China*. San Francisco: China Books and Periodicals.

Zweig, D. 1989. "Peasants and Politics." *World Policy Journal* 6, No 4 (Fall): 633–646.

MISCELLANEOUS TOPICS

Women and Gender Issues

Croll, E. 1983. *Chinese Women Since Mao*. Armonk, N.Y.: M. E. Sharpe, Inc.

Davin, D. 1988. "The Implications of Contract Agriculture for the Employment and Status of Chinese Peasant Women." Pp. 137–146 in S. Feuchtwang, A. Hussain, and T. Pairault (eds.). *Transforming China's Economy in the Eighties*. Vol. 1: *The Rural Sector, Welfare and Employment*. Boulder, Colo.: Westview Press.

Honig, E., and Hershatter, G. 1988. *Personal Voices: Chinese Women in the 1980's*. Stanford, Calif.: Stanford University Press.

Johnston, K. A. 1983. *Women, The Family and Peasant Revolution in China*. Chicago: University of Chicago Press.

Stacey, J. 1983. *Patriarchy and Socialist Revolution in China*. Berkeley: University of California Press.

Wolf, M. 1985. *Revolution Postponed: Women in Contemporary China*. Stanford, Calif.: Stanford University Press.

Population and Family Planning

Arnold, F., and Liu Zhaoxiang. 1986. "Sex Preference, Fertility, and Family Planning in China." *Population and Development Review* 12, No. 2: 229–230.

Croll, E. J. 1985. "The Single-Child Family: The First Five Years." Pp. 125–139 in N. Maxwell and B. McFarlane (eds.). *China's Changed Road to Development*. Oxford: Pergamon Press.

———. "The Single-Child Family in Beijing: A First-Hand Report." Pp. 190–232 in E. J. Croll, D. Davin, and P. Kane (eds.). *China's One Child Family Policy*. London: Macmillan.

Davin, D. 1985. "The Implementation of the Single-Child Family Policy in the Chinese Countryside." In E. J. Croll, D. Davin, and P. Kane (eds.). *China's One Child Family Policy*. London: Macmillan.

Freedman, R., Xiao Zhenyu, Li Bohua and Lavely, W. 1988. "Local Area Variations in Reproductive Behavior in the People's Republic of China, 1973–1982." *Population Studies* 42, No. 1 (March): 39–57.

Greenhalgh, S. 1986. "Shifts in China's Population Policy, 1984–1986: Views from the Central, Provincial and Local Levels." *Population and De-*

velopment Review 12, No. 3 (September): 491–515.

Greenhalgh, S., and Bongaarts, J. 1987. "Fertility Policy in China: Future Options" *Science* 235 (March 6): 1167–1172.

Poston, D. L., Jr. 1986. "Patterns of Contraceptive Use in China." *Studies in Family Planning* 17, No. 5 (September): 217–227.

Tien, H. Y. 1973. *China's Population Struggle: Demographic Decisions of the People's Republic, 1949–1969.* Columbus: Ohio State University Press.

Whyte, M. K., and Gu, S. Z. 1987. "Popular Response to China's Fertility Transition." *Population and Development Review* 13, No. 3 (September): 471–493.

Whyte, T. 1987. "Implementing the One-Child Population Program in Rural China: National Goals and Local Politics." Pp. 284–317 in D. M. Lampton (ed.). *Policy Implementation in Post-Mao China.* Berkeley: University of California Press.

Everyday Life in Contemporary China

Cheng Naishan. 1989. "No. 2 and No. 4 of Shanghai." Pp. 1–116 in Cheng Naishan. *The Piano Tuner.* San Francisco: China Books and Periodicals.

Huang Shu-min. 1989. *The Spiral Road.* Boulder, Colo.: Westview Press.

Whyte, M. K., and Parish, W. L. 1984. *Urban Life in Contemporary China.* Chicago: University of Chicago Press.

Zhang Xinxin and Sang Ye. 1987. *Chinese Lives: An Oral History of Contemporary China.* New York: Pantheon Books.

Crime and the Legal System

Baum, R. 1986. "Modernization and Legal Reform in Post-Mao China: The Rebirth of Socialist Legality." *Studies in Comparative Communism* 19, No. 2 (Summer): 69–103.

Leng, S. C., and Chiu, H. 1985. *Criminal Justice in Post-Mao China: Analysis and Documents.* Albany: State University of New York Press.

Li, V. H. 1978. *Law Without Lawyers: A Comparative View of Law in China and the United States.* Boulder, Colo.: Westview Press.

Munro, R. 1989. "Party, Politics, and Interference in the Law." *China Now,* No. 129 (Summer): 22–23.

ABOUT THE BOOK & AUTHOR

Since the death of Mao Zedong in 1976, critical changes have been occurring at all levels in Chinese society. This text, which views contemporary China from a geographer's perspective, assesses the questions inherent in such rapid evolution. How do the Chinese manage to provide enough food for more than a billion people? In what ways are they restructuring and modernizing their economy? How have they been able to provide mass access to such services as health care, education, and housing? The author also delves into the relatively unexplored realm of everyday life in the new China. Why do so many want to leave the countryside and move to the cities? How has life changed for women after centuries of Confucian oppression in China? And what does the future hold for China's many ethnic minority groups?

By providing answers to questions such as these, the book illustrates the centrality of geography to the study of China—a country where distance still acts as a major constraint on social and spatial interaction; where the population is so vast that the demand for resources almost always outstrips the supply; and where regional variations have produced a rich mosaic of human and physical characteristics.

Introducing students to the major concepts of modern geography, the author uses a series of case studies to illustrate the importance of geographical factors in the organization of production, distribution, and consumption in China. This accessible and comprehensive text will be invaluable as an introduction to China in all disciplines.

Christopher J. Smith is associate professor of geography and planning at the State University of New York in Albany.

INDEX

Annexation of rural counties; Food; Urban
self-sufficiency
Vogel, Ezra, 43–45, 48, 145, 152, 247, 248, 277–
278
Voice of America, 271
Von Thunen, Johann, 149, 230

Walder, Andrew G., 66, 67(Table 4.3), 282
Wang Anyi, 203
Wang Meng, 202
Warlords, 54, 55
Warring States epoch, 37
Water: demand, supply, and pollution, 180, 184,
186, 187(Table 10.2), 188. *See also*
Environmental policy
Weddings, 195, 196, 202. *See also* Gender and
socialist theory; Marriage
Wei Jingsheng, 259, 262–263. *See also*
Democracy movement; Democracy Wall;
Dissidents
Western decadence. *See* Morality
Whyte, M. K., and R. L. Parish, 44, 196–197,
252
Wolf, Margery, 197, 198, 199
Women
attachment to localities, 14
attitudes to and knowledge about sex, 37
and Confucianism, 35, 36, 37
in the countryside, 14
educational statistics, 196–197, 197(Table 11.1)
effects of market socialism on, 207–211
and equality in the labor force, 196, 197,
198(Table 11.2)
exploitation of, 196–198
Mao Zedong's views on, 195
"proper" roles for, 198–199
and the Revolution of 1949, 196, 198
and socialism, 195–196
See also Marriage; Patriarchy
Work groups, 19, 80, 83
Work points, 80, 82
Work units, 21, 101, 126, 147, 200, 222–223,
224, 251
Wugong Village. *See* Hebei Province
Wuhan, 140

Xiamen SEZ, 105. *See also* Special Economic
Zones
Xian (Shaanxi Province), 92, 140, 232
Xian (county) towns, 17, 139
Xinjiang Autonomous Region, 10, 117, 162, 176,
266

Yang, Martin C., 15
Yangtze River (Chang Jiang)
deforestation in the basin, 181, 183

as a dividing line in China, 1
multiple cropping, 72
population distribution, 117
Yantai, 243–244
Yenan
CCP headquarters, pre–Civil War, 195
the "mass line," 125–126, 256
"Yenan Way." *See* Yenan
Youth
"baby boom," 116
dating and courtship, 200–201
and sex, 37
Yue Daiyuan, 44–45
Yu Luojin, 37, 204, 264, 285
Yunnan-Guizhou Plateau (poverty in), 163–164,
165(Figure 9.3)
Yunnan Province
deforestation, 180–181
markets in, 172
son preference and contraceptive use, 132

Zero population growth (ZPG), 121, 125, 137
Zhang Dynasty (1480–1122 BC), 57
Zhang Jie, 22–23, 45, 205
Zhang Xian, 205
Zhang Xianliang, 9, 44, 178, 204, 206, 259, 263,
265, 268
Zhang Xin Xin and Sang Ye (*Chinese Lives*), 15,
85, 150–151, 196
Zhang Zilong, 52–53
Zhao Ziyang
accused of being a "splittist," 68
on market socialism, 62, 183
meteoric rise to fame ("helicopter" cadre), 65,
67
the political demise of, 67, 68, 113–114
on the "primary stage" of socialism, 111–112
on SEZs, 105–106
and Tiananmen Square demonstrations, 68,
262, 269, 270
See also Chinese Communist Party; Deng
Xiaoping; Economic reforms
Zhejiang Province, 162, 220
Zhengzhou, 92, 140
Zhongnanhai, CCP headquarters, 240
Zhou Dynasty (1122–221 BC), 57
Zhou Enlai
on birth control, 123
criticisms of, within the CCP, 57
death, 62, 260
and the Democracy movement, 238
and the Four Modernizations, 62
Zhu De, 62
Zhuhai SEZ, 105. *See also* Special Economic
Zones
ZPG. *See* Zero population growth